STRANGE STORIES, AMAZING FACTS

Reader's Digest

STRANGE STORIES, AMAZING FACTS

Stories that are bizarre, unusual, odd, astonishing, and often incredible

THE READER'S DIGEST ASSOCIATION, INC.
Pleasantville, New York   Montreal

About this book

While *Strange Stories, Amazing Facts* was being prepared for publication, we asked the staff to suggest a descriptive subtitle for the book. One member was enthusiastic about "a literary smorgasbord." Another strongly favored "a Disneyland for readers." Although cooler and, we choose to think, wiser heads prevailed and both proposals were vetoed, the metaphors are, in fact, apt.

This volume does offer an astonishing variety of subject matter, treatment, and tone. For example, "Will the Ice Age Return?" (a frightening and real possibility) and "Heaven's Artillery" (a story about meteorites) are enough to give one chills in a sauna, while "Bunga-Bunga" (an account of an elaborate hoax) and "Everything Has Its Price" (a tale of a remarkably persuasive gentleman who, among other felonious exploits, sold the Eiffel Tower and rented out the White House) would probably bring a smile to a wooden Indian.

In this book fascinating "hard" scientific articles about space exploration, solar energy, and the human body are companions with stories of psychic phenomena, vampires, and the curious superstitions of professional athletes. Wondrous discoveries about the earliest days of this planet are bound in with highly informed predictions about the world-to-be. History's greatest explorers, from the ancient Orientals to the astronauts, are found in the company of charlatans, real and fake artists, legendary beasts, and monumental eccentrics. The baffling questions about unidentified flying objects and the mysterious "clocks" that seem to govern all life on earth are discussed only a few chapters away from lighthearted articles about the evolution of our modes of dress and the origins of many of our most familiar phrases.

In short, we think you'll find this book a delightful companion—informative, funny, surprising, varied, thought provoking, unexpected. Here's your plate for the smorgasbord, your ticket to Disneyland.

The Editors

Contents

PART 3

PART 4

PART 5

PART

1

The universe . . . eternally fixed or forever exploding?

The enigma of
space

A DROP IN THE OCEAN OF SPACE. *When viewing his home against the backdrop of the universe, man feels humble. The earth (top left) is third closest to the sun and*

PORTRAIT OF THE UNIVERSE

How stars are born—from here to eternity

Looking at the sun and the stars is like gazing backward down a time tunnel. What is seen from the earth is not the stars as they are, but as they were when the light rays left the various heavenly bodies.

Light travels at 186,000 miles a second, and at this speed takes eight minutes to reach the earth from the sun. By the same token the closest star to the earth's solar system, Proxima Centauri, is seen not as it is but as it was 4.25 years ago.

With powerful telescopes it is possible to look back millions of years into the past of the universe and, by linking telescopes with sensitive photographic plates, even farther back—to a staggering billions of years ago.

With man's ever-increasing knowledge and use of more and more sophisticated equipment, we are more aware than ever that the earth is an insignificant dot when measured against the overwhelming backdrop of space.

The earth occupies third place from the sun in a system of nine planets—some with moons, others without—in orbit around the sun. This,

one of the smaller planets of the solar system. But the sun's vast empire is unimpressive when seen in its galaxy, the Milky Way (left), which contains innumerable suns, or stars. The Milky Way itself is insignificant when pictured against its neighboring galaxies (above), while in the infinity of the universe it is but a pinprick.

the solar system, is a tiny speck in a breathtakingly huge spiral, 100,000 light-years across, known as a galaxy.

This galaxy, in turn, is one of countless others in yet another system of galaxies so incredibly vast that it defies the imagination.

Distances between the earth and the nearest objects in space were first measured by a method of trigonometry known as parallax. This involves taking triangulated sightings on a star at six-month intervals or, in effect, using the diameter of the earth's annual orbit around the sun as the baseline of a triangle. If the baseline of a triangle and the angles at each end of it are known, the remaining dimensions of the triangle can be worked out.

Threefold success in 1838

Astronomers in the 17th and 18th centuries tried to calculate star distances by the parallax method, but it was not until 1838 that three astronomers, within a few months of each other, successfully and independently made parallax calculations of star distances.

Friedrich Bessel, director of the Konigsberg

DISTANCE LENDS ENCHANTMENT. *The most distant known quasar is 3C-295, in Boötes, photographed in 1960 at the Palomar Observatory.*

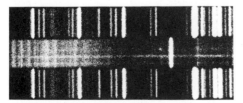

COLOR CLUE. *According to the red shift in this quasar's spectrum, it is 5 billion light-years away. Probably there are even more distant quasars.*

Observatory in Germany, measured a star called 61 Cygni as being just less than 11 light-years away; Thomas Henderson, Astronomer Royal for Scotland, announced that Alpha Centauri was 4.3 light-years from earth; and F.G.W. Struve, working at Dorpat in Russia, gave a value of the distance for Vega, now acknowledged to be 27 light-years away.

Later, the parallaxes of other stars were calculated, but beyond a distance of 100 to 150 light-years, the trigonometric method leaves an increasing margin of error—because of the very tiny angle at the apex of the triangles involved.

Star distances can, however, be measured by other methods, many based on how luminous a star is. To the naked eye all stars may seem white, or nearly so, but this is not the case.

In the constellation of Auriga, for example, the star Capella is yellow. Betelgeuse, in Orion, is reddish, and Rigel is slightly blue.

An analysis of the spectrum of any distant object in space reveals its chemical elements and the temperature at which they are reacting, as well as the speed at which the body is traveling. From these clues astronomers can get an idea of the true brightness of a star, and by correlating this to its apparent brightness, as seen on earth, make an accurate estimate of its distance.

The estimation of the speed of a distant object stems largely from a scientific principle laid down in 1842 by the Austrian physicist Christian Doppler. This principle—known as the Doppler effect—is best demonstrated by relating it to the whistle of an approaching train. As a train draws near, the pitch of the whistle climbs higher, until the train passes. Then, as it recedes in the distance, the tone falls.

The red shift

Two later 19th-century astronomers—Sir William Huggins in England and Hermann Vogel in Germany—independently made use of Doppler's principle.

When applied to light waves, the Doppler effect shows up in color. At the red end of the spectrum, light waves are longer; at the violet end, shorter. So, redness in light coming from a celestial body is taken to mean that it must be moving away from earth.

This phenomenon is known as the red shift. Conversely, light waves from a source that is *approaching* the observer tend to move up the spectrum toward the violet end, where they become stronger and more frequent.

The so-called radial velocities of many stars have been measured in this way. Thus, Sirius is approaching our solar system at 5 miles a second and Altair at 16. Aldebaran, on the other hand, is receding at 34 miles a second and Capella at 18.

Some other explanation for violet and red shifts in stars and galaxies may, of course, be possible. But most modern astronomers accept the principles of the Doppler effect.

In 1924 Dr. Edwin Hubble, of Mount Wilson Observatory in California, using the superior instruments then available, learned more about the red shift. He found that whole galaxies must be traveling away from earth at tremendous speeds. Hubble concluded that the whole universe is expanding, with everything in it moving farther apart from everything else. And as the galaxies move farther and farther away from our own, the radiation of light we get from them gets weaker and weaker. This, said Hubble, is why starlight is too feeble to illuminate our night skies.

The "Big Bang"

Why should the universe be expanding? The idea ties in with one of the main theories about the birth of the universe, expounded in 1930 by the Belgian astronomer Georges Lemaître. His was the "Big Bang" theory, which suggested that about 10 billion years ago all the matter of the universe was contained in a primal atom— which he vividly described as a superdense "cosmic egg."

This, he said, exploded, and its many fragments became galaxies—one of which contains our solar system—all moving apart at incredible speed.

Another popular belief—the "Steady State" theory—was advanced in 1948 by British cosmologists Hermann Bondi, Thomas Gold, and Fred Hoyle, who suggested that the universe is eternal and that it has always existed.

They said that matter is continuously created, apparently from nothing, at the rate of 62 atoms of hydrogen per cubic inch of space every billion years.

This is sufficient to form new galaxies to fill in the gaps caused by the expansion of the universe.

The "Pulsating Universe"

In 1965 the American astronomer Professor Allan Sandage adapted the "Big Bang" theory and developed it into his "Pulsating Universe" theory.

He suggested that the universe is created, destroyed, and then re-created in 80-billion-year cycles. At the moment, he said, the universe is only 10 billion years along in the expansion stage, and it will continue to expand for another 30 billion years before the galaxies overcome the force of the "Big Bang" and begin to contract.

Eventually, he maintained, moving at millions of miles an hour, they will converge and fuse again into their primal atoms, which will then explode once more to restart the cycle.

FACTS ABOUT OUR NEIGHBORS

OUTSIDE the earth's planetary system, the nearest star to the sun is Proxima Centauri, at a distance of 4.25 light-years. But it is by no means the brightest star in the earth's heavens. The four brightest are Sirius, the Dog Star (8.7 light-years away), far-distant Canopus (98 light-years), Alpha Centauri (4.3 light-years), and Arcturus (36 light-years).

The most distant body that can be seen with the naked eye from earth is the Great Spiral Galaxy in the star cluster, or constellation, known as Andromeda—more than 2 million light-years away. It appears only as a faint patch of light in the sky.

The largest star visible to the naked eye is probably Alpha Herculis, a red giant—the name given to stars that are losing their heat. The smallest known stars are about the size of planets—less than 10,000 miles in diameter. The smallest yet detected is Wolf 457, which, at 3/1,000 the size of the sun, is smaller than the earth. Some stars may even be less than 1,100 miles across. By the standards of the earth's solar system, the largest stars are enormous. The variable star VV Cephei, at 1 billion miles in diameter, for example, is 1,220 times the size of the sun. (A variable star is a pulsating star, growing bright, then dim.) The most densely populated area of the heavens is considered to be the central part of the Milky Way (the earth's galaxy), toward the constellation Sagittarius.

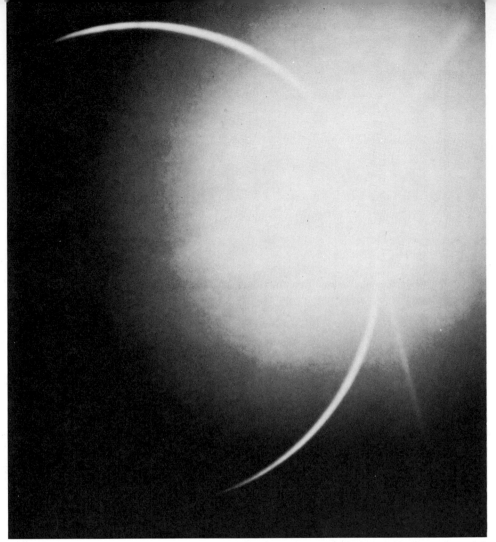

THE SUN ECLIPSED BY THE EARTH. *This photograph was taken from the* Apollo 12 *command module during its expedition to the moon in November 1969.*

THE SAVAGE SUN

It is a normal star, like millions of others

In the order of the universe, the sun is an ordinary, medium-sized star. Yet its energy and violence almost defy imagination.

It is a dense mass of glowing matter, a million times the volume of the earth, and in a permanent state of nuclear activity. Every second, 4 million tons of hydrogen are destroyed in explosions that start somewhere near the core, where the temperature is about 25 million degrees Fahrenheit.

More energy than man has used since the dawn of civilization is radiated by this normal star in a second.

The earth's entire oil, coal, and wood reserves would fuel the sun's energy output to the earth alone for only a few days.

Tongues of hydrogen flame leap from the sun's surface with the force of a billion hydrogen bombs. They are forced up by the enormous thermonuclear explosion at the core of the sun, where 564 million tons of hydrogen fuse each second to form helium. Matter at the core of the sun is so hot that a pinhead of it would give off enough radiation to kill a man 100 miles away.

Slow-burning bomb
The sun, therefore, is like a vast hydrogen bomb, burning slowly. It is only its vast size that makes its energy output so phenomenal. In fact, its output is about one-fifth that of the human body—in relation to volume.

Sometimes the sun's surface is partly covered by dark patches known as sunspots, thousands of miles across. They are probably caused by magnetic disturbances, but are not fully understood. From the sun's surface tens of thousands of fountains of blazing gas, called spicules, spurt out every second. They reach out 6,000 miles, then fall back within minutes.

The number of sunspots is greatest about every 11 years, and over the same cycle earthly phenomena of aurora variations, magnetic storms, and radio blackouts are observed.

Solar flares

Loops of bright gas, or prominences, arch 100,000 miles into the sun's outer atmosphere, or corona. But these are small compared with solar flares.

These eject electromagnetic waves, which travel at the speed of light and reach the earth in about eight minutes. They are followed by other particles which take half an hour to reach the earth. A day later, slower particles arrive.

One of the largest recorded flares occurred on November 12, 1960. A cloud of hydrogen, 10 million miles wide, stretching back 46 million miles, collided with the earth and started a violent chain of disturbances.

Aurorae, normally seen within 1,500 miles of the poles, displayed much more spectacular, shimmering colored ribbons than usual.

Two days later, teleprinters produced nonsensical messages, and radio communications were blacked out. Electric lights flickered as if a thunderstorm raged, yet the skies were clear. Some of these effects lasted more than a week.

A suggested explanation of these phenomena is that solar flares in some way send out nuclei of hydrogen atoms and electrons. Traveling at 400 to 600 miles per second, they begin to reach the earth's atmosphere about 50 hours after the flare and produce the disturbances.

THE SAD TALE OF HSI AND HO

ONE DAY a very long time ago a hungry dragon tried to eat the sun. The Emperor of China and his people were terrified. At first, a tiny bite was taken out of one side of the orb. Then a quarter, a half, and finally the whole sun had gone, and there was nothing but a circle of white light around the black space where the sun had been.

The frightened, but resourceful, Chinese knew what to do. They ran around in the strange twilight, shouting and screaming defiance at the dragon, beating drums, banging gongs, and whacking hollow wooden ducks until the startled dragon moved away. The sun was saved, but the Emperor, now more angry than scared, ordered that the Imperial Astronomers, Hsi and Ho, depicted here attending their Emperor in happier times, should be beheaded for failing to warn him in time of the dragon's approach.

Astronomers have long enjoyed the anonymous rhyme that has become their epitaph:

Here lie the bodies of Hsi and Ho,
Whose fate, though sad, was visible:
Being killed because they did not spy
Th' eclipse which was invisible.

The tale is but a myth—the astronomers' names derive from that of the sun's legendary mother, the goddess Hsi Ho. How long ago the first solar eclipse was observed is uncertain. But according to the Shang oracle bones (inscribed animal bones), the Chinese recorded one in 1217 B.C. Chinese scholars later decided that the sailing moon briefly hid, or "ate," the sun.

MYSTERIES OF THE MOON

Where a stone can lie untouched for 3 billion years

Even the rocks returned to earth by the Apollo missions have failed to answer the many puzzles of the moon. Still, today, it remains the strange satellite, which has been the source of myth and legend since prehistoric man looked at it—and wondered.

The moon is the earth's closest companion in its endless journey around the sun. The distance between the earth and moon is 239,000 miles. It takes 27.3 days for the moon to complete a full revolution around the earth, and it takes exactly the same time for the moon to spin once on its own axis. This means that the moon always presents the same face to the earth. So far, only the astronauts have seen its far side, although it has been photographed by satellite.

It was once thought that the moon was part of the earth and that it broke away, leaving a huge hole now filled by the Pacific Ocean. This theory has long since been discounted by mathematical calculations that show that the size of the moon and the volume of the Pacific do not correspond.

Probably, the moon and the earth were born about the same time—about 4.7 billion years ago. And they evolved from the same accumulation of dust and gases that went to give birth to the sun.

Russian probe

In October 1959 a Russian moon probe—*Luna 3*—circled behind the moon and took photographs that were later transmitted back to earth. As expected, the photographs showed mountains, valleys, and craters. But there was no sign of life. It is now known that the moon is entirely sterile—as it has undoubtedly been throughout its entire violent history.

Since 1959, more probes, including the manned U.S. Apollo missions, have circled behind the moon, and scientists now have detailed maps of its entire surface.

In July 1969 one of the most valuable cargoes in history was delivered to the Lunar Receiving Laboratory in Houston, Texas. It consisted of 50 pounds of rocks and dust brought back to earth by the crew of *Apollo II* from the moon's Sea of Tranquillity.

There were 46 rocks brought back by *Apollo II*—all from the top layer of the lunar surface.

They were small, ranging from the size of a pea to five inches long. At first glance they looked very much like ordinary earth rocks, but when they were examined under microscopes, startling differences appeared.

The lunar rocks were pitted with small, glass-lined pockmarks. Some were covered with spatters of glass that formed whitish patches on the surface. And the soil samples were made up of 50 percent glass—most of it sharp, angular, and without color. On earth very little glass is found in the soil.

Different proportions

All rocks, whether from the earth, the moon, or elsewhere, are basically composed of the same elements that existed in space before the solar system was formed. So what lunar scientists found in the moon rocks was not a difference in elements but a difference in proportions.

The ratio of uranium to potassium, for example, was 4 times higher in the moon rocks than in those found on earth and 15 times greater than in meteorite samples found on earth. In all, 68 of the more than 100 known elements have been found in moon rocks.

The puzzle of the moon has been heightened by researchers who tested the effects of moon dust on bacteria and plants. Certain bacteria were exposed to four lunar surface samples. On three of them there was no effect. But when they were exposed to subsurface samples brought back to earth by *Apollo 12*, they died. No explanation for the results of the tests has yet been found.

In other tests corn was exposed to the samples as representative of a complex plant, with no apparent effect. But simple algae exposed to moon dirt appeared to thrive on the "food" from space and grew greener for no explicable reason.

Gases from the sun

Scientists have already managed to uncover some information, however, which may lead to breakthroughs in man's knowledge of the universe. The moon rocks are now known to contain particles from the sun, embedded in them in the form of gases. And these gases may provide us with the vital key to how the sun works and how long it will sustain life on the planet earth.

One thing is certain. The moon is much more complicated than scientists had expected. It is not a kind of billiard ball frozen in space and time as had been thought. It was an active volcanic mass 4.6 billion years ago, which later stilled to an endless silence.

The first rocks found by the astronauts were more than 3 billion years old—and these turned out to be young by the standards of the moon.

At least one rock was 4.6 billion years old. On earth it is only by searching out remote crannies in Greenland that rocks approaching 4 billion years old can be found.

The other striking thing about the lunar rocks is that they have not been subjected to erosion by wind, water, and the other disturbances on earth. The rocks picked up by the astronauts had been lying there for 3 billion years without moving a fraction of an inch.

PACK UP YOUR TROUBLES. *Heavily laden astronaut Edwin E. Aldrin climbs down the ladder to set foot on the moon for the first time. The photograph was taken by fellow astronaut Neil Armstrong.*

ROCK OF AGES. *This five-pound rock, brought back by astronauts from the* Apollo 12 *mission to the moon, is 3 billion years old.*

PLANET	DISTANCE FROM SUN IN MILLIONS OF MILES	DIAMETER (Miles)	LENGTH OF DAY	LENGTH OF YEAR
MERCURY	36	3,025	59 days	88 days
VENUS	67	7,526	243 days (retrograde)	224.7 days
EARTH	93	7,926	23 hr. 56 min.	365.26 days
MARS	141.5	4,218	24 hr. 37 min.	687 days
JUPITER	483	88,700	9 hr. 50 min.	11.56 years
SATURN	886	75,100	10 hr. 14 min.	29.46 years
URANUS	1,783	29,200	10 hr. 49 min.	84.01 years
NEPTUNE	2,793	31,650	15¾ hr.	164.8 years
PLUTO	3,666	3,600 (?)	6 days 9 hr.	247.7 years

OUR NEAREST NEIGHBORS

The solar system in which we live

There is no general agreement about how the planets were formed. The most widely accepted theory is that about 5 billion years ago swirling clouds of matter began to condense. Through the action of centrifugal force, the heavier molecules were concentrated near the center of the eddies, and the lighter, gaseous material was thrown out toward the periphery. Such is the theory. What is *known* is that nine satellites began orbiting around the sun. These are the planets.

The earth we live on

The planet on which man lives is the third closest to the sun, with the third shortest orbit. It has the fifth fastest rotation, the fifth strongest gravity, the third hottest surface temperature, and the fifth greatest mass.

It also has something none of the others has—an atmosphere that can support life in all the diverse forms that exist on our planet. There may be satellites circling other stars in other parts of the universe that have the right ingredients for some sort of life to evolve, but the earth is the only one in the solar system.

Earth's distance from the sun (93 million miles) gives it a maximum temperature of 140°F (60°C). Harmful cosmic rays are prevented from reaching it by a magnetic field, known as the Van Allen belt, which traps these

MASS RELATIVE TO EARTH	ATMOSPHERE	SURFACE TEMPERATURE (Max.)
.05	None	(752°F)400°C
.81	Carbon dioxide, water, nitrogen	(932°F)500°C
1.00	Nitrogen, oxygen, water, carbon dioxide, argon	(140°F)60°C
.11	Carbon dioxide, water, nitrogen	(70°F)21°C
317.8	Hydrogen, helium, methane, water, ammonia	(−200°F)−130°C (cloud tops)
95.2	As Jupiter	(−256°F)−160°C (cloud tops)
14.5	As Jupiter	(−346°F)−210°C (cloud tops)
17.2	As Jupiter	(−382°F)−230°C (cloud tops)
.8 (?)	Not known	Not known

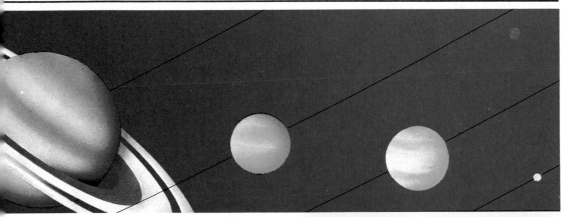

THE NINE PLANETS. *A scale drawing shows the size of the satellites in relation to the sun, part of which is seen curving in the background. The sun is vastly bigger than any of its planets.*

particles and holds them captive far out in space.

The tilt of the earth's axis produces the seasons; and the composition of the atmosphere—oxygen, nitrogen, water vapor, carbon dioxide, and argon—provides the ingredients vital for the sustenance of organic life.

Mercury, the smallest planet

Mercury is the smallest and least hospitable of the inner planets. Until recently, it was believed that Mercury's day was the same length as its

ASTRONAUTS' VIEW. *The earth is seen from* Apollo 11, 100,000 *miles away, on its journey to the moon. Africa can be clearly recognized.*

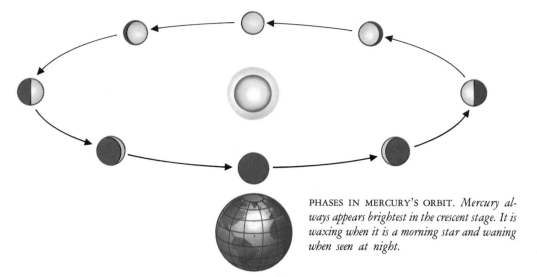

PHASES IN MERCURY'S ORBIT. *Mercury always appears brightest in the crescent stage. It is waxing when it is a morning star and waning when seen at night.*

year—88 earth days. Astronomers had thought that one side of the planet was always hidden from the sun, in permanent intense cold, while the other side, always under the sun's rays, was so hot that soft metals, such as lead or tin, would be boiled away.

But this belief has now been proved false. It arose through the coincidence that Mercury always presents the same face to the earth at the same point in its orbit around the sun. So the "cold" side of Mercury is not so cold after all. If ever an astronaut is able to take a trip to the planet—the distance ranges from 50 to 136 million miles, and the journey would take well over six months—he will find the temperature at night to be much the same as on a comfortable summer day back on the earth, 72°F (22°C).

Because Mercury's orbit around the sun is only half as much again as its rotation, the astronaut would have to wait up to 176 earth days for the scorching dawn. If he were in some way able to stay until "noon," the temperature would reach 752°F (400°C), and the mercury in his instruments would boil.

Assuming that the astronaut could somehow survive, the great weight of his insulating equipment would probably not hamper his movements too much. Because of Mercury's small gravity pull, a 150-pound man would weigh only 57 pounds.

A drive around Mercury
The planet's surface would be scorched hard, and there would be no seas or rivers to impede a vehicle throughout the 10,000 miles it would cover in a trip around the circumference.

Mercury's orbit is more elliptical than that of any other planet except Pluto, so the temperature varies from one Mercurian day to another. On one of the hottest days a visitor would see a cratered, rocky landscape under the blinding light of a huge sun. At night, since Mercury has no moon, only the stars and the distant luminosity of Venus and the earth would be visible.

The truth about Venus
Although it is much closer to the sun than is the earth—67 million miles, compared with 93 million—the surface of Venus is protected from the burning heat by a permanent dense cloud. Only 50 years ago astronomers visualized a planet teeming with life beneath this cloud—a kind of tropical, steamy jungle through which some of the more imaginative saw dinosaur-type monsters roaming.

Others even interpreted the halo sometimes seen around the dark edge of Venus as the glow of cities at night.

Now the Venusian clouds have been pierced by American and Russian space probes, and the fantasies have melted way. The reality is far different. Carbon dioxide envelops the planet, sealing in a temperature of 932°F (500°C) at the surface. Dust and ice crystals fuse together into a yellowish "smog" through which only occasionally a pale sunlight filters, making the rocks glow red.

All around is sand, littered with boulders scoured into weird shapes by constant dust storms. In the stifling heat nothing can grow. The ice particles in the cloud melt and turn to vapor long before they can reach the surface as rain.

Venus is almost as big as the earth, with a diameter of 7,500 miles compared with 7,900, and its gravity is slightly less. It rotates on its axis in the opposite way from the earth. So if it were possible for a man to land on Venus, the sun, if he were ever able to catch a glimpse of it through the "smog" shroud, would rise in the west and set in the east. There are no seasons, and as the planet takes 243 days to spin on its axis and only 224.7 days to orbit the sun, a Venusian day is longer than a year.

One of the biggest problems the scientists would have to solve before the three-month flight to Venus could even be thought of is the planet's enormous atmospheric pressure of 1,500 pounds per square inch, 100 times that of the earth's atmosphere. So even if an astronaut could survive all the other perils, unless he were protected in some way, he would be crushed to death.

Despite the harsh facts revealed by modern astronomers, Venus has always aroused the fanciful imagination. If only its permanent envelope of cloud were to disperse so that water could reach the surface, releasing free oxygen into the atmosphere, then indeed this gloomy, lifeless inferno might be transformed into something approaching the science-fiction writer's dream.

Mars and its "canals"

The first visitor to Mars may well bring back a specimen of the only organic life that exists in the solar system outside our world. But if he does, it will be no little green man. The sample is likely to be nothing more romantic than a primitive kind of moss.

The notion that Mars was so similar to the earth that it could be peopled by a race of men persisted until the 20th century. It was given a powerful impetus when, in 1877, the Italian astronomer Giovanni Schiaparelli reported the discovery of narrow, regular lines crossing the Martian deserts. He marked them on his map of the planet and called them *canali,* Italian for "canals."

Schiaparelli himself made no firm claim that these canals were artificially made, but the word "canals" stuck, and, fueled by music-hall jokes and science fiction, popular imagination easily

drew the inference that where there are canals there must be canal builders.

The American astronomer Percival Lowell also saw the *canali* and supported the theory that they were evidence of life. Intelligent Martians, he reasoned, had dug this vast system of canals to irrigate the deserts from the reservoirs of moisture held in the Martian icecap.

Lowell, who established an observatory in Flagstaff, Arizona, especially to study Mars, reasoned that the planet was undeniably short of water. Proceeding from the conviction that the canals were artificial, he came to this conclusion: "Mars is inhabited by beings of some kind or other: this is as certain as it is uncertain what those beings may be."

No Martians

Lowell's views fostered the fascinating picture of a world in which lived a highly cultured race, living in peace and toiling to conserve every drop of precious water.

But his theories were not accepted without opposition. It was pointed out that the polar icecaps must be very thin—not more than a few inches deep—and so could hardly be the source of a vast planetwide irrigation and pumping system. Moreover, other observers using telescopes as large and as powerful as Lowell's either failed to see the canals or surmised that they were natural formations.

Research carried out over the last 50 years has finally exploded the "Martian Man" theory. The "canals" are just geological cracks that imaginative astronomers have joined up into long, straight lines. Mars, in fact, is less hospitable to organic life than the Sahara Desert or the Antarctic continent.

Even so, the first man to visit Mars will see a fascinating new world, more closely resembling the earth than any other of the sun's planets. Mars does have an atmosphere, though not one that an earthman could breathe. The "air" is thinner than that at the summit of Mount Everest and is mostly carbon dioxide, with hardly a trace of oxygen. Mars is farther from the sun (141.5 million miles) than is the earth (93 million). So the sun would appear smaller on Mars.

The Martian day is half an hour longer than the earth's, but the Martian year is nearly twice as long as ours—23 earth months. The phenomenon of gravity would reduce an astronaut's weight by almost two-thirds. A complete circuit of the planet at its equator would cover more than 13,000 miles.

The explorer of Mars would land on an apparently lifeless surface, carpeted with brownish dust and pitted with craters. Mountains rise to perhaps three times the height of Everest.

If the spaceman landed near the equator at noon, he would find the temperature comfortably warm, about 71°F. At the poles he would find not a thick polar icecap but a thin layer of carbon dioxide, which in the spring turns to vapor. As the seasons change, cold winds rush in from the polar atmosphere to replace the rising currents in the equatorial zone.

It would be in the Martian spring that the first man from the earth would search for life. At this time, as the icecap retreats, observers on earth have seen expanding dark areas that appear to move toward Mars' equator.

It is possible that the explorer would radio back disappointing news. Once, it was thought that these dark areas were belts of vegetation, changing with the seasons. But a more likely explanation is that they are merely highland rocks that have been swept clean of dust by the strong winds.

Nevertheless, the spaceman on Mars could well find the hardy lichens that some scientists are confident grow there. These would be able to extract the water necessary for their existence from the rising vapor or even reach down to reserves of water below the parched surface. It is just possible that the "rocks" lying among the lichens may be, in fact, rounded, limbless ani-

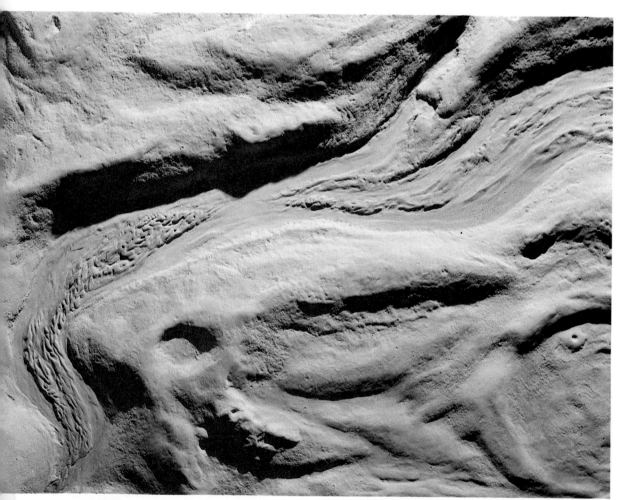

MARTIAN LANDSCAPE. *This dry channel on Mars is one of hundreds formed ages ago by water or volcanic flows. Picture is based on photographs taken by* Mariner 9 *spacecraft, which photographed the planet in detail in 1972.*

mals that can extract water from the iron oxide in the planet's red dust.

Jupiter—a mass of gas

It is safe to say that man will probably *never* land on Jupiter. For all the known facts indicate that there is nothing to land on. If Jupiter has a surface—and this is by no means certain—it is likely to be nothing more than a plastic slush of compressed hydrogen.

Jupiter, the biggest planet, is the most like the sun. It is composed primarily of gas and produces its own energy. The gases are hydrogen and helium, the basic building materials of the universe. Because of its great size, and therefore its immense gravity—it is bigger than all the other planets put together—Jupiter has retained its original hydrogen, which encircles it completely, making life impossible. Other

JUPITER'S RED SPOT. *A studio model shows the Red Spot (top) and its size relative to the earth.*

planets lost their atmospheric hydrogen when, heated by the sun's rays, it broke away from the gravitational pull.

But although hydrogen is the lightest substance known, Jupiter's gravity is so powerful, and the planet so remote (483 million miles) from the sun, that no external force has been able to tear away this shroud of gas.

When the sun, following the fixed pattern of the stars, expands and burns up the inner planets, the character of Jupiter may undergo a spectacular change. According to the latest predictions, the enlarged sun, with a greater gravitational pull, will then suck away Jupiter's

hydrogen, and the planet could then shrink to a dense globe of heavy elements. Life based on the element carbon would be possible on the surface, and Jupiter could become another earth.

But this is very much a glimpse into the distant future—about 7 billion years hence. In the meantime the giant planet will have to be explored from one of its moons. There are 12 of these, and the biggest, Callisto, is bigger than Mercury. From it Jupiter would appear as a massive disk covered with bands of swirling colored clouds.

In the unlikely event that a man could be equipped to penetrate Jupiter's atmosphere, he would first have to pass through the clouds that surround the planet. These are ammonia and methane, and as the explorer sank through them, he would see them condense into ammonia rain and snow. Before this rain could reach anywhere near the core of the planet, the ammonia would evaporate back into the clouds, giving off enormous discharges of electricity, which by comparison would make earthly lightning seem like sparks from a cigarette lighter.

Five thousand miles up, the pressure would be intense, and on the surface the astronaut would be 2½ times his normal weight. There would be no free oxygen to breathe at any stage of the journey. The clouds would have a temperature of −220°F (−140°C), colder than anything known on earth except some artificially produced liquid gases. The faint sun, so distant as to be just a flickering star, would rise and set every 9¾ hours.

For such a massive planet this rotation is astonishingly fast. The centrifugal force generated causes matter to be heaped up at the equator, so that the giant Jupiter is more flattened at the poles than is the earth.

Jupiter's journey around the sun takes 11 years. But this would have little meaning to a visitor, because, owing to its distance from the sun, there are no recognizable seasons.

The first astronaut to visit Jupiter would certainly be briefed to make a special study of the so-called Red Spot, which first appeared on astronomers' drawings as long ago as 1631. The Red Spot is so called because of its ruddy glow, which varies in intensity at different times, sometimes disappearing altogether. What exactly it is has long baffled observers. One guess is that it is a vast cloud of gas rising from Jupiter's "surface." Another is that it could be some form of solid matter floating in the planet's atmosphere. What is known beyond much doubt—because it has been carefully studied and measured through telescopes—is that the Red Spot is a very big spot indeed; it is estimated to be 30,000 miles by 7,000 miles.

The rings of Saturn

The most easily identifiable planet is Saturn. And, though faint, it can be seen without a telescope. What makes it so distinctive is its unique system of glowing rings girdling its equator. The rings are concentric, like those seen in a cross section of a felled tree.

It is a huge planet, 740 times the volume of the earth and only a little smaller than Jupiter. Like Jupiter, it is probably composed mainly of hydrogen and helium, with a core of the hydrogen in liquid or metallic form.

THE RINGS OF SATURN. *Partly covering the planet's northern hemisphere, the rings appear as a thin belt of light, casting shadow on the disk. This photograph was taken at Mount Wilson Observatory.*

THE SUPERSTAR THAT CAME IN WITH A BANG

The Crab Nebula in Taurus was named by the amateur astronomer Lord Rosse. Its light takes 4,000 years to reach the earth. The picture at far right shows how Lord Rosse actually saw the Crab through his telescope.

Saturn has four rings and 10 moons, one of them—Titan—almost as big as Mercury. From Titan the rings would be seen to be made of particles of ice-covered rock caught in the planet's gravitational pull. The rings have a total diameter of 170,000 miles but are less than 10 miles thick. It is possible that the rock particles are the remains of an 11th moon that was shattered by some cataclysm.

Landing on Saturn would present the same problems as a journey to Jupiter. And it would be even colder: -256°F (-160°C). Day on the planet would be a matter of just 10¼ hours, but a year on Saturn lasts about a generation in man's terms—29 earth years.

Uranus, no holiday planet

Everything about Uranus makes it a place to be avoided by a migratory race of spacemen in search of a new planet to populate.

The sun, because of its immense distance—1.7 billion miles—would appear only as a very bright star, and its rays, struggling through an atmosphere of ammonia and methane, would make no impact on the slushy surface of frozen hydrogen. The temperature is -310°F(-190°C). In these unpleasant conditions the astronaut would live, at most, only a single year of Uranian time; for a year on this planet is 84 times longer than one on earth.

Despite its vast distance from the sun, the fact that Uranus orbits in a plane at right angles to its axis gives it a variation of seasons, though the difference between them is rather more blurred than is the case on earth.

One of the most fascinating facts about Uranus is the manner of its discovery. A young amateur astronomer named William Herschel was busy at his homemade telescope one evening in 1781, carrying out what he called his "review of the heavens," when an unfamiliar luminous disk in the sky aroused his interest. When other astronomers worked out the orbit of the disk, it was realized that Herschel, without knowing it, had discovered a new planet—Uranus. He was rewarded by George III with a pension, gave up his job as a musician to devote his life to the study of the heavens, and became the first man to show how the stars are arranged to make up the Milky Way.

It's cold on Neptune

If a year on Uranus is an earthly lifetime, the journey around the sun that creates this yardstick of time takes the remote Neptune almost twice as long—more than 164 years. The planet spins on its axis once in 15¾ hours, and the sun is almost 2.8 billion miles away. So it is not surprising that the temperature is as low as -382°F (-230°C).

Mysteries of faraway Pluto

Very little is known about Pluto, the most remote of the sun's planets, 3.6 billion miles from the center of the solar system. Astronomer Clyde Tombaugh confirmed its long-conjectured existence at the Lowell Observatory in Arizona in 1930.

Its atmosphere, if any, cannot be analyzed with any accuracy; nor can any guesses yet be made about its surface temperature. But Pluto is almost certainly a cold, dead planet.

YANG WEI-TE, chief astronomer and the court official in charge of the calendar, prostrated himself before the Sung Emperor of K'hai Feng, the ancient capital of China, and said with modest pride: "I have observed the appearance of a guest star." But it was the end of that star, not the birth.

It was 1054, and the people of China were amazed as their heavenly "guest" grew as bright as Venus, its reddish-white color becoming visible even in daylight. Within a month it faded and was soon forgotten.

But what the Chinese observers had seen was the explosion of a massive star—called a supernova—in the constellation of Taurus. Today, the remains of that explosion are known as the Crab Nebula, a luminous shell of gas that is still expanding in all directions at 700 miles a second; it is a gigantic, white glowing cloud, whose violent borders are laced with red, feathery filaments.

It was rediscovered by astronomers after the invention of telescopes, and in 1758 the French astronomer Charles Messier, who drew up a catalog of star clusters and nebulae, called the faint patch of gas shining dimly in the heavens Messier 1.

Later, in the 19th century, the amateur astronomer Lord Rosse looked at the patch through his huge, homemade telescope at Birr Castle, near Athlone, in Ireland, and named it the Crab Nebula.

THE DREADED OMEN IN THE SKY

Comets meant fireworks in the heavens and disaster on earth

When they saw a comet in the sky, the ancients were stricken with dread. A ball of fire half the size of the moon, with a tail stretching across the sky, obviously boded ill for somebody. The skies were the home of capricious gods, and such a disturbance in the heavens must mean danger on earth.

Though the roles of comets as harbingers of doom are now discounted by most people, scientists are still intrigued by the phenomena. Like the planets, comets are in orbit around the sun. However, many of them fly so far away into space that they are visible from earth only once or twice in a century at most.

Although their composition is still a matter of conjecture, it is known that they are not solid like meteorites but are composed of small, icy particles and gases millions of times less dense than air.

Some scientists say that the head of a comet is like a "dirty snowball." Others retort that, if so, it is the sort of snowball thrown by a very nasty boy, because the particles are made of rock coated by ice.

However, it seems to be agreed that comets are flimsy objects that would not do much more than local damage in a collision with the earth.

The comet's long tail is believed to be composed of gas and dust, forced out of the head by radiation from the sun.

A comet does not give out light but reflects the light of the sun. It thus grows brighter as it approaches the sun and fades as it hurtles away into space.

Regular visitor

While there are some small comets that orbit the sun every two or three years, the only really bright one to be seen regularly is Halley's Comet. Watching it in 1682, Edmond Halley, Britain's Astronomer Royal, thought that this might be the same brilliant comet that had been recorded several times in the past. Checking with his records, he decided it did appear once every 76 years and was the same phenomenon that had preceded the Battle of Hastings.

Halley's discovery has proved a boon for historians, who can now often pinpoint the date of events described by the ancients as preceded by an ominous comet.

In 1973 high hopes were raised by the appearance of a hitherto unknown comet—named Kohoutek, after its discoverer, Czechoslovakian astronomer Lubos Kohoutek. It was expected to leave a fiery trail, and American astronauts orbiting the earth in the *Skylab* stood by to take spectacular photographs.

But everyone was disappointed. According to Russian scientists a coating of cosmic dust prevented Kohoutek's tail from forming for all the world to see.

HALLEY'S COMET IN 1910. *The most spectacular comet to orbit the sun regularly will next visit us in 1986.*

HALLEY'S COMET IN 1066. *King Harold of England sees the comet as an omen of doom.*

HEAVEN'S ARTILLERY

Meteorites and their constant threat to earth

As recently as October 30, 1937, the earth missed a major disaster. It happened when a minor planet, Hermes, weighing about 500,000 tons, passed within the orbit of the moon. A slight change in the angle of its course and it could have pierced the atmosphere and smashed into the earth with an explosion that could have obliterated an entire city.

The threat that the earth may be hit by a giant meteorite is with us constantly. Scientists estimate that about seven small meteorites bury themselves in the ground each year. Others hurtle into the sea.

Every day the earth is bombarded by rocks from space called meteoroids. Usually, they are small and disintegrate with the friction caused by their entry into the atmosphere. The result is the bright glow of their flight path, frequently seen streaking across the night sky.

When this happens, the meteoroid splits into meteors. If one of these meteors manages to penetrate all the way to the earth's surface, it is known as a meteorite.

Iron from the skies

Meteorites are composed either of stone or of an alloy of nickel and iron. Scientists believe they probably come from somewhere within our solar system and are the remains of comets and asteroids. (Asteroids are minor planets that have their orbits in the void between Jupiter and Mars.)

Twenty thousand years ago an iron-nickel meteorite, weighing an estimated 2 million tons, blasted a hole nearly a mile wide and 570 feet deep in the Arizona desert. Its destructive force was bigger than a 30 megaton H-bomb or 30 million tons of TNT.

On the morning of June 30, 1908, an enormous area of the Tunguska region of Siberia was totally devastated by what may have been a gigantic meteorite.

Shock waves from the impact were so violent that an engineer, who was 350 miles away on the Trans-Siberian railway, thought his engine had exploded.

Because of the site's remoteness, and the harsh terrain, it was not until 1927 that a scientific expedition was able to investigate the meteorite. The blast had flattened trees over

several miles, and effects were felt over 1,500 square miles, but no craters were seen. It is believed that the Siberian meteorite could have weighed 1 million tons. It broke up before it hit the earth at more than 90,000 miles an hour.

The biggest meteorite strike so far witnessed by man also occurred in Siberia, in 1947. Hundreds of people saw a brilliant ball of light as it sped southward across the sky, shedding a trail of sparks. Within four or five seconds it vanished, and then a giant pillar of brownish smoke, as if from a major explosion, rose 20 miles into the atmosphere.

On the slopes of the Sikhote-Alin Mountains, investigators found more than 100 holes, up to 75 feet across and 40 feet deep.

MILEWIDE CRATER. *A huge meteorite left this scar in the Arizona desert 20,000 years ago.*

The meteorite apparently broke up just before impact and strewed meteoric iron for miles. Scientists believe the meteorite weighed about 1,000 tons.

In parts of the Carolinas, 3,000 shallow pits surrounded by circular walls of earth are the result of meteorite strikes during the last 50,000 years. Everything in an area of 500 square miles was obliterated by the blasts and the heat they generated.

Fortunately, no populated area has yet been hit by a meteorite. If it were, the destruction and loss of life could be so great as to leave no one alive in the immediate vicinity to record the tragedy for posterity.

UNRAVELING THE TRUTH OF THE STARS

Long fight to put the earth in its place

The first man to suggest that our world was not the center of the universe, but traveled around the sun in company with the other planets, was a Greek, Aristarchus of Samos. He lived from 310 to 230 B.C., and his theory was so revolutionary that it was dismissed as absurd by most of the leading philosophers of his day.

Men had, of course, been gazing at the heavens since the beginning of time, and the accurate sitings of ancient monuments, such as the pyramids and Stonehenge, indicate that precise astronomical observations were being made by engineeers and priests at least 5,000 years ago.

But the ancients put forward no theory to explain the behavior of those celestial bodies whose movements they had plotted with such accuracy.

They simply assumed that the earth was the focal point of the universe and that the other bodies in space danced to the earth's tune. What the tune was and who composed it they regarded as an eternal mystery.

Aristarchus' methods of estimating the relative distances of the sun and the moon from the earth were essentially accurate—but his inability to make precise observations caused him to calculate the sun's distance from the earth at 1/19 of the true figure.

Rotating sphere

His calculations were based on those of the Greek mathematician, Pythagoras, who 100 years before had claimed that the earth was a sphere rotating on its own axis. This idea had been greeted with derision by learned contemporaries who believed the world was flat. So it is not surprising that Aristarchus, who was unable to prove his theory, was ignored.

No other theory of the universe was propounded until 400 years after Aristarchus' death, when Claudius Ptolemaeus, known as Ptolemy, came up with a much more acceptable explanation.

He deduced that the earth was the supreme body, lying stationary at the center of the universe. The sun and moon moved around it in circular orbits, along with the five visible planets—Mercury, Venus, Mars, Jupiter, and Saturn. This comforting notion instantly captured the approval of the authorities.

To explain the fact that the planets did not move in perfect circles, Ptolemy plotted a cumbersome system of smaller individual circles, or epicycles, which he believed they must follow while they were, at the same time, traveling around the central earth.

Although the Ptolemaic theory relied on many clumsy explanations, it formed the unquestioned basis of astronomy for 1,700 years —until Copernicus came to the fore in the 16th century.

A mere planet

Nicolaus Copernicus, born in Poland in 1473, was a devout churchman fascinated by astronomy. By the time he was 40, and after a lifetime's study of the heavens, he was convinced that Ptolemy's theory was wrong.

He devised a completely new theory in which the earth was a mere planet moving around the sun. But even though Copernicus had broken away from the central-earth dogma, one basic truth eluded him: Planets move in ellipses, not circles.

And he had another major problem. As a church canon he knew that his superiors would resist the idea of the earth losing its central role. Even a rumor of the new theory prompted the religious reformer Martin Luther to denounce Copernicus as a fool who wanted to turn the science of astronomy upside down.

Like the hapless Aristarchus, Copernicus had no telescope or any other mechanical means of proving his theories to skeptics. He was therefore reluctant to publish his great book of astronomical theories, *Concerning the Revolutions of the Celestial Bodies*.

When friends finally persuaded him to have the book printed in 1542, his misgivings proved justified. Without his knowledge the publisher had added a preface to the 400 pages of text, charts, and diagrams. This unauthorized introduction stressed that the book's theories were merely aids to calculations and need not be taken literally.

Happily, it is unlikely that Copernicus ever saw the book in print, for by the time a copy reached him in May 1543 he was dying.

MASTER ASTRONOMER. *Tycho Brahe sits alongside his quadrant, in effect a huge brass protractor, while at far right his student Johannes Kepler observes the stars. Two aides keep time and record findings.*

Strangely, the Catholic Church did not realize the implications of Copernicus' work until 73 years after his death, when the heretical astronomer Galileo unwittingly drew attention to it. The scandalized Vatican then placed it on its index of prohibited books—and there it remained until 1822.

The genius who was wrong

The church had influential backing for its views from the remarkable Danish nobleman Tycho Brahe, who was born in 1546. He could never accept the idea that the earth moved around the sun and intended his work specifically to prove the Ptolemaic theory correct. Despite this, he became the greatest observational astronomer since Aristarchus.

When Brahe was 30, the King of Denmark made him landlord of the island of Ven, in the Baltic, and provided him with enough money to build a house and observatory there.

From this lonely base, and using only a giant quadrant, Brahe made a 20-year study of the heavens and produced a magnificent and comprehensive star catalog, including tables that gave thousands of accurate "fixes" on the changing positions of the planets against their background of stars.

Brahe allowed nothing to interfere with his studies—particularly shortage of cash. To ensure that islanders paid their rents, he had a prison built into the observatory, and anyone threatening his supply of funds by defaulting on payment was promptly locked up.

Ven became a famous scientific center, and eminent visitors included James VI of Scotland, later James I of England. But the clamor of protest from irate islanders, constantly threatened with prison, eventually prompted the Danish King to withdraw his support.

An inexorable fate

Brahe went to live in Prague, where he engaged as his assistant the astronomical genius Johannes Kepler. In later years Kepler was to announce: "Tycho and I were joined by inexorable fate."

When Kepler studied the volumes of tables drawn up by Brahe, he found that the island astronomer had paid particular and painstaking attention to the movements of Mars. Kepler quickly realized that the observations demolished the long-cherished notion that Mars traveled in a circular orbit.

It was perhaps providential that Brahe died in 1601 while Kepler was still toiling with his figures regarding Mars—checking each complicated calculation as many as 40 times to ensure absolute accuracy. He spent five years at the task before he was confident that his earlier suspicions were correct: Mars, earth, and all the other known planets had elliptical paths—and, in defiance of Brahe's strongly held belief, they traveled around the sun.

Kepler, described by Albert Einstein as "an incomparable man," was then able to draw up his laws of planetary motion, upon which calculations are based to this day.

Toward the end of his life Kepler was put under surveillance as a suspected heretic, and people even spat at him in the streets. But when he died in 1630, the tide of science was running his way, despite opposition by the church.

Among Kepler's admirers was one of the most colorful characters in the history of astronomy—Galileo Galilei—the first serious astronomer to use a telescope and the last to be persecuted for claiming that the earth moved around the sun.

Galileo made his own telescope while he was teaching mathematics at the University of Padua in Italy. He used it to good effect, discovering, among other things, the moon's craters, some of Jupiter's satellites, sunspots, and the stars of the Milky Way.

Everything he saw convinced him that Aristarchus, Copernicus, and Kepler were right in

(*continued on page 33*)

THE STARGAZERS' TOOLS

From the pyramids to radio astronomy

About 5,000 years ago the Egyptians built what is still the world's biggest clock. It was designed to register time not only in hours but in days, seasons, and even centuries.

It is the Great Pyramid of Cheops, which was built in the 27th century B.C., and is the largest in the group of pyramids at Gizah on the banks of the Nile. These pyramids are the only surviving example of the Seven Wonders of the Ancient World. The Great Pyramid is probably the world's oldest astronomical observatory and still attracts scientific and occult speculation.

In 1853 the French physicist Jean Baptiste Biot visited Gizah and decided that the pyramid was a huge sundial. But it recorded more than just the time of the day, for the Egyptians had built it on such a scale, at such a latitude, and at such a precise angle that it could also indicate the precise day of the year.

On the ground adjoining the northern and southern faces, wide, level pavements, or "shadow floors," had been constructed. In the winter the pyramid would cast its shadow on the pavement to the north, and in the summer the highly polished southern face would reflect a triangle of sunlight onto the pavement to the south.

Accurate forecasts

The paving blocks had been cut in widths similar to the gradations by which each noon-day shadow or reflection succeeded its predecessor. Thus the days could be measured and such seasonal pointers as the equinoxes and solstices accurately forecast.

The equinoxes are the two times each year when the sun crosses the Equator, while the solstices are the two days when it is farthest from the Equator. (*continued on page 32*)

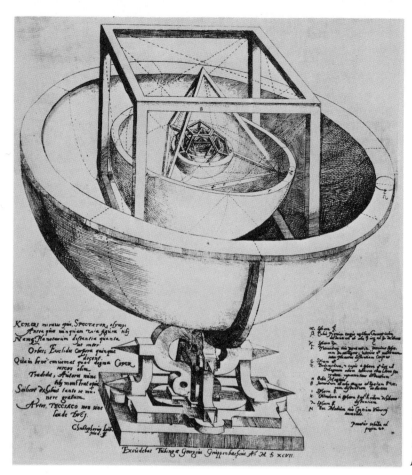

MODEL UNIVERSE. *Johannes Kepler worked out in miniature the spacing of the planets.*

TOMBS THAT TELL THE TIME. *As well as being burial chambers for the Pharaohs, the pyramids at Gizah were also designed as observatories—and giant calendars.*

THE FIRST RADIO TELESCOPE. *Karl Jansky built his telescope on a farm in New Jersey in 1931. He called the strange array of aerials and old car wheels his merry-go-round.*

The 19th-century British astronomer Richard A. Proctor put forward the theory that the Great Pyramid would have made an almost perfect observatory.

The descending passage that leads down to a pit in the heart of the pyramid was set at an angle of 26° 17′, the exact alignment to aim it at the Pole Star.

The Egyptians' Pole Star was not the present one. Over the centuries the gravitational pull of the sun and moon on the imperfect sphere of the earth moves the earth's axis very slightly. This means that the Pole Star changes every few thousand years. When the pyramid was built, the Pole Star was Thuban in the constellation of the Dragon. Today it is Polaris in the constellation of Ursa Minor.

But as the earth has moved, so the Great Pyramid has moved with it and aligned itself on the new Pole Star.

Proctor also pointed out that the pyramid's central grand gallery would have provided an ideal platform from which the priests of ancient Egypt could have observed and recorded the movement of stars and planets. By stationing observers at different levels in the gallery, an astronomer could track the movements of the stars, using the entrance as a guideline.

The enigma of Stonehenge

It is now thought that the building of Stonehenge—the great circle of giant stone slabs on Salisbury Plain in the English county of Wiltshire—was begun around 1900 B.C., about 800 years after construction of the Great Pyramid.

Until recently, Stonehenge was popularly believed to have been built by the Druids as a sun-worshiping temple and a site for human sacrifice. But modern archeology has deduced that the mysterious structure predates the Druids by more than 1,000 years and was in fact built in several stages over a period of 300 years.

The ditch and two banks that circle the complex are thought to have been built first—by Neolithic, or new stone age, people who arrived in Britain about 3000 B.C.

suggesting that the earth moved around the sun. But in 1616 Galileo was ordered by the church in Rome to stop supporting what had become known as the Copernican system.

Galileo publicly recanted and at once began work on a book called *Dialogue of the Two Chief World Systems*, in which the whole question was fairly discussed from the two opposing points of view. Before having the book published, however, he took the sensible precaution of getting clearance from Rome.

Yet, when the book appeared, the church summoned him to answer a charge of heresy, even though their own censors had approved the work. At his trial he was ordered to make a further public recantation. Kneeling, he read a statement pledging that he was ready to "curse, abjure, and detest" the theory that the earth moved around the sun. The alternative was undoubtedly the stake.

As a further precaution, Galileo was ordered to be cut off from the world in his villa at Arcetri. Visitors were forbidden, and the only people he was allowed to see were those who looked after his personal needs. To add to his troubles, the rebellious astronomer became totally blind in the later years of his life.

When Galileo died in 1642, the Pope forbade the erection of a monument over his tomb. But within 50 years the central-earth theory completely crumbled.

The picture widens

The Royal Observatory at Greenwich (England) was founded in 1675 on the orders of Charles II, who was eager to have a new catalog of stars compiled for ships' navigators. The building, designed by Sir Christopher Wren, was an immense success, but unfortunately the man chosen as official astronomer, the Rev. John Flamsteed, though a skilled observer and an almost obsessive perfectionist, was painfully slow at calculation.

He had only one assistant, who was thoroughly unreliable, and after 29 years of work the two of them had still not finished the catalog. Nevertheless, 400 copies were published in the incomplete form against Flamsteed's wishes. He got hold of 300 of them and publicly burned them in protest.

When he died in 1719, the catalog was still not ready—but by then the whole scheme was obsolete, for better navigational techniques had been perfected.

In 1781 an amateur astronomer, the young German-born William Herschel, made a most remarkable discovery while using his telescope at his English home. He spotted a small red disk

About 150 years later the Beaker people, a highly developed late stone age-early bronze age race, are credited with hauling and erecting the estimated 82 original bluestones, monoliths each weighing up to 5 tons, which they probably brought by sledge roller and barge from the Prescelly Mountains in southern Wales. The inner horseshoe of five trilithons—two uprights with a crossbar—in sarsen sandstone, was erected some 50 years later, probably by the bronze age Wessex people.

Then followed construction of the inner bluestone circle and horseshoe, with work ending about 1600 B.C.

In 1963 the American astronomer Prof. Gerald Hawkins claimed that he had finally decoded the mysteries of Stonehenge and that it could be described as a sort of prehistoric computer, its function being to make intricate calculations of sunrises and sunsets, the movements of the moon, and the eclipses of both sun and moon. Hawkins fed details of the structure's stone alignments into a computer and

SHADOWS AT STONEHENGE. *Some experts believe the ancients built it to plot the movements of the sun and moon.*

found that many related to the positioning of the sun and moon.

He suggested that by moving a marker stone around an outer circle of holes once a year, priests or astrologers could calculate suitable in the sky and sent a report, entitled *An Account of a Comet*, to the Royal Society.

Experts worked out the object's orbit and decided that Herschel had indeed found something unusual, but it was more unusual than a comet.

He had discovered the first new planet since Grecian times—a monster that took 84 years to circle the sun. It was named Uranus, and it earned Herschel a knighthood.

The sidereal day

When in 1931 a young radio engineer named Karl Jansky pieced together what he called his merry-go-round—a strange array of aerials attached to old car wheels—the result was the first radio telescope.

He built his telescope to investigate static—the hissing and crackling that plagues long-distance radio communications. He picked up plenty of static, but there was also a steady hiss that reached its peak exactly four minutes earlier each day. This matched the period of the earth's rotation in respect to the stars, as opposed to the sun—23 hours 56 minutes. Astronomers call this the sidereal day.

Jansky rightly concluded that he was picking up signals from the Milky Way.

An amateur astronomer, the American Grote Reber, built a steerable dish-shaped aerial 30 feet in diameter in the garden of his Illinois home.

He amplified and recorded the radio signals he received to produce the first crude "radio map" of the sky.

Reber focused radio signals by altering the angle of his receiver dish. The shape and size of a radio source were accurately assessed by interpreting its transmissions from various angles. Reber's studies revealed that the shapes of some sources were quite different from the way they appeared when viewed through a conventional optical telescope.

The 3,000-ton saucer

Among the scientists impressed by Reber's studies was an Englishman named Bernard Lovell.

He set up two trailers full of radar equipment in a field in Cheshire, England, to track meteors. Lovell's apparatus gradually developed into the great radio-astronomy observatory of Jodrell Bank. The observatory contains a giant saucer-shaped steerable radio telescope that weighs 3,000 tons and pirouettes on a circular railway track.

SEARCHING FOR GALAXIES. *The Earl of Rosse's telescope first enabled him to observe other galaxies in 1845.*

times for crop planting, predict weather cycles, or practice divination.

In 1845 the world's largest telescope was built in Ireland by an amateur astronomer, the third Earl of Rosse. It had a 72-inch metal mirror and was suspended between two stone walls. It was this telescope that made man realize that there are other galaxies beyond his own, for Lord Rosse discovered what appeared at first to be fiery Catherine wheels far out in space.

There are still no telescopes powerful enough to show these "spiral nebulae" in detail. Even the 200-inch Hale complex at the Mount Palomar Observatory in California is not up to the job. An extra-large reflecting telescope is sited on Mount Semirodriki, in Russia's northern Caucasus. The telescope's power comes from a unique 232.6-inch diameter mirror, and it collects 1½ times more light than the one at Mount Palomar.

The world's largest steerable radio telescope is at the Max Planck Institute for Radio Astronomy in Bonn, West Germany. Its dish has a massive 328-foot diameter. Radio waves from space are reflected to a receiver at the focus of the dish. The signal is then amplified and recorded.

WHEN A STAR DIES

Fifty tons in a matchbox

Near the brilliant Dog Star Sirius lies a faint dot of light, a much smaller star known as the Pup. Although it is smaller, the material at its center is so dense that one matchboxful would weigh 50 tons.

The Pup, or Sirius B, was first spotted through a telescope by Alvan Clark, an American astronomer, in 1862, although 30 years earlier the Prussian astronomer Friedrich Wilhelm Bessel had noticed deviations in the orbit of Sirius that led him to believe they were caused by another nearby star.

The two stars revolve once in 50 years around a common center of gravity. While the Pup has as much mass as the sun—enough to make Sirius wobble in its orbit—its diameter is only 24,000 miles, compared with 865,370 miles for the sun, so that the same mass is crammed into 1/27,000 of the sun's volume.

Abnormally small

In other words, the Pup is 27,000 times denser than the sun. Its surface temperature is 3,632°F hotter than the sun, and each square inch of the surface radiates 3¾ times more heat and energy than the sun, yet the Pup's luminosity is only 1/125 of that of the sun. It was these facts that first led astronomers to realize that the Pup is abnormally small.

The Pup was the first recorded of a class of stars now known as white dwarfs, though many more stars of this type have since been identified. Among the densest listed in the Astrographic Catalog is a star that is known as +70 8247. It is about half the size of the earth, but every cubic inch of it weighs 620 tons.

Astronomers believe that these exceptionally dense stars are in the final stages of evolution and are nearing extinction.

Birth of a star

Stars are thought to begin life by the condensation of clouds of gas and dust that shrink under the force of their own gravity as their cores heat up. Nuclear reactions begin, and the hydrogen of which they are largely composed is converted into helium, releasing energy and causing the stars to shine brilliantly in the heavens, just as the sun does.

The red giant stage

When the hydrogen supply runs low, further nuclear reactions begin, and the star swells, getting hotter and denser at the core and cooler at the surface. At this stage it is known as a red giant.

When all the nuclear reserves are exhausted, if a star is big enough, it may explode as a supernova. A smaller star may collapse under the force of gravity, and thereby become a white dwarf.

A white dwarf, therefore, is a dying star, with no means of reheating and no future but extinction. The next stage is for it to collapse still further and condense into a neutron star, shrinking so much that it forms a dense mass that would weigh about 20 billion tons per cubic inch.

OUR OWN SUN—A YELLOW DWARF

THE SUN is classified as a yellow-dwarf star, midway between the largest and the smallest stars and between the hottest blue-whites and the coolest red stars. Rigel, for example, is 60,000 times more luminous. The cool Antares, a red supergiant, is 27 million times bigger.

The nuclear reaction that keeps the sun shining involves a mass loss of about 4 million tons a second, but the volume of the sun is so enormous that it is not expected to expand into a red giant for at least another 8 billion years.

When this happens, the sun will cool but swell to dozens of times its present size, and if the earth is not actually swallowed up, life as it is now will not be able to survive. However, even if the earth's inhabitants of that time manage to protect themselves from the heat in some way, their descendants will have to cope with the extreme cold that will ensue when the sun reaches what is known as the white dwarf stage.

SIGNALS FROM OUTER SPACE

Stars that "broadcast" to the universe

The radio signal from outer space was weak, but it was being broadcast at precise intervals of 1.33730113 seconds. Prof. Anthony Hewish, who headed the group of Cambridge University astronomers who first heard it in 1967, said the signals were "as regularly spaced as a broadcast time signal."

Graduate student Jocelyn Bell had discovered the signals by accident while working with radio telescope equipment designed to record weak signals.

Despite their training and professional caution, the astronomers could hardly restrain their excitement. Could it be that some unknown civilization far out in space was trying to contact the earth? Again and again, they pinpointed the signals coming from the same spot in the sky, showing they came from outside the solar system.

But as the signals continued without variation for months on end, it was apparent that they had found a new kind of star—one that emitted regular but natural bursts of radio energy.

Visible pulsar

Since then, many more of these stars, now called pulsars, have been detected by radio telescopes, but so far only one has been tracked down as a visible star. Astronomers at the Steward Observatory in Arizona discovered it in 1969. Faintly flashing in time with its radio signals, it lies in the Crab Nebula, 4,000 light-years away.

An early theory was that a pulsar might be a rapidly vibrating white-dwarf star, a sun that had used up most of its energy and collapsed. But though they are small, even white dwarfs are not thought small enough to vibrate at sufficient speed to emit the signals.

Enormous density

Radio astronomers estimate that if a pulsar were as big as our sun—865,370 miles in diameter—the radio signal from its farthest point would take longer to reach us than one from its nearest point.

The result would be a continuous radio rumble, not a regular intermittent signal. Because the pulses are clear and precise—often coming over at a rate of 30 a second—the experts believe that pulsars must be quite small and that their atomic components have compressed to make their density enormous.

Pulsars are now believed to be the remnants of massive stars that have collapsed under the weight of their own gravity and imploded—that is, collapsed violently inward. They are so dense that on earth a single cubic inch of pulsar material would weigh 10 billion tons.

The rate at which a pulsar sends its signals depends on its rotation in space. A pulsar has a powerful magnetic field, and the magnetic pole may not coincide with the pole of rotation. As the star spins around, the earth comes regularly into the "emission beam," rather as a ship out at sea comes regularly into the rotating beam of a lighthouse.

But most pulsar signals appear to be slowing almost imperceptibly, and scientists expect that eventually they will go "off the air" and become untrackable.

BRIGHTER THAN A MYRIAD SUNS

Racing to the edge of the universe—and beyond?

Of all the objects in the sky, probably the most puzzling are the quasars. They were identified as recently as 1963, and as yet we have no real idea of their true nature. They are believed to be the brightest and the remotest objects known to man. But we cannot yet be sure that there has not been some major mistake in interpreting the evidence.

Astronomers are accustomed to surprises. But the discovery of quasars was wholly unexpected by scientists and aroused total astonishment. The Milky Way numbers 100 billion stars, many of them brighter than the sun. Yet one quasar is 200 times as bright as the entire Milky Way galaxy.

The first quasar was spotted through a telescope at Mount Palomar in California by the Dutch astronomer, Maarten Schmidt.

He was trying to find a Milky Way star, thought to be the source of unusual radio signals. At the charted spot in the sky he saw a point of light, but it was not a star. The object was so far away that its distance was estimated at 1 billion light-years. (A light-year, the distance traveled by light in a single year, is about 6 trillion miles.)

Moreover, the object showed what scientists call a red shift on the color spectrum. This was particularly significant, because it meant that it was rushing away from the earth through space.

When a train approaches a station, its noise rises in pitch, but as it recedes into the distance, the note falls. This is called the Doppler effect after the Austrian scientist who investigated it. A similar effect can be observed in stars, although in this case it is produced from light and not from sound.

Receding into space

If the light from a heavenly body is directed through a prism and broken up into a color spectrum, much information can be discovered about the star. If it is approaching the earth, the light waves will become shorter—a "blue shift." If the star is receding from the earth, the light waves will become longer—a "red shift"—a phenomenon comparable to the falling note that tells a listener that the train has passed.

The spectrum of Maarten Schmidt's quasar had a most pronounced red shift. The logical conclusion, therefore, was that this object was not only incomparably brighter than anything observed hitherto and the most distant body man had seen in the sky but it was also hurtling even farther outward into space at enormous speed.

The newly found object was named a quasi-stellar radio source, now shortened to quasar. Since 1963 about 200 quasars have been found—the last one by an international team of scientists working in Arizona in 1974.

This may be the most distant object known to man. It was estimated to be traveling away into outer space at more than 177,000 miles a second—faster than any previously observed quasar.

Some scientists think that quasars are formed by large numbers of stars exploding in quick succession.

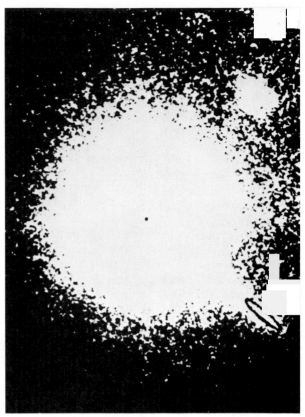

QUASAR 3C273. *The first quasar was found in 1963 by Maarten Schmidt, who was investigating radio signals from what he at first believed to be a star.*

Chain of exploding stars

To astronomers exploding stars are nothing new, for about once a century this type of explosion takes place in the Milky Way, resulting in a supernova, or exploding star that is suddenly much brighter than an ordinary one.

The theory is that quasars may be a chain reaction of supernovas, one exploding star causing another to go off like artillery shells in a blazing warehouse.

But this is by no means the only theory. It has even been suggested that the colossal release of energy by the quasars is caused by the collision of matter and antimatter, which is composed of the counterparts of ordinary matter—antiprotons instead of protons, for example.

But if we assume that the red shifts are true Doppler effects, caused by the hurtling of quasars into the outer fringes of space, we then face the question of whether space is infinite or not. Either concept is difficult for the human mind to grasp. We can imagine neither a boundary to our universe nor space going on forever.

Traveling faster than light

The farther away a quasar is, the faster it seems to be traveling. If this acceleration continues, there should eventually come a point where the quasar would be traveling faster than light.

In this case, its light and radio waves would never reach us, and it would pass beyond the boundary of the observable universe. The distance involved would be more than 10 billion light-years.

It may be that all the material in the universe was created at one particular moment (the "Big Bang" theory) and that the expansion which this initiated, and which we are witnessing in the quasars, will continue indefinitely. In this case the universe has a limited future before all galaxies and stars die away.

An alternative is the concept of the cyclic universe. According to this theory the outward rush of the quasars will reach a limit and will then be reversed. In the far distant future (perhaps 60 billion years from now) the stars will coalesce again into a single point.

In which case the universe will be reborn, and a new expansion will begin.

MYSTERY OF THE BLACK HOLES

Could they be universes running in reverse?

Imagine a star made of matter so dense that enough to go into a matchbox would weigh 10 billion tons. If a rocket is to escape from earth's gravity, it must reach a speed of about 25,000 miles per hour. But the gravity of this star would be so enormous that there would be no escaping from it even at 670,615,600 miles per hour—the speed of light. Indeed, light itself would not be able to escape, making the star forever invisible.

Such stars are believed to exist in the universe. Because light cannot leave them, no one has ever seen one, but astronomers have good reasons to suppose they are there. They are called black holes.

One of the first clues to their existence came from the odd behavior of a star called Epsilon Aurigae, a giant 60,000 times as bright as the sun. Once every 27 years this star fades to less than half its usual brilliance.

An invisible partner

Scientists know that Epsilon Aurigae has a partner that swings with it around a common center of gravity. The fading was presumably caused by the partner getting in the way of the view from earth. But why, in that case, does the partner emit neither light rays nor radio waves like other stars?

The answer seems to be that the partner is a black hole—invisible, small, but enormously heavy.

Scientists are able to explain how a black hole could be created. The heat of stars like the sun comes from continuous nuclear fusion—the process that goes on in the hydrogen bomb. After billions of years the store of nuclear fuel in the star begins to be exhausted. Then the star cools down and eventually implodes—that is, it collapses inward in a matter of seconds, with terrible violence.

A white dwarf

The sun will do this in about 8 billion years. It will end up as a small cool object called a white dwarf. But the forces of gravity in stars 1½ times the size of the sun are much stronger. When they implode, they squeeze smaller than white dwarfs, until the center becomes so hot that it explodes outward. The exceptionally bright mass that results is known as a supernova.

When this happens, a tiny part of the star remains at the center, fantastically compressed by gravity. This is known as a neutron star.

But there are much larger stars, some as much as 50 times the size of the sun. When one of these collapses, it will contract even smaller than the neutron star. If it is only two-thirds the size of a neutron star, the gravitational pull would be so strong that nothing could withstand it.

Not even light could escape, and even if the star was white-hot, absolutely nothing could be seen. For this reason the phenomenon is called a black hole.

Compared with the vastness of other objects

in the universe, black holes are tiny. For example, a collapsed star 10 times bigger than the sun would be compressed into a black hole less than 40 miles across.

Because they emit neither light nor radio waves, astronomers can only speculate about their presence by the behavior of neighbors under their influence.

Having so enormous a force of gravity, black holes suck into themselves any matter that comes into their part of the heavens. One theory even has it that they will eventually suck up everything in the entire universe.

Meanwhile, they are busy absorbing some of their neighbors. One supergiant star in the Cygnus constellation, called HDE 226868, which is believed to be paired with a black hole, seems to be losing clouds of swirling gas into its invisible neighbor.

Once it gets close to the black hole, the gas becomes invisible, entering what is called the "event horizon." There is a limit to the pull even of black-hole gravity, and there must come a point where light can neither escape nor be pulled back. On this event horizon, light would stand still or move very slowly.

An immortal spaceman

This raises the fascinating possibility that light images on the event horizon would go on being seen more or less forever. For instance, if an astronaut headed for a black hole, he might still be seen going through the event horizon for millions of years afterward.

However, the prospects of any man landing on a black hole are small indeed. Closing in on the event horizon, those parts of his spacecraft or his body nearer to the black hole would receive more pull from the gravity. The results would be to stretch him out into a streak miles long, while the compression would reduce his volume.

If the spaceman were able to observe a clock far away from the black hole, the hands would appear to move faster as he approached the event horizon, until he was unable to see them. As he went through the event horizon the hands would reverse and start to slow down; he would appear to be going backward in time, though the time as measured by a watch on his wrist would not change.

Once through the event horizon the spaceman would be unable to escape. In fact, the harder he tried to avoid his fate, the faster he would meet it, because the energy expended in the attempt would produce increased mass and hence increased gravitational attraction.

As the spaceman approached closer to the black hole, he and his spacecraft would be torn to shreds by the tremendous force of gravity long before the touchdown. In a small black hole, say one of twice the sun's mass, it would take only 20 millionths of a second for him to fall to the center. In fact, for the experience to have any noticeable duration, the black hole would have to be very large. Even in a black hole a million times the size of the sun, the falling process would take a maximum of only 10 seconds.

Backward through another universe

One mind-boggling theory is that if a man ever did enter a black hole and avoid destruction, he might find himself in another universe, traveling backward in time. This idea is based on the way in which a black hole appears to behave like the rest of the universe, only in reverse. For while the universe is continually exploding outward, a black hole is forever imploding, or turning in on itself.

And while science can explain matter compressed into an astonishingly dense pinprick, it cannot account for matter disappearing absolutely. Thus, as the universe represents a process of seemingly endless outward expansion, so the black hole represents inward expansion without a foreseeable limit.

It has been suggested that a black hole may exist in our own galaxy of stars; and some scientists even think that there may be a little one in the middle of the sun and that this is affecting the sun's production of certain kinds of radiation.

According to some theories, man could use a black hole to produce energy for his own purposes by directing matter toward it and storing the gravitational energy sent out by the black hole as it sucks the matter in. It would thus be used as a sort of cosmic garbage can, giving out energy for any unwanted rubbish thrown in.

But other scientists dispute the very existence of black holes.

Only one thing is certain. Black holes are one of the most intriguing concepts to come to man's attention during this century. And they are going to occupy the thoughts of astronomers for years to come.

The miraculous mechanism that is ourselves

The astonishing human body

•

THE MOST AMAZING MACHINE

All in a waterproof case

Engineers have never devised a machine to equal nature's supreme achievement: the human body. Athletes can sprint at almost 25 miles per hour, throw a ball at more than 100 miles per hour, high jump over seven feet. But even our everyday activities are powered by a system that, in its complexity and efficiency, would make the most sophisticated robot seem inadequate.

Take the circulatory system. Every minute of our lives the heart pumps 10 pints of blood—30 pints during brisk exercise—through about 60,000 miles of arteries, veins, and capillaries. An adult body contains between 8 and 10 pints of blood: The average for a man is about 10 pints, containing 25 trillion red cells (to carry oxygen) and 25 billion white cells (to fight disease). Some white cells have a life cycle of only 12 hours; red cells have a life of about 120 days.

The capillaries—tiny tubes servicing the bloodstream—have a total surface area that would cover a 1½-acre field. Not all are opened at once; otherwise all the blood in the body would drain into them within seconds, like floodwater into a swamp. Instead, local chemical changes and nerves to the muscular portion of microscopic blood vessels operate to maintain a cycle of opening and closing every few minutes.

One part of the body that needs blood all the time is the lungs. Their capillaries continuously take up oxygen from the tiny air sacs of the lungs, while releasing excess carbon dioxide.

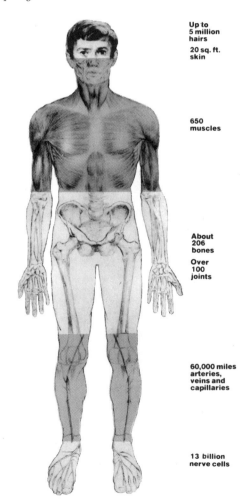

Up to
5 million
hairs

20 sq. ft.
skin

650
muscles

About
206
bones

Over
100
joints

60,000 miles
arteries,
veins and
capillaries

13 billion
nerve cells

During an average lifetime we breathe more than 500 million times.

Blood, it is said, is thicker than water. But, in fact, almost two-thirds of the body *is* water—10 gallons of it, or 60 percent of the average person's weight.

Fat people often like to think that a lot of their weight is due to water retention, but actually, fatty tissue is only 10 percent water.

A human being also contains an odd assortment of other substances: enough fat for seven cakes of soap, enough lime to whitewash a small shed, the carbon equivalent of a 28-pound bag of coke, enough phosphorus to make 2,200 matches, and as much iron as in a one-inch nail. There is also a spoonful or so of sulfur and an ounce of various metals—apart from iron.

A strange and motley collection. Yet the body cannot function efficiently unless it is all there. If, for instance, a person's diet is deficient in iodine, his thyroid gland enlarges, causing the dramatic swelling in the neck called goiter. In fact, all but one of the factors necessary to health—the oxygen we breathe—have to come from our food. This is why doctors say that we should have a varied diet throughout life.

A baby is born with 305 bones, but some of these fuse together later until there are about 206 (though the number can vary), operated by 650 muscles and more than 100 joints. The tendons anchoring muscle to bone are strong enough to stand a stress of eight tons per square inch, and the thigh bones take a strain of half a ton per square inch while walking.

All this wonderful complex of nature's machinery is encased in a flexible, waterproof covering—the skin. The average man has 20 square feet of it, which wears away and is replaced every few weeks. Set in the skin are up to 5 million hairs; each lasts about three years.

Nine thousand taste buds come to our aid in choosing what we like, aided by millions of nerve cells; 4 million "receptors" in the skin enable us to feel, distinguish hot from cold, and experience pain or comfort.

To achieve all this and to move itself about, the human body needs fuel. In the course of a lifetime the average person consumes 50 tons of food and at least 11,000 gallons of liquid. According to one estimate, if that person is a town dweller, he or she walks about 7,000 miles; a rural resident walks almost 28,000 miles.

CUT DOWN TO SIZE

| Old Stone Age man 5 ft 9 in. | New Stone Age man 5 ft 6 in. | Bronze Age man 5 ft 8 in. | Anglo-Saxons 5 ft 7 in. | Medieval Europeans 5 ft 6 in. | Modern man 5 ft 8 in. |

CONTRARY to popular belief, modern man is shorter than his earliest ancestors. Skeletal studies show that, with slight variations, over the ages we have lost an inch compared with the average five feet nine inches of old stone age man (400,000 to 8000 B.C.). The "midget ancestors" myth probably stems from the way in which medieval suits of armor are displayed. On the wearer's body the plates were more widely separated and so were "taller."

CONTROL ROOM

The brain and its workings

The world's most complex computer is composed of just three pounds of gray-white matter shaped rather like an over-sized shelled walnut. This is the human brain, whose billions of components control everything we do every moment of our lives; in a split second it has the ability to use literally millions of interconnections.

Each working part is a nerve cell known as a neuron, the primary unit of the brain's still unplumbed abilities. The brain's power seems to come from the interaction of the neurons, rather than from the neurons themselves. The neurons both receive electrochemical impulses and generate the power to transmit signals racing along the nervous system. These impulses move from one nerve to another, dispatching messages through the brain.

The body's central nervous system, the control room for thought and action, includes not only the brain but also the spinal cord, which is the link between instructions from the brain and every sense we have.

The brain's most obvious external features are two soft hemispheres that make up the cerebrum. Each hemisphere controls movement and registers sensations from the opposite side of the body.

In most people the left hemisphere is dominant, with the result that the majority of us are right-handed. In those who are left-handed, the right hemisphere of the brain is dominant. For this reason it is unwise to force a left-handed child to be right-handed. Even in ambidextrous people, one hand is usually dominant.

White matter beneath the cortex, the gray covering of the brain, makes up the hemispheres that are bridged by several tissue connections, the largest of which is called the *corpus callosum.* Most of the crossover of information between the hemispheres occurs through the corpus callosum; just how the information is transmitted is still under investigation.

Most information is stored subconsciously, so it is true to say that people are not aware of all that they know. However, this varies from one individual to another.

Recent research in the United States and Britain demonstrates clearly that each hemisphere is associated with different functions. The left, or dominant, hemisphere is concerned primarily with specific symbols, such as words and numbers, and therefore is especially important in speech, reading, writing, and calculations. The right hemisphere is concerned more with recognizing patterns. Happily, the exchange of data between the hemispheres via the connecting tissues makes it possible, in a sense, for the left hand to know what the right hand is doing.

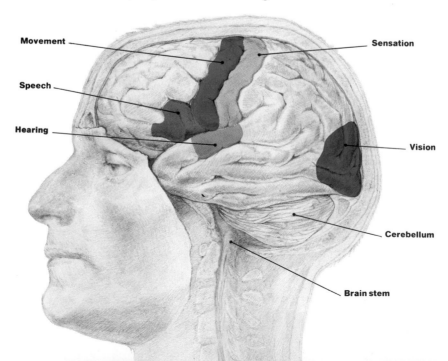

Beneath the cerebral hemispheres lies the cerebellum, the vital link between the brain and the spinal cord, which coordinates the actions of muscles and determines how fast they will work. The cerebellum also has two hemispheres of its own. It is associated with balance and muscular coordination.

Buried under these is the brain stem, which controls the heart, the lungs, and the digestive system. This portion of the brain has many connections with the lowest portion of the cerebrum, the hypothalamus, which appears to be very important in terms of our emotions.

The male brain is on the average slightly heavier than that of the female because men usually have heavier bodies than women.

The massive memory section in the cerebral cortex is believed to contain enough potential connections to receive 10 new items of information every second of life.

And the brain each day uses 100 times more connections than the world's telephone systems.

THE CURE OF MIND OVER MATTER

Ancient yoga principles in service of medical science

The system of self-control practiced for centuries by the yogis of India may well be an answer to some medical complaints that doctors have been unable to cure.

Doctors call it biofeedback, and its key is "patient, heal thyself." Researchers have found that with the initial aid of sensitive machines, some patients can control certain automatic or involuntary body functions once considered uncontrollable. The principle is mind over matter.

Doctors and scientists working in the United States and abroad say that some illnesses connected with the heart, brain, muscle groups, and the circulatory system can be controlled, if not cured completely, by biofeedback.

Although research is incomplete, one aspect of biofeedback is the ability of some individuals to learn to control alpha brain waves, one form of the electrical activity recorded from the brain on the EEG, or electroencephalogram. In an alert individual whose attention is fixed on something, EEG waves are fast and irregular; but relaxation and inattention are associated with development of the slower, regular alpha pattern. In some individuals the EEG can be "fed back," in the form of beeping sounds, for example, and the subject can increase the duration of the alpha rhythm periods, and thus promote his own relaxation.

Many years ago British doctors in India sent back reports that yoga followers could perform amazing feats, including marked slowing of their heartbeat, respiration, and metabolism.

The reason was that yogis had gained extraordinary control of their bodies and minds by exercise and mental discipline, or by a form of self-conditioning involving the biofeedback principle. It is likely that these reactions include the changes in brain waves already described, although the yogis of past years presumably were unaware of the existence of such electrical activity in the brain.

Like yoga techniques, biofeedback involves control of the autonomic system—the part of our nervous system that operates without conscious control, such as the systems controlling breathing, heartbeat, and blood pressure.

"My hands are warm"

In 1910 the German hypnotist Johannes Schultz found that when he taught patients self-hypnosis by having them talk themselves into a relaxed state, he had surprising results. When they repeated the phrase "My hands are warm," their hands did grow warmer.

In 1964 American doctors confirmed Schultz's early experiments, wiring volunteer housewives to instruments that monitored skin temperature. The women were then asked to relax and feel their hands getting warmer. Clearly and indisputably, the instruments registered an increase in heat from their hands.

This was a highly important experiment because it had supported the view that the autonomic system could be controlled.

Since 1964, however, doctors have made even more promising advances. The technique has been extended to the treatment of insomnia, anxiety, blood pressure, and asthma; and experiments are already being conducted on the relief of epilepsy, stroke paralysis, pains in the back, and migraine and tension headaches.

The essential part of such treatment is the feedback. This means that patients must be able to "tune in" to the particular body function over which they are trying to win control. Once the patient can see his heartbeats or brain waves recorded on an electric meter, or can hear them as a fluctuating tone, he is on his way to controlling them.

Asthmatics, for example, are sensitive to such irritants as dust, pollen, and fumes—but a lot of their trouble stems from their own nervous tension. An asthmatic patient is treated in a soundproof room and wired to an instrument called an electromyograph, which measures breathing activity. If he is relaxed, he hears only a slow clicking.

But he is then told to visualize dust, flowers, or whatever else can cause an attack. His response, at least in part, is what behavioral scientists call a "conditioned" one—he develops the symptoms of asthma without actually being exposed to the materials he is particularly sensitive to.

A part of his reaction is increasing muscle tension as the attack approaches, and this can be sensed in the experimental room by increased clicking from the electromyograph. However, the patient can learn to "decondition"—in other words, to relax his muscles when feedback tells him that he is getting unduly tense. This "deconditioning" appears to help in avoiding a full asthmatic attack.

In time, the sufferer may learn to recognize the muscle tension that signals an approaching attack of asthma, without depending on the electromyograph. He then can use the deconditioning he has learned to avert the attack, and thus may find himself leading a freer, fuller life.

SUPERFLUOUS PARTS

Our vestigial organs serve useful purposes

Until recent years a number of organs in the body were thought to be useless "vestigial" carryovers from earlier evolutionary ancestors. Currently, however, there is reason to believe that nature rarely is wasteful and that so-called vestigial or superfluous organs continue to serve useful purposes in man.

Present-day pediatricians generally believe that the tonsils and adenoids, once considered classic examples of organs not merely superfluous but actually undesirable, may have a useful function, blocking access of bacteria and other foreign material to the lungs and digestive system. They now advise removal only when the tonsils or adenoids become the site of repeated infections.

Not so long ago, many surgeons, while carrying out abdominal surgery, would casually remove an undiseased appendix as "a little extra favor to the patient." Now, however, some doctors believe that the appendix may have a role in the immunity systems of the body, and surgeons are not so eager to remove this organ at any convenient opportunity.

The thymus gland, long regarded as useless, now is known to have very important functions in the development of white blood cells and antibodies in a fetus and in an infant, although its role may be relatively minor after puberty.

Perhaps the most interesting questions about a "useless" organ revolve around the mysterious pineal gland or pineal body. Even the name is in dispute, because many scientists question whether it secretes materials as other genuine glands do. The pineal body looks somewhat like a pinecone or walnut. It is considerably smaller, but still is easily visible to the naked eye, when one finds it buried deep in the brain.

Its location, nearly in the middle of the brain mass, would seem to be very strategic, and it is not so surprising that René Descartes, the great 17th-century French philosopher, quite seriously suggested that it was the "seat of the human soul."

More modern scientists have learned that the pineal body in such amphibians as frogs can be affected by light transmission through translucent skin and an opening in the skull and is thought to release chemicals that affect skin pigmentation. The pineal body in some reptiles may have similar functions. But as one moves up the evolutionary ladder to mammals and man, the pineal body was believed, until recently, to have become vestigial—to serve no useful function.

Research during the 1960's, however, has reopened the whole question. In 1958 an American scientist, Aaron Lerner, discovered that the pineal body in mammals can synthesize or manufacture a substance called melatonin, and Lerner and other investigators found that the melatonin was made from serotonin, which is found in higher concentrations in the pineal body than anywhere else in the mammal.

Serotonin is an especially interesting chemical because, in other parts of the brain, it acts as one of several chemical "messengers" for normal brain function. The ability of LSD (lysergic acid diethylamide) to alter perception and to produce states similar to schizophrenia may be owing to its interference with serotonin in such brain areas as the hypothalamus, frequently regarded as "the seat of our emotions." There is no direct proof of a relationship between serotonin in the pineal body and serotonin in other parts of the brain, but the possibility that there may be a genuine relationship deserves further investigation.

There is, however, considerable evidence that the pineal body plays a role in regulation of reproduction. Exposure of female rats to light increases ovarian weight and the frequency of the estrus (mating) cycle, and thus facilitates reproduction. Two American endocrinologists, Richard Wurtman and Julius Axelrod, have presented data indicating that the pineal body is a link in this response. They have shown that injected melatonin inhibits the estrus cycle in rats, possibly by a mechanism involving the pituitary gland. Prolonged darkness has a similar effect. However, increased exposure to light appears to decrease melatonin synthesis in the pineal body while stimulating the estrus cycle. These effects are abolished by denervating the retina of the eye or cutting the nerves to the pineal body. Wurtman and Axelrod believe that the action of light on the retina somehow stimulates the nerves to the pineal body, thus slowing or abolishing release of melatonin, and reducing its inhibitory effect on reproduction.

While this view is not accepted by all scientists, and a similar mechanism has not yet been demonstrated in man, there does seem to be a good basis for thinking that the pineal gland is far from "vestigial" or "superfluous." This strange organ probably will never regain the lofty role assigned to it by Descartes, but a significant function in reproduction, and perhaps other functions, too, may become clear in the not too distant future.

THE BO TREE. *Buddha gained enlightenment under this fig tree, which is rich in serotonin.*

CATARACT SURGERY—AN OLD OPERATION

A COMMON cause of partial or total blindness is the cataract, the opacity of the eye's lens. The only known cure is its removal by surgery, a delicate and complex operation even today. Yet the cataract operation was performed centuries before glasses had been invented, and by men who had little knowledge of eye structure and only the crudest instruments. It is known that such operations took place in India about 3,000 years ago. Ancient Babylonia even set rigid surgeon's fees for the operation, and these payments ranged from 2 silver shekels for a slave to 10 shekels for a freeman. If the surgeon made a mistake and botched the freeman's operation, however, he had to pay a painful penalty—his hand was cut off!

THEY FEEL NO PAIN

But they're not so lucky as you think

Over the years doctors have documented a number of cases of individuals who have felt little or no pain. These people have had serious accidents or tolerated extensive surgical and dental procedures and reported that, at worst, "The experience was a little uncomfortable."

At first thought, inability to feel pain might seem like a fine thing. But pain, at least up to a point, is the body's warning of danger. The importance of the reflex to remove one's hand from a dangerously hot object is obvious. However, the agonizing pain of a heart attack or of a dangerously infected appendix is also a highly desirable warning sign.

Most people have known two distinct types of pain. The touch of a hot object or a cut in the skin is experienced as a quick, sharp pain, producing an immediate reflex response. Pain of this sort is recognized and transmitted by small, insulated nerves called A-delta fibers. The second type of pain, such as a bad toothache, is a persistent, aching, deep-throbbing sensation, carried from small, bare nerve endings along uninsulated C fibers to the brain.

The individuals who "feel no pain" probably have normal receptors in organs or at the body surface and normal nerve pathways to the brain. Their low sense of pain most likely is owing to some failure of "perception" within the brain itself—the message is there, but it just "doesn't hurt."

Objectively, normal individuals have different thresholds of pain. This can be measured by the amount of radiant heat shined on a person's forehead necessary for him or her to report the "prickling" pain carried by A-delta fibers. Normal individuals also have widely varying abilities to tolerate pain, but this has been shown to have very little relationship to the objectively measured "pain threshold."

The placebo effect

Some insight into low pain perception may be gained from hypnosis and from studies of what medical scientists call the placebo effect. It has been shown repeatedly that suggestible people can undergo painful procedures, including major surgical operations, under hypnosis. It is possible that the ability of fakirs and yogis to impale themselves on sharp objects and to handle hot objects or walk on coals is owing to a form of self-hypnosis.

"Placebo" is a term used for any normally inactive material, such as a solution of salt or sugar, which can exert none of the properties of a drug that has clear-cut beneficial actions. A classic study of placebos was carried out by members of the faculty of Harvard Medical School in the 1950's. Alternating injections of morphine, a potent analgesic, or painkiller, and salt or sugar solutions were given to more than 400 patients following surgery. While most of the patients experienced definite relief from pain with morphine, about a third of them also experienced distinct relief after injection of placebos.

A recent University of Florida study indicates that the ability of acupuncture to relieve pain in a variety of conditions, including arthritis, backache, and headache, may be due in large part to the placebo effect. More than 200 subjects were studied, and classical acupuncture techniques, in which the needles were placed along "meridians" specified by the ancient Chinese physicians, were alternated with random placement of the needles. More than three-fourths of the patients reported significant relief from pain, but there turned out to be no difference between the "classical" treatment and the random placement of the needles. Four weeks after treatment, about half of the subjects reported that their pain was as severe as before.

In their 1975 report the Florida investigators suggested that the benefits of acupuncture, while undeniable (although short-lived) in many of the patients, were owing in large part to the placebo effect.

From work of this kind it appears that many individuals have the ability, latent or well developed, to master pain by the psychology of "the way they look at it." In other words, much of the unpleasantness of pain may be due to the fact that we are conditioned to fear it or to perceive it as dreadful.

Clearly, a belief that something will relieve pain is enough, for many people, actually to relieve suffering. In time, perhaps most individuals will be able to learn to use this fact to make pain a less frightening experience.

THE PRICK OF A NEEDLE

The ancient art of acupuncture still yields results

During the past few years Western physicians and scientists have shown a sharp increase in interest in one of the world's oldest medical weapons: the Eastern needle technique of acupuncture. Properly used, acupuncture can relieve many patients of the pain of migraine headaches, arthritis, backaches, and ulcers. Patients have undergone major surgical operations, including appendectomies and Cesarean deliveries, with acupuncture as the only method of anesthesia.

Currently, Chinese medicine uses most of the principles and methods of Western medicine, especially in the areas of infectious diseases, public health, and surgery. However, Chinese doctors also rely on some of the ideas and methods developed more than 4,000 years ago and set forth in the world's oldest medical text: the *Nei Ching,* or *The Yellow Emperor's Classic of Internal Medicine.* This ancient book, translated into English and published in 1949, is in the form of dialogues between Huang Ti, the legendary "Yellow Emperor," and his chief physician. According to classical Chinese tradition, the book dates back to about 2600 B.C., although the work, most likely, is really a collection of lore from that time to a few centuries before Christ.

The philosophy underlying the *Nei Ching* is even more ancient and includes ideas from the *I Ching,* or *Book of Changes,* which Chinese tradition assigns to the legendary Emperor Fu Hsi, who is said to have lived about 2800 B.C.

This ancient philosophy holds that the universe is a battleground between two forces, yin and yang. Between them, yin and yang compose the world and everything in it. Yin is the negative aspect of things—the feminine, the passive, cold, and odd numbers. Yang is positive—masculine, the active, heat, and even numbers.

According to the theory, man, like everything else, is made up of yin and yang; normally, the two forces are more or less in balance. But when the body is hit by illness, they get out of equilibrium, so that some parts of the body have either too much or too little of one or the other. The needles of acupuncture are designed to restore the balance by blocking off or stimulating the flow of yin and yang.

The Chinese believed that yin and yang flow around the body through special channels called meridians, each of which is associated with one particular organ.

It is on these meridians—12 in all—that the 900 acupuncture points are placed. This is why the needles often seem to be so far from the organs they are trying to treat. The liver merid-

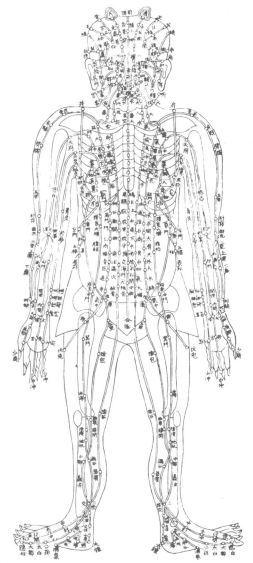

PINPOINTED. *An ancient Chinese acupuncture chart shows the positions of some of the 900 needle points on the network of "meridians."*

47

ian, for example, runs from near the liver down to the inside of the leg to the big toe; the pancreas meridian, from the waist to the left armpit; the one for the intestines, from the point of the chin through the navel to the groin. Only the heart meridian makes any immediate sense to Westerners. It runs from over the heart down the inside of the arm to the little finger of the left hand—exactly the path of the pain felt by many angina sufferers.

The Chinese also believe that each of the meridians is linked with a pulse—six on each wrist. And expert acupuncture diagnosticians are said to be able to feel all the pulses with such sensitivity that they can not only define a present illness but describe past ones and predict future ones, too.

Scientists have put forward several theories to account for acupuncture's effects. These range from the concept that the small pain of the needles distracts the patient from his illness, to the simple notion that it works because the patient believes it will.

Modern acupuncture uses steel needles instead of the traditional needles of stone or wood. And instead of twirling them about by hand to keep on stimulating the desired point, the job is normally done by running a weak electric impulse through them.

Otherwise the treatment has not changed.

THE FLEXIBLE BARRIER

Skin is tough and elastic—the perfect wrapper

An allover, skintight garment for a man or woman would require 6 yards of material 13 inches wide—and an extremely good tailor.

And yet every few weeks the natural processes of cell reproduction give each human being 20 square feet of new and perfectly fitting skin. This completely replaces the old one, which is continually being worn away by friction in such activities as bathing and moving.

Skin keeps moisture out and, at the same time, prevents the body—which is 60 percent water—from drying out. It acts as a barrier against dirt and germs. Together with underlying fatty layers, it rounds out the body's contours and provides a cushion against bumps and knocks. It is also very elastic, the perfect wrapper for our bodies.

There are three layers of skin: the outer epidermis, the middle dermis, and the subcutaneous layer. All the skin's vital structures are located in the dermis, the relatively thick underlayer. This is covered by the paper-thin epidermis, which has an outer part consisting of flat, dead cells. As the outer cells get worn away, new ones move up from the dermis, where they have been formed, to take their place in a never-ending succession throughout life.

There are millions of nerve endings below the epidermis. Many of these endings consist of specialized structures for the various sensations arising from our skin. These "receptors" detect at least five distinct sensations—pain, heat, cold, pressure, and touch. Every skin sensation is a combination of some or all of these.

In the sensitive areas, such as the fingertips or lips, there are as many as 1,300 touch receptors to every square inch of surface. Less sensitive regions, such as the shoulders, have only about 1/50 of that number.

A cooling system

In each square inch of skin there are 700 sweat glands releasing salty water, which evaporates and keeps the body cool.

Normally, the daily loss of water from the skin is about one pint, at a rate so low that it is called insensible perspiration. Active people working in a very hot climate, however, can lose three gallons or more of water in the form of sweat. That is why people in hot climates are advised to take salt tablets—otherwise, the loss of water and salt may be so great as to produce collapse because of heatstroke.

Apart from sweating, body heat can be lost through the skin by radiation. The heat is lost from blood pumped through yards of capillary blood vessels just under the skin's surface, producing a flushed appearance. Contractions of the same blood vessels prevent heat loss in the cold and make the skin turn white.

Goose pimples are caused by tiny muscles in the hair follicles that contract when a person is cold, thus producing bumps on the skin. Originally, the purpose of these muscles was to make the hair stand up, either to give a more fearsome appearance when fighting or for greater protection against the cold.

The skin also has bulblike hair follicles and oil-producing sebaceous glands—100 of them to every square inch. The oil lubricates the skin and hair, helping to make them waterproof.

Another major factor is melanin, a dark pigment that gives color to the skin and hair. Melanin also acts as a filter, keeping out the potentially dangerous ultraviolet light in the sun's rays, and it is the cause of a white man's skin tanning when exposed to sunlight. Clumping of the melanin—a hereditary trait in many fair-skinned people—causes freckles.

Like old clothes, skin goes "baggy" with age. It wrinkles because of lack of firmness and support from the fatty, subcutaneous tissue, which gradually disappears in most people as they grow older. Just as the skeleton shrinks and other organs function less efficiently, the loss of the fatty layer is due to the failure of the body to rejuvenate itself.

In effect, the skin becomes too big—and the wrinkled form is maintained and regenerated. Unfortunately, the skin does not shrink to fit the smaller model. Even in younger people, wrinkled skin, caused by prolonged stretching and sudden release, takes many weeks to return to normal; even then some wrinkling may remain. This is particularly the case after childbirth with some women.

That the skin copes with such unending assaults on the body by abrasives, sharp objects, sunrays, heat, and cold, yet allows us to remain healthy and efficient within, is one of man's most remarkable adaptations to his environment.

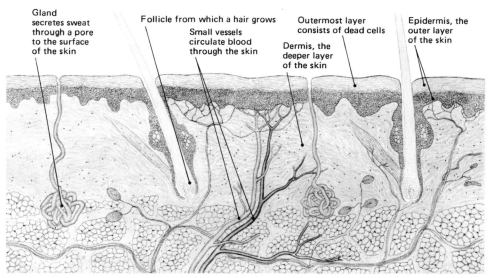

Gland secretes sweat through a pore to the surface of the skin

Follicle from which a hair grows

Small vessels circulate blood through the skin

Outermost layer consists of dead cells

Dermis, the deeper layer of the skin

Epidermis, the outer layer of the skin

CROSS SECTION OF SKIN. *The two main layers are the dermis and the epidermis. Passing through the dermis are hair follicles, ducts from sweat glands, and small blood vessels.*

WINDOW TO THE WORLD

HELEN KELLER (1880–1968) lived in a world of blackness and silence. Blinded and rendered deaf by a fever when she was 19 months old, she managed to overcome these appalling handicaps and then went on to become an internationally famous author and lecturer.

Creation of her window to the outside began when she was about 6½ years old and an instructor of the blind, Anne Sullivan, became her teacher. Miss Sullivan would spell a word into Helen's palm while the child felt the object with the other hand. The breakthrough came one day as the teacher spelled the word "water" while holding Helen's hand under a pump. Once Helen had made the connection between object and symbol, she progressed quickly, and her sense of touch became her eyes and ears.

THE BATTLING BODY

How it fights the invisible enemy

The body is a battleground in which a never-ending war is waged against disease-producing germs. The air we breathe teems with potential killers—bacteria, invisible to the unaided eye—which, fortunately, are normally quickly vanquished by the natural defenses of a healthy body.

Bacteria, or the even smaller viruses, can invade through any opening, such as the mouth, nose, and ears, or a cut or scratch in the skin. Illness or infection is caused only when they penetrate into the tissue or bloodstream.

The first defenses of the body are the outer skin and the membranes around the interior organs. Areas prone to invasion, such as the mouth and eyes, are protected by saliva and tears, both antiseptic liquids. Stomach acids, besides digesting food, kill off dangerous invaders that are often swallowed with it.

Once a germ has penetrated any vulnerable area, the body's "infantry," the white cells of the blood, spring to its defense. The average human body contains 25 to 30 billion of these. When germs invade, the white cells rally and multiply at the site of the infection and kill the invaders by absorbing and digesting them—hence the name phagocytes ("eating cells") given to these invaluable fighters.

Many phagocytes die in the battle that rages in an infected area, such as a boil. During the battle the germs release poisonous substances called toxins. These act as "antigens" and stimulate certain white and other cells of the body's RE (reticuloendothelial) system to produce the defense chemicals called antibodies.

Each antibody evolves to deal with a particular infection. In a lifetime the body may encounter as many as 100,000 different antigens, each one bringing forth the army of antibodies.

Even when the battle is won, the victorious body does not disband its antibodies. They persist in the bloodstream sometimes for life, being reinforced occasionally by fresh ones manufactured in the liver and the lymphatic system. So, if the same germs should return, the correct antibodies are ready and waiting to repel the attack. This is the natural defense system that gives the body immunity to a second onslaught of certain diseases.

Immunity to the common cold is short-lived, because there are so many different viruses causing it that the body can never build up a resistance to them all. Artificial immunization, or vaccination, has been developed as a defense against some diseases. The most familiar example is, of course, smallpox. The vaccine that the doctors inject contains the germs of cowpox, a closely related but less dangerous disease. These germs stimulate a reaction that produces a resistance to the much more dangerous disease.

Immunity acquired either through having had a disease itself, or through vaccination, is called *active* immunity. There is another kind of protection, called *passive* immunity, in which the body does not have to manufacture the defense antibodies for itself. This kind of immunity can be obtained by an unborn baby from its mother's bloodstream or from breast feeding in the first few days of a baby's life.

A WHITE BLOOD CELL *approaches a cluster of bacteria.*   *Contact is made with the enemy, and the deadly battle begins.*   *The white cell surrounds the invading germs and "eats" them.*

50

LARKS AND OWLS

The inner clock that rules our lives

Guess what time it is—without looking at your watch! The chances are you will be right to within half an hour. Or try waking up at a particular time—without an alarm clock. You'll probably be able to do that, too.

Just about everyone can do these things, with a little practice, because the human body has its own built-in clocks.

There is a complex series of interacting rhythms in nearly everything the human body does. It sleeps to a rhythm, eats to one, and even shows a rhythm in the electrical waves produced by the brain.

Three main rhythmic cycles affect body time: the daily rhythm of the revolving earth; the monthly orbit of the moon around the earth; and the yearly journey of the earth around the sun.

A perfect time sense

Not only mankind is affected by these great natural tides. All animals and plants feel them, too. Sometimes a body clock can keep accurate time to the precise minute, as in the case of the bean aphid, which can either lay eggs or produce live young, according to the season of the year and the length of the day. So perfect is this insect's adaptation to natural time that when the daylight lasts longer than 14 hours 55 minutes, live offspring are born to take full advantage of the extra warmth. If the day is shorter, the aphid lays eggs to hatch at a later time.

Man's time sense is both mental and physiological—the world over. He feels hungry every three to four hours. His brain cells show two-to-three hour cycles of activity. Even dreams run in cycles. During dreaming, the eyes, even under closed eyelids, show rapid scanning movements, much as they would in watching a movie or television. Measurements of this movement, during "rapid eye movement," or "REM," sleep, permit accurate timing of periods of dreaming. Based on this, man appears to dream in cycles of about 90 minutes.

Circadian rhythm

Man's natural rhythm of life is balanced between the length of the 24-hour solar day and the lunar day, which is 50 minutes longer. For this reason it is called the circadian rhythm, meaning, literally, "about a day." Under normal conditions the circadian rhythm is constantly influenced by the rising and setting of the sun. But people isolated from outside stimuli—such as prisoners kept constantly in cells without natural light—revert automatically to a longer natural cycle.

The circadian pattern seems to be controlled in part by the hypothalamus—an area in the base of the brain close to the pituitary gland. The hypothalamus can regulate pituitary secretions, and thus, in turn, the activity of a number of other endocrine glands. Effects on the cortex of the adrenal gland, and changes in release of an adrenal hormone called cortisol, appear to be especially important in certain kinds of rhythms. These mechanisms are highly adaptable.

Most humans do have contact with natural stimuli, and their slightly shorter version of the circadian rhythm is vitally important to them. Temperature, blood pressure, pulse, breathing, and hormone activity all rise and fall in time with the world's slow spin.

A cycle for illness

Similarly, ability, temper, and even resistance to infection are controlled by the circadian clock. This may be why some epileptics have seizures only at certain times of the day or why pregnant women get morning sickness.

Experiments have shown that mice injected with pneumonia germs at 4 a.m. survive better than those injected at any other time of day. This could be important to humans. If vulnerability to disease is rhythmic, then response to vaccination is likely to be rhythmic, too.

Circadian rhythms account for the difference between "owls," people who are wide awake at night and stay up late, and "larks," who rise early, do their best work in the morning, and go to bed early.

Lark and owl patterns

Both the lark people and the owl people have quite distinct rhythms, probably because of differences in the rhythm of their metabolism. The variation is important in that it shows an important difference in rhythmic patterns in members of the same species. Surprisingly, although owls go to bed later than larks, both groups tend to get up at about the same time. In larks body temperature and efficiency rise more quickly, but by evening they have "peaked out"; whereas owls at that time are still building to their peak.

Regular air travelers experience "jet lag"—a feeling of bewilderment and lethargy when they make rapid journeys from one time zone to another. The phenomenon is caused by the individual's circadian rhythm being out of step with clock time in his new part of the world. Gradually, he will adapt to new rhythms, but the process may take as long as a week.

The best known cycle is that of menstruation in women. This monthly tide of physiological change can alter a woman's moods dramatically and affect her susceptibility to illness. Men also follow a monthly cycle of hormonal activity, but its effects are less obvious.

Oysters sense the moon

A remarkable experiment with oysters shows that their rhythm is extremely persistent. Oysters were taken from Long Island Sound 1,000 miles inland in a sealed and darkened tank. At first, they continued to follow their normal rhythm, opening and closing according to the cycle of the tides on their home beach. But after 15 days their rhythm changed—to what it would have been if the sea's tides had washed over their new home.

They opened when the moon—which controls the tides—reached its highest point over their new location. This occurred despite the fact that the oysters were kept in a light-free tank, at a constant temperature, thus ruling out responses to lunar light or temperature change. One possibility is that they were responding to subtle changes in atmospheric pressure caused by the moon's gravitational pull.

In human beings, birth and death follow cycles. Most babies are born—and most heart attacks occur—between midnight and 6 a.m. More babies are conceived in August and September than in February and March. And science has even confirmed some of the age-old beliefs of astrology.

The cosmic rhythm

The sun's own cycle—the 11-year rise and fall of sunspots, which are dark smudges that can be seen on the sun at the same time as it hurls vast fountains of energy into space—also has its effects upon life. In the 1930's the Russian historian A.L. Tchijevsky claimed to have found a link between this cosmic rhythm and wars and epidemics on earth.

Maki Takata, a Japanese professor, discovered a relationship between human blood and the sun. He had developed a method by which gynecologists could check the menstrual cycles of women. This involved comparative tests of the albumin in the blood of both sexes. In January 1938 hospitals throughout the world that used the "Takata reaction" reported that the results were changing for men as well as women. Takata cross-checked and analyzed the results for 20 years and discovered that they changed primarily when a group of sunspots passed across the center of the sun: that is, when the sun was pumping a concentrated stream of radiation toward the earth. The burst of hospital reports corresponded to a sudden surge in the sunspot cycle after several years of quiet.

Takata also noticed that his test results showed a sudden change a few minutes before sunrise each day—as if the blood itself "foresaw" the break of day. "Man," Takata declared, "is a living sundial."

He could just as well have been talking about animals or plants. Whatever and wherever it is, life seems completely in step with a cosmic clock.

HOW THE COCKTAIL-PARTY EFFECT WORKS

THERE is always a confused clatter of sounds at a noisy party, but we can still hear our name if it is mentioned on the other side of the room. This ability is known as the cocktail-party effect. But it is not really our name we hear—only the sound. The ear transmits whatever sounds it hears to the brain, which then interprets them. Because of the familiarity of our name, we are instructed by the selective mechanism of the brain that we have heard it spoken above the other noises. The brain also interprets information from the other sense organs and tells us what we see, taste, and feel.

MALADIES OF FATE

Diseases that influenced the world's history

Abraham Lincoln was heartbroken when an unknown illness killed his mother. He was only nine, a poor boy living in a wilderness area that had no pasture, so the Lincolns' cow had to forage in the woods.

Lincoln never knew what malady had brought him such grief and so affected his life. But doctors know today. The science of medical detection has begun to catch up with the past.

In 1818 the aunt and uncle of Nancy Hanks Lincoln took to their beds with fatigue, stiffness of the legs, and red tongues. In a few days they were dead, and Nancy followed them to the grave shortly thereafter.

Their neighbors in Pigeon Creek, Indiana, spoke of the "milk sickness" and pointed to their cows, suffering from an ailment called the trembles. How right they were was shown in 1927, when the malady was identified.

Mrs. Lincoln died from drinking the milk of a cow that had eaten poisonous white snakeroot. If there is grass to eat, cattle shun snakeroot, so she was in fact the victim of poverty.

Only by sheer luck did the future American President avoid sharing his mother's fate.

The cancer of war

In 1887 the intelligent and likable Crown Prince Frederick of Prussia developed a growth on his left vocal cord. When early treatment failed, his German doctors diagnosed cancer and advised him to have his larynx removed. However, an eminent British throat specialist, Morell Mackenzie, said there was no sign of cancer, and the operation was, therefore, not performed.

On June 15, 1888, only 99 days after ascending the throne, Frederick died of cancer of the throat. His son, Kaiser Wilhelm, a far less intelligent man and a warmonger, thus began his fateful reign.

Many medical men believe that Frederick's life could have been saved if the German physicians had had their way, and the world might possibly have been spared the horrors of the First World War.

Death in the bath

The infamous Jean Paul Marat, one of the most ruthless leaders of the French Revolution, was stabbed to death in his bath in 1793. There is no mystery about how he died. His assassin was an idealistic girl named Charlotte Corday, whose sharpened table knife severed the aorta near his heart. But his habit of spending most of the day isolated in his bath made the killer's task considerably easier.

By studying contemporary accounts, doctors know that he suffered from pruritus and pityriasis simplex, itching skin diseases contracted during the years he had spent hiding in cellars and sewers. To obtain relief he would sit in his bath and write his rabble-rousing editorials.

The unbearable itching probably helped to inspire the venomous outpourings from his pen that led to the worst excesses of the revolutionary terror. It was ironic that it should also have contributed to his own death.

IN TIME OF PLAGUE

The disease that changed the course of history

The greed of fur trappers was responsible for the last major outbreak of bubonic plague, in which 60,000 people died in just seven months. It happened in eastern Siberia in 1910 after worldwide demand had quadrupled the price of marmot skins. The animal, a rodent whose skin is sold as a substitute for sable, had long been hunted by Mongols who knew of the strange illness that sometimes afflicted it.

No Mongol would hunt a sick animal, and, although the flesh and fat of a marmot were considered a delicacy, there was a local taboo that the lump of fatty tissue under the arm—an auxiliary lymphatic gland—should never be eaten. There was a legend that the gland contained the soul of a dead hunter, and the Mongols knew that this gland tended to become diseased. This disease sometimes infected humans, whom the Mongols left to their fate.

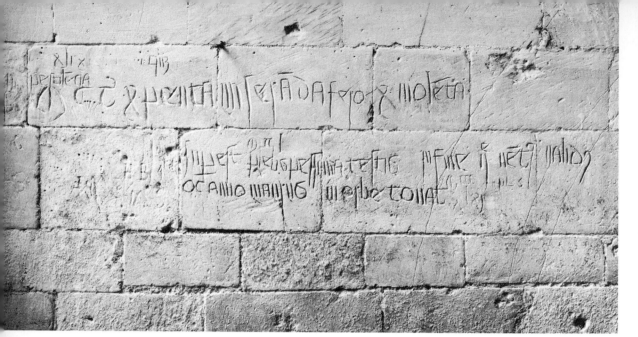

A TESTIMONY TO PLAGUE. *When translated, this Latin inscription scratched into the wall of a church tower in England tells of plague in 1350 and a storm in 1361.*

In 1910 thousands of Chinese moved into northern Manchuria to take advantage of the boom in furs. The Chinese thought it a stroke of luck when they came across a sick, easily caught creature. If a hunter fell ill, they nursed him tenderly, not knowing that the sickness he had contracted from the animals was bubonic plague.

The plague spread from the hunting grounds to the town of Manchouli, the terminus of the Chinese Eastern Railroad. Finally, it spread 1,700 miles along the rail route, killing tens of thousands of people.

Spread by fleas

Plague is normally a disease of rats rather than of humans. It is caused by bacteria—microorganisms not much larger than 1/1,000 of a millimeter—and it is carried from one rodent to another by fleas.

There are two main forms of the disease: bubonic and pneumonic. If fleas from an infected rodent bite a man, swelling occurs at the bite mark, under the arm, or in the groin. These swellings, or buboes, give bubonic plague its name. Pneumonic plague is contracted by breathing in the bacteria, for instance when handling an infected rodent; then it is transmitted from person to person on the breath.

During an epidemic, or a pandemic, as the greater epidemics are called, up to 90 percent of the population may be infected. Modern antibiotics can save most of those afflicted if treatment is begun within a few hours of the onset of symptoms. However, if treatment is delayed more than 12 to 24 hours, more than 50 percent of those who contract bubonic plague will die, and the mortality from pneumonic plague will be nearly 100 percent.

Man seems to have suffered from outbreaks of plague since the beginning of recorded time. In Babylon in 3000 B.C. there was a plague called Namtar. (Namtar was the demon of plague.)

Plague has wiped out so many hundreds of millions of people that it can definitely be said to have changed the course of history.

In A.D. 542 the most devastating plague the world has known began to spread from Egypt along the great trade routes. It traveled through Asia Minor to Constantinople, Greece, Italy, and even as far as the Rhine. The disease raged for 52 years. In that time 100 million people are estimated to have died—a large proportion of the then-known world's population.

With the decline of the Roman Empire came the breakup of the trade routes, and there were few reports of plague for about eight centuries. One, however, is mentioned by the Venerable Bede in his *Anglo-Saxon Chronicle*. He writes of a "great pestilence" in England and Ireland in A.D. 664 and specifically describes what could only be a bubo.

Graveyard for victims

Early in the 14th century missionaries of the Nestorian sect—a group who believed, among other things, that Christ had two natures—began to travel the new routes between Europe and Asia. Graves of missionaries dating from the years 1338 and 1339 have been discovered along the routes. Some of these wanderers were known to have caught the plague in Outer Mongolia, and this tragic fact, together with the presence of the common rat in Europe (first recorded in the 12th century), are believed to be the main causes of the Black Death that ravaged the European continent for the next 60 years and that continued to terrorize the world for nearly four centuries.

Terrible death

The term "Black Death," coined in the 14th century, comes from the medieval Latin use of the word "black," meaning "terrible."

In 1348 much of the population of Florence was wiped out by an outbreak of the Black Death that eventually spread throughout Italy. In that same year Pope Clement VI, who was then living in Avignon, proposed a pilgrimage to Rome. Just over a million people went on the journey of about 500 miles. Only 100,000 returned.

At the height of the epidemic, the Rhone River was consecrated to provide a graveyard for victims who could not be disposed of in any other way.

By the end of the 14th century, 25 million deaths had occurred—an estimated 25 percent of Europe's population. According to one estimate, there were 45 outbreaks of plague between 1500 and 1720. The most notorious reached London in June 1665.

One of the preventive methods used in London against the spread of the plague was to burn cats, dogs, mice, and rats. But this precaution was a case of too little, too late. By 1666 more than 68,000 Londoners had died, and Europe feared another pandemic.

But then, on September 2, 1666, fire broke out in the heart of London's most populous area. The fire raged for four days, leaving four-fifths of the city devastated. But the great blaze also wiped out the unsanitary conditions that had helped the contagion to spread.

Last major outbreak

The last major outbreak of plague in Europe occurred in Marseilles, France, in 1720. There are pictures and descriptions of plague doctors clad in thick clothes, leather gloves, and a mask with a beak containing herbs to ward off smells that they believed carried the disease.

No one knows why the plague nearly disappeared after the 18th century. But perhaps an adage of the time had something to do with it. The advice was that if the plague occurred in your area, "Go quickly, go far and return late."

ALL FALL DEAD

IN ALL innocence children have for centuries sung a nursery rhyme with strangely sinister undertones:

> *Ring-a-ring o'roses,*
> *A pocket full of posies,*
> *A-tishoo! A-tishoo!*
> *We all fall down.*

The song arose in the London streets in 1665 during an epidemic of plague. "Ring o'roses" refers to small, red rashlike areas on people infected with plague, or the Black Death. "Pocket full of posies" was a reference to the fact that from ancient times people believed that evil smells were the poisonous breath of demons who afflicted them with disease. Sweet-smelling herbs and flowers were thought to ward them off. "A-tishoo! A-tishoo!" During the plague sneezing was a symptom of plague victims. "We all fall down." As, indeed, thousands of people did—dead.

An estimated 25 million people died during the infamous epidemic of the Black Death, which swept over Europe in the 14th century.

In playing ring o'roses, children sing while acting out a sinister parody of the dread plague.

Secrets of the planet on which we live

Wonders of the natural world

•

EARTH'S INNER CRUCIBLE

Hidden deep in the earth's crust: a giant foundry

Beneath the thin crust of the earth is a dynamic smelting pot, in which are found all the basic metals used by man. The earth's interior is extremely hot. Only 30 miles down, where volcanic lava is formed, the temperature is about 2,200°F (1,204°C). At the center of the earth, known as the core, the temperature could be as high as 7,200°F (4,000°C)—a little less than at the surface of the sun.

The core is probably made of a dense material, possibly iron and nickel with small amounts of sulfur and silicon. It is also believed to consist of two parts: a solid inner core, about 820 miles in diameter, and a molten outer core, about 1,340 miles thick.

Expelled upward and outward from this natural crucible through fissures in the earth's crust, the metals and other minerals cool, crystallize, and form bodies of ore.

The outer core is surrounded by the mantle, an 1,800-mile-thick layer of heavy, dense silicate rock, rich in iron and magnesium. Above this is the world we are familiar with.

It is made of two types of crust—the oceanic and the continental. The oceanic crust is less than 200 million years old, found below the ocean basins, about five miles thick, and covered with various kinds of soft sediment deposited on the seabed.

The continental crust is about 30 miles thick and very much older—containing rocks that are as much as 3.5 billion years old—and has a varied composition, although most of it is granitic. This is the crust that forms the earth's land masses.

The layers of rock that are found on the continental crust contain the best record of the earth's history; for trapped in them are fossils. There are traces of palm trees in Britain, glaciers in Brazil, and marine life on the plains of Kansas. Whale relics lie on hilltops; for most parts of the world have been under the sea at least once in the distant past.

So far, man's direct exploration of the mysteries beneath his feet extends only as far as the deepest borehole ever drilled. This well, known as Baden No. 1, in Beckham, Oklahoma, reached a depth of 30,050 feet (5.69 miles) in February 1972.

Knowledge of the earth's deeper layers is based on intelligent guesswork and the study of pressure waves caused by earthquakes. These studies suggest that there are sudden changes in density in various parts of the earth.

One of these changes is called the Mohorovicic Discontinuity, or, more popularly, the Moho. Attempts to drill to the Moho have so far been prevented by the massive cost; but if drilling is attempted, it may be more economical to drill through the ocean crust, which is much thinner than the continental crust and the Moho is closer to the surface there.

Why should man want to drill into the earth? One reason is that one day it may be possible to harness the vast energies of the earth's internal furnace.

The Grand Canyon, a gash 1 mile deep, 4 to

PATTERNS OF THE EARTH'S PAST. *Cutting a deep slice out of the earth's crust to probe into layers of years gone by is a daunting operation. But nature has already done the job at Arizona's Grand Canyon, where it is possible to see rock formations dating back some 2 billion years.*

18 miles across, and 280 miles long, provides a good visual example of the upper layers of the earth. It was formed by erosion caused by the Colorado River, a slow, inexorable natural process that commenced about 10 million years ago.

Twelve major groups of rock are visible from the rim of the canyon. The bottom layers are quite different from any of the others. They are made of Brahma and Vishnu schist—blackish, heavy rock more than 2 billion years old.

A rich palette

Going up the chasm walls, the bands measuring the passing eras show distinct changes in color—the blackish schists, the pinkish hue of granite, and the whites and browns of sandstone. Perhaps the most striking is a gray-blue limestone belt about halfway up, which was formed about 335 million years ago. Above this are alternating layers of sandstone and shale, each 1,000 feet thick. They contain the fossils of insects, fern fronds, and the stubby-toed ancestors of today's frogs.

The next layer, pale-hued, seems to have been formed by windblown sands, indicating a long period of desert conditions. Near the top are yellowish limestone layers that must have been laid down in warm seas, judging by the number of marine snails, sponges, and corals.

Above these come the first traces of man—prehistoric tribes who arrived on the scene at least 10,000 years ago.

And there are many more layers to be built up in the future; for the earth is still young. Astronomers believe it will survive up to 10 billion more years before it is destroyed when the sun finally dies.

FROM THE CREATION TO NOW, IN 100 YEARS

MAN'S existence has occupied only a tiny fraction of the earth's history. It is almost impossible to visualize the vast sweep of time since the earth was born out of gas and cosmic dust 5 billion years ago.

Imagine the planet's history condensed into a single century. On the time scale produced by this leap of imagination, the oldest known rocks began to form at the dawn of year 15, and life in its most primitive form of bacteria and algae appeared in the year 26. Until the year 80 life evolved slowly as the continents drifted about, and it was not until eight years ago that the first amphibians struggled ashore. Dinosaurs were dominant three years ago, but by the following year they had become extinct.

Three weeks ago the first man emerged in Africa, using tools and walking upright. The last ice age ended two hours ago; the industrial revolution started two minutes ago . . . and three seconds ago man set foot on the moon.

WALL OF FIRE. *In 1973 a new volcano on the Icelandic island of Heimaey erupted, and the lava overwhelmed this fishing village.*

LEFTOVER. *White Island, in the Bay of Plenty (New Zealand), is part of the rim of a huge eroded volcano that has been invaded by the sea.*

MOUNTAINS OF FIRE

How volcanoes build and destroy

At about eight o'clock on the morning of May 8, 1902, the volcano of Mount Pelée in the French Caribbean island of Martinique erupted. Within three minutes the town of St. Pierre was totally destroyed. Every street and building was a ruin. Ships in the harbor were wrecked, the cathedral was flattened, and nearly 30,000 people died. Only two men survived—one of them a prisoner condemned to death. His cell was very strong, but the roof collapsed, and he was buried for three days before being rescued.

It was the worst volcanic disaster in this century. But there have been even more destructive eruptions. On August 27, 1883, Krakatoa, in the Sundra Strait between Java and Sumatra, erupted, killing 36,000 people. The eruption was heard 3,000 miles away, and the ensuing wall of water raised by the explosion sank dozens of boats.

The skies above Krakatoa turned murky yellow; then darkness fell. A rain of thick, black mud drenched Batavia, 100 miles from the island. Areas 40 miles away were smothered by a

BIRTH OF AN ISLAND. *The island of Surtsey was born on November 14, 1963. Eight days later the island was still growing.*

CRASH VICTIM. *The steam and gas that pour from Stromboli are caused by the collision of the African and European plates.*

THREE-MILE INFERNO. *Iceland's Helka (background picture) is a three-mile ridge that has erupted since 1104. In 1947 lava was thrown 20 miles up, and the dust covered 25 square miles.*

rain of ash that fell remorselessly at the rate of three feet an hour.

In one mighty explosion the volcano shattered its cone, and 5 cubic miles of dust was scattered over 300,000 square miles. When the lava had been expelled, the volcano collapsed and was invaded by the sea.

Eighty years later Icelandic fishermen watched a volcanic process take place and had another glimpse of how volcanoes helped to form the surface of the earth.

Capt. Gudmar Tomassón's boat was trawling off Iceland on November 14, 1963, when suddenly the sea started to "boil." Through a vast cloud of steam the black column of a volcanic

island rose above the surface. Within weeks the new island was 567 feet high and 1.3 miles long. It was named Surtsey, after a legendary Norse giant.

Following its violent birth Surtsey evolved gently. Birds were the first to arrive, bringing seeds with them. In June 1967 the first flower—a white sea rocket—bloomed. Sea currents brought more seeds, and within three years four kinds of plants and 18 of mosses were established. Fulmars and guillemots made the island their home. But it will not be a permanent home. Already Surtsey is shrinking as the sea wears away its brittle lava.

It will not be the first volcanic island to

vanish. In 1900 a 150-foot-long island appeared in Walvis Bay, South-West Africa. Three months later, as cartographers were preparing to enter it on their charts, the crew of a survey ship found that it had disappeared.

The lava that pours from volcanoes does not come from the earth's core. One of the sources is generally about 60 miles below the surface, where molten rock under pressure rises upward through the crust. When most of the molten rock has been ejected, volcanic eruption stops.

There are more than 500 active volcanoes in the world, and most of them are on the Ring of Fire that circles the Pacific Ocean. Outside this ring there is a chain of volcanoes running across the Atlantic from Tristan da Cunha through the Azores to Iceland.

Another group of active volcanoes, in the Tyrrhenian Sea, includes Vesuvius, Etna, Stromboli, and Vulcano.

ATLANTIS—LEGEND OR FACT?

The island that exploded an Empire

Once, a beautiful island, prosperous and powerful, dominated an Empire that stretched to Africa and Europe. Its inhabitants were technologically advanced and well versed in the arts of war, but they offended morality and as a punishment were overwhelmed by the waters of the sea, which swallowed them up.

So wrote the Greek philosopher Plato, and for centuries this story has provided material for romantics and poets, while defying the logic of history and geology.

Plato's name for this lost paradise was Atlan-

tis, and he placed it beyond the "Pillars of Hercules," which today we know as the Strait of Gibraltar. It was a land larger than Libya [Africa] and Asia, and could therefore have existed only in that vast ocean to the west of Greece—the Atlantic.

Plato's account was based on stories told by his ancestor, Solon, who in turn had heard them from Egyptian priests. According to them, the disaster had occurred 9,000 years before Solon's birth. But geological evidence shows that the Atlantic Ocean has existed in its present state for several million years and con-

WAS THIS ATLANTIS? *The island of Santorini is all that remains of Thera, which was destroyed by volcanic eruption in the 15th century B.C. Evidence points to its being Plato's fabled land.*

LOST WORLD. *Map shows Thera's location before it was destroyed by a cataclysm.*

tains no signs of a once-inhabited island sunk beneath its surface.

The civilization that Plato described closely resembled that of the Minoan Empire, which was centered on the island of Crete. It was a highly advanced society, with written laws and skills in metalworking and engineering.

Late in the 15th century B.C., this civilization disappeared, as abruptly and mysteriously as Plato's Atlantis. For centuries its disappearance puzzled scholars, who were unable to see how such a sophisticated society could be eclipsed in such a short time. But recent findings suggest that the Empire was destroyed by one great volcanic explosion.

It is known that the volcanic island of Thera, in the Aegean Sea, exploded in about 1470 B.C. The 4,900-foot mountain erupted with such violence that the central portion of the island collapsed into the rapidly emptied chamber 1,200 feet below the sea. The surrounding area, now known as the island of Santorini, was covered in a 100-foot-thick layer of volcanic ash, and it is beneath this layer that relics of the Minoan Empire have been found.

But how can this cataclysm be related to Atlantis? The simple answer may be that—as so often happens when history is translated or rewritten—Plato misinterpreted the writings of Solon. If the eclipse of Atlantis had occurred 900 years before the birth of Solon—not 9,000 years—then this would put the event close to the eruption of Thera. And Plato may well have incorrectly translated the size of Atlantis as 800,000 square miles instead of 80,000 square miles. An island of this size would fit neatly into the Aegean Sea.

Word confusion

Two other possibilities strengthen the belief that Plato made a mistake. The Greek word for "greater than" is very similar to the word for "midway." Was Atlantis, therefore, midway between Libya and Asia, not "greater than"? And were the Pillars of Hercules really the Strait of Gibraltar? Two promontories on the coast of Greece, near Crete, are also called Pillars of Hercules.

On the evidence available it seems the mystery of Atlantis has been solved.

Archeologists have uncovered a complete town in the ash of Santorini, and its similarities to the fabulous Atlantis leave little doubt that Plato's paradise is a legend no longer.

WHEN THE GEYSER BLOWS OFF STEAM

AMERICAN scientist John Rinehart has discovered that the timetable of geysers, some of which erupt at regular intervals of a few seconds to several hours, is changed at full moon and new moon.

A geyser is caused by heat deep in the earth warming up ground water in complex underground plumbing. Deep down at the bottom of the system the water is heated well beyond its normal boiling point, but it does not boil because of the immense pressure of the water. As it rises, some steam is produced, lifting the column of water, and the pressure is lessened. The water boils, and the geyser erupts.

Geologists believe that at times of full and new moons the earth's crust changes so much, because of the moon's gravitational pull, that the plumbing systems through which the steam travels are warped. As a result, the steam takes longer to reach the surface. This has altered the timetable of eruptions of one geyser by more than an hour.

Blast off! Yellowstone Park's Old Faithful erupts in a jet of superheated steam.

CHANGING WORLD. *The continents are still drifting today. Eventually—within 50 million years—Africa will split in two. North and South America will separate, and a great slice of the west coast will tear off on its own. The Indian subcontinent will slide eastward, and Australia will sideswipe Borneo. The Atlantic will widen, while the Pacific shrinks. The colored areas above show how geologists estimate these movements will develop.*

OUR JIGSAW WORLD

Continents that once were one

Look at a map of the world and it becomes clear that, if the continents could be moved around, as in some vast jigsaw puzzle, the bulge of Africa would fit snugly into the shape of the Americas.

As long ago as 1912, the close match between the outlines of the two continents helped to put a German meteorologist, Alfred Wegener, on the trail of a startling theory. He reasoned that the earth's seven continents had once been joined together in a single land mass—a supercontinent to which he gave the name Pangaea, meaning "all lands." Floating on a sea of viscous rock, they had drifted apart over hundreds of millions of years.

Wegener's theory made sense of the distribution patterns of many animals and plants, both living and extinct. For instance, many freshwater fish in South America have close relatives in Africa, and it is unthinkable that they could have crossed thousands of miles of open sea to get from one continent to the other. Monkeys, too, are found in the wild in South America and Africa, and they are hardly likely to have evolved separately in both places.

Despite clues like these, it took half a century before Wegener's theory was widely accepted. The evidence came from a study of magnetic patterns on the ocean floor. When the rock that forms the seabed is first laid down, it is molten, and iron-bearing minerals become magnetized, pointing toward the magnetic pole. Once the rock has solidified, these compasses are trapped in position and can swing away from the pole only if the rocks that hold them also move. It was discovered in the 1960's that the compasses of the ocean floor have pointed in different directions at different times.

Final confirmation came in 1968, when the U.S. research ship *Glomar Challenger* set off on one of the most fruitful voyages of scientific exploration the world has ever known. By drilling a series of cores up to 3½ miles deep in the ocean floors, the geologists on board the *Glomar Challenger* were able to build up a picture, not only of what happened in our planet's past but also of what is likely to happen to the earth in the future.

Our present system of seven continents, it is now believed, formed some 150 million years ago, when two supercontinents, which geologists have named Laurasia and Gondwanaland, began to break up and move gradually apart.

Both the land and the ocean floor rest on a number of separate plates, each made of rock 60 to 90 miles thick. It is these plates that are afloat, borne on a sea of highly viscous rock.

The plates move across the globe at a rate of between half an inch and six inches a year, and although this may not seem to be much of a speed, they move vast distances over the ages. Africa, for instance, was once over the South Pole. The coal of northern Europe and the deposits of oil in Alaska and beneath the North Sea could have been laid down only in the Tropics and have since drifted to their present location in the northern latitudes.

When plates collide, mountains can be formed, like folds pushed up in some enormous blanket. It was in this way that the Himalayas were created, when India, moving north at what in geological terms was the breakneck speed of 15 miles in a million years, crashed into Asia.

Where plates grind against one another, earthquakes are common. New material for the earth's crust is formed by molten rock bubbling up from cracks in or between the plates. In some places this produces volcanoes. In mid-Atlantic the molten rock that wells up from a rift thousands of feet deep has created a mountain range as high as the Rockies, the result of the European and African continents moving away from the American continents.

THE TILTING ISLAND

How Britain is recovering from the ice age

Britain's geography is changing. The island is tilting along a line running from Devon, through south Wales, and across the middle of England to north Yorkshire. Land to the north and west of the line is rising, that to the south and east is sinking.

During the ice age Britain was covered in ice from Scotland nearly to the north bank of the Thames. The enormous weight of ice pushed the land down, and even now, millions of years after the ice melted, northern Britain is slowly springing back into position—with the result that the other parts are sinking slightly.

All the countries bordering the North Sea are affected. For example, the west coasts of Denmark, northern Germany, Holland, and southeastern England are sinking, while Scandinavia is rising.

Geologists estimate that the rise or fall is about five inches every 100 years, although the rate varies considerably. London has slid 15 feet downward since Roman times, which partly accounts for the tide's advance up the Thames. During Roman times the river was tidal to London Bridge, but now it reaches 19 miles upstream.

Harlech Castle, on the coast of Wales, shows the opposite process. When the castle was built by Edward I in 1286, the watergate led directly from the castle wall into the sea, but today the sea is about half a mile from the walls.

PROUD AND ISOLATED. *Harlech Castle, built in 1286 with its watergate directly accessible from the open sea, is now about half a mile inland—because the area is rising.*

CONTINENTS IN COLLISION
Earthquakes can be more destructive than H-bombs

There are about 1 million earthquakes a year. Most are so small that they can be detected only with the most sensitive instruments. Others release enormous amounts of energy—the equivalent of 2½ times the size of the world's biggest thermonuclear device, a Russian test bomb of 58 megatons, detonated in 1961.

Earthquakes are caused by the movement of the 60-to-90-mile-thick plates of rock. There are about 12 of these plates that move about on the viscous rock in the earth's interior. Where two plates meet, there are faults in the earth's surface. The friction as one plate grinds along the edge of another leads to earthquakes and also causes the fissures through which molten rock rises up, forming volcanoes.

The most serious earthquakes happen along two belts—where plates are moving toward each other.

One of the belts is known as the Ring of Fire and almost completely circles the Pacific. It runs up the coast of South America, Mexico, and California to Alaska. Then it swings westward through the Aleutians and turns southward through Japan and the East Indies.

The second earthquake line is the Alpine belt, running eastward from Spain through the Mediterranean to Turkey, the Himalayas, and the East Indies. Here the African and Indian

LIVING ON THE EDGE. *Yungay, Peru, built below Nevados Huascaran, is near the line where the American and Pacific continental plates meet.*

A TOWN'S DEATH. *On May 31, 1970, friction between the plates caused an earthquake, and tons of ice, rock, and mud buried the town.*

This image of the San Francisco peninsula, made by radar

The 1906 earthquake left the newly built San Francisco City Hall a ruin. Masonry was stripped from the facade by the violent shaking, leaving a skeleton of structural supports.

plates are moving north, both of them grinding slowly against the Eurasian plate.

Stresses may also build up in faults for other reasons. One is the gravitational pull of the moon, which draws up the surface of the land by as much as one foot as the moon passes overhead. Then, when the moon passes by on its trip around the earth, the land sinks back.

When the stresses below the surface build up, the crust splits along fault lines, and vibrations spread out from the fault. The primary waves move at five miles a second along the line of the fault. Then come the secondary waves, which vibrate at right angles to the fault, causing the earth to buckle. These secondary waves effect the greatest damage to buildings.

The waves sometimes cause the ground to open and occasionally close. In 1692 the ground in Jamaica was seen "rolling like the sea."

Fissures opened, and people were swallowed in the cracks. Then the gaps closed over them.

By measuring the stresses building up along the faults, and by studying the time cycle of past earthquakes, it is possible for scientists to forecast approximately when and where earthquakes will strike.

At present it is not possible to prevent earthquakes. But there is hope. American researchers believe that the dangerous friction that builds up between two continental plates could be eased.

They suggest that boreholes, 2½ miles deep, could be drilled along the line of a fault and, one by one, filled with water, which would lubricate the plates as they pass each other.

Only buildings standing right on the fault would then be in danger, and sensible town planning could prevent even that.

CALIFORNIA'S TERRIBLE WOUND

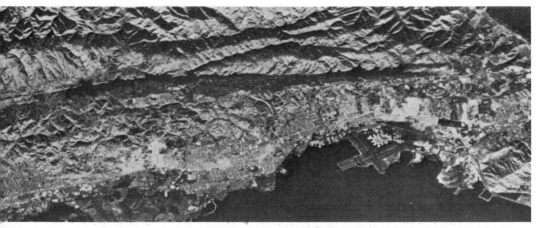

shows the San Andreas Fault as a dark, straight streak. The fault runs for 650 miles through California.

JUST before dawn on April 18, 1906, San Francisco was shaken by an earthquake. Buildings collapsed, and then, because the earthquake had ruptured water mains, fires roared through the city unchecked, devastating four square miles. Nearly 700 people died. The city was rebuilt, but some time in the future it could be destroyed again unless a way is found to prevent earthquakes.

San Francisco straddles the San Andreas Fault, the meeting place of the Pacific and American plates. The fault runs southeast to northwest, near the continental margin. The Pacific plate is edging past the American plate at a rate of a few inches a year, tearing a great area of California away from the mainland and into the Pacific. In 20 million years the site of Los Angeles, at present 400 miles south of San Francisco, will have moved almost as far to the north of it.

But the movement of the plates is not smooth. Every so often, the great blocks bind on each other, although the pressures pushing them continue. Eventually, something gives. There is a great convulsion, which results in an earthquake. This happened in San Francisco in 1906. Since then, all has been quiet.

MAN AGAINST THE DESERT

Sahara's burning sands on the move

The desert is on the move. Right across Africa the Sahara is creeping south at an average rate of half a mile a month—in some parts four times that fast.

A 4,000-mile belt below the desert is affected by drought. Animals die, crops wither, people starve. Survivors crowd into a dwindling area of savanna grassland, where overgrazing speeds the process. When rain does fall, it comes in sudden downpours that do more harm than good by washing away what topsoil there is.

Whole countries in the Sahel, the semiarid zone below the Sahara, are threatened with extinction. Weather experts predict that the earth is in for decades of low rainfall, which may turn richly cultivated areas into dust bowls.

What is causing this disastrous switch in the weather pattern? The reasons are not fully understood, but certain factors are accepted by many climatologists.

Basically, there has been a marked decrease in the supply of energy that generates the world's weather and moves it in great swirls around the globe. Both the North and South Poles have become colder, and this has had its effect on a ring of high-altitude winds, known as the circumpolar vortex, which circles the North Pole. The vortex has widened, and so shifted south, pushing in front of it belts of descending dry air that are believed to be the cause of the intensely dry Sahara region.

Because of the southward movement of the high-pressure belts, the rains are diverted to fall in the ocean or farther south in Africa.

Ocean currents, set in motion by the turning of the earth, also play a part in forming deserts. Icy currents from the polar regions come up against the edges of the continents. Winds blowing landward over these waters become cold and can carry little moisture, though they may bring fog and mist. What little moisture they have rarely condenses into rain.

Mountain barriers often trap rain and leave the country beyond them desiccated. Winds reaching Asia's Gobi Desert and the center of the Sahara have crossed enormous tracts of territory and deposited their water on the way.

Major changes in the world's patterns of weather are neither new nor permanent, although they may seem so when measured against a human time scale. It seems that, from 4000 B.C. to 2000 B.C., the Sahara was rich grassland. The earliest paintings found in the desert, executed on rock walls at Tassili in southern Algeria in about 8000 B.C., showed humans hunting buffaloes, elephants, lions, and antelopes. About 4000 B.C., later tribes painted their cattle grazing. Still later paintings

showed war chariots, Nile boats, camels, and bearded warriors with shields and spears, indicating that the inhabitants of Tassili knew of the Egyptians far to the east. The last tribes left about 2,000 years ago, and the area is now desolate.

Man has done much to spread the desert by his misuse of the soil. Cutting down trees, uncontrolled grazing, and overcultivation have created dust bowls where there was once rich land. Is man equally able to undo the damage? Given time, money, and skill, he can. The key is water—in the right place, in the right quantity, at the right time.

But it is not as simple as it seems. Lavish irrigation without drainage can draw salts to the surface and render the land incapable of growing anything—an expensive lesson that some Middle Eastern governments have learned in recent years. Dams can clog up with silt, and the tapping of rivers and deep wells can lower the water table seriously.

Ironically, there is enough water in the world to satisfy man's needs forever. The oceans hold 360 million tons of it for every person on earth. The problem is to make it drinkable by removing the salt. There are many ways of doing this—chemicals, distillation, or freezing.

The most successful, so far, is multistage flash evaporation, developed in Britain. Seawater is heated under pressure to prevent it from boiling. It passes through chambers where the pressure is lowered, causing the brine to boil and release salt-free vapor. The steam condenses on coils filled with seawater, which is warmed, to start the process all over again.

The inhabitants of Kuwait once collected their meager rainfall (less than six inches a year) in rooftop storage tanks or courtyard reservoirs and supplemented it with water brought by sailing vessels from Iraq and peddled in the streets from goatskin bags.

Now this enormously wealthy oil state can afford to distill tens of millions of gallons a day from the Persian Gulf and deliver it in a fleet of modern road tankers. As the distilled water has no taste, 5 percent of brackish water is added to provide taste and minerals.

In the Persian Gulf states, where temperatures over 100°F (38°C) are not uncommon, men grow vegetables in plastic-screened houses. The houses are kept cool by drawing air through a curtain of waste water, after it has been processed through the desalinization plant. Plants are fed with a water-nutrient mixture through plastic tubes. Tomatoes are ready for picking in three months, cucumbers in six weeks.

SANDS OF TIME. *Man is losing his battle against the desert. The Sahara is moving south, threatening the 4,000-mile Sahel belt with drought and starvation. Yet once, it seems, the Sahara had plentiful water; prehistoric drawings found on rocks indicate that game once abounded.*

EARTH'S FROZEN WATER SUPPLY

Masses of ice that form the world's glaciers

Nearly three-quarters of the world's total stock of freshwater is locked up in the form of glaciers—great rivers and ribbed sheets of ice, covering the poles and slowly chiseling pathways down the world's highest mountains.

In places the ice sheets are more than two miles thick. They are estimated to contain enough water to fill the Mediterranean basin six times over or to raise sea levels all around the world by 200 feet. If they melted, London, New York, Paris, and many other of the world's principal cities would be submerged.

A controlled manmade melting of the glaciers, however, could be beneficial. The Russians, with perhaps 10,000 mountain glaciers in their country, are studying ways of melting them to relieve droughts in central Asia. Then they hope to induce snow artificially in winter.

Glaciers are formed when more snow falls in winter than is melted in summer. As the amount of excess snow increases, year by year, the snowflakes at the bottom are pressed by the weight of those above, and they shrink, and the whole mass becomes denser granular snow. As the pressure mounts further, these in turn are recrystallized into granules of ice, roughly in the shape of a sphere. Eventually, these are compressed yet further into a rocklike mass.

If that were the end of the story, the glaciers would remain fixed to the spot. But, with gravity tugging at it, the rocklike mass behaves like a plastic substance, and the glacier starts to slide under the force of gravity.

Glaciers normally move a few inches a day, but some notable exceptions have been recorded. In 1966, at Mount Steele in the Yukon, a glacier was observed from the air to be traveling at two feet an hour.

About 25,000 years ago, in the last great ice

GOUGING VALLEYS OUT OF THE EARTH. *The vast glaciers of Alaska, some of them at heights above 10,000 feet, move inexorably across the landscape, creating deep valleys along their route. These glaciers cover about 3 percent of Alaska's total area.*

age, the glaciers advanced over the land. Most of Canada and northern Europe lay under a crushing weight of ice, and in the Southern Hemisphere even parts of Australia were in its grip.

Glaciers, moving relentlessly down valleys, plane off the rocks in their path, carving the valleys into U-shapes. When the glaciers began their retreat, about 18,000 years ago, the melting waters were sometimes trapped in valleys. North America's Great Lakes and Britain's Lake District were formed in this way.

The ice ages brought extinction to many species of animals but allowed others to expand their range, for it gave them a route over the frozen sea between continents. The ancestors of the modern horse, for instance, crossed from North America to the plains of Eurasia, more than 1.5 million years ago, using the land bridge over what is now the Bering Strait.

The same bridge was used, in the opposite direction, by the ancestors of the American Indians, who crossed from Siberia to Alaska to begin the colonization of America.

WILL THE ICE AGE RETURN?

The world is cooling—helped by man

Some scientists are convinced that the world's climate is getting colder every year, threatening a return to the conditions of the last ice age, which reached its peak about 18,000 years ago.

Geological and historical records leave no doubt that the earth's climate is constantly changing. From about 400 B.C. to A.D. 1300, the climate in Europe was much milder than it is today.

During the little ice age, from about 1300 to about 1890, glaciers advanced, and bodies of water in the northern latitudes, such as the Baltic Sea, remained frozen for long periods of time.

From 1890 to 1940 worldwide temperatures rose about 0.18°F every 10 years. Some animals extended their ranges northward, the sea was less frozen than before, and icebergs from Greenland did not penetrate as far south.

Since 1940 temperature has been dropping. According to a survey by the National Oceanic and Atmospheric Administration, the average ground readings for the Northern Hemisphere have, in the years from 1945 to 1968, fallen by one-half degree F. In the United States, east of the Continental Divide, temperatures in the last decade averaged one to four degrees cooler than in the past 30 years. Another study by the same agency noted that the amount of sunshine reaching the ground in the United States decreased by 1.3 percent between 1964 and 1972.

Dr. James D. McQuigg, director of NOAA's Center for Climatic and Environmental Assessment, points out that in crop-growing regions at higher latitudes an apparently small change in the average annual temperature may have sufficient impact on the length of the growing season to cause certain crops to be abandoned. He also notes that the range of year-to-year weather-induced variability in world production of wheat and other grain crops—the difference between production in a highly favorable weather year and that in a definitely poor year—is now equal to about 10 percent of annual world consumption. "In a real sense," he says, "the fact that we have a margin of reserves at all is the result of good luck with weather through a few most recent years."

Most experts would agree that the basic cause of cooling is a change in the amount of the sun's heat reaching the earth. How this change comes about and keeps the world in a recurring cycle of ice ages, followed by warm interglacial periods, has been the subject of a long debate among scientists. Many ideas have been proposed, but the one that seems to provide many answers and has much support was developed in the 1920's and 1930's by a Serbian physicist, Milutin Milankovitch.

In addition to spinning on its own axis and orbiting the sun, the earth also performs three other delicate motions. It wobbles on that axis, like a child's top about to come to rest; the axis itself changes the pitch of its tilt in relation to its plane of orbit; and, finally, the ellipse that the earth describes around the sun periodically becomes more circular. These movements are hardly violent—it takes 21,000 years for the earth to complete a simple wobble, for instance—but they are enough, according to Milankovitch's theory, to account for the great climatic changes that have occasioned the ice ages.

PATTERNS FROM THE SKY

The jewellike structure of snow and how it "speaks"

Countless billions of snow crystals have fallen on the earth, each a faultless piece of design; and, so far as is known, no two have ever been found to be identical.

Formed by the crystallization of water vapor in the air into geometrical forms, the shape of the crystals depends on the temperature of the air and the amount of water vapor it contains.

These crystals are always hexagonal, but they can take one of four basic forms: thin plates, thin needles, prisms, and star shapes.

Snowflakes form when simple crystals fall into a warm, lower atmosphere, melting slightly and bunching together.

On the ground, incidentally, snow speaks, or rather squeaks, its own comment on the temperature. The approximate temperature of snow can be measured by the sound that it makes underfoot.

A deep crunch means that the temperature is only slightly below 32°F (0°C). At 23°F (-5°C) the pitch rises, and the snow creaks

ANATOMY OF A SNOWFLAKE. *The shapes of snow crystals change with temperature and amount of vapor. Prisms and needles form from 18°F to 27°F. Warmer or colder temperatures produce plate and star shapes.*

higher up the scale. At 5°F (-15°C) the sound is unpleasantly high, like the highest notes on a violin being badly played.

A frost that is even more severe sounds like the scraping of a knife over a plate.

Hail is formed differently from snow. Liquid water is frozen around an ice crystal, which acts as the nucleus on which a hailstone is built. Small hailstones can be carried repeatedly through the freezing zone in the atmosphere by updrafts, building up successive layers like an onion.

When these become too heavy to be supported by the updrafts, they fall.

Freak accident

In 1930 five German glider pilots, carried into a thundercloud above the Rhön Mountains, bailed out of their aircraft. Carried by the strong upcurrents into the regions of supercooled vapor, the men became the nuclei of enormous hailstones. They were covered by layers of ice until finally they fell, frozen. Only one of the pilots, Guy Murchie, survived.

Hailstorms can damage crops so badly that farmers in Italy regularly fire 50,000 fireworks' rockets into potential hailstorm clouds to try to disperse them by shattering the hailstones before they fall.

Perhaps one of the world's strangest monuments, in eastern England, at Barton, Lincolnshire, commemorates a fierce hailstorm that occurred on July 3, 1883.

The inscription reads:

"In memory of the great hailstorm at Barton, July 3, 1883, 10.30 to 11 p.m. Ice 5 in. long, 3 in. wide—15 tons of glass broken—ice weighed 2½ oz."

The "ice" referred to the size of some of the largest hailstones.

The monument is built of bricks that were newly made and still hardening at the time of the storm. They bear the deep indentations made by the hailstones.

The United States suffered its worst snowstorm ever in 1921 when, at Silver Lake, Colorado, 75.8 inches fell in 24 hours.

Great Britain's highest recorded snowfall, at Tredegar, Gwent, Wales, totaled 65 inches in February 1963.

COOL, CLEAR, BUT ANCIENT, WATER

The unending cycle of earth's inexhaustible reservoirs

Earth retains all the water ever created—an estimated 326 million cubic miles of it. Water responds to a variety of powerful forces—the heat of the sun, the pull of earth's gravity, and the tidal forces of the sun and moon. The result is a natural cycle in which water has been used, purified, and reused for 3 billion years.

The accepted theory of how water was formed is that a chemical reaction between hydrogen and oxygen took place as the earth cooled. This produced H_2O, two parts hydrogen to one of oxygen. As the gases that formed the earth cooled and became liquid particles, a dense cloud blanketed the earth.

A 60,000-year downpour

When the temperature dropped, the clouds shed their water, a downpour that lasted for 60,000 years, filling the oceans and the lower land basins that were formed when the molten crust hardened.

Although water is still produced by manmade and natural processes, the levels of the oceans and the amount of water on the earth remain relatively constant. The amount of manmade water is relatively small, and water produced during the formation of volcanic rock is balanced by water lost in the weathering of minerals and when it is trapped by sediments.

About 97.2 percent of the earth's water lies in oceans, and 2.15 percent is held in icecaps and in the ancient glaciers of the high mountain zones.

The remainder of the water is spread over an area ranging from three miles below the earth's surface to seven miles up in the atmosphere.

Rivers and streams account for only 0.0001 percent, or 300 cubic miles. Other surface water totals some 55,000 cubic miles and is divided between inland seas and freshwater and saltwater lakes.

In addition, the earth has a reserve supply of some 2 million cubic miles of water below the surface. That in the upper layer, called the aeration zone, clings to soil and rocks, is absorbed by plants, or returns to the air through evaporation.

Lower-lying water, in what is called the saturation zone, feeds swamps, rivers, lakes, and wells. The Sahara Desert has an underground reservoir of some 150,000 cubic miles.

The atmosphere holds about 3,100 cubic miles of water—enough to cover the earth with one inch of rain if it fell at one time. This atmospheric water falls as rain and is replaced by evaporation every 12 days or so. Most rain falls in the sea or runs into rivers. About one-sixth soaks into the earth to nourish growth.

Wonders of water

Water has many unique properties. A skin forms, for example, where water meets the air. Water molecules are attracted to each other, and they squeeze together to form a dense layer. This phenomenon is called surface tension.

The same attraction of molecules also gives water its ability to climb uphill. Capillary action, as it is called, causes water to move upward through the ground, to the roots of plants, and through stems and leaves.

Water can also absorb more heat than almost any other common substance, without there being a considerable increase in its own temperature.

When a kettle of water is put on to boil, it is subjected to a temperature that would cause many substances to melt or burst into flames. But the water soaks up the heat until a temperature of 212°F (100°C) is reached; then the water boils, becomes a gas, and evaporates.

Another of water's unique qualities is that it floats when frozen because it expands at freezing point, becoming less dense. The force of water expanding as ice in the earth cracks rocks, helping to produce soil.

In arctic regions huge ice floes form and cover the surface of lakes and oceans with a protective insulating blanket, preventing further freezing. This helps life to go on under the blanket of ice.

There is no life, for instance, on the 16-foot-thick pack ice of the North Pole, but it teems in the ocean beneath.

If ice did not float, it would build up gradually from all the ocean beds and eventually cover our planet where it is cold in a solid glacierlike mass.

If this happened, life as we know it would then be unable to survive.

OCEANS WILD AND WIDE

The importance of the earth's great seas

Water covers 70 percent of the earth's surface—and in the ocean deeps is a dark, sunless world of spectacular canyons, great plains, and mountain ranges.

Huge areas of the ocean floors are plains that stretch for hundreds of miles at an average depth of 13,000 feet. Rising from these flat areas, called abyssal plains, are midocean ridges that girdle the globe, only occasionally breaking the surface to form islands. The Mid-Atlantic Ridge, reaching 10,000 miles from Iceland to the Antarctic, is by far the world's longest mountain range. Its highest peaks are the Ascension Islands, the Azores, and Iceland.

From the ocean floor in the mid-Pacific rises the world's highest mountain—the Hawaiian volcano Mauna Kea. It is 31,000 feet from base to peak—surpassing Everest by nearly 2,000 feet—but only the top 13,823 feet show above the surface.

Sunlight can penetrate to a depth of only about 800 feet, and many of the creatures that live in the perpetual midnight of the depths have evolved their own luminous lighting system. Their survival depends ultimately on a constant drizzle of food reaching the ocean floor—waste matter from the levels above.

Trenches are found on the floors of some oceans. The deepest known is the Challenger Deep, in the Marianas Trench, discovered by the British survey ship *Challenger* in 1873, off the island of Guam in the Pacific. It is seven miles deep.

Just as mountains are barriers to movement on land, so the ranges of the sea act as barriers to ocean dwellers. For undersea creatures have to keep to the levels for which they are adapted.

Most of the great land masses are skirted by continental shelves, which slope gradually for up to 200 miles before plunging steeply into the deep. Some parts of a shelf are scored by vast canyons. The Hudson Canyon, off New York, is 150 miles long and 16,500 feet deep. These canyons may be caused by avalanches of mud and water—called turbidity currents—that roll down the shelves to the ocean floor.

The oceans absorb heat from the sun and spread it across the world in the form of vast currents. They are also driven by the winds, which are themselves created by the sun's heat. All major currents move in a circular path, called a gyre, because of the earth's rotation.

One of the most powerful currents is the Gulf Stream, which, when it leaves the Caribbean, is 50 miles wide and up to 1,500 feet deep. This warm current broadens and flows across the Atlantic at a speed of about four knots. In the North Atlantic the flow divides, part of it flowing north past Scotland, while the other sweeps south.

The daily rise and fall of tides is caused by the gravitational pull of the moon and sun. The effect of each pull causes, in effect, a bulge in the ocean. When the sun and moon are pulling on the same side of the earth, large tides—the spring tides—occur. Neap tides, the smallest, happen when the sun and moon pull at right angles. The largest tides occur where the sea

A WALL OF WATER. *Monster waves like this can hit with a force of 3½ tons per square foot. Waves are ripples from a storm center, and the giants are created when ripple patterns are in phase.*

runs into bottlenecks, as in the Bay of Fundy on Canada's eastern coast.

Waves are whipped up far out to sea by wind. They move across the water, which rises and falls as the swell passes. In shallower water the wave rears up and breaks.

Waves in midocean often reach a height of 40 feet. In 1933 the USS *Ramapo* survived a 112-foot wave—the highest recorded.

The level from which altitudes are measured is called sea level. This is an average of the ocean levels, for in reality the sea is not level at all. If, for example, the Pacific Ocean were suddenly frozen in a calm, without a ripple on its surface, there would be "plateaus" and "depressions" in the water, with differences of as much as 60 feet. This is caused by variations of atmospheric pressure and by the effect of the tides.

WHEN THE SEA TREMBLES

The killer waves that follow an earthquake

On April 1, 1946, an earthquake shook the abyssal plain deep beneath the Pacific Ocean. The wave it generated traveled the 2,250 miles to Hawaii in 4 hours and 34 minutes, an average speed of 490 miles per hour. When it struck the town of Hilo, the wave was more than 45 feet high. It killed 173 people, injured hundreds more, and caused $50 million worth of damage.

The "tidal wave" was a tsunami, caused by the movement of the seabed in the earthquake. Tsunamis are the most terrifying waves of all, hurtling silently across the ocean to crash onto the nearest shore. Ancient monuments along the coast of Japan carry the inscription "When you feel an earthquake, expect a tsunami"—reflecting Japan's long history of tsunami disasters.

The word "tsunami" is Japanese and was adopted by scientists of other countries to replace the misleading term "tidal wave," since tsunamis are not tidal at all. The wave spreads from the center of the disturbance, like the ripples from a pebble tossed into a pond. But the waves generated are so long and in deep water the swell is so slight that ships do not notice them. The energy stored in the tsunami is only about one-hundredth of the total energy of the earthquake, but it can equal the power of a multimegaton nuclear weapon.

As the tsunami approaches the shore and gets into shallower water, its energy becomes more concentrated, and the wave height increases. Usually, the wave is preceded by a trough that sucks out water along the shore, beaching ships like an abnormally low tide.

The effects of a tsunami are nearly always terrifying—and sometimes extraordinary. In the Hawaii tsunami of 1946 it was reported that one house was plucked from its foundations, carried hundreds of yards, and set down again—so gently that the breakfast dishes did not spill.

After the 1946 disaster a tsunami warning system was set up in the Pacific—the ocean most affected. Seismographic stations distributed across the Pacific notify tidal stations whenever an earthquake is detected.

CREST OF THE GREAT WAVE OF KANAGAWA. *Tsunami near the coast of Japan is depicted by Hokusai, the great 19th-century printmaker. In the background is the cone of Fujiyama.*

THE MEDITERRANEAN WAS A DESERT

How the seabed revealed its secret

Six million years ago the Mediterranean Sea dried up, leaving a barren desert lying 10,000 feet below the level of the Atlantic. Then the ocean burst through the Straits of Gibraltar, and its water cascaded into the Mediterranean basin in the most spectacular waterfall the earth has ever seen.

It was like turning on a gigantic tap to fill a bath 10,000 feet deep and about 2,000 miles long. Ten thousand cubic miles of water poured through the gap in a torrent 1,000 times greater than Niagara. Even so, it took almost 100 years to fill the basin up to the level we know today, flooding vast areas and leaving only mountain peaks above the water to form islands such as Malta and Sardinia.

The evidence for this story has come from geological drilling into the bottom of the Mediterranean, carried out from the U.S. research ship *Glomar Challenger*. In 1970 the ship, which was amassing scientific data about the theory of how the continents have drifted apart, sailed through the Straits of Gibraltar and began to drill into the soft sediments lying in the seabed, 6,100 feet below.

Six hundred feet through the sediments, its crew of scientists found a layer of gravel— unusual for ocean beds.

More holes were drilled, and they revealed even more extraordinary findings. The types of rock that lay below the sediments were what geologists call evaporites; they are found only in places where seas have dried up.

The scientists were at first unable to believe that the Mediterranean had once been a desert. Yet was it so impossible? The climate of the region is dry, and, even today, the sun sucks up water from the surface of the Mediterranean faster than rain and rivers can fill it. Evaporation is at the rate of 1,000 cubic miles of water every year, and only the flow from the Atlantic keeps the basin full.

Suppose that at some time in the past the straits had closed, isolating the Mediterranean from the Atlantic. It would have taken only 1,000 years to dry up the Mediterranean completely, turning it into a deep parched canyon, something like Death Valley in California.

There was one final piece of evidence that clinched the argument. Seventy years ago a deep gorge was discovered in southern France, cut into granite and lying hidden beneath millions of years of deposits. It looked like the gorge of an ancient river, but it lay hundreds of feet below the level of the Mediterranean.

Although the scientists on board the *Glomar Challenger* did not know it at the time, an identical gorge lay at the other end of the Mediterranean, under the River Nile. Russian scientists had been mystified by it while building the Aswan Dam.

Only one explanation is possible: The gorges must have been cut by rivers flowing into the Mediterranean basin when the level of the sea was much lower than it is today. The rivers, flowing across what is now the bottom of the sea, had cut the gorges.

So the Mediterranean was once a sea and then a deep, hot canyon, dotted with isolated salt lakes. Then, after 1½ million years, it became a sea again, as the dam burst at the straits, and water rushed in from the Atlantic.

POWER BEYOND BELIEF

The devastating winds produced by earth's rotation

An average hurricane releases as much energy as several atomic explosions. Its power output in a single minute could keep the United States in electricity for 50 years.

But hurricanes cannot be harnessed. They pour their energy unfettered into the atmosphere, often spreading death and disaster across vast coastal areas.

The hurricane that struck Bangladesh in 1970 produced a tidal wave that killed at least 200,000 people. In 1900, in Galveston, Texas, a hurricane created storm tides that swept 6,000 people to their deaths. Another 1,000 people were drowned in 1954, when a large ferryboat was sunk by a hurricane in Hakodate Bay, in Hokkaido, Japan's northernmost island.

HURRICANE FROM ABOVE. *The 90-mile-per-hour hurricane Gladys was photographed in 1968 by the crew of* Apollo 7 *from a height of 113 miles above the surface of the earth. The hurricane was about 150 miles southwest of Florida at the time; in the background is the island of Cuba.*

A hurricane is created at sea. The water temperature must be at least 80.6°F (27°C), which means that northern latitudes are normally spared. The warm sea creates a funnel of air that rises to perhaps 40,000 feet, producing vast cumulus clouds. High air currents are distributed, and more air from below is drawn into the funnel. The earth's rotation gives it a twist, and the hurricane is born—a mass of storm winds up to 400 miles in diameter, swirling around at up to 200 miles per hour.

At the center of every hurricane is the eye, an area of warm, calm breezes about 20 miles in diameter, which appears to be created by centrifugal force thrusting the winds outward. Places hit by a hurricane have a brief period of peace while the eye passes; then turmoil resumes as the other half of the hurricane arrives.

Hurricanes are constantly recharged at sea, since the water's heat makes air rise faster and faster in the central funnel. But on land the forests and mountains slow it by friction, and it can no longer draw up water vapor to power its condensation heat engine. So hurricanes rarely last more than a few days on land.

The terrible tornado

The hurricane is the giant of nature's violent storms, but its cousin, the tornado, operates on a smaller scale and is even more destructive. A tornado springs up without warning and usually lasts less than an hour.

One of the most devastating in history ripped through Missouri, Illinois, and Indiana in 1925, leaving 800 people dead and nearly 3,000 injured; yet it was only 300 yards wide.

The winds were so fierce that buildings collapsed, many trees were uprooted, trains were overturned. Winds on the edges of a tornado can reach speeds of 500 miles per hour.

Tornadoes occur on hot, humid days in central areas of the United States, the West Indies, the South Pacific, and Australia. They are funnel clouds that start to rotate gently and within minutes start twisting violently. The funnel travels forward at between 25 and 40 miles per hour. In its center air surges upward at 100 to 200 miles per hour, which creates enough suction power to drag huge objects into the whirling spout.

DEVASTATING "TWISTER." *A funnel-shaped wind storm that revolves violently, the tornado can cause death and enormous destruction within minutes.*

AWESOME SPECTACLE IN THE SKY

The power that may have created life

From earliest times man has speculated about the great power and destructiveness of lightning. It has always been one of nature's most awesome spectacles, dramatically lighting the dark sky during a storm.

Lightning is, in scientific terms, a visible discharge of atmospheric electricity. When a giant spark leaps from one part of a thundercloud to another, it appears as sheet lightning. A spark traveling from a cloud to the ground produces forked lightning.

Collision of droplets

No one is quite sure how the electricity builds up; but many scientists believe it is caused by collisions between the innumerable water droplets in a thundercloud.

The theory is that when falling drops of water strike smaller drops, some of the energy in each small drop is transformed into a charge of positive electricity on the new, larger drop. The air around it then gains an opposite, negative charge.

As it falls, each drop grows bigger as moisture in the air condenses on it. When the drop reaches a size of about a fifth of an inch across, it splits in two, each half still carrying its positive charge.

If the drops fell straight to the earth, the charge would have no effect; but inside a thundercloud there are powerful drafts of air that carry the drops up, so that the whole process is repeated time and again. As the charge on each drop increases, the thundercloud becomes a gigantic accumulator, storing electricity.

Within about 15 minutes the electrical charge stored in the raindrops becomes so great that it breaks down the insulating effect of the air around it. It is then that the lightning flash occurs.

Flash heat

Thunder is caused when the flash heats the air around it to temperatures up to 30,000°F (16,666°C)—three times the temperature of the sun's surface—so that it expands and then explodes.

The sound of the explosion travels more slowly than the lightning flash; so by counting the gap between the flash and the thunder it is possible to estimate the distance of the lightning. A five-second delay equals a one-mile distance.

Frequent thunderstorms

It is estimated that in any one year throughout the world there are 16 million thunderstorms. As many as 1,800 take place at any given moment.

One of the worst tragedies caused by lightning was at Brescia in Italy, in 1769. A flash hit the state arsenal, exploding more than 100 tons of gunpowder and killing an estimated 3,000 people.

Lightning fire

Perhaps the most disastrous fire started by lightning was at San Luis Obispo, California, on April 7, 1926. The flames raged for four days, spread over 900 acres, burned nearly 3 million barrels of oil, and destroyed $15 million worth of property. Amazingly, only two people died.

Despite lightning's deadly power, however, the number of people killed by it each year is relatively small. In the United States the average number of deaths is 150.

Life-giving force

Lightning also has beneficial effects. It causes nitrogen and oxygen in the air to combine and dissolve in raindrops. When the rain falls to the earth and soaks into the soil, it provides plantlife with nitrates, which are a valuable fertilizer.

And lightning may have been one of the original causes of life on this planet.

In a fascinating experiment at the University of Chicago, scientists prepared a mixture of gases—hydrogen, methane, ammonia, and water vapor—all of which are thought to have been in the atmosphere after the earth was formed.

Artificial lightning, which is an electrical charge, was then sent through the mixture of gases.

As a result, complex compounds known as amino acids were formed. Such acids are known to be the basic building blocks of all forms of life on the earth.

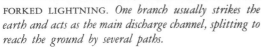

FORKED LIGHTNING. *One branch usually strikes the earth and acts as the main discharge channel, splitting to reach the ground by several paths.*

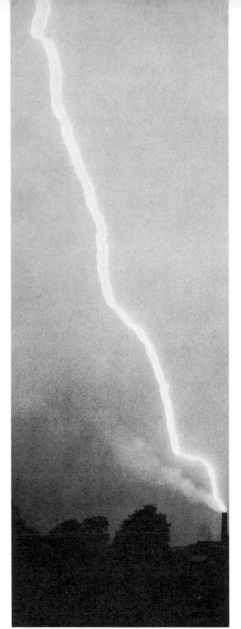

RIBBON LIGHTNING. *The strokes of this unusual type of electrical discharge to the earth are displaced as wind blows the channel sideways.*

BALL LIGHTNING. *Gas combustion could be the cause of this rare form of lightning, which appears as a ball about eight inches in diameter and lasts a few seconds.*

ILLUSIONS OF GRANDEUR

Cities, lakes, and mountains that vanish into thin air

In 1913 an American expedition, led by Donald MacMillan, set out to discover a mysterious arctic mountain range that had been sighted by the explorer Robert Peary. The party sailed as far as possible through the ice floes, then set out on foot over the ice until the vast mountain range, which Peary had called Crocker Land, came into view. But as the men moved toward it, the mountains receded; and when the men stood still, the mountains stood still as well.

Finally, as the sun disappeared below the horizon, the mountains dissolved to nothing, leaving only a vast expanse of ice. The men realized that they, and Robert Peary too, had been fooled by one of nature's strangest tricks—a mirage.

Mirages are usually associated with deserts, but they can appear anywhere. They occur when layers of air of different temperatures and different density are superimposed. The light waves are bent and refracted irregularly as they pass from an object through the unequal layers. The result is that it is possible to see objects that are far beyond the horizon.

The arctic explorers wasted much time and a great deal of money on their fruitless journey; but they at least survived. In the desert thirsty men have been driven mad by the sight of shimmering "lakes" that can never be reached. The Arabs call them Lakes of Satan.

Mirages in battle

Mirages have been recorded in battle. In 1798 Napoleon's army in Egypt saw a muddled landscape with lakes that vanished and blades of grass that turned into palm trees. So confused were they that the men are said to have fallen to their knees, praying for deliverance from the impending end of the world.

Gunners of the British artillery had to stop firing at one point during the desert campaign of the First World War, when a false landscape completely blotted out the enemy's position. On another occasion a German submarine captain, far from the east coast of the United States, saw New York City hovering above him as he peered through his periscope. He is said to have beaten a hasty retreat.

FIRE IN THE SKY

The dazzling spectacle of the auroras

The northern lights, according to Scandinavian folklore, are reflections from the golden shields of the warrior-maiden Valkyries as they escort the souls of dead heroes through the heavens to Valhalla.

Scientists have a less romantic explanation for the phenomenon. They believe that auroras are created in much the same way as pictures on a television screen. Television pictures are produced by a beam of electrons, which is focused onto a fluorescent screen by electromagnets. The earth's magnetic field has the same effect on charged particles coming in from the sun and focuses them onto the "screen" of the sky above the magnetic poles.

At the poles the magnetic fields are funnel shaped, and as the charged particles spiral down, they meet and excite atoms in the upper air. It is these atoms that cause the flashing lights of the aurora. Oxygen atoms produce the red, yellow,

and green lights; nitrogen produces violet, blue, or green.

An aurora appearing in the Northern Hemisphere is called aurora borealis, and in the Southern Hemisphere, aurora australis. Auroras are usually visible after the eruption of a solar flare, when a small part of the sun's surface suddenly brightens, causing a violent solar storm. During the storm the nuclei of atoms and electrons escape from the sun's atmosphere and shoot toward the earth, traveling at 400 to 600 miles per second.

The aurora's magnificent spectacle is seldom seen outside the polar regions; but it has been observed in the Mediterranean. Long ago, the Greek philosopher Aristotle wrote: "Sometimes on a fine night we see a variety of appearances in the sky: chasms . . . trenches . . . blood-red colors." He then went on to theorize that the air was turning into liquid fire.

THE SEASONING OF LIFE

The humble compound that flavored history

Common salt, the humble seasoning taken for granted at mealtime, is the stuff of history. It is so vital to human survival that wars have been fought over it, empires have been founded on it and have collapsed without it, and civilizations have grown up around it.

The word "salary" is a constant reminder of salt's importance. Roman legionaries were given a salarium—a salt allowance. Later, the word came to mean a cash allowance to buy salt. From this it was a short step to its present meaning.

Man realized from his earliest days that he had to have salt or perish. Without it the delicate salt and water balance in the body is upset, and death occurs through dehydration.

It began with stone age tribesmen following their cattle to salt licks—outcrops of salt rock the animals had located for their own survival. The humans carried salt from the life-giving rocks back to their caves, but eventually, they discovered a more reliable supply—brine salt springs.

Primitive cultures developed around these springs at such places as Droitwich in England, the Moselle region of France, and the Saale area in Germany. Over thousands of years entire forests were destroyed by man to provide wood fires for evaporating water from salt brines.

The demand for salt even altered landscapes. Ancient peoples created coastal lakes when they dug up sea-soaked peat, burned it, and retrieved salt by boiling the ashes in seawater.

While early Europeans were turning salt production into one of the first industries, similar operations were going on in other parts of the world. The earliest settlements in China were near the Yellow River saltpans. In the Jordan Valley villages grew up in about 8000 B.C. by the salt-laden Dead Sea and on Mount Sodom, which is also rich in salt.

Over thousands of years the development of transportation enabled people to move away from the salt sources. Early Egyptian farmers, for instance, were supplied by boat with salt from swamps at the mouth of the Nile.

The sea has always been the world's main source of supply, and significant phases in history have been directly influenced by its

SALT PANNING. *In some parts of the world, shallow salt-water pools are created by man to evaporate in the sun and provide salt that is panned for commercial use.*

SALT OF THE EARTH. *The areas of great salt concentrations in today's world are a clue to where yesterday's seas may have been.*

level. When oceans shrink, they leave behind coastal saltponds and salt-impregnated marshes. When the seas rise, they engulf these salt-rich areas.

In 500 B.C. the sea was at its lowest recorded level—three feet below its present line. It was then that the Greek and Phoenician civilizations reached their peaks. They had vast amounts of home-produced salt available for trade, and the Phoenicians increased their salt treasure by gathering stocks from as far away as Spain.

About 400 B.C. the Via Salaria, or Salt Road, came into being in Italy—and it still exists today among the oldest roads in the country. Salt was carried along it from Rome to the Sabine people in Italy's central regions.

The salt trade flourished for 1,000 years around the North Sea, the Mediterranean, and the Atlantic . . . but the sea was rising. By A.D. 500 it had reached three feet above today's level. In Europe trade declined as saltworks vanished under the encroaching waves.

Meanwhile, Arab lands, with access to the Dead Sea, enjoyed a new prosperity, trading salt for gold, marble, and other luxuries.

The Arabs' powerful role continued until the ninth century. Then the sea receded, and the English, French, and Dutch were able to start salt production again. The sea intervened in the 16th century by again flooding the saltworks along the coasts of Europe. Huge excavations on the east coast of England became lakes.

Hundreds of ships plied the oceans, carrying salt from nations with plentiful supplies to those hit by the flood. The traders realized that in parts of Africa their commodity was held more precious than human freedom, and salt developed into a powerful factor in the slave trade. Families in the salt-starved interior would sell children into slavery for a handful of salt.

Today the world consumes 169 million tons of salt a year—some from underground brine deposits, some from salt lakes or rock. But more than a quarter of the output is still from coastal pans, which are just as vulnerable to a rise in sea level as the pans that were submerged centuries ago. Our descendants hundreds of years from now will presumably be obtaining their salt from land now beneath the sea.

THE TREASURED METAL

The measure of wealth for men and nations

The world's currencies have revolved around gold for nearly 2,500 years—since King Croesus of Lydia struck the first pure gold coins. It is still the ultimate standard of wealth; yet nearly every country has gold in the ground, and there are at least 10 billion tons of it in the water of the oceans, waiting to be harvested.

One of the obstacles to recovering this vast natural treasure is its sheer elusiveness. In most places on land where gold appears, it is a mere fleck in the earth's crust. In the sea one of the heaviest concentrations is 10 milligrams of gold to 1 ton of saltwater; so 2,835 tons of water would have to be filtered to produce an ounce.

Even in a profitable mine, the rate of extraction can be as low as 1 part gold to 300,000 parts of waste rock.

Geologists are certain that every major goldfield in the world has now been discovered in the relentless hunt for what has been dubbed the "noble metal," but still the demand for gold increases.

It began when stone age men were attracted by shining specks in river gravel. They picked the specks out and found that they had acquired a heavy, pliable substance that could be hammered into pleasing shapes—the world's first gold ornaments.

What these early men did not realize was that their crude workmanship bore the stamp of eternity. Gold is impervious to the ravages of time. It is not tarnished by air, water, or most corrosives; and it can be melted down time and again without shedding any of its quality. A single ounce can be drawn out to make an unbroken wire 35 miles long—or hammered into a sheet 1/250,000 of an inch thick.

Gold is normally found in rock veins or sometimes just lying loose as nuggets—the prospector's dream. The veins filled fissures deep in the earth, which are gold-rich quartz, some of which was formed only 2 million to 10 million years ago. The loose gold nuggets were also trapped in rock at one time, but they escaped through erosion and were shaped into pellets as they were washed along streams and rivers toward the sea.

The biggest pure gold nugget ever found was 21 inches long and 10 inches across, and weighed more than 150 pounds. It was discovered in 1869 by two Englishmen, John Deason and Richard Oates, prospecting in Victoria, Australia. The huge nugget—dubbed the "welcome stranger"—was 98.66 percent pure gold. Deason and Oates sold it for almost $50,000.

The largest mass of gold ever found in a reef was the 630-pound Holtermann nugget, turned up in 1872 at a mine in Hill End, New South Wales. It yielded over 187 pounds of gold.

The famous California gold rush of 1848 was triggered off by a man named James Marshall, who discovered a piece of yellow metal stuck in a crevice of soft granite in a waterway at a mill located on the American River at Coloma, near Sacramento.

The Yukon stampede began in 1896, when gold was found among gravel near the Klondike River in a creek called Bonanza—a word that has come to mean sudden, unexpected wealth. But the greatest goldfield in the world had already been discovered thousands of miles away—and sold for exactly $50.

George Harrison, a prospector in South Africa, found traces of gold in the Witwatersrand basin. In 1886 Harrison was so poor that he sold his claim for $50. What he had given up for a pittance was the opportunity of becoming a multimillionaire, for The Rand was to become the world's major source of gold.

Forty-six years after Harrison's disovery, Emmanuel Jacobson and Allan Roberts began drilling on a farm called Aandenk, in the Orange Free State in South Africa. They reached 4,064 feet before their money ran out and they had to give up. In 1950 other prospectors continued the operation, and after going down only 400 feet more the gold-bearing Basal Reef of The Rand was opened up. Allan Roberts was so poor when he died that his friends had to pay for his funeral; yet The Rand, in which he and his partner had such faith, now produces more than 70 percent of the world's gold.

Tutankhamen's coffin

Probably the biggest solid gold object in existence is the innermost of three coffins of the Egyptian King Tutankhamen, which weighs 2,447 pounds. Other huge golden works from ancient times have long since disappeared, presumably melted down. One was a gold garment weighing more than a ton that adorned the statue of Athena on the Acropolis in Athens.

Many smaller treasures have passed down through history. Gold goblets dating from 2500 B.C. have been found at Ur, near the Persian Gulf. The Etruscans, who lived in central Italy from 900 B.C., were perhaps the greatest goldsmiths of all time, and they have bequeathed us a little bowl encrusted with 137,000 microscopic golden globules forming a peachlike bloom. It was not until 1933 that modern craftsmen learned this skill.

Today's goldsmiths cannot hope to tackle such impressive assignments as their predecessors—partly because the raw material is so expensive, but mainly because so much of it is now hoarded away as ingots in vaults.

At one time alchemists firmly believed that they could solve the supply problem by turning common metals into gold. Physicists now have the knowledge to create gold from lead or platinum by means of nuclear fission—but it would cost millions of dollars to produce just a golden pinhead.

So man must go on digging his precious metal from the ground, unless some practical technique is discovered, enabling him to extract gold from the sea. So far, it has eluded him.

Dr. Fritz Haber, a German chemist, conceived the idea at the end of the First World War to repay Germany's war debt from the gold in the North Sea. He tried and failed . . . but perhaps his ideas will be revived one day.

Weight	630 lbs.
Height	4 ft. 9 in.
Width	2 ft. 3 in.
Average Thickness	4 inches

LUCKY STRIKE. *The largest mass of gold in a reef was found in 1872 at a mine in New South Wales. It yielded 187 pounds of gold.*

THE ORIGINAL STONE

The Cullinan diamond, named after its finder, Thomas Cullinan, was the largest ever found. Discovered in 1905 at Pretoria, South Africa, it was bought by the Transvaal government in 1907 for £150,000 and presented to Edward VII on his 66th birthday. The life-size picture shows how the stone was split and cut into separate gems.

THE BIG SPLIT

THE HUGE diamond in Jacob Asscher's hand was an awe-inspiring sight, even for one of the world's most experienced gem cutters. It was 2:45 p.m. on February 10, 1908, and Asscher was preparing to break up the biggest diamond in history—about five inches across and nearly 1½ pounds in weight. Watched by a group of assistants at his company's headquarters in Amsterdam, Asscher laid a diamond cleaver along a meticulously plotted groove in the stone. The slightest miscalculation and he would have nothing but a worthless heap of diamond fragments. He rapped down a heavy steel rod . . . and the tool blade snapped. Asscher wiped his brow and called for another blade.

On his next blow the blade did its work. The stone fell apart—and Jacob Asscher fainted. When he recovered, he had two pieces of priceless stone, which he then cut into 105 separate diamonds.

THE SEVEN LARGEST PIECES

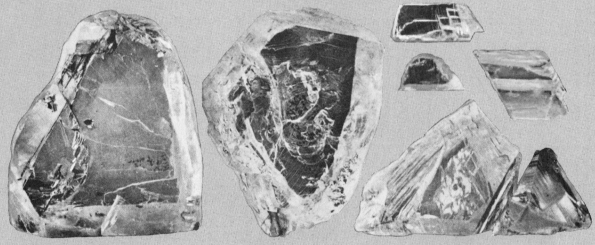

THE PRINCIPAL FINISHED GEMS

Set in
brooch worn by
the Queen Mother

Set in
pendant owned
by the Queen

Set in
Imperial State Crown

Star of Africa
in Queen's scepter

Set in
necklace worn by
Queen Elizabeth

Set in
Queen Mary's
crown

Set in
Queen Mary's
crown

JEWEL OF FIRE
The brilliant stone that lasts forever

The word "diamond" comes from the Greek *adamas*, meaning "invincible"—an apt description for the hardest substance on earth. The mineral is composed of pure carbon and is formed deep within the earth under enormous pressures and temperatures.

A diamond's weight is measured in carats, equal to one-fifth of a gram, and there are about 142 carats to the ounce. The word "carat" is believed to be derived from the carob bean, which grows on a tree called *Ceratonia siliqua*. The first two syllables of the name have apparently become transformed into carat.

It is the extraordinary "fire" of diamonds that makes them so attractive. A diamond splits up light as does no other gem, gloriously reflecting the colors of the spectrum.

To obtain this brilliance, the stone must be precisely cut and polished. First, the stone is marked for cutting by a planner, who is an expert on the correct cutting for its particular shape and atomic structure. He marks the stone with India ink to show where it should be cut.

Diamond cuts diamond

If the stone is to be cleaved, the cleaver cuts a groove, using another diamond as a cutting tool. He mounts the diamond in a holder and inserts a steel wedge into the groove. With a sharp blow from a mallet the diamond is split.

Sawing is done by means of a paper-thin disk of phosphor bronze coated with diamond dust. The disk spins at about 4,000 revolutions per minute and will cut through a one-carat rough stone in four to eight hours. The diamond is then faceted and polished, using diamond dust as the polishing medium.

The first major diamond discovery in South Africa was made in 1867 by a Boer child who pocketed an attractive-looking pebble he had found on the banks of the Orange River. It was a diamond weighing 21.25 carats.

Two years later prospectors rushed in when a shepherd boy picked up an even finer stone in the same area. He swapped it for 500 sheep, 10 oxen, and a horse. The man who made the trade sold the stone in turn for about $50,000. The stone, weighing 83.5 carats, was later cut and polished into a pear-shaped diamond for the Countess of Dudley.

When the prospectors moved in, they built a shantytown which they called Kimberley, after the British Colonial Secretary of the time. Some of the early diamond hunters quickly struck it rich, for the precious stones were lying in distinctive patches of yellow clay. Even when the topmost diamonds were harvested, there were more underneath in a layer of "blue ground," which was the prospectors' name for kimberlite.

Eventually, the adventurers gave way to commercial miners, who dug down thousands of feet to claw every available diamond from the ground. But after those initial simple treasure hunts, diamond mining became hard work. At Kimberley nowadays 1,000 tons of ground must be moved to yield just an ounce or so of diamonds. But the stones are so precious that even this vast turnover in waste material is still profitable.

The Koh-i-noor

One of the most famous diamonds, and certainly the one with the longest history, is the Koh-i-noor. It was first reported in 1304 as being in the possession of the Raja of Malwa in India. For the next 400 years it formed part of the treasure of the Mogul Emperors, until the Nadir Shah of Persia invaded India in 1739 and took the diamond. In 1849 it was discovered in the jewel house of Lahore, capital of Punjab, when that province of India was annexed by the British.

The East India Company presented it to Queen Victoria in 1850, but she was disappointed with its lack of fire and had it recut from its original weight of 186.5 carats to 108.93 carats. It is now part of the British crown jewels.

One diamond that did not end up in the crown jewels, although it passed through London, is the Orloff, which weighs 194.8 carats. This stone is reputed to have been the eye of a statue of Brahma in Mysore (India) at the beginning of the 18th century. A French soldier is said to have risked his life in 1750 to pry it out and sell it for about $10,000 to the captain of an English ship. The stone came to London, where a dealer bought it for about $60,000, and in turn it was sold in 1773 for about $450,000 to a

Russian, Prince Orloff. Revolutionaries found the diamond in Russia's imperial treasury in 1917, and today it is one of the prizes of the state collection in Moscow.

The Hope Diamond

During the French Revolution a stone weighing 67.1 carats, and known as the Blue Diamond of the Crown, was looted from Louis XVI. It was never seen again, but in 1830 a diamond was sold in London to Henry Hope. This stone, the United States' most famous diamond, weighs 44.5 carats and is certainly blue, like the one that vanished in France in 1792. The Hope Diamond is now owned by the Smithsonian Institution.

About five tons of diamonds are mined every year. Much of the production goes to industry, for diamonds are the only known natural material for cutting and fashioning hard metals.

As the mines are depleted, attention is being paid to the possibility of getting diamonds from the seabed. South Africa's Marine Diamond Corporation recovered more than 2,000 stones during its first 10 months of dredging for diamonds in international waters.

STRIKING IT RICH

Liquid assets beneath the ground

Edwin Drake, a former railroad conductor, seemed an odd choice to supervise the drilling of the world's first oil well when he was hired by George H. Bissell in the late 1850's. Drake struck oil in 1859.

A sticky, black mess bubbled to the surface at Drake's workings on the site of a former Seneca Indian village, 75 miles from Pittsburgh, Pennsylvania. The story goes that young John D. Rockefeller, sent by a commission house to investigate Drake's well, reported that it seemed to offer no real prospect of profit—a prediction he was to disprove in his own lifetime by becoming one of the world's richest men, with a fortune based on oil.

With or without Rockefeller's approval, the Seneca Oil Company was in business, heralding the end of man's dependence on whales as a source of oil.

Within a year the nearby town of Titusville had become a thriving community. Prospectors drilled thousands of wells to cash in on the possibility of extracting oil from the ground for light and heat. Oil is still produced in the area.

The hunt for oil in the ground had been launched to find a cheap substitute for whale oil in lamps. At first, petroleum was scorned as a valueless by-product, but by the turn of the century the emphasis was changed by the development of the automobile.

Although the commercial exploitation of one of the world's most valuable and conve-

MEETING THE DEMAND. *The City Field outside Los Angeles in 1895 was typical of the industrial congestion created by the world's newfound need for oil and its by-products.*

nient resources is a modern phenomenon, oil has been known for thousands of years. The Sumerians, Assyrians, and Babylonians used bitumen in 3000 B.C. as a building mortar and for fixing jewelry in place. The bitumen was formed after crude oil seeped up through the ground to the surface and was weathered by the sun.

During their wanderings the children of Israel were guided by "day in a pillar of cloud . . . and by night in a pillar of fire"—a perfect description of what happens when an oil seepage catches fire.

Later, the Persians and Arabs collected the oil itself and used it for lighting and for cleaning silk. By A.D. 300 oil was being used by the Chinese, who discovered it by accident when they dug salt mines in oilfields. Both the Chinese and the American Indians used oil as a medicine.

In 1271 the Venetian traveler Marco Polo described oil springs near Baku on the Caspian Sea, where for 1,200 years there had been a fire-worshiping cult around the "eternal fires"—oil seepages that burned day and night. But it was not until the 19th century that the true potential of such oil finds was realized.

In 1850, James Young, a Scottish industrial chemist, patented a process for manufacturing crude oil from bituminous coal and shale. He refined this oil into paraffin, and the product proved such a formidable competitor to whale oil that plants were set up rapidly near coal mines in Britain and other countries.

The next step was inevitable. Some manufacturers successfully experimented with oil obtained from seepage swamps, to bypass one of Young's production stages. The stage was set for Edwin Drake to start drilling to produce natural oil.

He was a fortunate man, for wherever oil is found, it is there only because of a series of accidents and geologic freaks. The substance is believed to be derived from the decomposed remains of countless billions of tiny aquatic plants and animals.

Over the ages they were changed into oil with the help of the weight of rock above them. Oil has been produced only in tropical latitudes. Deposits in Alaska, beneath the North Sea, and in other places far from the Tropics, have moved to their present sites with the drifting continents.

Oil can be held underground only where there is a perfect seal of rock above to keep it in place, and these oil traps are the reservoirs prospectors hunt for. But even with the most sophisticated instruments, it is impossible to be sure oil exists at a drilling site until a well is sunk.

At one time a successful strike was often heralded by a "gusher"—a huge jet of oil thrust to the surface by compressed natural gas. It could take days to get the jet under control. In 1901, for instance, one Texas gusher hurled 30 million gallons of oil to waste. There were only 14 million gallons left underground when the well went into normal production. But modern drilling techniques have overcome this hazard.

No matter how much waste is avoided, however, the amount of oil in the world is limited. A substantial proportion of all land-based oilfields is now thought to have been discovered.

It took millions of years for the oil deposits to be created; but in not much more than 100 years since Drake made his strike, one-third of the world's known oil reserves have been used up. It is unlikely the demand can be satisfied for more than another 100 years, no matter how much oil comes from beneath the seabed.

AUSTRALIA'S ETERNAL FIRE

THE FIRE that never goes out has been eating away an Australian mountain for thousands of years. It is in the Hunter Valley region of New South Wales, 15 miles north of Scone. Early explorers thought that the column of smoke came from a volcano, but investigation showed that the cause was a burning seam of coal, 500 feet below the surface. It is thought that about 2,000 years ago a tree, perhaps set on fire by lightning, fell onto the exposed face of the coal seam. This set fire to the coal, and over the years the fire has slowly smoldered along the line of the seam. Another theory is that the seam caught fire by spontaneous combustion—through the heat generated by the oxidation of sulfur pyrites. The local aborigines fear the place, yet associate it with the creator Bhaiami and his earthly mediator Turramulan, who speaks from the smoke.

SENTINELS OF MILLENNIA

Ancient trees that help to rewrite history

Before the founding of Rome, before the golden age of Athens, and about the same time as the pyramids were built, a seed germinated on a mountain in what is now California. The tree that grew from that seed is still alive—the world's oldest living thing. It is Methuselah, a 4,600-year-old bristlecone pine growing 9,000 feet up in the White Mountains.

There was another bristlecone even older than Methuselah. When it was cut down in 1964 for scientific study, it was found to be 4,900 years old.

Scientists estimate that a bristlecone may live for 5,000 years; so Methuselah may be around for another 400 years.

At the laboratory of Tree-Ring Research at the University of Arizona, scientists have compiled a chronology based on pine rings and other tree remnants. In this way, every year dating back to 6200 B.C. has been specifically identified.

Researchers also discovered a fossil tree line of bristlecone remnants above the current tree line on Mount Washington in eastern Nevada, as well as in the White Mountains of California. By examining damaged water-conductor cells, the scientists in California were able to pinpoint climatic conditions of years gone by, such as the freak cold waves in the summers of 1453 and 1601.

Pollen grains trapped in scar tissue adjacent to rings have been examined, so that a picture of plantlife in 1300 B.C. can be compared with that of A.D. 350.

These pines are, in effect, organic computers that automatically record the changing conditions of life on this planet.

Paradoxically, the oldest bristlecones live in the poorest conditions—steep and rocky land, 9,500 feet or more above sea level, with only thin soil, very little rainfall, and scant vegetation to carry ground fire.

In better conditions bristlecones grow faster, die earlier, and decay more quickly.

The ancient pines have also helped to bring about some startling changes in our reckoning of prehistory.

Radiocarbon readings of bristlecone pine rings year by year showed up discrepancies in the radiocarbon dating systems used to date archeological finds. Basically, the radiocarbon dating system involves measuring the amounts of carbon 14 remaining in a fossil and, by estimating the amount of carbon loss, calculating its age.

But this system was based on the assumption that carbon in the atmosphere, caused by radioactive bombardment, had remained constant. The examination of the pines suggested fluctuations of the amount of radiocarbon, creating discrepancies in the dating system.

A new, recalibrated system of dates, based on the bristlecone scale, was devised, involving

NATURAL HISTORIAN. *Dead bristlecone pines continue to resist the elements and enable man to date the events of his past more accurately.*

date discrepancies ranging from a few centuries to 1,000 years.

This is not simply a matter of correcting and reshuffling a few historical date inaccuracies. The revised system has weakened assumptions about the influence of ancient cultures upon each other.

For example, archeologist Colin Renfrew, of the University of Southampton in England, has said that some of the great stone tombs found in northwestern France and in Spain may be older than the pyramids. It has also been suggested, using the new dating system, that important, evolutionary trends in building and engineering and the use of metals may have originated in Europe and not, as hitherto supposed, in the East.

The implications are that early Europeans were not less creative than advanced civilizations elsewhere. It could mean, Renfrew suggests, that textbooks of prehistory will have to be rewritten.

At the University of California a scientist has been using the tree as an aid in checking the effects of bomb tests.

Thus, the bristlecone pine, a tree with a lifespan that exceeds the period of development of modern civilization, is helping man to learn more about his past, present, and, indirectly, his future.

THE MIGHTY AND MICROSCOPIC

Giants and midgets of the plant kingdom

The world's largest seeds resemble giant coconuts and for centuries were thought to come from the sea. They were washed up on the shores of the Indian Ocean, and, consequently, those who found them called them sea coconuts.

But with the discovery of the Seychelles Islands in the mid-18th century, the seeds, which weigh upwards of 40 pounds and are two or three times the size of coconuts, were found to come from tall nut palms that grow only on the islands.

For years Far Eastern Kings and Oriental potentates eagerly sought the seeds, thinking that they could be used as antidotes to poison.

The oldest and biggest

The largest plants in the world are the Big Trees (*Sequoia gigantea*) of California that live to be more than 3,000 years old. They are also the world's largest living organisms.

The Big Trees live in groves between 6,000 and 8,000 feet high on the western slopes of the Sierra Nevada Mountains. "General Sherman" in Sequoia National Park, California, is 272 feet tall, has a base circumference of 101 feet 7 inches, and is estimated to weigh 2,145 tons.

Cousins of the Big Trees, the west-coast redwoods (*Sequoia sempervirens*) are the world's tallest trees. These giants grow along the California coast, and the tallest is the Howard Libbey tree in the Redwood Creek Grove, in Humboldt County. It is 366 feet 2 inches tall.

What was the tallest tree of all time is a matter of conjecture. In 1872, in Victoria, Australia, lumberjacks felled a mountain ash that was believed to have been 500 feet tall. But there is no official record of this.

There are claims that the tallest-ever title should go to a Douglas fir felled in British Columbia in 1940 and said to have measured 417 feet.

The tallest nonsequoia alive today is also a Douglas fir, at Quinault Lake Park Trail, Washington. It is 310 feet tall.

The stoutest living tree is in the Mexican state of Oaxaca. It is a Montezuma cypress, called the Santa Maria del Tule, and has a girth between 112 and 113 feet at a height of about 5 feet from the ground.

In 1770 a European chestnut, known as the Chestnut of the Hundred Horses, measuring 204 feet in circumference, was found on the edge of Mount Etna in Sicily.

The seed of all these tremendous trees weighs only about 1/6,000 of an ounce.

The tiniest plants are, in fact, microscopic algae and bacteria, which are found almost everywhere.

Algae live on the surface of animals, in soil, in hot springs, in saltwater and freshwater, and on long-lying snow.

Bacteria are even more plentiful and are found in the human body, feeding on cells and on each other. These are so small that about 25 million of them could fit on the head of a pin.

Viruses even smaller

There are even smaller viruses that prey upon bacteria. But it is not clear, from a scientific standpoint, whether viruses should be classed among living things.

A virus cannot live until it gets into the cell of another living organism. It is not large enough to contain all the chemical information necessary to support its life processes, and the virus uses the chemicals it finds in the cells of its host.

They are so microscopic that many hundreds of viruses can live in the smallest plankton, minute plants and animals that float on freshwater and saltwater surfaces.

Planktons themselves are so small that 500 of them, laid side by side, would fit in a one-millimeter space.

But despite their size, some groups of plankton, such as a type known as *Coccolithophoridae*, are exotically beautiful. Each of these tiny plants has an outer armor of elaborately patterned scales made of chalk. They are among the smallest known plants in the world—at the other end of nature's scale from the trees of California.

BEAUTY IN MINIATURE. *One of the smallest plants,* Cyclococcolithus leptoporus *has an elaborate outer shell of patterned scales. They are so tiny that 500 would fit on a pinhead.*

REACH FOR THE SKY. *The Howard Libbey tree (second from right) is the world's tallest known tree. It is 366 feet 2 inches high—about 90 feet taller than its near neighbors, the Big Trees.*

GARDEN OF EXTREMITIES

The largest and smallest flowers

The world's smallest flower, and also the world's smallest flowering plant, is the Brazilian duckweed called wolffia. The whole plant can be less than 1/16 inch across and the flower about half that. The rootless *Wolffia punctata* has fronds only 1/35 to 1/50 of an inch long.

These tiny plants were first discovered by the French naturalist Hugh Algernon Weddell, who found them growing among the leaves of the largest flowering plant that lives in freshwater, the giant water lily *Victoria amazonica*. Named after Queen Victoria and the river on which it grows, this water lily is the fastest growing flowering plant. Its massive leaves can grow from a very small prickly bud to more than three feet across in as few as six days.

The world's largest flower is produced by the plant *Rafflesia arnoldii*, named after the two men who discovered it, Sir Thomas Stamford Raffles and Joseph Arnold. Rafflesia is parasitic on the roots of vines in the deeply shaded forests of Borneo, the Malay Peninsula, and other parts of Southeast Asia. It has no roots, leaves, or stems to speak of, but the flower itself can measure more than three feet across and is three-quarters of an inch thick. Resembling the heart of an enormous red cabbage, a bloom can weigh as much as 15 pounds.

Rafflesia is marred by its nauseating smell, resembling that of rotting meat. But the plant with the most repulsive smell is the tropical giant arum lily. The function of the smell is to attract flies to carry the pollen.

NATURE'S MASS PRODUCTION

UP, UP, AND AWAY. A spore is a single cell capable of development. Spores from an insignificant mold, *Cladosporium herbarum*—which have been caught by balloons as high as 90,000 feet above the earth's surface—are the most common.

Some of the larger bracket fungi, often found growing on old decaying trees, can keep up a daily spore production of as many as 30 billion for a period of five months.

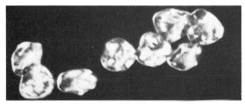

Pollen grains of the silver birch, here enlarged 300 times, cause most of the hay fever in Scandinavia.

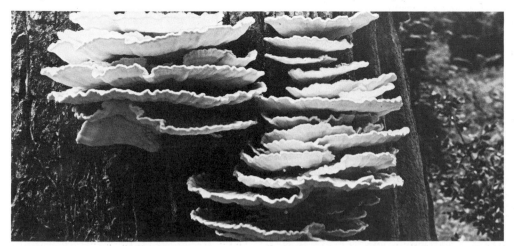

Bracket fungus is especially common in the United States on oak, birch, and other trees. This picture shows a sulfur polypore fungus, which causes rot in the heart of the tree.

THE FLESH EATERS

The predators of the plant world

A fly hovered over a small, white-blossomed herb, whose open leaves revealed an inviting red center. The fly descended to investigate, and that was a mistake—the last it ever made. For the open leaves sprang together, their comblike edges interlocking to form a death trap. Slowly, the trap tightened, and the Venus's-flytrap began to devour its latest victim.

The flytrap, a native of North and South Carolina, is one of a number of carnivorous plants that live by digesting animal proteins into simple, soluble amino acids. Its leaves are hinged at the center, and threadlike triggers set the trap. The moment an insect touches one of the triggers the trap is sprung, and the plant's digestive juices set to work on the creature.

The process usually takes about 10 days; then the flytrap opens its leaves again and ejects the indigestible parts, such as wings and scales.

A near relative of the Venus's-flytrap is the pitcher plant, found in the northern United States, which has small, pitcher-shaped containers hanging from its leaves. An insect is lured into the trap by the plant's exotic smell, and as it crawls over the slippery mouth of the pitcher, it loses its footing and falls into a pool. Stiff, downward-pointing bristles prevent the victim from climbing out, and it soon succumbs to the poisonous bath of digestive juices.

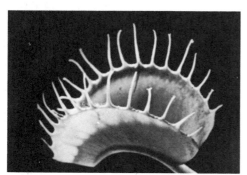

SETTING THE TRAP. *A Venus's-flytrap opens its leaves and waits for a victim. Insects are attracted by its blood-red center.*

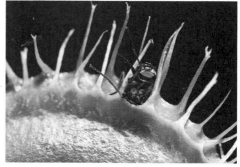

THE TRAP IS SPRUNG. *An unsuspecting fly has touched off the trap and becomes a meal for the carnivorous plant.*

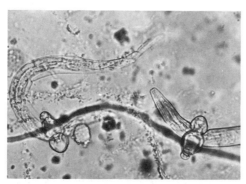

A LIVING SNARE. *Two nematodes are caught in the stranglehold of* Dactylaria gracilis. *The one on the right is freshly caught; the one on the left is almost entirely consumed.*

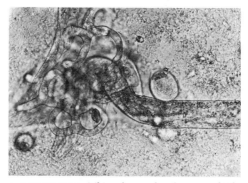

A STICKY END. *This eelworm has been caught by* Trichothecium cystosporium, *a fungus with adhesive networks. The creature's head is entangled with the fungal network.*

Remarkable trapper

Perhaps the most remarkable of the animal-trapping plants is the bladderwort, usually found in tropical regions. It grows in ponds and sluggish streams, rooting in the mud or drifting at the mercy of winds and currents. It is a long, slender plant with many-sectioned leaves, each carrying about a dozen small bladders. These are the traps, and the entrance is a door that can be pushed open from the outside but not from the inside. The insect does not enter by choice—it is sucked in.

Not all insect-catching plants use mechanical traps. Some employ a "flypaper" method. The beautiful sundew of North America, Australia, and South Africa is a sweet-smelling plant, with a flower that can kill an unwary creature.

Its pincushion center contains a strong glue, and when an insect alights, it becomes firmly stuck. Then the glittering heads of the pins curl over the victim—and the sundew begins its meal.

Similarly, the leafy butterwort, lying flat on the ground in moist and mossy areas, usually in the Northern Hemisphere, waits for its insect prey. When a moth or bee alights to feed, the plant exudes a sticky secretion to hold the insect. Then it emits an enzyme that digests the proteins over which the leaves have curled.

DO PLANTS HAVE EMOTIONS?

Sensitive creatures in the botanical world

In the fantasy world of Walt Disney cartoons, the creatures of nature perceive more than mere man. At the approach of danger trees draw in their branches; bushes shrivel; flowers close their blossoms; blades of grass send messages to fields far away. Saucer-eyed, children throughout the world anticipate the happy ending when the evil threat is overcome. Then the music surges; trees reach for the sun; flowers bloom; and the audience applauds the end of another make-believe episode.

Or is it make-believe?

Is it possible that plants know who loves them and who wishes them harm? Within the past decade several researchers have reported that plants do know who their friends are and react to threats—even going so far as to "faint" in the presence of a dangerous person.

Cleve Backster is one of the men working in this field. A lie-detector expert, Backster attached one of his polygraphs to the leaves of a philodendron and saw, to his surprise, that the tracing began to show a pattern typical of "the response you get when you subject a human to emotional stimulation of short duration."

In search of other reactions Backster decided to burn the leaf of the plant. While he was thinking about this, there was a dramatic upward sweep in the tracing pattern. He had neither moved nor touched the plant. Backster concluded that he had frightened the plant with his decision to burn it. Not only can plants feel things, he decided, they can also anticipate actions by reading people's minds.

Reports of Backster's philodendron experience were made public early in 1966. News coverage was vast, and a large percentage of the population apparently accepted the findings at face value. Owners of plants became, in various ways, servants of their botanical friends. Some devotees of the new cult even installed recorded-music systems so that their plants would not feel alone while their caretakers were away.

The belief that plants are capable of emotional response was not a short-lived fad. In 1973 Peter Tompkins and Christopher Bird's *The Secret Life of Plants* became a bestseller. Enlarging upon Backster's thesis, Tompkins and Bird stated that plants respond to speech, thoughts, and prayers. They felt they had proved that plants could count and alter their behavior.

The nature of their proof is what many scientists find questionable. Scientific evidence, they argue, is an accumulation of data derived from repeated experiments that can be controlled and recorded, not only by the initiators of a project but by researchers in laboratories anywhere in the world.

Backster, Tompkins, and Bird turn their backs upon these requirements. They say that "what makes plants live, or why, does not appear to be the purview of science." They maintain that some very sensitive people might be able to obtain the very same results as they. In short, the character of the researcher determines the results of the experiment.

Strange and mysterious creatures that share our world

The surprising animal kingdom

•

THE LONG AND THE SHORT AND THE TALL

Laws and limits of size

A favorite theme of science-fiction films is that ants or other insects, mutated by radiation, will grow to gigantic proportions and terrorize mankind. But nature prevents this nightmarish fiction from becoming a reality; for the size of every living creature on earth is limited by immutable laws.

It would be just as impossible to produce an ant the size of a horse as it would be to shrink a man to the size of a mouse or a bird. In both cases the change in size would alter the relationship between mass and surface area, producing new problems for the new-sized creature.

As the diagram on this page makes clear, double the size of an animal, and you reduce by half the rate at which it loses heat through its surface. Conversely, reduce its size by half, and it loses its body heat twice as fast. A man as small as a bird would have to do as birds do: spend most of his time eating or looking for high-energy food—assuming that, without feathers, he did not freeze to death in a few minutes.

The fact that large animals conserve body heat better than small ones explains why those that live in polar regions are generally bulkier than those that live in warmer climates. A polar bear, for instance, can grow to 11 feet tall and weigh up to 1,600 pounds—nearly twice the height and six times the weight of the Himalayan black bear.

Bulky animals that live in hot climates, such as elephants and rhinos, have to get rid of excess heat by wallowing in water and plastering themselves with cool mud.

An ant that reached the size of a horse, apart from overheating, would die of oxygen starvation, for insects have no lungs. Oxygen reaches their air sacs through tiny holes, called spiracles, in their bodies. In insects of normal size the air simply seeps through to the air sacs; but with an ant as big as a horse, it would take a wind of hurricane strength to force the air from its spiracles down to its internal tissues.

Even if the giant ant of science fiction somehow evolved muscle-powered lungs, it would not be saved. For its shell would need to thicken immensely if it were not to buckle under air pressure, with the result that it would crush the body it was meant to protect.

Apart from considerations like these, there

THE PROBLEM OF SIZE. *Imagine a man whose mass is one cubic unit (small figure). Double his height, and his mass increases eightfold, while his surface area increases only four times (large figure). His rate of heat loss through the skin will have been halved. Such an increase in size would cause overheating problems.*

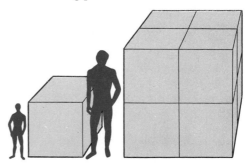

are many other factors that affect size. At one end of the scale, anything less than about 1/1,000 of a centimeter in diameter is at the mercy of the molecules around it. Molecules of air, for instance, are in constant motion, colliding with one another and with objects in their way. With large objects the collisions on one side are balanced by those on the other, producing the unfelt force known as air pressure. But if the object is infinitesimally small, the collisions are uneven, so that the smallest living organisms are kept in such an active state that they cannot control their environment.

At the other end of the scale, massive bulk brings its own penalties, not the least of which is the difficulty of finding food. The largest animal the world has ever seen, the 100-ton blue whale, needs 4 tons of food a day. It obtains this by sucking in thousands of gallons of seawater and straining out krill and other tiny organisms from this intake. No creature living on less widely available food could attain such a size.

The largest living organisms, the sequoia and redwood trees of California, get around the problem of finding food by manufacturing their own. Like almost all plants, they transform carbon dioxide into sugar and oxygen.

The drawback to being a plant, whatever its size, is again lack of control over the environment. No creature that has to move about can afford to be as large as these trees, for its appetite would then outstrip its food supply.

LARGEST, SMALLEST, FASTEST

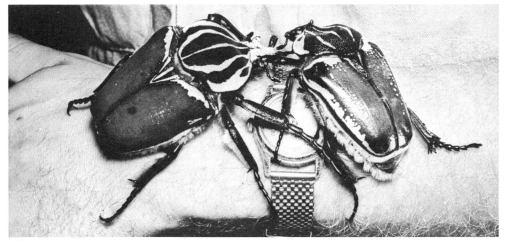

The Goliath beetle, measuring 4 inches across and 5.8 inches in length, is the world's largest known insect.

WHEN animal life first appeared on earth, some 2 billion years ago, it was in the form of single-celled creatures called protozoa. As more complex animals evolved, their need for an ever greater number of cells brought about an automatic increase in size. A man, for instance, has billions of cells: His very complexity sets a limit to how small he can be.

The largest and heaviest animals the world has ever seen are blue whales, some of which weigh more than 100 tons. The largest creature without a backbone is the Atlantic giant squid, which can weigh 2.5 tons and grow up to 55 feet long. The largest land mammal is the African bush elephant, which averages 5.6 tons; while at the other end of the scale the pygmy shrew of the Northern Hemisphere is rarely longer than 2½ inches from nose to tail.

The flightless North African ostrich is the largest bird, weighing up to 345 pounds and growing to nine feet tall. The smallest is the bee hummingbird of Cuba: 2 inches long with a 1.1-inch wingspan. The fastest creature is the spine-tailed swift, which reportedly can fly at speeds over 200 miles an hour. In the insect world the Goliath beetle weighs in at 3.5 ounces and measures 4 inches across and 5.8 inches long. The South American bird-eating spider, with a leg span of 10 inches and 3½-inch body length, is the largest spider.

THE SUPERSENSES OF ANIMALS

Nature's amazing communication systems

To a sparrow the human voice sounds something like the low rumbling of distant thunder, and the low notes produced by a bass singer may well be completely inaudible to the bird.

This is because the sparrow's hearing range is different from a human being's. Like many of the creatures in the world around us, it possesses the five senses of sight, hearing, touch, taste, and smell. These are heightened or diminished according to the creature's way of life.

In birds it is the sense of sight that has developed to an unusual degree. The high-soaring buzzard, which needs to be able to pick out a meal as small as a lizard or even a beetle on the ground below, has eyesight eight times as keen as a man's.

Animals that hunt by following a trail, on the other hand, often have poor eyesight but a keen sense of smell. Dogs, for instance, see a world that is blurred and devoid of color—apart from shades of gray—for they are shortsighted and have no color vision.

But a dog's sense of smell is to a man's what a symphony orchestra is to a penny whistle. An Alsatian has 220 million olfactory cells, compared with a man's 5 million, and experiments suggest that this makes it a million times better at detecting odors.

This does not mean that the sense of smell in humans is rudimentary. Most of us are equipped with a far more sensitive nose than we need in the modern world. The average human being can distinguish between more than 10,000 different odors and, if put to the test, could detect the presence of a single drop of musk inside a large concert hall.

Only one relevant smell

It is not always the ability to distinguish between a host of smells that is necessary to survival. There is a type of beetle larva that feeds on vine roots and is sensitive only to a single smell—that of carbon dioxide, which is given off by the roots of vines. Any other smell is irrelevant to the larva, but it will pursue the scent of carbon dioxide unswervingly through the ground until it reaches its goal.

The characteristic scent of every living creature is carried in molecules that leave the body in the form of sweat, breath, bodily wastes, and so on. With every step you take, you leave behind millions of sweat-borne molecules, which lay a scent trail.

Creatures that spend most of their time in the air cannot mark the ground with a scent trail; yet butterflies, in the mating season, can attract a mate from miles away by scent alone. The female butterfly carries a store of perfume weighing only 1/10,000 of a milligram, and she squirts minute fractions of it into the air. These scent molecules can be detected by a male seven miles away.

Echo-locating system

Just as remarkable is the echo-locating system used by bats to pinpoint their prey or obstacles in their way. Contrary to popular belief, bats are not entirely blind. Most can see in twilight; but in pitch darkness they rely on sending out high-frequency squeaks, some audible to the human ear, others inaudible. The returning echoes tell the bats the exact position of any obstacles.

In this way bats can flit about in great numbers without colliding. Even when they fly out of caves in the thousands, they respond only to their own individual echo signals and are not confused by their neighbors' noises.

How they manage to tune in so finely remains a mystery. Scientists have conducted experiments in which they tried to jam the radar signals of bats by drowning them with a volume of noise 2,000 times as intense and on the same frequency. It made no difference. Somehow, the bats managed to pick out their own echoes and ignore the foreign noise.

One of the oddest hearing systems in nature is that of the North American ichneumon fly. Its "ears" are in its feet, and it uses them to listen for the noise made by the larvae of the horntail thick-waisted wasp when they are chewing wood.

When the larvae of the fly hatch, they feed on the living bodies of the moth larvae. No other host is suitable. The female fly locates the moth larvae with deadly accuracy, both by her sense of smell and by running up and down tree trunks, listening with the hearing cells in her feet for the sound of chewing inside.

Many of the senses of animals are switched

A SNAKE'S SECOND SIGHT. *The deep pits between the red eyes of this bamboo viper of Formosa are organs sensitive to heat. They help it to find its warm-blooded prey, even in darkness. These extra aids were first observed in the rattlesnake by two American zoologists in 1952.*

on or off by a system of signals. Bees, for example, are first attracted by the smell of flowers; they can also distinguish them from leaves by their shape and color. But when bees have finished foraging, they are instinctively attracted to black dots—the flight holes of their hives—and no flower shape can lure them.

Bees are also sensitive to ultraviolet light, invisible to humans, which enables them to locate the position of the sun even when it is obscured by clouds. This helps them to navigate. On the other hand, there are parts of the color spectrum to which bees are insensitive. For instance, they can see red only as black.

The rattlesnake's "third eye"

The secrets of the animal world are being gradually revealed by patient observation and imaginative experiments. In 1952 an American nerve specialist, Prof. T. H. Bullock, of the University of California, discovered that rattlesnakes possess a "third eye."

When Bullock taped over a rattler's eyes, he found that it could still locate a mouse with uncanny precision. The organs responsible appeared to be two small dimples located on either side of the snake's head, between the nostrils and eyes.

In these Bullock discovered heat-sensitive cells that enabled the snake not only to locate living prey when its eyes were covered, or at night, but also to determine the size and shape of these creatures from the heat given off by their bodies.

Experiments have shown, too, that the frog has a completely economical and selective sense of vision, seeing only the objects necessary to its survival—a fly crawling within striking distance or an approaching enemy.

The eyes of most creatures produce pictures of objects on a layer of light-sensitive cells called the retina. These are transmitted to the brain, which forms a mental picture.

But a copepod crustacean, the Copilia, has a single, simple median eye that works on a different principle.

The eye consists of a few neurosensory cells partly surrounded by a cup of reflecting and screening pigments, innervated by a median nerve from the forebrain.

HOW SNAILS HELP TO SAVE LIVES

THE COMMON garden snail lays about 30 eggs a year, each of them the size of a large pinhead and each one a potential lifesaver. The snail's egg is a cheap, readily available, and stable source of a chemical that is used to determine blood groups. Normally, this chemical is extracted from human blood, but it takes the blood from five donors to provide as much as is contained in a single snail's egg. The contents of the egg are extracted and dissolved in a saline solution.

LIVING LIGHTS OF THE ANIMAL KINGDOM

Creatures that produce their own illumination

Only 4 percent of the energy output of an electric light bulb is light. The other 96 percent is given off as heat. The firefly, a tiny member of the beetle family, glows in the dark to attract its mate. It has an efficiency of over 90 percent, producing light almost devoid of heat.

Fireflies, which are found in the Tropics and parts of Europe and North America, produce their light through a chemical process that takes place in an organ near the tip of the abdomen. Light-producing chemicals and enzymes combine with oxygen to produce a bright glow. The insects, placed in perforated gourd lanterns, have been used in Brazil and China as a form of cheap lighting. The glow from six large fireflies can provide enough light to read a book. But attempts to produce artificially the "living light" or bioluminescence of animal life have proved more costly than orthodox electric lighting.

The glowworm, a member of the same beetle family, *Lampyridae*, also produces chemical light. The winged male possesses two tiny light-producing organs on the abdomen. The grub-like female has light organs in the tail segments of her body, whose powerful glow attracts the male. The larva of the glowworm becomes luminescent only in defense, when it is disturbed. Its light is a brighter green than that of the adult.

Many deep-sea creatures also employ bioluminescence, probably both as a mating signal and as a means of attracting prey.

In depths where light does not penetrate, sea anemones, sponges, coral shrimps, prawns, and squids can produce their own light. Other fish act as hosts to colonies of luminescent bacteria, which illuminate parts of their bodies from within. The bacteria emit continuous light, but the host sometimes has a means of shutting off the light, presumably when danger threatens. Possibly this is done by reducing the oxygen supply. The Indo-Pacific photoblepharon, a shallow-water fish, has a large white spot under each eye, rich in bacteria and blood vessels. A black fold of skin above the luminous spot can be lowered to shut off the light.

The bathysphere fish, so called because the pale blue, glowing spots along its sides resemble

---

NEW LIMBS FROM OLD

IN THE PAST starfish were dredged up from oyster and mussel beds (where they are predators), ripped apart, and thrown back into the sea in the belief that they were dead and could do no more damage. Far from it—the injured starfish grew new arms from the torn body parts to form two new animals.

Starfish are not alone in this curious habit of replacing bits of themselves. Crabs and lobsters are able to regrow a leg or claw they have lost in a fight. The earthworm can replace its head if it loses the front of its body. Lizards can grow a new tail—though a somewhat stumpy one—if necessary.

Some of the simpler animals have the ability to regrow complete new bodies from a minute part of the old. Planarian worms live both at the bottom of the sea and in freshwater under mud and stones. They are usually less than an inch long and look like small leeches. If the tail is cut off, a planarian will grow a new one. If the head is cut off, it will replace that. If a section is taken from the middle of the body, a new head and tail grows on each end. The head develops at the original front end and the tail at the original hind end, as if the piece "remembered" its position.

If the head is cut down the middle, each half replaces the missing part so that the flatworm ends up with two heads. If the head is cut several times and the cut edges not allowed to grow together, then a monster with 10 complete heads results. Planarians can be trained to contract when an electric light is switched on. Trained worms cut in half and allowed to regrow their appropriate missing bits were tested to see if they too cringed at the light—they did. Even the tail that regenerated a new head cowered when the light was switched on. Hungry, untrained planarians were fed chopped-up, trained worms. The hungry worms "learned" the light trick much quicker than worms fed on pieces of untrained worms. It was as if they had eaten the memory of their fellows.

the portholes of a diving bell, has two three-foot tentacles with luminous ends which attract the fish on which it feeds. Its long glowing teeth are also an invitation to inquisitive prey.

The tiny hatchetfish, on the other hand, emits from its body ghostly, greenish-white lights which resemble a row of teeth, deterring would-be enemies while it feeds undisturbed on its diet of plankton. The lantern fish uses the blue, green, or yellow luminous "buttons" along its body as a form of recognition and to attract a mate, while the anglerfish actually uses luminous lures as fishing rods to catch fish whose usual prey is luminescent.

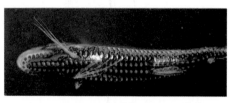

BEAUTY OF THE DEEP. *Many types of deep-sea fish, such as the* Chauliodus, *employ luminescence to lure prey and attract mates.*

NIGHT LIGHTS. *Both the male beetle and the grublike female glowworm have light-producing organs that they use as mating signals.*

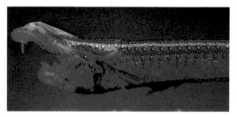

TRAVELING LIGHTS. *Light-producing chemicals combine with oxygen to produce the bright colors of fish such as the* Ichthyococcus.

Starfish, regarded as pests in mussel and oyster beds, were once dredged up, torn apart, and thrown back in the sea. But since the starfish can regenerate lost limbs, the process was ineffective. Here, a painted prawn is carrying off the arm of a starfish, which will grow another limb.

MARKSMEN AND TRAPPERS

Winners in a world where the unwary can end up as a meal

Many creatures have evolved ingenious ways of hunting and capturing their prey. The young ant lion, before it changes into a type of dragonfly, uses its abdomen as a plow to dig a hole in the sand in its desert habitat. Then it sits in the hole and waits for its prey: ants and spiders.

When one of these creatures approaches the hole, it disturbs the sand on the rim, and the ant lion goes into action. It places a grain of sand on its head and flicks it with unerring accuracy toward its target. This tumbles the creature into the pit, where it is quickly devoured. And the ant lion resumes its position, ready for its next victim.

The archerfish also claims its victims by

from its back, and the fish can bend this forward so that the tip is just in front of its mouth. On the end is the "bait," a fleshy, wormlike growth that wriggles convincingly. When smaller fish try to take the bait, the angler strikes.

Spider's trick

A cunning trick is used by one species of jumping spider. It spins a web across the mouth of the carnivorous pitcher plant, which feeds on insects that fall into the pitcher-shaped flower. The spider sits on its web and waits for insects to fall into the net. Thus the jumping spider catches its prey—and robs the plant of a victim at the same time.

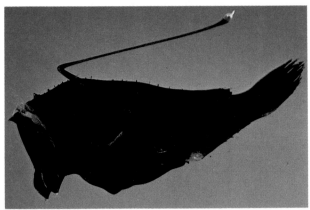

FISH-CATCHING FISH. *The anglerfish attracts its smaller victims with a special kind of lure—a fleshy, wormlike growth at the end of its rodlike fin.*

firing a missile. Swimming close to the surface in rivers in its native India and Australia, it seeks insects on the low-hanging branches of trees. When it spots a victim, the fish rises to the surface and fires a jet of water from its mouth, knocking the insect into the water.

This water-pistol effect is achieved by the shape of the fish's mouth. A groove runs along its roof, and when the tongue is pressed against it, a narrow tube is formed. Closing the gill flaps provides the pressure necessary for the archerfish to eject the water.

The deep-sea anglerfish uses a more subtle method. A long fin like a fishing rod grows

FLYING UNDERWATER

CLOSE to the rushing waters of mountain streams lives a sturdy bird, about the size of a starling, called the dipper. Found in many parts of the world, it is a truly aquatic creature with the ability to "fly" underwater. Using its strong wings, it has been known to dive into 20 feet of water and fly to the bottom, staying down as long as half a minute while it searches in the grit and sand for food.

It is thought that the dipper is able to walk on the bottom by setting its body at an angle against the current to obtain a planing effect that prevents it from bobbing to the surface until it has finished its meal. A movable flap over the bird's nostrils keeps out the water, and the eyes are protected by a membrane.

NATURAL MODESTY

Survival by camouflage—or bluff

The law of nature demands that every creature must have some form of defense—or die. Some have developed fearsome weapons with which to defend themselves; others use subtle disguises to escape attention.

Insects are the staple diet of many predators, and so they have become particularly adept in the art of disguise. In forests and jungles all over the world, the foliage and branches of trees are not all they seem; the stick insects merge with the twigs, a piece of fungus may be the cricketlike katydid, treehoppers look like thorns, and the leaf insect sways its body to resemble a leaf that is blowing in the wind.

The caterpillar of the elephant hawk moth goes one better. When threatened, it retracts its legs and rolls over, revealing a pair of false "eyes" that give it the appearance of the deadly pit viper.

One insect that can defend itself in a daunting and spectacular manner is the bombardier beetle. With a loud bang the beetle fires a jet of liquid, composed of hydrogen peroxide and quinol, at any would-be attacker. The European species is quite small; but in India they grow to two inches in length, and their deadly jet could cause severe pain to a man if it entered his eyes.

The infamous skunk also uses a noxious fluid to repel attackers, but it gives two clear warnings. It thumps the ground with its forefeet, and if this warning is ignored, it shakes its head from side to side in a disapproving manner. Finally, arching its black-and-white tail, it aims the tail toward its adversary and fires a jet

WALKING STICK. *These stick insects are almost indistinguishable in shape and color from the stems of the plants upon which they are feeding.*

NOW YOU SEE ME, NOW YOU DON'T. *A praying mantis waits motionless, camouflaged against a twig, ready to pounce on victims.*

BLOWING IN THE WIND. *Leaf insects not only resemble leaves in their coloring and veinlike markings but flap their bodies, imitating trembling, wind-blown leaves.*

FACE TO FACE. *An elephant hawk moth caterpillar takes on the appearance of a miniature snake in an attempt to scare off predators such as this toad that is threatening to eat it.*

of blinding fluid. The sulfurous liquid, known as mercaptan, does not kill, but any animal that has been on the receiving end gives the skunk a wide berth in the future.

When it comes to a standup fight, however, the musk-oxen use a formidable defense system. To protect their young from marauding wolves, they form a ring, like the battle phalanx used by the infantry of ancient times. With horns lowered, the ring of oxen wheels so that the adult bulls face the enemy, and any wolf that comes too close to the bulls is caught on the horns and tossed over the ox's shoulder, to be trampled to death by the oxen.

IF IT MOVES, IT'S MOTHER

VIENNESE zoologist Konrad Lorenz studied the behavior patterns of newly hatched ducks and geese and found that a greylag gosling will follow the first moving object it sees after hatching and adopt it as its mother. Lorenz's goslings have adopted various mother substitutes, including an Alsatian dog, a ball, and a block of wood.

Ducklings, on the other hand, reacted to sounds. Young mallards showed fear of anything other than an adult mallard, unless the call of the mallard was imitated.

KILLER THAT TIES ITSELF IN KNOTS

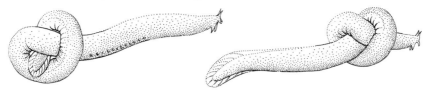

A hungry hagfish slides its tail into a knot around its slime-covered body and, when it attacks, rolls the knot forward to press against its prey.

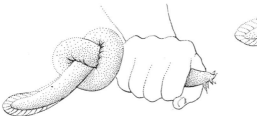

The hagfish's twisting knot can help it to escape if caught—although the slimy, rubbery creature has no known natural enemies.

A hagfish also uses its knot for leverage to tear flesh from its prey. Flexibility comes from a spine made of cartilage rather than bone.

THE HAGFISH ties itself in knots to become a killer. This slimy, eellike creature twists itself into a loop as it attacks another fish, then plunges its teeth into one of the fish's gills.

Once firmly attached, the tenacious hagfish begins a twisting action with the knot in its body, burrowing deeper and deeper into its prey until it is completely inside the other fish. Then the hagfish starts eating its dead or dying captive—from the inside—until the victim's skin and bones are all that remain.

The creature's name is thought to be derived from its sheer ugliness—like a jagged-toothed hag.

HIGH-POWERED HUNTERS

Fish that generate electricity

The electric eel, which lives in South American rivers, can generate electric power strong enough to light more than a dozen household bulbs. Its electric organs discharge up to 600 volts at a current of about two amperes to kill prey, such as fish and frogs, and to ward off predators.

The shock, which lasts only a split second, is generated from thousands of linked cells in the creature's tail.

The electric eel, sometimes six feet long, belongs to the South American knife fish family, and is more closely related to the carp than to the eel.

It continuously sends out weak electrical impulses from two additional electric organs, probably to detect unseen prey. The impulses create an electrical field around the eel, and an intruder's size and position are betrayed when the eel senses changes in the field.

Different species of electric fish are found in rivers and oceans in various parts of the world. Their voltages range from fractions of a volt in the African Mormyriform to several hundred volts in the electric catfish and electric eel.

The freshwater electric catfish of tropical Africa kills or paralyzes its prey with a shock of several hundred volts, emitted from a membrane that extends along its back.

Another shock producer is the disk-shaped electric torpedo, found in the Atlantic, the Indian Ocean, and the Mediterranean. These fish can kill or stun smaller fish, with their powerful discharge of current.

THE MATING SEASON

Finding a partner can be a serious—or deadly—occupation

Courtship among the animals has many strange forms and rituals, and finding a mate can often be a perilous business, particularly in the insect world.

The female praying mantis will eat anything that passes by—including a potential mate. Fortunately for the male, she can spot prey only when it moves, so he approaches from behind and freezes in his tracks whenever she moves her head. As soon as the female is distracted by another insect, the male seizes his chance, and

FINAL TOUCH. *With his mate already in the nest, the satin bowerbird adds one final decoration.*

mating takes place. Even then, however, his chances of escape are slim; for as soon as he moves away, his partner turns and makes a grab for him—often with fatal results.

Attracting a mate

Insects that lead solitary lives have the problem of finding another of their species to mate with, and the senses of smell or hearing are used to attract a partner. The male bumblebee makes his presence known by leaving spots of a scented chemical secreted from his mouth on leaves and twigs. When a female bumblebee finds one of these spots, she waits patiently for the male to return. When he does, they then mate, but the male dies shortly afterward.

The female moth also uses scent to attract the male. Glands at the rear of her body produce the scent, which she disperses by vibrating her wings. Carried on the breeze, this scent can be detected by a male as far as six miles away.

The mole cricket calls his mate with a chirping song made by rubbing his forewings together—and to make sure his song is heard, he builds his own kind of stereo amplifier. With his large, flattened forelegs he digs an underground nest with a twin-horned tunnel entrance. Then he sits at the junction of the horns and beams out his hi-fi message for any passing female to hear.

HIGH—SPEED SERENADE

These pictures show how the male fruit fly produces his courtship song—a serenade that lasts only 1/3,000 of a second. By making incredibly rapid upward wing movements, he emits a high-pitched sound that stimulates the female. If she accepts him, she buzzes in reply.

If speed is essential in finding a mate—and getting away again—the snail has a big disadvantage, but nature has compensated by making most species bisexual. Banded snails meet by picking up each other's slime trails, and courtship begins as they rear up and press their bodies together. During this embrace each fires a love dart—a chalky needle—into the other. This powerful stimulant enables them to mate for several hours.

Courtship and mating

In the world of mammals and birds, courtship is often of a more gentle and considerate nature. Elephants spend weeks in gentle loveplay before actually mating. A couple will stand for hours playfully entwining their trunks and engaging in a mock tug of war.

Female mammals often take the leading role in courtship. The tigress parades before her potential mate, flicking her tail across his muzzle in a tantalizing manner. The female giraffe canters with a peculiar gait that shows she is ready to mate. The female gnu drops to her knees and gives a suggestive nudge to any male that happens to wander past her.

Hard work for the bower

But for painstaking wooing, the Australian satin bowerbird has few equals. The male's glossy, blue-black plumage would be enough to dazzle any female, but he also tempts her with a home, or bower. Every year he builds or renews his elaborate parlor, using twigs and sticks firmly interlocked. It has two parallel walls of sticks extending upward about 12 inches and averages 2 inches in thickness.

The bird then sets about decorating the interior. First he paints the inside walls with a mixture of charcoal and saliva, using a wad of bark as a brush. Then he decorates the bower with brightly colored objects: flowers, parrots' feathers, berries, and manmade objects, such as tinfoil and pieces of glass.

When a female arrives near the bower, the male puts on a display, flashing his wings and emitting curious croaking sounds. Eventually, the female enters the bower, and, after she has made a few alterations to the "furniture," the male enters, and mating takes place.

The sole purpose of the bower is for courtship and mating. Once this has taken place, the female flies away, builds her own nest, and brings up her young.

BIRDS OF A FEATHER. *Weavers are among the most community-minded members of the bird kingdom. The social weavers of South Africa build their nests in huge "apartment blocks," high in the branches of trees. From 100 to 200 pairs of birds pool their resources to build these communal nests, which sometimes measure 10 feet high and 15 feet in diameter.*

The birds start by building a straw thatch roof; then each pair weaves a flask-shaped nest underneath. The entrance is a long tube, which discourages snakes and other predators from raiding the nest.

The village weavers, found in most parts of Africa, also build in colonies, but their nests are not joined together.

TURNING BACK NATURE'S CLOCK

Animals in cave paintings are brought to life again

Standing uncertainly on spindly legs was the most unusual foal the two zoologists had ever seen. But they were delighted by its strange appearance. For it was no ordinary foal—the zoologists, Heinz and Lutz Heck, had re-created an animal that had been extinct for 50 years.

The foal had all the characteristics of the wild tarpan, the stone age ancestor of the modern horse. These animals, mouse-gray in color, had roamed the plains and forests of Europe and central Asia for thousands of years.

The Heck brothers were able to report after many years' research: "We had our first primeval horse. An animal had been born which no man had ever hoped to see."

Unexpected characteristics appeared. When winter came, the foal's coat turned white—just

PREHISTORIC WALL PAINTINGS. *Artists who decorated cave walls at Lascaux in France, 10,000 to 30,000 years ago, recorded important details which were used by two Germans, Heinz and Lutz Heck, to breed the horses and cattle that once roamed Europe and central Asia. The tarpan (left) and aurochs (right) are shown, re-created.*

A SPECIES REBORN. *By crossing strains, the brothers bred back to the tarpan, the tough wild horse from which modern breeds are descended.*

CATTLE OF THE FOREST. *They also re-created the aurochs, cattle which inhabited the forests that covered Europe until the 17th century.*

as the coat of the ancient tarpan was known to have done.

Then, after another five generations of foals had been born, the animals developed another feature the Hecks had not expected—the hooves became incredibly tough, much tougher than those of any domestic or wild horse in the world. This was the hoof of the wild tarpan—a hoof which, although unshod, would not wear down, chip, or split.

The Hecks—Heinz was director of the Munich Zoo and Lutz was director of the Berlin Zoo—were confident they had proved their theory that it was possible to put evolution into reverse and breed back to extinct animals.

Correcting past changes

Lutz Heck explained: "We proceeded from the principle that no animal can be extinct whose heritable constitution still exists. This constitution may be crossed with other species of animals, it may have suffered changes through race formations, but if it still lives, with the aid of our present-day knowledge of heredity it can be brought back as a whole. Crossings can be bred out again, changes of race can be corrected by suitable selection."

So they followed a process used by their father when he ran the Berlin Zoo. He had mated an ibex—a wild goat—with domestic goats. Some of the goats' offspring had the color of the ibex, some the colors of the mothers. But some had the exact coloring of the bezoar, the wild goat of the Middle East, one primeval ancestor of domestic goats.

The last tarpan had died in captivity in 1887, and to build up an exact picture of the animal, the Hecks traveled to many parts of Europe, studying medieval records, fossil remains, skeletons—even the drawings of primeval horses made 10,000 to 30,000 years ago by stone age men on the walls of the Cap Blanc and Lascaux caves in France.

In the first breeding in Munich some 40 years ago, the brothers used stallions from Poland, known to be descendants of the tarpan. These they crossed with carefully chosen domestic mares from Iceland, Scotland, and Scandinavia. When the first foals were born, the brothers checked carefully for tarpan characteristics—then mated the most suitable animals. Heinz reported: "In the second breeding there appeared our fabulous foal." Today there are herds of tarpans in zoos and sanctuaries in Europe and the United States.

Using the same techniques, the Hecks also set out to re-create the aurochs, the fierce ancestors of present-day cattle. Aurochs, which weighed up to a ton, died out in the 17th century. After 10 years a calf was born that had all the characteristics of the aurochs. Today there is a complete herd in the Munich Zoo.

Thanks to the Hecks, the ancient tarpan and aurochs live again.

THE SURVIVOR

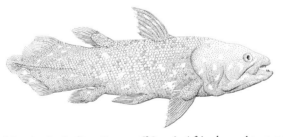

IN 1938 fishermen working in the Indian Ocean off South Africa brought up a strange, metallic-blue fish almost six feet long. It had large, thick scales covering its body and strong, fleshy fins which it probably used to propel itself along the bottom. Later, when it was brought to Prof. J. L. B. Smith, the eminent marine biologist, for identification, he commented: "My surprise would have been little greater if I had seen a dinosaur walking down the street." The professor was understating the case, for the creature was a coelacanth, a fish known before only as a fossil. As such, it occurs in rocks 400 million years old—200 million years older than the dinosaurs.

Examination of these fish—several other specimens have been caught in the last decade—shows that they differ hardly at all from their fossil forebears. With hearts more primitive than those of other vertebrates and brains only 1/15,000 of their body weight, they belong to an ancient era.

Four stages in the process of getting a very small African egg-eating snake outside a very large egg are shown. First, the snake sizes up the job.

This snake, which lives solely on eggs, opens its flexible jaws. They will distend, if necessary, to four times the circumference of its body.

The snake, only about two feet long, has engulfed an egg that is more than double its own diameter. Saliva flows freely to slide the egg down.

The snake is ready to start digesting its food. Sharp internal spines on the backbone will break the shell, which will then be regurgitated.

THE POISONERS

Fangs and stings can bring rapid death

In 1963 a Tasmanian woman was bitten on the foot by a small insect. Fifteen minutes later she was dead. The creature that inflicted the fatal wound was a black bulldog ant, one of the deadliest producers of venom.

Venom is used by some reptiles, spiders, scorpions, and fish to kill or paralyze their prey. In reptiles it is a modified form of saliva that also acts as a predigestive juice, enabling snakes to devour and digest animals larger than them-selves. The venom is usually injected into the bloodstream through hollow fangs similar to hypodermic needles. The poison is in sacs at the base of the fangs and is forced out by the reptile's biting action as it attacks its victim.

Animal venoms fall into two groups: hemo-toxic, which cause blood cells to clot and destroy the walls of blood vessels; and neuro-toxic, which act on the nervous system and may affect the heart muscles and breathing system.

These paralytic venoms are generally used by creatures that wish to preserve their victim, either for consumption later or as a food supply for their unborn young. Solitary wasps stun caterpillars and other larvae, then lay their eggs on the paralyzed bodies, which will serve as food for the young. The amount of poison to be injected must be precise, to ensure that, though immobilized, the creature does not die.

Many spiders paralyze their prey, then wrap it in a silken shroud for later consumption. But some are killers and can be dangerous to man. The black widow is highly poisonous, though deaths from its bite are rare. Other spiders that have killed humans are the brown recluse spider of the southern and central United States, the funnel web spider of New South Wales, the red-back spider of Australasia, and the South African button spider.

Scorpion venom usually paralyzes rather than kills, but some scorpions, such as the *Androctonus australis*, can inject a lethal dose from the sting in their tails. Between 1936 and 1950, they killed 377 people in Algeria.

One of the strangest poisons is in the green maritime worm. The female carries a poisonous sticky substance on her skin. If the young worms swim about normally, they grow to become females. But if they happen to land on a female's skin, the sticky poison changes the young worms into microscopic males.

An estimated 40,000 people die each year from snakebite, 75 percent of them in India. Most of the deaths are due to the king cobra. It has even been known to kill elephants, by striking at the tender tips of their trunks.

Australia has some of the world's most poisonous snakes, though the average death toll is only six every year. The southern Australian tiger snake has venom so deadly that only .609 milligrams will kill a man. The diamondback rattlesnake of the southeastern United States produces enough venom to kill 30 people.

One of the most powerful poisons is manufactured by a frog, the kokoi of Colombia. When the frog is injured or under stress, its skin releases a substance known as batrachotoxin. If injected, 0.1 milligrams of the poison could kill a man. (The toxin would have to be injected, however; in nature the frog is practically harmless to man.) The toxin makes the kokoi distasteful to its predators.

Blue-water killers

The deadliest of all animals live in the sea. One of the most terrifying is the blue-ringed octopus of the Pacific. Its venom, injected through its horny beak, is so potent that a bite can kill a man within two hours. Although scientists have discovered the chemical makeup of the venom, it acts so quickly that antidotes are useless. Many people presumed drowned were probably victims of the octopus.

The sting of the sea wasp, a type of jellyfish, is even worse. It attacks the nervous system and can cause a victim to break into a fierce sweat, go blind, gasp for breath, and die—all within minutes. Some biologists have classified this creature's poison as the most potent of all. In the last 25 years 60 people have died from sea-wasp stings while bathing off beaches in Queensland, Australia.

The stonefish, found in Indo–Pacific waters, injects neurotoxic poison through 13 spines in its back. The stings cause excruciating pain, delirium, and sometimes death. In the same region lives the venomous cone shell. At least five men have died from the effects of the paralyzing fluid which the creature injects through a needlelike tooth.

ONE THOUSAND EGGS A DAY

THE QUEEN termite grows 100 or more times bigger than her subjects, as she develops into a massive egg-laying machine. She spends her entire life in a chamber in the most secure part of the nest, where she is fed by worker termites. A mature queen, fertilized at intervals by her consort, can lay as many as 1,000 eggs a day, at the rate of more than one a minute.

Both queen and consort secrete an acid that other members of the colony lick. This prevents them from developing the power to reproduce. If the queen becomes sterile, she is denied food and dies of starvation. Her body is then devoured by her subjects. Deprived of the contraceptive fluid, a female of the right age develops the ability to reproduce and so becomes queen. If a consort becomes sterile, he is replaced in a similar way by a young male.

AS LIGHT AS GOSSAMER

How man has learned to exploit insects

Gossamer threads spun by spiders are incredibly flimsy—about 1/5,000 of an inch in diameter—and weigh so little that if a spider could spin a single thread long enough to encircle the world, it would weigh no more than six ounces.

In 1710 French entomologist René de Reaumur was asked to look into the practicality of a spider-silk industry. He found that while it took 2,500 silkworms to produce one pound of silk, 265 times as many spiders would be needed to obtain a similar amount. In fact, spider silk is too sticky and fragile for most commercial purposes, though man still finds uses for it.

The silk from two common European spiders, *Araneus diadematus* (the garden spider) and *Zygiella atrica*, was widely used to mark the center of the field of vision on telescopic gunsights from the early 1930's until fine wire was introduced soon after the Second World War. Some microscope manufacturers still use spiders' silk for the same purpose, although it has been largely replaced by wire or photo-etched lines.

The silk is gathered by holding the spider, gently pulling the thread hanging from its spinnerets, and winding the fiber onto a card. It is workable even after two years' storage.

The Papuans of New Guinea use the huge, flexible web of the tropical orb spider as a fishing net. The spider spins its web—up to eight feet across—between trees, and the Papuan fisherman scoops it off with a pliable stick bent into a loop with a handle. A gummy substance coating the silken threads acts as a natural waterproofing, and the readymade net is strong enough to bear a one-pound fish.

Insects in industry

Many other insects provide raw materials for human use. Cochineal, the brilliant crimson dye used in medicines, cosmetics, and candy, is obtained from the dried, pulverized bodies of the scale insect, *Dactylopius coccus*, which lives on cactus plants in Mexico and Peru. The insect's "scale" is a body covering that protects its eggs after the insect dies.

Another scale insect, *Laccifer lacca*, exudes a sticky resin that is made into shellac, an important industrial resin used in varnishes, polishes, and sealing wax. It is also used for making inks, linoleum, and electric insulation material.

The scale insect, *Trabutina*, may well have been responsible for providing the manna that the Israelites ate during their 40 years in the wilderness. The exact nature of this food cannot be established from its Biblical description, but one theory among entomologists is that it was a sweet honeydew secreted by *Trabutina*.

Yet despite the many benefits that scale insects have unwittingly conferred upon mankind, they have their drawbacks. They live by sucking the sap from plant tissues and are among the most destructive of crop pests.

HARNESSING A BIRD'S NATURAL SKILL

For centuries Japanese fishermen have harnessed the remarkable food-hunting skills of the Japanese cormorant to provide them with their catches. This remarkable bird, a highly skilled hunter, is trained to swoop down on a shoal of fish, snatch its prey, and carry it back to the fishing boat. A leather collar fitted tightly around the cormorant's neck stops it from swallowing the fish it has snapped up for its masters. The

A WHIFF OF THE SEA

A whale's indigestion yields fabulous rewards

The sperm whale has been the principal target of the whaling industry for more than 200 years. Its great square forehead contains as much as 500 gallons of the purest oil which, until the development of refined mineral oils, was the finest lubricant known. Early hunters believed the fluid to be the animal's sperm, and from this error the whale was named.

But useful as this oil is, it does not begin to compare in value with the evil-smelling black lump of matter that the whale occasionally regurgitates from its intestinal tract. Ambergris, or gray amber, as it is called, is thought to be produced from the irritation caused by the hard beaks of the thousands of squids that the sperm whale swallows whole.

Ambergris is most often found floating in the sea. After exposure to sun and air, it pales in color and develops a pleasant fragrance of its own, though its chief value lies in its ability to fix other perfume ingredients and make them last longer.

Ambergris is usually found in lumps of no more than a few ounces; in 1912, however, a record amount of 1,003 pounds was discovered in a whale's intestine. It was sold eventually in London for about $100,000.

HUNTER OF EDEN

The whale that killed for man

One of the most remarkable partnerships between animal and man came to an end one day in 1930, as the tide gently deposited the carcass of Old Tom the killer whale onto a beach in New South Wales.

Each winter, for many years, Tom and his companions had appeared off Twofold Bay and waited for their human allies—the whalemen of the little township of Eden—to row out and join them. The killer pack would seek out their gigantic quarry—usually a humpback or fin whale—and drive it into shallow water.

The killer whales worked with great skill. With the boats standing by, two killers seized the victim's tail to stop it from flailing about, while two more swam beneath its head to prevent its escape by diving. Then the remainder of the pack closed in, each one in turn hurling itself out of the water onto the creature's sensitive blowhole. At last, stunned and breathless, it rolled on the surface until the whalemen plunged their lances home. Dying, it slid beneath the waves, and, as it did so, the killer whales fought over their reward—the tongue and lips of their victim. The whalemen waited for a few days until the carcass rose to the surface and then towed it ashore.

Old Tom showed an uncanny understanding of the whalemen's methods. Even when there were no boats at sea, the pack would surround a whale, then detach two or three of their number to raise the alarm in Eden by slapping the offshore waters with their flukes. When the boats put to sea, the killers would guide them to the fray.

After Tom's death the pack forsook Eden forever. In any case, more sophisticated whaling methods were replacing the old rowing boats and hand-held harpoons, and the industry gradually died out in the town. But Tom is not forgotten; to this day his skeleton is one of the Eden Museum's proudest exhibits.

fisherman gently squeezes the bird's throat to release the catch. A contemporary photograph (left) and an 18th-century print (below) show how little the technique of men and birds has changed.

DEEP CONVERSATIONS

The dolphin's wonderful sonar system

For thousands of years dolphins were known simply as playful creatures that seemed to have a fondness for human company and were thought to save swimmers in distress by nosing them to the surface.

But it has recently been discovered that a dolphin's brain is as large or larger than a man's, and that, although a dolphin has no vocal cords, it has a vocabulary of at least 32 distinct sounds, including clicks, whistles, creaks, barks, rasps, squeals, and groans.

A dolphin makes these sounds by forcing air past valves and flaps located just below its blowhole. Every dolphin has its own distinctive voice.

Like a bat in a cave, this bottle-nosed mammal navigates by emitting sounds and picking up their echoes. In an experiment at the Oceanic Institute in Hawaii in 1950, blindfolded dolphins were able to determine the size, distance, and rigidity of an object by listening to the sound waves bounced off it.

They could also distinguish between two spheres differing in size by only a quarter of an inch when the objects were 10 feet away. A dolphin's hearing is so acute that it can pick up an underwater sound from 15 miles away.

With their ability to isolate, interpret, and remember sound signals and the messages they represent, dolphins can deduce navigational information, discover the position of other members of the schools and discuss strategy with fellow hunters.

They have a strong herding instinct, living in schools of up to 1,000 and showing a great reluctance to desert any member of the school that is in trouble.

Distress alarm

A dolphin in danger or distress will emit a short, sharp, high-pitched whistle that acts as an S O S. Its companions will nose it to the surface if it needs air, and there are cases on record of a dolphin being supported in this way for four days.

The instinct to nose an injured companion to the surface is probably maternal in origin, for when a baby dolphin is born, it has to be nudged to the surface by its mother to take its first breath. It is from this behavior, too, that the legend has grown that dolphins will try to save a drowning man.

Their extraordinary ability to communicate with one another has encouraged scientists to experiment with trying to teach dolphins human speech. But although they seem to recognize a few commands and can give a plausible imitation of human laughter, they have not yet mastered the intricacy and complexity of the human voice.

HUNTING BY TRAP AND TRICKERY

The intuitive cunning in staying well-fed

Spiders are the favorite prey of the hunting wasp, but the trapdoor spider keeps itself safe from attack by digging an underground retreat with a tight-fitting door.

Using its powerful jaws, the spider excavates a vertical shaft about 12 inches deep and 1½ inches in diameter. The walls of the tunnel are lined with a sheet of silk, and the trapdoor is built up with layers of silk and soil.

Above the door a layer of leaves and moss camouflages the entrance, and, as an extra precaution, the spider holds the door shut from the inside with its claws. It even makes special holes on the inside of the door so that it can get a proper grip. In some species the trapdoor is toothed so that it gives an exact fit. In part the trapdoor is undoubtedly protection against enemies, but it also serves to shield the insect's burrow from dust and vegetable rubbish.

During the day the trapdoor spider remains in its hideaway; at night it cautiously emerges to catch its prey. Any passing insect is quickly seized and taken below. The spider seldom leaves its home completely, preferring to stay just outside the entrance, holding the door open with its back legs to guard against being locked out. When it retreats to safety with its prey, it pulls the door closed behind it.

INTELLIGENCE OR ADAPTABILITY?

The monkey that could drive a tractor

A rough measure for comparing the intelligence of different animals is the ratio of the weight of the brain to that of the spinal cord.

The ratio for a cat is 4 to 1; for a monkey, 8 to 1; and for a human being, 50 to 1. The animal with one of the highest ratios after man is the marmoset, a South American monkey, with 18 to 1.

Among mammals, primates (men and monkeys) are the most intelligent, followed by flesh eaters and grazing animals.

But, like human beings, individual animals can be brighter than their fellows. For instance, Johnnie, a rhesus monkey kept by Lindsay Schmidt on his farm in Australia, learned to drive a tractor and to follow simple instructions, such as "turn right" and "turn left."

Monkeys can also teach each other. Japanese scientists lured a troop of macaques to a supply of sweet potatoes. It was the monkeys' habit to remove sand sticking to the vegetable by rubbing it. One of the monkeys, however, found it was more effective to wash the potatoes in a brook. The other monkeys soon picked up the practice.

Some monkeys have learned that the easiest and fastest way to separate grains of wheat from dust and sand is to throw handfuls of the dirt into a stream or pond and wait until the wheat grains float to the surface.

Among other animals with high levels of intelligence are dogs, horses, lions, tigers, and elephants. Their ability to learn can be seen from the tricks they are taught to perform in circus rings.

CLEAN FOOD. *A Japanese macaque finds that dipping sweet potatoes in a brook is the best way to wash off grit and sand.*

A QUICK MEAL. *A monkey teaches its young how to separate wheat grains from sand and grit by throwing handfuls of dirt into a nearby pond.*

NATURE'S UNDERTAKER

ANOTHER creature with a strange job is the Necrophorus beetle, more popularly known as the sexton beetle. When a small animal dies, the smell of death attracts the black-and-orange beetle, which then sets about its task. By lying on its back beneath the corpse, the male beetle moves it to a suitable burial place. Then, with the aid of the female, it digs a hole into which the body slowly sinks. Using some of the animal's fur as a nest, the female lays eggs in a tunnel from the burial chamber. When the eggs hatch, the grubs feed on meat from the scavenged body—until they themselves hatch, grow, and become adult and go into the world to continue as nature's undertakers.

ANIMAL ARTISANS

Making up for nature's shortcomings

It has often been said that one of the most important distinctions between man and the rest of the animal kingdom is that he alone uses tools. This is not accurate, however, because many animals use tools.

The chimpanzee, for example, strips a twig of its leaves and uses it to dig into an ant heap. The disturbed ants bite the twig, and the chimpanzee quickly pulls it out to lick off the insects. The chimpanzee also chews leaves into a kind of sponge, which it uses to soak up drinking water from shallow puddles.

Another tool user is the woodpecker finch of the Galápagos Islands. It lives on insects from tree bark, but unlike the woodpecker it does not have a long, sticky tongue to lift them out. So the finch snaps off a cactus spine and, holding it in its beak, digs out the insects.

Insects also use tools. The weaver ants of southeast Asia and Australia construct their nest by sewing leaves together with silk produced by ant larvae. One ant takes a larva in its mouth, while rows of workers hold together the leaf edges. Then the "weaver" moves to and fro, joining the leaves.

Several animals use stones as tools. The European hunting wasp uses them to flatten the sand in which it has buried its eggs. The European song thrush holds the rim of a snail shell in its beak and hammers it against an "anvil" stone to break the shell. The Egyptian vulture breaks open ostrich eggs by picking up

MOBILE HOME. *This shrimp pushes through the sea the empty body of a salpa that it has hollowed out to make a baby carriage.*

BACKSTROKE. *A sea otter lies on its back in the water, hammering a shellfish against a stone balanced on its chest.*

LUNCH BREAK. *The tool-using woodpecker finch snaps off a cactus spine to poke into tree bark for the insects on which it feeds.*

stones in its beak and repeatedly dropping them on the eggs until they break. The dwarf mongoose of Africa throws eggs backward through its hind legs against a rock.

The sea otter also uses stones to get at its food, and does so with considerable skill. It balances a stone on its chest while swimming on its back and hammers shellfish against this anvil.

Further down the scale of marine life, the shrimp *Phronima* is a unique tool user. It makes a baby carriage for its young by scraping out the barrel-shaped body of another sea organism, the salpa. The shrimp then lays its eggs in the pram, and pushes it around until the eggs hatch and the larvae are ready to swim off.

THE DEMOLITION EXPERTS

Nothing is indigestible to the voracious termite

Frail and virtually blind, and no bigger than a grain of rice, the termite is one of the world's most extraordinary builders —and one of its most effective demolition experts.

Guided almost wholly by smell and touch, some species extend their nests above ground level to form giant anthills.

Some of the largest of these termitaria are to be seen in northern Australia, between Mount Isa and Darwin. Here, millions of termites have produced a strange tourist attraction —thousands of "cathedrals" with rocklike spires from 12 to 20 feet high and 10 feet in diameter.

In parts of Africa pillars and mounds built by termites may reach up to 30 feet high and be 100 feet in diameter. Inside is an intricate system of tunnels and connecting spaces spreading over several acres. To build on such a scale takes a termite colony at least eight years.

Virtually all termites, male and female, are sterile. But after the colonies have existed for some time, sexual forms of the species are produced. These "nymphs" (a term applying to both sexes of termites) have wings and have the important function of ensuring that termite life survives by establishing new colonies. How they judge when the moment for departure from the native colony has arrived is a mystery, but when it comes, there is a flurry of activity. Workers bore tiny holes to the outside of the

TERMITE SPIRES. *This 20-foot high "cathedral" discovered in Australia took a colony of hardworking termites about eight years to build.*

mounds and build minute takeoff platforms.

One by one the nymphs flutter away. Probably only one in a million survives—lizards, frogs, birds, and other insects eat the rest.

When a female, exhausted from a flight that may not have taken her more than 100 yards, touches down, she must find a mate. She releases a scent, and when a male appears, a strange ritual begins. Both termites hunch up their bodies and break off their wings. Then they search for a nesting place in the soil or in rotting wood. The female selects the spot, and two days of frantic burrowing begins. A few days later a dark, moist nest is completed, and mating proceeds. A new termite city has been founded.

Appetites extraordinary

The destructive dry-wood termites burrow in wood above ground. They damage forests and often cause wooden structures to collapse without warning. When termites tackle a joist, a rafter, or a tree, they gnaw away on the inside, without damaging the exterior surface of the wood or the bark. Only the shell remains.

Colonies of termites have been known to chew through tires, lead sheathing on telephone cables, and even billiard balls. They can also exude a liquid over tin that causes rust.

A termite colony may contain a population of 3 million and is run on ruthlessly totalitarian lines. Ruled by a queen, most termites work 24 hours a day until death. And the strict conditions necessary for life for these specialized insects make death a daily proposition. Without constant warmth and moisture termites die in a matter of hours. If all other dangers are avoided, they are eventually eaten by their kin. In the event of a food shortage, termites will eat their own young.

Gardeners in darkness

Most of the population are workers who look after the nest and the eggs and collect food. Deep inside the nest the workers tend a fungus garden that yields the cellulose essential to the termites' diet. Each night columns of termites venture out to collect wood and grass, which is pulped by the termites' jaws, mixed with fecal matter, and spread on the garden. Vital heat is also generated as the fungus grows, absorbing excess moisture.

Soldier termites differ from the workers in that they are armed either with powerful mandibles for seizing and fighting or with a mechanism in their foreparts that ejects poison.

Most of the time soldiers patrol the maze of tunnels in the nest. But their most important role is to defend the colony against invasion by ants.

When marauding ants find an opening, they pour in and carry off hundreds of termites and eggs. But the sightless termite soldiers fearlessly and instinctively attack the bigger and more powerful ants. Some will grab the enemy with their jaws. Others exude a gummy substance that irritates the ants' bodies and tangles their legs and antennae.

While the battle rages—a battle whose orders seem to be passed telepathically—thousands of termite workers go into action, sealing off the battle area from the rest of the nest. The workers wall up the tunnels by cementing minute fragments of soil into place. The soldiers will die fighting in their effort to shut out the enemy. The colony usually survives.

WEAVERS OF DEATH

Silken traps that are stronger than steel

Long ago, it is said, there was a girl named Arachne who wove so beautifully that she excited the envy of the goddess Athena. Despite divine warnings, she rashly persisted in her excellence, so Athena turned her into a spider. To this day the spider family is classed as *Arachnida*, and in the intervening years they have lost none of their namesake's skill.

For sheer artistry the spider's web is without equal. It is a home with food trap attached, made from silk sometimes only 1/1,000 of an inch in diameter. With this unbelievably fragile material, spiders are able to calculate stresses and strains on their intricate webs, measure angles, and weld "joints."

Silk for all needs

Spiders make silk to meet their every need —each kind produced by a series of organs called spinnerets. A coarse, dry silk is used to create the permanent frame of the web, and a sticky type to form the wide carpet that traps insects. Then there are dry "pathways" that the spider uses to run from its base at the center of the web to inspect captured prey. The spider also spins a thick, often brightly colored silk in which it encases its eggs for safety.

Some of this exquisite gossamer is stronger than steel—supposing that steel could be drawn out to the same diameter. It is about the most delicate solid in the world, with the exception of a snowflake. These silk threads can also be stretched by as much as one-fifth before they snap.

Seven kinds of spider silk are known; and although no spider can produce all seven, every spider can create at least three, and most can create four. Each spinneret opens through a different shaped tube. To use it, the spider does not have to stop and think any more than one has to think to select the muscles that will snatch one's fingers from a fire.

Not all the 40,000 species of spiders spin webs; of those that do, the best spinners are usually female. Frequently, the males produce only temporary "bachelor" dwellings of poor-quality silk. There are thousands of types of

BEES WITH A STING OF DEATH

AMERICAN SCIENTISTS have warned that swarms of killer bees are advancing up through South America and approaching the U.S. border. Their violent behavior has proved fatal to animals, and human deaths have also been reported. The bees were bred by accident in São Paulo, Brazil. African bees were being crossed with gentler European bees to improve productivity, when 26 European swarms escaped, each with an African queen. The United States is now trying to develop a vigorous but less aggressive strain of bees that can be released in Central America to breed out the savage strain.

webs, the simplest being the cobweb—a shapeless, dingy mess made by the common house spider.

One of the most familiar, yet most spectacular, examples of the spider's skill, is the orb web that is made by many species, including the garden spider. This has a central hub with a number of radial threads linking it to nearby plants.

Immediately surrounding the hub is a short spiral of silk that joins the radials and looks something like the grooves in a phonograph record. After a short gap a second spiral begins, extending outward in some places almost to the extremities of the radials.

It takes a spider about 4½ hours to spin a web, including brief rests. When the web is completed, any flying insect that touches its sticky threads is doomed: No matter how the trapped creature struggles, it can only become more and more entangled.

Monitoring vibrations

In the daytime the garden spider stays hidden and uses a "dragline" connected to the web to monitor vibrations created by its victims. In the evening the spider moves to the web and lurks in its central lair, ready to run out along one of its safe paths when movements indicate that some prey has been trapped.

The spider immobilizes a victim by injecting it with venom that causes instant paralysis. The insect is then either devoured on the spot or wrapped in a silken shroud and carried to the center of the web to be eaten later. The spider can take food only in liquid form, so it bathes its prey in digestive juices that turn the insect's inner parts to liquid.

Spiders are the best insect killers known and will also prey upon each other. Even mating is fraught with danger, for the larger female sees her suitor only as an advancing meal. For this reason the male approaches courtship with great caution. First, he spins a small silken parcel and deposits sperm cells on it. Then he absorbs the cells into leglike attachments near his head and sets out to find a suitable mate.

Male spiders use various techniques to avoid being devoured during their brief courtship. Some vibrate the threads of the female's web in a particular way to establish recognition, then mate by depositing the sperm onto the threads. Fertilization occurs as the female absorbs the sperm as she moves over the web—without ever making contact with the male.

The males of some species placate the females by wrapping a fly in silk and presenting it to them. The male crab spider is even more cautious. He crisscrosses the female with threads until she is stuck helplessly to the ground. The silk he produces for this purpose is known as the bridal veil.

The number of eggs produced varies according to the species—some lay 10, others as many as 2,000. Most females live for a year and mate only once, but during this time they produce several batches of eggs. These are laid on a small web and cocooned in silk.

When the spiderlings emerge, they travel considerable distances by a method known as ballooning. Each one climbs to the top of a blade of grass and produces a long strand of silk, which is carried away by the wind with the spiderling attached. Some spiderlings have been carried as high as 14,000 feet on this journey to find a new home.

THIMBLE-SIZED IGLOO

The tiny false scorpion constructs an igloo-type nest little bigger than a thimble. The quarter-inch-long creature, a distant relative of true scorpions, has no tail or sting and surrounds itself with sand grains and fragments of wood and stone that are cemented together with a coating of fine silk threads. The dome rises until only a small hole remains, out of which the false scorpion emerges to forage for new materials. Finally, this too is sealed, and the internal walls are lined with further quantities of silk before egg laying or molting begins.

TINY BUT DESTRUCTIVE

When ant battalions go foraging for food

The ant is one of nature's busiest creatures. There are at least 10 trillion ants in the world, constantly toiling to perpetuate their species. This instinct for survival sometimes creates havoc, particularly in Africa and South America, where huge battalions of army, or legionary, ants march in search of food. They eat and devastate everything in their path with their enormous sickle-like jaws.

In one horde there might be 100,000 ants —most of them blind. They will strip a house and garden of everything edible, including domestic animals. Once, a tethered horse was reduced to a skeleton in three hours.

Aggression is also a characteristic of the Amazon ants, which raid the nests of other ants to capture slaves. The hunters, who are unable to feed themselves, spend days scouting an objective and marking out escape routes. Then they attack and carry off pupae. When these hatch out, they gather food for their masters.

The Argentine and fire ants prey even more viciously on fellow ants. When they move to a new area, they exterminate the existing ant population for food.

Red wood ants are also killers, but they hunt other insects and will sometimes slaughter creatures much larger than themselves, such as centipedes.

Other ants live on vegetable substances. The parasol ant of South America mixes saliva with finely shredded leaves to form a compost, on which a fungus is grown inside the nest. The harvester ant builds granaries and stocks them with grain collected from cornfields. This food is eaten in winter.

MINUTE BUT MIGHTY BUILDERS

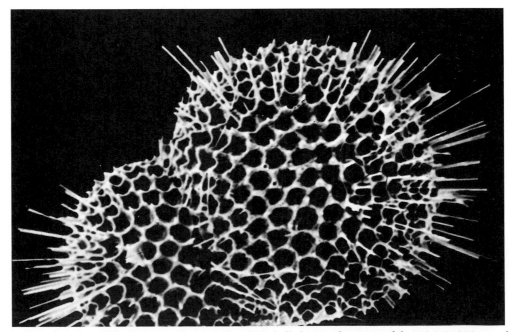

Look at the White Cliffs of Dover or the 1,000-foot-thick chalk deposits along parts of the Mississippi River and you are seeing how minute animals, each with a shell only about 1/60 inch wide, can form huge thicknesses of rock. These creatures, like the one above, are called foraminifera. They are mere specks of protoplasm existing in shells perforated with holes, through which strands of protoplasm project to trap food. When the creatures die, their empty shells sink to the bottom of the sea where, over millions of years, they combine to form vast chalk deposits.

HARSH START IN LIFE

Chicks that have to make a double breakthrough

A double obstacle faces an African hornbill chick of the genus *Tockus* when it enters the world. It must break out of its shell; then it has to demolish the walled-up entrance to its specially built "nursery."

The female lays between one and six eggs in a tree-trunk cavity and blocks up the entrance from the inside with cement made from clay and saliva. The bird leaves a hole just big enough for her mate to be able to feed her.

For five weeks she incubates her eggs, and when they hatch, she breaks through the wall, leaving her brood behind. The bird repairs the damage at once—often helped by the chicks on the inside.

When the chicks are strong enough, they attack the wall with their beaks and emerge into the outside world.

LABOR OF LOVE

Birds that build their own incubators

B reeding chicks is a lifelong labor for the mallee fowl of southern Australia. The hen lays an average of one egg a week for six months, and she spends another five months of the year helping her mate to construct and tend their nest, which is really an elaborate incubator.

The pair first dig a pit 2 to 3 feet deep and about 10 feet in diameter, then fill it with leaves, twigs, and bark. After rain has soaked the debris, the birds cover it with soil or sand.

Work for father

As the compost rots and heat rises, the cock regularly probes the mound with his beak to check the temperature. When this reaches 91°F (33°C), the hen lays her first egg. Her mate opens the mound, puts the egg into position, and carefully rebuilds the structure to make it ready for the next laying.

He also has the job of keeping the incubator at an even temperature. In early spring, when the leaves rot rapidly, he uncovers the eggs each morning to let air circulate around them. In summer he adds soil to the mound to insulate it from the sun's heat.

Later in the year, when the weather is cooler and the rotting ceases, he uncovers the mound early in the day to let the heat reach the eggs.

Each egg needs 50 days' incubation, which means that, while the hen is still laying, other eggs are hatching out.

The chicks have to make their own way to the surface, tunneling through almost three feet of soil to reach the open air. This may take as long as 15 hours; they then stagger to the nearest bush to rest and take shelter.

The chicks have to fend for themselves from the day they hatch, for they are totally ignored by their parents. They can fly within 24 hours of leaving the egg.

When the nesting season ends, the cock and hen have just one month's rest before the whole cycle begins again.

FINERY FROM THE SILK OF A SEAFOOD

THE FIELD OF CLOTH OF GOLD, the meeting place in 1520 of Henry VIII of England and Francis I of France, was so named because the tents and nobles' apparel were made of golden cloth. Their tunics were made from the "beards" of mussels, bundles of short, tough threads secreted by a gland in the mollusk's foot. The threads are discharged as a thick fluid, which sticks firmly to the rock or gravel where the creature lives. They harden almost immediately, yet are flexible enough to allow the mussel to swing around with the movement of the tide. The silky beards of the 12-inch-long fan mussels, *Pinna nobilis* and *Pinna fragilis*, found on the shores of the Atlantic Ocean and Mediterranean Sea, were woven into cloth. The finely dressed gentlemen were the beneficiaries

LIVING IN HARMONY

In sea and on land, some creatures exist by mutual consent

The laws of nature are often harsh and cruel, but some groups of animals have learned to live together in peaceful coexistence. The zoologists call this symbiosis, from the Greek words for "life together."

The European hermit crab is one example. It uses a discarded whelk shell to protect its soft body but often shares its home and meals with a rag worm. Sometimes another lodger, a parasitic anemone, attaches itself to the shell.

The rag worm is usually a reluctant guest, becoming trapped in the shell when the crab moves in; but the anemone lives on the hermit's borrowed shell and remains to share the shell with its next occupant when the hermit crab moves to a larger shell.

Strangely, the crab neither tries to eat the rag worm nor dislodge the anemone, and the latter's stinging tentacles form a useful protection against marauders.

Another sea creature that hitches a lift is the remora, a tropical fish that lives with the deadly shark. The remora attaches itself by means of a suction disk on its head and lives on the parasites that attack the shark's skin. Sometimes it detaches itself to feed on scraps from the shark's kill and is totally ignored by its host.

Interdependence is carried to extremes by the bitterling, a minnowlike fish found in European and Asian rivers, and the mussel. In April, when the female bitterling is ready to spawn, the male guides her to a mussel, and she releases her eggs into the mussel's siphon, or breathing tube. The eggs are fertilized by the male and are then hatched out within the mussel's shell.

The mussel, in turn, fosters its offspring on the fish. While the bitterling is spawning, the mussel discharges its larvae, which grip the fish's tail or fins. The bitterling's skin grows over these tiny passengers, and three months later they emerge as perfectly formed mussels.

On land symbiosis is found among the

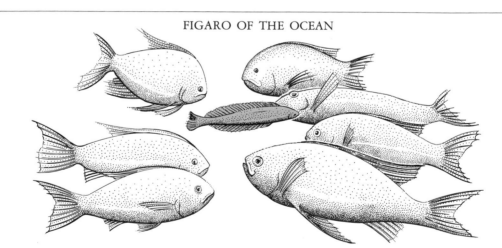

FIGARO OF THE OCEAN

THE CLEANER, or barber, fish make their living, as many humans do, by offering a service to others. And they find that it pays to advertise. Working in groups, the tiny fish base themselves in a crevice near a brightly colored sea anemone or sponge.

This performs the same function as a barber's pole, attracting customers for their grooming service. Shoals of larger fish line up to be cleaned, and the barber fish are rewarded with food. They eat through the patches of dead skin, parasites, bacteria, and fungi on their visitors.

The larger fish cooperate throughout, raising one gill cover to let the cleaner in and opening the other to let it out when its work is done. Even sharks and other deadly species allow the cleaners into their mouths without harming them.

Fish that live out at sea, such as the ocean sunfish, may travel far to obtain this cleaning service.

tiniest and largest of creatures. Bluebottles, dung beetles, and ants are often inhabited by mites, which live on the food particles adhering to their host's mouth.

Riding piggyback is a favorite occupation of some birds, to the mutual advantage of rider and ridden. The carmine bee-eater rides on the kori bustard through the tall grass of the African savanna. The bustard, a bird that stands over three feet tall, disturbs flies and other irritating insects, and the bee-eater swoops down to capture them.

Similarly, the cattle egrets in Africa perch on the backs of buffaloes, antelopes, zebras, or rhinoceroses and snap up the insects disturbed by the animals' hooves. The birds are thereby ensured of a constant supply of food, while relieving the animals of irritating pests. But they also give another service.

When anything that may threaten their safety approaches, they fly up, and their flashing white wings act as a warning signal to the herd.

The oxpecker, or tickbird, also stays close to a buffalo, living on the ticks that infest the animal's hide. Some birds become so attached to an animal that they will stay with it constant-ly, even to the extent of courting and mating on its back.

Perhaps the most remarkable example of coexistence is that of the plover and the Nile crocodile. The crocodile is renowned as a voracious reptile that will snap at anything that comes within range of its powerful jaws. Yet the plover can enter that gaping mouth and act as a "dentist"—cleaning the scraps of decaying food from between the crocodile's teeth.

The farmers

In most animal partnerships the relationship is one of mutual convenience, but in the case of ants and aphids, the ants act as "dairy" farmers. When aphids suck the sap from plants, they leave behind a sticky substance called honeydew, which is a favorite food of some species of ants. By stroking the aphids with their antennae, the ants induce them to produce more honeydew; and to ensure a copious supply of the liquid, they herd the insects together. In the autumn the ants collect the aphids' eggs and care for them in their nests. When the young hatch in spring, the ants carry them above ground to "graze" on plants.

THE KAMIKAZE RODENTS

The lemmings' four-year death cycle

Everyone probably has heard the legend of the lemmings—how every four years frenzied millions of these little rodents hurl themselves from Norwegian cliffs and beaches into the sea to drown.

The lemming, a small hamsterlike creature with a short tail, is normally shy and scarce. But lemmings' lives follow a strange four-year cycle. In the first year their reproduction is slow, but it builds up during the second and third years, and by the fourth the females are almost contin-ually with young. And then panic—seemingly caused by overcrowding—takes hold, and they quit their habitat in millions in a desperate search for more living space.

The maniac rush goes on until the lemmings find their flight barred by a river valley or a fiord. Driven by desperation, they plunge in madly; but although they are fair swimmers in calm water, even the smallest waves overwhelm them, and they perish. Thus they provide their own harsh means of population control.

IS THIS HOW WE LEARNED TO WALK?

HOW was it that our far-off ancestors developed so large a brain and learned to walk on two legs? Dr. Sydney Britton, a zoologist, may have found the answer when he installed a chimpanzee named Bonga on a small island. When there was snow on the ground, Bonga walked upright, apparently to keep her body from getting cold and wet.

Dr. Britton believes that long ago our ancestors reacted in the same way. Coincidentally, there was an increase in the size of the brain—and the long process of man's evolution began.

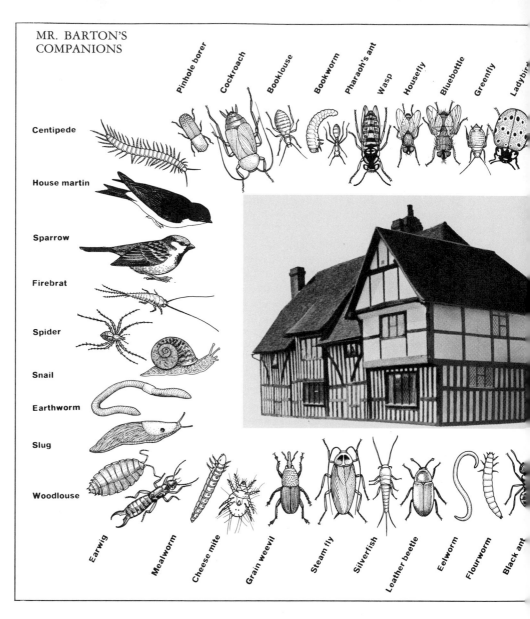

MR. BARTON'S COMPANIONS

Pinhole borer · Cockroach · Booklouse · Bookworm · Pharaoh's ant · Wasp · Housefly · Bluebottle · Greenfly · Ladybird

Centipede

House martin

Sparrow

Firebrat

Spider

Snail

Earthworm

Slug

Woodlouse

Earwig · Mealworm · Cheese mite · Grain weevil · Steam fly · Silverfish · Leather beetle · Eelworm · Flourworm · Black ant

YOU ARE NEVER ALONE

The teeming life that shares our homes

Like most people, John Barton's son wanted a little privacy, so his father cleared some forest land in Kent and built a secluded farmhouse for him. The young man moved in with his family and servants in 1555.

But they were not the first occupants. Pinhole borers and all kinds of wood beetles were already there in the hundreds, eating away at the beams and woodwork. Families of birds, bats, worms, and insects were quick to move in too. Three years after the house was finished, it had 1,092 tenants—only 7 human.

The history of the squatters of Barton's End, as the house was called, has been traced by zoologist George Ordish. He studied the many surviving documents relating to the house, its structural changes, and the varied lives of its human inhabitants. From them, and his knowledge of animal life, he could deduce the principal animals living there in different years and estimate their numbers.

After the first wave of invaders, noctule bats and the smaller pipistrelle bats arrived in the loft. They ate some of the wood-boring beetles,

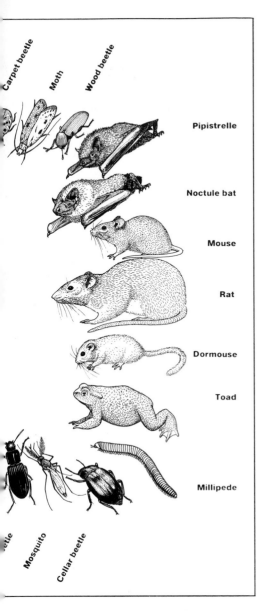

Carpet beetle

Moth

Wood beetle

Pipistrelle

Noctule bat

Mouse

Rat

Dormouse

Toad

Millipede

Mosquito

Cellar beetle

A cellar was dug in 1630 with a loose-fitting trapdoor outside the house. This proved a handy entrance for toads, as well as more insects and spiders, although the toads fed on the spiders, keeping the numbers down.

On the other hand, the replacement of the thatch roof by tiles in 1660 reduced the volume of life in the house. Even so, earthworms, woodlice, snails, centipedes, millipedes, slugs, and aphids all thrived, and there were more than 3,000 living creatures in the house.

The larvae of moths devoured the family's furs and woolens, the carpets and upholstery, the stuffed birds in glass cases, leather harnesses, book covers, and even the corks in the wine bottles. Many things had to be shared with the carpet beetle, leather beetle, cellar beetle, earwig, and Pharaoh's ant.

When books in the library grew slightly damp, bookworms, booklice, and silverfish arrived to eat them—and the wallpaper. The kitchen, of course, swarmed with life—cockroaches, silverfish and their relatives, the firebrats. The larder housed and fed grain weevils, mealworms, flourworms, black beetles, and steam flies; eelworms wriggled in the vinegar, and cheese mites gave flavor to the Stilton.

By 1860 the population of Barton's End had reached its peak—119 species plus *Homo sapiens*. More people now came to stay, which meant that many of the rooms were kept warmer for longer periods. The total population rose to about 3,300, including common houseflies, mosquitoes, black ants, bluebottles, ladybirds, and various wasps. And this total refers only to visible creatures. It omits the tens of thousands of mites to be found in any house.

The changing natural history of Barton's End is typical of country houses. Because of central heating, synthetic fabrics, vacuum cleaners, and pesticides, nature is kept largely at bay.

At the last census of Barton's End, only some 450 inhabitants were estimated—an average number for a well-scrubbed modern home.

but brought their own insect parasites to keep up the numbers. Sparrows nested under the eaves, and house martins built on the walls.

Mice moving in from the fields were the only rodents, but rats and dormice visited occasionally for meals.

THE BIRDS THAT WENT TO WAR

ONE of the heroes decorated in the First World War was a pigeon that carried vital messages through the artillery fire around Verdun in 1916. The bird—one of thousands used by the French—died after a particularly hazardous trip and was awarded a posthumous Legion of Honor for its courage. In the Second World War, British aircraft dropped boxes of homing pigeons behind enemy lines by parachute. The birds were used by Resistance fighters to fly messages to London.

Huskies—the toughest, most faithful dogs of all

The Eskimo sled dog, or husky, is one of the hardiest animals on earth and is still the most reliable form of overland transport in the 2-million-square-mile frozen wastes of Canada's Northwest Territories.

Without the husky the rich fur and mineral resources of the North could never have been developed, and the nomadic Eskimo might never have survived. At various times, doctors, missionaries, and the Royal Canadian Mounted Police still have to depend on the sturdy creatures in the more remote areas.

The current strains of the husky belong to a number of breeds, including the pure, original strain of northern Canada, the malamute of western Alaska and the Siberian husky, imported when the Russians occupied Alaska.

The dogs stand about 25 inches high, are 44 inches long from nose to bushy tail, weigh between 60 and 100 pounds, and have coarse hair under which is another coat of oily wool 2 to 3 inches thick. This enables the dogs to endure immense cold (temperatures as low as −50°F) without shelter.

Eerie howling

Both the male and female are built for hard work, with deep, wide chests, muscular necks, and powerful legs. Their tough, padded feet can negotiate jagged rock and broken ice that would split the hooves of a horse.

The dogs' eerie, protracted howls tend to make people think they are domesticated wolves, and, although the husky did branch out from the wolf's family tree thousands of years ago, it is the wolf's bitter enemy. Even when starving, huskies will not eat wolf flesh.

Huskies will, however, mate with wolves. But a male will be killed by the rest of his pack if he returns after doing so; a female will be unharmed.

The dogs have immense strength—a team of 12 to 15 huskies can pull the average Eskimo's sled weighing about 1,100 pounds fully loaded. So long as the nomadic Eskimo can move from one hunting ground to another, he can live well. If he can't move, he will perish; so his life depends on the faithfulness and efficiency of his husky team.

An Eskimo will rarely part with his pack and will frequently risk his life for them. Many Eskimos have died trying to free their dogs when thin ice has broken under a heavy sled.

Pups are trained by introducing them one or two at a time to the sled team. With tough competition from its veteran teachers, an eight-month-old pup will learn quickly. Although the dogs may have toiled together for years as a team, they will fight over food and for the favors of the females.

Boss dog

Eskimo husky teams are usually harnessed in a "fan-hitch"—each dog being separately tethered to a six-foot walrus or seal-hide pull rope, hauling abreast of one another in a fan formation. A "boss dog" runs backward and forward around the formation, nipping the legs of shirkers and urging the team forward.

The lead dog, often a bitch, works with a quiet determination, feeling out thin ice and sometimes leading the team back to base when the driver has lost his bearings in a blizzard.

Food is the team's greatest incentive because it is always scarce. The dogs need rich fats, muscle-building meat, and plenty of vitamins, all of which are available in the flesh of the arctic seal. But when the dogs are let loose to fend for themselves in the two-month arctic winter, they readily return to camp when the weather turns cold because they have a hard time existing on a scanty diet of shrimps, mussels, and birds' eggs, or any dead creature cast up by the tides.

Great endurance

The husky's apparent ferocity at feeding times is countered by its amazing devotion and self-sacrifice. Often, the dogs can cover 25 miles a day at about seven miles an hour without feeling it. Subzero gales can freeze the dogs' faces or lungs, slushy snow can harden and cripple their feet, and sometimes the animals have to be destroyed.

Eskimos now are taught to feed their dogs a full ration all year long, to breed them properly for strength and intelligence, to inoculate them against sickness, and to isolate them when they fall sick—the kind of care richly deserved by the breed that helped develop the arctic wastes.

PART

2

The marvels of science

.

MOON VOYAGER

The awesome complexities of Saturn 5

Blasting off a Saturn 5 rocket is the equivalent of setting off an explosion under a naval destroyer balanced upright on its stern and blowing it more than 30 miles into the air—but so smoothly that no fragile object on board is broken.

The rocket, the biggest operational one in the world, was designed and built to get man to the moon. It has 2 million parts, and—for a launching—each is monitored electronically from a control center three miles from the launching pad. At the control center 400 men and women sit watching television screens and instrument panels. But the final word rests with three small computers on board the rocket. Two of them must vote "yes" before a clock starts ignition in the engines and the rocket lifts off.

The stages assemble

The Saturn 5 is constructed in three sections, each made in a different part of the United States and transported by water, road, or air to the John F. Kennedy Space Center in Florida to be put together. Final assembly and checkout is done in the vast vehicle assembly building and takes at least four months.

The first stage—138 feet tall, 33 feet in diameter, and weighing 134 tons without fuel—is placed upright on a six-legged platform alongside a servicing tower. The second stage—81 feet 7 inches tall and weighing 43 tons—is lifted on top by crane.

Stage three—58 feet tall and weighing 16 tons—is hoisted on top. Finally, the spacecraft itself, which carried three astronauts to the moon, is placed on the very top. An *Apollo* spacecraft is 82 feet high and gives a height of about 360 feet to the total space vehicle.

The whole rocket is fitted together vertically and moved to the launching pad, with its service tower clamped onto it.

The "crawlers" that carry out this huge task are the world's biggest land vehicles. There are only two, both at the Kennedy Space Center. Everything about them is colossal. They weigh 3,000 tons each, are 131 feet long and 114 feet wide, have a crew of 10 in a driving cab at each end, and make the nine-hour journey to the launching pad at a majestic two miles an hour.

Each crawler has 16 electrical motors and engines, including two diesel engines, which develop 2,750 horsepower. Then there are generators, hydraulic power units, and electric motors for driving the tracks. Starting up a crawler takes 90 minutes; the manual on how to do it is 39 pages.

Each link of the eight caterpillar tracks weighs a ton, and the special roadway to the firing pad sinks an inch each time a laden crawler passes over it.

As the crawler and rocket move slowly toward the pad, a complex jacking and leveling system keeps the ungainly load level. When the rocket is at last unloaded it is filled with 12 million gallons of liquid hydrogen, liquid helium, and liquid oxygen. The fuel is poured into cold-storage tanks so well insulated that ice cubes would take eight years to melt in them. With the fuel loaded, the weight of the rocket is increased to 3,000 tons—heavier than a destroyer—and it sinks 16 inches into the brick-lined pad.

Power for liftoff

There are 11 main engines on a Saturn 5 for upward thrust and another 24 for control. Each of the five engines in the first stage weighs 10 tons and consumes 3 tons of fuel a second, pushing with the combined power of 30 diesel locomotives. Together they generate 160 million horsepower. They take the rocket about 38 miles up and boost its speed to more than 6,000 miles an hour. Then the second-stage engines ignite, raise it to an altitude of more than 100 miles, and increase its speed to 15,000 miles an hour or more.

The fuel pumps need turbines generating 300,000 horsepower—twice the engine power of a liner.

The third stage contains only one engine, but it can be restarted. This engine is used to send a spaceship to the moon. It can boost speed to 25,000 miles an hour.

Saturn 5 has made 13 almost perfect flights. The first men to land on the moon were lifted off the earth by Saturn 5.

When the next flight of this gigantic rocket will be is uncertain. Two rockets are in storage, but there are no plans for launching them.

BLAST-OFF. *A Saturn 5 rocket rises from the launching pad at the Kennedy Space Center.*

A WORM'S EYE VIEW *of the world's biggest land vehicle, the 3,000-ton crawler that moves Saturn 5 to its launching pad at a speed of two miles an hour.*

HEAT FROM THE SEA

Uses for hydrogen fusion

There is enough hydrogen in one gallon of seawater to provide as much heat as 10,000 electric space heaters running for one hour. Scientists all over the world are now trying to harness this energy by a process similar to one that occurs on the surface of the sun. This is called continuous thermonuclear fusion and involves causing hydrogen atoms to rush together and release vast amounts of energy. The process is vastly more powerful than the energy created by nuclear fission, which involves breaking uranium atoms apart. Nuclear fission was used in the first atom bombs.

The fusion has already been achieved to a degree in the hydrogen bomb. But H-bombs, like the sun, are an example of uncontrolled thermonuclear fusion. What the scientists are seeking is a way to harness the energy safely for peaceful purposes.

Hydrogen nuclei do not fuse readily, but if the temperature of their surroundings is increased sufficiently, they rush together, and fusion takes place. But raising the temperature is not easy. About 212 million degrees Fahrenheit is required and has to be maintained for about one second to start the reaction. Once the hydrogen atoms are fusing, the reaction has to be contained so that it does not explode and allow the energy to escape and be wasted.

So far, the nuclear scientists have been unable to maintain the reaction for more than a fraction of a second, but they are confident that the problems can be overcome and that by the year 2000 the first thermonuclear power station will have begun operation.

The sea will provide an almost unlimited supply of hydrogen, and it can be simply and cheaply extracted.

While a modern coal-fired power station needs 10 trainloads of coal a day, a thermonuclear station could operate for a day on the hydrogen from one single truckload of water.

FUEL CELLS—LIGHTWEIGHT ALTERNATIVES TO BATTERIES

A MAJOR problem in space travel is providing power to use inside the spaceship. It is needed for instruments, heating and cooling systems, computers, radios, TV cameras, and other equipment. A trip to the moon would call for something like 40 tons of car batteries and a generator.

The hydrogen-oxygen fuel cell is a lightweight alternative that also provides drinking water as a by-product. Three fuel-cell power plants, each consisting of 31 cells, were installed in each *Apollo* spaceship that went to the moon.

A fuel cell is a type of battery that makes electricity instead of storing it. A hydrogen-oxygen mixture, or oxygen acting on a fuel such as carbon, creates current at two terminals. As long as the gases are fed in, the cell continues to produce electricity. In the *Apollo* spacecraft both gases combine to form water as they produce current in the cell. Because hydrogen and oxygen can be produced from water, the cycle can theoretically go on indefinitely. However, since the energy released in the cell is less than the energy required to produce the gases from water, cells are normally powered from gas cylinders.

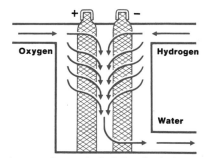

The layout of a typical fuel cell—hydrogen and oxygen combine in a chemical solution, releasing electrical energy through the terminals.

Fuel cells offer many possibilities: electric trains that need no overhead wires or live rails; buses and cars that do not emit fumes; silent generators and lightweight power packs for spacecraft.

The main problem in adopting the cell for use in everyday life is cost. Although hydrogen and oxygen are available cheaply, catalyst materials —which help the reaction—are expensive.

BOATS ON CUSHIONS OF AIR

Christopher Cockerell reversed the vacuum cleaner

In 1950 a British mechanical engineer named Christopher Cockerell had an idea to make boats go faster, by using a vacuum cleaner.

Working from his boatyard, he first borrowed his wife's vacuum cleaner, then cut a slot in the bow of a punt, reversed the motor of the vacuum cleaner so that it blew instead of sucked, and squirted air beneath the boat. The result was that the friction of the water flowing past the punt was decreased.

Some months later he found that by blowing air through open-ended cans of different sizes on kitchen scales he got vastly different readings. The same mass of air though a narrow can exerted up to three times as much thrust as when it was blown through a wide can.

In that moment Cockerell laid the foundation for the first new form of transport since the jet plane. He called it the Hovercraft.

Cushions of air

Nine years later the first experimental Hovercraft—the SR–N1—was launched from the Isle of Wight. It amazed the world by skimming over the water at 25 knots and moving effortlessly between land and water because it rode on a cushion of air. Today, more than 140 of the machines are in operation, and some of them are as large as ships.

Many of the early problems of the Hovercraft—noise, high running costs, limitations of use during rough seas—have been largely overcome. The challenge to designers of the future will be to develop a more efficient propulsion unit than the engines that are used in most Hovercraft. One suggestion is that very large Hovercraft might be driven by atomic power.

Cockerell knighted

In 1969 Cockerell was knighted for his invention, the principle of which has now been applied to other spheres of activity. Engineers have developed a strange assortment of vehicles for carrying people and cargoes where no other transport can go and for lifting heavy objects.

Hover trailers have been used to lay pipelines across swamps in Holland and Germany and to carry heavy machinery across paddies in Bangladesh. Other equipment has been developed for moving crashed aircraft off runways, while hover platforms are being developed to carry oil-drilling rigs over difficult terrain such as the Alaskan tundra.

Small Hovercraft are also proving reliable for high-speed shallow-water surveys, in places as far apart as the dikes of Holland and the Amazon River. Others are undergoing trials as coastal patrol craft, police patrol launches, and fire-fighting tenders.

HOVER BEDS FOR SEVERE BURNS

ONE OF THE most unusual applications of the hover idea is the hover bed, which is used to support badly burned hospital patients on a cushion of air. It was designed by a British biomechanical engineer, Dr. John T. Scales, and a team of engineers, who thought it would be a good idea to turn the Hovercraft upside down and blow air upward so that a patient could be supported on air.

Until new skin begins to form on his raw flesh, a severely burned patient can suffer agonies from the contact of his bed under the pressure of his own weight. If he could be floated on air, his new skin could form without being rubbed.

After many experiments a bed was designed to support a patient indefinitely and at the same time blow sterile air over him. Trials proved this was a particularly effective way to treat patients who had been badly burned.

The hover bed lifts patients into the air and is especially useful in treating burns.

MAN AND SUPERMAN?

Steel muscles can give men the power of giants

One day you may see a motorist in a traffic jam get out of his car, go to the trunk, take out a large metal frame, strap it around himself, and use it to carry his car.

In theory it is already possible, because of "mechanical muscles" which engineers are developing to give men the strength of giants. These are frames with a system of levers and linkages that a man can strap to his arms, waist, and feet to amplify his movements. This technique mimics the man's actions but feeds back

IN ACTION. *A mechanical muscle mimics and amplifies the driver's arm and leg movements.*

extra strength, so that he should be able to lift more than half a ton with ease.

Another mechanical muscle, the Unimate, does not work from the human frame but needs to be taken through a series of operations only once to remember and repeat them. It can store 200 separate actions in its magnetic tape memory, and it works tirelessly for 24 hours a day, with a consistency and an accuracy far beyond that of the best human worker.

Learning by mistakes

Some Unimates used in diecasting have been given the first vestiges of senses—a system that checks the temperature of a casting. If it is not right, the machine starts an alternative series of operations.

Other robots with sensory equipment have been devised, but they have so far not been programmed for elementary tasks. It seems incomparably easier to design a computer that will solve problems beyond the reach of the most brilliant mathematician than to design one that will empty ashtrays, because ashtrays come in so many shapes.

Ordinary robots can do only what they have been told in a programmed set of instructions. But another and more advanced type, the automaton, can actually learn by its mistakes. Few have been built, but one that seems extremely promising is the American-designed Perceptron. When the machine is completed, it will have no instructions built in but will have a sense of logic and an instinct to solve problems.

The possibilities for a successful machine of this type are enormous. Already psychiatrists envisage a time when Perceptron could be driven mad, so that in curing it they could learn how to treat the human mind.

POSSUM—THE BREATH OF FREEDOM

IT IS POSSIBLE to dial a telephone number, open a front door, or switch on a light without lifting a finger by using Possum, electronic equipment made to help severely disabled people. A sequence of lights on a display board is operated by blowing on a stem pipe. When the light flashes on over the panel designating the desired appliance, the user stops blowing and sucks. The release of pressure activates the gadget. A code of sucks and blows enables disabled people to operate an electric typewriter at up to 40 words a minute.

SOUNDS OF SILENCE

Engineering's invisible tool—ultrasonics

Some of the world's most interesting and useful sounds cannot be heard at all. Ultrasonics—the "too high to hear sounds"—can be used to drill, cut, weld, clean, and inspect for cracks and flaws. Like all sounds, they travel in waves through the air or any other medium, but they have a far higher frequency than the sounds we hear.

Human ears can detect sound waves that vibrate from 20 to 20,000 times per second. Bats can hear up to 50,000 vibrations per second. But when scientists talk about ultrasonics they can mean billions of vibrations per second.

Special vibrators produce these high-frequency sounds. One, the transducer, is made by sandwiching a thin slice of quartz crystal between two metal plates and passing an alternating electric current through it. When this happens, the crystal alternately expands and contracts by a tiny amount—but enough to generate the pressure waves needed. Ordinary sound waves spread in all directions, but because of their high frequency, ultrasonics can be more easily directed into a beam and made to do useful work.

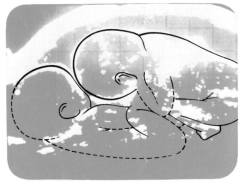

SOUND PICTURE. *Twins (outlined) are revealed in the womb by an ultrasonic beam.*

They can clean weeds and barnacles from the hulls of ships just as a car engine will vibrate off a loose nut. They can be used to detect invisible cracks in metal because the sound waves travel at a different speed through the crack than through the metal. Dishes and clothes can be washed with them because of the pulsations they set up in liquid. And doctors can use them to examine the unborn child in its mother's womb.

CROWNING TRIUMPH

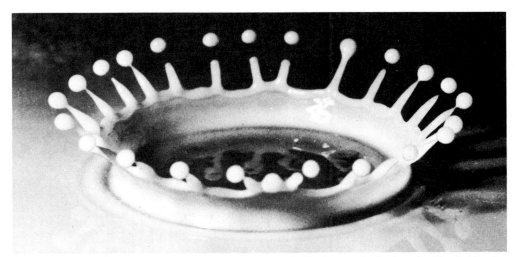

An American scientist, Dr. Harold Edgerton, took this remarkable photograph of a drop of milk splashing into a bowl in 1937, at an exposure of 1/10,000 of a second. Through his research into stroboscopes, or flashing lights, Edgerton helped bring about high-speed photographic techniques.

ANCIENT MYSTERY. *A fragment of the Dead Sea Scrolls is darkened and indecipherable.*

MODERN REVELATION. *Infrared photography clearly reveals the centuries-old text.*

ARTFUL DODGES

How science can restore great works of art

In 1965 a Liverpool (England) art gallery had a 19th-century painting of Dante's meeting with Beatrice flown to Rome for an exhibition. But the painting, by Henry Holiday, was put in an unpressurized hold, and on arrival the canvas was half bare—a pile of tiny flakes of paint lay in the crate. The canvas had shrunk due to changes in air pressure.

Fortunately, Rome boasts one of the top centers for restoration, and there the jigsaw puzzle of paint fragments was reglued on a new canvas.

Rome's Central Institute of Restoration was set up by the government in 1941 because it was felt that many private restorers did more harm than good. Paintings can be damaged by fungus, mold, smog, insects, and moisture. When a painting arrives at the institute, black and white, infrared, and ultraviolet photographs are taken of it. Infrared photography allows the restorers to see through the outer layers of paint, occasionally disclosing signatures. Ultraviolet rays show up retouching and repainting.

If it is suspected that there are previous compositions under the surface, the painting is X-rayed. Torn canvases are glued and ironed onto new fabric backings. Wooden-panel paintings are treated with deadly methyl bromide gas in a sealed chamber to kill off lice or their eggs.

After cleaning, missing parts of the surface of paintings are filled in, and retouching is done.

BLUE MOON . . . AND SUN

BOTH THE MOON and the sun can appear blue, as happened with the sun in 1883 after the volcanic eruption of Krakatoa in Sundra Strait and in 1950 when the moon appeared blue throughout the Western Hemisphere after a forest fire in British Columbia, Canada. The reason is that particles in the air come between the source of light and the observers; the red light scatters and the beam of light becomes richer in shorter wavelengths (blue and violet) than in longer (yellow or red) wavelengths.

A WINDOW TO THE BRAIN

A MACHINE has been developed that can take three-dimensional X-ray photographs of the human brain. It allows doctors to see for the first time a living brain in cross section.

Developed by Godfrey Hounsfield, an English computer engineer, the machine has the added benefits of providing fast, more accurate and detailed diagnosis (which should reduce hospital costs), as well as lessening radiation risk to patients.

A wide variety of disorders can be detected by the machine, which scans the brain with X rays and is linked to a computer and a Polaroid camera. The effects of a stroke, the presence of tumors, cysts, or skull injuries can be diagnosed within minutes.

By comparing segments of the brain at different levels, the depth of a tumor can be determined. In addition, the machine is capable of identifying tumors as small as 1.5 millimeters in diameter, which means that surgery can be performed quickly, before the tumor grows.

The scanner takes only four minutes to rotate halfway around the patient's head in 180 steps of one degree each. At each step, 240 readings are taken from a narrow beam of X rays.

Then, the 43,200 readings from each "slice" are fed into a small computer, and from these a picture is formed on a television monitor screen. The picture is available a mere six minutes after scanning and may be studied either immediately on the screen or later in a photograph or computer printout.

The patient remains fully conscious throughout the procedure, and merely lies flat on his back with the top of his head in the scanning aperture. The completely painless process does not entail any of the discomfort of other tests which involve injecting air and chemicals into the head. Also, the patient must be kept in the hospital for at least 24 hours. Perhaps the greatest advantage to both doctor and patient is that the new system eliminates a great deal of exploratory surgery.

THE WHOLE PICTURE

Lasers are the key to 3-D television

Holography, a system of creating pictures to give a three-dimensional effect, has been developed in the United States and Britain. Literally meaning the "whole message," it has been described as the photographic equivalent of hi-fi in music. Its development was made possible by the invention, in 1960, of the laser, which turns ordinary light—a jumble of colors radiating in all directions—into a single, intense wavelength.

In holography light from a laser is split into two beams. One is pointed at the scene to be recorded, and the other, called a "reference" beam, is directed toward a special photographic plate. The light reflected from the scene to be recorded and the reference beam mix to form a hologram, which is recorded on the emulsion of the special photographic plate. To the naked eye, it is a meaningless blur, but when another laser beam is shone onto it from the back, it springs to life: a perfect three-dimensional reproduction of the original.

A hologram contains many optical details too fine for the human eye to take in. Holographic pictures can even be taken through a microscope, which is why scientists envisage many different applications for it such as processing information. A hologram the size of a postcard could store all the information in 3,000 telephone directories.

A LEAP IN THE DARK

A HUMAN BEING can now see better in the dark than a cat or an owl—thanks to a device known as an image intensifier. It consists of a tube through which the images of objects at night are made brighter by electrons focused on a phosphor screen, on which is built up a brighter reproduction of the original picture. The device can be used for military operations at night, for driving at night without headlights, to observe the habits of nocturnal animals, and to intensify X-ray pictures.

CLEAR AS GLASS
New uses for one of man's oldest discoveries

Since man first began to explore the ocean depths, one of the major hazards has been the enormous pressures that exist in the sunless world beneath the sea. For every 33 feet of descent, the pressure increases by 15 pounds per square inch. The record depth reached in a steel bathyscaphe is 35,800 feet, by a U.S. Navy team in 1960. Had it been possible to descend much farther, they would have run the risk of the bathyscaphe, *Trieste,* being crushed by the weight of water above it.

But a new era in undersea exploration is promised by submarines made of glass. For glass can withstand much higher pressure than steel. The reason is that the microscopic faults and scratches on its surface "knit together" under pressure.

This principle is being exploited by scientists such as Taylor Pryor, director of the Oceanic Foundation in Hawaii. His aim is to use glass vessels to put men 20,000 feet below the surface of the Pacific to study prospects for ocean farming—aquaculture. At this depth the pressure is almost 4½ tons per square inch, but the explorers will run no risk of being crushed, and they will have perfect all-around vision.

TARGET PRACTICE. *Soldiers demonstrate the bullet-resistant Triplex glass.*

Fine glass filaments are used to twist light in any direction. This concept, known as fiber optics, enables doctors and engineers to see around corners inside the human body or machines. The flexible filaments—no thicker than a human hair—transmit light along their entire length. When hundreds of them are bundled together like a strand of spaghetti, it is possible to look through one end and see out of the other even if the glass cord is knotted. These vision tubes are used in medicine for inspecting lungs and stomach walls. In industry they allow engineers to study inaccessible parts of engines.

Fiber ends can also be placed in spots where it is inconvenient to mount electric bulbs. For instance, some traffic signs mounted high above highways have their bulbs at ground level where they are easily maintained, and the light is carried aloft through the glass tubes.

Technologists are experimenting with a telephone cable made up of glass strands that will carry thousands of conversations, transmitted along a light beam.

Glass has been manufactured for 4,500 years, and its extraordinary qualities are constantly being put to new uses.

Soft as silk

Glass can be spun into fibers fine enough to produce material as soft as silk. It can also be made so tough that it is six times stronger than steel or so heat resistant that on the nose cone of a missile it will withstand the intense heat of reentry into the atmosphere.

The flight-deck windows of the Concorde supersonic airliner must cope with temperatures ranging from −58° to 248°F (−50° to 120°C). The crew sits behind 1½-inch-thick glass pressure panels that are protected by an outer shield made up of six ¼-inch-thick glass panes. Each pane is coated with gold two-millionths of an inch thick, to conduct heat to the windshield.

The Leonardo da Vinci cartoon in London's National Gallery is protected by the sort of anti-bandit glass that has become a standard fitting in many banks, post offices, and jewelers. Two sheets of glass are bonded together with a tough plastic filling that resists intense shocks —such as an attack by a smash-and-grab raider

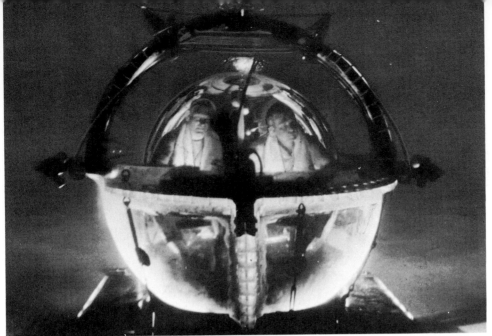

ALL-GLASS BATHYSCAPHE. *Ocean scientist Taylor Pryor and an assistant try out a glass vessel that he hopes will allow his team to investigate depths of up to 20,000 feet in the Pacific.*

or a bullet. A fierce blow will shatter the glass but not the plastic.

Reaction to light

Photochromic glass is clear in darkness but turns dark in daylight—a characteristic that may be exploited in future house and car building, with windows being made to act as automatic shades, depending on the sunlight. Molded glass fiber has been used to replace damaged 1812 stonework.

Some architects are now designing glass-walled houses that would never need painting because the color would be baked into the glass.

TRANSMITTING PHONE CALLS VIA GLASS

SO MUCH information has to be exchanged at high speed in the modern world that the airwaves and telephone lines are being stretched to their capacity. A new communications system that uses lightwaves as a medium for telephone communications holds promise of solving the problem. The voice is transmitted on pulses of light sent through glass fibers.

The sending of signals by light was made possible by research, done in the 1950's, on the use of new light sources—lasers and tiny, light-emitting diodes no bigger than a salt grain. Hair-thin glass fibers were designed to carry the light, and minuscule photodetectors were developed to convert light pulses into electrical signals that could then be made part of a nationwide telephone communications network.

In 1977 this complex new system of lightwave communication was installed experimentally in a downtown section of Chicago. In a year-long test, each lightguide was connected at one end to a transmitter module containing either a laser or diode light source. The other end of the lightguide was connected to a receiver module containing the photodetector.

During the experiment this amazing system proved a single pair of lightguides is able to carry 672 simultaneous conversations. A lightguide cable containing 144 fibers is only a half-inch in diameter, and has the capacity to carry some 50,000 simultaneous conversations. Because such cables are so much lighter and smaller than the conventional copper cables, they can also be used to interconnect the frames of electronic switching systems in much less space and at far less cost.

The Bell System network, which developed this new lightwave communication system, expects to put it into general operation by the end of 1980. The system can also be used to transmit computer data and television video signals.

YOU ARE WHAT YOU EAT

"Artificial" protein may sustain life

Cholesterol-free bacon, steak manufactured from beans, milk made out of petroleum-eating bacteria—these and other exotic foods are already here, or soon will be. They are the by-products of a revolution in food technology.

But why artificial food when the genuine article can be grown the old-fashioned way? The answer is people: 3.9 billion in the world right now, with 3 billion more due by the year 2000. And people need food, especially food with the body-building compounds known as proteins. To Americans protein has traditionally meant meat. But it takes five to seven pounds of vegetable protein in the form of feed to produce a single pound of animal protein in the form of beef, pork, eggs, or milk.

Even the "have" nations cannot afford such extravagance indefinitely, while the "have-nots" are already in trouble and soon could be desperate. The answer may lie in fabricated protein foods, particularly synthetic meat.

The first of the new foods has already reached the grocery shelves of Europe and America in the form of "ham," "sausages," and "bacon." Their main constituent is soybeans. Technically dubbed textured vegetable protein, it is also known as "spun" meat because it is made by a spinning process similar to that used to manufacture rayon.

The first step in making textured protein is the preparation of a "soup" of dissolved soybean, wheat, and oat protein. The soup is forced through a metal die with many tiny holes called a spinnerette. The resulting filaments of protein are then coagulated in a special chemical bath, colored, flavored, and pressed into shape. The finished product looks like meat, tastes like meat, and even chews like meat. The chief differences are that it contains no cholesterol, has 75 percent less fat, and sells for about half the price.

The market for textured vegetable protein is big and getting bigger. In 1975, 188 million pounds of spun meat were used in the United States, most of it as meat extender in the National School Lunch Program (30 percent textured protein is permitted in the meat dishes). Within five years the market is expected to increase tenfold to almost 2 billion pounds a year.

At present, soybeans are the major source of vegetable protein, but this may change rapidly. "Corn could be the next big one," an agriculture expert has said, and one firm is already planning to go into the business of making protein from corn germ.

Work is under way in every corner of the world on a bewildering variety of other protein sources. Food engineers in Chile and Argentina are looking into the protein possibilities of sunflower seeds. A California outfit is churning

ALTERNATIVE TO MEAT. *Synthetic bacon and sausages, rich in vegetable protein and low in fat, are now on supermarket shelves. Technologists believe such fabricated protein food may someday feed the world's hungry billions.*

out 10 tons of protein a day from alfalfa. A factory for making protein flour from cottonseed is in operation in Lubbock, Texas. In Canada an Alberta farm cooperative is gearing up to produce some 3,500 tons of protein a year, using rapeseed as the source. Elsewhere, sugarcane waste, potato stalks, pea vines, beet tops, wood pulp, and even water hyacinths are being studied.

For the day after tomorrow scientists are planning high-protein dishes with no animal *or* vegetable basis at all. Results can already be seen. A pilot plant in Minnesota is producing

10 million pounds of protein-rich yeast per year, using natural gas as "food." And near Moscow the Russians are busily converting oil into protein with the assistance of strains of microorganisms that have a sweet tooth for paraffin.

Almost all artificial protein is presently being used to feed livestock rather than humans. People, apparently, aren't paying as much attention to science and statistics as to their own tastes and traditions, which are still very much on the side of real meat, milk, eggs, and cheese. By the year 2000, though, world hunger may change all our minds.

MICROBES IN MAN'S SERVICE

A revolutionary answer to pollution

One of the 20th century's major problems, pollution, may soon help scientists find a solution to one of mankind's greatest needs—how to feed our over-populated world.

Researchers in microbiology believe that human and industrial waste from large towns and cities can be converted into nutritious food for animals.

The researchers have found that certain kinds of microbes can be stimulated to exceptional growth by feeding them a mixture of oxygen and phosphorus. When treated in this way, the microbes develop the ability to live on almost any "foodstuff" available to them. It is the scientists' plan to develop large factories where armies of microbes would be kept in special tanks into which would be dumped waste of many kinds.

As the microbes attack the waste material, a kind of fermentation process is started, and the first beneficial side effect is that the fermentation produces gases—especially methane, which can be used either as an ordinary domestic fuel, or can be fed to the microbes to continue the

stimulation of growth, or can be used to power the plants on which the microbes grow.

Later in the fermentation process, when the waste material has been largely disposed of, scientists find that the water remaining is rich in many kinds of minerals that can be used to support the growth of plants, such as algae.

These plants may in turn be used directly as animal foodstuffs or may be fed to such creatures as earthworms, which can themselves be used to fatten fish and chickens for human consumption.

The use of microbes in this way is a never-ending process, for as long as some form of waste is available, microbes will go on reproducing and will never die. The more they are fed, the more they reproduce themselves.

Scientists who have been engaged in research work in this field have also found that selected strains of microbes can be developed to eat certain kinds of rocks or minerals and to ignore others. It is possible that before the end of this century armies of microbes can be pumped down mine shafts to eat up bedrock and leave behind only the required minerals.

NEW USE FOR OLD BODIES

MAN'S NEWFOUND ability to keep bodies functioning with the use of heart, lung, and kidney machines has led to a startling proposal by Columbia University sociologist Amitai Etzioni. He, like Dr. Willard Gaylin, who formulated the idea, wants "cadaver farms" set up, using bodies that are technically dead—with no brain waves being registered over a prolonged period but with the other organs intact. Machines would keep organs functioning to produce vaccines and blood for purposes of transfusion.

MILLION-DOLLAR BRAINS

Machines man devised to do his thinking for him

Computers of one sort or another have been around for nearly 5,000 years. The Babylonians invented the first about 3000 B.C. This was the abacus, a sand-covered slab used for mathematical calculations. About 600 B.C. the Chinese, and later the Greeks and Romans, used a bead-frame style abacus. But the first automatic calculating machine did not appear until 1833, when an Englishman, Charles Babbage, invented his "analytical engine," which was designed to calculate logarithms and, in theory, the position of the moon.

The Second World War gave impetus to computing, and the first computers using modern principles were developed at the University of Pennsylvania and at the German Aircraft Research Institute to calculate the trajectories of shells.

It was not until 1951 that the first commercial computer was put to work on the U.S. census. Shortly afterward, the International Business Machines Corporation (IBM) began producing computers commercially.

Every computer has five basic units that enable it to perform vast numbers of complex calculations at fantastically high speed. The input unit "reads" information fed into the machine; the data store holds the information—usually on either magnetic tape or disks—until needed; the arithmetic unit selects stored information and performs calculations; the control unit coordinates the processes; and the output unit produces the results of each operation.

The world's most powerful computer, the Control Data Corporation's CDC 7600, can perform 36 million flawless operations a second.

Computers have been used to compose music, create art designs, play chess, and even to find that Shakespeare used the word "love" 2,271 times in his collected works.

At the Massachusetts Institute of Technology computers are sorting waste materials to decide what can be recycled. And at the University of Texas a computer has been programmed to simulate human behavior. It responds to objects with fear, anger, or attraction, and simulates actions of withdrawal, approach, attack, or indifference.

Computers do have limitations. They have no intuition and can work only by sheer logic. They are incapable of solving a problem that is beyond human intelligence, because humans must provide information for every calculation and give instructions for working it out.

Nervous breakdowns

Several hard-working computers have had "nervous breakdowns." One clicked away all night trying to do an impossible task, then "collapsed." It had been trying to divide by zero.

Another computer that has shown sensitivity is the British ERNIE, the Electronic Random Number Indicator Equipment that picks Premium Bond lottery winners. One day, as a film star was about to perform ERNIE's monthly switching-on ceremony, bagpipes were heard in the street. ERNIE showed every sign of switching itself on. Apparently, the pipe music had struck some sympathetic chord deep in ERNIE's "heart."

LANDING GEAR

Ingenious devices that keep aircraft on the right track

An RAF Varsity transport plane touched down on an airfield at Suffolk, England in 1949—and made flying history. For the pilot had not laid a finger on the controls. Instead, he used the first automatic landing device.

The search for a way of landing "blind" began in earnest during the Second World War. Too many bomber pilots and crews, their missions accomplished and fuel tanks low, were at the mercy of the weather when they came in to land. So a team of scientists was set up in England to try to find a solution.

They took as their starting point a method called instrument landing system. Twin radio beams, transmitted from the ground, gave an airplane its angle of descent and relative position to the approaching runway.

However, the system needed the pilot's unswerving concentration and was useless below 200 feet. So the scientists developed a radio altimeter coupled to the automatic pilot, which leveled the aircraft just above the runway.

Even after the 1949 demonstration, it took years before automatic landing was reliable enough to be used regularly and accurately. Only in 1962 was the system considered safe enough to build into an operational aircraft.

Another electronic miracle, the Decca Navigator, helps a plane thread its way through the world's crowded skies. The Navigator also grew out of a wartime need—guiding a ship safely and accurately through a sea full of peril. The Navigator was invented in Britain by an American, Chicago-born William O'Brien. He got the idea just before the Second World War, and the British Admiralty gave him the backing he needed to develop the system.

Lifesaving ripples

Radio navigation beacons then in use had one big snag—they told a navigator he was on the right path, but they did not tell him exactly where he was on it.

O'Brien's idea ran something like this. Suppose three men were stationed around a pond, with a fourth suspended over the center, and at the same moment each dropped a pebble into the pool.

The four ever-widening circles of ripples would form an orderly lattice, and anyone on the pond, if he were a good enough mathematician, could fix his precise position by using the ripple intersection pattern on a chart.

O'Brien planned to do the same with radio beacons. Three set up at the corners of a triangle, with the fourth "master station" in the middle, would produce a similar grid of radio waves.

The Admiralty was intrigued. A test of the system in 1942 proved that the beacons did everything O'Brien said they would. By D-day in June 1944, the navy had set up beacons along the south coast of England, and O'Brien had produced 27 receivers, made largely from old gas-meter parts.

The success was phenomenal. Thanks to the first Decca Navigator, not a single ship was lost in the landings in France.

Today, the Decca Navigator system is worldwide. Forty chains of radio beacons cover 7 million square miles of the earth's surface. The

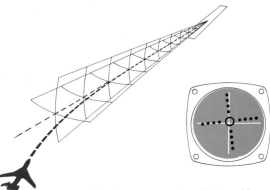

HOW IT WORKS. *If the plane stays on the path formed by the crossing beams, it will be guided home. The instrument shows divergences.*

receivers, too, have come a long way. Using a computer the size of a shoebox, they pick up and instantly digest as many as 4,000 instructions, and then plot an aircraft's or ship's course on a map unrolling automatically.

The advantages for aircraft are enormous. Because of the lack of precision of most navigational systems, huge amounts of airspace must be allotted to each plane. Aircraft over the North Atlantic, for example, must stay at least 110 miles apart. Approach paths to major airports must be 10 miles wide.

But the fantastically accurate Decca system is not obstructed by mountains or buildings and can locate a runway to within 40 yards.

Now, because of this precision, it is possible for planes to fly both ways down a 10-mile air corridor, thus doubling the capacity of existing airlanes. And 12 aircraft fitted with the Navigator could fly safely in airspace presently used by only one plane.

CRASH REGISTER. *"Black" boxes, or flight recorders, are sensitive but tough devices containing multichannel wire or tape machines that store vital information about aircraft performance. When an aircraft crashes, the box helps investigators find out what happened and why.*

137

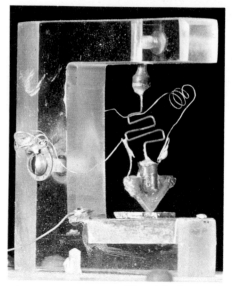

THE FIRST TRANSISTOR. *The original germanium-based electric circuit (pictured twice its size).*

THE MINIATURIZATION of electric circuits—and everything that depends on them, from tiny hearing aids to computers, slimline television sets, and spaceships—would not have been possible without the invention of transistors in 1947.

The three Americans responsible—William Shockley, John Bardeen, and Walter Brattain—were all awarded the Nobel Prize for Physics. They worked for the Bell Telephone laboratories in New Jersey where they were intensively studying the properties of germanium and silicon, the simplest materials of semiconductors.

The basic discovery of the three researchers was that an electric current running through one pair of contacts on a tiny piece of germanium or silicon could be controlled by a much smaller current through another contact on its surface. Thus the device could be made to amplify by a factor of 100 or more. One application was the use of the transistor in high-speed electronic switching systems at telephone exchanges.

PINHEAD ELECTRONICS

Here is the news . . . on a radio cuff link

I t is now possible to listen to the radio—on your cuff links. A British electronics firm makes the tuned-in cuff links as a gimmick to give to visiting VIP's. But the technology that makes this miniaturization possible has more practical uses—including some sinister ones.

RADIO LINK. *This cuff link is a radio amplifier. When connected to a power supply, it can pick up broadcasts.*

Miniaturization has made practical a radio set that will fit into a matchbox, a television set with a five-inch screen, a computer that will go into your pocket, and a pill containing a tiny radio transmitter, which can be "fed" to a suspect and will then give out signals so that he or she can be constantly tracked.

The secret of such minute devices is in the development of integrated circuits.

The process starts with electronic engineers designing a circuit that is drawn on a chart and then reduced photographically to, say, the size of a pinhead. The "picture" of the circuit is then printed on a slide that is made into a mask. This is put over a tiny sliver from a crystal of silicon, and through lines cut in the mask, the silicon is etched to reproduce the lines of the circuit. The transistors and other components are deposited on the circuit. Then workers using binocular microscopes solder fine gold wire less than 1/1,000 of an inch thick onto the ends of the circuit, so that it can be connected to other components in the finished article.

Using this technology, a computer, which 20 years ago occupied a room and needed refrigerators to keep it cool, can be reduced to the size of a typewriter.

BOOK IN MINIATURE. *Actual size (16 millimeters) of pages in this book as they would appear in a retrieval system. But with microfilm, it is possible to photograph the entire book on just two frames.*

MICRODOT PIGEON POST

First miniature photographs failed to save Paris

Napoleon III had been captured, France was in chaos, and the invading Prussian Army had surrounded Paris. It was then, at the height of the 1870 siege, that the first practical use of microphotography was conceived.

The hard-pressed garrison holding on in Paris needed to get messages to the French commander in chief outside the Capital. But the information was too bulky to smuggle through the army lines.

Then an inventor named Prudent Dagron remembered the work of an English optical manufacturer, John Dancer. In 1853 Dancer had reduced a page of *The Times* to a dot, 1/16 inch across.

Dagron suggested that the vital messages should be printed, then photographed and reduced. How would the film be carried? Dagron's answer to this was less of a technological breakthrough. "Pigeons," he said. The idea worked although, in this instance, it did not save Paris from capitulation.

Dagron used the collodion process utilized by Dancer. (Collodion was a liquid used to cover photographic plates.)

When the messages had been photographed, the negative was reduced and printed onto plates. The processed emulsion was stripped off and wound into a thin tube that was fastened to the tail of the pigeon. Up to 3,000 messages were recorded on one plate, and 18 of the emulsion films could be carried by one pigeon. When the pigeon landed at its home cote, in Paris, the films were transcribed, using a lantern projector.

Sixty years later Kodak began working on a semiautomated method of photographing documents for filing. By the 1930's banks and some newspapers were keeping records on film and, in 1938, under the threat of war, the British Museum stored 35-millimeter films of some of its most valuable books. Espionage, too, found the process useful.

War, and the threat of war, led to another advance in the 1950's. Research into materials that could shield the eyes of troops exposed to the glare of an H-bomb led scientists to a number of compounds that change color when exposed to radiant energy.

The compounds, called photochromic, form the basis of an experimental microfilm system being tested. Molecules of light-sensitive organic dye are integrated into the film emulsion, so that when images are transferred onto it they can be read as soon as light falls on them. The film does not need developing.

Using this system, a bank clerk can, at the press of a button, flash on a screen in front of him any one of 160,000 signatures.

Reductions in size of 40,000 to 1 are possible, reducing a 300-page book to postage-stamp size.

NEW SOURCE OF ENERGY. *An intense laser beam eats its way through a thin razor blade.*

THE DEATH RAY THAT SAVES LIFE

Widespread uses being developed for laser beams

A beam that was once thought to have potential as an invisible death ray has turned out to have countless peaceable uses. It can measure the distance between the earth and the moon to within six inches; burn holes in a piece of metal in a few seconds; transmit a three-dimensional television picture —or cut a man's suit from a length of cloth.

The beam can even be used in the most delicate eye surgery to weld back detached retinas or to destroy tumors in some of the eye's blood vessels, and also to remove tonsils.

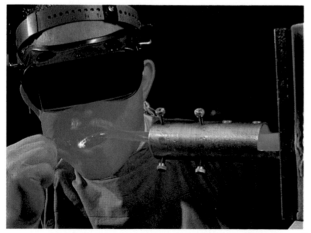

AN END TO PAIN. *Laser beams can pinpoint and painlessly destroy decayed areas of a tooth.*

The beam is shot from a "laser," a device named from the initials of its title, Light Amplification by Stimulated Emission of Radiation. Much of its development in the 1960's was secret because defense scientists thought it could be used as a weapon of war. Theoretically, a laser beam could kill a man or knock out an aircraft.

But, happily, the amount of energy needed to project a powerful beam any distance ruled it out as a means of destruction. Laser beams are used to guide bombs to their targets and as rangefinders for artillery. But they are not practical enough to be lethal weapons.

The laser is a device that stimulates the atoms of the substances fed into it to give out radiation in an intense beam of energy—it may be visible or invisible light energy. All the rays are of the same wavelength or color. They remain concentrated and are able to penetrate objects or be beamed over great distances with a minimum of spreading.

Excited molecules

The idea first occurred to Prof. Charles Townes, of Columbia University. In 1954 he found that he could excite the molecules of ammonia gas by bombarding the gas with microwaves at a frequency of exactly 23,870 megacycles a second. The molecules jumped about so that they gave out a very much more uniform flow of energy than they had taken in.

Townes and his research team built a device that they called a "maser," standing for Microwave Amplification by Stimulated Emission of Radiation. The device was a highly sensitive, interference-free radio amplifier of the type being used in radio telescopes and space radio communications.

But masers operate in only one part of the energy spectrum. Townes and others turned their thoughts to the part bordering the frequency of light.

Potential of light

Light is made up of all the colors of the spectrum. At one end there is blue; at the other, red; and at the extremes there are ultraviolet and infrared, which cannot be seen but can be felt as warmth. Townes reasoned that, if he excited suitable atoms that are situated between two mirrors, some of the light that is normally given off by the atoms would be trapped between the two mirrors. This would then reflect back and forth and in so doing cause much of the remaining light to be given off by the atoms in the form of an intense beam.

He published this theory in 1958, and engineers competed to make the first working laser. The race was won in 1960 by Theodore Maiman, a young physicist working at the Hughes Research Laboratories in California.

He used a ruby as the heart of his laser. It was not, in fact, very efficient, and now other substances are used, notably gases such as helium and neon.

THE COLOR NO ONE SEES
Infrared warning meant no landing on Mars

New developments in the study of infrared rays have enabled astronomers to measure the density of the atmosphere around Mars, doctors to make earlier diagnoses of cancer, and explorers to devise better equipment for polar expeditions.

Infrared rays are the invisible light that emanates from beyond the red of the visible spectrum. Their existence became known in 1800 when an English astronomer Sir William Herschel measured the colors of the spectrum with a thermometer. He found that the bands of light became warmer as he approached the red band at the end of the spectrum. When he placed the thermometer beyond the visible red streak, into an area where no apparent light existed, the temperature rose higher still.

Herschel had found a new kind of light that could not be seen but could be detected by its temperature. He named it infrared, meaning below the red.

Practical use of his discovery came about only in recent years. Space officials scrapped plans for using parachutes alone to land on Mars when measurements of the planet's infrared radiation showed the atmosphere was too thin to permit a soft landing.

British doctors found in 1961 that breast cancers were slightly warmer than normal tissues. This led to the first medical infrared camera, or thermograph, which is now widely used to aid cancer diagnosis, indicate the depth of burns, detect hidden bruises in unconscious patients, and pick up early signs of one type of stroke before it occurs.

Scientists testing the efficiency of arctic clothing found that body heat loss soared where clothing wrinkled near the thin metal of zippers. Thanks to heat photography, arctic workers are now more warmly clad.

OUT OF THE DARK. *An infrared "heat" camera reveals the face of a man hidden in darkness.*

CHEATING DEATH BY FREEZING

The remarkable science of ultracoldness

In an underground storage site near Los Angeles, a dozen men and women lie in capsules that look like giant vacuum flasks. Their bodies are wrapped in aluminum foil. Remove the foil and a thin layer of frost covers their faces. An icy mist of liquid nitrogen clings around each body.

These people have been dead for some years. But centuries from now attempts may be made to bring them back to life again. They chose this odd method of entombment in the hope that, at some time in the future when medical science has advanced far beyond today's standards, they will be thawed from their deep-frozen state and cured of the diseases that killed them.

In their lifetimes these men and women were pioneers of cryogenics—the science that paved the way for the first serious attempt to conquer death by the use of freezing. It is based on the study and application of very low temperatures. Though cryogenics began as more of a craze than a science, it may one day enable man to travel to the distant stars and help him to discover a cheap, almost limitless supply of energy.

The first known example of cryogenics, in 1626, had an unhappy ending. The English philosopher Francis Bacon stuffed a chicken with snow, so that he could observe the effect of the cold in preserving its flesh. Unfortunate-ly, Bacon caught a chill from the snow and died from it soon afterward.

In the 19th and early 20th centuries, scientists found that if gases were sufficiently cooled they turned into liquids. If these supercooled liquids are applied to metals, the metals become brittle; steel shatters to powder at one blow of a hammer. In addition, metals in this state are better conductors of electricity.

The discoveries lay unexploited for 50 years. But with the space age came the need to build rockets that could carry enough fuel for journeys in space. Cryogenics supplied the answer. Oxygen, hydrogen, and nitrogen in liquid forms were all used as rocket fuels—and as they were tested, more uses were found for them.

Near absolute zero

Several of the most far-reaching discoveries have been in the use of liquid gases to cool metals to near absolute zero, $-459\,°F$ $(-273\,°C)$ —the lowest temperature that can be recorded anywhere in the universe. It is the temperature at which all molecular activity ceases.

One such use of cryogenic cooling is in the food industry. Liquid nitrogen, which has no taste or smell, gets fresh farm produce into a frozen state far faster than conventional refrigeration methods and so preserves the flavor better. Meat, shellfish, and bread are now being preserved in this way.

So, too, is blood, for cryogenics has meant that blood can be banked indefinitely. The blood cells, if soaked first in an antifreeze agent, are undamaged by rapid freezing to −320°F (−196°C).

Freezing human bodies

Research into the rapid freezing of blood, as well as human sperm and skin tissue, led to the craze for freezing bodies in the hope of bringing them to life again—and to those corpses lying in beds of liquid nitrogen near Los Angeles.

Some of the corpses have been there since 1967. They could be there for hundreds of years because, if the person died from a particular form of cancer, it could take that long before an effective cure is found.

Apart from a cure for cancer (and the hope of such a discovery accounts for several of those bodies awaiting a new life), adherents of cryogenics are also believers in the possibility of rejuvenation. It is little more than a dream now, but future scientists may make it come true. In that hope some of the bodies will be left in limbo until their inhabitants can be not only cured but also be made young again.

The cost of dying to live again is high: anywhere from $7,000 to $15,000 to be put in a state of "cryogenic suspension" and about $700 a year for "storage" costs.

Scientists say the chances of these people having cheated death are slim. For cryogenics is just not advanced enough to freeze the entire brain and other tissue fast enough to avoid the destruction of vital cells. Even so, science may well learn to conquer that problem, too.

NEW LIFE AHEAD? *Inside the capsule is a corpse, deep-frozen. It may someday be brought back to life, perhaps rejuvenated, and, if possible, cured of the disease that killed it.*

Feats of building and engineering

THE SHOWPLACE OF FRANCE. *The Palace of Versailles was built at the expense of the nation. It typified the vanity and arrogance of Louis XIV, who satisfied his whim with complete disregard for the cost in money and human misery. Louis, when not fighting wars, personally supervised the building of the palace and gardens, which took 50 years to complete. More than 30,000 workmen were employed at one time, many of whom were unpaid or forced labor. The gardens alone cover an area of about 250 acres.*

THE GREAT PALACE

France's monument to a King's vanity

A King's vanity helped to bankrupt a country—and gave the world one of its most beautiful follies. The King was Louis XIV of France. The folly was the Palace of Versailles.

The palace, which became the center of the French court and government, started as a humble hunting lodge where Louis' father, Louis XIII, could retreat from the rigors of the French court. In 1627 Louis XIII built a modest chateau at Versailles. After his death his son decided to replace the chateau with a lasting monument to his own vision of himself as the "Sun King."

The work began in 1661, and the place chosen for "the greatest palace on earth" was an architect's nightmare. The fine, sandy soil caused some foundations to sink, and the entire surrounding area was wild and inhospitable.

Louis XIV was obsessed with Versailles. For 50 years, when not engaged in fighting wars, he personally supervised the building of the palace and gardens, undeterred by the cost, human misery, and loss of lives involved in the project.

At one time, more than 30,000 workmen were employed at Versailles, and many of them were unpaid or forced labor. The conditions in which they worked and lived led to epidemics, and hundreds died. Fatalities on the building sites were frequent, and the fevers emanating from the marshes took a heavy toll. Even Louis was embarrassed by the number of deaths, so he expressly forbade his courtiers to discuss the subject.

Nothing but the best

Time, ingenuity, and expense were never spared. The area became the workshop of France. Large forests were planted, and statues of marble and bronze were brought to the site to embellish the magnificent formality of the gardens.

Occasionally, Louis brought the entire French court from Paris to Versailles to admire the progress of the buildings. The courtiers had to sleep on half-built floors or wherever else they could find accommodation in the area.

To fulfill his ambition, Louis employed the best architects in France. Louis Le Vau began by improving the original Louis XIII buildings.

Then, in 1678, Jules Mansart took over and remodeled the main section of the palace, building the two north and south wings, creating a 667-yard facade with 375 windows.

The task of finding the money was given to Jean Baptiste Colbert. He tried to recoup some of the money invested in the project by building factories to manufacture the many elaborate trappings for Versailles.

Colbert appointed Charles Le Brun, the King's favorite artist, as director of the factories that turned out furnishings not only for Versailles but also for the other royal palaces in France. Le Brun prepared the designs, which ranged from the painted ceiling of the Galerie des Glaces (the Hall of Mirrors) to the design of metal door locks at Versailles.

The linens, silks, furniture, carpets, and other luxuries were displayed to foreign visitors.

Flowers for the King

The gardens, which cover an area of about 250 acres, were the work of André Lenôtre. Louis had a passion for flowers. He imported 4 million bulbs every year from Holland—when he was not at war with the Dutch.

Two star attractions were the Grotto de Thetis and the Menagerie. The grotto was encrusted with pebbles and shells and contained an organ that worked by waterpower. Another feature was the concealed water jets, which sprayed unsuspecting admirers. The Menagerie was contained in a small chateau and housed a collection of exotic animals and birds.

In the gardens Louis built the Grand Canal, 200 feet wide and a mile long, where ornamental gondolas and other boats were kept. In 1684 Mansart built the Orangerie, importing fully grown orange trees for the purpose.

But the most splendid features of the gardens were the fountains and waterfalls. These required an enormous water supply and a huge pumping station. The Machine de Marly was built between 1681 and 1684 to bring water from the Seine River. It was not a success, and an effort was then made to divert the course of the Eure River. The cost in lives and money was vast, and the project was halted in 1686 because the troops that were being used as labor battalions were needed for war.

Eventually, the waters of the plateau between Versailles and Rambouillet were collected and fed to the gardens through a system of channels.

Magnificent but unsuitable

The entire court moved to Versailles in 1682, and it remained the royal residence until 1789. Louis' court was as grandiose as his palace. It consisted of 20,000 people, including 9,000 soldiers who were quartered in the town of Versailles. One thousand courtiers and 4,000 servants lived in the palace, but the magnificent rooms and galleries were unsuited to ordinary needs. The building was virtually impossible to heat and had practically no sanitation.

After Louis XIV's death his great-grandson, Louis XV, made further additions to Versailles. He built the Petit Trianon, which later became a favorite retreat of Louis XVI's Queen, Marie Antoinette.

Louis XVI added a suite of apartments for Marie Antoinette, but the power and influence of the Palace of Versailles ended with the French Revolution of 1789. After the Revolution the furniture and fineries were sold or stolen, and the palace was neglected. Restoration work was carried out in the middle of the 19th century by Louis Philippe, with help from the United States.

Versailles became a museum, dedicated to "All the Glories of France."

THE MACHINE DE MARLY

THE LACK OF a water supply was always a problem at Versailles. There was never enough to slake Versailles' insatiable demand. In the gardens Louis XIV demanded water for 1,400 fountains. The volume of water required rivaled the amount needed by the whole of Paris.

Whenever the King walked in the grounds of Versailles, servants operated the controls so that the fountains were playing. The overseer was liable to a fine if the fountains failed to work.

Louis' search for an adequate supply of water inspired amazing schemes and inventions—of which the best known was the enormous Machine de Marly. Work started on the machine in 1681. Its purpose was to raise a constant supply of water from the Seine.

Fourteen enormous water wheels, each 36 feet wide, moved 221 pumps to bring water 177 yards up the hillsides from the Seine. But after its completion in 1684, work began on an aqueduct to carry the water to two reservoirs near Versailles.

The machine suffered frequent breakdowns and required costly repairs.

IMMORTALITY FOR PHARAOH

All Egypt toiled to build Cheops' tomb

Egypt is a treasure house of engineering miracles, both ancient and modern. No two feats demonstrate this 5,000-year link more dramatically than the building of the Great Pyramid of Cheops around 2700 B.C., and in the 1960's the internationally organized rescue of the massive rock temples of Abu Simbel from the rising waters of the Aswan High Dam.

The Great Pyramid rises as high as a 42-story modern building and covers 13 acres of desert.

Within this solid stone structure there is room for St. Paul's and Westminster Abbey in London, St. Peter's in Rome, and the cathedrals of Florence and Milan. It contains enough stone to build a 10-foot wall around the whole of the boundaries of France.

Channels in the rock

When the ancient Egyptian engineers began to build this massive structure, they first had to establish a truly horizontal surface for the foundation. They did this by cutting channels in the rock, filling them with water, and then, on a calm day, sticking in rods and measuring the waterline.

With the aid of this giant spirit level they then cut the surface of the rocks down to the waterline.

Many thousands of masons, quarrymen, and laborers toiled for 20 years to build the tomb on the Giza Plateau for the Pharaoh, Cheops.

Its stones range in weight from 2½ to 15 tons; in total they number an awesome 2½ million.

Yet the men who quarried these stones and raised them into position used no mechanical aids except the lever, the roller, and the inclined plane. (The wheel, though probably known, was impractical, and sledges were used for transport through the sand.)

Without possessing any fine measuring instruments, the Egyptians achieved an astonishing degree of accuracy.

The corners of the pyramid are almost perfect right angles, and the sides precisely face the four main points of the compass—north, south, east, and west.

The ancient architects almost certainly managed this remarkable feat with the use of astronomical observations.

Originally, the building was encased in blocks of white, polished limestone. A few casing stones that survive near the base are so exquisitely cut that a piece of paper cannot be inserted between them.

The building of the Great Pyramid was a highly organized and coordinated effort.

From the Nile, a quarter of a mile away, a great stone causeway was built, sloping gently upward to the lip of the plateau.

This construction alone took almost 10 years. Along its slope work gangs hauled huge chunks of stone on wooden sledges, using thick, strong ropes made from plaited reed.

Central core

Quarrymen worked at three widely separated parts of Egypt. The stone for the massive central core of the pyramid was cut from the coarse desert sandstone of the Giza region itself.

From the east bank of the Nile came the limestone for the casing. The granite that lined the inner galleries and burial chamber was hewn from rock at Aswan, at the first cataract of the Nile, and was floated 600 miles downriver on huge barges—an enormous operation. The Aswan quarrymen used mallets of dolerite, a stone harder than granite, to roughly cut the blocks.

At the pyramid site masons accurately trimmed the blocks to their final shape, using abrasives to give them their final high polish.

Liquid mortar

Gangs hauled the stones up a long supply ramp, to put them in place. At the lip of the ramp, where the last layer of stones had been laid, each block was slid into position on a bed of liquid mortar, which also acted as a lubricant.

As the pyramid rose, the ramp was lengthened, for the slope had always to remain the same to ensure that the building's dimensions were correct.

Skilled craftsmen were employed all through the year. But the unskilled men only worked for three months a year—in the autumn, when the Nile had its annual flood.

While these agricultural workers—about 100,000 of them—waited for the flood to subside before planting their crops, they were put to work on the building of the pyramid.

Channels in the rock and mud walls around the base held water that acted like a spirit level.

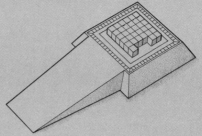

The causeway was built for hauling construction materials above ground level.

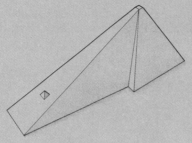

With the core of the pyramid finished, the causeway touched the apex, providing a gradient.

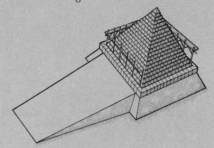

The ramp was dismantled progressively as the stonework was dressed from the top down.

The names of some of the gangs and overseers have survived, painted roughly on the limestone surfaces.

Started from the top

By the time the entire inner core was laid, the pyramid had become totally hidden, surrounded by ramps.

The final task of facing the pyramid with its overlying skin of limestone was begun at the top.

As the casing stones were fitted, the ramps were gradually removed until the moment arrived when the great building stood revealed on the plateau in its glistening white coat.

In the heart of the pyramid, more than 140 feet above the desert floor but still far beneath the peak of the building, is the King's Chamber, a cell that is lined with polished granite.

At one end of the room, set into the floor, was a stone sarcophagus, intended to be the last resting place of the mummified body of the Pharaoh, Cheops.

Cunning engineering

The Grand Gallery, adjoining the King's Chamber, is an extremely cunning piece of engineering. It was originally intended to solve the problem of sealing the royal burial place permanently.

Huge "plug blocks" were stored on the floor of the gallery, resting on temporary timber supports.

After the immense and colorful funeral procession had followed Cheops' body to the pyramid, workmen released the blocks, which slid down the gallery's slanting floor and jammed the entrance.

The workmen escaped down a near vertical tunnel, which was then sealed. Cheops' body seemed safe from intruders for all time.

The plundered tomb

In fact, man was to prove over the centuries that his ability to plunder burial places of ancient kings matched his ability and skill in constructing them.

In the ninth century A.D. Arab workmen tunneled through the pyramid and found only a rifled sepulcher. Later, Arab rulers stripped away most of the limestone casing to use in the building of their mosques.

Of the 36 major pyramids built, only the Great Pyramid and one or two others remain almost in their original state, despite many hundreds of years of plunder and exposure to extremes of temperature.

The Great Pyramid of Cheops remains today as an enduring monument to man's skill—and to his longing for immortality.

HOLDING COURT
Removals on a royal scale

Three enormous statues of the god-king Ramses II now gaze across the 20th-century manmade Lake Nasser from their original 3,200-year-old rock temples. They survive because of a spectacular removal job.

In 1963 these and other antiquities faced destruction from the rising water behind the Nile's new Aswan Dam. The most important priceless treasures were the Ramses temples.

A Swedish engineering firm devised a plan to move the Small Temple with its statues of Queen Nefertari and the Great Temple with those of Ramses—three complete and the 67-foot seated, but broken, fourth one. The engineers managed to cut away some 330,000 tons of cliff and shift most of the temples.

The total operation cost $40 million. It took 4½ years to cut the temples into 1,050 pieces—some weighing 33 tons. This mass of material had to be reassembled piece by piece 690 feet farther up the sheer rock face.

Egypt then decided to raise the waterline, so all the Small Temple blocks already rebuilt were dismantled and resited seven feet higher. To preserve the cliffside background, a dome with a span of 195 feet was built over the Great Temple and, above it, a manmade mountain of rocks and rubble. By the end of 1967 the Great Temple dome was in place. The rockfill was made from ground level.

There remained one important task—a special treatment to camouflage the mile-upon-mile of cutting on the joints along the surface of the temples. Today, the colossal stone guardians of the temples have been expertly restored to match their former majesty.

MOVING A ROYAL FAMILY. *Colossal statues of the god-king Ramses II (above left) were cut into blocks (above right), moved to another site, and reassembled (below) in a $40-million scheme to save two ancient temples from the rising waters of the new Aswan Dam on the River Nile.*

CHINA'S ANCIENT BULWARK

The wall that has stood for 2,000 years

Of all man's achievements, the one that qualifies for the title of the greatest construction work attempted by human hands is the Great Wall of China. And it certainly is great, stretching about 1,600 miles from Pohai Bay westward well into Kansu Province, where the ancient Silk Road crosses into the wilderness of Central Asia.

The Ch'in Emperor Shih Huang Ti began the wall in 214 B.C. to protect his vulnerable northern border, where the frontier was open to raids by the fierce Mongol horsemen of the Hsiung Nu—the Huns who, centuries later, were to topple the Roman Empire. Tens of thousands of criminals slaved in relays to complete the defense, and Chinese legends say that more than a million died before it was finished.

Branch lines

A defensive wall was not a new idea. Centuries before, kings and princes had built walls around their cities. What Shih Huang Ti did was to join up three sections of those old border walls to form one continuous defense system surrounding his whole Empire.

In places branches leave the main wall for local defense—sometimes there is a double or triple line of defense. In a number of areas the wall is simply earthen; in others it becomes a rampart of rubble faced with brick or stone.

Did it work? In an age without artillery, walls would and did keep invaders at bay. But the wall had to be garrisoned, and maintaining a steady defense force was almost impossible in China at that time.

Universal fame

Shih Huang Ti died only four years after the work was begun, but his successors carried on the task. The wall was repaired and extended, giving it a height of 30 feet in places, with 40-foot towers every 200 yards and ramparts 32 feet thick.

So, after more than 2,000 years, the zigzag climb through the hills to the north of Peking still presents an intimidating spectacle to the observer on this earth—and perhaps beyond—for the Great Wall was the only manmade object big enough to be seen from space by U.S. and Soviet astronauts.

BORDER BARRIER. *Below are the magnificent ramparts and watchtowers of the Great Wall, which winds over desolate northern China.*

CITY OF THE MAYAS

The splendor of a little-known civilization

Little known, but barbarously magnificent, the Empire of the Maya Indians in the Yucatan peninsula (now part of Mexico) flourished at a time when Europe was still weltering in the bloodshed and chaos of the Middle Ages.

Many of the Mayans' great stone cities and ceremonial centers, hidden for centuries by the encroaching jungle, were joined by a network of fine causeways with level, paved surfaces from 8 to 30 feet wide. The longest ran 62.3 miles in three arrow-straight sections from Cobá to Yaxuna, cutting through forests and swamps. The construction was simple but durable—a core of rubble laid between stone retaining walls and pressed with heavy stone rollers, then surfaced with a white cement.

Now freed from the jungle's hold, the cities stand as monuments of a mysterious past. One of the most memorable is Chichén Itzá, a place of haunting grandeur.

In Yucatan, a dry land with seasonal rains, centers grew up around huge, open wells because they yielded a year-round supply of drinking water. The discovery of two especially wide and deep pools led to the founding of Chichén Itzá in the fifth or early sixth century. Mayan culture flowered there, but it collapsed about 987, when the Toltecs occupied the city and made it their Capital.

During the 11th and 12th centuries Chichén Itzá reached the height of its fame and prosperity. Mayan traditions were retained, and the Toltecs built remarkable stone temples, halls, and colonnades that blended Toltecan and Mayan design. The Thousand Columns, ranked around a five-acre plaza containing a huge temple covering an acre and rising to a height of 75 feet, date from this period. Round about are columned halls, sunken gardens, terraces, and pyramid temples.

Like all Mayan cities, Chichén Itzá also had its Ball Court, a rectangular enclosure 272 feet long and 199 feet wide, where two teams played pok-a-tok, a game something like basketball. Each side struggled to send a heavy rubber ball through the opponents' goal. The goals were vertical stone rings on opposing walls. Pok-a-tok was played at a furious pace, sometimes so violently that players died during the game.

Reliefs carved in stone walls of the Ball Court show the decapitation of a ballplayer, and along a nearby platform are carvings of skulls skewered on sticks. The game seems to have been ceremonial, with religious overtones, and it may be that the losers lost their lives

SERPENT GUARDIANS. *These enormous columns stand at the entrance to the vast Temple of the Warriors at Chichén Itzá in Mexico.*

STEP PYRAMID. *The Castillo pyramid is made of huge blocks of cleverly worked stone. It was abandoned in the 15th century.*

The city is also famous for its Well of Sacrifice, a deep pool linked to the Grand Plaza by a 900-foot causeway. Into this pit people may have been thrown alive to propitiate the gods in time of drought. Many skeletons have been recovered from the well.

Chichén Itzá's greatness ended suddenly. For 200 years the city served as the Mecca of the Toltecan world, but it was abruptly deserted by its inhabitants about 1224, when the Itzá warriors arrived. The Itzás moved in as squatters; toward the middle of the 15th century they too were driven out, and Chichén Itzá was abandoned forever.

SPLENDOR IN THE JUNGLE

The fabulous home of a god-king

In 1861 a French naturalist, Henri Mouhot, was marching along a forest path in the jungle of northern Cambodia when, high above the treetops, he saw three tall stone towers. They were the pinnacles of Angkor Wat, one of the most splendid temples in all Asia, and the first sign of the fabled lost city of Angkor Thom. This, the Capital of the great Khmer Empire, had been abandoned 500 years before, to lie hidden and forgotten in the folds of the all-embracing jungle.

Even in ruins Angkor has a disconcerting impact. Surrounded by a wide moat once stocked with crocodiles, backed by a high defensive wall with earthen ramparts, the city was founded by King Jayavarman II, who lived from A.D. 770 to 850. Declaring himself a god-king, he set out to build a Capital to declare his power and the wealth of his Empire.

Each side of the square moat is two miles long, and the area inside the walls could contain all of ancient Rome, with room to spare. Yet few people lived there—it was simply the royal, religious, and administrative center of the Capital. The people of the city had their homes in two huge suburbs outside the walls, beside artificial lakes along the banks of the nearby Siemreap River.

Four broad causeways cross the moat, leading into the city through huge triple-towered gateways. The arch of each gate was built tall and wide enough to allow the royal elephants to pass, each beast carrying a howdah and large ceremonial sunshade to protect imperial heads.

Terrace of the Leper King

The four roads meet in the very center of the city, in a great square bounded by two carved terraces, the Royal Terrace and the Terrace of the Leper King. Opposite them are ranged the 12 elaborately carved Towers of the Cord Dancers. Flights of steps lead through the terraces to the lawns and pavilions of the royal gardens and tombs.

PARADISE LOST. *The noble towers of Angkor Wat reach toward the sky, their image reflected in a shimmering pool. For 500 years the temple lay forgotten in the Cambodian jungle.*

The chief glories of Angkor are the wonderful sandstone carvings: Each causeway is bordered by parapets carved in the shapes of gods and giants supporting mythical creatures. Every gateway is covered in elaborate sculpture, and the towers are crowned with triple-headed heraldic elephants.

The royal terraces are crowded with figures of kings and queens, princes and princesses, lions and elephants, and figures from Hindu religious epics. Other carvings portray almost every kind of activity of a highly civilized society, in a style so lifelike that movements seem interrupted only for an instant.

Noble monument

Yet perhaps Angkor's most noble monument lies a mile outside the walls of the city—Angkor Wat, one of the most beautiful and famous shrines in the world. Built by the 12th-century King Suryavarman II, under whose rule the Empire and city reached their height of prosperity, it is surrounded by a four-mile-long moat in an almost perfect square. The temple is a bewildering complex of lakes and libraries, cloisters and galleries, shrines and stairways. Behind the central sanctuary wall the lowest gallery contains a frieze of vivid carvings from legends and Hindu holy books. It stands eight feet high and stretches right around the gallery's half-mile circumference. Above this the pyramid-shaped temple climbs in three stages to the central cluster of five towers, the tallest of which is 215 feet—these were the signposts that guided Henri Mouhot to the city's ruins.

Not defensible

What happened to Angkor? Less than 30 years after Suryavarman's death, in 1177, it was captured and sacked by Cham invaders from Laos. Two years later the Chams were conquered by King Jayavarman VII, but the city's days were numbered.

In the following century and a half, the Empire was invaded by the Thais from the west and the Mongols from the north. The Thais captured Angkor in 1369, 1388, and again in 1431. Despite its forbidding ramparts, the city was indefensible.

Finally, the elaborate rice-producing irrigation system on which Angkor depended was destroyed, and in 1434 the Capital was moved to a site near Phnom Penh, and Angkor was left to the jungle.

STREETS AHEAD

The road network that lasted 2,000 years

The Roman Empire, at its height, stretched from the Persian Gulf to the Humber in Britain. Fifty thousand miles of first-class roads in Britain and Europe made rapid travel possible, and a quarter of a million miles of local roads connected forts, legionary camps, towns, villages, harbors, and signal stations with the main road system.

The main roads carried the postal services, set up by Emperor Augustus, as well as all the commercial traffic of the Empire.

Five-day mail

The regular postal services could cover 100 miles a day, so a letter from the garrison on Hadrian's Wall near the Scottish border could reach London in less than five days. Vital messages carried by relays of mounted dispatch riders traveled up to 200 miles in a day and a night. Julius Caesar once traveled 800 miles in eight days.

Road building held first importance among Roman enterprises. Only men of the highest rank were entrusted with their construction and maintenance. The costs, for the time, were high: It has been estimated that one Roman mile (9/10 of the present mile) of the Appian Way cost the equivalent of $13,500 to build. (In comparison, however, a mile of modern highway costs approximately $3 million.)

Roman engineers built along straight lines, with little regard to topography. Mountains were cut through, valleys filled, and marshes bridged. Even seas did not daunt them, for roads were pushed to the water's edge and then continued on the opposite shore.

From Rome 29 great roads radiated out to the corners of the Empire. Wide stone embankments four or five feet high provided them with drainage and helped to maintain them in good condition for many centuries. The roads themselves were 14 to 16 feet wide, enabling the

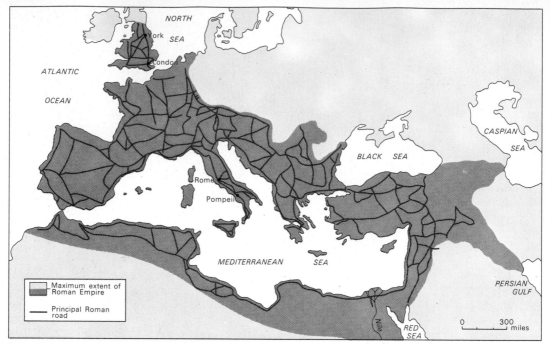

HIGHWAYS OF AN EMPIRE. *The Roman Empire covered most of Europe and parts of North Africa and the Middle East. An intricate network of roads linked the farthermost outposts with Rome.*

RECOVERED FROM THE ASHES. *The excavated ruins of Pompeii have revealed some fine examples of Roman road building. The ruts worn by chariot wheels can be seen in the photograph above.*

widest, most unwieldy carts to pass each other. Flanking the road itself were two elevated sidewalks for pedestrians. Construction was methodical and well thought out. The topsoil was removed, the foundation of heavy stones fitted by hand, then layers of small stones, broken tile, brick, and chalk held together with mortar were laid. The surface, cambered for drainage, was of flat stones cemented into place and bordered by curbs on each side.

Along the road milestones were erected giv-

ing the distance to the nearest town. At regular intervals along the route were posting houses, where relays of horses were stationed, and inns for overnight stops. The local communities, with great resentment, paid for the upkeep of the roads.

The Roman road network was so efficiently planned, and the roads so well built, that the system lasted for nearly 2,000 years and was the fastest transport system until the coming of the railways.

Rome's race—Rome's pace

A traveler between London and Rome during the height of the Roman Empire needed to take only 13 days for the journey. Nearly 2,000 years later, on his recall to England from Italy to be Prime Minister, Robert Peel took exactly the same length of time, although he traveled posthaste all the way.

In the United Kingdom several of the old Roman roads are still in use. Watling Street, which runs from Dover to London and on to Wroxeter, is built on Roman foundations. Dere Street runs from York to Melrose in Scotland, via County Durham. Sarn Helen East runs through the Welsh countryside and was built to serve the Dolaucothi gold mines.

The road system that was originated by Britain's conquerors, to enable them to maintain control over her hostile native population, continues to benefit the British 19 centuries later.

154

THE GLORY THAT WAS ROME. *The arena floor has long fallen in; but the rows of storerooms and wild beast cages underneath the Colosseum are still well preserved.*

BREAD AND CIRCUSES

Rome's mighty stadium, where games were played to the death

Towering above the bustling traffic of Rome, the enormous bulk of the Colosseum still stands as a link with her mighty imperial past. The games held there dominated social life in the ancient city—a cruel and spectacular mixture of wild beast hunts, gladiatorial combats, mock battles, and fights between condemned men and wild animals. It was the policy of Rome's rulers to provide such circuses—and bread—to keep the unruly citizens quiet.

At first the games were held in a stone amphitheater with wooden seats, built in 29 B.C. This was destroyed in Nero's great fire, and the Colosseum was built on the site of Nero's own Golden House by his successors, the Emperors Vespasian and Titus. Despite legend, Nero never saw the Colosseum, which opened in A.D. 80, many years after his death.

The oval arena, nearly 100 yards long, was built over a complex of underground passages and animal cages. Flanking it, tiers of stone benches rose to a height of 160 feet and provided room for 50,000 spectators. The lowest row of seats was for senators and high-ranking citizens only, and in the center stood the imperial box, with boxes nearby for the consuls and vestal virgins. The higher tiers were for the patricians, and above them sat, or stood, the plebeians—the common people.

During wild beast fights a strong fence was erected around the arena; and to protect spectators from the sun, the seats were screened by awnings, which were swung into position by sailors of the Imperial Navy.

The great opening ceremony lasted 100 days. Nine thousand wild beasts were killed, as well as gladiators and sailors who took part in a naval battle. The arena could be flooded to a depth of five feet for these naval *naumachiae*, but it was difficult to keep it watertight. However, there is no record of Christians ever being put to death at the Colosseum.

The glory crumbles

During the sixth century the amphitheater fell into disuse, and earthquakes in the 13th and 14th centuries badly damaged it. The stone was used for other buildings, and many statuettes that stood in wall niches were stolen.

Restoration began in the 19th century; but all that remains now is an empty shell of stone and brickwork—and the memory of the blood-lust of ancient Rome.

IMPOSING AND IMPREGNABLE. *Krak des Chevaliers dominates a vast area of the Syrian desert. This was the formidable obstacle in the way of invaders on the road from Damascus to Tripoli and Jerusalem. Perhaps this Crusader fortress was impregnable; it was never taken by direct attack.*

MIGHTIEST CRUSADER FORTRESS

It fell to the guile of a Muslim Sultan

Krak des Chevaliers—Crag of the Knights —a fortress of astonishing strength, with towering defenses and walls dozens of feet thick—yielded at last in 1271 ... to a humble pigeon.

The castle was built by the Crusaders on a spur in the Syrian Desert for the strategic purpose of guarding the road between the Muslim city of Homs and the Christian city of Tripoli at the eastern end of the Mediterranean. A small castle, occupied by a Kurdish garrison, had stood on the site when the Crusaders arrived in the 1090's. This passed into the hands of the Christian Count of Tripoli, who in turn gave it in 1142 to the Knights of the Hospital of St. John of Jerusalem. In the next 150 years the knights constructed a stronghold of such immensity and ingenuity that it withstood at least 12 Saracen attempts to storm it.

Krak des Chevaliers was built in two stages. The outer curtain of walls and an inner castle of small, square buildings came first. In 1202 an earthquake damaged many of these inner buildings, and a massive redesign was undertaken. This included the huge inner, or second, series of fortifications, plus the distinctive round-house look of many of the buildings. Wherever possible, the plunging contours of the spur were used to tactical advantage.

Weak points

But two weak points needed special treatment: the main entrance and the exposed south side, which opened onto a plain. The knights solved the second problem with a formidable wall of masonry composed of three huge linked towers, further strengthened by an apron of rubble and masonry, in places 80 feet thick, that made mining almost impossible. The problem of the entrance was met in an even more ingenious way. The path leading to it was made to zigzag up the steep escarpment, so that any invader had to cross and recross a concentrated line of fire. A hairpin bend, followed by the fortified main gates themselves, compounded the invaders' misery.

And if attack was a waste of life and limb, siege was equally futile. Like all great Crusader castles, Krak was provided with vast storage spaces for food and water—enough to keep a full-strength garrison of 2,000 men alive and fighting for at least a year, while a relieving army marched to the rescue.

Fall of the fortress

Krak seemed impregnable. Even the great warrior Saladin had turned away. In 1271, however, another Muslim conqueror stood at the gates of the castle: the Sultan Baybars (the name means "panther"), with an Egyptian army. Krak was the last defense in his way to total domination of what had been the Crusaders' kingdom.

By this time the castle was seriously undermanned. A year before the Eighth Crusade had failed, and reinforcements from the West were out of the question. Nevertheless, the handful of fighting monks left in command of the garrison's mercenaries were tenacious warriors, and Baybars still had to pierce layer upon layer of defense to get to them.

The Sultan set to work with fanatical determination. After weeks of heavy mining, the southwest tower of the outer curtain collapsed, and the attackers rushed in, only to find the huge inner defenses towering above them.

Conquest by trickery

Baybars, refusing to accept defeat or the probability of a lengthy siege, turned to trickery. Arab historians record that he used a carrier pigeon to send a forged letter into the castle. The message purported to come from the Grand Masters of the Hospitallers in Tripoli and ordered the garrison to surrender since no help could be sent to them.

The order was obeyed, and Krak had fallen at last, though its strongest fortifications had never been put to the test.

Baybars chivalrously permitted the garrison free conduct to Tripoli.

Today the castle stands in a remarkable state of preservation and is considered one of the finest examples of military architecture. In the words of Lawrence of Arabia, Krak des Chevaliers is "the most wholly admirable castle in the world."

NO PLACE TO HIDE

The strongest walls have proved no match for ingenuity

Fortifications have played a vital part in military history, from the earthen ramparts of iron age hill forts to the steel-and-concrete emplacements of the 20th century. Yet however impregnable these fortresses may have been, a wily enemy has usually found some way of breaching their walls.

In Biblical times the Assyrians were particularly skilled at walling cities and battering down enemy fortifications. Later the Romans perfected the art. When the Roman general Flavius Silva successfully attacked the Jewish rebels in the fortress at Masada, his engineers built a siege wall of 3,800 yards and then erected 12 towers on it, at irregular intervals.

Constantinople, the greatest city of Europe in the Dark Ages, had three sets of walls, with a moat 60 feet wide and 20 feet deep. Behind this was a row of battlements; 60 feet farther back was another wall, studded with 96 towers at 200-foot intervals; and inside this was a third wall with another 96 towers, each set between a

pair of towers of the middle wall and reaching twice the height. This was certainly a daunting obstacle for any enemy. But the warriors of the Fourth Crusade penetrated the defenses by throwing bridges across from ships to the battlements and setting fire to as much of the city as they could reach.

Era of the fortress

The art of fortification reached its peak in the Middle Ages, when the great stone-walled castles sprouted like mushrooms all over Europe. Before the advent of gunpowder, these fortresses could hold off an attacker for months, sometimes years, but even the strongest fell to a determined foe.

The Chateau Gaillard, built by King Richard Coeur de Lion near Rouen in France, had three lines of defense, consisting of ditches and walls studded with towers. The castle stood in a commanding position on a hill overlooking the town of Les Andelys and is considered to be one

STRIFE WITHIN THE FORTIFICATIONS. *The fortified city of Constantinople fell partly because of internal strife during the Fourth Crusade. The best troops mutinied because of arrears in pay, and the city surrendered when the moat, walls, and towers were breached by invaders.*

of the most powerful fortresses ever constructed.

In 1203, Philip II of France laid siege to the castle, then held by Roger de Lacy for King John of England and, having taken Les Andelys, began to seek ways of making life uncomfortable for the defenders.

Successful siege

Trenches were dug to cut off the castle's water supply, and siege engines were brought up to batter the outermost wall. In time the wall was breached, and the attackers poured through. A party of men climbed the castle's drains and emerged behind the second wall, where they were able to lower the drawbridge between the middle and outer defenses. Finally, they started digging under the inner wall. The defenders dug countertunnels, and furious battles took place underground. But at last the wall, now thoroughly undermined by both sides, collapsed into the moat, and the castle fell to the French.

The emergence of gunpowder spelled the beginning of the end for the stone-built castle. Forts became steel-and-concrete emplacements, sunk deep into the earth and invulnerable to direct hits by the heaviest of shells—until the invention of the airplane and tank changed the pattern of war once again.

CHATEAU GAILLARD. *These few remains can still be seen near Rouen. The long siege staged there in 1203 reduced the castle to a ruin.*

HEART OF THE VATICAN
Centuries of craftsmanship created perfection

Few of the world's great buildings can have had so many fingers in its architectural pie as the Basilica of St. Peter in Rome.

From the time it was planned by Pope Nicholas V in the 15th century, it took nearly 350 years to complete. During that time a succession of Popes and architects left their mark on it.

Although it was Nicholas V who first decided to replace the original basilica built by Constantine the Great in honor of the apostle Peter, the first tangible move did not come until 1505. In that year Pope Julius II thought of building close to the basilica a mausoleum to contain a vast monument to himself. He had already asked Michelangelo to execute it, and expense was no object.

Building demolished

After changing his mind several times, Julius abandoned the idea of a separate tomb and decided that the old basilica must be completely rebuilt. He brought in the architect Donato Bramante, who first demolished Constantine's building—and everything in it. Bramante threw out tombs, statues, mosaics, icons, and altars, and employed 2,500 men for many weeks on the work of destruction. But although he was an architect of genius, Bramante was too hasty to be thorough and too casual to supervise his workers properly. After his death, faults appeared in the building, which were costly to put right.

After Pope Julius died in 1513, his successor, Leo X, appointed Raphael as the new architect. He made radical changes to Bramante's design, but when he died, six years later, he had done little more than erect one or two columns and continue the correction of Bramante's faults.

Delay, then new life

In 1521 Leo died, and a later Pope, Clement VII, made Baldassare Peruzzi chief architect. He built much in Rome but almost nothing in the neglected St. Peter's. Grass and weeds grew in the crevices of Bramante's piers and arches, but the next pontiff, Paul III, breathed new life into the project. He pilfered funds given by Spain for a crusade against the Turks and appointed first Antonio da Sangallo and then Michelangelo as architect. The great Florentine was then 72 and had long ago completed his ceiling in the Sistine Chapel.

Michelangelo produced his first model for St. Peter's in 1547 and soon began building. But when Paul died in 1549, however, the zest that Michelangelo had inspired in the builders began to fade. Pope Paul IV encouraged Michelangelo, but the architect's age was beginning to tell, and he made many mistakes. His death, in 1564, led to another spell of confusion, and little was done to the building during Pius IV's time.

Pius V's successor, Gregory XIII, made progress but, like so many before him, not so much as he had hoped. Then Sixtus V ascended St. Peter's throne in 1585, and work on the great project began to move again. He did far more than any of his predecessors and was almost entirely responsible for building the dome designed by Michelangelo.

It was Sixtus who ordered the construction of the Sistine Hall and Vatican library—built by Domenico Fontana in 1588. The library was originally founded between 1447 and 1455 by Nicholas V, with a nucleus of 340 volumes.

At last, the finishing touches

In 1594 Pope Clement VIII celebrated the first Mass at the new high altar. Then came another unproductive period, until Pope Urban VIII (1623-44) brought in the architect Giovanni Bernini, who built the canopy over the papal altar, put up the bell towers, and decorated the naves.

The last addition was the sacristy—in 1784—and, with that complete, St. Peter's was finished. But it was then nearly 200 years since Sixtus built the dome, 238 years since Michelangelo worked on the great piers that support it, and 338 years since Nicholas V set out to replace the ancient basilica of Constantine.

Considerably expanded during the 17th and 18th centuries, the library suffered severely when numerous manuscripts were taken to France in 1798.

Today the library contains some 60,000 manuscripts, 7,000 incunabula, 100,000 engravings and maps, and more than 900,000 books.

AMERICA'S BIRTHDAY PARTY

Architecture, art, and Little Egypt, too

Authorized by Congress in 1890 to commemorate the 400th anniversary of the discovery of America, the Columbian Exposition was to become the most successful of all world's fairs in the United States.

Like a city of marble (actually constructed of staff, a far less costly material), 150 neoclassic buildings rose on 686 acres along the shore of Lake Michigan in Chicago. The landscape was laced with canals and reflecting pools, and interspersed with such statuary as Daniel French's 65-foot-tall "The Republic."

The Chicago Fair, as it came to be known, cost $27 million; it was formally opened on May 1, 1893, and closed on November 1. More than 27 million visitors from the United States and the 72 participating nations thronged to see the wondrous sights.

The major emphasis of the fair was on American artistic achievement. Visitors saw the works of such American artists as Frederic Remington, Thomas Eakins, John Singer Sargent, and Winslow Homer.

While the emphasis of the exposition was decidedly cultural, many visitors were, perhaps, even more impressed with the fair's enormous midway, where they spent their time riding the gigantic Ferris wheel, laughing giddily under the blaze of lights supplied by George Westinghouse to demonstrate the capabilities of his new AC (alternating current) power system, and ogling the shocking gyrations of Little Egypt.

Little now remains of the Chicago Fair; it was partly destroyed by fires in January and February of 1894. Its influence, however, was felt for decades. It had an enormous effect upon American cultural values and was of tremendous importance in advancing city planning.

RIDING HIGH. *The exposition's Ferris wheel, the first ever built, had a diameter of 250 feet, and each of its cars carried 40 passengers.*

LURE OF THE MIDDLE EAST. *Decorated with a replica of the Sphinx, the Streets of Cairo building featured Egyptian artifacts along with the notorious dancer Little Egypt.*

HIT OF THE FAIR. *Probably the biggest attraction of the exposition was Little Egypt, whose sensual "hootchy-kootchy" dance scandalized and delighted the visitors.*

ON THE RIGHT LINES

The railway system that showed the way to safety

Right from its opening in 1841 the Great Western Railway was different from other British railways—thanks to its brilliant, but unorthodox, engineer, Isambard Kingdom Brunel. In a pioneering age Brunel had his own personal style. Faced with the necessity of boring a tunnel at Box Hill for the Great Western's main London to Bristol line—a difficult, dangerous, and expensive undertaking—he did it on a precisely calculated alignment. It is said that on one day a year, June 21, the sun shines directly through the length of the 1¾-mile tunnel.

To carry the line across the Thames at Maidenhead, Brunel built a shallow-arched brick bridge—which his colleagues insisted would never carry the weight of a train. Yet more than a century later the bridge is coping with trains 10 times the weight of those in Brunel's time.

While all the other railway companies laid their lines with the rails 4 feet 8½ inches apart, Brunel had other ideas. He set the Great Western's tracks seven feet apart, wide enough for engines and carriages to be slung between the wheels, giving them much greater stability. This broad gauge served the company well, and for half a century it ran expresses at top speed, almost without a hitch.

Even when mishaps did occur, the broad gauge proved its worth. In 1847 a driving wheel on the Exeter to London express collapsed at top speed on an open viaduct near Southall, yet not a single wheel jumped the rails.

Brunel's problems in building the line were enormous, but he was undaunted. A cutting through Sonning Hill, Berkshire, had defeated two contractors, but despite torrential rains that flooded the excavations, the tireless engineer urged on his team of 1,200 laborers and 196 horses until the 2-mile-long, 60-foot-deep cutting was completed.

The last and probably the greatest of his railway engineering triumphs was the Royal Albert Bridge at Saltash, Cornwall, over the formidable Tamar River, 1,100 feet wide and 70 feet deep at high water. Because the river was used for shipping, Brunel had to give ample clearance—and an assurance that he would not obstruct the channel with scaffolding.

His final design was for two 465-foot spans, supported by one central pier, at a level of 100 feet above the high-water mark. When the railway company ran short of money, Brunel decided to put only a single stretch of line across the bridge. Today, although the track has been replaced by standard gauge, the bridge remains a one-line crossing from Plymouth.

In May 1859, after the opening of the bridge, Brunel had his first and last sight of the finished structure. Seriously ill from overwork, he was carried across his bridge on a platform truck.

ALL CHANGE. *A print from 1846 shows the chaos as passengers and luggage are shifted from Brunel's broad-gauge express to the narrow-gauge train at Gloucester, the end of the line.*

CANADIAN PACIFIC

The track that created a nation

The Canadian Pacific Railway (CPR) was not only a great construction achievement, linking the western and eastern seaboards of Canada, it was a project that created a nation.

In 1867 the eastern provinces of Ontario, Quebec, New Brunswick, and Nova Scotia formed the federation of Canada, to offset the threat of a U.S. invasion from the south. But British Columbia on the Pacific coast remained vulnerable, while Saskatchewan and Alberta were still part of the Northwest Territories. As an inducement to get British Columbia into the federation, the Canadian Parliament guaranteed a transcontinental railroad in 10 years.

Six millionaires formed Canadian Pacific, and for $25 million, 25 million acres of choice western land, a 20-year exemption from tax, and other guarantees, they promised to build the railroad. William Cornelius Van Horne, a railway superintendent from Chicago, was appointed construction boss. He urged work gangs into rapid progress across the prairies and then took 12,000 men and 5,000 horses into the icy wastes north of Lake Superior to begin digging, blasting, and bridging.

When dynamite supplies ran out, Van Horne built three emergency factories. At one stage three miles of granite had to be excavated to make 900 yards of progress; swampland swallowed up three locomotives, and one particularly difficult mile cost $11 an inch.

Soon Van Horne had spent $27 million over his budget, and creditors began clamoring for cash. An applicaton for a fresh grant of $35 million was ignored by Parliament. The CPR seemed on the verge of ruin when, inadvertently, Louis Riel, a half-Indian anarchist, saved it—by stirring up a rebellion in Saskatchewan.

Van Horne guaranteed to transport 4,000 soldiers to the scene on his unfinished railway within 11 days. He did it, and they crushed the rebellion.

The speed of the operation awakened the nation to the value of Van Horne's project, and fresh funds were raised.

As work gangs moved east and west toward each other, a scouting party found the final link in the chain—the northwest land passage, avoiding four ranges of impassable mountains. Tunnels were blasted, valley walls were shored up, and on November 7, 1885, 4½ years after taking over the job, the gangs drove in the last spikes.

At the western terminus Van Horne ran his tracks to a spot on Burrard Inlet called Port Moody, 12 miles east of Vancouver, the railway's present terminal. A CPR team dragged a post-office shack to a spot in Alberta, and the bustling cattle town of Calgary grew up around it.

The official opening date of the railway was July 4, 1886, when the Pacific Express, the first through passenger train, completed the 2,891-mile journey from Montreal to Port Moody.

Today Canadian Pacific is an industrial colossus, embracing an airline (C.P. Air), shipping fleets, hotels, and resorts. Its subsidiary operations reach into practically all aspects of the nation's life.

THE ROARING U. P. TRAIL

The workmen who won the West

It was not the best time or place to build a railroad in the United States. The Civil War was being fought, and marauding Indians roamed the central plains. Yet in 1862 Congress passed an act for building the Union Pacific, the railroad that opened up the West.

It was agreed that the Central Pacific Railroad Company of California should work east from Sacramento, and the Union Pacific west from Omaha, Nebraska. Work began in 1863.

The Central Pacific men, under the supervision of a dry-goods storeowner, Charlie Crocker, were faced with the solid granite slopes of the Sierra Nevada only 80 miles from their starting point. The Union Pacific gangs, under Gen. Grenville Dodge, had to cross the territory of hostile Sioux and Cheyenne Indians, who were already resentful of the white man's "talking wire" telegraph network and convinced that the railway would ruin their hunting grounds.

Supplying materials for one mile of track at Dodge's end meant 40 wagonloads of supplies from the Missouri River, about 50 miles away. Oak ties, at a cost of $3.50 each, had to be brought from Pennsylvania 800 miles away.

But by the end of 1866 the Union Pacific had laid 300 miles of track, and the Central Pacific had conquered the 7,000-foot Sierra.

Most of Dodge's men were Irish. Crocker's gangs were mainly Chinese, of whom he remarked to those who doubted the Orientals' ability to do the job: "They built the Great Wall of China, and that's the biggest run of masonry in the world."

In the severe winter of 1866–67, many workers froze to death or were killed in avalanches in the Sierra. In February 1867 a 12-day blizzard buried a shack of workers in 60-foot drifts.

The two lines eventually met at Promontory Point, Utah. The eastbound team had covered 690 miles and the westbound gang 1,086 miles. And so, by an eventual linkup of the Union Pacific with the railroad network in the East, a coast-to-coast service was established.

On May 10,1869, a ceremonial mahogany tie with a silver plaque was laid at Promontory Point—only to be quickly broken up by souvenir hunters. Two locomotives met at the site to mark the occasion, and several commemorative spikes, including one made of gold, were hammered home—and then quickly withdrawn for safety. Dodge's Irishmen and Crocker's Chinese had truly won the West.

CHARGE OF THE RAILROAD BRIGADE

How an army of laborers saved the British Army at Sevastopol

Who were the real heroes of the Crimean War? Not the Light Brigade, whose famous charge threw away Europe's finest cavalry on a worthless objective because of a mistaken order. They received the glory, but the unsung heroes were a group of railroad workers who rescued an army 100 times their number from defeat and death.

In the late autumn of 1854, British forces were laying siege to Sevastopol, chief naval base on the Crimean peninsula. Delay and bungling had allowed the Russians to reinforce the city's defenders, and Lord Raglan's 30,000 soldiers were suffering from cold and disease.

As the Russian winter tightened its grip, the single road to the port of Balaklava broke up. Deliveries of food, water, clothing, and medicine petered out.

Fortunately for the army, the great railroad builder Samuel Morton Peto was a Member of Parliament. Peto, his brother-in-law Betts, and his greatest rival Brassey offered to build a railroad to supply the troops without making a penny of profit. They proposed a force of 250 laborers, 30 foremen and masons, 80 carpenters, 20 blacksmiths, and 10 enginemen. All were to be formed into a civil engineer corps, entirely separate from the army.

The Prime Minister, the Earl of Aberdeen, agreed, and the party left Liverpool on December 21. During the following month 23 other ships carried more men and supplies to Balaklava.

They took everything, from picks and shovels to cranes and pile drivers, wagons and engines to ropes and rails.

The raw winter weather was nothing new to many of the workers—fresh from railroad building in Canada and the United States. They built an encampment of warm, solid huts and laid five miles of track, all in the first 10 days. The army was amazed. In the words of Capt. Henry Clifford, they could do "more work in a day than a regiment of English soldiers do in a week."

Within six weeks they laid a double-track main line from the harbor to the hills overlooking Sevastopol, seven miles away. But with branch lines to outposts the total network covered 29 miles. Once finished, it was handed over to the army.

The trains, drawn by horses, steam locomotives, and stationary engines hauling wagons by wire ropes, carried 112 tons of food a day, plus ammunition, clothing, and medical supplies.

By April the army was reequipped, and in September, following British and French assaults, the Russians abandoned Sevastopol. For the railroad workers, saving an army from destruction was, very nearly, all in a day's work.

CLEOPATRA'S NEEDLE

The priceless piece of Egyptian flotsam

The strange-looking vessel, abandoned and wallowing in the Bay of Biscay, carried a priceless treasure—Cleopatra's Needle, a 3,500-year-old Egyptian obelisk.

Several British individuals had subscribed about $75,000 for the needle—actually made for Pharaoh Thotmes III—to be shipped from Alexandria to London, but it looked now as if it would end up at the bottom of the sea.

The obelisk's specially designed cigar-shaped container ship, the *Cleopatra,* seemed in danger of sinking. The steamship towing it, the *Olga,* sent six volunteers in a boat to take off the *Cleopatra's* crew. But the boat was swamped, and the volunteers drowned. Eventually, the *Olga* drew alongside and rescued the *Cleopatra's* five crewmen and their skipper—then cut the towrope, leaving the vessel adrift. Five days later

a steamship spotted the *Cleopatra* floating undamaged off northern Spain and towed the vessel to the port of El Ferrol.

The brothers John and Waynman Dixon designed and built the *Cleopatra* around the 70-foot-long, 200-ton obelisk at Alexandria. When completed, the *Cleopatra* was a 93-foot-long iron cylinder, 15 feet in diameter, with 10 watertight compartments. Bilge keels, a cabin, bridge, and rudder were riveted on, and the vessel floated.

After the *Cleopatra's* narrow escape, the steamship *Anglia* was sent to fetch it. In January 1878 the two ships sailed up the Thames to the cheers of crowds. That September the needle was winched into position on the Thames Embankment to commemorate Britain's victory over Napoleon, 63 years earlier.

COSTLY SHIPMENT. *Cleopatra's Needle (left) was shipped from Egypt to London—at a cost of $75,000 and the lives of six seamen, drowned in the process.*

MOMENT OF TRIUMPH. *Made for Pharaoh Thotmes III in 1460 B.C., the obelisk was placed on the Thames Embankment (right) in 1878 to commemorate Britain's victory over Napoleon.*

CLEOPATRA'S BARGE. *A specially designed cylindrical ship, the* Cleopatra, *was built around the needle to float it from Alexandria to London. After the operation the vessel was sold for scrap.*

DITCH ACROSS THE DESERT

De Lesseps achieved what others only dreamed about

Almost 4,000 years ago the ancient Egyptians built waterways across the Isthmus of Suez, a neck of land 100 miles wide separating western Asia from Egypt. But the waterways fell into disuse and were filled in A.D. 767 after an Arab invasion.

Napoleon discovered the remains and dreamed of improving trade routes by linking the Red Sea and the Mediterranean.

It was in 1859, thanks to the genius of a French diplomat and politician, Ferdinand de Lesseps, that work started on a new waterway. Though he was not a trained engineer, he had been haunted by the idea of the canal since his youth.

From striking the first blow with a pickax, De Lesseps spent 10 dedicated years supervising the massive operation that involved the excavation of about 97 million cubic yards of earth.

De Lesseps first established an artificial harbor at Port Said as a base and had a canal dug from the Nile to the isthmus to provide freshwater for the 20,000 laborers.

Working from north to south, De Lesseps' scheme involved carving a 30-foot-deep channel across the land, connecting up lakes en route. The Great and Little Bitter Lakes in the south were reconnected with the Red Sea and flooded with seawater. The canal joined these with Lake Timsah.

Three thousand camels carried drinking water for the workers across the desert to Lake Manzala, where it was sent by barge to Port Said. Local fishermen were recruited to scoop out a channel through the lake by hand. They worked by day, and slept on rafts at night. At the height of the operation, an estimated 80,000 fellaheen, or peasants, were employed, each being paid up to three piasters (about six cents) a day.

From 1863 until 1869, when the canal was opened, the labor force was gradually withdrawn, in favor of mechanical dredgers and digging equipment.

During October 1869 a French steamer, *Louise-et-Marie,* became the first oceangoing vessel to sail through the canal. But the official opening was on November 17, when representatives of almost every European royal family attended an inauguration fete.

A little before midnight on opening day, an unfortunate accident occurred. An Egyptian frigate ran aground, 18 miles from Port Said, and threatened to prevent the ceremonial sail through of ships from many nations, including France, Russia, Austria, Italy, Britain, and the United States.

Dispatches to Paris carried the news that the opening would have to be postponed. The next day the fleet of ships was only five minutes from the site of the incident when De Lesseps was informed that the canal was clear.

The total length of the canal is 103 miles, 21 of them through the lakes. It has an average width of 656 feet.

The total cost of the project was an estimated $105 million.

This was more than twice the original estimate, but it was a tiny sum compared with the value of the canal to world trade.

SHIPWAY TO THE PACIFIC

First a battle had to be won against yellow fever

As early as 1517 the Spanish explorer Vasco Núñez de Balboa saw the possibility of a canal across the narrow waist of Central America, connecting the Atlantic and Pacific Oceans.

But 400 years passed before the sea journey from New York to San Francisco was cut from 13,000 miles to 5,200. The French in 1879 tried but failed to build a canal, and within 10 years the French Panama Canal company collapsed, owing to bankruptcy, lack of planning, and the deadly yellow fever.

It was not until 1898, during the Spanish-American War, when the United States had to send the battleship *Oregon* nearly 13,000 miles from San Francisco to Cuba, that the value of a transcontinental waterway was appreciated.

In 1903 the United States gained permanent

control of a 10-mile-wide Canal Zone, after paying $10 million to the new Republic of Panama, plus, from 1913, $250,000 a year. In return, the United States guaranteed the independence of Panama.

The greatest obstacle to building the canal was disease, and in 1904 Col. William C. Gorgas, who had successfully combated yellow fever in Havana, took charge of improving sanitary conditions. Areas of brush and grass where disease-carrying mosquitoes swarmed and bred were cleared during the first two years.

The Americans excavated about 184 million cubic yards of earth. The French had removed 78 million cubic yards, but only 30 million of these were usable in the new canal.

More than 43,000 men were employed at the peak of construction, and the main work was completed in 1914. On August 15 of that year, the SS *Ancon,* a passenger-cargo vessel, made a complete trip through the canal, from the Atlantic to the Pacific. But landslides prevented further use for a few weeks. The canal was formally opened on July 12, 1920.

The canal, with its approaches, is 50.72 miles long. There are three steps at the Pacific end and three on the Atlantic side, equipped with locks 1,000 feet long and 110 feet wide.

Because the Isthmus of Panama runs from east to west and the canal cuts across it diagonally, a ship going from the Atlantic to the Pacific emerges 22 miles *east* of the Caribbean entrance.

Some 14,000 oceangoing ships travel through the Panama Canal every year, each paying a toll of about $4,000 to $5,000.

A ship usually takes eight hours to go through the canal. Experts estimate that the waterway may reach a capacity of 25,550 ships a year by early in the 21st century.

EXCAVATING AT MIRAFLORES. *At the height of construction of the Panama Canal, more than 43,000 workers were employed.*

SURVEYING. *Work on the Panama Canal was difficult and hazardous in swampy jungles infested with disease-carrying mosquitoes.*

GIANT WITH A JINX

The Great Eastern *was decades ahead of her time*

Isambard Brunel had successfully designed two ships, the *Great Western* and the *Great Britain,* when he began to consider the idea of a ship large enough to steam to Australia and back without refueling. He found a backer in the Eastern Steam Navigation Company, formed in 1851 to trade with India, Australia, and countries of the Far East.

Everything about the ship, the *Great Eastern,* was of staggering proportions. The overall length was 692 feet, and the breadth of the hull over the paddle boxes was 118 feet. Two sets of massive engines drove the 56-foot-diameter paddle wheels and the 24-foot screw. The vessel's displacement was 32,000 tons. The hull was constructed in the form of a huge box

THE GREAT EASTERN. *Designed by Isambard Brunel to carry 4,000 passengers, the ship became a success only after it was converted into a cable layer.*

girder, with a double frame and skin. Water-tight bulkheads divided the hull into 10 com-partments, each 60 feet long.

The ship was built at the yards of David Napier in London. The Thames at that point was too narrow to permit a lengthways launch, so the hull was built broadside to the river. But moving the huge craft to the water created problems that kept the ship high and dry for many weeks, while the costs escalated and Brunel became ill as a result of worry and overwork.

The first launching attempt, on November 3, 1857, was abandoned when a man working on one of the checking drums was killed by a winch handle spinning suddenly and hurling him into the air. The second attempt, on November 19, was a little more successful, and by the end of the month the ship had moved a total of 33 feet 6 inches.

Eventually, the ship was eased into the water, on January 31, 1858, but its troubles were not over. On a trial run to Weymouth a steampipe burst, wrecking one of the funnels and killing five stokers. When the news reached Brunel, who was by then extremely ill, it proved too much for him, and he died a few days later, on September 15, 1859.

The Eastern Steam Navigation Company was unable to bear the heavy costs of the delayed launch, and the vessel was taken over by a new concern, the Great Ship Company. The new owners tried, unsuccessfully, to use the *Great Eastern* on the transatlantic route. But the ship's accommodations for 4,000 passengers were never filled, and on two voyages it suffered severe damage, once in a midatlantic storm and again when the ship hit an uncharted reef at the entrance to Long Island Sound.

These two accidents cost $650,000 in repairs, and the ship was put up for sale. It was bought by three former shareholders of the Great Ship Company who chartered it to the Telegraph Construction Company for use as a cableship.

Successful career

So, at last, the *Great Eastern* embarked on a successful career. In July 1865 it left Ireland to lay a new cable across the Atlantic. After 1,200 miles the cable snapped, and all efforts to retrieve it failed. The following year the ship set out again, this time to succeed, and then went on to recover the cable it had lost the previous year. Having proved itself in a new role, the *Great Eastern* laid cables from France to the United States, Bombay to Aden, and along the Red Sea.

When its cable-laying days were over, the *Great Eastern* was used for a time as a floating exhibition and amusement park at Liverpool. Oddly enough, this ignominious fate had been predicted by a cartoonist when the ship was launched. In 1888 it was broken up on Mersey-side, and nearly 20 years passed before another ship, the *Lusitania,* approached the *Great Eastern*'s displacement.

PLUTO AND MULBERRY

Two ideas that helped win a war

In spite of Hitler's succession of lightning victories in 1940, one prize still lay beyond his grasp. For all the toughness and efficiency of the German troops, the English Channel was a formidable barrier—even though the British forces were so painfully weak that resistance could have been easily overcome once his troops were ashore.

Yet when the Allies faced the same task in reverse four years later, the opposition they faced was even more daunting: heavy fortifications and an army that, though stretched to its utmost, was still one of the world's best.

Given command of the channel, and the air above it, the problems of landing the first wave of troops on enemy soil were straightforward enough. But once the Germans woke up to what was happening, and mounted a full-scale counterattack, then everything would depend on landing masses of reinforcements and—even more important—keeping them supplied.

But all the harbors were strongly defended. Capturing even one would divert men and equipment from the main invasion; and even if the attempt succeeded, the Germans could destroy port installations so thoroughly that they would be unusable for weeks.

Only one answer

The Allied planners searched for an answer, but the conclusion remained the same. The invaders had to have a harbor—and if capturing one would take too long, then they would have to take one with them. And so it was that the harbors, code-named "Mulberry," were born—prefabricated ports of breakwaters, jetties, and pontoons, where ships could tie up to unload, and floating ramps, upon which trucks could be driven to the beaches.

As the invasion fleet of more than 4,000 ships headed toward the coast of Normandy in the early hours of June 6, 1944, the components of two Mulberry harbors went with them. Tugs towed caissons and sections of concrete-and-steel pontoons, making up seven miles of piers and jetties. Sixty block ships, which would be maneuvered into position and then scuttled to build an outer harbor wall, followed the invaders. Each harbor weighed 750,000 tons; each had the capacity of the port of Dover.

Avalanche of men

In the first six days of the invasion, the Allies managed to land a third of a million men on French soil, backed up by 54,000 vehicles and more than 100,000 tons of stores. On June 19 a storm in the channel wrecked the American Mulberry harbor and severely damaged the British port at Arromanches. Swift work by engineers soon had the British port operational again, and a week after the storm, the Americans captured Cherbourg.

Although the port was extensively damaged, more block ships were sunk outside the harbor to extend the port area, and it was soon able to

ELABORATE CAMOUFLAGE. *Careful precautions were taken to disguise the British end of the pipeline. The first and fourth structures are pump houses.*

MULBERRY SUCCEEDS. *Allied war vehicles drive onto a Normandy beach from a steel roadway supported on concrete floats.*

take over as the major supply port. By the end of the first three months 2 million Allied troops had been landed, with 3½ million tons of ammunition and half a million vehicles.

Invaders' lifeblood

These, however, were only part of the lifeblood of a modern army—without fuel any offensive would soon grind to a halt. But tankers and fuel trucks were extremely vulnerable to accidents and enemy action, and they tended to monopolize harbor space.

So the planners came up with another idea —Pluto. The initials stood for "pipeline under the ocean," and the idea was astonishingly simple. Specially modified tugs towed huge drums wound with continuous lengths of flexible piping, and as the drum rotated, the pipe unwound to sink to the seabed.

Eleven pipelines were laid across the channel, mainly between Dungeness and Boulogne, and by April 1945 a total of 3,100 tons of fuel was being delivered every day—without a single conventional tanker being necessary.

TUNNELS OF DANGER

Men faced death to drive new pathways beneath the ground

For merchants and military conquerors alike, climbing over mountains is a long and laborious business, and for centuries the Alps formed an almost impassable barrier between France and Italy. It was not until the middle of the 19th century that an all-out attempt was made to link the two countries by tunneling, and even then many engineers predicted that such a feat was impossible.

The idea of an Alpine tunnel had occurred to the spice merchants of Genoa and Turin as long ago as the 15th century. Their project was a two-mile dig through the Col di Tende, the main mountain barrier between Genoa and Nice, which would speed the progress of their mule trains. Explosives were not then in use, and the only method of cutting through the mountains was to light fires under rock to heat it, then to pour on cold water to crack it. This was an ingenious method, but the rock had to be removed by hand, and progress was slow.

Finally, history overtook the diggers; Vasco da Gama sailed around Africa to the Far East and pioneered the way for Portuguese ships to smash the Italian spice monopoly.

Abandoned for 300 years

The partially dug tunnel was abandoned for 300 years, until the King of Piedmont in northeastern Italy ordered work to start again. But the French Revolution brought the work to a halt. Twenty years later the arrival of the railroad changed the picture dramatically, and once again the kingdom of Piedmont took the initiative with a scheme for a seven-mile tunnel under the Mont Cenis Pass.

A French engineer, Germain Sommeiller was given the task of drawing up the plans, and his problems were many. The tunnel would be nearly a mile underground at its deepest point, where the temperature of the rock would reach 117°F (47°C), and the choking fumes from the gunpowder charges would have to diffuse through miles of tunnel. Sommeiller found the answer with the introduction of the compressed-air drill, which sharply reduced the need for blasting.

Volcanic mountains

In 1857 digging started from both sides of the Alps, but until the compressors were ready, the men had to use the old methods. The rate of advance during the first few years was nine inches per day.

When compressed-air drills at last went into action, they were even slower, until Sommeiller installed compressors that were driven by water. Above the compressor station a dam was built, and water descending from it drove water wheels, which in turn operated the compressor.

At last, on Christmas Day 1870, the two tunnels met, and when the final breakthrough was made, the misalignment was less than 18 inches. The cost was $15 million and 28 lives.

Tunnel building is still difficult and dangerous, even with modern aids. The Tanna tunnel in Japan was planned to take the Tokyo-Kobe main line of the Imperial Japanese Railway through the volcanic mountains of the Izu Peninsula, 60 miles southwest of Tokyo. Work began in 1918 and was to be completed within seven years.

In fact, the project took 16 years, during which time 70 men died. Flooding was the major problem, and drainage tunnels had to be dug on either side of the bore. On November 26, 1930, the mountain was hit by an earthquake, and for three years work was held up while the torrents of water drained away. But, eventually, in 1934, the two borings met.

Under rivers

Mountains were not the only barriers to man's progress. Rivers divided the land, and before modern bridge-building techniques were developed, the only way to link the banks of a wide river was by tunneling.

In 1825 it was decided to join the north and south banks of the Thames by digging the world's first underwater tunnel. The work was entrusted to the engineer Marc Brunel, famous father of an even more famous son, Isambard Brunel. In 1818 the elder Brunel had patented a tunneling shield that consisted of cast-iron frames 21 feet high and 2 feet wide, with three platforms on which the excavators worked. Six frames were placed side by side against the work face, and as the men dug away at the soft earth, the frames were moved forward 4½ inches at a time. Behind the excavators bricklayers lined the semicircular tunnel with brickwork.

As the tunnel progressed, water seepage caused problems. The foul waters of the Thames—then an open sewer—carried disease and death. In May 1827 the river burst through the tunnel roof, but without loss of life.

Financial difficulties beset the Thames Tunnel Company from the beginning, and the flooding delayed the operation disastrously. But, eventually, the work was completed, and in March 1843 the first horse-drawn carriage passed through the tunnel. Later it was used by the railway, and today it still forms part of London's underground railway system.

EARLY PLANS TO TUNNEL UNDER THE CHANNEL

THE FIRST proposal to link England and France by tunneling under the channel was made in 1802 by the French engineer Albert Mathieu. He suggested that relays of horses could pull coaches through a candlelit tunnel between Dover and Calais in under an hour.

A start was made at Abbot's Cliff, near Folkestone, in 1881. The remains of this venture can still be seen; a dank 7-foot-high, 879-yard-long tunnel behind a locked wooden door on a sea-swept ledge of the coast of Kent.

Design suggestions for the "chunnel," as the newspapers have christened it, have been many and elaborate. They have included the cast-iron submarine railway (above) with steeplelike observation and ventilation towers, put forward by French engineer Hector Horeau in 1860.

A few years ago France and Great Britain announced a new project to build a chunnel to be completed by mid-1980 at a projected cost of about $2 billion. But it was abandoned in 1974.

SPANNING THE WAVES

The problems of bridging troubled waters

Water has always been one of the most formidable barriers to the progress of land transport; and bridges have been one way of taking a shortcut.

Stone bridges go back to prehistoric times, but with the arrival of iron technology in the 18th century, bridge builders were able to design spans of unprecedented length.

The advent of the railways in the mid-19th century brought an urgent need for long bridges of great strength, and one of the most impressive was the Britannia Tubular Bridge over the Menai Strait between northern Wales and Anglesey.

Designed by Robert Stephenson and Wil-

MENAI BRIDGE. *The 1850 bridge, between Anglesey and north Wales, was one of the world's strongest tubular iron structures.*

liam Fairbairn, it employed the box-girder principle and consisted of two continuous wrought-iron tubes that carried the railway tracks. Placed side by side, these tubes formed a rigid and immensely strong structure, which carried trains 12 times heavier than those for which it was designed.

There were four spans, supported by three towers, and the two main sections were 459 feet long and weighed 1,500 tons each. The length of the bridge was 1,841 feet, and it stood 100 feet above the water. When it was opened in 1850, it was the longest railway bridge in the world. It was severely damaged by fire in 1970.

In the mid-19th century U.S. engineers, faced with far greater problems, began building bridges of steel. The famous Brooklyn Bridge, which carries traffic over New York's East River, was completed in 1883. It has a span of 1,595 feet and is suspended from four steel cables. Its designer, John A. Roebling, devised a cable-spinning method used on all big suspension bridges subsequently built in America.

Demands of the automobile

With the coming of the automobile, bridges were required to carry all kinds of traffic, but for sheer carrying capacity few can equal that of the Sydney Harbor Bridge. Not only is it one of the world's largest steel arch bridges but also it has the widest highway. Two railway tracks, eight lanes of roadway, a footpath, and a cycle track soar 172 feet high, spanning 1,650 feet.

Of all civil engineering challenges, the bridging of Lake Maracaibo in Venezuela must rank as one of the most difficult. A bridge of more than 5 miles in length was required, and, to allow shipping to pass through, the central spans had to be 150 feet above the water. To complicate matters, the whole area was affected by tropical storms and earthquakes.

Designed by R. Morandi of Italy, the bridge was finally completed, on schedule, in 1962. In three years a structure of supreme complexity had been built under the most arduous conditions. It consists of a quarter mile of embankment, 20 spans of 40 yards each, another 77 spans of 50 yards each, the main spans of 80 yards, and five high center spans of 260 yards, each slung from 300-foot towers.

In the United States the desire to get there quicker led to the building of yet another bridge in New York harbor. The Verrazano Narrows Bridge runs from Staten Island to Brooklyn and at 4,260 feet is the longest suspension bridge in the world.

But to satisfy the demands of the motorist, no structure can beat the complicated bridge-tunnel system crossing the Chesapeake Bay. It stretches for a total of 17½ miles and contains 12 miles of low-level bridgework, two high-level steel bridges across shipping channels, four manmade islands, and two mile-long tunnels— all to save 1½ hours of driving time.

RESERVOIR BELOW THE SEA

How Hong Kong tapped a saltwater inlet

A large part of Hong Kong's water supply is stored below sea level. A sea inlet, Plover Cove, was blocked off to make a reservoir holding 37 billion gallons of drinking water.

This gigantic reservoir was the brainchild of Hong Kong waterworks engineer Tommy Morgan. His department faced a serious problem. The colony's water supply was hopelessly inadequate for its growing population, and water was already rationed to eight hours a day. While sailing in Plover Cove, Morgan suddenly saw the mountains and peninsula surrounding him as three of the four sides of a natural reservoir.

Within two years the $200 million project was launched. Engineers had to dig a trench in the sea bottom 7,000 feet long and 600 feet wide, at depths of 60 to 95 feet. Nearly 15 million tons of rock and rubble were dropped into the trench for the dam's foundation.

There was one moment of anxiety. In 1968, when the last few yards of the dam's rockfill remained to be closed, the escaping waters surged through at a rate of nearly seven miles an hour. Any greater velocity would sweep the fill away. Luckily, the rocks held, and the gap was closed.

Within three months about 25 billion gallons of saltwater were pumped from the cove, leaving a mud-cake desert. Drought slowed the buildup of freshwater in the new reservoir, and for some time the water from Plover Cove remained unpleasantly salty. But the project later proved to be so successful that the reservoir's capacity was enlarged to 50 billion gallons.

MOON POWER AT SAINT-MALO

The world's first major tidal power station

For centuries men have dreamed of harnessing the power of the rising and falling tides. Now, near the ancient French town of Saint-Malo, on the English Channel, the dream is a reality. The Saint-Malo site, spanning the estuary of the River Rance, tempted power experts because some of the world's highest tides—raising the sea level as much as 44 feet—occur there. Twice a day the waters surge up the estuary and then back again, reaching a maximum volume of about 280 million gallons a minute.

In the early 1940's a French engineer, Robert Gibrat, saw Saint-Malo's potential for producing hydroelectric energy. He was influenced by documents and patents going back to 1737, showing ideas for utilizing the tides.

Gibrat spent 20 years researching the project, finally persuading colleagues in Electricité de France of its worth.

In 1961 engineers began the formidable task of building a half-mile barrier across the Rance. They had to overcome a unique problem. When building a conventional river dam, the stream is simply diverted around the site. At Saint-Malo the engineers had to contend with a tremendous two-way daily flow. To cope with this, they built two coffer dams, one on each bank of the river and each with its own system of locks, which allowed the tide to pass. In the middle they constructed a temporary lake.

The lake was then drained, and over the dry riverbed was built the central dam wall. The wall contains 24 uniquely designed turbines that work in either direction—i.e., they are driven by both the incoming and outgoing tides. Each turbine can supply the electrical needs of about 15,000 people.

After five years' work and an expenditure of $175 million, the station was opened in November 1966. It now functions for at least 14 hours a day.

This braking action on the tides has had one strange side effect. Scientists have calculated that it has imperceptibly slowed the earth's rate of revolution.

Throughout the world there are only a few sites where the differences between low and high tides are great enough to produce power on a large scale. At one of these, the Bay of Fundy, in eastern Canada, plans are well advanced to build a Saint-Malo-type station.

SUPERSCULPTURE

Man's attempts to immortalize himself

The building of giant statues has a long and awe-inspiring history, leaving us with a permanent record of man's efforts to immortalize himself or to pay homage to his gods or his country in stone or metal structures.

The Colossus of Rhodes soared 105 feet and stood guard in the harbor on the Greek island of Rhodes. It was justifiably classed as one of the Seven Wonders of the Ancient World.

Work on the great bronze statue, by the sculptor Chares, a pupil of Lysippus, was begun in 292 B.C., and this unmistakable landmark and guide to shipping took more than 12 years to complete. But, tragically, its very size turned out to be its downfall.

The island of Rhodes was ravaged by an earthquake in 224 B.C., and the huge statue toppled and was smashed to pieces. The massive fragments lay where they had fallen for almost 900 years until, in A.D. 672, the chunks of bronze were finally sold for scrap and carted away by the buyers to be melted down.

An Emperor's vanity

The Romans, too, thought on a large scale and never did anything by halves. Predictably, they were lovers of giant statues, none more so than the megalomaniac Emperor Nero.

He summoned the sculptor Zenodorus, who was then working on a statue of Hermes in Gaul, and ordered him to drop everything and come to Rome to start work on an enormous statue of the Emperor.

When it was finished, the sculpture measured 106 feet from top to toe. However, Nero's bid to create a permanent reminder of his greatness did not survive his suicide in A.D. 68—when the statue was promptly dedicated to Apollo, chosen as a personal god by Emperor Augustus.

But even the grand-scale statues built by the Romans and ancients are dwarfed by those created in modern times.

The Statue of Liberty—officially entitled "Liberty Enlightening the World"—stands at the entrance to New York harbor, an enduringly impressive first sight of America for the seagoing traveler.

It is by the sculptor Frédéric Auguste Bar-

tholdi and measures an awesome 305 feet from the base of the pedestal to the tip of the torch's flame. The pedestal is a granite and concrete structure, but the figure itself, which measures 151 feet 1 inch, is made of copper sheets over an iron framework. It was engineered by Alex-

FRENCH GIFT. *The Statue of Liberty in New York harbor was designed by Bartholdi and was given to America by the French people.*

andre Gustave Eiffel, creator of the most famous of all Parisian landmarks.

Gift of the French

Costing approximately $250,000, the statue was presented to the Americans by the French people to commemorate the birth of the United States and the friendship between the two countries. Dedicated in 1886, the statue incorporates viewing galleries in the torch and head. However, the torch gallery has been closed for several years.

An elevator runs to the top of the pedestal . . . from there the energetic visitor can climb the stairs inside the body to reach the lady's head.

But the prize for sheer height goes to the figure "Motherland," which is the tallest statue in the world, and stands on Mamayev Hill, outside Volgograd in Russia. It was designed in 1967 by Yevgeyi Vuchetich to commemorate the Battle of Stalingrad. The female figure itself measures 270 feet from its base to the tip of the sword clenched in its right hand.

Just to prove that the rivalry of the two Great Powers extends beyond weaponry and sporting events, the American sculptor, Felix de Welton, is now working on an ambitious plan to build a replica of the Colossus of Rhodes—with one big difference. De Welton's version will stand 308 feet—203 feet taller than the original version.

Faces in stone

The desire to carve figures in stone is an inherent part of man's nature that originated with the cavemen. But no one has taken this desire to such satisfying and impressive lengths as the American sculptor Gutzon Borglum.

In 1916 Borglum began to carve a gigantic head of Gen. Robert E. Lee on the sheer, 650-foot face of Stone Mountain in Georgia. The work, commissioned by the United Daughters of the Confederacy, was intended to include the figures of Stonewall Jackson, Jefferson Davis, and a procession of Confederate soldiers. The head of Lee was unveiled in 1924, but Borglum then had a difference of opinion with the United Daughters of the Confederacy and quit the project.

The work was taken over by Augustus Lukeman. He worked on it until 1928 but made little progress during this time—and actually destroyed the gigantic head.

In the meantime Borglum had moved on to other undertakings and had begun work on the mammoth project for which he is most famous.

Into the craggy rocks of Mount Rushmore, in the Black Hills of South Dakota, he carved the heads of four great Presidents of the United States of America—Washington, Lincoln, Jefferson, and Theodore Roosevelt. Each of the massive figures measures 60 feet from the chin to the top of the forehead.

Before the great work was completed, Borglum had patched up his quarrel with the United Daughters of the Confederacy and had agreed to resume his work on the carvings. But he died before this could be achieved.

GREAT PRESIDENTS. *These giant carvings were made in the craggy face of Mount Rushmore. Each face measures 60 feet from chin to forehead.*

INFLATING THE BUBBLE-BUILDING BOOM

THE HANDYMAN of the future may have not only to check the air pressure in his car tires—but also in his house, garage, greenhouse, and, in the case of the more affluent, swimming pool. All this could come about if the present boom in bubble building continues. Instead of a rigid structure, a skin of thin fabric is held in place by internal air pressure, created by a blower. If the blower stops running, the building slowly goes flat.

The idea is not new, for it was patented in 1918 by Frederick William Lanchester, one of the pioneer British car makers. But it was developed only in the Second World War when engineer Walter Bird, of Cornell University, was asked to find a solution to the problem of protecting radar antennae in northern Canada from frost. The cost of bubble building can be as little as one-fifth that of traditional structures. Versatility is the main attraction. They can be used to cover tennis courts, and as warehouses and greenhouses. The first residential bubble house was built in the United States.

LIVING LITERALLY on top of each other has led to the great American skyscraper cities of New York and Chicago. But the beginnings of the skyscraper can be traced back to the days of the Roman Empire, when architects designed five-story blocks, with shops at ground level and balconied homes above.

Most famous of the modern skyscrapers was the Empire State Building, completed in 1931. At 1,250 feet it towered above New York until it was overtaken in 1970 by the twin 1,350-foot towers of the World Trade Center.

In 1973 the World Trade Center was knocked into second place by the Sears Tower in Chicago, 100 feet higher, at 1,450 feet. The Sears Tower has 110 stories and provides office space for 16,500 employees on 101 acres of floor space. More than 17,000 tons of refrigeration equipment maintain a year-round controlled temperature. Planned for the future is its own electricity substation below ground level, which will not only provide power for the building but will boost the entire system in the surrounding city center.

A five-story Roman block, second century A.D.

WHITE ELEPHANT OR A WONDER?

The story of Sydney's controversial opera house

Australia's Sydney Opera House, in its magnificent harbor setting, is the biggest and, many people think, the best piece of abstract architecture in the world. It is one of the world's most expensive buildings and has been called a white elephant, a King's palace, an unjustifiable extravagance, and a wonder of the world.

Its original estimated cost, when work started in March 1959, was about $10 million, and it was planned to be completed in two years. By the time it was opened by Queen Elizabeth II in October 1973, it had taken longer to build than any other modern building, and its costs had soared to $150 million—and were still rising, for union troubles had delayed peripheral work. Access roads and car parks had yet to be built and the site's 5½ acres paved.

Sculpture in the round

The story of the opera house began with an international competition for its design, which was won by Danish architect Jørn Utzon. He envisaged it from the beginning as a piece of sculpture, which could be seen in the round.

It stands on a peninsula jutting into the Sydney harbor, just in front of the famous bridge, and can be seen from every side. Because the shore slopes steeply behind it, and there are

GRACE. *Designed as a sculpture, the shells of the Sydney Opera House sit majestically over the waters of the harbor, like a ship at sea.*

176

Manhattan, New York City...the world's most famous skyline.

Sears Tower, 1973.

numerous skyscrapers to the west, the opera house can also be seen from above. The most striking features of the building are probably the 10 shells that make up the roof. The highest of the shells soars 221 feet above the harbor.

Self-supporting concrete

When Utzon first conceived the idea, he envisaged true shells—thin skins of self-supporting concrete. But when work started, he found he had to design massive arches for support.

The result was that the cost of the building rose dramatically, and the shells took on a heavier appearance. Not surprisingly—since their total weight amounted to 26,800 tons—it is the heaviest roof in the world.

Utzon never saw the shells completed. He resigned from the project in 1966 in the midst of a furor over rising costs.

His place was taken by a group of four Sydney architects, with Peter Hall as design architect. Hall faced the awesome task of de-signing the great glass walls that close in the shells at each end, for when he took over only the first stage of the building had been completed. But perhaps his biggest task was the interior, which in 4½ acres had to accommodate a concert hall, a theater for opera and ballet, a drama theater, a recording room for the Sydney Symphony Orchestra, and a movie theater. He solved most of the difficult problems well, but the opera theater turned out to be too small for its purpose and is not expected to make a profit.

More expense on the way

Utzon's white shells sit majestically over the harbor as he conceived them, despite gloomy predictions by his critics that they might fall down. Visitors standing on the terrace below them feel they could be aboard a yacht at sea.

Public lotteries paid for the building, but more money may still be needed, for the magnificent but controversial opera house promises to cost almost as much to run as to build.

RECYCLING RUBBISH

RUBBISH IS being used as a valuable raw material in the production of energy for the city of Nashville, the capital of Tennessee.

A plant that cost $16.5 million went into operation in February 1974, to start converting hundreds of tons of rubbish at a time into enough energy to provide heat and air conditioning for 38 Nashville office buildings. Truckloads of trash from the city are fed into an incinerator pit and then into a furnace, where they are burned to convert water into high-pressure steam. The steam is then used to spin the rotors of turbines, and so generate electricity.

Weird and wonderful answers to the problems of living

Man's amazing inventions

.

ANCIENT PENNY-IN-SLOT MACHINE

The Greeks had a drachma for it 1,900 years ago

The coin-operated machine—almost a symbol of our own age—was first designed by the Greek scientist Hero, who lived in Alexandria during the century after Christ.

It was planned as a holy-water dispenser in temples. The water was contained in an urn with a short dispenser pipe leading out from the bottom. The upper end of this pipe, inside the

STEAM ENGINE. *With this design, which spun the sphere by feeding steam into the jets, Hero beat James Watt by 1,700 years.*

urn, was closed by a plug fixed to one end of a horizontal bar that pivoted like a seesaw. When a coin was put into a slot at the top, it dropped down a chute onto the other end of the seesaw. For a few seconds the seesaw would tip and, lifting the plug from the pipe, allow the water to pour along a trough into a goblet. As soon as the coin—a five-drachma piece—fell into the bottom of the urn, the seesaw would return the plug to the end of the pipe and shut off the water flow.

A similar principle is used to this day in the simpler coin-operated machines, such as candy-bar dispensers.

Hero's extraordinary genius made him a prolific inventor. The author of important books on mechanics and engineering, he had a mind that soared away from figures on paper to practical applications of science—and to parlor magic.

Forerunner of the computer

Hero is credited with one of the earliest calculating devices, the odometer. This was a mileage meter with wheel and worm gears encased in a box and mounted on a carriage. Hero's odometer is considered part of the mechanical tradition that produced today's computer.

Hero also made a surveyor's instrument, the *dioptra*, that was a combination level and device for measuring angles. It is notable not only for its refinements over earlier instruments but for being the first-known equipment to have interchangeable parts.

In addition, he invented a screw press to extract olive oil and grape juice, worked to improve the *gastraphetes*, a powerful crossbow of classical times, and described how an organ might be operated by an air pump.

Parlor magic

Oddly, most of his inventions were toys to entertain guests or perhaps impress worshipers. Hero built innumerable automatons, including mechanical birds that sang and puppet shows with rising and falling curtains, all worked by strings.

Even more impressive was his use of steam or hot air to operate some of his creations. Among his toy models was a steam turbine called an *aeolopile*—a hollow sphere rotated by steam escaping through a pair of jets. It demonstrated the power of steam 1,700 years before it was harnessed for practical use.

Remote control

One of Hero's most spectacular designs was a model of a temple with doors that opened and closed by remote control, mystifying beholders. The secret was that when a fire was ignited on the temple altar, it heated air in a chamber inside. The expanding air was then forced down a pipe into a water-filled vessel below. This pushed water out of the vessel, along a tube, and into a bucket attached by rope to spindles connected to the base of the temple doors. Weighted down by the water, the bucket descended, so turning the spindles and opening the doors. When the altar fire was put out, the

SLOT MACHINE. *Coins fed into an urn tilt a seesaw, displace a plug, and allow but a few seconds' flow of water. Designed as a holy-water dispenser for temples, it was similar in principle to today's slot machines.*

air in the chamber cooled, contracted, and reversed the whole operation, sucking the water from the bucket and allowing a counterweight to fall and close the doors.

It is not known how many of Hero's designs were actually built, but the details of them, contained in his books, leave no doubt that he was centuries ahead of his time.

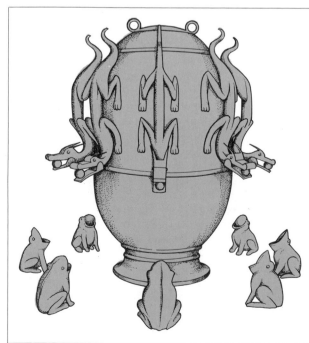

THE DOOM-WATCH DRAGONS

THIS ornate and fanciful object is not a tea urn but an early earthquake alarm, invented in A.D. 132 by the Chinese astronomer Chang Heng. It was indirectly the forerunner of the modern seismograph, which measures earth tremors.

When a shock occurred, a pendulum inside the eight-foot-high vessel would swing in the direction of the tremor and tilt one of eight horizontal arms, opening the jaws of one of the eight dragons around the outside. A ball would then fall from the dragon's mouth into the mouth of the frog beneath it.

The dragons and frogs were aligned at even intervals like the points of the compass, so the released ball would indicate the direction of the earthquake.

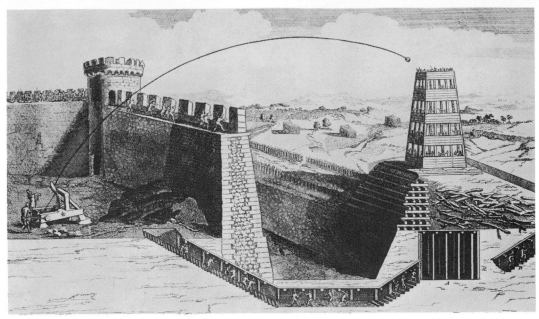

MEDIEVAL MISSILE LAUNCHER. *Besieged troops use a catapult, powered by twisted coils, to bombard an assault tower with great boulders while tunnelers attack from below.*

GUNS WITHOUT GUNPOWDER

Deadly weapons that devastated cities

Long before the days when the Western World began to use explosives, armies had a whole range of devices for hurling missiles at enemies.

One of the most powerful was the ballista, which was employed by the ancient Greeks. Built like a huge crossbow on a frame, it could shoot a five-pound wooden bolt more than 500 yards.

At the siege of Rome about A.D. 537, a Gothic chief was pinned to a tree by a ballista bolt, and when Paris was besieged by the Vikings three centuries later, a bolt passed clean through three Norsemen in succession.

Backing up the ballista was the catapult—the equivalent of the modern mortar—which lobbed rather than fired missiles.

The catapult had a lever arm with a cup for a missile at one end, and the engine's power resided in the springy ropes or coils used to pull the arm back. These ropes, which were twisted until taut, were made of animal sinew or rawhide, or human hair, which was even better because of its elasticity. When the arm was released, it flew upward and struck a crossbar, sending the missile 500 yards or more.

The ballista and the catapult (including the "scorpion," which had a sling attached to the lever arm) were used until the 12th century.

In the Middle Ages a new engine of war came into use—the trebuchet. This machine was similar to the catapult, except that it used a counterweight instead of torsion for power. Some trebuchets were colossal. With throwing arms 50 feet long and counterweights of 10 tons, they could hurl 300-pound boulders more than 600 yards.

Stones were not the only missiles fired. As far back as 400 B.C., pots of liquid fire had been used in warfare, and in the seventh century A.D. the precursor of napalm came into being. Called Greek fire, it was a mixture of sulfur, naphtha, and quicklime, and its most alarming property was that water only caused the flames to burn more fiercely. This fearful concoction was regarded as the ultimate weapon in the early Middle Ages, and it was used with terrifying effectiveness by Leo III in the 717 conquest of Constantinople.

Other tactics were more subtle. Missile engines were sometimes used to terrify the enemy by hurling dead opponents or live prisoners into their midst. Rotting carcasses of horses were also fired into besieged cities in the hope of spreading pestilence—an early form of germ warfare. At the siege of Carolstein in 1422, the garrison was showered with 200 cartloads of manure.

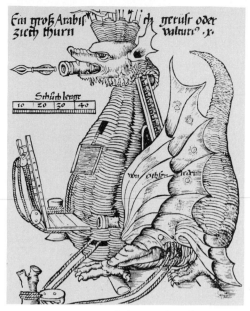

CREATURE OF WAR. *A siege machine designed in 1472, with drawbridge, "gun," and turret.*

FIREPOWER. *The man aiming the trebuchet (top) is lifted off his feet by the weapon's force.*

One of the last recorded uses of a trebuchet was at the siege of Rhodes in 1480, when the Turks brought up heavy guns to batter the defenders. In desperation the beleaguered Christians built a trebuchet, and with it they managed to silence the Turkish siege artillery.

But the days of the trebuchet were over. Explosive black powder, possibly first used by the Chinese, became known in the Western World in the 13th century, and the first guns, which were appallingly unreliable, were invented early in the 14th century.

HOW ARCHIMEDES SET THE ENEMY ON FIRE

ARCHIMEDES, the mathematician and inventor who lived more than 2,000 years ago, may have used solar energy as a weapon. According to several ancient writers—including Plutarch and Anthemius of Tralles—he reflected sun rays onto the Roman fleet when it sailed against his hometown of Syracuse between 215 and 212 B.C. and set the ships on fire.

But their descriptions were discounted by later historians. In 1973, however, Dr. Ioannis Sakkas, a Greek engineer, carried out a series of experiments that proved that the idea was workable.

He focused 50 bronze-painted mirrors on a small rowing boat and reflected the sun's rays onto it. Within seconds the craft began to smolder, and after two minutes it burst into flames.

Prof. Evenghelos Stamatis, a Greek authority on Archimedes who saw the experiment, said later he had no doubts that the inventor had used solar energy.

In a 1973 experiment to prove that Archimedes, the Greek inventor, had used the sun's power to defeat the Romans, 50 Greek sailors were given oblong mirrors that they focused on a small boat, setting it on fire. When Archimedes carried out the same operation, he may have used concave burning mirrors, or possibly shields of polished bronze. The Roman ships are reported to have been routed by Archimedes' device.

THE GENIUS OF LEONARDO

Tanks and aircraft designed 500 years ago

The many-sided genius of the 15th-century artist and engineer Leonardo da Vinci produced schemes for a host of modern inventions, hundreds of years before their time—including road vehicles, aircraft, and weapons.

Leonardo (1452–1519) was a man of many talents—painter, sculptor, musician, architect, military engineer, and scientist. But it was as an inventor that his ideas were most prolific.

He produced designs for a vehicle propelled by a system of gears and springs, as in a toy car wound with a key. He planned a tank with sloping sides to shield it against artillery.

His military designs included a rapid-firing gun, exploding shot, and a giant crossbow. He

MACHINES OF WAR. *Leonardo's design for a system of military flails (top). The revolving blades would have swept the horseman's enemies from his path. Below: an armored vehicle, driven by operators turning cranking handles and protected from artillery fire by steeply sloping sides.*

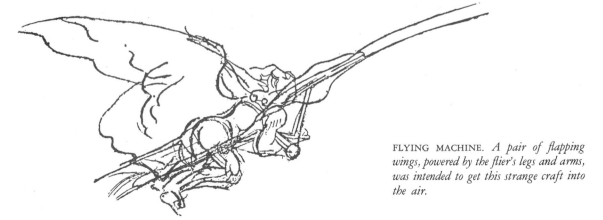

FLYING MACHINE. *A pair of flapping wings, powered by the flier's legs and arms, was intended to get this strange craft into the air.*

even proposed stench bombs to be shot by a bow or catapult.

Leonardo also tackled the problems of the frogmen of his day and produced schemes for a diving suit with a breathing tube like a snorkel.

He turned out the first known design for a parachute, something like a square tent, and worked on several plans for flying machines.

His designs for a ship of the air included a vertical-takeoff aircraft, using an aerial screw similar to the modern rotor of a helicopter. Still another showed a retractable landing gear.

His ingenuity was irrepressible and sometimes resulted in bizarre contraptions.

Sadly, Leonardo lacked the temperament to carry through most of his schemes. His designs for new machines, and his scientific observations, were set down in thousands of pages of drawings, sketchily annotated in mirror writing. (He was not only left-handed; he wrote from right to left.)

He died with his work unpublished, leaving his conclusions to be rediscovered by others—often hundreds of years later.

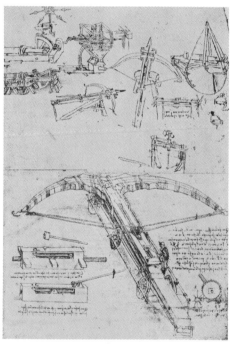

GIANT CROSSBOW. *This massive machine dwarfs the operator (lower right), who was to load and fire it using cogs and pulleys.*

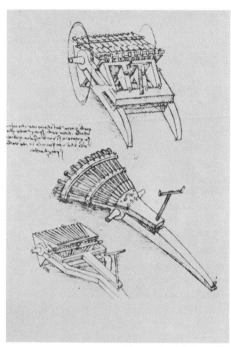

RAPID-FIRING GUNS. *Alternative designs for semiautomatic weapons. Each employed several barrels firing in quick succession.*

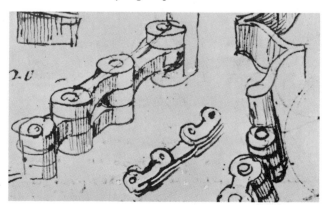

IRREPRESSIBLE INGENUITY. *Leonardo's inventive powers even extended to articulated chains. The drawings anticipated much later inventions leading to the familiar bicycle chain.*

ON VICTORY'S TRACK

How the modern tank was developed

The tank, as we see it smashing through defenses in war films or in news programs, seems a brilliant example of modern inventiveness and military engineering. Yet the concept of a vehicle strong enough to carry guns or missiles, while protecting its own crew from enemy fire, is far older.

An armored battle car was first proposed by Guido da Vigevano in 1335 and sketched by Leonardo da Vinci in 1484.

But even before Leonardo, armored wagons had proved themselves in battle, and with devastating effect. Their innovator was Count Jan Žižka, leader of the Protestant Hussites of Bohemia. In 1420 Sigismund, the German King and nominal head of the Holy Roman Empire, invaded Bohemia—and Žižka was waiting with his wagon fort. This was a heavy, horse-drawn farm wagon armored with sheets of iron. The crew fired crossbows and guns through loopholes pierced in the side.

Žižka's tactics were astonishingly original. Because his wagon forts were slow and cumbersome, his strategy was to force the enemy to attack at a disadvantage. In his defense tactics Žižka used the wagon forts in much the same way that modern generals deploy their tanks. Dug in behind a ditch, linked together by chains, the wagon forts made a formidable obstacle to any advance.

Žižka, with a mere 25,000 men, crushed Sigismund's invasion force of more than 100,000. For the next 14 years the Hussites

FIRST TRUE TANKS. *Armored wagon forts with crews firing through loopholes helped the Hussites to repel the Germans.*

demolished their enemy. But despite the success of mobile artillery, it was not reintroduced until 200 years later by the King of Sweden.

In 1855 the armored car evolved a stage further when a British inventor named Cowan patented a turtle-shaped vehicle based on the steam tractor. In 1899 F. R. Simms fitted a Maxim machinegun to a four-wheeled armored motorcycle.

The modern monster

The ultimate battlewagon, the modern tank, with its caterpillar tracks and heavy armor and guns, was invented by Ernest Swinton in 1915 to be used against the Germans during the First World War. The English and French began to make tanks simultaneously, but the British tanks were the first to go into action, on September 15, 1916.

The first tanks sent to France were given their name because, for security reasons, their packing crates were labeled WATER TANKS.

BATTLEWAGON. *Horse-drawn carts carried crews armed with pikes, bows, and early guns into battle in the 15th century.*

THE SQUARESHOOTER

A machinegun that dealt two sorts of death

One of the world's first machineguns fired two types of bullets: round ones for shooting at a Christian enemy; and square ones, which were more damaging, for killing Turks, as Muslims were once called.

The inventor, a London lawyer named James Puckle, designed the flintlock machinegun in 1718 for use on board ships, claiming in his patent application that "it discharges so often and so many bullets and can be so quickly loaded as renders it next to impossible to carry any ship by boarding."

The gun was not the most portable of weapons, however. It was heavy, with a bore of 1½ inches and a barrel nearly 3 feet long. The barrel, mounted on a tripod, had a firing drum with from six to nine chambers, which could be hand-revolved by the gunner.

At a public demonstration in 1722, a Puckle gun discharged 63 bullets in seven minutes. The impressed authorities put the weapon into production, but it proved cumbersome and hard to load in action, and the Puckle gun was soon no more than a military curiosity.

Three examples survive: one in Copenhagen and two in the Tower of London. Both London models, one of brass and one of iron, are fitted with the square firing chambers.

THE MIGHTY, INVULNERABLE MOUSE

THE HEAVIEST TANK ever built weighed 180 tons and stood almost 20 feet high. Its armor at the front was 12 inches thick. Code-named the Mouse, it first appeared in 1944, after the German Army's tank divisions had been badly mauled on the Russian front.

Hitler realized he could never hope to match the masses of Russian tanks ranged against his forces. So he briefed Dr. Porsche—designer of the Volkswagen Beetle—to produce a land battleship, a tank that would pack a heavier punch than any enemy tank, yet remain completely invulnerable to enemy fire, thanks to massive armor protection.

To move this enormous bulk, it had a 1,500-horsepower diesel engine driving an electric generator that fed the power to two motors mounted in each hub of the monster's giant caterpillar tracks.

The Mouse was completely watertight with its hatches closed. It could cross the bottom of a river 40 feet deep, with its engine switched off to conserve power and its electric motors fed by cable from another tank on the riverbank.

But its size and weight were the Mouse's undoing. Its top speed was only 12 miles an hour, and when it drove along roads on a test, the vibration cracked foundations, smashed cobblestones, and shattered windows in all the towns and villages it passed through. Also, the pressure on its tracks was enough to cause it to sink into anything but the driest ground. So finally, the project was dropped.

THOSE MAGNIFICENT MEN

The uncertain struggle for the skies

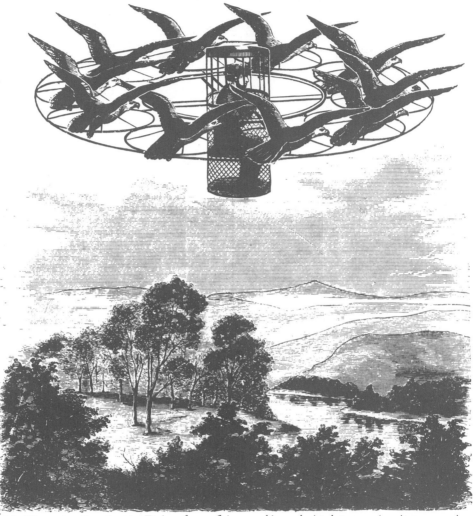

STRICTLY FOR THE BIRDS. *Design for a flying machine submitted to an American magazine anonymously in 1865. So far as is known, the 10-eagle-power device never flew.*

The ascent of man has always been a precarious affair, particularly in the early days when most attempts to get off the ground were clumsy efforts to emulate the action of birds in flight. A Benedictine monk is said to have jumped from a tower, wearing wings, about A.D. 1000. He reportedly broke both his legs, and there is no record of his making a further attempt to defy gravity.

Examples of Leonardo da Vinci's studies in the 15th century include drawings of a parachute and a helicopter model.

Looking forward to lift-off

A hundred and fifty years after Leonardo da Vinci, inventors began thinking of power sources to obtain lift-off. In 1670 Francesco de Lana, a Jesuit priest, designed an airship with four vacuum cylinders "to wreck ships at sea, or houses could be set on fire by fireballs dropped from the sky." Because he was a peaceful man, he abandoned the idea, which was just as well, for he had overlooked the fact that vessels emptied of air would need to be strong enough

FLIGHTS OF FANCY

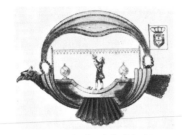

Magnets were supposed to help lift this aircraft off the ground. It was designed by Barthélemy Laurenço de Gusmão in 1709.

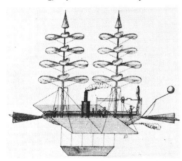

Rubber bands acted as springs on the wings of this birdman's design by Bréant in 1854. The rest was up to the energy of the would-be flier.

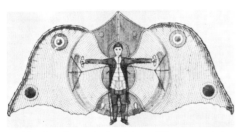

This highly sophisticated failure by M. G. de la Landelle in 1863 combined propellers, inclined planes, parachutes—and hope.

d'Arlandes, soared to 300 feet in the Montgolfier hot-air balloon and made a journey of five miles over Paris.

Balloons across the channel

In 1785 the first crossing of the English Channel was achieved, with rather less dignity than such a historic occasion deserved. The balloonists, Jean-Pierre Blanchard and his American backer, Dr. John Jeffries, sat in a car slung beneath the giant hydrogen-filled balloon. It was hoped that an arrangement of flapping wings and a propeller would drive the balloon to its destination.

The launch from the cliffs of Dover went without mishap, but six miles off the French coast, the craft began to lose altitude. The aeronauts first shed their equipment and finally most of their clothes. These desperate measures worked, and the happy pair landed in a forest 12 miles inland, clad only in their underwear.

It is unlikely that the flapping-wing arrangement on the Blanchard balloon contributed in any way to its progress, but it was one of the earliest attempts at air propulsion. As soon as balloon flight had become a reality, the designers turned their attention to controlled flight, and some very remarkable and quite impractical devices were proposed. These ideas ranged from

ANIMAL ASCENTS. *In 1798 a Frenchman, Margat, put his white stag, Coco, in a hot-air balloon's gondola and took him for a ride over Paris.*

to resist the external air pressure, and so would be too heavy to fly anyway.

It was another century before man finally rose triumphant, borne aloft by the hot-air balloon of the French Montgolfier brothers. Joseph Montgolfier is said to have conceived the idea of using hot air while watching smoke from a fire curl up a chimney. He took paper bags—he was a paper manufacturer—held them above the flames, and watched them rise gently to the ceiling. On November 21, 1783, two Frenchmen, Pilâtre de Rozier and the Marquis

BIRDMAN. *German glider pioneer Otto Lilienthal tested his models from 1891 to 1896. He made many hundreds of successful flights of up to 250 yards in his graceful craft before he was killed in 1896 when his glider crashed.*

Blanchard's hopelessly small propeller to hot-air jets, steam jets, and even gunpowder.

Possibly the most eccentric idea came from an anonymous American designer who wrote to a science magazine in 1865 suggesting that eagles could be used to carry a man. He designed a harness for the birds, each tethered to the rim of a circular frame, with the passenger seated in a basket in the center. Ten sets of reins were provided to steer the birds, with a set of cords to make the birds fly higher or lower. The inventor did not say where one would find 10 eagles obliging enough to cooperate with this scheme.

An idea that comes a close second in the eccentricity stakes was that proposed in 1885 by another American, W. O. Ayres. A forerunner of the vertical-takeoff "flying bedstead," it was to be driven by seven propellers, six for lift and one for propulsion. Foot pedals provided the drive for two of the lifting propellers, and compressed-air motors drove the other four. The propulsion screw was operated by a hand crank, as were the rudder and elevator controls. Inevitably, steam power was considered as a

power source by some inventors, and one, Hiram Maxim, inventor of the machinegun, built a steam-powered biplane test rig in 1894. The wings were 125 feet across, and two propellers were driven by powerful steam engines that consumed 12 gallons of water a minute. At its first, and only, trial the machine left its launching rails briefly before being brought to a stop.

Tragedy after soaring success

In contrast to Maxim's snorting giant were the silent, graceful gliders built by Otto Lilienthal, a German. In 1891 he started gliding experiments, controlling the craft by shifting his body. He made more than 2,000 jump-off flights of up to 250 yards before he died in 1896. His glider sideslipped into the ground, breaking his back.

Another silent spectacle was the first parachute descent, made on October 22, 1797, by a young Frenchman named André Garnerin. He hitched a gondola and a parachute to a hydrogen balloon, rose to 3,000 feet, and then released his device from the balloon. The canopy, 23 feet across, opened perfectly, but the descent

PEDAL POWER. *Dr. Ayres hoped to use pedaling, cranking, and compressed air.*

FLYING BEDSTEAD. *A 1953 rig designed by Rolls-Royce to test vertical takeoff.*

had realized that an aircraft must have fixed wings and a separate propulsion system, and his work between 1799 and 1809 laid the foundation for the whole of modern aerodynamics. He designed and flew gliders with curved wings, rudders, and elevators, and proved that fixed-wing aircraft were possible.

One hundred years later the Wright brothers made history's first successful powered flight at Kitty Hawk, North Carolina, on December 17, 1903. They made four flights that day: The first lasted only 12 seconds, but the fourth lasted 59 seconds and took them 852 feet.

Soon afterward the Wrights built the world's first practical airplane, the Flyer III. A biplane with a 16-horsepower engine, it was able to bank and turn and fly for half an hour.

In 1908 Wilbur Wright demonstrated an improved model in France, flying 60 miles in slightly less than two hours.

The Wright brothers revolutionized the approach to aviation: The initial problems of powered flight were solved.

As the threat of the First World War loomed, the race between rival nations for air power began in earnest.

proved uncomfortable. Garnerin swung like a pendulum, and he was violently sick, but he landed safely.

Progress on more satisfactory lines was taking place in other directions, however. The airship began to emerge from the balloon, and in 1852 Henri Giffard, a French engineer, built the world's first working dirigible. The airship, 132 feet long, was driven by a steam engine developing three horsepower. Giffard made his first flight from Paris on September 24, 1852, and traveled 17 miles at a top speed of 6 miles an hour.

Airplanes around the corner

But not until the end of the century were the practical possibilities of powered lighter-than-air craft demonstrated, by a Brazilian, Alberto Santos-Dumont, and by German Count Ferdinand von Zeppelin. In 1900 Von Zeppelin flew the world's first rigid dirigible and achieved a speed of 20 miles an hour.

In the field of heavier-than-air machines the groundwork had been done by Sir George Cayley, truly the father of aerial navigation. He

MADONNA AND HELICOPTER

A 15th-century French Madonna and Child shows the infant Jesus holding what looks like a toy helicopter that works by pulling on a string wound around a spindle. Surprisingly, toy helicopters were made as far back as the early 14th century.

TOPS FOR IDEAS

How a child's toy revolutionized navigation

Airliners fly on automatic pilot and navigate with great precision around the globe; ships keep a relatively even keel in rough seas; and submarines find their way through the ocean depths—all thanks to a child's toy and an imaginative American, Elmer Ambrose Sperry.

While watching a child's spinning top on a summer day in 1905, Sperry was asked by one of his children: "Why does it stand up when it spins?" It gave him the germ of an idea, which, eventually adapted as the gyrocompass, revolutionized sea and air navigation.

Sperry borrowed a school's electrically powered gyroscope, which was used to demonstrate the rotation of the earth on its axis, and studied it. He began to wonder if the action of the gyroscope—whose axis retained its position whichever way the frame was moved—could be put to practical use by modern engineers.

Later, on a sea voyage to Europe, he was thrown out of his berth during a storm and thought that the gyroscope could be used to steady a ship. After three years of tests he produced the first full-scale stabilizer for the U.S. destroyer *Worden.*

Basically, the principle involved in the use of a gyroscope as a stabilizer is that the gyro's constant axis helps compensate for the movements of a ship and, to some extent, reduces its tendency to roll.

In 1908, using the same principle, Sperry produced the gyrocompass, which stayed on true north and was unaffected by any magnetic influences. First used in 1910, it was quickly adopted as standard equipment by the U.S. Navy.

Further developments from Sperry's ideas followed: the automatic pilot, which, through a system of tiny gyroscopes, can keep a plane on course in clouds or darkness; a direction finder for use in drilling; and a bank indicator, which indicates whether a plane is following a straight course or turning, and by how much.

At his death at the age of 69 in 1930, Sperry had more than 400 patents to his name.

SEEDING THE RAIN CLOUDS

When cannon fire failed to start a downpour

In the 18th and 19th centuries it was noted that it frequently rained after battles in which there had been heavy cannon fire. This was taken to mean that the loud bangs had sent shock waves into the clouds and caused "rain formation."

So early attempts at rainmaking, aside from the rain dances of primitive societies, involved the firing of artillery or the launching, from a large cannon or mortar, of explosive grenades into the clouds.

Some exponents of this technique, lending an authentic air to an otherwise scientifically unproven theory, made inflated claims for their efforts. They suggested that their methods would cause only rain and prevent hail, high winds, and forest fires.

Daniel Ruggles, an American inventor, used a hot-air balloon in 1880 to lift an explosive charge into the clouds, usually before an obviously imminent downpour.

Rainfall is naturally caused by water droplets or ice particles combining in clouds until they are heavy enough to fall. A French meteorologist of the 1930's seeded clouds with ice crystals from an airplane, thinking this would help the formation of snowflakes that would then fall. A light snow followed.

In 1946 two American scientists at General Electric, Irving Langmuir and Vincent Schaefer, found that seeding clouds with pellets of dry ice (solid carbon dioxide) worked even better.

In 1947 another General Electric scientist, Bernard Vonnegut, developed a more economical rainmaking technique—spraying clouds with silver iodide crystals, which then serve as nuclei for snowflakes.

Other nations, such as Australia and Israel, are also trying to "make rain." Israel has claimed that it has substantially increased its annual rainfall.

THE DEADLIEST WARSHIPS OF ALL

No land target in the world is now safe from submarines

In May 1955 the U.S.S. *Nautilus* slid smoothly beneath the waves off New London, Connecticut. Eighty-four hours later it surfaced off San Juan, Puerto Rico.

The vessel's record-setting trip of 1,602 statute miles marked the U.S. Navy's *Nautilus* as the world's first true submarine, perfectly at home under the sea and able to operate for months without either surfacing or touching land to refuel.

In 1957 the *Nautilus* continued its pioneering by making the first trip under the arctic icecap. The next year it made a 2,000-mile voyage under the North Pole from the Bering Strait to Greenland.

Slightly over five years after the *Nautilus* revolutionized underwater travel, the U.S.S. *George Washington,* while submerged off Cape Canaveral, Florida, launched a Polaris missile that flew 1,100 miles downrange and landed precisely on target. On that day, July 20, 1960, man's destructive power was vastly extended; now a vessel under the seas could hit any land-based target in the world.

Nuclear fuel

The key to this awesome development is nuclear power—for propulsion and destruction. The *Nautilus* and the even larger and more efficient Polaris-armed submarines have a nuclear reactor that superheats water under pressure. This water is passed through a heat exchanger so that water in a secondary plumbing system is changed into steam, which then turns a turbine to drive the vessel. In 10 years of underwater prowling, the *Nautilus'* nuclear power plant

used only about 12 pounds of uranium fuel; almost 10 million gallons of fuel would have been needed if the ship used diesel engines.

These amazingly self-sufficient craft, described as "a breathtaking microcosm of American technology," are equipped to obtain two essentials for their existence from the ocean: oxygen and salt-free water. Generators draw an endless supply of oxygen from seawater, and stills extract freshwater from brine.

Knowing that these vessels, despite their advanced technology, depend on the physical and mental well-being of their crews, the navy provides the best possible living conditions: air-conditioning, excellent food, freshwater showers, automatic washers and dryers, movies, hi-fi systems, and library facilities.

The nuclear sub's control center is a highly sophisticated combination of gyros and computers, which, among many other things, can give the craft's location in a split second. Other computer systems plot the trajectories for the Polaris missiles and fire them, locate enemy surface and underwater craft, and control the firing of torpedoes.

Missile carriers

The Polaris-armed submarine, of which there are more than 30 on station today, carries 16 missiles having a combined explosive power exceeding that of all bombs dropped by the Allied and the Axis Powers in World War II.

The Polaris, the first long-range ballistic missile to be launched from a submarine, can carry a nuclear warhead 2,500 miles. Compressed air shoots it from its launching tube and

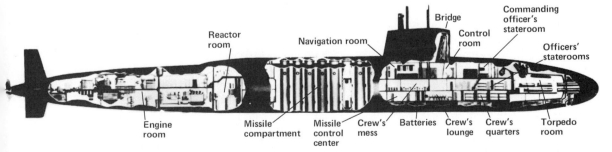

NUCLEAR SUBMARINE. *Diagram of a nuclear fleet ballistic missile submarine shows the various compartments are well separated for safety's sake. The crew's quarters are situated well forward, with the nuclear reactor aft; the missiles with nuclear warheads are located in between.*

into the air. Then a two-stage rocket ignites and lifts the Polaris into a set trajectory and sends it streaking through the stratosphere. Finally, the rocket drops off while the missile zeroes in on its target.

The ancestry of the nuclear submarine can be traced back several hundred years.

In 1620 a Dutch chemist, Cornelius van Drebbel, reportedly submerged in a wooden boat covered with greased leather and propelled by oars.

First combat submarine

The first sub to go into combat, however limited, was the one-man *Turtle,* built by David Bushnell during the American Revolutionary War. Sgt. Ezra Lee, busily cranking a propeller, took the *Turtle* under a British warship in the New York harbor. But when he tried to attach a bomb by drilling a hole in the ship's bottom, its copper sheathing balked him. Both the *Turtle* and the bomb bobbed to the surface; Sgt. Lee escaped, and the bomb exploded harmlessly.

Early submarines

In 1800 Robert Fulton, of *Clermont* fame, demonstrated his submarine, the first *Nautilus,* for Napoleon. The French dictator, at first intrigued, lost interest in Fulton's invention when it failed to sink a British ship during a trial period.

During the Civil War, Confederate marine engineers built the *H.L. Hunley* from an iron boiler. It was propelled by eight men turning a crankshaft attached to a propeller. The *Hunley* sank three times during tests, drowning her crews. But on February 17, 1864, the *Hunley* rammed a torpedo into the Union warship U.S.S. *Housatonic,* on blockade duty outside the Charleston, South Carolina, harbor. The warship plunged to the bottom, and the *Hunley,* the first submarine to sink an enemy vessel, went down with its victim.

In the 1880's and early 1890's, European naval experts tried propelling submarines with steam, but their engines could not operate underwater.

Submarines using electric motors powered by storage batteries performed well, but their range was severely limited because their batteries could not be recharged at sea.

Then in the 1890's two American inventors, John P. Holland and Simon Lake, independently hit upon the idea of taking a gasoline engine out of the newfangled horseless carriage and installing it, along with batteries, in a submarine. When the subs were on the surface, their gasoline engines propelled them at a respectable speed and recharged their batteries. These batteries then provided the power when the vessels submerged.

The *Holland* was bought by the U.S. Navy in 1900, and Lake's *Protector,* launched in 1902, won him contracts from Russia, Austria, and later the United States.

Underwater vision

Lake's greatest contribution was to enable the sub to see when underwater. Until he arranged a collection of prisms, mirrors, and lenses to make a periscope, a submarine had to poke its conning tower above water in order to see, making it vulnerable to attack.

During World War I the Germany Navy, which was no match for Britain's fleet on the surface, went underwater and did tremendous damage to the British merchant marine with U-boats. By this time all subs were powered by diesel engines, which were more efficient and less likely to cause an explosion than a gasoline engine.

Both Germany and the United States used the submarine with deadly effect in World War II, but these craft still had a serious weakness. They had to surface to recharge their batteries and were then vulnerable to patrol bombers using detection gear that pierced the darkness and fog to pinpoint a sub.

Breathing tube

The Germans sought to solve this problem with the *schnorchel* (their slang for "snout"). It was a breathing tube that permitted the sub to run its diesels underwater and recharge its batteries. But these tubes still could be spotted by planes as they cut a wake through the water, and they could also be spotted by radar at night.

Today the problems of propulsion, navigation, and concealment have been solved by the U.S. Navy's deadly nuclear submarines. The Soviet Union also has nuclear subs capable of spreading ruin over the world.

Robert Fulton had hoped that his *Nautilus* would make naval warfare so destructive that nations would eschew it. That state of affairs, envisioned by Fulton, now confronts all the peoples of the world.

SHIPS WITH ROTATING SAILS

In the 1920's the Germans planned to return to wind propulsion

In 1925 the nautical world was startled by the appearance of ships apparently propelled by gigantic cotton bobbins. Their German inventors believed that these vessels were a major breakthrough in sea transport.

Experiments at the University of Göttingen in 1922 gave Anton Flettner, a German engineer, the idea for the revolutionary rotor ship. He had found that wind pressure on a revolving disk was very much greater than pressure on a stationary disk. Rotor ships operated on this principle of propulsion.

The ships had two rotors, each turned by a small engine at its base. The pressure of the wind on the upended cylinders could be increased by revolving them, and the pressure point could be altered also. A beam wind could be used to push on the rear surface of the cylinders, thus driving the ship forward instead of blowing it sideways.

Long before anyone thought of applying the principle to ships, players of ball games had noticed the phenomenon and had even turned it to their advantage. In baseball a pitcher spins the ball so that the air pressure upon the spinning surface curves the ball's path and deceives the batter. Tennis players and others do the same.

The Flettner rotor ship was said to be faster than sailing ships, cheap to run, and efficient to crew. It could fight its way through storms, using only the power of tiny gas engines, no bigger than those used in small cars. An ordinary sailing vessel is required to take down all canvas in a hurricane, while the rotor ship could continue sailing.

On transatlantic voyages rotor ships reached speeds of 17 knots. They were small vessels—about 600 tons—with their two rotors looking like enormous funnels, 65 feet high and 10 feet in diameter.

Cheap to run

Rotor-ship enthusiasts predicted that all the world's shipping would soon be using rotor power. The advantages the rotor ship had over conventional sailing ships were simplicity and economy in handling. The Flettner ship was 80 percent cheaper to run than sailing ships. Whereas several dozen men would be required to handle the sails, a single man could control the speed of the rotors. The rotor ship could also be turned or reversed simply and quickly.

But less than 20 years later the revolutionary new ships were broken up for scrap. The ships had all developed serious mechanical problems because of the rotor's incessant vibration. And they had proved unreliable because of their dependence on wind power.

ROTOR IN MANHATTAN. *Anton Flettner's rotor ship, the* Baden-Baden, *weathered several heavy gales on its transatlantic voyage from Hamburg to New York in 1926. Propelled by two rotating yellow towers, the ship caused a sensation in America.*

SIR HENRY BESSEMER, the British developer of a revolutionary steel-making process, was a constant traveler to the Continent—and a very poor sailor. So he designed a "swinging saloon," which, with the help of a naval architect, R. J. Reed, was incorporated in a new cross-channel steamer, the *Bessemer*. The saloon was balanced amidships on a central pivot and was supposed to remain on an even keel regardless of the ship's motions. But at sea it rolled violently, and the passengers fared worse than those on the upper deck. So Sir Henry introduced a hydraulic brake, to check the motion of the saloon, but this worked even worse than the pivot. The saloon was then locked in position, and the ship was used as a conventional steamer. Unfortunately, it was virtually unsteerable, and on its first trip it collided with the piers at Calais and Dover. Sir Henry sold the ship for scrap, but the saloon found a home at a horticultural college in England. It was "sunk" there by a German bomb in the Second World War.

ALARM TO THE ADMIRALTY

Glass-shutter signals from Portsmouth to London

At the end of the 18th century, bad food, inhuman treatment, and appalling living conditions roused more than 50,000 men of the Royal Navy to mutiny.

On April 13, 1797, an informer on HMS *Sovereign* at Portsmouth told an officer that mutiny was imminent, and only minutes later British Admiralty authorities were handed a message: "Mutiny brewing in Spithead."

The signal had been flashed the 70 miles from Portsmouth to London in three minutes, by means of a remarkable signaling system devised by George Murray in 1795.

Coded messages were sent along a series of relay stations, about seven miles apart and operated by men equipped with telescopes and a special signaling apparatus. This was a large, wooden frame divided into two columns of three shuttered apertures, rather like a window with six panes of glass. The operator pulled a lever to open a shutter and reveal a square of daylight.

Different combinations of opened shutters represented a letter or even a complete word. At night lanterns were used to replace shutters.

The relay stations were on the tops of church towers or hills, with each one in sight of those on either side in the chain. The system linked London with Deal, Portsmouth, Plymouth, and Yarmouth.

ICEBERG AIR BASES

Cold feet only in the Treasury

In the early years of the Second World War, German U-boats were sinking thousands of tons of shipping every month. Convoys escorted by warships were the usual form of protection, but the best defense of all against submarine attack was aircraft patrol.

Aircraft did not have the vast flying ranges and flight-refueling techniques of today, so air cover was limited to within only a few hundred miles of friendly Atlantic coasts.

Pyke's manmade icebergs

Then, in 1942, an English inventor named Geoffrey Pyke put forward a possible solution: giant, manmade icebergs that could be used as floating mid-Atlantic airstrips. These might also be used as halfway refueling stops when ferrying new warplanes from the United States.

Pyke's ice ship would be 300 feet wide and 2,000 feet long—a hollow ice hull like a rectangular box. Aircraft would land on the upper surface, beneath which would be hangars, workshops, crew's quarters, and a refrigeration plant.

The project was named Habakkuk, after a minor prophet in the Old Testament. Habakkuk 1:5 says: "For I am doing a work in your days that you would not believe if told."

Secret research work was begun on lakes in the Canadian province of Alberta. There, during the construction of small-scale prototypes, it was discovered that the addition of 10 percent wood pulp made the ice as strong as concrete and as easy to work as wood.

But there was a snag. When it was found that Habakkuk would cost at least as much to build as a conventional aircraft carrier, enthusiasm waned, and the project was abandoned.

READING FOR THE BLIND

System devised for military use at night

Until 1819 lettering for the blind consisted simply of raised characters of the alphabet made of wood, lead, twigs, or even pins and needles arranged in pincushions. Valentine Haüy, founder of the Royal Institute for Young Blind Persons in Paris, made three-inch-deep letters from cloth.

In 1819, the same year that a 10-year-old blind boy named Louis Braille enrolled at the institute, a French artillery captain tried to interest the Academy of Sciences in Paris in a new system he described as "night writing."

Capt. Charles Barbier de la Serre had devised an alphabet of raised dots and dashes on strips of cardboard that soldiers could "read" with their fingertips when in action at night.

He eventually took his method to the institute, but, because his system consisted of a complex arrangement of 12 dots to each letter, it was not a success.

Braille, now a teenager, became interested in Barbier's system and simplified it. From this he soon developed the now internationally used Braille system.

FLOATING SERPENT

THE "FLOATING SERPENT" is a flexible barge—an alternative to tankers and pipelines as a method of carrying crude oil from wells to distant refineries. It was invented in 1956 by a British scientist, W. R. Hawthorne, who called it Dracone—the Greek word for "serpent." The huge vessel, made of rubber-proofed cloth, could be filled with oil and towed, just beneath the surface of the water, by a tanker. The idea was later adapted as a means of taking freshwater to remote Greek islands. But as an oil carrier, the Dracone was abandoned. It had two drawbacks: It could be towed only at slow speeds and was not suitable for large shipments—quite apart from the pollution risk if it should burst and spill oil in the ocean.

PEDAL FOR THE SHORE

An invention to prevent that sinking feeling

Once the bicycle had developed to the stage where it was powered by pedal cranks and a chain drive, many inventors adopted this propulsion for other vehicles.

One of the most remarkable of these was a one-man, pedal-driven life preserver for use in case of shipwreck. It was invented in 1895 by a Frenchman, François Barathon, and consisted of a saucer-shaped metal dish containing an inflatable rubber bag and some machinery.

The survivor sat on the bag—which kept him and the machine afloat—and worked two sets of cranks, one with his hands and the other with his feet. The cranks turned two propellers, one placed vertically to keep the craft stable and the other to push from behind.

THE FIRST HOTROD

An idea that ran out of steam

The first steam carriage to transport passengers on a highway was designed by Richard Trevithick in 1800. Despite warnings by James Watt that the boiler would explode, the engine ran on a steam pressure of 60 pounds. Watt was opposed to high-pressure engines—his engines seldom ran on more than seven pounds—and said that Trevithick deserved hanging for introducing such a device.

The vehicle had its first outing on Christmas Eve 1801, and three days later Trevithick invited some friends to take a ride. The journey ended abruptly when the carriage broke down, so the travelers made for the nearest inn where they warmed themselves with mulled ale. But the boiler fire was still burning merrily, and when the party returned, the carriage was a smoldering wreck.

A WATERTIGHT CASE

Saving life at sea was an obsession with the Victorians. Many bizarre and impractical ideas were put forward, but one with possibilities was the suitcase-life jacket.

Invented by a German named Krenkel in the 1880's, the case had circular panels in the lid and base that could be quickly removed. The user then fitted a watertight rubber seal into the hole and pulled on the case to encircle his body.

Such a device would probably have kept its wearer afloat for several hours. Moreover, it had the added advantage that a gentleman could politely raise his hat to any lady who happened to be floating by.

HOW MANY MILES TO THE GALLEON?

IN THE AGE of invention one thing that the innovators knew all about was harnessing the wind.

Several road carriages were designed to use this form of power, and one of the most efficient was the sail carriage invented by a Frenchman.

The vehicle was tried out in Paris in 1834 and required a crew of sailors to man the rigging, in addition to the coachman and postilion on regular coaches.

The carriage was called *L'Eolienne*, after Aiolos, the Greek god of the winds, and on its first run it showed an impressive turn of speed.

Steering the carriage must have been a terrifying experience, as the "driver" had no control over its speed.

Stopping the vehicle seems to have been entirely overlooked by the inventor.

Devices such as this were never practical and soon gave way to the steam carriage and later the automobile.

HORSE OF A DIFFERENT COLOR

When the first steam streetcars were introduced in San Francisco in the 1870's, horses panicked at the sight and sound of these snorting monsters. For a while, chaos reigned in the city streets as horse-drawn vehicles careened in all directions whenever a streetcar came into sight. But an inventor named S. R. Mathewson provided the answer. He built a streetcar in the shape of a horse, which could travel at eight miles an hour. The engine, patented in 1876, was gas-fired so that there would be no belching smoke to frighten the horses. Apparently, the idea worked, because order was restored.

FIRST CAR—FIRST CRASH

And the inventor lands himself in court

Nicholas Cugnot, a French artillery officer, was the world's first motorist. Within minutes of starting, he had the world's first motoring accident. And he became the world's first convicted dangerous driver.

His three-wheel vehicle appeared in 1769. A steam-driven, two-cylinder engine drove the front wheel, and Cugnot said his contraption would carry four people at a speed of just under two miles an hour.

But the weight of the huge copper boiler on the front of the carriage made it almost impossible to steer. On its maiden run the machine ran into and demolished a stone wall.

Undismayed, Cugnot spent the next year building a larger version as a gun carriage for the French War Ministry. He demonstrated the new machine on a Paris street. The military observers were impressed, particularly as Cugnot promised that it could carry five tons.

But the steering again let him down, and as he tried to turn a corner, the carriage overturned. The ministry lost interest—and Cugnot lost his freedom. Magistrates sent him to jail and impounded his machine.

By the time he was able to think of modifications, France was in the grip of the Revolution. He moved to Brussels, where he died in 1804.

Cugnot's ill-fated gun carriage was later rebuilt and remains his only monument—in the Paris Conservatoire des Arts.

THE IMPOSSIBLE DREAM

Man's quest for free power

The first law of thermodynamics says, in effect, that you cannot get something for nothing—but that has never stopped people from trying. It is scientifically impossible to build a machine that will run without an external energy supply, yet for centuries inventors have persisted with designs for perpetual-motion machines.

One of the most common was a gravity-operated overbalancing wheel. If a weight is attached near the top of an upright wheel, the wheel will rotate until the weight reaches the bottom. If it were possible to arrange a series of weights around the wheel so that those on the way down were farther from the wheel's center than those on the way up, the result would be an overbalancing wheel that would keep on turning.

Leonardo's attempt

Such a device was designed in the 13th century by the French architect Villard de Honnecourt.

His wheel had seven pivoted hammers that stuck out on the falling side and folded in on the rising side.

Even Leonardo da Vinci designed one in the 15th century, using four radial arms. At the end of each was a metal sphere containing a little mercury. The shifting weight of the mercury was supposed to keep the wheel turning.

A balanced wheel will keep turning for some time, simply because it slows down very gradually. This explains the apparent success of an overbalancing wheel, 14 feet across, built in the 17th century by Edward Somerset, Marquis of Worcester. It was started by hand, then rotated on its own for the few minutes that observers were permitted to watch. But once they had left, fricton began to slow it down until it eventually came to a complete halt.

And back to square one again

Other "perpetual motion" machines used liquids. One naive effort, proposed by the Abbé de la Roque in 1686, consisted of a funnel with its long stem curved around and upward in such a way as to discharge any liquid in it back into the funnel. The inventor hoped that the weight of the water in the funnel would force liquid up around the stem and back into the funnel and function indefinitely.

The fact is that the only way to force water up such a funnel is to install a pump—which would defeat the idea of perpetual motion. For the truth is that you cannot get something for nothing—particularly from machinery.

DELIVERING THE
MAIL—BY AIR

A practical use for the air-tube railway in February 1863. The first mailbags are sent speeding on their way from the post office's Northwestern District Office at Eversholt Street, London, through a pneumatic tube, to Euston Station. Inset: A 1914 variation of Brunel's system—the prototype of the electric train that now moves the mail around London in a similar way.

TRAINS THAT COULD RUN ON AIR

Early attempts to develop air-driven trains

Trains have been powered by steam, diesel oil, electricity, and, experimentally, jet and rocket engines. But in 1844 Isambard Kingdom Brunel, the great British inventor, built a train that was driven by air.

His plan was to pull a train along a tube between the tracks. The lead coach was attached to the 15-inch-diameter pipe by means of a piston arm.

Huge pumping engines every three miles along the track extracted air from the pipe in front of the train, and the pressure behind the piston forced it along.

Brunel built an experimental section of pipe on the South Devon Railway. But the copper and leather pipe valves corroded in the salty air and were chewed away by rats.

Seventeen years later another British inventor, T. W. Rammell, designed a system in which the whole train was blown and sucked along a tube. But the idea of huge tubes crisscrossing the country was unrealistic, and in 1870 pneumatic railways went underground.

That year a 312-foot-long model subway opened in New York beneath lower Broadway. Its 22-seat cars were driven like sailboats, by a blast of air.

But in 1880 electric trains seemed more promising, and the long search for a railway that could run on air was abandoned.

CYCLING ON AIR

JOHN DUNLOP, a Scottish veterinary surgeon living in Ireland, wanted to find a way to protect his son's tricycle from damage on cobbled roads. Robert Thomson, an English civil engineer, had already designed and patented a hollow rubber tire filled with air or horsehair in 1845. But Dunlop was looking for something better, and in 1888 he made a pneumatic tire with a rubber outer casing and an air-filled inner tube, inflated through a valve. This was the first inflatable tire containing air under pressure. André and Edouard Michelin first used the pneumatic tire on motor vehicles in 1895, and five years later the Dunlop Rubber Company produced its first automobile tire.

WORDS ALONG A WIRE

The telephone evolved from attempts to aid the deaf

By an odd coincidence the first message transmitted by telephone, an instrument that has proved such a great boon in emergencies, was a cry for help from its inventor.

At the moment Alexander Graham Bell was ready to test his invention for the first time, he accidentally spilled some acid on his clothes.

So the first words his assistant, waiting in the basement of Bell's home, heard over the receiver from his employer, who was in the attic, were: "Mr. Watson, come here! I want you!"

Bell, born in Edinburgh in 1847, had been trying to design a machine for communicating with the deaf when he stumbled on the basic principles for a telephone. He found that when an iron diaphragm was vibrated by the human voice, close to a magnet around which was a wire coil, a weak current was created. This could be transmitted along a cable to a corresponding diaphragm.

Although Bell is generally acknowledged as the inventor of the telephone in 1876, several others worked to develop a telephone before him, notably the German Johann Philipp Reis, who claimed success in 1861. And in 1871 an Italian, Antonio Meucci, filed a caveat for an invention of his made in Havana in 1849.

But it is doubted that Bell's predecessors transmitted articulate speech, and the German patent office later decided Reis had not invented a "speaking telephone."

Bell later went on to invent the gramophone record, the photophone—which was the forerunner of film soundtracks—the electric eye, and the induction balance.

BELL'S ORIGINAL TELEPHONE. *One of the adman's early attempts to sell it to the public. An extract from the material accompanying this high-powered advertisement reads: "Its employment necessitates no skilled labor, no technical education, and no special attention."*

THE BONE DIGESTER

THE PRESSURE COOKER, found in many kitchens today, was invented some 300 years ago by a young Frenchman, Denis Papin, while working in London to develop a steam engine. His bone digester, as he called it, was a cylinder with a clamped-on lid and the first automatic safety valve, also his invention. In 1679 Papin put on a demonstration dinner for the Royal Society, and the great architect Christopher Wren, who found the meal delicious, requested a booklet on how to use the cooker. Papin wrote that it would render "the oldest and hardest Cow-Beef" as tender as the choicest cut, and it would preserve the flavor and nutrients of meats and vegetables. But it was not until the Second World War that pressure cookers became popular with housewives who were eager to economize.

A LINK BETWEEN CONTINENTS

The first Atlantic cable: a monument to one man's courage

The first successful transatlantic telegraph cable, laid in 1866, was a tribute to the vision and dogged perseverance of a single man, a New England-born entrepreneur named Cyrus W. Field. A highly successful New York paper merchant who had retired from the business with a considerable fortune in 1852 at the age of 33, Field first became intrigued by the possibility of laying such a cable in 1854.

Field first wrote to Samuel F. B. Morse, the inventor of the first practical telegraph, and to Matthew Fontaine Maury, of the National Observatory in Washington, D.C., who was the foremost oceanographer of his day. Both were enthusiastic, and Maury told Field that a recent survey of the North Atlantic had providentially revealed the existence of a submarine plateau between Newfoundland and Ireland that seemed "to have been placed there especially for the purpose of holding the wires of a Submarine Telegraph."

Delighted with this encouraging news, Field set about raising capital. His persuasive talents must have been awesome, for within the year he had been promised help from the British Navy in surveying the route and laying the cable, as well as a pledged subsidy of $14,000 a year from the British treasury until the line was finished. His efforts to obtain financial help from nongovernmental sources were also successful.

Flies in the ointment

His own countrymen were less enthusiastic. In March 1857, however, Congress narrowly passed a bill granting an annual subsidy and providing a ship to help lay the cable.

Back in England, the cable itself was being rushed into production. It was ready by July 1857. Two ships, the British man-of-war *Agamemnon* and the American frigate *Niagara*, had been engaged to lay it out. (The cable's bulk and its weight of one ton per mile made it far too cumbersome for a single ship to carry.)

On August 6 the *Agamemnon* and *Niagara* set sail from Valentia Bay on the Irish coast. The plan was for the American ship to pay out its line as far as midocean; there the British vessel would splice on its section of cable and complete the westward journey to Newfound-land. But the paying-out mechanisms aboard both ships were crude, and 335 miles out to sea the *Niagara*'s section broke—$500,000 worth of cable plummeted to the bottom of the ocean. The two ships returned to Ireland with their remaining cable still aboard.

For the second attempt, in June 1858, a different technique was tried: The *Niagara* and *Agamemnon* met in mid-Atlantic and spliced their cable ends together; then the two ships set off in opposite directions—the American frigate toward Newfoundland and the British ship toward Valentia Bay. But the second effort proved as disastrous as the first. After three breaks in the cable both ships returned to Valentia Bay.

A short-lived success

After a gloomy meeting of the Atlantic Cable Company's board of directors in England, during which several members resigned in exasperation, it was reluctantly agreed that one last attempt should be made. On July 29 the *Agamemnon* and *Niagara* made a final rendezvous in mid-Atlantic and began paying out their cable; this time few on board had much expectation of success. But in spite of repeated near-disasters, both ships arrived at their destinations on the opposite sides of the Atlantic on August 5, 1858, and a halting message was tapped out from the *Niagara* in Newfoundland to the *Agamemnon* in Valentia Bay.

Such a totally unexpected success created wild outbursts of enthusiasm in both the United States and England. A vast celebration was given in Field's honor on September 1 by the jubilant citizens of New York City. But unbeknownst to the celebrants, the cable—which had been working only intermittently from the beginning—had ceased functioning that very day.

When the news came out, public reaction was scathing. Some even suggested that the cable had never actually been laid and that the whole enterprise was merely a gigantic stock manipulation on Field's part. In Britain a commission of inquiry was set up by the Board of Trade, and its report, made in 1860, was surprisingly optimistic: Provided suitable care was taken in the manufacture, laying, and maintenance of a new cable, there was no reason that it should not prove successful.

The final triumph

In 1865, after scores of cable designs had been submitted to and tested by the Atlantic Cable Company, a new line was built. It was 2,300 miles long, heavily armored, and more than an inch in diameter, with a conducting core three times as large as that of the original cable. Altogether it weighed almost twice as much as the 1858 cable but was considerably more buoyant, and luckily, a giant steamer, the British ship *Great Eastern*, the largest vessel afloat, was available to carry this 5,000-ton burden.

When the *Great Eastern* steamed ponderously out of Valentia Bay on July 23, 1865, Field

TRY AGAIN. *Businessman Cyrus W. Field finally succeeded in laying the transatlantic cable.*

and Thomson were aboard, and this time their expectations for success were justifiably high. But the troubles continued. There were three electrical failures in the cable because the overly brittle iron casing sheared off and pierced the wires. In the third instance the weakened cable suddenly snapped, and more than a thousand miles of telegraph line went slithering to the ocean bottom. The ship returned to England.

The latest expedition had failed, but this time failure did not mean catastrophe. The new cable was perfectly sound except for its iron armoring, but this could be improved; and the *Great Eastern* had performed superbly.

By 1866 Field and his colleagues in Britain had ordered 2,400 miles of new cable with an improved armoring of galvanized iron, and on Friday, July 13, 1866, the *Great Eastern* again steamed away from the Irish coast. This time, despite the date, the expedition proceeded with almost uncanny smoothness, and on July 27 the mighty ship, "gliding calmly in as if she had done nothing remarkable," dropped anchor in front of the telegraph house at a place appropriately called Heart's Content on the Newfoundland coast. The *Great Eastern* had not only brought the cable safely across the Atlantic; she had also managed to retrieve the 1865 cable from the sea floor, 2½ miles down, and splice it to the new line—so that two telegraph cables now linked Britain and the United States.

Vindicated at last, Field gratefully tapped out the following telegraph message from Newfoundland to New York:

Heart's Content, July 27. We arrived here at 9 o'clock this morning. All well. Thank God, the cable is laid and in perfect working order.
Cyrus W. Field.

NEXT TO GODLINESS

The inventor who took a deep breath to success

The vacuum cleaner is considered to be a recent invention, but the Victorians had a machine that used bellows to suck up the dirt. Two people were needed to operate it, one to hold the nozzle and the other to operate the bellows. Often it would blow dust out again, but one successful model used water as a filter. This type was so well made that some of them are still in use.

In 1901 a new railway-car cleaner was dem-onstrated at St. Pancras Station, London. It worked on the principle of blowing out the dirt rather than sucking it up. The demonstration did not impress the choking, dust-covered onlookers. But one of them, Hubert Booth, was set thinking. When he got home, he lay on the floor with a handkerchief over his mouth and sucked hard. The dust trapped in his handkerchief convinced him that sucking up dirt instead of blowing it out was the right principle;

an efficient cloth filter in the cleaner would trap dust but let air through.

A "noisy serpent"

Booth's first practical machine was so big that it had to be drawn by a horse. It stood in the road and sucked dirt from houses through a long hose, but the inventor had difficulties with the police because his "noisy serpent" caused passing horses to bolt in terror.

To this day, however, all cylinder vacuum cleaners rely on Booth's principle.

His vacuum cleaner came just 25 years after the first practical carpet sweeper had been marketed by an American china-shop owner named Bissell. Bissell suffered terribly from headaches, and, convinced they were caused by the dusty straw in which his china was packed, he invented a sweeper.

It was a huge commercial success—but it did not cure his headaches.

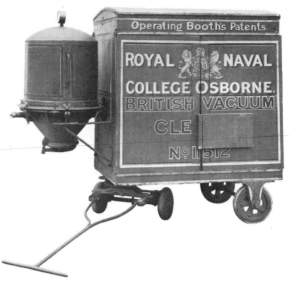

EARLY CLEANER. *This 1905 machine had electrically driven pumps to provide the suction. The cylinder on the end contained the filter.*

THE WIRE THAT CHANGED THE WEST

Cattlemen first hated it, then adopted it

In the early 1800's cattle still roamed free over the prairies and plains of the western United States, making scientific breeding impossible and creating the law of the open range, which allowed free access to water and grazing lands but discouraged farming.

Settlers did attempt to mark their property and protect their crops from cattle and wild animals, but traditional fence-building materials, such as stone and wood, were scarce. Convinced that without suitable fencing large-scale agriculture on the Great Plains was impossible, many farmers gave up and returned to the East.

Then at the 1873 DeKalb County (Illinois) Fair a farmer named Henry Rose exhibited a contraption to keep a troublesome cow from straying. After hammering metallic points into a strip of wood, he attached the strip to his fence. When the cow brushed against it, the sharp points drove her back into her pasture.

The attachment might have remained only a curiosity, but it inspired another farmer to experiment with a cheap and dependable wire-fence design, which would be known as barbed wire, bob wire, and the devil's rope.

Joseph F. Glidden, a New Hampshire-born farmer who had worked his way to DeKalb between 1842 and 1844, created an armored fence made of wire, with barbs placed at regular intervals. He used a coffee grinder to make the barbs. He turned the mill full cycle and wound a piece of wire into an eye; clipped the wire, leaving two sharp points, or barbs, extending in opposite directions; and then strung the barbs on another piece of wire.

To lock the barbs in place, Glidden decided to use two wires instead of one, twisting them around each other and employing a grindstone as a twisting device. He began to manufacture the wire in DeKalb on November 1, 1873, and was awarded a patent on November 24, 1874.

From 1873 to 1900 about 400 different types of barbed wire were devised, but Glidden's "The Winner" design remained the most popular. A new fencing industry grew quickly, from 10,000 pounds made and sold in 1874 to 80.5 million pounds by 1880, as barbed wire proved an effective enclosure for animals, was relatively inexpensive, easily transported, and quickly strung.

Range wars broke out as cattlemen protested the fences, but in the 1880's they began fencing off their own land to allow for selective cattle breeding. The open range was history.

MIGHTIER THAN THE SWORD

Blot was blessing in disguise

Fountain pens were born out of sheer exasperation. In 1884 Lewis Edson Waterman, an insurance salesman, had just won an important contract from several rivals. Waterman handed his client a fine quill pen and a bottle of ink to sign the contract. The pen spattered the document; Waterman hurried away to find another form . . . and a rival stepped in and completed the deal.

This incident spurred Waterman to design the first practical fountain pen with a controlled flow of ink. He applied the principles of capillary attraction—by which sap defies gravity and rises in plants. In the piece of hard rubber linking the pen's ink reservoir and the nib, Waterman cut a hair-thin channel. This ad-mitted a small amount of air into the ink chamber, keeping the internal air pressure in balance, so that the ink leaked out only when pressure was put on the nib.

The first Waterman pens were filled with an eyedropper, a technique soon replaced by the development of flexible rubber sacs, which drew in ink after the air had been squeezed out.

The modern fountain pen can be traced back to a simple reed or bamboo stem used by the ancient Greeks and Egyptians, and to the quill pens of the Romans.

The term "fountain pen," indicating that the pen contained a reservoir, was first used in England in 1710, but they were on the market in Paris in 1656.

THE MULTIMILLION-DOLLAR ZIP

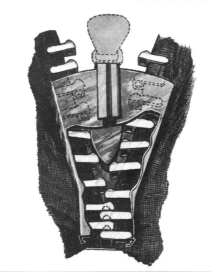

SADLY, the original zip fastener, invented in 1893 by Whitcomb L. Judson, a Chicago engineer, did not live up to its trade name, C-Curity. Its interlocking teeth would spring open or jam.

Then, in 1913, a Swedish-born engineer, Gideon Sundback, turned Judson's unreliable brainstorm into a multimillion-dollar industry. Sundback devised a series of cups on the backs of the interlocking teeth (left), which made it possible for them to enmesh more firmly and reliably.

Sundback's modified zipper has been used in many trades and professions—from agriculture to medicine. It has been fitted on boots for sheep in foot-and-mouth infected areas, and an Austrian surgeon sewed one into a patient's stomach for easy examination. Today more than 250,000 miles of zippers are manufactured every year.

CORSET REBELLION

NO ONE CAN SAY FOR SURE who first invented the brassiere, but in 1914 a New York debutante designed one and was paid $15,000 for the patent. In the years since, the invention has made untold millions of dollars for manufacturers all over the world, and at least $15 million for the corset company that bought the patent. The debutante, Mary Phelps Jacob, had an inventive mind and a deep resentment for the corsets that imprisoned women of her time. One night she and her French maid constructed a brassiere out of two handkerchiefs and some ribbon. Her friends liked the idea, but she failed in her own attempts to market the bra commercially.

DINNER-TABLE RAILROAD

"The meal now standing at platform. . . ." Things never quite went this far in the home of Frenchman Gaston Menier in the 1880's. Nevertheless, dinner was a strange and wonderful affair. Meals were brought straight from the kitchen to the table by the electric railroad pictured below. Carriages bearing the food ran on a four-rail track and were controlled by the host. No servants were needed, nor did guests have to pass the dishes from hand to hand. The train could carry 50 pounds of food at up to two miles an hour. It gave the meal "particular liveliness and intimacy," said one guest.

ELECTROPATHIC BELT

Shock therapy, Victorian style

Victorian England was obsessed with the idea of a "sound mind in a healthy body." Especially the latter! Health gadgets—a few useful, some harmful, most useless but harmless—abounded.

Girls with prominent ears wore "Claxton's Ear-Cap" as they slept. Rheumatic sufferers underwent excruciating treatment on "Zander's Mechanical Exercisers." Sedentary adults bought mechanical horses that simulated riding and came with sidesaddles for women.

But one of the oddest inventions was "Mr. C.

B. Harness's Electropathic Belt." This battery-operated appliance, strapped around the midriff, delivered a series of mild electric shocks. An advertisement proclaimed that the belt "acts upon all organs of the body, rarely failing to alleviate most of the disorders resulting from local or general debility."

It could also "improve the figure and prevent chills," not to mention that it renewed "exhausted nerve form" and cured hysteria. But the one thing it could not do was to survive in the face of advancing medical knowledge.

BLOODLESS SHAVING

WHEN safety razors were introduced in 1903, the public bought 51 razors and 168 blades. The following year, 90,000 razors and 12.4 million blades were sold. The first step toward safer shaving had been taken by a Frenchman in 1771, and in 1828 the Sheffield Company of England produced a razor with a guarded cutting edge. In 1895 King C. Gillette, a Boston bottle-cap salesman, hit on the idea of using wafer-thin slivers of steel that were held in a safety clamp and were so cheap they could be thrown away instead of sharpened. It took eight years to iron out the technical difficulties of mass production—then the shaving revolution was on.

THE CHESS-PLAYING TURK

Ingenious robot or elaborate joke?

Baron Wolfgang von Kempelen was a mechanical genius who intrigued 18th-century Europe with his automaton, which—dressed as a Turk—could not only play chess but win every match it played.

It was never revealed at the time that the Turk was a fake—and the baron a trickster with a dazzling sense of the outrageous to match his considerable mechanical ability.

The Turk was built in Vienna in 1769 and sat behind a chest, four feet long, two feet wide, and three feet high. In front of him was a chessboard on which he challenged all comers, shifting the pieces with unerring movements of his left hand.

Touring Europe's courts

Before each game the baron would open all the chest's compartments, revealing levers, gears, drums, and cylinders.

Emperor Joseph II of Austria sent the Turk on a tour of Europe's courts where it duly beat its royal opponents, including Empress Catherine of Russia and Napoleon—whose chess does not seem to have equaled his military strategy.

A widely held belief was that the chess was played by a series of talented midgets!

The truth was that a man squeezed into the chest and manipulated the Turk. He kept in touch with the game through a series of magnets attached to the base of the pieces. Below the board small iron balls were suspended by threads. The balls stuck to the roof of the chest because of the magnets above them. When the chessmen were moved, the hidden accomplice could follow the game by watching the balls also moving.

The facts about what the baron always regarded as a "mere trifle" to amuse the Austrian court were not known until after Von Kempelen died in 1804, and the automaton was taken to the United States. It was eventually bought by the Chinese Museum in Philadelphia, where it was destroyed by fire in 1854.

MACHINE OR MIDGET? *Von Kempelen's chess player in all his Eastern glory. The opened doors reveal the baron's puzzling array of levers, gears, drums, and cylinders. But skeptics alleged that the chess was played by talented midgets.*

OPEN THIS END

Today's can opener has a long history

A can of veal, taken on Sir William Parry's Arctic expedition in 1824, was labeled "Cut round on the top near to the outer edge with a chisel and hammer." The can was the product of Britain's first cannery, set up in London, in 1812, but the pioneers of canned foods had given little thought as to how their product should be opened.

AN ARCTIC SURVIVOR. *This can of veal was once part of a ship's "iron" rations. The problem of opening it was solved by the carpenter.*

Bryan Donkin, a partner in John Hall's Dartford Iron Works, adapted the idea of Nicolas Appert, a French confectioner who is generally regarded as the "father of canning." Appert had sealed food in glass jars, then boiled it. This process won him a French government award with which he established the first cannery—the House of Appert—in 1812.

Donkin used iron cans coated with tin, and by 1818 he had supplied 27,779 pounds of preserved meat to the British Admiralty. As an alternative to the hammer and chisel, a Frenchman, Angilbert, proposed in 1833 to modify the can so that it could be opened by melting the solder around the lid. Another French inventor, Bouvet, suggested a steel wire soldered between the lid and the body of the can, which could be removed by applying heat.

The first can openers were elaborate mechanisms, used by shopkeepers before the can was handed over to the customer.

The introduction of tinplate in the 1860's made the cans easier to open, paving the way for small can openers. The earliest of these was the bull's-head type, still used today, which had a steel blade attached to a cast-iron handle.

After that a variety of shapes and sizes were patented—from scissor-handled types to the butterfly-screw models still in use.

HATS OFF TO THE INVENTORS

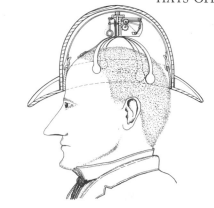

THE VICTORIAN male's custom of raising his hat to ladies had its drawbacks. A gentleman laden with parcels, for example, would first have to set them down. But in 1896 James Boyle of the state of Washington invented a self-tipping hat. The wearer simply nodded to activate a lifting mechanism in the crown. Boyle noted that the device could also be used for advertising; a sign or placard could be placed on the hat, and the novelty of its movement would attract attention. In 1912 the Canadian Patent Office recorded another self-raising hat. It worked hydraulically by squeezing a rubber bulb.

TEETHING TROUBLES

Once, only the upper set could afford upper sets

False teeth are at least as old as the Etruscans, the rulers of central Italy before the Romans. Human skulls with false teeth carved from bone and ivory and with gold bridgework have been discovered, dating back to 700 B.C.

But for centuries the dental skills of the Etruscans were forgotten, and generations of men and women suffered agonies from toothache and looked old before their time because of the sunken cheeks that resulted from losing their teeth. When England's Queen Elizabeth I lost her front teeth, she resorted to stuffing layers of cloth under her lips to fill out her face.

For many years medieval quacks preserved the myth that worms in the gums caused toothache and decay, and often made a public entertainment of their "treatment" and extractions—without anesthetic. Usually, a clown capered and gestured to keep the crowds amused, while an assistant held down the patient and the quack yanked out teeth. Sometimes, an assistant would bang a drum to drown out the cries of agony.

Hand-carved dentures

By the end of the 17th century, crude dentures, hand-carved in ivory, were available to the rich. The mouth was usually measured with compasses, and individual false teeth were tied to their neighbors with silk threads.

Full sets for the lower jaw were made, but top sets were difficult to keep in place.

As the demand for new teeth increased, the poor would often sell their teeth to the rich to buy food and clothing. But some of the more flamboyant figures of the English court commissioned ornamental teeth in silver, gold, or agate.

Even at this stage, however, the teeth had to be removed when eating.

Teeth transplants

Some fashionable women had their gums pierced with hooks to keep their dentures in place. But early in the 18th century, a Parisian dentist named Fauchard made upper and lower sets, coupled together with steel springs. This kept the upper set in position, but closing the mouth required quite an effort.

For a time during the 18th century, transplanted teeth became popular, with donors' teeth being wedged into sockets made in the recipients' jaws.

Shortly before the French Revolution, an Italian dentist, Guiseppangelo Fonzi, practicing in Paris, manufactured individual porcelain teeth set in gold or platinum plates. These were introduced to England by a Frenchman, Dubois de Chémant, late in the 18th century.

In 1817 Anthony A. Plantou is reputed to have introduced porcelain teeth to the United States, and shortly afterward, J. Leon Williams improved the appearance of artificial teeth by molding the plates to the contours of the face. Sets became available in three basic face shapes: square, tapering, and oval.

Teeth from the dead

Even with the introduction of artificial teeth, human teeth continued to be used. Aging dandies wore "Waterloo teeth"—extracted from the dead at the 1815 battlefield of Waterloo. Teeth from the dead of the Civil War (1861–65) were also shipped to England.

From 1845 a much-improved type of porcelain tooth was made by Claudius Ash, an American dentist who disliked handling dead people's teeth. Ash introduced vulcanite—a composition of sulfur-hardened rubber—to the casting of gums in which the teeth were set.

As molded plates fitted better and were firmer, suction pads and coil springs were eventually discarded.

At one stage before the turn of the century, cheap celluloid teeth were introduced. But they were highly inflammable, and at least one man is said to have suffered when his teeth caught fire while he was smoking.

Modern denture plates are often made from plastic acrylic resin, although porcelain is still preferred for the teeth.

In the late 1950's an American chewing-gum company, which was trying to solve the problem of its product sticking to false teeth, produced teeth to which their gum would not stick. The dentures were coated with polytetrafluoroethylene (PTFE), the substance now widely used in many ways—from the finish on nonstick frying pans to artificial arteries.

QWERTY—THE TYPIST'S BURDEN

The machine with the deliberate flaw

The job of the typist is made unnecessarily difficult owing to a deliberate flaw in the basic design of the typewriter itself—the curious layout of its keyboard letters.

As long ago as 1714, Queen Anne granted a patent to an Englishman named Henry Mill for the manufacture of a machine "whereby all writings whatsoever may be engrossed on paper or parchment so neat and exact as not to be distinguished from print."

THE FATHER OF QWERTY. *"A blessing to mankind—and especially to womankind,"* Christopher Sholes said of his invention, the modern typewriter.

No one knows how Mill's invention worked, or even what it looked like, but there were others throughout the world who worked on the same idea.

The first American patent for something like a typewriter was granted in 1829 to William Austin Burt, of Detroit, for "Burt's Family Letter Press." Four years later Xavier Projean, of Marseilles, France, produced a "Machine Criptographique." It would, he said, record words "almost as fast as one could write with an ordinary pen." Credit for the first modern typewriter, however, belongs to Christopher Sholes, a newspaper editor who lived in Milwaukee in the 1860's, and two associates, Carlos Glidden and Samuel Soulé. On the Sholes' model, as on present-day manual typewriters, each character was set on the end of a metal bar that struck the paper when its key was pressed. The keys were arranged alphabetically.

Keys to success

But there was a snag. When an operator had learned to type fast, the bars attached to letters that lay close together on the keyboard became entangled with one another. Sholes' way out of the difficulty was to find out which letters were most often used in English and then to position them on the keyboard as far from each other as possible.

This lessened the chance of clashing type bars. In this way was born the QWERTY keyboard, named after the first six letters on the top line of letters.

Delighted with it, Sholes wrote, "A blessing to mankind—and especially to womankind."

BRAMAH'S LOCK

ONE OF THE 18th century's most prolific British inventors was a Yorkshire farmer's son, Joseph Bramah. Among his brainchildren were beer pumps, a toilet, a machine for numbering banknotes—and his famous lock. He patented the lock in 1784—11 years after he walked 170 miles from Yorkshire to London to seek a living. Until then, any lock—cheap or costly—could be picked by anyone with a little skill. Bramah claimed that his barrel-shaped lock, with 494 million possible combinations of notches, was totally burglar-proof. He was so confident that he offered a 200 guinea prize to the first person who could pick it. The prize went unclaimed for 67 years until an American locksmith, Alfred Charles Hobbs, finally picked the lock—after a month's work. Nevertheless, the design was so effective that the Bramah lock and variations on its design are used to this day.

Daring and epic journeys

·

SOUTH OF THE MIDDAY SUN

How the Phoenicians rounded Africa—and proved it

Nobody believed the Phoenicians when they claimed—2,000 years before the Portuguese explored West Africa—that they had sailed around the Dark Continent from Suez to the Strait of Gibraltar.

The most incredible part of their story was that, as they had rounded the southern tip, the midday sun had been to the north of them. Every man in the ancient world knew that the sun was *always* in the sky's southern half. And so it is—in the Northern Hemisphere.

Even the great Greek historian Herodotus, who reported their story 150 years later, dismissed such a notion. Yet the Phoenician adventurers undoubtedly did make the journey they claimed. And what convinces modern scholars is the very detail that led the ancient world to believe they were telling a pack of lies: the report of the sun on their right at midday as they sailed west around the Cape of Good Hope.

The Pharaoh's idea

Not even the exploring Phoenicians could have guessed that what was always true of the sun's position in the north temperate belt of the Mediterranean was never true south of the Tropic of Capricorn. It would never have crossed their minds to invent such an unlikely story unless they had seen the phenomenon.

The voyage itself was planned by an Egyptian Pharaoh, Necho, about 600 B.C. He became intrigued by the possibility of sailing from Egypt's east coast on the Red Sea to Alexandria on its north coast. Rather than build a canal across the desert (as Ferdinand de Lesseps did 2,450 years later when he built the Suez Canal), Necho thought it would be a fairly simple journey to follow Africa's southern coast around to Morocco.

Because his own people were not great seafarers, he hired crews of Phoenicians together with a small flotilla of their own 50-oared sailing ships. He ordered them to sail down the Red Sea and around Africa to the Pillars of Hercules, now known as the Strait of Gibraltar.

Rowing into the unknown

The Phoenicians were happy enough to be hired, because they were eager to find a new route to their western markets, avoiding waters controlled by their Greek rivals. But neither they nor Necho had any idea of the shape or the vast size of the continent they were to sail around.

According to modern reconstructions of their voyage, the Phoenicians set off in November—rowing to the eastern tip of Africa at Cape Guardafui before turning southwest with the monsoon winds.

For month after month they pushed on down the coast—farther than anyone before them—constantly expecting the coastline to sweep around to the west and north and point the way home. But to their dismay it did not.

Instead, they noticed anxiously that the sun was slipping across the sky to their north. And the polestar from which they took their bearings vanished altogether. The explorers must have despaired until, finally, the coast swung west.

They plowed on along the 500-mile tip of the continent until, in May of the year after they set out, they rounded the Cape of Good Hope and the coast dropped away to the north.

The relieved crews stopped to plant some of the wheat they had taken with them. In December they sailed northward—and each day the sun climbed higher and higher in the sky.

At long last, home

It took them at least 10 more grueling months to fight their way around Africa's huge northwest bulge, and they made another long stopover somewhere in Morocco to restock their food supply. At last they sighted the familiar Strait of Gibraltar.

More than two years and 13,000 miles after they cast off in the Red Sea, the Phoenicians sailed triumphantly up the Mediterranean to Egypt—only to wait 2,000 years for vindication.

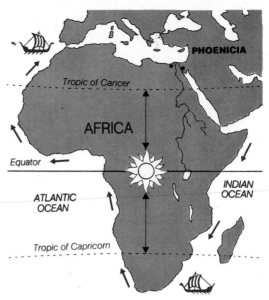

SUN TO THE NORTH. *A map of Africa shows the relation of the sun to Gibraltar and the Cape of Good Hope. The sun never moves north of the Tropic of Cancer or south of the Tropic of Capricorn. Thus, to the observer in the Mediterranean the sun is always to the south, while to a sailor rounding the Cape of Good Hope it is always in a northern direction.*

OVER THE EDGE OF THE WORLD

The man who shone a light on the Sea of Darkness

Beneath the cliffs of Cape Bojador, on Africa's west coast just south of the Canary Islands, the Atlantic boils and foams in constant fury. Seas crash into unseen gullies and explode like geysers into spume-laden columns.

Beyond this point lay the Sea of Darkness, a maelstrom inhabited by monsters and the spirits of dead mariners—the end of the world. The cape marked the point of no return.

Such were the terrifying reports that chilled the souls of European sailors in the 14th and early 15th centuries. Their fear was so great that it slowed the pace of exploration down the west coast of Africa.

Then, in 1434, a Portuguese mariner named Gil Eannes, urged on by Prince Henry the Navigator who chafed at this barrier to discovery and scoffed at the superstitions, resolved to find out what really did lie south of Bojador.

Gil Eannes dealt with the fears of his crew with reason and common sense as he set course for the end of the world.

The results must have surprised the fainthearted among his crew, for there was no threatening promontory and no treacherous reef—only an innocent coastline. Shoals of sardines flashing in the water gave the appearance of silver seas. The ocean swelled as winds conflicted with currents, and wind-blown desert sand occasionally darkened the sky as they sailed southward.

Rounding the low cape, Gil Eannes and his crew found nothing unusual: There was no sinister whirlpool; there was not even a monster in sight.

Their fears now behind them, they followed the coastline for another 30 miles. Then, landing on a sandy shore 900 miles from home, they spotted a familiar plant, rosemary. They gathered a bunch for their prince and turned back to the north.

It had taken 15 attempts over a period of 15 years for the Portuguese sailors to summon courage and sail beyond the legendary edge of the world. Gil Eannes' bold venture opened a door to a new surge of discovery by other Portuguese navigators, and the remaining thousands of miles of Africa's west coast were mapped in less than 70 years.

THE MAN WHO DISCOVERED BRITAIN

He described frozen seas—but few believed him

On his return from a sea journey north to the Atlantic about 300 B.C., the Greek explorer Pytheas said of Britain: "The island is thickly populated and has an extremely chilly climate. . . ." Of its people he found them to be "unusually hospitable, and . . . gentle in their manner. . . . Their diet is inexpensive and quite different from the luxury that is born of wealth. . . . It [Britain] has many kings and potentates, who live for the most part in a state of mutual peace."

Yet few believed him. Unfortunately, nothing remains today of Pytheas' book, *The Ocean*. But his contemporaries knew of it, and most of them regarded his descriptions of the strange things he saw as masterpieces of fabrication. For centuries most scholars remained tongue in cheek when they wrote of his "discoveries."

But from the recounting of his voyage by the historian Diodorus and the geographer Strabo, both of the first century B.C., we are able to reconstruct his trip.

Pytheas was the first Greek to visit and describe Britain and its people and, possibly, to sail within sight of the Icelandic coast.

The Britons, Pytheas reported, "are simple in their habits, and far removed from the cunning and knavishness of modern man . . . they do not drink wine, but a fermented liquor made from barley, which they call *curmi*."

At the time of his epic journey, the northern waters of the Atlantic were unknown to Pytheas' contemporaries. How could they—familiar only with the warm waters of the Mediterranean—believe that he had seen chunks of ice floating in the ocean? Or that farther north the sea was entirely frozen and the sun never set?

Pytheas became a subject of controversy, for although the Greek scientist Eratosthenes and a few others believed him, the attitude of most was typified by Strabo who ridiculed Pytheas' claim that, a day's sail from an unknown northernmost land called Thule, he had encountered a congealed sea. "As for this substance," Strabo wrote, "he affirms he has beheld it with his own eyes."

Whether Thule was Iceland or Norway is still debated. The congealed sea, most modern scholars think, may have been a glaze of fragmented drift ice.

Pytheas' voyage covered 7,000 miles. He circumnavigated Britain and in various places went ashore, where he saw people harvesting grain and tending cattle. In Cornwall he visited tin mines, and he touched the coast of Denmark in search of amber.

On his return home he said that Ireland lay to the west of Britannia. Strabo disagreed, placed it north of Scotland, and was believed.

Belatedly, Pytheas has been recognized as a great explorer and the first to reach the northern seas.

THE TRAVELS OF MARCO POLO

A 25-year adventure to the Empire of Kublai Khan

The sight was breathtaking for a young man barely in his twenties. There before him was a city more magnificent than any he had ever seen before. He considered that its beauty might lead an inhabitant to imagine himself in paradise. There were landscaped highways, public parks, marinas, and canals with hundreds of arched bridges—many of them so high that vessels with masts could pass beneath. There were underground drainage systems, police and fire brigades, and a postal service.

Quite staggering . . . especially for a youth who lived 700 years ago. He was Marco Polo, one of history's great travelers, and the magnificent Hangchow was just one of the cities within the mighty Empire of Cathay (the ancient European name for China).

Marco Polo wrote in his diary of Hangchow's preeminence over all other cities in the world. To him it was even more beautiful than the Emperor's Capital of Peking or Marco's own Venice.

Marco was one of a widely traveled family. His father, Nicolo, and uncle, Maffeo, had already made the trip to China, and before they had started back to Venice, the Emperor had made them promise they would return. They did in 1272 and took the then 17-year-old Marco with them.

Their three-year journey was arduous. They sailed to Ayas, a busy port in southeastern Turkey, and then traveled by caravan across the entire width of Asia. Their route took them through Iran and northern Afghanistan, over the high Pamir Plateau, along the lower Silk Route, and then across the Gobi Desert into Mongolia. At last, in May 1275, the Polos reached Kublai Khan at his summer Capital just north of China's Great Wall. That autumn they accompanied him to his winter Capital, Peking.

Marco described their fight to climb frozen mountain ranges and their battles against torrential rain, sandstorms, floods, and avalanches. In Afghanistan they were delayed for a whole year when Marco became ill. Bandits and local wars forced them to make many detours and new plans.

Stones that burned

He later wrote of the wondrous sights and strange people they encountered. He was amazed by the "veins of black stones [coal] which, when lighted, burn like charcoal and give out a considerable heat." He saw "a substance spurting from the ground and used for burning in lamps [oil]," and examined "a material which could be spun into thread and woven into a cloth that would not burn when thrown into a fire [asbestos]." He described crocodiles as "huge serpents ten paces in length with jaws wide enough to swallow a man" and yaks as "wild cattle that may be compared to elephants." Coconuts were "nuts the size of a man's head, pleasant to taste and white as milk."

The Emperor was so impressed with his young guest that he took him on hunting trips on royal elephants and gave him the run of his opulent marble palaces and summer resorts. Marco was dazzled by the gilded carvings, art treasures, and the elegant courtiers of the Emperor's world. He wrote that emissaries were sent out every two years to find 100 or more beautiful concubines to fill the harem.

Marco was the first Western man to describe China and its bordering countries, the first to outline a route across the Asian continent, and the first Westerner to see the Pacific Ocean.

ADVENTURER EXTRAORDINARY. *Marco Polo wearing the Tartar costume in which he reappeared in Venice after 25 years of travel in Asia. On his deathbed he said, "I have not told half of what I saw."*

While his father and uncle amassed a fortune by trading, Marco spent 17 years working for the Emperor, who made him his personal emissary and sent him on missions across the Empire. He visited such places as Indochina, Burma, and Tibet during this period. Later he served three years as Governor of the rich city of Yangchow, a center of arms manufacture, with 24 towns under his jurisdiction. And, it is possible that he became commissioner in the Emperor's imperial council in the Capital, but the records are not clear.

By then, however, the ruler was past 70 years of age, and the Polos decided they might not be safe under any of his rival successors when he died. Early in 1292, in boats specially fitted out on the Emperor's instructions, they sailed from the port of Zayton.

FLOURISHING TRADE CENTER. *The Polo family set off from their home in Venice in this scene in a 1338 French manuscript. They were spurred by the already thriving trade in goods from the Orient.*

When they arrived in Venice—after an absence of nearly 25 years—no one recognized them, not even their own servants, who refused them admission to their own villa. They had long ago given their masters up for dead.

To convince people that they were not impostors, the three Polos were hosts at a banquet, and after their still-doubting guests had been wined and dined, the Polos produced their travel-torn Tartar clothes, then dramatically cut the seams to let a shower of precious gems fall out.

This was considered to be conclusive evidence of their claims, for who, they thought, but the Emperor of Cathay could have provided such riches?

Probably the world would never have heard about Marco's travels if it hadn't been for the fortunes of war. Three years after his return to Venice, the city clashed with its rival in trade, Genoa. Marco, who served as a "gentleman commander" of a galley, was captured and thrown into a Genoese jail.

Happily, he managed to use the time wisely. Employing the notebooks he had kept for Kublai Khan to refresh his memory, he dictated his memoirs to a fellow prisoner. When the volume of his travels, *A Description of the World,* was first published, it was denounced as a pack of lies.

Even on his deathbed in 1324, a priest urged him to retract some of his tallest tales. With his last breath Marco declared: "I have not told half of what I saw."

MASTERS OF THE PACIFIC

The Polynesians navigated the great ocean by sense of touch

Throw a stone into a large lake, and the pattern of ripples set up will be disturbed by any rocks that break the surface. Given a chart of the ripples, it would be possible for someone with a knowledge of mathematics to calculate the rocks' positions.

Enlarge the pond to the size of an ocean, substitute waves for ripples and islands for rocks, and it is still possible to apply the same principles to pinpoint the location of an island 100 miles away.

Some 2,500 or 3,000 years ago the ability to

read the messages of the waves in this way helped a race of master navigators to reach and colonize almost every habitable island in the vastness of the Pacific.

The Polynesians had no maps to guide them, no compasses, no sextants, no telescopes, not even a written language through which to hand down the lessons of experience. Yet over a period of 1,000 years they populated a huge triangular area covering more than 12 million square miles from Easter Island in the east, to Hawaii in the north, and New Zealand in the south.

They were able to do so because of their knowledge of the stars and their sensitivity to the sea. They noticed that when waves hit an island, some were reflected back in the direction from which they came, while others were deflected at angles around the island to continue in altered form on the other side. Investigating the phenomenon further, they acquired sufficient knowledge of the behavior of the waves to be able to reckon the location of an island possibly 50 to 100 miles away.

When the Polynesians first showed their *mattangs*, odd-looking webs of interlocking bamboo sticks to foreigners, the Western seafarers thought they were a primitive sort of map. But they were something quite different—devices for instructing boys in the principles of wave motion. The *mattang* demonstrated all the basic patterns that waves can form, and with its help a young navigator could learn to interpret the different wave movements.

Sense of touch

It was an intricate science and an intimate one, for it was not possible to read the waves from a height—a high cliff or an airplane. The Polynesian sailor had to be so close to the waves that he could feel their motions.

He would go to the bow of his canoe, crouch down in the hull, and literally feel the different sets of waves below. Within minutes he would be able to determine the position of the nearest island, intervening reefs, and other islands.

Of course, the Polynesians did not ignore the visible signs of a tropical island, which appear long before the island itself comes into view. Birds and flotsam indicate land—and often the direction in which it lies. And a stationary cloud bank on the horizon means there is an island anywhere up to two days' sailing away.

For local use maps of individual islands and

groups were made, showing islands with shells or pieces of coral fastened to shaped sticks.

Mysterious origins

Using these methods, the Polynesians explored most of the Pacific. Yet where they came from originally is a mystery, for their culture cannot be traced back to the Asian continent, and they were definitely not South American. It is known that nearly 3,000 years ago they passed through Fiji in Melanesia, settled in Tonga, and then moved on to Samoa.

Isolated from the plagues that swept the mainland, populations exploded, and an island's food resources soon became exhausted. And so they moved again—their women, children, animals, fruits, and seedlings as carefully guarded as possible against the elements.

About 2,000 years ago they reached the Marquesas. From there they made voyages to Easter Island, Hawaii, and New Zealand.

They traveled these vast distances in pairs of 60- to 80-foot dugout canoes, made with stone and shell tools, and lashed together with a deckhouse between them. Although the Polynesians spread throughout the Pacific, they remained a single culture, so that to this day a Maori visiting Hawaii can understand the local language.

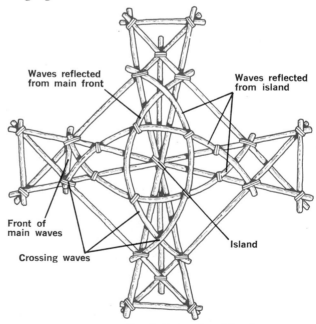

Waves reflected from main front

Waves reflected from island

Front of main waves

Crossing waves

Island

AID TO NAVIGATION. *Interlocking webs of bamboo sticks*—mattangs—*were used by the Polynesians to teach the science of wave motion.*

THE WESTWARD URGE

The men who discovered America

Few lands have been discovered as often as America. According to various claims, voyages to the New World had been made by the Phoenicians, Irish, Vikings, Welsh, and Chinese long before Christopher Columbus reached the Caribbean in 1492. And, of course, most scholars agree that America was discovered thousands of years ago by Asians who crossed the narrow Bering Strait to Alaska, then spread south and east across North America and on southward to South America. Columbus called these people Indians because he thought he had reached India.

The Chinese claim was made in recent years by a Peking University professor who asserted that five Chinese had sailed the Pacific to Mexico in A.D. 459. A sixth-century legend of the Chinese tells of a Buddhist monk, Hoei-Shin, who sailed 4,000 miles east from Japan and found a continent called Fusang. Was this America? No one has answered this question.

Junks could have been blown across the Pacific to the coast of America, but if they were, no trace of these wind-tossed ships and their crews has been found.

Did Irishmen reach America?

Historians have established that Irishmen discovered and settled Iceland and were driven out by Norsemen about A.D. 870. Did the Irish sail on to America? Samuel Eliot Morison, unsurpassed chronicler of voyages and voyagers, writes that the sagas describing Norse discoveries call a certain land near Greenland "White Man's Land" or "Ireland the Great." One Icelander named Bjorn was said to have sailed west about the end of the 10th century and vanished. Many years later, another Icelander, Gudlief Gunnlangson, was deposited by a western gale in a country where he was seized by natives who seemed to speak Irish. Their aged leader, whom Gudlief recognized as Bjorn,

LANDFALL? *The 30 miles of sand at Cape Porcupine in Labrador may be the "wonderful beaches" beyond the sea described in Viking sagas about the Norse expeditions to Vinland.*

ON COURSE. *This steering oar on a restored longship, used on raids in Europe, is 1,000 years old.*

rescued him from these "rough Irish" and sent him on his way.

Another Norse saga tells of captives in a western land who reported seeing white people who "wore white garments and yelled loudly, and carried poles before them to which rags were attached." Comments Morison: "Just what an Irish religious procession would have looked like to Indians! But if Irishmen did reach America in the ninth and tenth century, they never returned, and left no trace. . . .Some day, perchance, authentic Irish relics will be found in northeastern Canada; but until that time comes we have only these elusive stories of an Irish colony glimpsed vaguely through northern mists."

The elusive Welshman

Even more elusive is the legend of the Welshman, Prince Madoc ap Owain Gwynedd, who is supposed to have landed on the shores of Mobile Bay in 1170 and left behind, with the Indians, the Welsh language. On this shaky foundation of fact or fancy was built the theory that the light-skinned Mandan Indians of the upper Missouri River were descendants of Welshmen. Explorers of the West and scientists have exploded this theory, but it still titillates the imagination of some students of America's past.

Discovery by Norsemen

The Norse discovery of the New World rests on a sound foundation of documentary evidence, ruins, and burial grounds found in Greenland and archeological findings in Newfoundland but not on any solid proof of Norse settlements on the North American mainland.

In the 8th to 10th centuries the bold, adventuresome Norsemen made a living raiding the coasts of Europe. For these hit-and-run raids they used the long, narrow Viking warships, swift and maneuverable. For trading, they used a short, one-masted vessel about 40 to 60 feet long, called a *knorr.* In these ships they made incredibly long voyages, using neither maps nor compasses. Instead, they navigated by the sun and stars, and used their knowledge of the behavior of seabirds to estimate where and how far the nearest land was.

According to ancient accounts, a Norseman named Bjarni Herjolfsson was blown off course on his way to Greenland and sighted America in A.D. 986. Some 15 years later, so the sagas

go, Leif (the Lucky) Ericsson, the son of Eric the Red, who had discovered and colonized Greenland, paid a visit to Norway. There, Leif was converted to Christianity and was ordered by King Olaf to carry the faith back to his homeland. In 1001, soon after his return trip to Greenland, Leif decided to find Bjarni's flat woodlands. He came to a "place where wild grapes and self-sown wheat grew," which he named Vinland the Good. He built huts and spent the winter there and then sailed back to Greenland.

The mystery of Vinland

Seven years later Thorfinn Karlsefni, a Greenland trader, tried to establish a colony in Leif's Vinland. He landed at Leif's settlement with about 250 colonists. But in three or four years, after a clash with the natives, whom he called *skrellings,* Karlsefni returned to Greenland.

Historians have speculated endlessly about where Vinland was. If Leif found wild grapes, he could have been in Nova Scotia or possibly Cape Cod. But the findings at L'Anse aux Meadows in Newfoundland seem to establish it definitely as the site of Leif's colony.

Relics or jokes?

The discovery of other "relics" argue that Norsemen may have moved inland to Ontario about A.D. 1000 and into the Red River Valley of Minnesota in 1362. A "Viking" sword, an ax, and an iron handle of a shield discovered in a grave in Ontario were authenticated by experts, but Samuel Eliot Morison believes these relics were planted by a practical joker. He also ascribes to pranksters the Kensington Stone, found in Minnesota. It purported to describe in runic characters the massacre of Scandinavian explorers by Indians in 1362.

Finally, Columbus

Finally, in 1492, Columbus sailed the Atlantic and reached the New World, although he didn't know it and spent several years trying to locate the Asian mainland.

Still the experts and would-be experts continue to debate and write about the earliest discoverers of America. Perhaps Mark Twain hit the nail on the head when he observed: "The researches of many commentators have already thrown much darkness on this subject, and it is probable that if they continue we shall soon know nothing at all about it."

NEW WORLD WAS FOUND BY MISTAKE

The arrogance and stubbornness of Columbus showed the way

As Ferro, the most westerly of the Canary Islands, faded astern, the crew of the square-rigged little sailing ship piously crossed themselves. Before them lay the open Atlantic—the great and terrifying unknown.

Only the captain was undismayed. He ordered his men to sail due west day and night for 2,400 miles and, in case land was not sighted by then, kept a false second log to show his crew. In it he deliberately underestimated the distance sailed.

Four days later the compass needle began to veer west of north. The crew was confused and asked questions about the route. The captain was as unsure as they, but he covered his doubts by saying that the polestar was causing the needle to fluctuate. The earth's magnetic variations were then unknown, and he did not know that the compass was, in fact, working perfectly.

The ship sailed on with its two accompanying vessels—across a seemingly limitless ocean. The name of the ship was the *Santa Maria,* and its captain was Christopher Columbus.

With every passing day Spain was farther away, and the crew became increasingly anxious about the chances of getting home again. Their nerves were raw as they continued toward an unknown destination. But Columbus sailed onward, despite threats of mutiny.

Driftwood and birds

After 32 days out of sight of land, and 69 days out of Spain (they had set sail on August 3, 1492), they spotted some branches with green leaves. On the next day, October 12, the small fleet arrived at an island called Guanahani by its dark-skinned natives. Columbus renamed it San Salvador, or "Holy Saviour," and claimed this Bahamian island for Spain.

To the end of his days Columbus firmly believed that the islands he found were off the eastern coast of Asia. But he remains in history as the man who, against great odds and with little support, opened the New World to European adventurers.

Many of the so-called facts popularly accepted about Columbus are untrue. For example, he was not the only man of his day who believed that the earth was round and not flat. Most scholars and men of science also shared this view.

Nor was it the belief that the world was flat that at first made King Ferdinand and Queen Isabella of Spain refuse to back the Genoa-born sailor's project of trying to find new sea routes to the Indies.

Spain had been fighting constant wars with the Moors when Columbus asked for royal patronage, and they were not eager to spend more money on a purely speculative venture.

Extravagant demands

Then, in 1491, when Columbus made another approach—he had already been rejected by John II of Portugal—it was his extravagant and audacious demands that made Queen Isabella reject him. Columbus had asked to be named Admiral of the Ocean Sea and viceroy of all lands he discovered, with the right to 10 percent of all treasure he might find on the voyage.

It was finally only the jealous rivalry for discovery between Spain and Portugal that prompted the Queen to change her mind and give him all he asked.

So, with about 90 men, including a doctor for each ship and a translator whose Arabic Columbus thought would be helpful in China or Japan, the *Santa Maria* and her attendant ships, the *Pinta* and *Nina,* set sail on the world's most famous voyage of discovery.

On reaching the New World, Columbus spent many weeks sailing among the beautiful Caribbean islands. Then, on Christmas Day, the *Santa Maria* was wrecked on a reef off Haiti, and so in January, Columbus headed back to Spain on the *Nina.*

He made three more voyages to the New World—on the fourth he steered along the coast of Central America, searching for a strait into the Indian Ocean, for he believed he had reached Malaya.

Eventually, through ambition and arrogance, he fell out of royal favor and, racked with arthritis, he died on May 20, 1506, an almost forgotten and a deeply disappointed man.

Ironically, the huge continent he had discovered was named after his friend, Amerigo Vespucci, an Italian merchant and explorer, the year after Columbus died.

218

LAST VOYAGES OF CHRISTOPHER COLUMBUS

was reinterred in Santo Domingo, in what is now the Dominican Republic. Then, in 1795, when Santo Domingo fell to France, it is thought he was removed to Havana. But in 1902 the admiral was disturbed once more and returned to Seville —or so it was thought.

In 1877 another vault was discovered beneath the Cathedral of Santo Domingo, containing a coffin bearing the initials "C.C.A.," believed to represent "Cristóbal Colón, Almirante [Admiral]." Within, an inscription read "Illustrious and famous gentleman, Don Cristóbal Colón." Dust supposedly from this coffin was enclosed in two lockets (above) and was put up for sale in 1973, but bidders were skeptical. It is believed, however, that his authentic remains are in the Cathedral of Santo Domingo.

COLUMBUS, adventurer extraordinary, died at Valladolid, Spain, in 1506 and was buried in a church there. Three years later his coffin was removed to Triana, near Seville; 32 years after that his body

THE WORLD'S WORST CORNER

Sailing men who have lived to tell the tale of Cape Horn

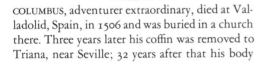

On all around-the-world voyages, one frightening, natural obstacle looms ominously—the worst corner of the world. Cape Horn, the bleak, southernmost tip of the South American continent, was once the only ocean passage between the Atlantic and the Pacific and is a focus for the worst nautical weather of the Southern Hemisphere.

Winds blowing across the wide wastes of the South Atlantic for thousands of miles are deflected by the mountain wall of the Andes through the narrow gap between Cape Horn and the South Shetlands. Waves blown along by endless westerly gales, backed by a steady eastgoing current, force a huge volume of water through the same narrow cleft in the opposite direction. As the seabed rises sharply, rollers build to frightening heights—to 120 feet or more.

Heavy seas and strong headwinds might last for months on end. In the days of sailing ships, the Horn was a terrible challenge—men froze or fell overboard, ships ran aground on rocks or collided with icebergs. In December 1905 a ship called the *British Isles* took more than 10 weeks to fight her way through these waters, a time that was by no means unusual.

For yachts and other small sailing ships these

remain the most dangerous seas in the world. Certainly yachtsmen have braved them: Chichester, Rose, Blyth, Knox-Johnston. But, as they have freely acknowledged, they were lucky in not meeting the Horn at its worst. However seaworthy, however well-handled a yacht may be, there comes a stage where waves are simply too big for a small ship to cope.

In January 1957 Brigadier Miles Smeeton, his wife, Beryl, and their friend John Guzzwell set out from Australia in the 46-foot ketch *Tzu Hang* to round the Horn the "easy way"—from west to east. It was a venture that nearly cost them their lives. After seven weeks, running hard before strong westerlies, they were approaching the Cape.

Increasing violence

By St. Valentine's Day (February 14) the sea was white with breakers and the wind so strong that all sails were taken in, and the boat ran on under bare masts with 360 feet of rope trailing astern to hold her in check.

The barometer had begun to rise, signaling better weather, but the wind continued strengthening. The waves started breaking with increasing violence, until one higher and steeper by far than all the rest caught *Tzu Hang* from astern, hurled her end over end, snapping both masts off at the deck, tearing away the cabin roof, half filling her with water, and hurling Beryl Smeeton into the sea, despite her safety harness and lifeline.

Yet all three survived. Beryl managed to swim back to the waterlogged yacht, and the three were able to bail out most of the water and patch the hole with planks from a bunk, a locker door, and spare sails. Then, with the weather improving, they improvised a makeshift mast and sail and ran for shelter toward the Chilean coast. After 1,500 miles they reached Talcahuano, where the damage was repaired.

In December, Miles and Beryl Smeeton set sail again. By Christmas Day they were well on their way to the Horn for the second time. But once again the barometer dropped, and the wind and sea kept rising as *Tzu Hang* raced southward. This time the white breakers were hitting her beam on. Once again the barometer stopped falling when the storm reached its peak, but at 4 a.m. on December 26 the yacht was hit by another monstrous wave and rolled over, this time sideways.

Once again the masts were snapped, the cabin hatches torn away. Yet once again the Smeetons survived. Just as before, they bailed out the water, rigged emergency sails, and headed for shelter—this time 1,100 miles away at Valparaiso.

The *Tzu Hang* had been savaged by Cape Horn weather twice in succession—yet the Smeetons were running with the wind and sea behind them, in the middle of the summer.

Bravery in a small boat

To sail against such violent winds and mountainous waves is well-nigh impossible in a small boat. Yet a Frenchman, Marcel Bardiaux, sailed single-handedly around Cape Horn, in a tiny, 30-foot, home-built boat, from east to west in midwinter.

On May 7, 1952, Bardiaux approached the Horn by Le Maire Strait, between Staten Island and the coast of Tierra del Fuego. When the wind blows against the tide, the breakers in this wild stretch of water are big enough to threaten steamers, so Bardiaux hoped to time his entry at slack water, when conditions would be at their calmest. But strong winds had held him back. It was 14 degrees below freezing, and there was a storm on the way. He was desperately tired and decided to rest. The only possible anchorage was a small bay, on the mainland coast. There was a heavy sea running, and the bay was swept by fierce currents; the only shelter was a small pool at the end of a narrow channel, studded by rocks. It was pitch dark, and the tide was rushing Bardiaux's boat out of control toward the waiting reefs. All he could do was heave three anchors overboard and tie a mooring rope to a nearby rock.

Frozen sails

When the weather calmed, he ran his boat on a sandbank, so that he could sleep for the first time in three days. After 10 hours he was off again—but after heavy snowfalls during the night, his sails were frozen stiff, and he had to soak them in seawater to make them pliable.

Without warning, hurricane-force winds battered his vessel, and when Bardiaux went below to fetch a sea anchor, two huge waves rolled his yacht over.

Sails, cabin shelter, and everything breakable were smashed or swept away, the hull was full of water, and Bardiaux was soaked to the skin—a serious problem with the temperature well below freezing.

But before changing into dry clothes, Bardiaux trailed his mooring rope astern as a makeshift sea anchor while he bailed out the water. He hoisted spare sails, but it was another 10 hours before he could anchor properly. By then, he was suffering from severe frostbite and exposure.

Freezing spray

After a two-day halt the Frenchman returned to the attack on the Horn—blinded by freezing spray and hail. He tacked for 48 hours against snow-swept wind and sea, and on one occasion conditions became so bad that he had to boil water, kettle by kettle, to thaw out his sails.

Then, at 12:30 p.m. on May 12, Bardiaux looked astern through half-closed eyes and saw a headland through the driving snow. It was a steep land mass streaked with snow running down into narrow gullies. Bardiaux realized that he was looking back at Cape Horn. He was safely around the corner at last.

AUSTRALIA'S FIRST SETTLERS

Mutinous and fugitive murderers

Australia's first European settlers may have been two Dutch mutineers who were set adrift off the western coast in 1629—159 years before the first English fleet arrived in Sydney Cove on January 26, 1788.

In 1628 the Dutch merchant ship *Batavia,* commanded by François Pelsaert, left Holland with a United East India Company fleet, bound for the East Indies. The ship carried valuable cargo, including 12 chests of money, jewels, silverware, and other merchandise.

The ships became separated in a storm, and just before sunrise on June 4, 1629, the *Batavia* struck a coral reef in the Wallabi group of the Abrolhos Islands off western Australia. She broke into pieces a week later.

The ship's complement of about 300 people—some of them adventurous men and women bound for the Indies in search of fortune—struggled ashore on two of the low, barren islands. Most of the provisions were salvaged, but there was an acute shortage of water, and Pelsaert, after a vain search, sailed in a dinghy to seek assistance in the East Indies.

With him were the skipper of the *Batavia,* the chief mate, other officers and men, two women, and a baby. They made the dangerous 2,000-mile voyage in about a month, arriving on July 5, 1629.

The Governor of Batavia (now Djakarta) lent Pelsaert the yacht *Sardam* to go back and rescue the castaways.

But during Pelsaert's absence one of the *Batavia*'s crew, Jerome Cornelius, had assumed command of the survivors, who were scattered over three islands. With several accomplices Cornelius planned to seize the rescue ship and, taking the money chests and jewels, embark on a career of piracy. Those who would not join him were to be disposed of.

Meanwhile, one party of survivors, led by Webbye Hayes, had found water on a distant island and lit three fires to signal their success. The same day Cornelius ordered a general massacre in which 125 men and women were brutally killed. Some had their throats cut; others were hacked or clubbed to death, or drowned.

Wearing gold- and silver-embroidered velvets and elegant silks, the mutineers drank great quantities of rum and wine. Cornelius, who had appointed himself "captain-general," wore a red jacket, richly trimmed with gold.

Warned by refugees

But he realized that he would not be safe until Webbye Hayes and his men had been eliminated. However, refugees from the massacre, who had escaped by swimming or on rafts, warned Hayes, and he was able to beat off two attacks.

Cornelius then tried to negotiate a peace treaty, to which Hayes agreed on condition that he and his party would be allowed to leave the island unmolested. In return, he agreed to surrender a small boat to Cornelius. Cornelius immediately broke the treaty and secretly sent letters to men on the island, trying to persuade them to desert Hayes. These men showed the letters to Hayes, and when Cornelius visited the island with a handful of followers to discuss terms, he was attacked and captured.

The fight between the loyalists and the mutineers was still raging when Pelsaert returned in the *Sardam*. Hayes alerted him, and when the mutineers tried to board the *Sardam*, they were seized. Each was tried by the officers of the *Sardam*, put in irons, and tortured. Cornelius had both his hands cut off before being hanged on Seal Island.

Two mutineers, however—Wouter Loos and a boy named Jan Pelgrom de By—were set adrift in a small boat. Neither was heard from again, but rumors arose that they had landed on the mainland.

Certainly, light-skinned aborigines who might have been descendants of the marooned Dutchmen were seen in the various coastal areas of western Australia.

For many years it was believed that the site of the *Batavia*'s wreck was on the extreme tip of the Abrolhos, but in 1963, Dave Johnson, a fisherman, discovered the hulk 45 miles to the north.

On the islands divers found coins, a seal, sword hooks, keys, glassware, and two macabre relics—a human ankle bone and a male skeleton with a twisted jawbone and sword cleft on top of the skull.

A FAMILY'S BID FOR FREEDOM

Fear and desperation sowed seeds of hope

Famine swept through New South Wales, Australia. The harvest had failed, grain stocks were low, and there was strict rationing among the convicts in the penal settlement at Sydney.

Many of the hungry convicts, transported to Sydney Cove in 1788 to found the colony, tried to escape. Some thought they could walk to China, which they believed was connected to

AUSTRALIA BOUND. *Mary and William Bryant were among the first lot of convicts to be sent by ship to the colony, which was 12,000 miles away.*

the Australian mainland. They either died from exhaustion or were killed by hostile aborigines. Others took to the sea, and few of these were ever heard of again.

But among those who chose the sea route and who succeeded in making one of the most daring escapes were William and Mary Bryant.

They had been convicted, independently, at Exeter (England) in 1786: she for stealing a cloak and for street robbery with violence; he for "interrupting revenue officers in the execution of their duty." Mary Broad, as she was then known, had been condemned to death at the age of 21, but the sentence was commuted to seven years in the colony. William Bryant, 27, a Cornish fisherman, had also been transported for seven years.

They had sailed on the *Charlotte*, and during the eight-month-long journey she had given birth to a daughter whom she named after the boat. Four days after their arrival, the couple had married. A year later she had given birth to a boy whom she named Emanuel.

Inspired by Captain Bligh

Frightened of impending famine, they decided to make a bid for freedom by sailing to the island of Timor 3,254 miles away. Bryant was inspired by Capt. William Bligh's amazing feat of rowing across the Pacific in an open boat after a mutiny aboard his ship, the *Bounty*.

Through his job with the harbor fishing fleet, Bryant acquired a small single-masted boat and, with their children and seven other convicts, set sail on March 28, 1791, under cover of night.

They steered north along Australia's eastern coast, navigating through mountainous and gale-whipped seas with amazing skill. Often their attempts to land to carry out repairs or look for food were thwarted by hostile natives.

Crossing the Arafura Sea, the escapees skirted the coast of Timor and more than two months later, on June 5, arrived at Kupang. There, Bryant told the Governor that they were survivors of a brig wrecked off New South Wales.

But the party began to quarrel, and the Governor became suspicious. Then in September 1791 a Captain Edwards and some of the crew from HMS *Pandora*, which had been wrecked in the Torres Strait while searching for the *Bounty* mutineers, reached Kupang, and the Governor had Bryant, his wife, and companions arrested. They were taken, in irons, to Batavia, on the island of Java, and there both Bryant and his baby son died. On the way to Cape Town three more of the party died, worn out by their adventures.

The remaining four convicts with Mary Bryant and her daughter were then transferred to a London-bound ship. The child died en route, and when the ship reached Portsmouth in June 1792, the survivors were sent to prison.

Nearly a year later, and on the insistence of writer James Boswell who heard of their plight, Mary Bryant was given a pardon. Six months later the four men were granted their freedom.

THE COCKLESHELL HERO

Doctor "shipwrecked" himself to prove a theory

Robinson Crusoe was lucky. When he was shipwrecked, he found a desert island that enabled him to stay alive until rescue came.

Thousands of seafarers have been less fortunate. In peace and especially in war, men have pulled away from sinking ships in lifeboats only to die of thirst or starvation.

Their plight so appalled a French doctor, Alain Bombard, that he resolved to do something about it. Many of these deaths, he believed, were unnecessary. A castaway adrift without food or water, with only an open boat and his own resources, should be able to keep himself alive far beyond the known limits of human endurance in such a situation.

The method he chose to prove his theory was one that scientists have used for centuries: He made himself the guinea pig. On October 19, 1953, he set off from the Canary Islands in a 15-foot rubber cockleshell of a boat to cross the Atlantic to the West Indies. To make the experiment as realistic as possible he took no provisions—not a scrap of food, not a drop of water.

Bombard did not accept the popular belief that drinking seawater sends a thirsting castaway mad and hastens his death. His theory was that shipwrecked men who suffered this fate had made the mistake of not drinking seawater until their bodies were already dehydrated.

From the time he set off, he was careful to drink 1½ pints of seawater every day, supplemented by water squeezed from fish caught with a makeshift harpoon. To ensure he did not fall a victim of scurvy, he trailed a net of closewoven cloth in which he scooped up plankton. One or two teaspoonfuls a day of these tiny organisms, which float on and near the surface of the water, provided the vitamins to reinforce his meager diet.

Almost at the start of his voyage a storm nearly wrecked his tiny craft. His sail was ripped, and his spare was torn away; he had to repair the original with needle and thread.

After a fortnight his poor diet, combined with constant drenchings, caused him to break out in a painful rash.

Hair raising

The storm led to the most hair-raising experience of all. Diving overboard one day to retrieve his single comfort, an inflatable cushion, which had blown away, he was horrified to discover that his sea anchor, a parachute-type canvas gadget used to slow the boat down, had fouled in its trailing rope and the dinghy was rapidly drifting away. Suddenly, the contraption righted itself; the "brake" worked, and he managed to haul himself back on board.

But his biggest disappointment came on the 53rd day when he hailed a ship to ask his position—and found that he had another 600 miles to go.

He thought of giving up. His experiment in survival had already been vindicated. But a meal on board the ship revived his spirits, and he decided to continue.

He reached Barbados on Christmas Eve, having sailed more than 2,750 miles in 65 days. He had lost 56 pounds, but he was alive and well. He had proved his point.

SEND IT BY BOTTLE

Messages can cross the world sealed with a cork

Paolina and Åke Viking were married in Sicily in the autumn of 1958, thanks to a far-traveling bottle. Two years earlier Åke, a bored young Swedish sailor on a ship far out at sea, had dropped a bottle overboard with a message asking any pretty girl who found it to write.

Paolina's father, a Sicilian fisherman, picked it up and passed it to his daughter for a joke. Continuing the joke, Paolina sent off a note to the young sailor. The correspondence quickly grew warmer. Åke visited Sicily, and the marriage soon followed their first meeting.

Surviving hurricanes

Fragile as it is, a well-sealed bottle is one of the world's most seaworthy objects. It will bob safely through hurricanes that can sink great ships. And for most practical purposes glass lasts forever. In 1954, 18 bottles were salvaged from a ship sunk 250 years before off the English coast. The liquor in them was unrecognizable, but the bottles were good as new.

It is impossible to predict the direction a bottle will take. Of two bottles dropped together off the Brazilian coast, one drifted east for 130 days and was found on a beach in Africa; the other floated northwest for 190 days, reaching Nicaragua.

Speed is also bound to vary according to wind and current. A bottle might be completely becalmed or, if caught up by the Gulf Stream at its raciest, might travel along at four knots and cover as many as 100 miles a day.

The longest voyage

The longest bottle voyage ever is thought to have been made by a bottle known as the Flying Dutchman. It was launched by a German scientific expedition in 1929 in the southern Indian Ocean. Inside was a message, which could be read without breaking the bottle, asking the finder to report where he found it and throw it back into the sea.

It apparently caught an eastgoing current, which carried it to the southern tip of South America. There it was found, reported, and thrown back again several times. Eventually, it moved out into the Atlantic, then again into the Indian Ocean, passing roughly the spot where it had been dropped, and was cast ashore on the west coast of Australia in 1935. It had covered 16,000 miles in 2,447 days—a respectable average of more than 6 nautical miles a day.

Charts compiled from bottles

When he was postmaster general for the American colonies, Benjamin Franklin realized that, because their whaler captains knew the currents much better than their English counterparts, American ships were crossing the Atlantic much quicker than the British mail packets. He therefore compiled a chart using both the whalers' lore and information he obtained by dropping bottles into the Gulf Stream and asking the finders to return them. The information he recorded is little changed today.

Since then both the British and U.S. Navies have used bottles extensively to compile intricate current charts. And the movement of oil slicks, mines, and even fish have been predicted with the help of seaborne bottles.

Of course, a number of bottles have been dispatched containing strange messages. Elizabeth I once received an intelligence report by this means and was so disconcerted to find it had been opened by a boatman at Dover that she appointed an official Uncorker of Bottles and decreed that no unauthorized person might open a message-carrying bottle, on pain of death.

In 1875 the crew of the Canadian bark *Lennie* mutinied and murdered the officers. A steward who was spared because he could navigate steered them to the French coast, telling them it was Spain, and surreptitiously dropped several bottles over the side revealing the whole story. The French authorities found one, boarded the ship, and arrested the surprised mutineers.

Torpedoed destroyer

A message found on a beach in Maine in 1944 read: "Our ship is sinking. SOS didn't do any good. Think it's the end. Maybe this message will get to the U.S. some day." It was identified as coming from the USS *Beatty,* a destroyer torpedoed with heavy loss of life somewhere off Gibraltar on November 6, 1943.

In 1953 a bottle was found in Tasmania 37 years after it had been dropped overboard by

FÜHRER'S END?

This message floated in a bottle in the North Sea for a year before being found on the Danish coast on November 26, 1946. It claims that Adolf Hitler did not die in the bunker in Berlin but lost his life aboard the German U-boat Nauecilus, *which sank on November 15, 1945, after colliding with a wreck near Gedser lightship on the way from Finland to Franco's Spain. The message, probably a fraud, is written on a page allegedly torn from the* Nauecilus *log.*

two Australian soldiers on their way to France in a troopship.

The mother of one of the soldiers recognized the handwriting of her son who had been killed in action in 1918.

Delayed message

The strangest case was perhaps that of Chunosuke Matsuyama, a Japanese seaman who was wrecked with 44 shipmates in 1784. Shortly before he and his companions died of starvation on a Pacific coral reef, Matsuyama carved a brief account of their tragedy on a piece of wood, sealed it in a bottle, and then threw it into the sea.

It was washed up 150 years later in 1935 at the very seaside village where Matsuyama had been born.

HORSEBACK TREK FOR HELP

Farmer's 10-day ride brought relief to besieged town

Shortly before midnight, Dick King and his Zulu servant boy stole quietly into the darkness and crept unseen to South Africa's Durban harbor. There they were rowed out, their horses swimming behind them, to Salisbury Island. Behind them lay a beleaguered British garrison fighting desperately for its life. Ahead stretched 10 days of hardship and hazard—10 days that helped to shape the history of South Africa.

The date was May 24, 1842. Durban was then little more than a sprinkling of scattered homes and farmsteads occupied by British settlers who had founded the town in 1835.

But in August 1841 a group of Boer farmers, after leaving the British-ruled Cape Colony, proclaimed their own Republic of Natal. They were followed by a force of 250 soldiers sent by the Governor of the Cape to reoccupy the territory and reassert British control. Furious, the Boer farmers threatened to drive them out of Durban. The British, outnumbered by more than six to one, fought back fiercely and dug in for a siege. Chivalrously, the Boers allowed the women and children to be evacuated to a cargo ship in the bay. Meanwhile, supplies and food for the fighting men left behind were running out.

The situation was desperate. Somehow word had to get to Grahamstown, a British base some 300 miles south across a wasteland of wild, mostly undeveloped country.

Dick King, a 30-year-old farmer, knew that only a man with his hunting skills and knowledge of the country could stand a chance of getting through—and even his chances were slim. But he volunteered, and with his servant boy, Ndongeni, saddled up on Salisbury Island, in Durban Bay—chosen because at low tide the sea swept out and exposed a wide stretch of sand that he might cross and so outflank the Boer lines where they thinned out toward the coast.

The route to Grahamstown was crisscrossed by creeks and rivers. There were no railroads, bridges, or roads. Snakes and crocodiles infested the low-lying areas, and there were lions and savage warrior tribes on the veld.

Worst of all, Boer patrols might turn up anywhere. So, for safety, King and his companion slept and rested during the day and traveled at night. Sometimes they had to dismount and swim across rivers, leading their horses behind them.

After 200 miles Ndongeni could take no more. Then King himself, hungry, weary, and sick, became too weak to sit in the saddle and had to take two days to recover his strength.

He struggled on alone. But his horse reached the limit of endurance. At Butterworth a friendly trader exchanged it for a fresh mount.

The last great hazard of King's ride was Kaffirland, a bush territory peopled by hostile natives. Fortunately, King spoke their language and was able to persuade them to allow him safe conduct.

On June 4, 11 days after he had set out, he rode up the main street of Grahamstown to the

CITY'S HERO. *A tribute to Dick King, whose epic ride saved the town's British garrison from disaster in 1842, is in Durban.*

military headquarters and delivered his message to the commander. A month later he was back in Durban with the seaborne troops who relieved the beleaguered settlement.

DR. LIVINGSTONE'S DARK CONTINENT

He took faith and science to the ends of the earth

The man who opened up more of the world's surface than anyone else in history owed his success to a burning faith, a medicine chest, and unfailing good manners.

Wherever Dr. David Livingstone traveled in unexplored Africa, he always treated the Africans with courtesy—even the witch doctors, whom he called his "professional brothers."

It was only by chance that Livingstone ever came to Africa. Born in 1813 in Blantyre, Scotland, he was sent to work in a local spinning mill at the age of 10. By working 12 hours a day, he paid his way through medical school in Glasgow to become a missionary doctor in China.

But his hopes were dashed by the Opium Wars, which made it impossible for him to work in China. In 1840, at the age of 27, he decided to go to Africa instead.

In the 19th century most of Africa's 11.7 million square miles were totally unknown. To Europeans and Americans it was the Dark Continent, a place of impenetrable, disease-ridden jungle inhabited by savages and ferocious animals.

When Livingstone first went to Africa, he had no interest in exploration; he traveled only to establish his Christian missions and provide medical assistance. But within a few years he was gripped with wanderlust. As he later wrote, "The mere animal pleasure of traveling in a wild unexplored country is very great."

Exploring the unknown continent

On foot, by canoe, and sometimes on ox-back, he traveled thousands of miles through the lower third of the continent. With him he always carried a medicine chest, a Bible, and a "magic lantern," a crude slide projector for illustrating his missionary lectures.

Livingstone had great facility with languages, fine powers of observation, insight, and more rapport with the Africans than had most white people of his time. These qualities enabled him to give the outside world its first intelligent and sympathetic view of African cultures.

He also brought to light the horrors of the slave trade run by the Arabs and Portuguese. Sickened by what he saw, he vividly reported it and stirred Europe into action to help bring it to an end.

In addition, Livingstone sent careful charts and geographic reports back to the Royal Geographic Society in London, and he made note of strange medical cases and health problems. He reported that the bite of tsetse flies brought "certain death" (a type of sleeping sickness) to cattle, horses, and dogs, and observed that "Myriads of mosquitoes showed, as they probably always do, the presence of malaria." He survived his own bouts of the disease with doses of quinine.

Livingstone soon became convinced that if Africa was to be Christianized it would have to be done by Africans. The duty of white men, he felt, was to introduce commerce that might one day supplant the profitable slave trade.

Livingstone never completely abandoned his role as a missionary doctor, but his discovery of the Zambezi River in 1851 was the turning point in his career.

He had married the daughter of a fellow missionary in 1844, and they had several small children, one of whom had died of fever in infancy. Now, wishing to be unencumbered and free of worry about his family, he took them to Cape Town and sent them off to England.

First to cross Africa

Alone and free, he learned to use a sextant and chronometer and began to explore for a great navigable waterway which would open Africa to Europeans who would bring Christianity and commerce with them. In the next few years he traveled from the Atlantic coast of Angola to

THE DRAMATIC MEETING. *The American Henry Stanley (left) greets the Scotsman who explored the Dark Continent. But Dr. Livingstone was an exhausted man, and two years later he was dead.*

the coast of Mozambique, becoming the first white man to cross Africa. Sailing back to England in 1856, he was received by an enraptured world, and his first book, *Missionary Travels and Researches in South Africa*, was an instant bestseller.

Soon Livingstone went back to his beloved Africa, this time as "Her Majesty's Consul" for eastern Africa. He had broken with the Missionary Society, and now he headed a large expedition with the aim of opening up territory for industry.

But Livingstone was bogged down with the problems the expedition presented. He felt impeded by the dozens of straggling bearers, the tons of supplies, and the large English riverboat sent along. He was a poor leader, querulous and stubborn, and his relationship with his English associates became impossibly strained. A total disaster, the expedition was terminated in 1863.

Search for the Nile

Later, in 1866, he started out again, on a quest for the Royal Geographic Society—to search for the source of the Nile River.

Livingstone was exhilarated, for once again he was on his own, with only a small retinue of Africans. But again he was plagued with problems. Some of his bearers fell ill, and a few deserted out of fear of the slavers and the warlike tribes of Tanganyika (now Tanzania). His medicine chest was stolen, and soon his own health broke down.

Suffering agonies from malaria, hemorrhoids, and dysentery, but tenacious in his determination to track down the Nile, he explored the great watershed around Lake Tanganyika. Finally, his supplies and energy exhausted, he and his little party lay up in the village of Ujiji, on the eastern shore of Lake Tanganyika.

Enter Stanley

Meanwhile, the world had become alarmed about him. His flow of letters had ceased, and no one knew whether he was dead or alive. In February 1871, reporter Henry Morton Stanley, on assignment from the *New York Herald*, set out to find Livingstone.

Stanley himself was a remarkable character. A penniless Welsh waif, he had shipped to New Orleans as a cabin boy, then drifted into journalism, and had become a star reporter.

Stanley started out from Zanzibar with a large caravan and bountiful supplies. Following up rumors of the doctor's whereabouts, he reached Ujiji village nearly nine months later, on November 10. There Stanley saw the emaciated figure of the explorer, standing in the clearing before his tent and staring in astonishment at the search party that had come so far to his rescue. The meeting between the two men has since become legendary—and something of a vaudeville joke. But the historic moment was charged with suppressed emotion, as Stanley conveyed in his autobiography: "I walked up to him, and doffing my helmet, bowed and said in an inquiring tone—'Dr. Livingstone, I presume?'

"Smiling cordially, he lifted his cap and answered briefly, 'Yes.'

"This ending all skepticism on my part, my face betrayed the earnestness of my satisfaction as I extended my hand and added, 'I thank God, Doctor, that I have been permitted to see you.'

"In the warm grasp he gave my hand, and the heartiness of his voice, I felt that he also was sincere and earnest as he replied, 'I feel most thankful that I am here to welcome you.' "

"Much work to do"

Stanley's rescue came none too soon, for Livingstone was very ill. Nevertheless, he refused Stanley's invitation to return to the certain triumph that awaited him in London. "I still have much work to do," he said. After four months Stanley left, and Livingstone, now well supplied with medicine and food, pressed ahead in his search for the Nile.

But he was a dying man. In the coming months he became so weak that, at times, he was carried on a litter. Wandering in circles, he came to a village in Ilala District on the edge of a swamp. There on the morning of May 1, 1873, his bearers found him kneeling by his bedside in an attitude of prayer, his head resting on his hands. They could not rouse him.

From village to village the message was spread. Africans came by the thousands to pay their last respects. His personal servants, Susi and Chuma, knew that the doctor's own people would want his body for burial. But first they removed his heart and buried it where it belonged, in the soil of Africa.

It took nine months for Susi and Chuma to make the perilous trip to the coast with Livingstone's remains. From Zanzibar a British steamer brought the body home, where it was laid to rest in Westminster Abbey.

THE FLOATING SCOTSMAN

Canoeist who opened up Canada

While his companions watched in silence, the 29-year-old Scot mixed vermilion pigment with grease and scrawled across a rock his title deed to one of the most prodigious feats of exploration in North America's history: "Alex Mackenzie from Canada by land, 22d July 1793." The rock may still be seen—a memorial to the first white men to cross the continent north of Mexico.

Mackenzie was born at Stornoway in the Hebrides, Scotland, in 1764, but he grew up in America where his father took him after his mother died. He went to school in New York and Montreal and then joined the North West Company, a firm of Montreal-based fur traders, who sent him to their most westerly outpost at Fort Chipewyan, now in Alberta.

Lure of the West

Having traveled there by canoe, his enthusiasm for exploration was aroused. He shared his company's ambition of reaching the Pacific and reaping the harvest of sea-otter pelts then being monopolized by Russians from Siberia.

Poring over the scrawled charts and notes of a trailblazer named Peter Pond, with whom he had spent a winter, Mackenzie reckoned that the rivers flowing northward must eventually turn west and empty into the Pacific, providing a northwest passage. So, on June 3, 1789, with 13 companions in three canoes, he started north on a river ending no one knew where. His surmise was false; the river did not turn west. Instead it took him to the Arctic Ocean. The vast Mackenzie River system, as it was later named, was now on the map of Canada.

But the discovery only disappointed the young Scotsman. The road to the Pacific still eluded him.

During the winter of 1791–92 Mackenzie studied geography and navigation in London. Then, in the fall of 1792, he rejoined his men at an outpost they had begun to build on the Peace River, beyond Fort Chipewyan. And there they wintered.

Not until May was Mackenzie able to proceed, with nine companions and 3,000 pounds of supplies, all tucked into a 25-foot birch-bark canoe.

The going was easy until the party encoun-

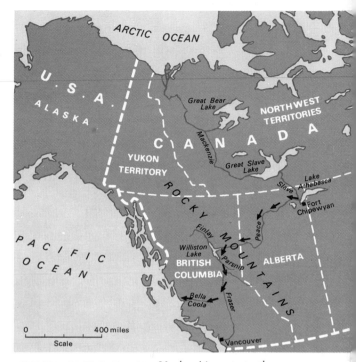

HOW THE WEST WAS WON. *Mackenzie's route to the Pacific across the unmapped continent is shown.*

tered the furious waters of the Peace River canyon, which runs for 25 miles into the Rocky Mountains. The rapids tore at the strained canoe, and it had to be poled, dragged by rope, or carried along the slippery cliffs.

Mackenzie's choice

Soon after they had passed the canyon and relaunched the canoe, the party was faced with a huge fork in the river—flooded when the Williston Lake dam was built.

Should they turn northwest along the wide and safe-looking main channel (now the Finlay River) or strike south on the narrow, swift, and dangerous tributary (now the Parsnip River)? Mackenzie remembered the words of an old Indian who had told him that the branch to the north poured out of the impenetrable mountains where no man could travel. Against the unanimous advice of his crew, he chose the southern tributary.

It was very hard going, and the men were again grumbling when the canoe was stopped

229

by a party of Sekani Indians. Through his interpreters Mackenzie discovered that the river went south and joined another that flowed into the "Stinking Lake."

Across the Great Divide

This was the party's first rumor of saltwater. They pushed on until the river dissolved into a maze of small brooks. On June 12 the canoe was lifted from the water and carried over a low rise to a small lake. White men had at last surmounted the Continental Divide.

After wrecking the canoe on a rock and patching it up with bark, the pioneers finally reached the Fraser River, which bore them safely west.

Suddenly, a flight of arrows showered from the bank. Mackenzie ordered his crew not to shoot and stepped ashore alone and unarmed. His daring gamble succeeded, and the Indians accepted presents of beads and knives from him.

He had discovered the warlike Carriers, a people from whom he learned that the Fraser did eventually reach the ocean but that there was a quicker route due west overland to another river.

Though it was midsummer the men shivered as they left the canoe to cross the snow-packed mountain passes on foot, and it was 13 days before they descended into the warm valley of the Bella Coola River. Friendly Indians lent them two canoes, and, on July 20, the 10 men paddled through a labyrinth of islands into the Dean Channel, a coastal inlet north of Vancouver Island.

Two days later Mackenzie scrawled his message on the southeast face of one of the rocks and began the return journey. This took a mere 33 days, and on August 24 he was back in Fort Chipewyan. He had beheld both the Arctic Ocean and the Pacific Ocean, and he had come back without the loss of a single life.

GATEWAY TO THE WEST

Two men who opened up the route to the Pacific

A rifle shot fired on the bank of the Missouri River on May 14, 1804, signaled the beginning of one of history's epochal journeys of exploration. And it was the first under U.S. auspices to reach the Pacific coast by traveling overland from the East. The trip took two years and four months, covered about 8,000 miles, and strengthened American claims against those of Britain, Spain, and Russia to Oregon country in the Northwest.

On January 18, 1803, President Thomas Jefferson had secretly asked Congress to vote money for an expedition beyond the Mississippi River—territory then largely owned by France. Congress had quietly authorized the spending of $2,500. Within a few months, however, the purchase from France by the United States of the vast Louisiana Territory, stretching westward from the Mississippi to the Rocky Mountains, transformed Jefferson's surreptitious fact-finding trip into a great public enterprise. Congress voted additional money, and Jefferson at once briefed his 28-year-old secretary, Meriwether Lewis, whom he had already chosen to head the expedition, and directed him to select a coleader. Lewis picked his friend and senior officer in the Northwest frontier cam-

paign, Lt. William Clark, the youngest brother of the famous George Rogers Clark.

No explorers were ever given more explicit instructions than these men. Jefferson ordered them to explore the Missouri and Columbia Rivers to locate "the most direct and practicable water communication across the continent for the purposes of commerce." They were to study "the general face," topography, and products of the country and record latitudes so that a map of the region could be made. They also were to study the Indians and report everything about them—even their pulse rates.

The expedition sailed from its winter camp near St. Louis. The explorers traveled in a 55-foot, 22-oared keelboat with a large sail and in two pirogues—canoelike boats. There were 29 men in the permanent detachment, most of them trained frontiersmen who had enlisted in the army. An additional party of seven soldiers and nine boatmen were to accompany the expedition as far upriver as the Mandan Indian towns, to lend a hand in transport and beef up the expedition during that part of the journey when Indian trouble might be expected.

These extra men proved useful in the exhausting struggle against the Missouri—row-

THE WIDE MISSOURI. *The expedition, led by Lewis (right) and Clark, spent the winter of 1804–05 in this Mandan settlement on the banks of the frozen Missouri. Though decimated by smallpox introduced by white trappers, the Indians were friendly and helped the explorers on their way.*

ing, poling, and towing the boats with only slight help from favorable winds. And when the expedition later was menaced by Teton Sioux, the explorers' willingness to fight caused the Indians to back off.

On October 27 the expedition reached the Mandan towns near present-day Bismarck, North Dakota, and spent the winter of 1804–05 there. When the permanent detachment headed westward on April 7, 1805, it consisted of 32 persons, including interpreter Toussaint Charbonneau and his young wife Sacajawea, a Shoshone girl who had been captured five years before by the Minnataree.

At the Great Falls of the Missouri they spent a back-breaking month portaging around the rapids, then moved on to the Three Forks of the Missouri. They traveled up the most westerly stream, which they named the Jefferson, and crossed the Continental Divide via Lemhi Pass. Sacajawea proved invaluable as a guide, and her brother, a Shoshone chief, provided horses for the explorers.

This good fortune was followed by days of hardship, as the men were battered by snowstorms and sickened by a diet of dried salmon, boiled roots, and stewed dog. Finally, they reached the Clearwater River, where they built canoes for the trip down the Snake and Columbia Rivers. The Columbia finally brought the party to the Pacific on November 15, 1805. While they wintered at Fort Clatsop on the Oregon coast, Indians swarmed around; their use of such phrases as "damned rascal" proved that English traders and sailors had been there earlier.

In March 1806 the explorers began their homeward journey. As they approached the Continental Divide, Lewis and Clark separated to search again for that elusive water route to the Pacific. Clark explored the Yellowstone, and Lewis headed for the Great Falls of the Missouri, during which time he had his only fight with the Indians—killing two Blackfeet.

The expedition was reunited near the junction of the Yellowstone and Missouri and made an easy passage down the Missouri to St. Louis, arriving on September 23, 1806. The expedition had lost only one man, by illness.

Lewis and Clark brought back valuable scientific data and inspired a generation of fur traders and trappers. These mountain men thoroughly explored the Far West and later guided settlers on the Oregon and California trails.

ACROSS THE WORLD IN 169 DAYS

The race that proved the automobile was here to stay

Six awe-inspiring contraptions were lined up across 43rd Street, in New York City, and their combined din was overpowering. They were recognizably automobiles, although one was fitted for a mast and sail and another carried skilike runners. As well as pneumatic tires, most had high, steel-studded wheels, and all carried food and medicine chests, picks and shovels, repair tools and spares, and firearms.

Perched on top of these remarkable machines were men in furcoats, bearskin caps, arctic boots, and goggles. Three of the vehicles bore French colors, one German, one Italian, and one American. It was February 12, 1908. This was the start of the first transcontinental automobile race.

Route without roads

The route was across the northern United States and then by ship to Alaska, where the plan was to drive across the Bering Strait on the ice. From there the cars were to cross Siberia and eastern Europe and finish up in Paris. It was a race that only supreme optimists were likely to enter, for there were virtually no paved roads in the United States outside the cities, and Siberia was almost devoid even of tracks.

But though the automobile was only 18 years old, the manufacturers were eager to show what it could do. Two newspapers were cospon-sors, *The New York Times* and *Le Matin* of Paris. The *Times* was particularly enthusiastic and proclaimed: "Over this route, the traffic of the world will some day move." But skeptics were more numerous, and among them was the London *Daily Mail*, which said: "The motorcar, after woman, is the most fragile and capricious thing on earth."

Of the six contenders, Germany's *Protos* looked the most formidable—a 60-horsepower monster manned by army engineers. Next biggest was the American *Thomas Flyer*, also 60 horsepower. Italy's *Zust* and two French cars, *De Dion* and *Moto-Bloc*, had 40 horsepower. The other French entry was the tiny 12-horsepower *Sizaire-Naudin*, whose drivers predicted that they would skim over snow and mud.

Substitute mechanic

Each car had two drivers and a mechanic. And perhaps of all of them the most unprepared was the young mechanic aboard the *Thomas*, George Schuster. He had never intended to enter the race. He had been sent by the Thomas factory to deliver the *Thomas* to the starting line. But when at the last minute the chosen mechanic withdrew, Schuster eagerly changed his clothes and climbed aboard.

More than 200,000 people crammed into the Times Square area to see the start of the race at 11:15 a.m., in a crescendo of banging motors,

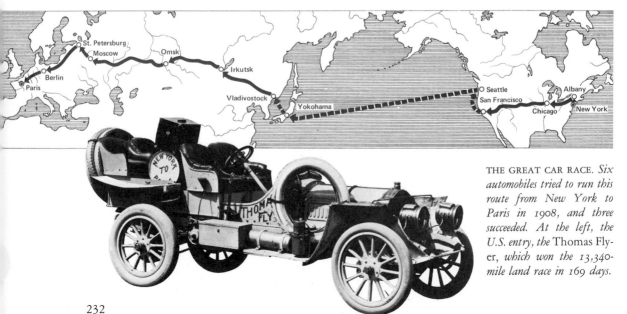

THE GREAT CAR RACE. *Six automobiles tried to run this route from New York to Paris in 1908, and three succeeded. At the left, the U.S. entry, the* Thomas Flyer, *which won the 13,340-mile land race in 169 days.*

horns, cheers, and brass-band music. Escorted by 200 cars, the racers swung north onto Broadway. For eight miles cheering crowds lined the streets. Then the escort dropped away, and the six cars roared off up the Post Road toward Albany.

At Hastings, 18 miles from the start, the *De Dion* plowed into a snowdrift, and it took half an hour's shoveling by all the crews to clear the road. At 8:20 p.m., the *Thomas* rumbled into Hudson, 116 miles from Times Square, trailed by the *De Dion* and the *Zust*. The *Protos* managed only the 74 miles to Poughkeepsie, while the *Moto-Bloc* and *Sizaire-Naudin* were at Peekskill, just 44 miles from the start.

The next day the *Thomas* and the *Zust* established themselves in the lead, while the little *Sizaire-Naudin* had a net loss of four miles, having taken a wrong turn and headed south. Then it tore out its differential gear on a rock and withdrew from the race.

West from Albany the drivers, despairing of the mapped route, took to the Erie Canal Towpath. The crews filled ditches, reinforced a bridge, and rolled away 80 huge logs that blocked their progress. On the fourth day the *De Dion* and *Thomas* pulled the *Zust* out of a swamp.

Sleds to the rescue

South of the Great Lakes snowdrifts made the road impassable, and Montague Roberts, out in front in the *Thomas*, paid $1,000 to have 10 teams, dragging sleds, harden the route for 100 miles.

The *Thomas, De Dion,* and *Zust* were crossing Illinois, while the *Protos* and the *Moto-Bloc* were still struggling though Indiana. The road across Iowa was a ribbon of mud, sometimes two feet deep, and this ultimately proved too much for the *Moto-Bloc*.

News of the crazy adventure had captivated Americans. People lined the route to cheer and give aid. Straw fires lit the way at night. Boucier St. Chaffray, driver of the *De Dion*, wired his backers: "I can't spend money. They give me everything." And Omaha's militia turned out to welcome the leading *Thomas* with a salute from eight guns.

In the mountain states, though, the crews were on their own and sometimes had to spend hours scouring the rocky, snow-swept surface for possible routes. Eventually, on March 24, behind a raucous parade of local motorists, the *Thomas* rolled through the decorated streets of San Francisco. The 3,836 miles from New York had taken 42 days. But the second-place *Zust* was still groping through the mountains of Utah; the *De Dion* was in Granger, Wyoming; and the *Protos* was even farther behind.

Quicker by rail

When the *Thomas* arrived in Alaska by ship, the locals laughed at its crew's plan to cross the Bering Strait. Not one of them could remember the strait solidly frozen. Back in New York the red-faced committee sent out frantic telegrams. The *Zust* and the *De Dion* were shipped from San Francisco to Seattle. The *Protos*, still well short of San Francisco, accepted a 15-day penalty and was taken to Seattle by rail. The *Thomas* returned to join them, and all four were shipped to Vladivostok in Siberia to resume the race.

At Vladivostok, St. Chaffray withdrew, deciding that his *De Dion* was too worn to risk what lay ahead. But on May 22 the remaining three were off again. The *Protos* was now in luck and forged steadily ahead while the *Thomas*, lost in a wild mountain maze, spent two days finding its way back to the route by stars and compass. Then it began to gain, overtaking the *Protos* 1,900 miles from Vladivostok. Meanwhile, the *Zust* was steadily losing ground.

The Germans and the Americans exchanged the lead half a dozen times on the plains of Siberia. But on July 20 the *Protos* rolled into St. Petersburg four days ahead of the *Thomas*. It was inspected by the Czar and awarded a $1,000 prize for winning the race across Russia.

The 2,587 miles from St. Petersburg to Paris offered the best roads of the entire race, and the *Protos* covered the distance in eight days. But because of its 15-day penalty it was not to be the winner. At 6 p.m. on July 30 the *Thomas* roared to a halt outside the offices of *Le Matin*. It had won by 11 days' driving time.

The stand-in was the hero

George Schuster, the young mechanic who had set out five months earlier to deliver the car to the starting line, was the hero of the day. He had become codriver with George Miller, when the other starting driver had dropped out.

The *Thomas* had covered about 13,340 miles in 169 days. The *Zust* reached Paris two weeks later. Three of the six starters finished. They had demonstrated what the automobile industry hoped to prove: The car had come to stay.

THE ATLANTIC CHALLENGE

Lindbergh's great gamble paid off

Shortly before 8 a.m. on May 20, 1927, a frail silver monoplane, straining under its heavy load of 450 gallons of fuel, took off from Long Island's Roosevelt Field. The aircraft was the *Spirit of St. Louis*, and the lone aviator at its controls, a tall, taciturn young man named Charles A. Lindbergh, Jr., was beginning a 3,600-mile flight across the Atlantic to Paris that would capture the imagination of the world as few events have ever done.

Lindbergh's historic flight was the longest solo nonstop airplane flight yet attempted and the first from New York to Paris. It was the fact that the young Minnesotan was flying alone that created an unprecedented outpouring of hero worship.

Lindbergh's dream of trying a solitary New York to Paris flight had been born more than a year earlier, when he was flying for the U.S. Air Mail Service on the St. Louis–Chicago run. It seemed to him that a solitary flier had the best possible chance: To achieve maximum range (a critical factor in those days, when few planes could fly anywhere near 3,600 miles nonstop), an aircraft must be mercilessly stripped of all excess weight, including crew. Lindbergh was only 25, but he had more than four years of intensive flying experience behind him—as a barnstormer, mail pilot, test pilot, and flying cadet in the U.S. Air Service Reserve.

The "Spirit of St. Louis"

The young flier's enthusiasm must have been infectious, for by February 1927 he had succeeded in acquiring financial backing from a group of St. Louis businessmen. He went to San Diego to order a plane built to his specifications. For two months he worked closely with designer Donald Hall of Ryan Airlines to produce the sleek, single-seat monoplane that would soon be immortalized as the *Spirit of St. Louis* (named to honor Lindbergh's backers).

Range was crucial. For example, almost all direct forward vision was sacrificed so that an extra fuel tank could be fitted into the plane's nose. A periscope, he decided, would be adequate for takeoff and landing. The small cabin was well to the rear, built into the fuselage so as to add no additional wind resistance.

The finished plane had five fuel tanks and a range, remarkable for the time, of 4,500 miles—more than ample for the Paris flight. Every ounce of excess weight had been ruthlessly discarded; the *Spirit of St. Louis* carried no sextant or radio, no lights or flares.

On May 10, 1927, Lindbergh left San Diego for New York, with a quick stopover in St. Louis, on a record-breaking flight—his time from California to Curtiss Field on Long Island was just over 21 hours. Two other planes were already there, awaiting clear weather in order to compete for the Orteig Prize of $25,000 for a successful transatlantic flight: the big trimotor *America*, commanded by the famed polar explorer Richard E. Byrd, and the *Columbia*, to be flown by Clarence Chamberlin and Lloyd Bertaud. The competition was formidable.

During the final endless days of waiting for the weather to clear, Lindbergh spent considerable time dodging the attention of reporters. All his thoughts were concentrated on final preparations and that most crucial question of all: the weather, which had been foggy and stormy over the Atlantic ever since his arrival.

"LONE EAGLE." *Charles A. Lindbergh, Jr., with his single-seat monoplane,* Spirit of St. Louis, *set an aviation milestone by solo flying the Atlantic in 1927.*

JOURNEY'S END. *The* Spirit of St. Louis *at Le Bourget Airport, near Paris, after Lindbergh's epic flight. The field had been illumined by the light from thousands of automobiles to show the lone pilot where to land.*

Takeoff from Roosevelt Field

On the night of May 19, Lindbergh received news that the weather was suddenly clearing over the ocean. After snatching a few hours' restless sleep at his hotel (the last rest he would get until Paris, as it turned out), he decided to risk a morning takeoff.

The morning was wet and dreary. After an alarmingly sluggish takeoff from Roosevelt Field, the *Spirit of St. Louis* suddenly gained power and soared smoothly northeastward over the New England coast. The pilot had checked and rechecked every detail of the Mercator projection charts on which he had worked out his northward-curving "great circle" route to Paris—over New England, Nova Scotia, and Newfoundland; then 2,000 miles across the empty northern ocean to the Irish coast; and finally a hop over England and the channel to Paris and Le Bourget Airport.

Lindbergh was well on his way, his plane flying smoothly over the open Atlantic between the coasts of Massachusetts and Nova Scotia, when he felt the first stirrings of the overwhelming fatigue that would plague him throughout the flight.

Night was falling, he had already been in the air 12 hours, and he had left the last landmark behind. From here until he struck the coast of Ireland, he would have to rely utterly on his compasses, his charts, and his own well-honed instincts—all the while battling sleep. Now came the most dangerous part of his flight, with icebergs below and fog swirling ahead.

Somehow the long night of flying through storm and fog over a black featureless sea passed by. When Lindbergh was 19 hours out of New York, the sky began to lighten, and he swooped down low over the choppy Atlantic to revive himself, slapping his own face as hard as he could in a desperate effort to stay awake. Finally, after he had been in the air 27 hours, he sighted a fleet of small fishing boats below. The men aboard, presumably terrified by the sudden silver apparition, huddled below decks, peering blankly at Lindbergh as he dove down low to yell: "WHICH WAY IS IRELAND?" He received no reply. But shortly thereafter, with Newfoundland 16 hours behind him, he sighted the Irish coast. Despite fatigue and the long night of blind flying, he was only three miles off his projected course—and 2½ hours *ahead* of schedule!

Landing in a human sea

The *Spirit of St. Louis* at last crossed the French coast over Deauville. Night was falling, and the plane's Wright engine was running smoothly. Lindbergh was now wide awake. Ahead of him in the soft evening sky he saw the glow of Paris and the unmistakable shaft of the Eiffel Tower.

He knew only the general location of Le Bourget—just northeast of the city—and he began to look for runway lights. But what Lindbergh finally saw was not a revolving beacon, or the usual warning and approach lights, but a vast irregular pattern of thousands and thousands of pinpoint lights. Puzzled, he slowly circled the airport before beginning his descent, finally realizing that those myriad lights represented thousands of automobiles clustered beside the landing field.

It was not quite 10 p.m., Paris time; Lindbergh had been flying for approximately 33 hours. Gently, the *Spirit of St. Louis* descended onto the dark runway (the plane had no lights, and Lindbergh touched down beyond the area lighted by the waiting cars) and came to a stop.

Its pilot was about to taxi back to the hangars at the lighted end of the airport, when he discovered that the entire field ahead of him was covered by an immense swarm of running human figures. Stepping out of his airplane, he announced, simply, "I am Charles Lindbergh," and was immediately engulfed by a crowd gone wild with joy.

SURVIVAL WITH SHACKLETON

Six men battled against the Antarctic Ocean

In March 1916, 28 desperate Britons stood shivering on the beach of an ice-covered, barren island in the Antarctic Ocean. For the past two years they had been members of a transantarctic expedition and had grown weak and sick in an 1,800-mile battle against a wilderness of snow and limitless ice floes—great glacial monsters that had crushed and sunk their ship, the *Endurance*, five months before. Only a few days before they had cast off in their three remaining small boats from the drifting floe that had been their home; their leader had laid his course for Elephant Island, southeast of Cape Horn. Now even that dreary refuge had to be abandoned.

Gales that swept the unsheltered shore were whipping their tents to shreds; the food supply of penguin meat and seaweed was dangerously low. Freezing and hungry, the men turned again—as they had repeatedly through this whole nightmarish ordeal—to the man whose courage and calmness had thus far preserved them.

Tall, broad-shouldered, with an angular face overhung by dark brows, Sir Ernest Shackleton looked like a great brooding rock, the sort of rock men cling to when hope has almost gone.

"We have got to reach a point where we can get a ship," he said quietly. It was a forlorn hope to make a long journey in a small boat, but he asked for volunteers. Every man offered to go.

Five men were chosen to accompany Shackleton on the 800-mile journey to South Georgia, one of the Falkland Islands, through the worst ocean in the world, in a boat only 22 feet long. They were Worsley, captain of their crushed ship, Tom Crean, Timothy McCarthy, McNeish, the carpenter, and Vincent, the boatswain. They caulked and ballasted the *James Caird*, a light, buoyant, double-ended craft, and stiffened its keel with the mast from another boat. Then they got ready to push off.

Two men fell overboard in the launching. Then a rock drove a hole in the hull, which they plugged with a marlinespike. Finally, they took on stores and set sail.

It was bitter going. A gale sprang up that drove the craft back nearly to the ice pack. It

UNENDURABLE. *The inexorable power of the Antarctic ice grips Sir Ernest Shackleton's research ship* Endurance. *Pressure from the countless millions of tons of ice cracked its beams like matchsticks.*

was a grave setback, and Shackleton said: "Skipper, if anything happens to me while those fellows are waiting, I shall feel like a murderer."

But the boat plowed on. Under the canvas deck was a cramped space reached only by a struggle over provisions and ballast, and at the end the only solace was a wet sleeping bag into which a man crawled wearily. Going to bed was as unpleasant as getting up.

"Every swell coming toward us towered like an over-arching wall," Shackleton wrote later. "We were getting soaked every three or four minutes. A great sea would break over us, making us feel that we were under a waterfall. Then, before the next wave broke, we would get several minor seas that would just cover the boat and wet us again. This went on day and night. The cold was intense."

Shackleton, suffering terribly from sciatica, remained cheerful. Worsley had to be held up on each side by a man while trying to get a sight, so that he would not go overboard with his sextant. Late one afternoon, through the constant mist that blurred the sun, he saw land—South Georgia!

That night a terrific gale catapulted them toward the coast. They were so thirsty they could hardly swallow, their lips were split, the

LAST REST. *Shackleton died of a heart attack in the Antarctic. He was buried in South Georgia.*

spray shot from the boat high into the air, and the wind howled remorselessly. They bore down on a tiny island, and it was a question whether they would hit it or round it into calmer water. "She'll do it," said Worsley. "Of course she will," Shackleton replied. "She's damned well got to."

Next day he proposed to land on the island and then hike across it to the whaling station on the other side. No human being knew what lay behind those glaciers and ice-covered mountains of South Georgia. But Shackleton was determined to try the route; if his boat were crushed against the rocks going around by water, the men back on Elephant Island would die.

They went ashore at King Haakon's Sound and found a cave. Baby albatrosses were caught and killed for food; the men were so hungry that they ate the bones. Nearby was a stream of water that tasted like nectar. Leaves and moss made a bed on the stones. For the first time in two weeks they could relax and sleep.

On May 19, 1916, the weather cleared, the moon shone, and Shackleton, Crean, and Worsley started across the island, leaving behind three men unfit for travel. Worsley steered the group by his compass, and they roped themselves together. They found themselves in blind passes, made their way almost down to the sea and had to turn back, and once teetered on the brink of a gigantic chasm, 200 feet deep and 200 feet wide.

Finally, they reached a ridge so steep they could sit on it and dangle their legs over each side. Fog and darkness had cut off retreat. If they did not move, they would freeze to death. Cutting steps down the icy mountainside was so slow as to be useless. After a moment Shackleton said: "It's a devil of a risk, but we've got to take it. We'll slide."

"We each coiled our share of rope into a pad on which to make our glissade," Worsley later recalled. "Shackleton sat on a step he had carved, and I clasped him around the neck from behind. Crean did the same with me, so that we were locked together as one man. Then Shackleton kicked off.

"We seemed to shoot off into space. For a moment my hair fairly stood on end. Then suddenly I felt a glow and knew that I was grinning! I was actually enjoying it. We were shooting down the side of a precipitous mountain at nearly a mile a minute. I yelled with excitement and found Shackleton and Crean were yelling too. It seemed ridiculously safe. To hell with the rocks!

"Little by little our speed slackened, and we finished up at the bottom in a snowbank. We picked ourselves up and solemnly shook hands all round."

When the trio finally reached the whaling station, having crossed South Georgia in 36 hours, they were so wild looking that the commander did not recognize them. Shackleton's hair had turned silver. When Worsley went back to King Haakon Sound to rescue the three men left there, they too did not know him. A bath, a shave, and some decent clothes had made a great difference in his appearance.

All the men on Elephant Island were found well—with the exception of one lad whose toes had been amputated. They had lived for 4½ months under two overturned boats, beaten by hurricanes, and pelted with ice from the mountains. Thus ended the last long expedition of Ernest Shackleton.

The record of his odyssey on sea and land still stands as the greatest Antarctic adventure of all time. His achievement is best reflected in the words of a fellow explorer: "For scientific leadership, give me Scott; for swift and efficient travel, Amundsen; but when you are in a hopeless position, when there seems no way out, get down on your knees and pray for Shackleton."

THE SAILOR WHO DARED AND DIED

His epitaph was a centuries-old letter

Spray freezes in the air, crystallizing all over a ship and capable of capsizing it with the weight. Shards of ice, razor sharp, cut through clothing and draw blood. Any man who grasps a rail with an ungloved hand is liable to strip the skin from his palm. Anyone falling overboard would die from the piercing cold in minutes.

This is the Barents Sea, named after the Dutchman Willem Barents who challenged it, and was killed by it, nearly 400 years ago.

On June 13, 1597, a great wind blew out of the west across a frozen island. Inside a makeshift shelter a Dutch officer wrote: "The best and strongest of us are so weak with the great cold and diseases that we have so long time endured, that we have but half a man's strength; and it is to be feared that it will rather be worse than better, in regard of the long voyage that we have in hand, and our bread will not last longer than to the end of the month of August . . . ."

The letter was signed by Captain Heemskerck, Pilot Willem Barents, and the crew, and

SHELTER FROM THE ARCTIC WINTER. *Barents and his crew built a hut for themselves and stocked it from their ice-locked ship. The structure was in ruins when it was found by a party of whale hunters nearly three centuries later.*

stuffed up the chimney of their hut. Then the 15 men stepped into two small boats and rowed out to sea.

The letter was found there almost three centuries later, in 1871, when a party of Norwegian whalers rowed ashore from their ship to the barren island of Novaya Zemlya. It recalled an almost forgotten saga of man's struggles against the savagery of the northern sea.

Barents, commissioned as pilot by Dutch merchants to discover the fabled North East Passage to the Indies, set out with two ships in May 1596. After rounding the coast of Spitsbergen, he found pack ice blocking his way north and decided to turn east and round the northern tip of Novaya Zemlya, as he had done once before. The captain of his other ship, Jan Rijp, refused to follow because of the risk.

Locked in the ice

As Barents' lone vessel rounded the tip of the island, it became terrifyingly obvious that Rijp had been right. The pack ice closed in and finally choked the ship. As it was August, Barents and his crew faced the problem of how to survive the arctic winter.

They built a hut of driftwood on the island and stocked it with food from the ice-locked ship. They killed arctic foxes for fresh meat. For freshwater they melted snow.

Cold was a nightmare. Even though they huddled close to the stove, which they kept burning day and night, their backs were always coated with frost. They warmed their beds with heated stones. Somehow, all but two of them survived the winter.

Then came the spring, bringing sunshine that lengthened into a few hours a day. The ship by then had been crushed into a near wreck by the ice. Their only hope was to escape in the two open boats.

Barents himself was by now weak from scurvy and almost certainly had a premonition of his fate. But no one expected to survive, so they prepared letters to tell the world their story, one letter to go in each boat and one to be left behind.

The little boats struggled around the northern tip of the island and headed south. Almost immediately, a storm battered them, and they had to drag the boats onto a large ice floe. There, on June 20, Barents died.

When the storm abated, the others struggled blindly on, sometimes having to drag their boats across the ice when it blocked their way. Once, the ice gave way under one of the boats: Most of their stores tipped out and were lost. Scurvy added its torments to the cold and hunger, but after weeks at sea they sighted some Russian fishermen who sold them food.

After traveling 1,600 miles across the Arctic in open boats and surviving appalling hardships, the little band eventually reached the Kola Peninsula near Murmansk. There, with his ship, was Capt. Jan Rijp, a more wary mariner, who had paid due respect to the ferocity of the Barents Sea—and who lived to sail another day.

TRAPPED AMONG THE ICE FLOES. *Barents and his men abandoned their ship and struggled over the ice to Novaya Zemlya. Barents had realized too late the wisdom of Capt. Jan Rijp's decision to turn back.*

RELAY RACE WITH DEATH

Children's lives were in the hands of the tough trappers

Dr. Curtis Welch looked down at the small boy, twisting and turning on the bed in a delirium of fever. The doctor's face was serious—for there was no longer any doubt about what was wrong with six-year-old Richard Stanley.

The boy had diphtheria, a disease that attacks the throat and blocks the respiratory passages. Dr. Welch had no way of knowing how many of Richard's playmates might already have contracted the disease. All he knew was that an epidemic would sweep through the little town of Nome, Alaska.

Dire need for serum

It was January 1925. Although an antidiphtheria serum had been available for some time, it was still in the development stage, and stocks were low.

Within 24 hours Richard Stanley was dead, and several new cases had been reported. Dr. Welch immunized known contacts with his own tiny stock of serum, which was soon exhausted.

More serum was desperately needed. The lives of dozens, perhaps scores, of children in the town were at stake. Getting further supplies to Alaska from the United States was a relatively simple matter. A shipment was on its way within hours. But it was when the serum reached Alaska that the real difficulties of transporting it began.

The nearest railway station to Nome was at Nenana, more than 1,000 miles away. Between the two towns lay a wilderness of snow, ice, and forest, through which the fastest transport was sled and dog team. Normally, the trip took two weeks at the least.

Plea for help

But the stricken town could not afford a two-week delay. On January 27, two days after the outbreak was first reported, newspapers all over the United States carried the story and a plea for help from Nome's mayor, George Maynard.

At noon that same day a tall, bearded trapper, Wild Bill Shannon, walked into the sheriff's office at Nenana. He suggested that the trip to Nome could be made in one week instead of two by doing it in relays. For between the two

towns there were 15 small trading posts, and at each there was an experienced trapper who could be called on to help.

Shannon volunteered to take the serum to the first post, where he would hand it over—and so it would go on, with a relay of trappers driving themselves and their teams to the limit, day and night.

That afternoon a metal case containing 30,000 units of serum arrived at Nenana. Shannon secured it to his sleigh and set out on the first leg of the journey—to Tolovana, 50 miles away.

He drove his seven huskies mercilessly, hour after hour. Darkness fell, bringing bitter cold and a razor-edged wind, but Shannon refused to take shelter. Ice rimmed his face and eyes, half blinding him.

He reached Tolovana shortly before midnight, and his dogs collapsed exhausted in the snow, as he handed over the container to trapper Dan Green. Green set out at once with his own team toward Manley Hot Springs, another 50 miles up the trail.

Gold prospector

Meanwhile, another dog team had set out from Nome, in the opposite direction. Its driver was 30-year-old Leonhard Seppala, who had come to Alaska to prospect for gold and who was reputedly the fastest teamster in that part of the territory.

Unaware that help was already on its way, he had decided to make a dash for Nenana, pick up the serum, and try to make the 1,000-mile return trip nonstop, relying on fresh dog teams picked up at the trading posts.

Dan Green arrived in Manley Hot Springs on the morning of January 28 and handed over the serum to trapper Johnny Folger. Folger covered the 30 miles to the next post, at Fish Lake, in only three hours.

So it went on, mile after mile, station after station. Meanwhile, day and night, Leonhard Seppala battled eastward through icy winds and snowstorms, from the other end of the trail.

The rescuers meet

By daybreak on January 31, Seppala had covered 200 miles. Suddenly, through eyes bleary with

THE LONG TRAVERSE. *Using sleds like these, relays of trappers covered 1,000 miles in 144 hours (inset map), carrying the serum that saved the children of the Alaskan town of Nome.*

fatigue, he saw another team approaching. It belonged to Henry Ivanoff, who had set out from the post at Shaktolik the previous day and who was suffering badly from frostbitten feet. Seppala took the serum and turned back.

It was an agonizing journey for his stalwart dogs. When the team was halfway across Norton Sound, a blizzard swept down. The swirling whiteness blotted out everything, forcing Seppala to rely on instinct alone as he pushed his dog team onward.

Early on February 1 Seppala reached Golovino, a tiny settlement on the far side of the sound. He was now only 100 miles from Nome, but the snow, ice, and subzero temperatures had taken their toll of both man and dogs. Reluctantly, Seppala handed over the serum to prospector Charlie Olson.

Last lap

At eight o'clock that evening Olson arrived in Bluff, 30 miles along the trail, and passed over the serum to another prospector, Gunnar Kaasen. Kaasen—who had taken part in one of Roald Amundsen's polar expeditions a few years earlier—was well known throughout the

territory. So too was his lead dog, Balto, a Siberian half-wolf, renowned for his skill and ability to outfight any other dog unlucky enough to cross his path.

Kaasen set out into the darkness at a fast pace as Balto followed the snow-covered trail unerringly. Kaasen was to have rendezvoused with a relief team, standing by in a trapper's cabin, but with no sure knowledge of its whereabouts he bypassed it.

Timely arrival

At 5:30 on the morning of February 2, with a snowstorm raging, Kaasen reached the outskirts of Nome. The dogs collapsed, and Kaasen—his face torn by ice particles, temporarily blinded, and almost unconscious—had to be chipped from the sleigh. The serum was a frozen block.

The epic race—1,000 miles of mountain, forest, and valley, through storm and gale-force winds in temperatures of 50° below zero—had taken 144 hours.

Apart from little Richard Stanley, the terrible epidemic of diphtheria had claimed only one other victim.

241

TRAPPED IN A WHITE HELL

A bumper catch, then the trawler itself was caught

The announcement that appeared in several local newspapers one gray morning in February 1923 was brief and final: "The steam trawler *Sargon* is now much overdue and must be presumed lost with all hands. She was last sighted off North Cape on February 2 by another Standard Fishing Company vessel, and appeared to be homeward bound."

A few weeks earlier the crew of the Grimsby trawler *Sargon* had been hailed as heroes. Off the Norwegian coast, in darkness and fearful weather, they had spotted a faint distress rocket. Skipper John Patton ordered full speed ahead, and, battered by mountainous seas, the *Sargon* turned in the direction of the signals.

Hours later the wintry dawn revealed a ship in distress, rolling helplessly in the heaving sea. It was the Scottish trawler *Ethel Nutton,* and her drenched, exhausted crew was clinging to the icy rigging. Patton saw that it would not last another half hour—and cursed in frustration. For the *Sargon*'s lifeboat had been carried away by the crashing waves, and there seemed to be no way of saving the doomed men.

Across the raging water that separated the ships, he yelled: "My boats have gone! I'll come as close as I can. Fasten lines to yourselves and throw the ends to my men as we come past!"

Leap to safety

Patton allowed the *Sargon* to drift broadside on toward the crippled *Ethel Nutton,* knowing that if the hulls of the two ships touched for even a moment, they would be wrecked. But, using all his skill, he maneuvered the *Sargon* until it was just a few yards astern of the *Ethel Nutton.* With a strength born of desperation, the men on the listing trawler hurled their lines. On that first attempt three were dragged to safety through the sea. Five times John Patton repeated the maneuver, and on the last attempt the two ships were so close that men were able to jump from the *Ethel Nutton* onto the *Sargon*'s slippery deck. All the *Ethel Nutton*'s eight men were safely aboard.

When the *Sargon* landed the survivors at their home port of Granton in Scotland, Patton brushed aside all attempts to make him a hero, and 24 hours later the *Sargon* put out to sea once more, following a course that would take it around Norway's North Cape to the fishing grounds of the White Sea.

After one brief sighting by another trawler on February 2, 1923, the ship vanished. In April it was officially written off—and the dependents of the gallant crew of 12 filed claims for insurance and compensation.

But even as their loss was being mourned, the men of the *Sargon* were still very much alive—fighting for survival in one of the sea's most gripping dramas. The epic began on January 28, a week after the trawler had reached its destination in the White Sea. The fishing was poor, and Skipper Patton had just made up his mind to head for home when he ran into an unexpected shoal of fish. He was running short of fuel, but he could easily refill his bunkers in the Norwegian port of Tromsö.

It turned out to be the biggest catch Patton had ever made. The following evening, low in the water with the weight of fish in its hold, the *Sargon* at last turned its bow southward, bound for Tromsö, then the Humber—and home. But

BLUE FOR DANGER. *The fierce beauty of the*

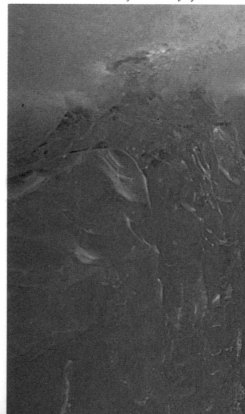

242

floating ice and fierce winds held it back; coal in the bunkers dwindled and at last ran out.

With the darkness came another menace: violent squalls of snow that reduced visibility to nil. For 10 days they raged, pushing the *Sargon* northwestward, out of the shipping lanes.

There was no coal to feed even the galley fire. Huddled in one small cabin, the men tried to keep themselves warm by burning anything that would catch fire: tarry fishnets, paneling, wood from their bunks. But still the temperature dropped as the trawler went on drifting northward, at the mercy of wind and sea.

Fit of depression

Late in February the weather cleared—and the sea around the *Sargon* froze solid. Food supplies ran out, and the men were forced to live on a monotonous diet of fish. For days they lay motionless in the cramped cabin.

Patton spent most of his time calculating the *Sargon*'s position by taking bearings on the stars—until one day in a fit of depression he threw away his sextant, certain that death was imminent. After that, there was no way of telling where they were.

On April 1, Patton went up on deck, and his despair deepened. Across the western horizon appeared what seemed to be a line of snow-capped mountains—monstrous, towering icebergs grinding their way toward them.

Hour after hour the crew could only watch helplessly as the mountain range of ice loomed closer and closer, accompanied by a noise like approaching thunder. With a sudden roar the ice field that gripped the *Sargon* shattered under the enormous pressure. The trawler lurched, throwing the men off their feet, and it wallowed in the water.

For hours, on all sides, giant slabs of ice reared up into the air and collapsed again with a fearful crash. Like a cork the *Sargon* bobbed helplessly around amid the white masses.

Then the miracle happened. One moment the *Sargon* was scraping past a wall of ice. The next she was in the open sea. The danger was behind her.

The *Sargon* drifted for four days, but on the fifth a ship was sighted—the German trawler *Schleswig Holstein*. The *Sargon* was towed to Reykjavik and from there, battered but proud, sailed back to Grimsby under her own steam. After four months John Patton and his crew had come back from the dead.

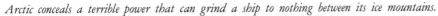

Arctic conceals a terrible power that can grind a ship to nothing between its ice mountains.

Detectives with spades and aqualungs

The quest for
the past

•

THEY FELL INTO THE FUTURE

Monster skeletons were found in a coal mine

Fragments of bones of a prehistoric monster known as the iguanodon had been found in different parts of Europe during the 19th century, but a complete skeleton had never been found. Then, astoundingly, in 1877–80, skeletons of the giant reptiles were found—down a Belgian coal mine.

The discovery—at Bernissart, near the French border—was the greatest find of the 16-foot-tall monsters that roamed the countryside 120 million years ago. And their eventual reconstruction showed that scientists' previous conceptions of the iguanodon had been wrong.

The 20 or so iguanodon skeletons—many of them complete—were the remains of a herd that had probably been swept by a raging flood into what was then a deep ravine. Mud poured into the ravine with them, covered the bodies, and preserved them in the excellent condition in which they were found.

In 1822 the first evidence of the creature that became known as the iguanodon was the fragmentary remains of a reptile more than 20 feet long. They were discovered by Mary Ann Mantell in the English county of Sussex.

Reconstructing the past

The name iguanodon—it simply means iguana tooth—was given to the creature by Mrs. Mantell's husband, a geologist and physician. He found that the teeth were similar to those of the iguana lizard but larger.

Many remains have since been found—particularly in the South of England and the Isle of

---

THE EARLIEST MAMMAL SKELETON

THE HISTORY of the mammals is well documented in the fossil record as far back as 80 or 90 million years ago. But the mammals go back much farther, into the mists of antiquity, about 200 million years ago when the great dinosaurs were making their first appearance. Until a few years ago, however, the only evidence of mammals from that far back consisted of teeth and jaws and parts of skulls—never a complete skeleton.

Then, in 1966, a remarkable discovery was made by Ione Rudner, a researcher from the South African Museum in Cape Town. She was helping a team of paleontologists unearth dinosaur remains on a hillside in the Orange River Valley of Lesotho when she noticed a tiny white "blob" on a cliff face. Thinking it was unimportant, one of her team flicked it onto the ground. But Mrs. Rudner was curious; she looked at the fragment under a magnifying glass and found that it had teeth.

In the next few months the entire skeleton of the tiny shrewlike creature was carefully removed from the encasing rock. For the first time the skeleton of a mammal from 200 million years ago was available for scientific study.

FOUR-LEGGED FALLACY. *These reconstructions in London's Crystal Palace Park were based upon fossils found in England in 1822. But later evidence showed that the iguanodon walked on two feet and was not horned.*

Wight, both formerly fertile delta areas where the tall, cumbersome beasts are believed to have died after being trapped in mud.

Tidal action in these areas during the following centuries broke up the skeletons and moved parts of them considerable distances. This may account for the fact that not one complete skeleton has been found in England.

A mockup of the iguanodon, built around the remains found by Mrs. Mantell, was constructed in the grounds of Crystal Palace in south London between 1853 and 1854 and still stands there today. It was then imagined to be a creature that moved on all fours, with a spiked horn on the tip of its nose. But the Belgian finds proved this concept to be incorrect.

Today in the great hall of the Royal Museum of Natural History in Brussels there are more than 20 iguanodon skeletons, some mounted in a standing position and others in the tumbled poses in which death had left them. These are restored as two-footed creatures. The spiked bone is not a nose horn but the last joint of two enlarged and spiky "thumbs" that helped the creatures to defend themselves and to tear down the vegetation which they ate long ago.

WHAT IT REALLY LOOKED LIKE. *From skeletons found in a Belgian coal mine in 1877–80, paleontologists were able to construct this more accurate concept of the 120-million-year-old reptile.*

245

BIRDS AS TALL AS ELEPHANTS

Powerful, but flightless—and now extinct

An old cart horse that collapsed and died while hauling a load of wood led to one of the world's great paleontological discoveries.

When New Zealand farmer Joseph Hogden and his son, Rob, began to dig a hole in which to bury the animal, they found a mass of strange-looking bones. The find—in Pyramid Valley, North Canterbury, in 1936—turned out to be the remains of several extinct wingless birds unique to New Zealand, the moa.

When paleontologists excavated the site, they found about 800 skeletons of the moa birds to the acre over the three-acre swamp. Never before had so many nearly complete sets of the birds' bones been found.

Long puzzled by the concentration of moa skeletons in New Zealand's sinkholes, naturalists have finally concluded that the unwary birds fell through the peat crusts of these swampy deathtraps and became mired, over the course of thousands of years.

About 25 species have now been identified, ranging from a bush bird about the size of a turkey to the giant moa, *Dinornis maximus*, which, reaching a height of 13 feet, was taller than any other land dweller except the giraffe.

At some crossroads of evolution the ancestors of moas began to rely for their survival on strength and then running speed. It was at this point that, in an "evolutionary burst," they lost the power of flight.

During the first years of excavations at Pyramid Valley paleontologists who flocked there collected 50 skeletons, including 17 of the *Dinornis* species, as well as several of the smaller moas and a few giant eagles.

Also found were the fragments of an unlaid egg, which had become free of the remains of a decomposed moa and broken into 200 pieces. Reconstruction work, which took months, showed that the egg was seven inches long by five inches in diameter.

Moa bones found in lava at some sites have been estimated to be 2 to 8 million years old. But it is known that two species of moa were alive when the first Polynesian settlers arrived in New Zealand around A.D. 1000, for their bones have been excavated from ancient Maori campsites.

NEW ZEALAND'S "DODO." *The giant moa,* Dinornis maximus, *stood up to 13 feet tall. It could not fly but relied on its strength and speed to ward off enemies. Complete skeletons of the moas were found in Pyramid Valley in 1936. It is believed they met death when they fell through peat crusts and were mired in swampy mud.*

246

MAN EXISTED 3.75 MILLION YEARS AGO

Theories upset by recent finds in southern Africa

In the 1970's three discoveries were made in Africa that sent shock waves through the anthropological world, for they challenged long-cherished theories concerning the origin and evolution of the human race.

One was the finding in Kenya of a human skull and bones below a layer dated about 2.8 million years ago. The second was the discovery that a cave in southern Africa, on the border between Swaziland and Natal, had been inhabited by men of modern type—possibly as long ago as 100,000 B.C. The third was human teeth and jaw bones found in Tanzania that were reported to be 3.75 million years old.

According to previous evolutionary doctrine, the first primate that could be called man, *Homo erectus*, did not evolve until about a million years ago. Yet the bones dug out of deposits in the East Rudolph Basin in Kenya not only were dated to nearly 3 million years ago but were far more modern in shape than the bones of man's presumed, less-developed ancestor.

Some biology textbooks said that probably the only humans in existence 75,000 years ago were beetle-browed Neanderthalers. But the remains unearthed in Border Cave in southern Africa were undoubtedly those of man's own species, *Homo sapiens sapiens*, who had been thought to have appeared about 35,000 B.C.

Tool making

Equally disconcerting were the artifacts found with the fossils. They indicated that men had developed intellects and had embarked on the road to civilization many thousands of years earlier than had been believed possible. The Border Cave dwellers had manufactured a variety of sophisticated tools, including beautifully worked agate knives with edges still sharp enough to slice paper.

They also held religious convictions and believed in the afterlife. The body of an infant had been given rudimentary ceremonial burial. They must have spoken a well-developed language, for such abstract ideas as immortality obviously cannot be conveyed by grunts and gestures.

Inspired detective work by two young South African prehistorians, Adrian Boshier and Peter Beaumont, led to important discoveries at Border Cave. In December 1970 they unearthed some 300,000 manmade objects and charred animal bones, many of creatures long extinct.

Charcoal from an overlying ash level, which was more recent than the stratum in which the child's skeleton was discovered, proved to be more than 50,000 years old. Stone implements and ground ocher appear right down to bedrock, suggesting the possibility that the cavern had been occupied for the past 100,000 years.

Bedding survived

The atmosphere of the cave had remained ideal for preservation during the ages. Even twigs, leaves, grass, and feathers brought in for bedding had survived. "Practically everything we found was three times older than the books said it should have been," Boshier observed. The discovery of stone arrowheads places the invention of the bow more than 50,000 years ago, whereas its appearance in Europe had previously been dated at only 15,000 B.C.

Carefully notched bones, from a 35,000-year-old level, may indicate that man had learned to count.

On the evidence of 500,000-year-old skulls found in Java and near Peking, many scientists had been convinced that man originated in Asia and drifted westward. Africa, it was thought, played no part in this evolutionary scheme.

African genesis

Despite Prof. Raymond Dart's discovery in 1924 of a far more ancient creature in Africa, the hypothesis held sway until it finally crumbled under a wealth of discoveries made by the British anthropologists Louis and Mary Leakey in Tanzania's Olduvai Gorge.

In 1959 they astonished the world by finding the nearly 2-million-year-old skull of a cousin of Dart's creature. In 1960 they found part of the braincase and lower jaw of another prehuman, together with chipped stone tools he had undoubtedly used for making weapons. They gave this creature the name of *Homo habilis* ("handyman").

Later that year they found fragments of a more advanced being, *Homo erectus*, the first man definitely known to have used fire. He later was found to be of the same species as Java and Peking man, but half a million years older.

In 1975 Mary Leakey reported further finds of prehumans in Tanzania that were established by radioactive dating to be 3.75 million years old.

Today Africa, not Asia, is favored as the most likely birthplace of the human race. It may be possible to trace the origins of *Homo erectus* back to the 2.8-million-year-old bones discovered in Kenya by the two anthropologists' son, Richard Leakey. Although the braincase of the Kenya creature is small, its whole shape is remarkably reminiscent of modern man's.

It may be years before anthropologists can fully evaluate the significance of these discoveries. But from the evidence it seems clear that modern man evolved far earlier than has been realized and that most probably it was in Africa that the miracle of human development had its genesis.

UNEXPLAINED SCENE FROM TASSILI. *Tableaux like this, painted thousands of years ago in the Sahara, record the lives of a forgotten people.*

WHY NEANDERTHAL?

CROSSING A WIDE green valley in West Germany's Rhineland, a motorist could be excused for expecting to see heavy-browed cavemen stalking mammoths or dragging women about by the hair. For a road sign reads: "Neanderthal"; and the Neander Valley is where bones of "Neanderthal man" were found in 1856—a so-called missing link between man and the apes.

Workmen quarrying for limestone dug up the bones and presented them to a local science teacher and naturalist, Johann Fuhlrott. When he started to assemble them, he realized that they had belonged to a creature that was beetle-browed and stoop-shouldered and walked upright. Fuhlrott was convinced that the bones belonged to a primitive human being.

The doctrine of evolution had already gained wide acceptance in scientific circles, and because of the ape's resemblance to man, some naturalists had begun to link them in the evolutionary process. Other scientists, however, were repelled by the association of man and ape; and most

people regarded the doctrine of evolution as simply blasphemous.

Fuhlrott showed his findings to the noted German anthropologist Prof. Hermann Schaaff-hausen, of Bonn. Schaaffhausen was astounded and described the skeleton at an 1857 meeting of natural scientists at Kassel, Germany. Fuhlrott addressed the society later that year and was greeted with outrage and derision.

In 1859 came a scientific bombshell in the form of Charles Darwin's *Origin of Species*, expounding the theory that natural selection was the operational factor in the evolutionary process. His implication that the theory applied to man as well as to other creatures shook thousands of people.

The controversy over the very notion of the Neanderthal man, which Darwin's book seemed to support, raged on for years. English biologist Thomas Huxley, a leading exponent of the Darwinian theory of evolution, declared that the Neanderthal skull was the most apelike yet found in the quest for man's past.

It was not until after Fuhlrott's death in 1877, and the discovery of similar fossils in Belgium, that Neanderthal man was accepted by anthropologists. Other fossil discoveries since then have helped to establish that the Neanderthalers lived from about 70,000 to 35,000 years ago.

The missing link comes to dinner in a 19th-century jibe at Darwin's theory of evolution.

WHEN THE SAHARA WAS GREEN

Civilization that flourished long before the Pharaohs

A caravan of Tuareg nomads silently led their camels into a camping ground on a stony plateau in the Sahara. With them was a young German explorer, Heinrich Barth, on his way to Lake Chad.

Glancing around at the steep sandstone cliffs that hemmed them in, Barth saw with a start that they were covered with remarkable carvings of bulls, buffaloes, ostriches, and people. The lines were incised in the rock with great firmness, and yet the figures were light and graceful. Struck by the absence of camels in the scenes, Barth noted that it was evidence of a state of life very different from today's.

Ancient art gallery

What Barth had discovered that day in 1850 was part of an art gallery 8,000 years old: the record of peoples, long-forgotten, who inhabited the Tassili plateau and neighboring foothills in the central Sahara when it was a green and fertile region.

It was not until 1933, however, that Tassili rock art was brought to the world's attention by a young French officer, Lt. Charles Brenans. Wandering amidst the Tassili's desolate hills and gorges, he came upon miles of engravings—and magnificent paintings. Glowing softly in ocher, violet, russet, and warm white were scenes of simple family life, of hunting parties, of strange gods, and religious rites. Painted warriors carrying round shields and lances race across the walls in chariots. Peaceful herdsmen wearing aprons and Egyptian-style headgear drive cattle with long, curved horns.

Some of the animals and birds depicted are long extinct. Others—the elephant, the rhinoceros, the giraffe, and the ostrich—can now only be found in the grassy plains 1,000 or more miles to the south.

Expedition organized

The French explorer and ethnologist Henri Lhote was among those who were inspired by the sketches made by Brenans, and he rushed off to find Tassili.

Several years later Lhote, with the backing of French scientific and government agencies, assembled a team of artists and photographers to return to the plateau. By 1957 Lhote's team had taken back to Paris 16,000 square feet of copies and photographs of the paintings.

Preserved in the dry desert air were records of several ages. The oldest scenes show a dark, possibly Negroid people, hunting giraffes, rhinos, and elephants with bows and arrows and lances. There are enormous half-human figures, possibly gods, painted a spectral white.

One, 19 feet high, has a head like a turtle and strangely positioned eyes, very much like those in paintings by Picasso.

Later pictures show far more lifelike figures. Rounded, well-muscled legs, decorative tribal scars, belts, anklets, and rings are depicted.

Banquet scenes

There are banquet scenes, wedding ceremonies, a woman pounding grain for flour, a hut being built, a family with a pet dog, children asleep under an animal-skin blanket, and other domestic scenes.

Between 5000 and 4000 B.C. it seems this people were gradually supplanted by a paler, copper-skinned race. These invaders added their own portraits to the gallery, in hunting scenes showing sheep, giraffes, and antelopes.

Still later paintings—from the second millennium B.C.—depict soldiers wearing bell-shaped tunics and riding in horse-drawn chariots. One guess is that they are the "People of the Sea" mentioned in ancient Egyptian records, who tried to invade Egypt from Crete or Asia Minor.

It is possible that, having been defeated, they settled in Libya and roamed as far west as the Tassili plateau.

A dying land

As the watercourses dried up, the population of Tassili dwindled, and little was added to the cave art. Finally, about 1000 B.C., the people yielded to the encroaching desert and moved away.

Then there was silence. The desert dust blows through the abandoned site, and for thousands of years, as Empires rise and fall in other parts of the world, the brilliant portraits of vanished races stare emptily from the sun-blasted rocks of Tassili-n-Ajjer.

ART GALLERY OF 17,000 YEARS AGO

How a little girl's find shed fresh light on prehistoric man

Nine-year-old Maria de Sautuola wandered deeper into the cave at Altamira in northern Spain, while her father, an amateur archeologist, was digging near the entrance.

Suddenly, from a side chamber, came the young girl's muffled screams: "Bulls! Bulls! Papa, come quickly!"

Her father, Marcelino, dropped his pick and raced into the cavern. His daughter stood there pointing excitedly at the ceiling of the cave. He raised his lantern, and there, painted in browns, reds, yellows, and black on the 60-foot by 30-foot ceiling were pictures of prehistoric bison—magnificent artwork dating back many thousands of years.

There were 17 of the bison on the ceiling in lifelike poses: pawing the ground, lying down, bellowing, dying of spear wounds. Around them were pictures of wild boars, a horse, a doe, and a wolf.

When Sautuola explored farther into the network of caves, he found scores of other paintings of animals, many of which were extinct or had disappeared from western Europe centuries earlier.

The year was 1879. At first, Sautuola's finds were dismissed by archeologists as forgeries—a plot to discredit Darwin's theory of evolution. The archeologists could not believe that such sensitive work could have been done by a primitive people thought of as savages and hardly better than the apes.

But the paintings turned out to be among the greatest discoveries of prehistoric art, most of them dating from 15,000 to 10,000 B.C.

In 1902, some 14 years after Sautuola had died, the archeologist Abbé Henri Breuil visited the caves and unearthed animal bones bearing engravings almost identical to those on the ceilings.

The authenticity of the paintings was no longer in doubt, and the caves were hailed as the "Sistine Chapel of prehistoric art." What was also remarkable about the paintings was their state of preservation. More than 100 other grottoes, decorated with stone age paintings and engravings, have been found in southern Europe, most of them in northeastern Spain and southwestern France. But many had faded and deteriorated with the ravages of time and weather.

The Altamira paintings had been done in pitch-black caves, discovered only shortly before Sautuola's visit, in which the temperature and humidity had remained constant. Ventilation was good but not excessive, and the moisture content of the air was sufficient to keep the colors from drying out and scaling off. They had been sealed off for centuries by rockfalls. Similar paintings at Lascaux, in southern France, suffered more damage in the 15 years they were open to the public—through perspiration, body heat, and micro-organisms introduced by visitors—than they had in all the previous thousands of years.

Young people were also instrumental in discovering the great prehistoric art gallery at Lascaux.

There, in 1940, 18-year-old Marcel Ravidat led three friends to a hole made by an uprooted tree that he had spotted a few days earlier while walking his dog. The youths enlarged the hole, and Marcel dropped down through it to the floor of a cave, about 18 feet below.

Finest primitive art

By the light of a few matches, he saw glimpses of beautiful wall paintings. The next day the boys returned with lanterns and discovered an array of horses, bulls, bison, deer, and other creatures.

The boys reported their find to the Abbé Breuil, and today the Lascaux cave paintings take their place with those at Altamira as some of the finest examples of primitive art ever discovered.

They include a chamber known as the Hall of the Bulls, with masterly drawings executed in ebony blacks and dark reds. In other compartments are hordes of horses and antlered deer heads, all exceptionally lifelike.

Like those at Altamira, it is clear that these are not the work of primitive savages but of sensitive artists—a far cry from the popular concept of stone age man. Executed over a span of 15,000 years or more and perhaps going as far back as 28,000 B.C., they include a range of

styles, from simple engravings to vividly colored paintings, often strikingly realistic.

Food gatherers

The people who produced this art are known as the Cro-Magnons, the name given to the stone age people of Europe between 32,000 and 10,000 B.C. They lived by gathering plants for food and by hunting, but they were also inventive and creative. Archeological study of them shows a succession of distinct cultures, the last of which was that of the Magdalenians, who lived from about 15,000 to 10,000 B.C.

The paintings were made by first engraving the outlines with a pointed piece of flint, then adding color. The artists had no greens or blues but may have got black and violet-black from manganese oxides, charcoal, or soot. Brown, red, yellow, and orange hues came from iron ore that was ground to powder with stones or bone mortars and pestles, then mixed with animal blood, or fat, and plant juices. The paint was applied in several ways: by finger, brushes made of fur, feathers, or the chewed ends of twigs. The artists also used pads of lichen and moss or blew paint through hollow reeds.

Done with artificial light

At Altamira, where the finest Magdalenian art has been found, ocher crayons made with tallow have been found. The paintings were executed with infinite care in dim chambers where daylight could barely penetrate, pointing to the use of artificial light; and stone lamps have been found. The ceiling paintings also indicate that some form of scaffolding was used.

Many archeologists think the cave paintings may have been part of a ritual to cast a spell over the beast to make it easy prey. The early people may also have believed that something of the prowess and strength of their prey was passed on to them through the medium of painting.

But the paintings may also have been used for instructing young hunters in how to kill: Many show spears thrust into an animal's most vulnerable spots.

The last of the great paintings were probably executed about 10,000 B.C., when the last ice sheet retreated, the climate warmed, and the Magdalenians left their caves to live in the open. During the next 4,000 years their descendants struggled to adapt to the radical changes in the environment. Slowly, they learned to farm, but, sadly, they lost their artistic skills.

KING TUTANKHAMEN'S GOLD

The long hunt that led to a treasure house of history

Howard Carter was growing desperate. For nearly 25 years he had searched for the tomb of the young King Tutankhamen. Now money to finance his quest was running out. He faced mounting skepticism, and even derision, from his colleagues.

What made the prospect of failure harder to bear was that the English scholar remained convinced that the tomb was somewhere in the Valley of the Kings, site of the ancient Capital of Thebes, for there were inscriptions about Tutankhamen in the nearby temple at Luxor. He believed, too, that the tomb had never been looted, for no relics had ever been reported.

But all he had found, after the first 10 years of searching, were jars and some clothing bearing the King's name. Since then Carter had explored nearly the whole floor of the valley but had found no trace of the Pharaoh, who had died at the age of 18.

PORTRAIT IN GOLD. *Covering the head of the young King was a stylized mask, executed in gold and jewels.*

As Carter trudged through the dawn-cool sand to his diggings, he thought again of his patron, the amateur archeologist Lord Carnarvon, and remembered their last meeting at the peer's home in Hampshire, England.

Carnarvon had wanted to call off the search. "It has cost me a fortune," he told Carter. "I can't afford it."

But Carter pleaded with him to finance one last try. "Howard," Carnarvon said, "I'm a gambler. I'll back you for one more toss. If it is a loss, then I am through. Where do we begin?" Carter showed him a map of the valley, indicating a small area not yet explored as it was on the approach to the tomb of Ramses VI. "There," he told his patron. "It's the last place left."

Now, as he approached the diggings, Carter reflected that this looked like the dismal end to his dream. He and his workmen had found nothing but the rubble of huts that had been used by the laborers building the tomb of Ramses VI. For three days they had hacked at the rubble and found nothing.

When Carter reached the site, his foreman, Ali, ran over. "We have uncovered a step cut into the ground," he said. Within two days they had cleared a steep staircase that led down to a sealed door. Carter immediately cabled Carnarvon:

AT LAST HAVE MADE WONDERFUL DISCOVERY IN VALLEY STOP A

DOORWAY TO THE PAST. *Beneath the sand of the Valley of the Kings lay a steep flight of steps untrodden for millennia.*

"WONDERFUL THINGS." *Howard Carter saw these treasures by the flickering light when he peered into the tomb through a hole chipped in the sealed door in November 1922.*

THE SEAL. *This sealed the door of the tomb beyond which lay a treasure store that human eyes had not looked upon for more than 3,000 years.*

MAGNIFICENT TOMB WITH SEALS
INTACT STOP RECOVERED SAME
FOR YOUR ARRIVAL
CONGRATULATIONS

The date was November 6, 1922.

After Carnarvon arrived, it took them several more days to break through the door and clear a rock-filled passage. Then the two men stood together in front of a second sealed door.

It was Carter's moment of truth. As Carnarvon peered over his shoulder, Carter chipped at the door until there was a hole big enough for him to flash a light in and take a look. He wrote:

"At first I could see nothing, the hot air from the chamber causing the flame to flicker. But as my eyes grew accustomed to the light, details of the room emerged slowly from the mist: strange animals, statues, and gold—everywhere the glint of gold.

"For the moment—an eternity it must have seemed to others standing by—I was struck dumb with amazement; and when Lord Carnarvon, unable to stand the suspense any longer, inquired anxiously, 'Can you see anything?' it was all I could do to get out the words: 'Yes—wonderful things.'"

The sepulcher consisted of four rooms containing caskets, vases, a gold-plated throne inlaid with precious stones, gems, furniture, clothing, and weapons. In the burial chamber itself, flanked by two black statues, were four gold shrines, one inside the other, and a sarcophagus containing a nest of three coffins.

The inner one, of solid gold, held the mummified body of Tutankhamen, wrapped in a jewel-studded shroud. Over his face was a gold mask inlaid with quartz and lapis lazuli. Across his neck and breast was a garland of cornflowers, lilies, and lotuses. After 3,300 years in the sepulcher, they still had a tinge of color.

The tomb's contents made up a complete capsule of the daily life of the legendary Pharaohs in Egypt 1,350 years before Christ. For Carter and his long-suffering patron Carnarvon it had been a long and frustrating hunt. But the final rewards made it all worthwhile: the most splendid of archeological discoveries.

BODY SNATCHERS OF 1500 B.C.

Priests exhumed Kings to foil the tomb robbers

By dead of night the priests slipped through the shadows of the valley where the Kings of ancient Egypt lay buried. Quietly, they broke into the rock-hewn sepulchers and lifted out the mummies.

One by one they rewrapped the bodies, recoffined them, and then carried their macabre burdens along a path over the cliffs to a new, secret resting place.

It was the priests' last attempt to beat the robbers who for centuries had been looting the treasure-stocked tombs of Egypt's Pharaohs.

Even pyramids with cunningly designed interiors had been stripped. The Egyptian rulers stopped building them and about 1500 B.C. began to have their tombs cut into the cliffs of the valley at Thebes—now known as Luxor—with the entrances concealed.

The architect Ineni, who designed the first of these sepulchers for Thutmosis I, boasted in his own epitaph: "It was a great work. . . . I shall be praised [for it]."

But the robbers went on winning, even penetrating tombs with mazes of passages and dead ends and chambers left unfinished to make it appear that the work had been abandoned.

Charged with the responsibility of keeping the bodies of their rulers inviolate for their life

THE CURSE OF THE PHARAOH

WHEN HOWARD CARTER and Lord Carnarvon opened the tomb of Tutankhamen, they set off a chain of mystery. Several of those connected with the discovery died violent or unusual deaths—victims of the so-called Pharaoh's curse.

The sinister superstition is based on unconfirmed reports of a chilling series of happenings on the very day when the two archeologists and their party had first penetrated the entrance to the tomb in November 1922. As the last man climbed back into the sunshine a sandstorm is said to have sprung up and swirled over the mouth of the cave. As it died away, a hawk, the royal emblem of ancient Egypt, was allegedly seen soaring over the tomb to the west—toward the mysterious "Other World" of Egyptian belief. The spirit of the dead Pharaoh, said superstitious people, had left his curse on those who had violated his tomb.

Five months later Lord Carnarvon, then 57, was bitten by a mosquito on the left cheek. The bite became infected, and weakened by blood poisoning, he contracted pneumonia. As he died in a Cairo hotel at 1:55 a.m., all the city lights went out. At the same time, back home in England, Carnarvon's dog howled—and died.

Strangest of all, doctors who later examined Tutankhamen's mummy reported finding a scablike depression on a spot on the left cheek corresponding to the location of Carnarvon's mosquito bite.

The curse was blamed also for the deaths of several others who had visited the tomb. For example, Carnarvon's half brother, Aubrey Herbert, died of peritonitis. An Egyptian prince, Ali Farmy Bey, whose family claimed descent from the Pharaohs, was murdered in a London hotel, and his brother committed suicide. George Jay Gould, an American railway tycoon, died of pneumonia in France, reportedly after catching a cold in the tomb. The Hon. Richard Bethell, who helped Carter to catalog the treasures, was thought to have committed suicide at the age of 49. A few months later, in February 1930, his father, Lord Westbury, hurled himself to death from his London apartment. An alabaster vase from the Pharaoh's tomb was in his bedroom. In the seven years after the discovery of the tomb in 1922 a dozen people who had been concerned with it in one way or another died strange deaths.

But one man continued to scoff at the legendary curse of the Pharaoh—the one man who might have had most reason to fear it. Howard Carter died in March 1939—of natural causes. Yet when Egypt agreed to send the Tutankhamen treasures to Paris for an exhibition in 1966, its director of antiquities, Mohammed Ibraham, dreamed that he would face terrible danger. He fought the decision up to one last meeting in Cairo with the authorities concerned. As he left the meeting, he was knocked down by a car. He died two days later.

after death, the custodians of the royal tombs realized that they could not hope to protect them while the sites were so well known—especially since the systematic looting was thought to be organized by court officials.

The guardians tried once more to secrete the mummified Pharaohs and Queens. Removing them at night, they hid 13 in the tomb of Amenophis II in the valley and carried 36 others up the clifftop path out of the valley. The mummies were lowered into a small chamber at the bottom of a 30-foot shaft in a deep cleft in the rocks, and then the opening was sealed and camouflaged. For 30 centuries the secret tomb at Deir el Bahri was undetected.

In 1880–81 funerary objects from the 21st Dynasty began appearing in Egyptian antique markets, arousing the suspicions of Sir Gaston Maspero, keeper of the Cairo Museum. He traced the "leak" to a family that had found a tomb in 1871 and had since been selling their plunder in Luxor.

An informer led Maspero's assistant, Emil Brugsch, to the rifled tomb. Brugsch was lowered down a deep shaft into a chamber. Dazed with wonder, he saw before him the bodies of 36 of the greatest Pharaohs.

A few years later, in 1898, the other 13 mummies were found in the tomb of Amenophis II. On the wrappings of each mummy, the ancient priests had left a ticket identifying the ruler and recording his successive burials and burial locations.

Thus authorities had eloquent testimony to the vain efforts of the priests to find a tomb safe for eternity for their deceased rulers.

SCROLLS FROM THE DAYS OF JESUS

An Arab boy found the world's greatest manuscript treasure

Muhammad adh-Dhib, a 15-year-old Bedouin boy, was searching for a stray goat in a desert region at the northwestern edge of the Dead Sea, when he saw a narrow opening in a rocky cliff. He threw in a few stones—and heard something shatter.

Thinking it might be hidden treasure, he brought a friend, Ahmed Muhammad, to the spot, and together they squeezed through the opening into a cave 26 feet long and 6 feet wide. In it, among pieces of broken pottery, they found a number of tall, cylindrical clay jars.

Excitedly, the boys wrenched off the lids, but instead of the gold or precious stones they expected, they found only some dark, musty-smelling lumps of material wrapped in linen. These consisted of 11 scrolls made of thin strips of sheepskin, sewn together, and coated with gummy, decomposed leather.

The scrolls—between 3 feet and 24 feet long, when unrolled—were covered on one side with columns of an ancient Hebrew script. The boys were disappointed but managed to sell them to a dealer in Jerusalem for a small amount of money. That was in 1947.

What the boys had discovered turned out to be one of the greatest of manuscript treasures—the Dead Sea Scrolls. Although an employee of the Department of Antiquities in Palestine at first described the scrolls as "worthless," five of them were bought the following year by the Syrian Orthodox Monastery of St. Mark in Jerusalem. The other six were bought by the Hebrew University there.

When the St. Mark-owned scrolls were examined by Dr. John Trever, acting director of the American School of Oriental Research in Jerusalem, he found that one contained the Book of Isaiah from the Old Testament. And the archaic lettering suggested that the scrolls dated back to before the time of Christ.

Unprecedented discovery

As there was no other extant book of the Old Testament in Hebrew known to be more than 1,300 years old, it was truly an astounding discovery.

Dr. William Albright, historian and archeologist at Johns Hopkins University, examined photographs of parts of the Book of Isaiah and dated the scroll to around 100 B.C. It was, he declared, an "absolutely incredible find—the greatest manuscript discovery of modern times."

Other archeologists and Bedouin tribesmen began combing the area around the Dead Sea, and by 1956, 10 more caves were discovered to contain scrolls and fragments.

Experts at the Chicago Institute of Nuclear Studies burned fragments of the linen in which the scrolls had been wrapped in the first cave and carbon-dated it from around 167 B.C. to A.D. 233.

As find after find was made, it became clear that the scrolls formed part of a large library that had, for some reason, been hidden in the wilderness.

Ruins of monastery

Excavations less than 600 yards from the original cave uncovered the ruins of a monastery, known as Khirbet Qumran, which once housed an obscure religious sect. In the writing room of the monastery's community center were found a long writing table and bench, two inkpots, and a jar like the ones found in the first cave.

It appeared that the members of the Qumran community had hidden the documents at the approach of the Roman 10th Legion, about A.D. 68.

Most of the documents and fragments found—some of them no larger than a postage stamp—are in Hebrew. But there are a few fragments of the Septuagint in Greek. They represent more than 500 books, including all the books of the Old Testament except Esther. In addition, there are commentaries on the Old Testament and texts documenting the life and disciplines of the community.

Little-known sect

The descriptions of the Qumran community's everyday life tally with what is known of the Essenes, a Jewish religious sect of those times with a membership of about 4,000. The Roman historian Pliny wrote that they lived on the western shore of the Dead Sea—the region where the monastery was unearthed. The site is assumed to have been their headquarters.

The scrolls have given Biblical scholars new insights.

Christian beginnings

Some of the documents, including the sect's *Manual of Discipline,* have revealed surprising similarities between the Essenes and the early Christian movement.

Admission to Essene brotherhood required candidates to renounce former ties and worldly possessions. Members lived austerely and strove for purity of thought, humility, and gentleness. Their rituals included baptism with water, symbolizing spiritual cleansing upon repentance, and a sacramental supper. The orders lived communally, and leadership rested with a group of 12.

Scholars are mystified about the identity of the "Teacher of Righteousness" mentioned in the scrolls.

But they are struck by the number of expressions and ethical ideas that parallel many in the New Testament, especially the references to "The Way" and to the struggle between the forces of "Light" and "Darkness."

Some believe that John the Baptist was an Essene, and it has been suggested Jesus was too. If so, he eventually broke away from the legalistic sect that upheld Mosaic law as the way to salvation.

Scholars are still busy piecing together and studying the thousands of scraps of manuscript. It will be years before the Dead Sea Scrolls yield all their secrets.

TREASURE CAVES. *Hidden from the advancing Roman legions, the scrolls lay in the dark depths of these caves for nearly 1,900 years.*

MASADA : JEWISH ROCK OF DEFIANCE

The Zealots chose mass suicide rather than surrender to Rome

As the Roman 10th Legion prepared a final assault on the rock plateau fortress of Masada in the year A.D. 73, the band of Jewish Zealots trapped inside came to a terrible decision.

Rather than surrender and submit to the cruelty of Roman retribution and slavery, they chose to die by their own hands.

The martyrdom of the Zealots was recorded by the Jewish historian Flavius Josephus. According to Josephus, their leader, Eleazar ben Ya'ir, made a heroic speech: "It is very plain that we shall be taken within a day's time. . . .

"Let us die before we become slaves under our enemies, and let us go out of the world, together with our children and our wives, in a state of freedom. . . . Let us therefore make haste, and instead of affording them so much pleasure, as they hope for in getting us under their power, let us leave them an example which shall at once cause their astonishment at our death, and their admiration of our hardiness therein."

Ben Ya'ir ordered the entire fortress to be burned (except for the ample food stores, for the Zealots wanted to show that they were acting from pride and religious belief, not out of desperation).

Then the married men slew their families. The survivors cast lots to choose 10 men who would kill the rest of the garrison. The 10 cast lots again to choose one who would kill the others. Then he killed himself.

The Romans surged over the walls—and encountered "perfect silence." Crossing the grounds, Josephus wrote, they "met with the multitude of the slain, but could take no pleasure in the fact, though it were done to their enemies. Nor could they do other than wonder at the courage of their resolution, and at the immovable contempt of death which so great a number of them had shown. . . ."

MASADA FROM THE AIR. *Perched on a high rock table rising 1,300 feet from the western shore of the Dead Sea in Judea, Herod's fortress seemed invincible.*

Of 967 Jews, only 7—2 women and 5 children—survived to tell the story. They had hidden in caverns, and the Romans who found them were so moved that their lives were spared.

Masada is therefore one of the great stories of a people's struggle for independence. Yet the story had long been regarded as suspect since the only account came from a Jew, Josephus, who had been nowhere near the battle scene.

The evidence was found in 1963, in one of the most difficult excavations ever carried out. Five thousand volunteers from all over the world participated under the direction of Prof. Yigael Yadin, Israel's foremost archeologist.

Masada is an enormous flat-topped outcrop of rock, 23 acres in area, on the Judean plain near the Dead Sea.

About 30 years before the birth of Christ, it was fortified as a citadel by King Herod the Great. A man who lived in constant fear of treachery, Herod built great walls and towers around the summit and a network of aqueducts and cisterns, huge underground chambers with stairs cut out of solid rock.

On the escarpment Herod erected palaces and an opulent three-tiered pleasure villa. It was a retreat that was both safe and luxurious. After Herod's death Roman soldiers garrisoned there until A.D. 66 when the Zealots under Menahem rebelled against Roman rule. Four years later, when the rebellion was all but crushed, Masada alone held out.

Vengeance of Rome

The Roman procurator of Judea, Flavius Silva, marched against Masada in the year 72 at the head of the formidable 10th Legion. By early 73 he had built a containing wall around the citadel so that no man, woman, or child would escape the vengeance of Rome.

Then he set about his campaign of attack. The only possible approach was by a spur on the western flank, and he began to build a great earthen ramp up toward it. By the spring the ramp was ready and was capped by a stone siege tower, and the Romans moved in their catapults and battering ram. It was only a matter of time. Masada was doomed.

Nineteen centuries later the excavators uncovered evidence of the Zealots' desperate last day—food stores that had not been set on fire and a heap of bronze coins that had been used like ration coupons.

In the debris of various structures they found fragments of 14 scrolls, each of which could be dated with some certainty from the early first century B.C. to the years preceding A.D. 73. They contained excerpts from the Biblical Books of Deuteronomy, Ezekiel, Psalms, and parts of the Apocrypha. One bore a sectarian text similar to that of the Dead Sea Scrolls.

At a strategic point overlooking the direction of the expected Roman assault, the archeologists found 11 pieces of pottery, each with a name inscribed on it, apparently all by the same hand. On one was the name Ben Ya'ir.

Was it possible that along with the 10 lots there had been an 11th—that of the heroic leader Eleazar ben Ya'ir? And that he was the last man left alive, to die by his own sword? A man of his caliber would hardly have shrunk from the terrible task he had asked his followers to perform.

Today, Masada is preserved by the Israelis as a sacred place. And every recruit to Israel's armed forces now makes this vow: "Masada shall not fall again."

THE PRINCESS AND THE CRONE

The ancient tomb's secret of a suicide pact

About 50 miles northwest of the Chinese city of Sian a cluster of 17 flat-topped pyramids rises boldly from the surrounding fields. This is the great burial field of T'ang royalty, and here, nearly 1,300 years ago, a young princess was buried. She was Princess Yung-T'ai (meaning Eternal Peace), who lived during the T'ang dynasty of A.D. 618–907, often described as China's golden age.

The story of her life and death is tragic, even after the passage of so many centuries.

In the year A.D. 700, the 16-year-old Princess Yung-T'ai was married to a high-born member of the T'ang court, a commander of the second rank of imperial carriages. Soon after her marriage she became pregnant, and her future in a brilliant world of pomp, extravagance, and exquisite works of art seemed secure.

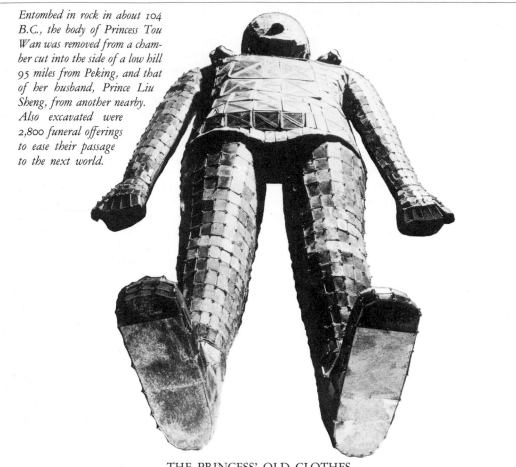

Entombed in rock in about 104 B.C., the body of Princess Tou Wan was removed from a chamber cut into the side of a low hill 95 miles from Peking, and that of her husband, Prince Liu Sheng, from another nearby. Also excavated were 2,800 funeral offerings to ease their passage to the next world.

THE PRINCESS' OLD CLOTHES

THE CHINESE Princess Tou Wan died more than 2,000 years ago, and, because she was buried in this jade suit, it was thought she would achieve immortality. Her husband, who reigned from 157 to 141 B. C. and who preceded her in death, was given a similar shroud, and they were laid to rest in vast tombs hollowed out of a rocky hillside. When their remains were discovered in 1968, they created a sensation because of the great wealth of the 2,800 funeral offerings that surrounded them. But most spectacular of all were the jade suits, each made up of more than 2,000 tiny plates of thin jade, sewn together with gold wire. To the nobles of the period jade symbolized power, and gold symbolized physical incorruptibility. But while they were right about the precious metal, the mortal body of the princess herself had crumbled to dust.

But it was also a world that was dominated by Yung-T'ai's grandmother, the Empress Wu, who had clawed her way to the Dragon Throne of China by murdering the former Empress and pickling her limbs in wine as a warning to any would-be rivals. Not without cause, she distrusted the entire court and imagined plots on every side.

One day, in the year 701, one of the palace's many informers overheard the young Princess Yung-T'ai laughing with her husband and brother at some aspect of court life they found absurd. The informer took the story to the Empress, who saw in it the birth of a palace intrigue. At once, she ordered that the three young people must die.

Imperial decrees of this nature were backed by a strict protocol. All three knew what they must do, and on October 8, 701, they committed suicide.

The princess and her story faded from human memory until, one day in 1960, the Chinese authorities decided to excavate at least one of the pyramid tombs in the T'ang burial ground near Sian. They did not know the names of any of the occupants, only that they were members of the T'ang dynasty. One tomb was picked at random, and with their choice the long-forgotten princess took her place once more on the world's stage.

When the archeologists made their first soil survey around the pyramid to determine where the entrance shaft lay, they discovered another shaft running vertically right beside the base of the pyramid. It was obvious that tomb robbers had dug their way in to plunder the tombs that lay below.

Death of a thief

One of the robbers was still there. The Chinese archeologists found his skeleton lying on top of debris that filled an underground passageway 50 feet down. His skull had been smashed by an iron ax that lay nearby, and his share of the gold, jade, and silver treasures was scattered around his bones.

The tomb chamber had been ransacked—it is thought, within 20 years of the burial—and the great stone sarcophagus had been scarred by crowbars, its heavy lid split, and all its contents rifled.

Only the bones of the dead had been left. But they had also left untouched the niches that lined the passage to the chamber. These were crammed with T'ang pottery—items that to the robbers were without value but to modern eyes are priceless.

Their entry had also left undisturbed wall paintings depicting the dazzling life in the T'ang court.

The archeologists still did not know who the occupants of the robbed tomb had been, until they came across a great stone slab lying in the passageway. This slab was inscribed with the epitaph of the Princess Yung T'ai.

After the Empress Wu was forced to abdicate in 705, her son, the rightful Emperor and father of Yung-T'ai, ascended the throne. Soon afterward the Empress died, and her son, still sorrowing over the tragic death of his children and son-in-law, ordered that their bodies should be exhumed from the humble graves in which they had been placed and be given instead a royal burial in the heart of the T'ang cemetery.

The Emperor also tried to rewrite history. The T'ang history books had all recorded the name of Yung-T'ai and her unjust death. Perhaps in an effort to obliterate this memory, the inscription placed on the tomb by her father simply records that the former Princess Yung-T'ai of the great T'ang dynasty had died—in childbirth.

LADY OF THE LAND OF SILK

She died 2,000 years ago after eating melons

She was no great beauty. She was about 50 and stout—probably due to overeating. She had a deformed back and hobbled with a stick. But when the Lady Tai died around 150 B.C., she was buried in a style that gave her exhumation in 1971 something of the excitement surrounding the discovery of the legendary tomb of Tutankhamen.

The Marchioness of Tai was the wife of the Prime Minister to the Prince Ch'ang-sha in the Hunan district of central China. A post-mortem examination more than 2,000 years later revealed that she was prone to hardening of the arteries and died of heart failure brought on by colic—not surprisingly, since her stomach contained 138 melon seeds.

Not a romantic end, but as befitted the wife of a very important personage she was given a funeral that rivaled those of the Pharaohs.

Her tomb came to light when workmen were digging the foundation for a new hospital. In the grave they discovered a hexagonal wooden coffin. It was insulated by a thick charcoal jacket and hermetically sealed so efficiently with china clay that the body inside was well preserved.

She was swathed in 20 silken cloaks and wraps, and the tomb was lavishly supplied with everything that so rich and important a lady might require on a long journey. There were plates of meat, fish, and fruit, jars of wine, and even beef soup. There were bowls, boxes, and jars, superbly decorated specimens demonstrating the fine work of Chinese lacquer craftsmen.

The Lady Tai's wardrobe for the afterlife included a patterned silk gown, skirts as light as gossamer, socks, slippers, coats, combs, all carefully wrapped in perfumed sachets. Every item was carefully checked and inventoried on 312 slips of bamboo.

But the objects that most interested the archeologists were the silks. The Lady Tai had lived in the period when China's fame as the land of silk had spread to the farthest outposts of the known world, when long camel trains plodded the famous silk route across the Hindu Kush and through Samarkand to the markets of the Roman Empire.

The tomb, at Ma-wang-tui near Hunan, yielded by far the best specimens of these matchless silks ever found—more than 50 rolls stored in basket-weave boxes and still preserved by the dry atmosphere. One of the most exciting of these relics was a silk banner that had preceded the funeral cortège, painted with scenes of the heavenly world and the underworld. In the center was a painting of the marchioness herself.

Figurines for company

No servants had been slaughtered so their spirits might accompany their mistress to the next world—as had been the custom in earlier times. Instead she was attended in death by 162 wooden figurines of maids and other members of her household, including musicians who were provided with a 25-string zither and bamboo flutes.

The government of the People's Democratic Republic of China did not share the delight of its own archeologists in this treasure trove. An official censoriously declared: "The fact that the lady's husband used so much labor and wealth . . . for the burial of his wife shows how brutally the feudal ruling class oppressed and exploited the laboring people."

THE SEARCH FOR TROY

A boyhood dream with a golden ending

Heinrich Schliemann was only seven years old when his father gave him the Christmas present that changed his life and fashioned an important chapter in the history of archeology. The gift was an illustrated book containing a picture of Troy in flames, after it had been captured by the armies of the ancient Greeks.

From the moment he saw that picture, one passionate, devouring obsession filled Heinrich's young mind: to find the remains of Troy and prove to a skeptical world that Homer's account of the siege of Troy was really true and not just a poetic fancy. This would seem to be an almost impossible goal for a poor pastor's son who worked as a grocer's messenger boy. Yet to equip himself for his task he taught himself classical Greek so that he could read Homer in the original. He also had to acquire a fortune; within a few years he had built up a career as a merchant from which he was able to retire in his early forties.

Then, romantic as ever, he persuaded the Archbishop of Athens to find him an ideal wife, a Greek bride who would fill his four conditions of perfection: She must be poor; she must be young and beautiful; she must have a devoted nature; and she must be familiar with the works of Homer. Surprisingly, in 1869 he found such a paragon—Sophia Engastromenos, a lovely Athenian still in her teens.

Buried cities

With the names of Hector, Achilles, and Ajax still resounding in his mind, the 47-year-old Schliemann and his bride set off for the Dardanelles, to track down Homer's "windy plain of Troy."

He flung himself into the search with characteristic energy and recruited an army of 100 workmen.

Schliemann believed a local tradition that the site of Troy was on Hissarlik, a 162-foot-high mount, mainly because it fitted with his knowledge of Homer, and it was known to contain ruins. Archeology was not then the exact science it is today, nor had Schliemann tried his hand at excavation before.

His workmen simply dug a deep gash into the steep northern face of Hissarlik to see what lay beneath. Soon Schliemann was faced with a bewildering jumble of ruins, which were later identified as the strata of nine separate settlements, one above the other.

Schliemann went on digging until eventually he lay bare what he was sure were the 20-foot-high ramparts of the lost city—the very walls from which Paris watched the advance of the Greek armies come to avenge the kidnapping of Helen.

Helen of Troy's treasure

On June 14, 1873, after two years' work, a dazzling prize spread before him—an astonishing hoard of 8,700 pieces of golden jewelry—most glorious of all, a diadem made up of 16,000 pieces of solid gold, which hung from the brow to the shoulder.

With tears of joy in his eyes, he crowned his lovely wife with the diadem, hugged her, and cried: "Darling, this is the most beautiful moment of our lives. You are Helen of Troy reborn!"

An ecstatic and romantic rainbow's end—but Schliemann was wrong. The buried city he had found was not Troy, but one even older. And the diadem, dating from around 2300 B.C., had been worn by another princess more than 1,000 years before Helen was born.

Scholars today believe that Homer's Troy was destroyed about 1200 B.C., and they have identified it with the third stratum from the top. Schliemann had worked right through its ruins as his army of workmen burrowed down through the layers.

Chasing a star

The treasure he had found belonged to another city, buried near the bottom of Mount Hissarlik. Later he recognized his mistake.

Nevertheless, archeologists have given him the credit for finding the site of Homeric Troy, and for discovering a more ancient city of a prehistoric bronze age culture as well. It was a worthy epitaph for the grocer's boy who dedicated his life to chasing a star—and found it.

FOUNDATIONS OF A LEGEND. *The ruins of a Roman theater, or senate house, on the site of the ancient city of Troy, are shown above. Romanticized by the poet Homer, the ancient city was found by a former grocer's boy with a dream.*

IN THE SHADOW OF VESUVIUS

Pompeii—a city embalmed in lava

The man lay in the cobbled street, his hand still closed around a fistful of gold coins. Perhaps he was a thief; perhaps he had saved the money. No one will ever know. Whatever his claim to the gold, it was his fate to hold it in his palm for more than 1,500 years—buried by layers of volcanic ash until his body was uncovered in the 18th century.

He was a citizen of Pompeii, the summer resort for wealthy Romans near the Bay of Naples, which was wiped out in one horrifying day, when Mount Vesuvius erupted on August 24, A.D. 79. But in destroying the city, the volcano also preserved it for all time.

Shopkeepers were closing their wooden shutters for lunch. Girls were gossiping at a corner fountain. A baker had just slid 81 loaves into his oven. In a wine shop a customer paid his money for a drink. Then an earthquake struck.

The barmaid did not pick up the money. The loaves were left in the oven—they can still be seen, burned to a crisp, in a Naples museum.

Most fled at once, for the earthquake was only the first sign of danger. But others were bound to the city by ties too strong to break.

One group was uncovered sitting reverently at the funeral feast of a friend. Others dug to bury their valuables—and were buried themselves. Some hid in their houses. Even more loaded their belongings into carts—only to be trapped in the bottlenecks of Pompeii's narrow gates.

By the time Vesuvius fell quiet, 28 hours later, Pompeii was buried 20 feet deep in lava, and 2,000 of its 20,000 people were dead.

ROW OF DEATH. *All over Pompeii men, women, and children like these were trapped by choking ash as they fought to escape the doomed city—and lie frozen forever in their last moment of agony.*

The city and its tragedy were for centuries largely forgotten. Then in 1748 the King of Naples' engineer, Alcubierre, set about inspecting a 150-year-old tunnel that had been bored to bring water from the nearby Sarno River.

By luck he sank his first shaft into Pompeii's business quarter and unearthed a brilliant wall painting. Another of his discoveries was the body of the Pompeian with the fistful of gold. Alcubierre went on vigorously, if somewhat haphazardly, excavating the site.

Then in 1763 a German cobbler's son, Johann Winckelmann, became fascinated by the secrets of Pompeii. He became an expert on its history. But the snobbish officials who controlled the site would not let him visit it.

Winckelmann went on all the same, studying the finds and bribing a foreman to let him look at the site. By hard-won scholarship he turned a miscellaneous jumble of relics into a record of six centuries of life in the ancient Roman seaside resort. But Winckelmann was murdered by a chance acquaintance in Trieste in 1768.

It was another century before an Italian archeologist, Giuseppe Fiorelli, founded the present scientific policy of moving forward slowly—house by house and street by street—to make sure that nothing was lost in excavation.

For, amazingly, two-fifths of Pompeii is still to be uncovered. The unknown that still lies in its ashen shroud may be yet more breathtaking than the known.

THE TRIBE THAT INVENTED ZERO
Rise and fall of the Mayas' jungle empire

They were an agricultural people who never grasped the principle of the wheel. Yet they rose to artistic and intellectual heights that possibly no other culture in the ancient Americas attained.

They could calculate the movements of heavenly bodies and predict lunar eclipses far in the future with amazing accuracy. Yet they could not build a simple arch.

Their writing was still in a crude picture form, but they had books, made of long strips of bark paper, which they folded like an accordion into pages. Their system of mathematics was unrivaled even in ancient Egypt. They could count in millions and used the concept of zero 1,000 years before the Europeans.

The Mayas of Central America built up a civilization that was both splendid and barbaric, a culture whose sudden decline remains one of the most puzzling in history.

Unknown past
How they developed from simple village communities of farmers and fishermen around 1000 B.C. or earlier into a mighty culture, spreading through British Honduras, El Salvador, Guatemala, the Yucatan Peninsula, and the southern states of Mexico, is not clear. But they did; in fact, Mayan pottery from Belize has been carbon dated to 2600 B.C.

Gradually, the Mayas developed a distinctive class system of hereditary nobles, rulers, and priests; free, working commoners; and slaves—usually prisoners taken in battle.

Their mathematics used only three symbols: a dot for one, a bar for five, and a shell shape for zero. Yet it enabled them to calculate in hundreds of millions.

STAIRS TO THE GODS. *This temple-topped Mayan pyramid is at Tikal, in Guatemala.*

For some unknown reason they took the year 3114 B.C. as a starting date for computing astronomical events and the passage of time. So brilliant were they in astronomy that they developed the most accurate calendar in the world in those times. They had a 365-day year divided into 18 months of 20 days each, plus a 5-day period called Vazeh.

During their Golden Age, between A.D. 300 and 900, the Mayas built magnificent cities with wide boulevards and plazas. Their architecture was of startling beauty, with temple-crowned pyramids silhouetted against the brilliant jungle foliage.

Once it was thought that the cities were ceremonial centers where only the ruling class lived, while the peasants dwelt in the outer city and on farms. But recent investigations indicate that this was not necessarily so.

For some unknown reason, Mayan civilization disintegrated about the beginning of the 10th century, and their cities were left aban-doned. There have been plenty of theories to explain the downfall. One suggests that their agricultural system collapsed as the soil became exhausted and unproductive, resulting in a sharp decline in urban population. Others suggest earthquake, disease, wars, or invasion from the Mexican uplands. Or there might have been a revolution by the commoners and slaves against their overlords. Perhaps the workers saw nothing to be gained in producing luxury goods or beautiful artifacts to be deposited in graves.

Some scholars have suggested that about the year 900 the theocratic elite lost control, and a social and economic leveling occurred by means of a peasant revolt.

The magnificent cities were abandoned, and in the next few centuries the Mayan civilization that had flowered so brilliantly was finished. In the process of resurrecting Tikal, the largest of the Mayan cities, archeologists hope to learn the reasons why.

LOST FORTRESS OF THE INCAS

Where the beautiful Chosen Women hid from the conquistadors

For more than 300 years tales of a lost Inca city, situated in the Peruvian Andes, were considered little more than folk-lore. It was said, but not really believed, that the survivors of the Inca dynasty fled to these forbidding peaks in 1533 to escape slaughter at the hands of the Spanish conquistadors.

High in a saddle between two peaks, the Incas were said to have built an impregnable fortress city.

Explorers searched for the city in vain. They crisscrossed the wild jungles and mountains near the Inca capital, Cuzco, but found nothing of great interest. Disappointed, they abandoned the search, convinced that no such city could exist.

But Hiram Bingham, a young assistant professor in Latin-American history at Yale University, was determined to prove them all wrong. He had made an earlier reconnaissance of the unmapped region but had found only minor ruins. In June 1911 he mounted yet another expedition. Accompanied by two friends and some Indian helpers, he set off by mule train along the Urubamba Canyon, following up yet another lead.

One rainy July morning Bingham's party sat disconsolately, debating whether to go on with an expedition that seemed doomed to failure, when the innkeeper pointed straight up the mountainside across the river. There, he indicated, they would find ruins.

The ever-optimistic Bingham set out with only the innkeeper for company. The two men and their mules scrambled across the river and up the 2,000-foot slope. They met two Indians who gave them water and casually spoke of some fine terraces and some old houses and walls "just around the corner."

After so many disappointments Bingham was still dubious. But not for long. He rounded the hill, and there the lost city stood, more beautiful than he had imagined.

There was a flight of about 100 perfectly built terraces, hundreds of feet long and 10 feet high, each covered with soil carried laboriously up from the valleys. The city was a complex of white granite buildings, large enough to hold 2,000 people and impregnable to attack from below. Why or when Machu Picchu was built is unknown, but it is thought that it was constructed in the early 1400's as a bulwark in the

LANDSCAPE GARDENING. *So that the fortress city could grow its own food, the Incas hewed terraces from the rock and filled them with topsoil carried up from the valleys by an army of laborers.*

heart of a region newly added to their empire.

The city was a masterpiece of construction. Centuries ago the Incas had moved granite blocks uphill without the aid of wheels. Each block was cut in an irregular shape, and each dovetailed exactly with its neighbors.

The fate of the city's last occupants remains a mystery. Strangely, the population seems to have been mostly women. A later party, again led by Bingham, discovered 174 skeletons in the burial caves, and 150 of them were female. Bingham offered this explanation:

The Incas maintained numerous convents all over the empire in which the most beautiful virgins were trained to serve the nobility and assist in religious rites. Some became the Incas' concubines; others were brides of the sun, a number of whom became sacrificial victims.

Bingham believed that as the Spanish advanced, these girls, called the Chosen Women, were taken to the citadel for safety. There they could perform their religious rites and pray for the hated invaders to be driven from the land.

But in 1533 the Spanish executed the Inca ruler Atahualpa, and in another generation the Incas were a vanquished people. As the years passed, the women grew old and died, and the men guarding them drifted away. In time the jungle again crept over Machu Picchu, leaving no one to tell of its baffling history.

CITY IN THE CLOUDS

Did ancient Egyptians inspire pyramids in the Andes?

Long before the Spanish conquistadors overran western South America—in fact, even before the Inca empire arose—the mysterious city of Tiahuanaco already lay in ruins. Its people had vanished, and only their tumbled monuments remained to tell of the skill of their master builders, the men who raised stone castles in the sky.

Tiahuanaco stood south of Titicaca, one of the world's highest lakes, 2½ miles above sea level, in Bolivia on the Peruvian border. It flourished from about 100 B.C. to A.D. 1000. Its inhabitants left no written records. Almost all we know about them comes from Indian legends recorded by the Spanish 400 years ago.

The Tiahuanacans had no beasts of burden, no wheels, or even rollers, and their only tools were of stone. Yet they transported enormous boulders from the nearest quarry, 25 miles over rugged terrain and across the lake, to their city. There, the blocks were ground to an accuracy of one-fiftieth of an inch, and built into vast, enigmatic structures.

Ruins of several great buildings still stand on the site. Largest is the Akapana, a natural mound, artificially shaped and faced with masonry, 700 by 700 feet, and 50 feet high. Nearby is the Kalasasaya, 440 feet square. In one of its walls is a block weighing 150 tons. Remains of many other works litter the area.

Over a gateway of the Kalasasaya is a carving that provides a clue to the origins of Tiahuanaco's civilization. It depicts the creator-god Kon-Tiki (whom the Incas later called Viracocha) with tears on his cheeks. According to Indian legend Kon-Tiki was a man. He and his followers were white-skinned, blue-eyed people who arrived at Tiahuanaco about A.D. 500. They taught the Indians architecture and agriculture and erected stone statues.

About 500 years later, the legends say, Indians from the coast invaded Tiahuanaco. Most of the white people were slaughtered, but their leaders and a few others escaped to the shore and sailed away across the Pacific Ocean.

Another clue is a statue of a man, twice life-size, near the Kalasasaya. Now called the Bishop, it holds an object that looks like a book, yet books were unknown in South America before the Spanish conquests in the early 1500's.

From these clues and legends, and from archeological evidence, scientists have sketched an outline of Tiahuanaco's history. Two sets of outsiders took part. There was already a primitive culture in the area when the first group arrived, about A.D. 500. The newcomers were probably peaceful bearers of an advanced civilization who taught the natives new skills. Within 200 years Tiahuanacan influence spread over an immense area, from Ecuador to northern Argentina, as well as the coast of Peru.

The second wave of invaders, about A.D. 1000, wiped out the great city. Its empire lay in fragments for 200 years until the Incas reassembled it by their continent-spanning conquests.

No one knows the identity of the white-skinned strangers who raised Tiahuanaco to its heights, or where they disappeared to. There are many theories.

Long before the Christian era the Phoenicians were sailing the Atlantic Ocean, and by 500 B.C. they had colonized the Canary Islands. They may have reached Brazil, and their descendants could have crossed the continent to the Andes. In 380 B.C. the Greek historian Theopompus wrote of an immense island west of Gibraltar. Possibly a Phoenician sea captain had told him of South America.

According to Irish legends, St. Brendan crossed the Atlantic in the sixth century A.D.

No one claims that the saint visited South America, but Irish monks were bold seafarers. In their frail "curraghs" of saplings and hides they sailed at least as far as Iceland and Greenland. Was the Bishop a pious father, breviary in hand, and Kon-Tiki the Man of Sorrows, as the Indians imagined him?

But South America's west coast is more accessible from Asia than from Europe. Chinese annals tell of a voyage by Buddhist monks in A.D. 500 to a land far away across the Pacific Ocean. There are indications that a Japanese fishing boat landed on the Ecuadorian coast in about A.D. 1100, probably blown off course by storms. The Chinese, more advanced than the Japanese at that time, could well have made the trip intentionally, 600 years earlier. The Bishop may have been a Buddhist monk.

A fascinating theory was advanced by the Norwegian Thor Heyerdahl. He showed not only where the white people could have gone after leaving Tiahuanaco but where they might have come from originally. He based his proposal on history.

In about A.D. 1480 an Inca emperor and his army are said to have made a long voyage over the Pacific in a fleet of rafts made of balsa (a very light wood that grows in the Andes). Such rafts had been used since time immemorial by the coastal Indians. Building a balsa raft, which he christened the *Kon-Tiki*, Heyerdahl sailed from Callao, Peru, west to Raroia Islet, near Tahiti. This was his demonstration of how the Tiahuanacans could have fled to Polynesia. For evidence that they had actually done so, he pointed out the uncanny resemblance between the stone statues and buildings on many Pacific islands and those at Tiahuanaco.

In 1970 Heyerdahl built a vessel of papyrus reeds, of the sort used by the ancient Egyptians, and in this craft, the *RA II*, crossed the Atlantic from north Africa to Barbados, in the West Indies. By this daring voyage he showed how people could have reached America from the Eastern Hemisphere in ancient times. Settling first in Guatemala and Mexico, they would have colonized South America as time passed. And it is now generally accepted that civilization was brought to South America from Central America.

If Heyerdahl is right, then white strangers built the city in the clouds—men of the Old World brave enough to sail the oceans in boats of reeds and on log rafts.

EL DORADO

The name that deluded treasure hunters for centuries

For centuries the hearts and minds of men have been held enthralled by El Dorado, the legendary city of gold, a treasure house hidden somewhere in the Andes.

Hundreds of fortune hunters have trekked through the jungle and the High Sierras—and died in the quest.

Surprisingly, El Dorado was not a city at all but a man.

The legend of El Dorado first reached the world through the Spanish conquistadors, who invaded Central America under Balboa as early as 1513.

As they plundered their way into South America, the Spaniards and other Europeans heard tales of the sun-worshiping Chibcha Indians who lived in the 8,600-foot-high plateaus near present-day Bogotá, the capital of Colombia. The tribe, it was said, venerated gold as the sun god's metal. They wore golden ornaments and for centuries had covered their buildings with sheets of the precious metal.

Some Indians spoke of a holy lake somewhere in the mountains, a lake that was full of gold. Others told of meeting a golden chieftain in a city called Omagua.

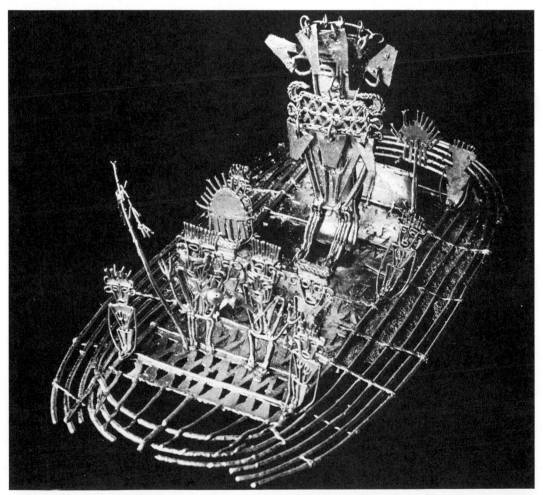

GLORIOUS CHIEF. *The exquisitely wrought golden model of the raft that carried El Dorado shows the rowing figures with their backs to the chief, so that their eyes may not see his glory.*

As the tales spread, El Dorado came to be thought of as a city of gold; it was even shown on ancient maps of Brazil and the Guianas, though its exact location was vague.

In the 1530's the Germans and Spaniards sent several expeditions into what is now Colombia to seek El Dorado. But the mountains were nearly impassable, and they were forced to turn back when they ran out of food. More than half the men were killed in skirmishes with Indians, and all the expeditions came to grief.

But the legend of the fabulous city still tantalized fortune hunters, and the very words constantly on their lips, "El Dorado," became synonymous with "The Golden Place," and its true meaning, "The Gilded One," was ignored.

The Gilded One

The Chibchas worshiped not only the sun but a being who lived in the lake. Some said it was the wife of a chief who had thrown herself into its waters centuries ago, to escape a dreadful punishment, and she had survived there as a goddess. Indians from all around made pilgrimages to present offerings to the goddess of the lake, and at least once a year the lake became the center of an elaborate ceremony.

The tribesmen would smear their chief with sticky resin and blow gold dust over him until he glistened from head to foot—literally an El Dorado. Then he was conducted in a magnificent procession to a raft on the edge of the lake. The raft was rowed to the middle of the sacred Lake Guatavita. Plunging into the icy water, the chief rinsed the gold off his body while the others cast in priceless offerings of gold and emeralds.

Lake Guatavita is a real lake. But supporting evidence for the Gilded One remained elusive until 1969, when two farmworkers found an exquisite model raft made of solid gold in a small cave near Bogotá. On board the raft were eight tiny oarsmen—rowing with their backs to the regal golden figure of their chief.

Yet Guatavita still refuses to yield its golden treasures. Many efforts have been made to drain Guatavita—by the Spanish, the French, the English (including Sir Walter Raleigh), the Colombians, and finally by the Americans. But although some gold and emeralds were found in the muddy banks, the icy depths of the lake were never plumbed. So far as is known, the offerings of El Dorado—the Gilded One—are still at the bottom of the sacred lake.

SIGNPOSTS ON THE FACE OF THE DESERT

ONLY FROM THE AIR is it possible to get a proper view of the strange patterns that were etched on the face of the Nazca Desert in Peru more than 1,000 years ago. On a 40-mile-long plateau above the irrigated settlements where they lived, the Nazca Indians scratched out on the sun-baked, barren ground geometric patterns and spirals and the shapes of giant lizards, birds, and cats.

The figure on the left resembles an eight-legged spider 150 feet long. The arrowlike shape on the right, equally mysterious, has been compared with the appearance of a long-billed hummingbird. Equally puzzling are the geometric figures—angles and triangles, lines running dead straight for up to five miles—which scar the face of the desert. Some scholars think these may have been astronomical signs or religious symbols. But because these gigantic designs can only be viewed in true perspective from the air, scientists still wonder how the Nazcas worked out their proportions.

THE FIRST AMERICANS

The migrants from Asia 40,000 years ago

José Cortés was digging a drainage ditch when he struck something hard with his spade. Scooping some earth away, he uncovered a huge curved tusk. Nearby was another, and both were attached to the enormous skull of the long-extinct mammoth.

José's farm was in Tepexpan, 20 miles northeast of Mexico City, and the year was 1950. Two years later, when Mexican paleontologists investigated the fossil, they were dumbfounded to find a projectile point in the fossil's rib cage. In the next few days other tools—scrapers—were turned up.

Victim of hunters

Apparently, the mammoth had become bogged down in a marsh, making it an easy victim for a band of hunters armed with stones and spears. But had men existed in America as long ago as the mammoth? Work stopped, and an announcement of the find went out to the archeological world.

The discovery supported earlier work of anthropologist Helmut de Terra. Digging in the same area in 1947, he had found the skeleton of a man. Because its bones were alongside those of a mammoth, De Terra decided that the Tepexpan man, as he called him, had lived possibly 11,000 years ago. But De Terra's claim had been dismissed by others with a charge of sloppy excavation work.

Men from Asia

The new discovery proved him right, and spurred new research into the peopling of North America. It is now thought that the first men arrived on the continent from Asia up to 40,000 years ago, walking to Alaska across the Bering Strait, which at that time was a land bridge.

This theory is based on recent discoveries of simple tools made of stone or animal bone in the Yukon Territory, Alaska, and Mexico. Scientists believe that many of these tools—projectile points, cleavers, and scrapers used to dress hides for clothing—date back 30,000 to 35,000 years.

Astonishingly, men were existing in America at a time when mammoths, mastodons, 20-foot sloths, gigantic saber-toothed cats, camels, a species of horse, and lions larger than the African lions all roamed the countryside.

Hunting animals and seeking a pleasant environment, men wandered southward and probably reached southernmost South America more than 8,000 years ago. And, after the melting of the ice sheet about 12,000 years ago, they gradually spread across North America.

The world's first farmers seem to have emerged in Asia about 10,000 B.C., and in the next few thousand years men began to live settled lives in many parts of the Old World. Just when the early Americans turned to agriculture and began to live in communities is not known for sure. But there is evidence that by 5000 B.C. pumpkins and squash and other crops were grown in Central America and Peru.

And in some other areas a reliable supply of fish or meat enabled people to adopt a semisettled way of life.

By then the mammoth and other huge animals had become extinct. Able to adjust to his changing ecology, man succeeded in outliving them all.

THE STONEHENGE OF THE U.S.A.

MYSTERY HILL has been called the Stonehenge of the U.S.A. It is a jumble of 22 stone beehive structures and walls, covering about 12 acres in Salem, New Hampshire, about 40 miles north of Boston. At the site a horizontal granite slab weighing nearly five tons has been found; it is called the Sacrificial Table—on the speculation that victims were sacrificed there in ancient rites. Investigators have found high, pointed stones along the walls that seem to follow the alignment of the stones at England's Stonehenge. Some wonder whether these are the ruins of a religious center built at the time of the Druids in Europe. Others believe they are the ruins of an old farm. About 150 similar sites have been found in New England.

THE SEA GIVES UP A GHOST

How a worm led the way to a ship's grave

August 10, 1628, was a great day for Stockholm. The city filled with patriotic, excited crowds as news spread that the *Vasa*, the mighty man-of-war named after the Swedish royal family, was to sail at last.

King Gustavus Adolphus II himself had ordered its construction. Intended to carry 300 fighting men as well as a working crew of 133, it displaced about 14,000 tons. Forty acres of timber had gone into its construction.

It was a 180-foot square-rigger, and 64 bronze cannons were mounted on its three decks.

Now the great warship was ready for the sea. It was 4 o'clock in the afternoon. To the cheers of the crowds onshore and the thunder of the fleet's guns fired in salute, the *Vasa* weighed anchor and slid gracefully away.

Then came disaster—sudden, startling, and total. A squall blew up in the bay, and the ship listed to port. Before the crew could haul the guns to redistribute the weight, water was pouring in through the square, open gunports of the lowest deck. In minutes the sea closed over the *Vasa*. There were few survivors.

Discovery under the sea

It was not until almost 300 years after the loss of the ship that two clues, which at first seemed insignificant, led a determined young man to pull off one of the most spectacular coups in the history of underwater exploration.

The first clue was the shipworm, a voracious mollusk with a pincer beak, which has plagued wooden ships since man first ventured to sea.

Cruising off the west coast of Sweden in the late 1930's, Anders Franzen, who was then just 20, came across some flotsam riddled with shipworms. This seemed odd to Franzen who, accustomed to sailing in the Baltic, had never before seen timber so badly worm eaten.

He investigated and learned that the Baltic is not sufficiently salty for the worm to flourish. So he reasoned that the *Vasa*, which had sunk in Baltic waters, might still be intact.

After the Second World War, Franzen, who had dreamed of salvaging an old ship, gleaned every scrap of information available about the *Vasa* and the place where it had sunk. He swept the harbor floor with grapnels and drag wires—

bringing up nothing but old bedsteads and all manner of junk. For four years his prize eluded him. But all the time he was getting closer.

Oak turned black

Then the second clue that was to guide him to his goal fell into his hands. Sounding the harbor floor in 1956, his core sampler—a device for picking up samples of the seabed—struck something. He raised the line and brought up a piece of ancient, black oak. Franzen knew that in these waters it took 100 years for the oak to turn black, so he must have stumbled upon an old ship. Could it be the *Vasa*?

Franzen's hunch was confirmed by naval divers, who found the *Vasa* 120 feet down, wedged up to its waterline in 16 feet of mud.

The first stage in the salvage operation was to tunnel through the mud and pass steel cables under the ship, suspended from pontoons, and

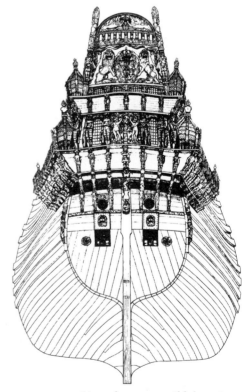

NAVAL GLORY. *More than 1,000 gilded carvings—of heroes and saints, surmounted by the Swedish royal arms—graced the ship that never left the harbor.*

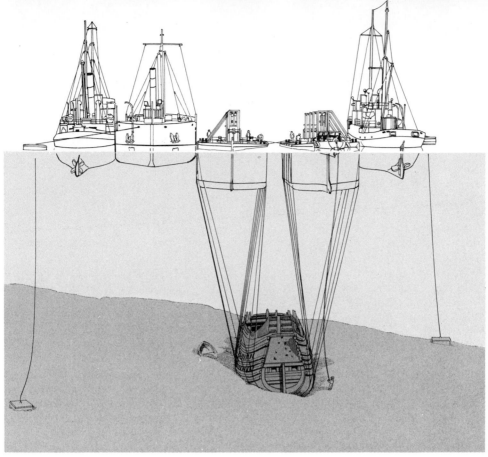

RAISING THE WRECK. *After divers had passed steel cables under the* Vasa, *it had to be "bounced" into shallower water and raised by two inflatable pontoons and a system of hydraulic jacks.*

then, by raising and lowering the pontoons, "bounce" the hulk free and into shallower water. This took two years.

Next, divers closed all the gunports, plugged every possible leak, and finally brought it up to the surface on April 24, 1961, with cables, pontoons, and a system of hydraulic jacks.

Today, the *Vasa* rests in a specially built museum in Stockholm and is continuously sprayed with steam and chemicals to keep its timbers from warping. The museum also contains personal effects of the crew. Chests, clothes, weapons, utensils, and coins make up a superb picture of the 17th-century seaman's life.

The *Vasa*'s resurrection was a triumph of underwater discovery and salvage.

THE WRECK OF THE "MARY ROSE"

"The more cooks, the worst potage"

The crew's last terrible cries of despair echoed across the waters of the Portsmouth harbor. Thousands of spectators stood, rooted in anguish, as the gaily bannered *Mary Rose,* pride of Henry VIII's navy, rolled over and sank before their eyes.

One of the onlookers, the young wife of Admiral Sir George Carew, fainted into the arms of a nobleman of the court; she had just watched her husband die.

It was July 19, 1545. France and England were once more at war, and a 200-strong French invasion fleet stood in line of battle off the Isle of Wight. Becalmed, the English fleet lay along the coast from Portsmouth to Gosport, praying for wind. Their plight was desperate, for the French oared galleys were able to close in and fire on the English more or less at will. But suddenly wind and tide changed together, and the English streamed out to meet the French. The formidable flagship, the *Great Harry,* led the vanguard, followed by the *Mary Rose.*

THE SCENE OF DISASTER. *This engraving helped Alexander McKee in his search for the wreck of the* Mary Rose. *In the center are the masts of the sinking ship; in the foreground is Henry VIII on horseback.*

Henry VIII and his court crowded the battlements of Southsea Castle, eagerly awaiting the result of the action. Below them on the coastal plain was the militia of the southern counties, ready to repel any invader who got ashore.

Before these thousands of spectators, the *Mary Rose* came around before the wind, gallantly heeling as its sails filled. Its lower gunports, just 16 inches above the water, were already open for action. With the helm hard over, the port dipped under, and in an instant the ship was on its beam end and sinking rapidly.

Handful of survivors

Within minutes only its topmasts stood above the surface; 700 men, hopelessly trapped, had gone to their deaths. There was only a handful of survivors.

The cause of the disaster is still disputed. The *Mary Rose*'s 91 heavy guns were run out, which may have affected its stability. It seems likely, too, that some of the guns were badly secured. As the ship heeled, they may have broken loose and careened down the sloping deck, increasing the list still further.

But witnesses testified later that the vessel had been grossly mishandled. One account said that it was a matter of "the more cooks, the worst potage"—each of the mariners on board considered himself fit to be a shipmaster in his own right, and none would take orders from another.

Certainly this view is borne out by Sir George's last words, shouted to his uncle, who was commanding a nearby ship: "I have the sort of knaves I cannot rule."

Salvage fails

The great sea battle dwindled to a skirmish, neither side being prepared to commit itself. Almost immediately a massive salvage operation was set up, and there was every hope that the *Mary Rose* would be quickly hauled up and restored to the fleet.

The ship's recovery was especially important to Henry, for he had ordered its construction in 1509 when he first came to the throne at the age of 18. It had been named after the King's sister, Mary Tudor, and his family emblem—the rose —and it was still considered one of the most formidable warships afloat at the time.

However, its 700 tons proved too much for the primitive salvage equipment of the day, despite the assistance of divers from Venice.

The *Mary Rose* was forgotten until one day in 1840 when a diving team, led by John Deane, working on the 18th-century wreck of the *Royal George,* was asked by some fishermen to free their nets, which had become snagged underwater close by. Deane dived and found the net hooked around some ancient timbers. His curiosity aroused, Deane explored the site and discovered five brass cannons dated 1535 and 20 iron guns, which he had hauled to the surface. Once more, the *Mary Rose* was in the public eye.

274

Ship's rediscovery

But somehow it was forgotten again until 1965, when naval historian and amateur diver Alexander McKee set out to find it. He suspected that the ship's hull, buried in mud for the last four centuries, might still be intact and that it might be possible to bring it up.

Such an operation had only been accomplished once before when, in 1961, Swedish marine archeologists lifted the 17th-century *Vasa* from the bottom of Stockholm's harbor.

With a small team of divers McKee managed to locate the *Royal George*, but after scouring the area he was forced to conclude that the *Mary Rose* lay somewhat farther away than the records suggested.

So he turned to contemporary accounts of the actual sinking and particularly to an engraving taken from a 16th-century painting. But the original painting had long since vanished, and there was a danger that the engraving, made in 1773, was not an accurate copy.

Marked on an ancient chart

McKee had already formed a clear idea of the general area in which the wreck lay, when unexpectedly he came across a chart of 1841—the year following Deane's discovery. There, right in the middle of McKee's search area, was a mark pinpointing the *Mary Rose*.

McKee and his associates, exploring the site with the very latest sonar equipment, found a wreck 200 feet long and 75 feet wide, although it lay 20 feet beneath the seabed. It was larger than McKee had expected for an Elizabethan warship, but in 1970 a single timber and an iron gun were dug out of the mud. The gun was proof that this was the *Mary Rose*.

Bones under the sea

On the first dive of the 1971 season, McKee found that during the winter the mud had shifted so much that a considerable amount of planking had been revealed. As more of the hull was exposed, bones were found, as well as pieces of leather that might have been clothing.

McKee is now eager to have the wreck moved to an underwater dock, so that excavation can continue without the problems caused by sea and weather.

His dream is that one day the old ship will be raised and exhibited in a specially built hall alongside Nelson's *Victory* in the Portsmouth dockyard. Such an operation, he thinks, might take 20 years and $15 million to complete.

A fitting memorial

This might be a small price to pay in exchange for the answers to ancient mysteries. No one knows how 16th-century warships were constructed or how they were armed. The *Mary Rose* may tell us. Once again, thousands of people will come to see it—a fitting memorial to the 700 men who died in the public's gaze so long ago.

PIECES OF EIGHT!

Treasure fleet of the Spanish Main

On any morning after a storm on Florida's Atlantic coast, treasure seekers can be found studying the wet sand in the hope of uncovering something washed up from the Spanish wrecks that litter the offshore reefs and shallows.

It is estimated that along the state's coastline there are between 1,200 and 2,000 wrecks. Many date from the time when galleons laden with treasure sailed the Spanish Main.

From the middle of the 16th century until well into the 18th, convoys would assemble in Havana, sail through the Strait of Florida, and ride the Gulf Stream north. Then off the Carolinas they could pick up the westerlies, which would blow them back home to Europe.

In May 1715 two small fleets under the command of Generals Ubilla and Echevez joined forces at Havana.

In its heyday the Spanish Navy had mustered as many as 100 ships for its annual transatlantic convoy. But by the 18th century, against British, Dutch, and French competition, it was past its prime.

The combined fleets at Havana in 1715 comprised a niggardly 11 ships, and not one of them was really seaworthy. The best of Ubilla's five vessels was a former English warship, the *Hampton Court,* which had been captured by the French and presented to Spain.

Nevertheless, there was much treasure for the ships to carry—including a cargo of precious works of Chinese craftsmen shipped across the Pacific and then carried over Mexico on mule-back.

Seams leaking

By the time they were loaded at Havana, all 11 ships were so low in the water that their seams leaked. And when they sailed on July 27, it was dangerously close to the hurricane season.

For two days they sailed through calm seas under a clear sky north toward the Bahamas. Then, ominously, thick clouds filled the sky, and visibility became almost nil. At night the wind rose, the ships began to roll, and passengers and cargo were thrown about. In the morning the sky was black, the heat unbearable,

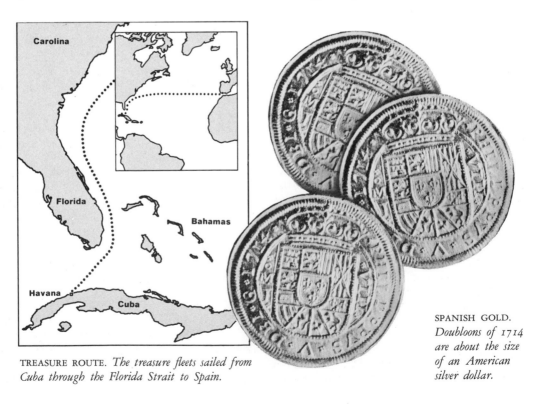

TREASURE ROUTE. *The treasure fleets sailed from Cuba through the Florida Strait to Spain.*

SPANISH GOLD. *Doubloons of 1714 are about the size of an American silver dollar.*

and purplish squalls could be seen on the horizon.

As the fleet entered the Strait of Florida, the wind doubled its force. The ships were caught between the sharp coral reefs of the flat Florida coast and the dangerous Bahamas Bank.

No more than three days out of Havana, the hurricane broke in full force. With their heavy hulls and short rudders the ships could not maneuver before the storm, which blew them rapidly toward the Florida coast. Masts snapped, and the decks became a mass of splintered wood and sodden rigging.

Sole survivor

Those who were not swept overboard knelt and prayed. Ubilla's flagship hit a reef first, and the rest quickly followed. Ten ships went down; the only one to survive was the *Grifon,* whose captain had disobeyed orders and sailed farther out to the northeast and was thus able to run before the storm.

More than 1,000 men were lost, together with silver, gold, and other goods valued then at nearly $20 million. Some of the survivors lucky enough to be swept up on the shore took what they could of the small amount of washed-up treasure and vanished with it to the interior. Others made rafts and reached St. Augustine, about 300 miles up the coast.

The Spaniards quickly sent eight ships from Havana and St. Augustine to set up a large-scale salvage operation. They established a camp on Cape Canaveral and a storehouse to hold the salvaged valuables. Using divers who simply held their breath and carried heavy stones to speed their descent, they brought up millions of pieces of eight.

Pirates rob the camp

Then news of the disaster reached Jamaica, the haven of English pirates. Two of these, Capt. Edward Teach, better known as Blackbeard, and Capt. Henry Jennings, attacked the Spanish camp, and Jennings alone got away with thousands of pieces of eight. Despite this the Spaniards returned to Havana in 1719 with about a third of their treasure.

The rest lay undisturbed for almost 250 years, when the wrecks became the site of one of the longest and most lucrative of all the Florida treasure hunts.

The searches, still continuing, brought worldwide fame to an amateur Florida treasure

seeker named Kip Wagner. Wagner moved to the Florida coast in 1949 and became interested in Spanish wrecks after hearing stories from friends who had looked for coins on the beaches. After buying himself an army-surplus mine detector for $15, he found a large number of coins dating from 1649 to 1715 on a stretch of beach between Sebastian and Wabasso, about 25 miles south of Cape Canaveral. From where the coins lay, he formulated theories about the positions of the wrecks. The coins were concentrated in small watercourses at various points along the shore. He wondered whether a different wreck lay off each point.

Rare-book discovery

Wagner and a colleague, Dr. Kip Kelso, conducted extensive research in libraries and institutes in the United States, and Kelso located a vital volume in the rare-books section of the Library of Congress. It was called *A Concise Natural History of East and West Florida* and was published in 1775. It described the wreck of the Spanish fleet in 1715 and mentioned "pistareens and double pistareens, which kinds of money probably yet remaining in the wrecks are sometimes washed up by the tide."

The pair got in touch with the curator of the Spanish naval records in Seville, who provided 3,000 microfilmed pages of ancient documents. When deciphered, these revealed the entire history of the 1715 disaster, the salvage work, and the rough locations of many of the wrecks.

It seemed that Wagner was on the track of the sunken Spanish convoy, but there were many years of work ahead. The operations were made more difficult by the weather on the Florida coast, which permitted salvage work for only a few months each year.

Wagner began by searching for the Spanish salvage team's base camp and store at Cape Canaveral; then after many days of combing the higher ground behind the beach with his mine detector, he located a ship's spike and a cannonball. He excavated and charted what turned out to be a half-acre site, finding more cannonballs, fragments of Chinese pottery, and a gold ring richly encrusted with seven diamonds.

Wagner knew from the records that a wreck lay off the camp. He spent many days floating on an automobile inner tube with a homemade face mask, peering through the silt and seaweed before he detected a cluster of cannons. Diving down, he found a large anchor. This was his first wreck, and now that he knew what these ancient relics looked like from above, he lost no time in chartering a plane from which he could scan the reefs and shallows for others. His aerial search was a success, and he charted the locations of a number of wrecks.

In 1959 Wagner assembled some friends, most experienced divers, and they formed what he called the Real "8" Company, Inc. (The piece of eight was the old Spanish peso of eight reals.) They also obtained the right from the state of Florida to keep 75 percent of what they salvaged. Using an old launch and a homemade sand dredge, they worked hard for six months without finding anything.

The team was losing enthusiasm and was on the point of breaking up when at last one member surfaced clutching six wedges of silver. Overjoyed, the others dived over the side to see what they could find on the ocean bed.

Carpet of gold coins

Over the next few weeks 15 wedges were found before Wagner decided to move the group to a different wreck. From then on his dreams of treasure moved rapidly toward fulfillment.

The first day's work on the second wreck yielded a staggering haul of silver coins, esti-mated to be worth $80,000. Then, one day after a storm, Wagner took his young nephew beach-combing. Wagner was picking up coins when his nephew found a gold chain. It was 11½ feet long and made up of 2,176 links. Attached to it was an exquisite gold dragon whose open mouth formed a whistle. A gold toothpick was hinged to its back, and the tail served as an earpick. This was identified as having belonged to General Ubilla and was sold for $50,000.

Finds continued over the years, and the group expanded. Perhaps its most amazing underwater feat was the salvage of 30 pieces of Chinese porcelain in near-perfect condition. The Spaniards had packed the delicate bowls and cups in a special clay called petuntse.

On May 31, 1965, the group was using a machine they had developed themselves. By directing a powerful jet of water downward from their boat's propeller, the treasure seekers blasted a crater in the sand without disturbing the precious objects that they were now confident were resting on the seabed.

As the water cleared, Wagner and his colleagues were spellbound to find themselves looking down at a carpet of gold that spread as far as they could see. In 1967 Wagner auctioned off the treasure for more than $1 million.

THE MOST VALUABLE FIND EVER

WHEN EDWARD TUCKER and his brother-in-law Robert Canton, salvage men working in Bermuda, spotted some cannons in a deep sand pocket between two reefs, they thought little of it. They lifted the cannons and some other objects that had come from an old Spanish wreck and sold them to the Bermuda Monuments Trust. It was not until five years later in 1955, when they returned with better equipment, that they began to find more interesting treasure.

Painstaking research identified the wreck as the Spanish ship *San Pedro*, which had sunk about 1595. In and around it Tucker and Canton found more than 200 silver coins, some assorted jewelry and gold bars, and other items.

But the most exciting find by far was a golden crucifix, three inches long by two inches wide, set with seven perfectly matched emeralds. It was identified as a pectoral cross and is thought to be the most valuable piece of Spanish treasure recovered recently from the Western seas.

This bishop's pectoral cross is thought to be one of the most valuable items ever recovered from the sea.

PART

3

Ancient defenses to counter perils of the unknown

Strange customs and superstitions

.

NEVER ON A FRIDAY

Man has done many strange things for the sake of luck

Not only was the ship called the *Friday* but its keel was laid on a Friday, and for good measure, it was commanded by a Captain Friday. The British Admiralty had decided to expose the absurdity of one of the Royal Navy's most cherished superstitions—that Friday is an unlucky day. Their plans might well have worked. But on its maiden voyage—on a Friday—the ship disappeared with all hands. No trace was ever found.

The Admiralty has consistently denied that this story is true, but its denials are unimportant; generations of British seamen have accepted every word of it. For superstition cannot be overcome by logic. In many cases it is a survival from those primitive religions in which man worshiped the wild elements in the pious hope that they might help him in his struggle for survival.

For instance, touching wood for luck reflects early man's belief that every natural object—a tree, for example—was inhabited by a particular god. The significance once attached to fire and iron lingers on today with the carrying of a piece of coal or a small replica of a horseshoe as a good-luck charm.

To spill salt meant misfortune, because for centuries it was the only means of preserving meat in the winter.

For some early peoples it was essential that the home be blessed with kindly spirits. The focal point was the hearth, the part of the house where, according to the Romans, household gods lived. In western Europe the area around the fireplace was thought to be the home of the "brownies" and other fairies who brought good luck to the household. Some even thought they helped with the chores.

It was unwise to offend the fairies. In their attempts to appease the spirits, housewives in the Western Islands of Scotland would leave part of the fire burning in the hearth to keep the fairies warm through the night.

When a family moves to a new home, it is still traditional in some parts of Britain to take the embers from the old fireplace and burn them in the new one. Housewarming parties are a development of this old custom.

Kitchen folklore

Superstition also dominated a woman's work in the kitchen. Some housewives believed a meal would be spoiled if the food was stirred "widdershins"—that is, against the sun's course. In order not to offend hens and so stop them from laying, no eggshells were thrown on the fire.

No implement has more superstitious connections than the knife. Made of iron, it is thought to be a protection against evil of many kinds. This may stem from a time long ago when people armed with weapons of stone or bronze were overcome by sharp-edged—and apparently magical—swords of iron.

Another belief is that if two knives are crossed on a table, a quarrel is indicated unless a second person uncrosses them.

TEMPTING FATE MONTHLY. *On the unlucky 13th of every month, the Eccentrics Club would meet at a London club and deliberately defy popular superstitions. Umbrellas were opened indoors, salt was spilled, ladders were walked under, and waiters poured drinks into cracked or broken glasses.*

There were many superstitions about bread. It was thought disastrous if bread did not rise in the oven, for it was believed that the Devil lurked inside unrisen bread. For this reason a cross was cut in the top to help the bread rise and also let the Devil out. But when cutting bread, it was considered foolish to slice off both ends of a loaf, since the Devil would be able to fly all over the house.

Even the table has superstitious significance. If a white cloth is left on a table during the night, the household will soon be in need of a shroud.

Above all, 13 people should never be allowed to sit down to eat at the same table. This superstition is generally associated with the Last Supper, when 13 were present, including Judas Iscariot, Christ's betrayer.

But the belief is older than Christianity. In Norse mythology 12 gods were feasting when the spirit of strife—Loki—appeared and provoked a quarrel that ended in the death of Balder, the favorite of the gods.

Outside the house further dangers lurk. One of the most widely known superstitions is the one about not walking under a ladder in case a tool or a pot of paint falls from above. One explanation is far older than that. Anyone walking between the ladder and the wall is

breaking the triangle—the early Christian symbol for the Trinity.

Another theory on the origin of the ladder superstition suggests that it was once associated with the gallows. One method of hanging was to turn the victim off a ladder so that he dropped "under" the ladder to the rope's end.

Chickens and fowl generally have long been regarded as reliable guides to what fortune holds. The Romans were frequently consulting their entrails, but self-confidence seems to have a lot to do with consulting fowl. On one occasion a Greek admiral was told by his soothsayers that the holy fowl refused to eat, which was a bad omen. He replied tartly: "Well, let us see if they will drink." He tossed the lot overboard, engaged the enemy, and won a resounding victory.

Some superstitions transcend national boundaries; others are peculiar to one country or race.

Scotland: Three swans flying together mean a national disaster. Red and green should not be worn together. It is unlucky to stand with your back to the edge of the door or to throw vegetables onto the fire. Love letters should not be mailed on Christmas Day. Carrying a spade through the house means that a grave will soon be dug.

CONFOUNDING THE DEVIL. *The clocks on the church at Mosta, in Malta, were set differently to confuse the Devil.*

Ireland: It is unlucky to use broken tombstones for the walls of a cottage. But it is wise to take care of the "fairy fort"—a tree in the center of a field. And it is lucky to spill a drink on the ground—a relic of the ancient custom of pouring a libation to the gods.

Malta: It was the custom for churches to have two clock faces, one showing the correct time and the other a false one, to confuse the Devil about the time of the service.

Ibiza: Priests are not allowed to board fishing boats, probably because of a vestigial respect for the pre-Christian sea gods.

Iceland: It is unlucky to shoot a seabird that follows a boat. An unmarried person who sits at the corner of a table will not marry for seven years. A pregnant woman who drinks from a cracked cup is risking her baby having a harelip.

Holland: When touching wood, it is necessary to touch the unpainted underside of, say, a table. People with red hair bring misfortune (a belief common to lands invaded by the Danes).

China: Any death by accident or foul play is to be feared, since the ghost may seek revenge on the seventh night. Sweeping out a house expels all good fortune—especially if done on the Chinese New Year.

Nigeria: Sweeping a house at night brings bad luck, but a good sweeping first thing in the morning gets rid of evil spirits. If a man is hit with a broom, he becomes impotent unless he retaliates seven times with the same broom. Sweeping after a person leaves the house gets rid of all bad spirits.

Japan: A comb picked up with the teeth facing the body is unlucky. Killing a spider in the morning is destroying a human soul. Most cats bring bad luck.

But as well as national superstitions there are other types of superstitions. For instance, a Jewish child must not be watched while he or she sleeps (because of the similarity to the death vigil). Nor must the child be shown its reflection until he or she has grown a tooth.

Gypsies believe that it is dangerous to eat food that has been stepped over or drink from a stream that a woman has walked over. And all caravans must be burned after their owners die.

It is easy to dismiss superstition as absurd, but only those who can break a mirror without a second thought are fully entitled to do so.

THE MAN WHO BOUGHT THE BLACK SEA

PRINCE URUSSOF, a Russian nobleman, had a family superstition that was initially very expensive but ultimately very profitable as well. While he and his beautiful young bride were honeymooning on the Black Sea, the wedding ring slipped off her finger and disappeared beneath the waves. The prince, remembering the family belief that the loss of a wedding ring caused the loss of the bride herself, did the only thing he could. He bought both shores of the Black Sea from hundreds of owners for more than $40 million. He reasoned that if he owned both shores he owned the sea itself and everything that lay at its bottom.

When the prince died, his heirs no longer needed to own the ring. So they sold their property on the shores of the Black Sea for $80 million.

THE FIRST REAL CHRISTMAS CARD. *It was designed by J. C. Horsley in 1843. The Christmas-card vogue caught on when the new postal services made it possible to send greetings this way.*

THE HOLY TIDES

The ancients had their own celebrations long before Christ

Christmas and Easter, although the greatest festivals in the Christian calendar, are celebrated with customs that originated in superstition and heathen rites hundreds of years before Christ was born.

Even the dates owe more to pagan practices than to the birth and resurrection of Jesus. It was not until the fourth century that December 25 was fixed arbitrarily as the anniversary of the Nativity—because the pagan festivals from which so many Christmas customs spring were held around that time.

And Easter, still a movable feast despite much pressure to allot it a specific date, falls according to the phase of the moon that the pagans long ago decided was the appropriate time to venerate their gods.

Although Christianity has swept the world in a relatively short time, as the histories of great religions go, the early missionaries faced an uphill task. The pagans were reluctant to give up their false gods and ancient practices.

So the missionaries, unable to convert them easily to an entirely new code of worship, did the next best thing. They took the pagan festivals as they were and gradually grafted the observances of the new faith onto these festivals and the rites and customs surrounding them.

December 25 was not called Christmas until the ninth century. Until then it had been the Midwinter Feast, a combination of the Norse Yule Festival and the Roman Saturnalia, both of which took place in late December.

Weeklong feast

The seven days of Roman feasting were an occasion for exchanging presents—one of the pagan customs that was gladly incorporated into Christmas. Even the sternest advocates of the new faith could not eradicate the notion that Saturnalia was a time for merrymaking. The Romans used to switch roles with their slaves, who were encouraged to elect their own "king" for the holiday. He would preside over a great banquet, at which the master would wait on him and his fellow servants.

A similar idea survives in the armed forces in Britain, where it is still an honored tradition for the officers and senior NCO's to serve the Christmas dinner in the lower ranks' mess. The reason Christian practice could never go the whole way with the Roman custom is that the

EASTER IN HUNGARY. *It was a Hungarian custom for village boys to call on eligible girls and sprinkle them with water "to make them good wives."*

unfortunate slave "kings," after their brief exaltation, were put to death.

When the Normans invaded England in 1066, they introduced into the Christmas festivities a mock king, called the Lord of Misrule, whose job was to ensure that the celebrations were conducted in the old pagan style.

Wearing paper hats and using firecrackers are throwbacks to the wilder excesses of ancient Rome. Yule logs and candles belong to the Norse tradition: They were symbols of fire and light, bringing welcome relief in the cold and darkness of the northern midwinter.

In the centuries that followed the Norman Conquest, as Christianity gained a firmer hold, carols and the Nativity play were added. And Father Christmas evolved as a mixture of the red-robed Lord of Misrule and St. Nicholas (Santa Claus), the patron saint of children.

The mistletoe

Mistletoe, a plant sacred to the Druids, was hung outside Viking homes as a sign of peace and welcome to strangers.

The custom of kissing under the mistletoe has been traced to the Roman Saturnalia. It has also been associated with certain primitive marriage rites.

The modern custom seems to have been confined to the English-speaking world. In England the Christmas mistletoe is burned on Twelfth Night because if this were not done it was feared that boys and girls who had kissed under it might never marry.

Even in relatively modern times, Christmas has not always been celebrated with unmixed enthusiasm. Under the 17th-century Puritan regime in England it was attacked because of its heathen associations, and Cromwell's soldiers were ordered to tear down seasonal decorations.

The prohibition spread to North America, where it remained in force until 1836 when the straitlaced descendants of the Pilgrim Fathers finally overcame their distaste, and December 25 was proclaimed a national public holiday.

Easter, like Christmas, was set by the early Christians to fit smoothly into the pagan timetable. In this case they chose the spring festival of Eastre, the Germanic Goddess of Dawn, held around the vernal equinox—the date when day and night are of equal length.

"One a penny, two a penny . . ."

Hot-cross buns, eaten nowadays by many people during Lent, are also a survival from pagan festivals. Both Greek and Roman women used to bake little "magic" wheat cakes. Two such buns, each with a cross on it, were found in the ruins of Herculaneum, destroyed when Vesuvius erupted in A.D. 79.

The origins of the Easter egg go back even further in history. Most of the ancient civilizations regarded the egg as the seed of life and fertility or a symbol of reincarnation. So it is not surprising that it was adopted along with the spring festival as a reminder of Jesus Christ's resurrection.

Egg rolling

The egg rollings of today are leftovers from the days when farmers hopefully rolled eggs across their fields to ensure good crops.

In Washington, in the early 1870's, so many children used the White House grounds for this pastime that the turf suffered and the game was transferred to the Capitol terrace. Mrs. Rutherford Hayes, the President's wife, took pity on the many disappointed children and again put the White House lawn at their disposal. From this beginning, Easter Monday egg rolling at the White House has become a national institution—a good example of a modern holiday custom that has its roots far back in pagan history.

TRICK OR TREAT. *Halloween is now a festival for youngsters who dress up in outlandish costumes for a night of fun. But Halloween began as a Christian holiday to honor all the saints and counteract autumn pagan celebrations.*

ALL HALLOWS' EVE

When ghosts, demons, and witches are abroad

Like Christmas and Easter, the festival of Halloween originated in a pagan celebration, even though its name derives from the Christian festival of All Hallows' or All Saints' Eve.

It was introduced in the seventh century to commemorate all those saints and martyrs who had no special day to themselves and was held on May 13. But in the eighth century All Hallows' Day was moved to November 1, to counteract the pagan celebrations held on that date.

October 31, the eve of November 1, was the last night of the year in the ancient Celtic calendar and was celebrated as the end of summer and its fruitfulness. It was a festival that the Celts of northern Europe marked with bonfires, to help the sun through the winter.

Winter also called to mind the chill and blackness of the grave, and so it was a time when ghosts would walk, and supernatural spirits, warlocks, and witches would hold their revels.

Only since the late 18th and early 19th centuries has Halloween developed into a festive time for children, with costumes, lanterns, and games. Before then it was regarded as a night of fear, and wise men, respectful of hobgoblins and wandering demons, stayed indoors.

In the 17th and 18th centuries, however, it was customary for "guisers"—people in weird masks and costumes—to go from house to house, singing and dancing to keep evil at bay, or to go about as representations of the ghosts and goblins of the night.

Trick or treat

This custom has survived today in many parts of the world, as a children's masquerade. In the United States costumed children go from door to door in a ritual known as trick or treat. They usually carry a sack and threaten to play a trick on householders if they are not given a "treat," in the form of candy or cookies.

The Halloween lantern, made from a hollowed-out pumpkin or turnip with a candle inside it, is a relic from the days when food offerings were made to the spirits of the dead.

THE BECKONING BELLS

Witches feared them; ghosts fled from them

Church bells that call people to prayer were once believed to have supernatural powers. In many Roman Catholic lands in the Middle Ages, when a new bell was consecrated and installed, gifts were presented to it, and the event was celebrated with much eating and drinking.

When England was ravaged by the Black Death in the 14th century, ringing the church bells was widely believed to help to dispel the plague. Almost three centuries later Dr. Francis Hering, in *Certaine Rules, Directions, or Advertisements for the Time of Pestilential Contagion,* advised: "Let the bells of cities be rung often: thereby the aire is purified."

The ringing of bells at a funeral was once supposed to drive away the dead person's ghost. When the ancient Romans held their feast in honor of members of the family dead in the month of May, it was customary to ring bronze bells and intone: "Ghosts of my fathers, go forth." In the *Roman Pontifical* the ringing of bells is recommended for expelling "the gibbering specters of the dead."

Many legends have told of bells being rung without human aid. Alexandre Dumas, in his *Pictures of Travels in the South of France,* said that in 1407 unearthly noises, including the chiming of a bell, were heard just before the collapse of the ancient bridge over the Rhone River.

Until the middle of the 18th century it was believed in Breslau, Poland, that if the cathedral bell rang by supernatural agency one of the canons would die.

Witches' role

Witches, who were said to fear church bells, were often credited with removing them from their belfries at night. In England a bell that had been dropped in the river by seven witches is said to have been heard tolling from under the water during great storms.

As recently as 1852 all the church bells were rung—unsuccessfully—in Malta to disperse a severe storm; and in the same century the bells were rung at a parish church in England, in the hope that their spirit would overcome "the spirit of the lightning."

THE FOOD OF LOVE

It has taken some strange forms—and still does

If an ancient Greek went for a walk with the udder of a hyena tied around his left arm, he was confident that no girl would be able to resist him. Even if this should fail, he could work a still more powerful love magic with calf's brains, hair from a wolf's tail, snake bones, the feathers of a screech owl—or even bits of human corpses.

Through the ages both sexes, of all races, have sought some kind of love potion. Women of ancient Rome brewed concoctions so strong that they were ruled dangerous and illegal.

The poet Lucretius was popularly thought to have been driven mad by one such potion; and according to the historian Suetonius, Emperor Caligula suffered a similar misfortune. According to gossips of the day he was thrown into a fit by potions administered by his wife in an effort to retain his affection. There is no record of the ingredients used.

In ancient Byzantium (later Constantinople), around 400 B.C., cakes made from asses' milk and honey were eaten on the recommendation of Hippocrates, the Greek "father of medicine." Honey is still highly esteemed by some as an aphrodisiac, though without any scientific support.

Many of the oldest love potions were made from flowers and herbs. Usually, to achieve the best results, they had to be gathered on Midsummer's Eve.

The herb mandrake has been the subject of many superstitions and was reputed in the Bible to have the quality of a fertility drug. The Book of Genesis records that the childless Rachel bargained with Leah for some mandrake that Leah's children had picked while playing in a field.

In Merrie England of the 16th century, marigolds—sometimes known as summer brides—

were regarded as a symbol of constancy and lasting love. They are still popular with some brides today when they choose their wedding bouquets.

Worried women in southeastern Europe in the Middle Ages employed a more complex means of correcting a husband or boyfriend with a wandering eye. They dug up earth from around his footprints and sowed marigold seeds in it. If this did not bring him back to fidelity, nothing would be effective.

About the same period cyclamen and fern seeds put into cakes were recommended as "a good amorous medicine." But a girl had to be very careful not only to gather these seeds at the critical time—Midsummer's Eve—but also to collect them in exactly the right way.

This meant that a Bible had to be placed under the plant and the seeds shaken into a pewter dish with a hazelwood fork. She was not to touch the plant itself. Otherwise, instead of winning romance, she was likely to be tormented by demons.

The amorous tomato

Many items of ordinary diet have been prized more for their qualities of stimulating the mating instinct than for their health-giving properties—and many still are.

The ancient Greeks used to bake their bread in phallic forms, believing that this would give them prowess in love. People ate eggs in the past for the same reason, because the egg was regarded—and still is—as a symbol of procreation and new life.

When the potato was introduced into Spain in 1534, it is said to have fetched up to $1,250 a pound as a love food.

The tomato was for centuries similarly esteemed, possibly because one of its many early names, *pomo d'ore* ("golden apple") became corrupted into *pomme d'amour* ("apple of love"). In England love apples were frowned upon as being conducive to excessive passion. Rumors were circulated by the Puritans that they were poisonous, with the result that they went out of fashion for 200 years. It was not until around 1830 that the tomato returned to favor as an item of food.

Lovers through the ages are recorded as having eaten spices, because they are hot and said to arouse amorous passion. Many seafoods—for example, the oyster, octopus, and red mullet—have been, and to some extent still are, favored, possibly because Aphrodite, the goddess of love, emerged from the sea.

Magic of the rhino

One of the most long-cherished beliefs in the realm of love lore, and one that remains relatively unshaken in the East, centers on the magical qualities of powdered rhinoceros horn.

Because of the insatiable demand for it, the Indian rhino was hunted almost to extinction, and about 60 years ago the authorities had to establish a government sanctuary to preserve the species. But the superstition lingers on, and rhino horn is still prized as an aphrodisiac in India and the Far East.

Another delicacy highly esteemed in the Orient as a love stimulant is bird's-nest soup, made from the unique substance that sea swifts exude from their mouths in order to make nests.

There is not a shred of scientific evidence that any of these love charms, potions, and philters—ancient or modern—has the slightest use in producing the desired result, but some people continue to believe in their efficacy nonetheless.

THE SACRED RATS OF KARAI MA

MORE THAN 100,000 rats swarm over the marble courtyard of a temple near the city of Bikaner in the Indian state of Rajasthan.

Karai Ma, the goddess to whom the temple is dedicated, is also the goddess of a caste of professional poets, who are called Charans. Whenever a Charan dies, according to the legend, he returns to the temple as a rat; and every rat that dies in the temple returns to earth as a Charan poet. If one of the temple rats crawls over the bowed head of a believer, it is taken as a good omen for his versifying in the future.

But if anyone should accidentally step on a rat and kill it, the penalty is a fine of silver equal in weight to that of the dead poet he has gone to revere.

LOVE AND MARRIAGE

How different peoples love, honor, and cherish

When two women of the Choroti and Chaco tribes of Paraguay want to marry the same man, they don tapir-skin boxing gloves and fight it out between them.

Girls from the Trobriand Islands, near Papua, begin their love overtures in a different way—by going up to the man of their choice and biting him. In fact, courting habits, both ancient and modern, involve the most complicated rituals and taboos.

A cold-climate courting custom known as bundling was popular in New England, as well as Holland, Switzerland, Scotland, and Wales. It allowed couples to lie in bed, provided that they were clothed and wrapped separately in blankets.

In 19th-century rural Scotland pregnancy was almost the rule for brides. A royal commission of 1868 established that 9 out of 10 women were pregnant on their wedding day in Scotland, a situation hardly in accord with the highest Victorian precepts.

In other societies, however, betrothal sometimes involved complete separation of the intended couple. A girl betrothed to a chieftain or other dignitary in the Solomon Islands in the Pacific was kept imprisoned in a cage, sometimes for years, under the watchful eye of her father, until her wedding day.

On the German island of Borkum in the mouth of the Ems River, an ordeal by smoke and water was once the punishment meted out to a man who had been courting a girl but was dilatory in naming the day. Young men of the village would surround his house and block the chimney, filling the place with smoke. Then they would remove the roof tiles, climb inside through the loft, and challenge the lover: "Are you engaged?" If he said he was, the whole village celebrated, but if his answer was "No," he would be dragged at the end of a rope three times through a pond.

Many of the present-day wedding customs that we take for granted are really born of age-old traditions. For example, the wedding veil was introduced by ancient Greeks and Romans to protect the bride from the evil eye of a jealous rival suitor.

The wedding ring, in general use in Christian marriages by the ninth century, dates back to the ancient Egyptians. The ring is placed on the third finger of the bride's hand because it was thought that this finger carried a vein leading directly to the heart. Made from gold, the most enduring of metals, the wedding band is supposed to confer upon its wearers a perfect and lifelong union; hence the superstition that a broken wedding ring is a portent of disaster.

Homemade underwear

The trousseau derives from the Old French *trousse*, or small bundle of valuables that was originally paid to the husband. Until a century ago in most parts of the Balkans, the bride was expected to provide her groom with sets of underwear that she had made herself.

The practice of throwing rice and confetti at weddings has its origins in an old Greek fertility rite of showering sweetmeats over the couple.

LOVE SPOONS. *These 18th-century wooden spoons were carved by youths in Wales as love tokens. A young man calling on his sweetheart was made to carve wooden spoons for her parents—to make sure his hands were kept occupied until the marriage took place.*

288

The act was also meant to confer prosperity on the pair.

In the Celebes, or Sulawesi Islands, of Indonesia, the belief is that unless the groom's soul is bribed with a shower of rice, it will fly away after the wedding and never return.

Feasting has always been a way of cementing kinship. At Malay weddings the bride and groom feed each other continuously during the ceremony with uncooked rice. And in marriages in New Guinea the bride and groom share a newly killed pig, or at least as much of it as they can eat. Similarly, Bushmen of South Africa gorge themselves with eland, a type of antelope, and leave nothing but the bare bones.

The Western idea of giving out pieces of wedding cake to guests originated in a Roman custom of breaking bread over the head of the bride to ensure prosperity. Each guest would then take away a portion of the broken bread.

Among the Lambodis, a seminomadic tribe of parts of central and northeast India, marriage is an occasion for lament. The morning after the wedding, the bride traditionally stands on the back of a bullock and wails her regret at leaving her father, mother, and family.

Aphrodisiac drink

In many societies the consummation of the marriage is more important than the ceremony itself—to the family, as well as to the bride and groom. The term "honeymoon," when the consummation takes place, derives from an old northern European custom of drinking honeyed wine, or mead, as an aphrodisiac during the first month of marriage.

A Greek-Cypriot custom is to roll a chubby baby boy up and down on the bridal bed before the consummation to ensure the couple will be blessed with healthy male children.

It was once customary among the peasants of Languedoc, in France, for friends to burst into the bridal chamber and offer the groom and bride soup from a chamber pot. The soup was meant to endow the couple with vigor, so ensuring that their marriage would be quickly blessed with children.

Newly married couples of 17th-century Brittany were expected to wait three nights before consummating their marriage. The first night was dedicated to God, the second to St. Joseph, and the third to the groom's personal patron saint.

The Yezidis of northern Iraq are consider-ably less restrained. They lock the couple in a room, and after consummation the bridegroom knocks three times on the door, which is opened by the priest, who fires a gun as a signal for general acclaim and the commencement of the festivities.

Conjugal claims

When a young man of the Todras tribe of Nilgiris, a district of Madras, marries, his brothers have conjugal claims on the bride because she is considered to have married the family. If the bride becomes pregnant, a ceremony known as *Pursutpimi* is performed to fix paternity. After a discussion among the potential fathers, the man chosen presents the bride with a symbolic bow and arrow under a kiaz tree, in the presence of an elder. Any further children are also considered to be those of the man first selected in *Pursutpimi*—including those born after his death—until some other man performs the ceremony.

GETTING TO KNOW YOU. *This water-pouring ceremony is aimed at helping a Hindu bride and groom to become better acquainted.*

BELIEFS OF ANCIENT MARINERS

The legends of men before the mast

In the 18th century it was common punishment for a sailor to be given 24 or more lashes for being drunk on duty. Old hands at the game of cheating authority had some words of advice for newcomers: "Get a crucifix tattooed on your back." Not only would the bosun's mate flinch from laying his whip onto the face of Christ, but the lash itself, it was believed, would cringe away.

Yet in other legends of the sea, Christian symbols, and parsons too, are feared because they bring bad luck.

Faced with the perils and mysteries of the sea, sailors have adopted beliefs from anywhere and in anything that seem to work. Animals, birds, names, even an action as apparently harmless as whistling can be dire omens at sea.

The beliefs are taken so seriously that the British Admiralty still takes enormous care in naming the ships in the fleet. Reptile names, for instance, are almost completely banned nowadays. For the navy has in the past lost four *Vipers*, four *Serpents*, a *Cobra*, an *Adder*, an *Alligator*, and a *Crocodile*—as well as a pair of *Snakes*, two *Dragons*, and a trio of *Lizards*.

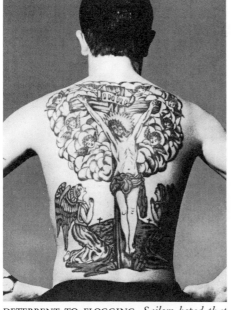

DETERRENT TO FLOGGING. *Sailors hoped that tattoos of a crucifix would avert the lash.*

Sailors have their own religious observances. The salute to the quarterdeck that the sailor makes when coming aboard has its origin in the time when a crucifix hung there.

But some fishermen will stay ashore for the day if they meet a priest or a nun on the way to the harbor. In the Faeroe Islands, between Norway and Iceland, whale hunters believe that their prey will get away if a boat with a minister aboard sails between them and the shore.

Even reading aloud or quoting phrases from the Bible at sea carries a terrible risk, except during a burial. As he was marched up to stand beneath the yardarm gallows in 1707, a condemned sailor shouted the words of the 109th Psalm: "May his days be few; may another seize his goods! May his children be fatherless, and his wife a widow! . . . Let there be none to extend kindness to him." The ship was the *Association*, the flagship of Adm. Sir Cloudesley Shovell. Later the same year the *Association* and two other ships sank off the Scilly Isles with the loss of 2,000 men.

According to legend, Sir Cloudesley, the man who had passed sentence on the sailor, was washed ashore unconscious—and buried alive. The woman who found him on the beach of St. Mary's Island confessed on her deathbed that she had murdered the admiral and hacked off his fingers to obtain the rings he wore.

In the days of sail, dead mariners were believed to be reincarnated in the bodies of petrels and seagulls. If one of these birds appeared over the ship in midocean, it was a sign of storms to come.

The bird that was regarded with the most awe was the huge albatross of the southern seas. To see one meant that a storm was certainly coming. To kill one brought an eternity of bad luck, as Coleridge recounts in his poem "The Rime of the Ancient Mariner."

In 1959 the cargo ship *Calpean Star* had to carry an albatross on its way from the Antarctic to a German zoo. When the ship docked at Liverpool with engine trouble, the crew walked off, claiming that the bird was responsible for a catalog of misfortunes on the voyage. Only after the bird died in its cage a day later was the captain able to find another crew to take the *Calpean Star* out of port.

Mentioning rabbits and pigs at sea is also unaccountably taboo. Sailors instead refer to pigs as Grecians or Jacks.

Perhaps most curious of all, whistling is banned. The logs of modern liners show that, even during the past 50 years, seamen were disciplined for breaking the taboo. Whistling was thought to encourage high winds and was allowed only when the ship was becalmed or shrouded in mist.

Another way to get rid of mist or buy a calm is to throw a coin overboard. When a storm blows up near the Bishop Rock lighthouse off the Scilly Isles, the keepers "blame" someone, who then has to hurl a coin into the sea.

It has long been believed that a drum owned by Sir Francis Drake possesses strange powers. When he was dying—off the coast of Panama in 1596—Drake ordered his drum to be sent back to his home near Plymouth (England), where it hangs still.

Drake vowed on his deathbed that if anyone beat upon it when England was in danger, he would return to defend his country. But the legend has changed through the years. Now, the drum rolls out ghostly warnings on its own.

It is said that the drum gave a growl when Napoleon was brought as a prisoner to Plymouth following the Battle of Waterloo. And it has been heard three times in this century: once in 1914 when the First World War started; four

DRAKE'S DRUM. *The drum is thought to sound by itself when England is in danger.*

years later aboard the flagship *Royal Oak*; and once in the Second World War, during the retreat from Dunkirk.

In 1918, as the German fleet steamed into Scapa Flow to surrender, a drum began an echoing tattoo somewhere within the *Royal Oak*. The commander himself made an unsuccessful search of the ship. But no sign of the drummer was found.

When the *Royal Oak* dropped anchor, the drum's victory roll stopped—as mysteriously as it had begun. Drake was at rest once more.

LOOK BACK IN ANGER
The power of the evil eye

People who use the expression "if looks could kill" are unwittingly reviving the once almost universal belief that the human eye had the power to injure or destroy an enemy. This fear is believed to have arisen from a primitive terror of being watched by wild animals, hostile tribesmen, evil spirits, or jealous gods who resented human success.

Before the development of medical science, disease and death were often attributed to the evil eye. Young children and animals were particularly vulnerable.

The evil eye was held responsible for male impotence and female frigidity. It was also thought that someone with the evil eye could blight crops.

Men and women with a physical deformity who might be suspected of envying their neighbors were considered the most likely possessors of the evil eye. This particularly applied to

PROTECTING THE DEAD. *Ancient Egyptian coffins bore painted eyes to protect the dead.*

hunchbacks and dwarfs. Those with a squint, or eyes set at uneven levels, or those whose eyebrows met, were also suspected.

In Africa the Congolese Lugbara tribesmen believe an evil-eyed man can be identified by his squinty eyes and bad-tempered disposition. He should quickly be placated with presents of beer and tobacco.

During the 16th and 17th centuries, when witches were said to destroy their victims by the power of the evil eye, hundreds of women were executed solely on the evidence that someone had died after receiving an angry look from them. The judges were so fearful of being bewitched when passing sentence that it was not uncommon for the accused to be led into court backward. Methods of protection against the evil eye—or "overlooking," as it was called in Britain—took a variety of bizarre forms.

In the Near East and Turkey passages from the Koran were painted on the outside walls of houses to provide a sacred barrier against the eye's influence. The symbol of the eye, which even today can be seen painted on the bows of fishing boats in some ports of the Mediterranean, was also supposed to counteract the effects.

Bunches of sage were used for protection in Portugal, and garlic was used throughout southeastern Europe, particularly among the Slavs and Greeks.

PROTECTING THE LIVING. *Maltese fishing boats have an evil eye painted on their bows—to shield the ship from other evil eyes.*

The Rwala Bedouins of northern Arabia carry two marbles wherever they go—one black, for protection by night; one white, for daytime insurance.

Throughout 18th-century Europe red—the symbol of blood and good health—was believed to protect the wearer against the evil eye. Italian brides covered their heads with a large red veil. In Rumania oxen had red rags tied to their horns. And Scottish tenant farmers tied red ribbons to the tails of their livestock or bound crosses of wood from the sacred rowan tree with strands of red thread.

Antidote—a hangman's rope

In the days of public executions it was common for a spectator who believed himself to be bewitched to buy a used rope from the hangman and burn it to ashes. These were mixed with cold water and swallowed to offset the dangers of the evil eye.

People who were convinced that their misfortunes were caused by the evil eye often attempted to return the curse to its source by throwing water upon the footprints of the person they suspected.

No one, it seems, was immune from possessing the power of the evil eye.

King Alfonso of Spain was reputed to have the evil eye. In 1923 he paid an official visit to Italy. Several sailors of the fleet sent to greet him were washed overboard; there was an explosion in one of the submarines; an ancient cannon fired in the King's honor blew up, killing its crew; and a naval officer with whom the King shook hands collapsed and died shortly afterward.

During the King's tour of Lake Gleno a dam burst, drowning 50 people and making 500 homeless.

The Italian dictator Benito Mussolini, who was terrified of the evil eye, refused to meet Alfonso personally and conducted all negotiations through an intermediary.

Similar fears persist today, for at the United Nations some delegates still turn away when they see eyelike designs. Their anxiety has given rise to a story that the peacocks that once roamed the lawns of the United Nations headquarters in New York City were removed to allay the peril of the evil eye.

The truth is more prosaic. The climate did not suit the imported peacocks: They died and were never replaced.

WHISTLING UP TROUBLE

The hidden charms—and taboos—in show business

First-night telegrams, congratulating actors on their performances, are usually stuck on dressing-room mirrors. If they turn yellow quickly, it is considered a sign that a production will enjoy a long run.

But on the final night of a show they must be taken down after each actor's last entrance. Some are torn up, especially if the show has not been a success. Others are kept in the hope that the "good luck" will carry on.

To many actors, the phrasing of the first-night message is very important. For example, it is considered acceptable to wish an actor a "great opening" or that he "knocks the audience for a loop." But to hope he has "a good run" is a jinx.

Most actors have a great belief in luck, crediting it with an ability to store itself in an object and reemerge when required. For instance, if an actor uses soap belonging to a "lucky" colleague, it is thought that some of the luck may rub off on him. To abandon something lucky, on the other hand, is risky. An actor who leaves soap behind in a dressing room may never be employed again.

Many actors cherish good-luck charms: a talisman or doll associated with a previous good run. The British actor John Mills has a lucky black cat, given to him by the late Sir Noel Coward, which he always keeps in his dressing room at the theater or film studio.

If something continually brings good luck, its use can turn into a habit. Hollywood star John Wayne, for example, likes to appear with the six-gun he used in his first Western, *The Big Trail* (1931). James Stewart wore the same hat all through his career, even when it began to fall to pieces.

In the theater actions, as well as "good luck" tokens, are considered important. For instance, though theater cats are pampered as lucky mascots, it is a very bad sign if one happens to run across the stage during a performance.

While umbrellas and combs are not in themselves unlucky, to open an umbrella or drop a comb onstage is asking for trouble. And if someone is knitting anywhere near the stage or in the wings, the actors must beware.

Some of the most curious actions take place offstage, often in the dressing room. For example, an actor will rarely look over the shoulder of a colleague into a mirror. And to spill the contents of a makeup box is unlucky. But perhaps the worst omen of all is someone whistling in the dressing room, for this means that one of the cast will soon be out of work.

An actor who inadvertently whistles must either curse loudly and vehemently or leave the room and knock before reentering. And anyone who fails to do this spontaneously must be sent out and made to turn around three times before returning.

Actors are superstitious about their work on the stage or film set. Because it is considered very bad luck, the last line of a play is not delivered at rehearsals. A smooth-running dress rehearsal is considered unlucky, while one with problems portends a good opening.

As the barrier between the actor and his audience, the curtain is highly symbolic, and there are a number of taboos about it. To look out through the curtains is always unlucky.

Unlucky yellow

Curtains that are part of the set must never be yellow. In fact, theatrical designers have to avoid yellow whenever they can, because it is an

TRUSTY SIX-SHOOTER. *Actor John Wayne prefers always to use the six-gun he had in his first Western film.*

unlucky color for many actors. Peter Sellers, though, dislikes anyone wearing purple onstage.

The fact that peacocks are especially abhorred by actors may be due to their vivid colors, or to an association of the many "eyes" of a peacock's tail with the "evil eye." Whatever the reason, their feathers, and any representation of them or reference to them, are taboo onstage.

As recently as 1974 bad luck plagued a "peacock" production that millions of viewers had been following on British television. Union trouble interfered with some BBC productions, and "The Pallisers" series, which had a peacock as its opening screen symbol, had to be taken off with the last two episodes still to run.

Apparently, however, the peacock curse does not cross oceans. When color television was introduced in the United States, the National Broadcasting Company, heedless of the superstition, chose a brightly hued drawing of a peacock as the new network symbol. During its use, there were no particularly dire results, or at least none that could be blamed on the bird.

THE TRUTH ACCORDING TO MARX

COMEDIAN Groucho Marx has his own, highly individual interpretations of the many popular superstitions that still survive, both inside and outside show business:

When a person's nose itches, it's a sign that it should be scratched.

A black cat crossing your path signifies that the animal is going somewhere.

Thirteen at a table is unlucky when the hostess has only 12 chops.

Singing before breakfast is a forewarning of a fight with a neighbor—if the neighbor is trying to sleep late.

Throwing salt over the shoulder is likely to give the impression that the man who throws the salt has dandruff.

Finding a four-leaf clover is a sign that you have been down on your hands and knees.

To get out of bed on the wrong side probably means that you have had too much the night before.

To carry a rabbit's foot is a sign that you are a good shot with a gun—or have a friend who is.

When three men get a light off one match it is indicative of the fact that they have only one match or are Scotsmen.

TAPPING HIS WAY TO VICTORY

Even the greatest sportsmen rely on rites and rituals

The world's tennis crowds had never seen a player quite like Art Larsen, an American. As he stood to serve, the gangling, nervous left-hander, perhaps the most superstitious sportsman of all time, would tap the court several times with his foot and his racket. Then he would bounce the ball . . . then tap-tap . . . bounce the ball again . . . tap-tap, tap again—and finally serve.

As he walked around the court between points, Larsen would tap baselines, sidelines, the umpire's chair, the net—almost anything that there was to tap. The crowds of the early 1950's called him Tappy Larsen and loved every minute of his performances at the major tennis tournaments.

Did his superstitions work? In 1950 Larsen became the American singles champion at Forest Hills.

For sheer prematch tension few sports can beat the buildup to a boxing title fight. Possibly to calm their minds, many fighters therefore follow extravagant and eccentric rituals.

Gloves and horseshoes

Former world heavyweight champion Joe Louis always insisted on having his left glove put on and tied before the right one. Bob Fitzsimmons, light-heavyweight boxing champion in the early 1900's, saw to it that a horseshoe was nailed up at his training camp. More recently, former heavyweight champion Ezzard Charles decided that his wife had a lucky dress and insisted that she wear it to all of his fights.

Henry Cooper, former British, Commonwealth, and European heavyweight champion, never polished his boxing shoes after a fight because following a bout early in his career he did so and lost. The world light-heavyweight champion of the mid-1960's, Willy Pastrano, used to tie his wedding ring to his left shoelace as a lucky mascot.

Baseball players have been known to be superstitious about their superstitions: They will not even talk about them. Often, to the distress of their teammates, many players refuse to have their uniforms washed during a winning streak. On the day of a game a superstitious pitcher will repeat everything he did the last day he won, even eating the same breakfast.

Other players firmly believe it helps to scratch away a bit of the baseline with a shoe spike. Some hitters cross themselves when they go to bat. Others refuse to step on the foul lines.

Empty barrels

During professional baseball's early days it was believed that seeing a truckload of empty barrels brought good luck. A New York Giant player named Mike Donlin spotted such a load before a game and made four hits that day. He mentioned his good luck to the manager, John J. McGraw, who said nothing but saw to it that the same truckload of empty barrels passed the entrance to the Polo Grounds each morning until the Giants left home for a road trip. Donlin made more hits, and the Giants won 10 consecutive games.

Another baseball player, Joe Dugan, third baseman for the New York Yankees, believed it was bad luck for him to throw the ball directly to the pitcher. He always threw the ball to another player to return to the pitcher, unless there was a chance of putting a runner out.

Football players are notoriously superstitious. After a winning season they have been known to request the same numbers on their uniforms for the following year.

Azam Khan, the Pakistani who was world squash champion four times from 1958 to 1961, believed it was unlucky to wear or use anything new for a championship game. Days beforehand he would start preparing by wearing in shorts, shirts, and shoes, and practicing with an ample supply of rackets.

Fish story

Anglers, too, have long-standing customs. Some will throw back the first catch of the season if it is female, probably because they think that females are the weaker sex and a bad omen for the rest of the season.

In professional sports it is sometimes hard to distinguish superstition from a touch of show business. A classic example of this is that for years South African golfer Gary Player wore all-black outfits, even in the hottest of climates. Player insisted that black brought him luck—but there is little doubt that it also made him instantly recognizable to the spectators.

HANDS OF FATE

The giveaway signs of a seasoned gambler

If a man at a card table sits bolt upright, picking up his cards in a strange way and breathing on them, the chances are that he is a seasoned gambler. For gamblers, with their unswerving belief in Lady Luck, are the most superstitious people of all.

The obsessive gambler who allies superstition with expertise breathes on his cards because, though he may not consciously realize it, he shares the primitive belief that the breath contains the essence of the soul. So by breathing on his cards he is projecting his powers into them.

Ritual blessings

A true gambler will never cross anything—not even his legs. He will always pick up his cards in the same way. He will give his dice a precautionary rub, performing much the same symbolistic ritual as when he breathed on his cards. The folklore of gambling is colorful, comprehensive, and enshrined in rules such as these:

He who wins the first game will win the third.

To play cards on a table without a tablecloth is unlucky.

Never play before 6 p.m. on Fridays.

To make a man win, stick a pin in his coat.

If playing for money, walk straight from the table, then make a round turn.

Many gamblers have their own private superstitions, and they probably owe their origin to someone's experience. But most gamblers' superstitions seem to be merely the result of man's desire to formulate laws—even to govern the one factor that obeys no law: chance.

However, consider the following: If a gambler plays cards with a cross-eyed man, whether his partner or his opponent, he will lose; a man who lends money at play will lose, but if he borrows, he will win.

Do cross-eyed men make people nervous? Lending money certainly does. And a nervous gambler is likely to lose. He may also show his nerves, thereby giving substance to some other superstitions: To drop a card on the floor is a bad omen; to sing while playing cards is a sign of losing.

People who are worried sometimes relieve their tension by singing. They frequently drop things. Perhaps the superstition that says it all is: To get into a passion or foul temper when playing cards will mean more bad luck, for the demon of bad luck always follows a passionate, evil-tempered player.

The gruesome superstition at Monte Carlo that after a suicide all those playing against the bank will win perhaps reflects a loss of concentration by the croupiers.

Whether there is a psychological explanation or not, there is always a great rush to exploit the tragic news.

SMOKE SIGNALS OVER ROME

The puff that means "Long live the Pope"

When a new Pope is elected, the eyes of the world are focused on Rome. Millions of people, Catholics and non-Catholics alike, anxiously await the cardinals' decision, which is formulated in a ceremony wrapped in secrecy and age-old custom.

No television cameras scan the ballot chamber, no reporters canvass the opinions of the voters. No one outside knows who the successful candidate is until the telltale plume of white smoke, signifying a decisive result, puffs from an iron chimney in the Vatican. Then a cardinal proclaims the name of the new Pope from a balcony to the crowd waiting patiently below.

A period of from 15 to 18 days after the death of the old Pope is devoted to the obsequies in St. Peter's Basilica. During this time the cardinals—the senior prelates of the Roman Catholic hierarchy—will have been assembling in Rome from all over the world.

Then begins their solemn conclave, the series of secret discussions and votes that will eventually determine which of them is to wear the Fisherman's Ring, symbol of authority of the man to whom 552 million Roman Catholics owe obedience. The ring is usually made of gold

SECRET BALLOT. *Cardinals have traditionally met and talked for days behind sealed doors in the Vatican before voting for a new Pope.*

BURNING QUESTION. *Smoke from this chimney relays the news. A separate alarm system informs the Vatican press corps of the decision.*

and set with a precious stone—a new ring is made for each new Pope. The tradition of the Fisherman's Ring is centuries old, though it is not known who the first Pope was to wear it.

To preserve the security of the conclave, the doors of the meeting place are walled up, and any necessary communication with the outside is by means of closely guarded turntable boxes in the walls, which enable messages, food, and other necessities to be passed in secrecy. As the voting goes on, the ballot papers are counted by three canvassers, chosen from among the cardinals and changed for each vote.

A ballot is indecisive unless it gives a candidate a clear majority of two-thirds of the votes plus one. Otherwise the ballot papers are mixed with wet straw and burned, producing the black smoke that signals no result.

Finally, often after many days, the cardinals vote the necessary decisive majority, and the papers are mixed with dry straw and burned. Then the excited cry resounds in St. Peter's Square: *"White* smoke! Long live the Pope!"

The traditional account is that wet and dry straw is still used for the ceremony. However, there were complaints in 1958 when the election of Pope John XXIII was announced with a tiny, grayish puff of smoke. During the election of Pope Paul VI in 1963, it is said that the cardinals bowed to the demands of the media and used black and white smoke bombs.

Although the smoke tradition goes back for centuries, it is only recently that any significance has been given to the color. When the people of Rome spotted white smoke, they knew they had a new Vicar of Christ.

HOMAGE TO A DEAD QUEEN

IN THE Portuguese city of Coimbra, a macabre ceremony is said to have taken place in the late summer of 1360. On the King's orders the highest dignitaries of the land came forward one by one and kissed the hand of a skeleton seated upon a throne. It was that of the Castilian Princess Inês de Castro, beloved mistress of the newly crowned King Pedro of Aragon. Inês had gone to Portugal in 1342 as lady-in-waiting to Pedro's wife. Pedro was then heir to the throne, and when he fell in love with her, his father, King Alfonso, feared intrigue and had her beheaded.

For the time being Pedro was obliged to suppress his grief and rage. But on becoming King five years later, he had the hearts torn out of her assassins. And he made the court do obeisance to the skeleton of Inês de Castro as Queen of Portugal.

Rituals to stop the dead from returning

Man has always been of two minds about death. On one side is the bright figure of St. Peter at the gates of heaven; on the other, the dark specter of the Grim Reaper.

Funeral ceremonies have always reflected both images. Some people have laid offerings in the graves of their loved ones to make their life in the next world easier; others have put stakes through their hearts to make sure that they never come back.

In the East one of the earliest ways of satisfying both requirements was cremation. The soul or spirit was helped on its way up to heaven by the flames, while the body was destroyed so that it could not haunt the earth.

Soul destroying

But in Christian countries cremation was outlawed for many centuries because it ran counter to the doctrine of bodily resurrection. That was the reason medieval witches were burned at the

PIONEER OF CREMATION. *Dr. William Price, an eccentric Welshman, paved the way for modern crematoriums.*

stake—to destroy both their bodies *and* their souls.

In Britain cremation began to gain acceptance fewer than 100 years ago, when Dr. William Price, an eccentric Welshman who believed himself to be an arch-Druid, cremated his own son. Price was prosecuted in Cardiff in 1884, and his acquittal—because the judge ruled that cremation was legal, provided it caused no nuisance to others—paved the way for modern crematoriums.

Burial, on the other hand, was designed to preserve the body, either because of the Christian belief in the Day of Judgment or because the physical body was thought to be needed in the afterlife.

The internal organs of Egyptian Pharaohs were carefully removed and embalmed separately from their bodies. Then, before the tomb was finally sealed, they were placed in the coffin beside the mummy; this was to ensure that the dead King would be physically complete in the next world.

It has been common for centuries to lay possessions to rest along with the dead. And archeologists have been able to tell from the gifts that were chosen what sort of afterlife was expected.

The Egyptians expected a rich and luxurious life after death, so they buried ornaments and household objects with their dead. The Vikings could not imagine a heaven in which there was no fighting, so they buried their heroes with weapons for use in Valhalla.

The gifts also had the purpose of making the dead person so content with his new world that he would not be tempted to return to the old one. Wreaths of flowers were meant originally not only to honor the dead with beauty but to act as a magic circle to contain the departed soul and stop it from wandering.

For similar reasons ancient Greeks laid a coin in the grave to pay the fare for the ferry across the Styx to Hades. In Scandinavia shoes were bound to the feet of a corpse to ease the long tramp to the next world. And the Zuni Indians bury bread so that the dead warrior will not go hungry and come back looking for food.

In extreme cases the custom has been extraordinarily expensive—for example, the fabulous treasure buried with the young Egyptian King Tutankhamen—while others were positive holocausts. At the funerals of ancient Scythian Kings like Darius and Arianthus (ca. 550 B.C.), scores of wives, slaves, and horses were buried alive to serve them in the afterlife. Only 100 years ago many Hindu wives accepted the custom of suttee—throwing themselves onto the funeral pyres of their husbands so that death did not part them. The British in India were still trying to stamp the custom out early in this century, although in some states it has been banned by law since 1829.

The Chinese have a much cheaper way of sending possessions and valuables through the vale of death. They burn paper replicas of them at the funeral.

The Tibetans, who believe in reincarnation, put as much stress on the "art" of dying as on that of living. When a person dies, an elaborate ritual is performed that involves reading the *Bardo Thödol,* the Tibetan Book of the Dead, to the corpse. The idea is to instruct the dead person in the mysteries that lie ahead before his return to earth in a new life.

Safely below ground

Tombstones also had originally the dual purpose of consigning the dead to the care of a god and of keeping them safely below ground. The cross has been used since the earliest times to mark graves, as an alternative to the ring cross of the ancient sun worshipers. Later, when the cross became the central symbol of Christianity, the ring cross was adopted as the symbol of the early Celtic church. The marking of graves at all, however, was mostly confined to wealthy people until the latter years of the 16th century.

Even the alignment of the grave has been important in speeding the departed soul on its way. Some old Welsh tribes used to bury their dead upright so that their souls could more easily ascend to heaven.

Often, Christian graves are laid east to west, so that they point toward Jerusalem. In Japan, however, the dead are laid with their heads toward the north—and the superstition has persisted so strongly that even now Japanese travelers sometimes use a compass to avoid the unlucky position at bedtime.

Death has not always been seen as the great leveler of men. In some churches in Scotland and northern England the northern part of the cemetery was reserved for criminals because it was considered unlucky, and the east was set aside for the saintly because it was closest to the Holy Land. The gentry got the southern end; the common people were huddled in the west.

Suicides have been particularly harshly treated. As self-murderers they were banned from being buried in consecrated ground, and until 1823 in England—when the law was changed—one who committed suicide was buried at a crossroads with a stake through the heart. This was because it was believed that people buried outside a churchyard would come back as malign ghosts to torment the living, unless they were tethered to one spot by a stake. Even if the spirit did get free, it would be confused by the choice of roads.

THE COLORS OF DEATH

DEATH IS associated with different colors in different societies.

In the West mourners traditionally wear black. In China white has always been acceptable, because it represents happiness and prosperity in the next world. Gypsies used to wear red at funerals to symbolize physical life and energy. Red was also the color representing death in the Celtic world and foretelling disaster.

Moslems believe that the souls of the just assume the form of white birds. This idea spread to Europe in the Middle Ages, and mourners in England wore white for centuries before black became the fashion.

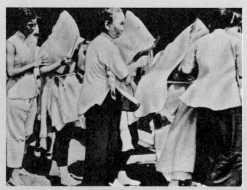

To the Chinese the hereafter is thought of as a new life of happiness and prosperity, so at funerals white has always been an acceptable color to wear.

THE SCREAMING SKULLS

Strange beliefs in the power of the death's head

Among primitive people of many races the human skull was regarded with superstitious awe. They believed that the skull housed the soul.

Headhunters preserved the skulls of their fallen enemies as trophies of war. Scandinavian warriors drank from skulls, hoping to acquire the martial valor of their foes. The ancient Celts decorated their shrines with skulls.

Widows in the Trobriand Islands of Papua impaled their dead husbands' skulls on poles as a kind of keep-out sign or sometimes used them as pots.

Skulls have always had an important role in witchcraft and black magic. They figured prominently in an English trial in 1612 in which Anne Chattox, head of a Lancashire family of witches, was accused of digging up three skulls from a churchyard to use in some ritual or demoniac recipe. She was hanged.

But skulls have not always been just the passive instruments of the sorcerer's craft. At Wardley Hall in Lancashire, the skull of a 16th-century Catholic martyr, Father Ambrose Barlow, is on view at the head of the staircase, and an old legend warns that should it be disturbed it will emit blood-curdling screams.

In the 17th century a girl named Anne Griffiths, who lived at Burton Agnes Hall in Yorkshire, was attacked and savagely beaten by robbers. As she lay dying from her injuries, she expressed the curious wish that her head should be buried in the home she had loved so well. She was, nevertheless, buried in the village churchyard. After the funeral terrifying groans and the sound of mysterious crashes and slamming doors were heard in the house. The dead girl's skull was exhumed and bricked up in a wall off the staircase. Since then, Burton Agnes Hall has been at peace.

Broken promise

The most curious of all skull legends in Britain is that of the screaming skull of Bettiscombe Manor, in Dorset, ancestral home of the Pinney family. The story goes that during the 18th century a Pinney who had been living in the West Indies returned home with a Negro slave. Shortly afterward the slave died, after making his master vow that he would be buried in his homeland, the Caribbean island of Nevis. But the squire apparently broke his promise, and the man was buried in the local churchyard. Soon, passersby were terrified by blood-curdling screams from the grave. The present owners of the manor, however, Mr. and Mrs. Michael Pinney, believe that the slave's dying wish was fulfilled—and that the legend was largely the invention of Judge J. S. Udal, a 19th-century antiquarian.

Mrs. Pinney says: "We believe the skull was found in a Celtic shrine behind the manor and brought into the house as a good-luck charm around 1690 to 1694. Judge Udal visited the island of Nevis in 1897, where he heard the tale of the slave who had gone to England. On his return he assumed the skull belonged to the Negro and read a paper about it to the local antiquarian society."

In fact, when the skull was examined by an expert it was said to be that of a girl and was 2,000 years old. Yet the legend remains that if it is ever removed from the house, the skull will scream, and the person who removes it will die within the year.

UNHAPPY SKULL. *Although forensic evidence refutes the original legend, respect for the skull's power lingers on at Bettiscombe Manor, in Dorset, England.*

THE MOUSE THAT DREW A MAP

Divine guidance via the animal kingdom

A group of generals gathered around a map spread on a table in their headquarters, anxiously following the progress of a mouse. Its feet had been daubed with ink so that every movement traced out a trail on the map. It was not some impish soldiers' game but a desperately serious conference on military strategy.

The year was 1796, and the Austrian campaign against Napoleon was going badly. The generals were worried and at a loss to know what to do. In desperation they decided to resort to a weapon as old as war itself—the use of a living creature to obtain guidance or knowledge of the future. But the mouse failed to indicate a way to victory, and Napoleon annihilated the Austrian forces.

Mice, cats, cockerels, animal bones, vegetables, even parts of the human body—all have been used in methods of divination throughout the world. Superstitious people who see a black cat as a good-luck omen if it crosses their path at the start of a journey are using an old one, dating back thousands of years.

The ancient Greeks, always careful to ensure that the gods were on their side in any important venture, would draw a circle and divide it into 24 sections, each containing a letter of the alphabet and a grain of corn. A cockerel was put in the center of the circle. The order in which he picked up the corn spelled out the message of the gods.

People who sometimes say, "I'm certain of such and such a thing, I feel it in my bones," might be surprised to know that, probably quite unconsciously, they are claiming powers similar to those of primitive seers. For this is a saying that has survived the custom of strewing animal bones on the ground and studying what is revealed by the way they fall.

It is also reminiscent of a divination method still practiced by the tribal medicine man in Guatemala, who addresses his question to a spirit supposed to live in the calf of his right leg. The spirit residing within signals "yes" to a question by causing the calf to twitch. If nothing happens, the spirit is saying "no."

Nature's products not only have been used to search for the secrets of the future but as a key to present truth as well.

This explains the use of a few peas to decide whether a person accused of theft was guilty or innocent. In parts of Europe in the Middle Ages the peas would be spread on a table under an upside-down basin, and all the suspects were made to walk up to the table in turn. The peas were the key witnesses in this identity parade. They would, so it was believed, bounce up and down when the guilty person stood near.

Handmaiden of justice

This curious belief in pea power is no great surprise, for magic was the handmaiden of justice for hundreds of years, even in the Western World. Britain and most European countries were greatly preoccupied with witches in the 16th and 17th centuries, and the methods by which suspects were "tried" often savored of witchcraft.

One favorite means of settling whether a suspected witch was guilty was to tie her up and throw her into a river or pond. If she sank, she was quickly rescued and declared innocent. But if she floated, she was condemned, for it was held that water would reject a child of Satan. Records do not show how many "innocents" drowned.

Fire and water have always been held in special veneration as instruments for reading the future. In ancient Rome poppy seeds were thrown into a fire and secrets disclosed by the way they burned. In the modern world there are still homes where a coffin-shaped cinder shooting from an open fire is seen as a warning of an impending death in the family.

The water method of foretelling the future has usually been based on the simple principle underlying the witches' ordeal: sink or swim. A custom among the Populuca Indians of Mexico, for instance, is to throw tiny balls of incense into jars of water. If the balls float, the answer to a particular question is "yes."

Until fairly recently, it was a widespread practice in New England for a girl to read her romantic future by writing her boyfriends' names on separate slips of paper and putting them in a bathtub of water.

The first slip to rise and float would be the one bearing the name of the young man she would eventually marry.

301

SECRETS OF THE TAROT

The future revealed at the turn of a card

The tarot is a pack of 78 elaborately decorated cards that can be used for games or for fortunetelling and divining. They were probably introduced to Europe by gypsies in the 14th century and are believed to be the forerunners of modern packs.

The 78 cards are divided into two arcana (from *arcanus*, meaning "mystery"): the major arcanum of 22 trump cards; and the minor, of 56 cards, itself consisting of four suits of 14—cups, coins, swords, and wands. These suits may represent four classes of medieval society: cups or chalices for the clergy; coins for merchants; swords for the nobility; and wands or staffs for the peasantry. As in modern packs, there are 10 numbered cards in each suit, but there are 4 face cards—knave, knight, queen, and king. The major arcanum consists of ornate picture cards. The meanings of the ones pictured above follow.

Top row, left to right: folly; subtlety; mystery; fruitfulness; power; marriage; love and beauty; providence; courage; prudence, but also treason; destiny or success.

Bottom row: rightness; wisdom or sacrifice; destruction; moderation; violence; calamity; loss or privation; hidden enemies and terror; happiness; outcome or renewal; assured success.

THE LOVERS. THE CHARIOT. STRENGTH. THE HERMIT. WHEEL of FORTUNE.

THE STAR. THE MOON. THE SUN. JUDGEMENT. THE WORLD.

Some believers in the supernatural think that the whole pack represents a system of philosophy that embraces the true nature of man, the universe, and God. They believe that they can gain insights into these mysteries by setting out the cards and meditating on them.

More popularly, however, the cards are used for fortunetelling. One method is to shuffle the cards, then lay them out in a pattern known as the Tree of Life, based on an ancient Hebrew symbol. The cards are placed in 10 piles of seven, face-down, and the rest are put aside. Each pile represents a different aspect of the inquirer's life, and each card has a particular meaning. As each card is upturned, its symbolism is interpreted in relation to the position in which it falls—health, knowledge, and so on.

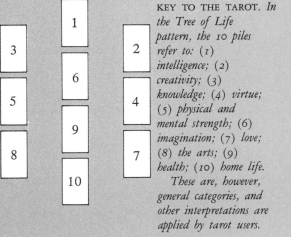

KEY TO THE TAROT. *In the Tree of Life pattern, the 10 piles refer to: (1) intelligence; (2) creativity; (3) knowledge; (4) virtue; (5) physical and mental strength; (6) imagination; (7) love; (8) the arts; (9) health; (10) home life.*

These are, however, general categories, and other interpretations are applied by tarot users.

303

ANIMALS THAT BROKE THE LAW

They had to answer for their crimes in court

Punishing animals that break the law is a practice as old as the Bible. According to the Book of Exodus: "When an ox gores a man or a woman to death, the ox shall be stoned."

It was not only four-footed beasts that fell foul of the law. Offenders have included horseflies, moles, caterpillars, locusts, snails—and a Russian goat that was banished to Siberia at the end of the 17th century.

The first recorded "animal" trial was in A.D. 864, when the Diet of Worms decreed that a hive of bees that had stung a man to death should be suffocated.

St. Bernard was preaching in a French church in the 11th century when a swarm of flies irritated him with their buzzing. He excommunicated them on the spot. The next day heaps of flies had to be shoveled out of the church—killed, it is suspected, by an overnight frost.

More often it was the larger animals that were brought to justice. In 1639 a horse was sentenced to die at Dijon in France for throwing its rider and causing his death.

Birds, too, were not immune from the law. In 1471 a chicken in Basel, Switzerland, was found guilty of laying a brightly colored egg "in defiance of natural law." It was burned to death at the stake as "a devil in disguise."

Murderous swine

Pigs roamed the village streets in France in the Middle Ages—a freedom that the law sometimes held them to have abused. One was hanged in 1394 in Normandy for eating a child. A sow and her six piglets were accused of a similar crime in 1547. The sow was executed, but her piglets were spared because of their youth and the bad example set by their mother.

One of the most merciful sentences was that pronounced on some moles that were the subject of criminal proceedings at Stelvio, in northern Italy, in 1519. The moles were accused of damaging crops "by burrowing, so that neither grass nor green thing could grow." They were required "to show cause for their conduct by pleading their exigencies and distress."

They did not turn up in court in answer to the summons and were sentenced in their absence to exile. But the court, in its mercy, promised them safe conduct "and an additional respite of 14 days to all those which are with young, and to such as are yet in their infancy."

Animal trials were normally conducted according to established legal procedure, and some lawyers made a reputation as defense counsel. The trial of a bear that had ravaged some German villages in 1499 was delayed for more than a week for legal arguments, on a submission that it had a right to be tried by its peers—in this case a jury of fellow bears.

Counsel for the rats

Bartholomew Chassenée, a French lawyer, made a reputation with his skillful defense of some rats that had destroyed a barley crop in 1521. When his clients failed to appear, he successfully argued that the summons was invalid: It should have been served on *all* the rats in the district. When the new summons also was ignored, Chassenée pleaded that "evilly disposed cats" belonging to the prosecutors were intimidating them and demanded a cash guarantee that the cats would not molest the rats on their way to court. The prosecution refused to give this guarantee, and the case was dismissed.

Animals have appeared in court not only as felons in the dock but also as witnesses in murder trials. In Savoy in the 17th century it was believed that God would give an animal or bird the power of speech rather than allow a murderer to escape justice. So, if a man accused of committing a murder in his own house swore his innocence in front of his own domestic animals and they made no protest, then he was acquitted.

One of the strangest "animal" cases was that of the Italian caterpillars that were asked to appear in court in 1659 on charges of trespassing and willful damage to property. A copy of the summons was nailed to a tree in each of the five districts where the damage had occurred.

The accused were asked to return to the woodlands and to refrain from destroying the crops. The court in fairness conceded the caterpillars' right to enjoy life, liberty, and the pursuit of happiness, provided that their behavior did not "destroy or impair the happiness of man."

CRIME AND PUNISHMENT. *A pig, dressed in human clothes and tied to a wheel, is publicly flogged. This was a scene common in medieval France, where free-roaming pigs sometimes broke the law.*

Some 50 years later a community of Franciscan monks in the Brazilian state of Maranhão complained that termites were eating their food and gnawing their furniture. The termites, summoned to explain their conduct, were allocated a lawyer who made an eloquent speech on their behalf. He pointed out that the termites were the original owners of the land and pleaded that their industry put the monks to shame.

After a long trial the judge arrived at a compromise verdict, which was read aloud to the termite hills. The judgment was, in effect, that both parties were bound over to be of good behavior: The termites should stop worrying the monks, and the monks on their part should not harass the resident termites.

In the 19th century American families plagued by rats would send them a polite letter asking them to leave. All proper courtesy was observed by coating the letter with butter and molasses and "posting" it in the rats' warren.

Trials of animals survived in Europe into the present century. The most recent was in Switzerland in 1906, when two brothers and their dog were tried for murder. The men were sentenced to life imprisonment. The dog was condemned to death.

As recently as 1974 in Libya, a dog was tried for the crime of biting a human and sentenced to a month's imprisonment on a diet of bread and water. It served its sentence and was released: Justice was seen to have been done.

AFFLUENT SOCIETY IN THE DESERT

If leisure has a value, the Bushmen are well off

In today's world unlimited leisure is a luxury that most people attain only after a lifetime of hard work. Yet there are communities that provide ample leisure for people of all ages.

The people who have time on their hands are those who are in many ways still living in the stone age—the Hadza of Tanzania, the Pygmies of Central Africa, some of the more inaccessible tribes of South American Indians, the Nuniamut Eskimos, and a few other remote groups of hunter-gatherers.

All told, they number only about 0.001 percent of the world's population of 4 billion. Yet if affluence is measured by the amount of leisure a society affords its ordinary people, they are the most affluent on earth.

According to the "leisure" theory, the bulk

of the human race took a wrong turn about 12,000 years ago, when agriculture was invented, somewhere between northern Greece and Iran. Once leisurely hunter-gatherers, they became farmers, obliged to accept the discipline of working to a timetable imposed by the seasons and their animals' needs. The Bible makes the point when it records Adam's banishment from Eden for eating the forbidden fruit: "And you shall eat the plants of the field. In the sweat of your face you shall eat bread till you return to the ground."

Food was there for the picking in Eden—as it usually is for the world's most primitive peoples. The Bushmen of Africa's Kalahari Desert, for example, can gather all they need in an average "working week" of 12 to 19 hours. Research has shown that one group lives mainly on mongono nuts, which give them a daily protein diet equal to 14 ounces of steak. Other edible plants and animals are abundant. They even run their own form of welfare state. The young and the old are not expected to work but are supported by the 20 to 60 age group.

In Tanzania the Hadza tribe has an even easier time. It has been calculated that the average Hadza spends less than two hours a day finding food. The men spend most of their time gambling.

It may be argued that the hunter-gatherer way of life is precarious and that a primitive community can be wiped out by a few lean years. But the facts suggest that in all except the very worst droughts primitive peoples are better equipped to survive than their more advanced and harder working neighbors.

In Botswana, on the fringes of the Kalahari, a quarter of a million cattle died in 1966 in one of the worst droughts ever to afflict southern Africa. Starvation faced remote farming tribes that were beyond the reach of a U.N. relief program. Then the Bushmen, who plant no crops and raise no cattle, came to their aid. Their womenfolk showed the farmers' wives where to find the wild plants and nuts on which the Bushmen lived. Faced with a crisis, the agriculturalists survived by returning to mankind's oldest way of life.

DEATH—OR HONOR?

FROM A rickety tower of bamboo and vines more than 90 feet tall, men of the Pentecost Islands in the South Pacific dive into the air, with liana creepers tied around their ankles. It is a semi-religious ceremony called the Gol and is intended to demonstrate the divers' courage.

The nearer to the ground a man can swing, the greater his courage. The lianas are cut so that the diver will swing only inches from the ground.

Early in 1974 the Queen and other members of the British royal family were at a Gol ceremony when one of the divers' vines snapped. The man broke his back and died later.

All that saves the man from certain death are liana vines tied to his ankles. Sometimes the vines stretch, and the diver crashes to the ground.

TOP HAT, WHITE FACE—AND SKULL

The dread ritual of voodoo

For hours on end the ritual chants are repeated to the incessant beat of the wood and skin drums. The rhythms become faster and faster. Perspiring dancers, visible in the night by a glowing fire and candles in the forest clearing, are exhausted. But still they whirl around, arms flailing, eyes glazed with excitement, mouths contorted with exertion and ecstasy.

Suddenly, all activity ceases. Only the flames from the fire and candles flicker. A figure in black clothes and a top hat emerges from the shadows of the trees. His face is painted white, and in his hands are a rod and a skull. He lifts his head up and screams a name into the night: "Baron Samedi, Baron Samedi." The drums end their silence. The dancers spark into action. The chants continue their weird message.

Lord of the underworld

This is how a tourist would see a voodoo ritual on one of a dozen islands in the Caribbean, in some parts of Brazil, or in certain areas of the Deep South in the United States.

The contortions of the dancers are caused by the voodoo gods possessing their subjects. The man in the hat is the high priest, and the name he has screamed is that of the lord of the underworld, the king of the voodoo cemetery spirits.

The word "voodoo" comes from the African word *vodun*, which means "sacred object, spirit, or god." It was transmitted to Haiti by African slaves from Guinea and Dahomey in West Africa.

Voodoo is a blend of beliefs derived from the West African religious cults, Catholicism, and the debased ceremonial magic of the grimoires or textbooks of ritual magic in France of the 18th century.

The wood and skin used in the drums during the rite, in which Baron Samedi's name is shrieked, are primarily symbolic of resurrection. Such is the hypnotic effect of this frenzied worship that participants have later been genuinely unable to remember what happened.

Walking dead

One of the more gruesome facets of voodooism is belief in zombies, or the walking dead.

Such "beings" are very real to many of Haiti's superstitious population. They believe that a magician can restore the dead to life—as slaves. The zombie belief made many converts during the great labor shortage in Haiti's sugar plantations in 1918. To cash in, sorcerers were alleged to have exhumed corpses, revived them, and sold them as slaves.

But some authorities believe that these "slaves" were people who had been drugged into a coma, taken for dead, buried, then dug up again, and revived with other drugs. Before selling their victims, the sorcerers first cut out their tongues, so that they could not reveal their origins. The practice was so widespread that a law was introduced treating the administration of soporific drugs as murder. Several so-called sorcerers were allegedly tried and hanged for the crime.

A form of community "devil dancing," still practiced in some remote villages in southern India, seems akin to the dark rites of voodoo. But it has only one distinct purpose—to "charm" away the dreaded disease of smallpox.

People infected by smallpox were believed to be transformed into devils, a superstition strengthened by the hideous pockmarks and delirium characteristic of the disease.

Professional devil dancers are hired by families to induce the "devil" to switch to one of the dancers. These "exorcists" are people who have developed immunity by contracting smallpox and surviving.

Mask with tusks

The dancers usually wear a costume of leaves and a brass mask with tusks and features exaggerating the symptoms of smallpox. They drink large quantities of a locally brewed strong liquor called arrack and dance with violent contortions to the beat of drums.

At the climax of the dance, the chief dancer severs the head of a goat with his sword and then drinks the blood gushing from the animals' neck. Other dancers will bite off the heads of cockerels, gyrating with the birds still dangling from their clenched jaws.

Once the dancers believe they are possessed by the "devil," they run off into the countryside—taking the disease away with them.

FIRE WALKERS OF THE WORLD

Is pain banished by religious ecstasy?

The mastery of man over flames has for many centuries been an essential part of many religious and magical rites. Holy men in Fiji and Sri Lanka and even in the Balkans traditionally have the power to walk unharmed and without flinching across red-hot stones or coals.

On the tiny Fijian island of Beqa, the gift of fire walking was, according to legend, granted to Tui-na-iviqalati, a prince and leader of the islanders, who caught an eel that transformed itself into the god Tuimolawai.

The god begged to be spared and promised to make his captor into the greatest fisherman or warrior. The prince refused. He was already both these things.

INTO THE FLAMES. *Western science can offer no rational explanation why fire walkers should not be burned. Perhaps faith is the answer.*

The god then offered him immunity from fire. The pact was sealed. A pit was dug and lined with stones, which were heated by a fire that burned for four days and nights. Tuimolawai invited the prince to lie on the stones and cover himself in fire to achieve complete immunity. Tui-na-iviqalati, not trusting the god, replied that he would be content merely to walk on the glowing stones.

Fire walking in Beqa is performed by a priest, called a *mbete*, and his novices. He is said to be a direct descendant of Tui-na-iviqalati.

A 15- to 20-foot-diameter pit is dug, usually 4 to 5 feet deep. A great pile of logs and stones is placed in it, and as the logs burn, the stones sink into a compact layer. The *mbete* tests the stones by scattering dried leaves. They instantly explode in flame. The stones are ready. The *mbete* then leads the fire walkers slowly over and around the glowing stones, and they emerge unscathed.

A similar ceremony takes place annually at a small fishing village north of Colombo in Sri Lanka. There, beside an old Hindu temple, a pit is filled with coals so hot that the men tending the fire have to douse themselves with water.

The walkers are then led to the pit by a priest who is first to cross it. He does so with unhurried dignity. The procession follows and moves across the coals at a rather faster pace—without mishap.

Another similar ceremony is performed every year in some villages of southern India, notably at Udaipur. Once the fire pit is prepared— usually 15 feet by 6 feet and 3 feet deep—the heat makes it impossible for spectators to approach closer than 30 feet.

In the Balkans a Greek sect, the Anastenaria, practices fire walking to honor the feast day —May 21—of St. Constantine and St. Helena.

Western science can offer no rational explanation as to why fire walkers should not be badly burned. Doctors examined fire walkers in Fiji and Sri Lanka. Their soles were not burned, and they still had normal sensitivity.

It seems that the walkers are able, as a result of long religious training, to put themselves into a profound trance, in which they feel no pain and need fear no harm. The explanation could be the simplest and oldest of all—faith.

THE THROWAWAY SOCIETY

To demonstrate their wealth, the Kwakiutl Indians destroyed it

In most societies the world has known, amassing wealth and worldly goods has been a sure passport to status. But less than 100 years ago, there existed in Canada a society in which a man's social standing was decided in exactly the opposite way—by how spectacularly he could ruin himself.

This extreme example of the throwaway society flourished on the northwestern coast of Canada and the United States from the mid-19th century until well into the 20th century, reaching its peak among the Kwakiutl Indians of Vancouver Island. Their chiefs publicly burned food, blankets, canoes, and ornaments in the ceremony of potlatch, a word that means "giving."

The Indians of the Northwest lived in a society obsessed by rank and would arrange elaborate potlatch feasts to mark any significant event.

The birth of a chief's heir, the marriage of an important man, a dispute about who should be a tribe's next chief—all of these were celebrated or settled at a potlatch, with feasting, speech-making, and gasps of astonishment at the more spectacular examples of conspicuous waste.

The American traveler and scholar Franz Boas described a potlatch among the Kwakiutls in the 1890's that began with gallons of precious oil being poured liberally onto a fire. Then a chief named Nolis outdid his rival by throwing onto the fire seven canoes and 400 blankets. There was such a blaze that the great cedarwood feasting hall had all its roof boards singed and was nearly burned to the ground.

At some earlier potlatches human lives were sacrificed. But even the beheading of a slave did not bring a man as much honor as breaking up a copper plaque.

These decorated plaques, beaten from lumps of ore, were for the Indians the highest and most desired forms of wealth. Individual plaques were given names, and a chief who destroyed one earned enough respect to last him for the rest of his life.

One famous Kwakiutl copper plaque, which went by the appropriate name of Causing Destitution, was almost beyond price. It cost 20 canoes, 20 slaves, 10 smaller plaques, 20 lynx skins, 20 marmot skins, 20 mink blankets, and much more.

Chief Tlatilitla ensured his supremacy among the Kwakiutls by breaking up such a plaque and giving the pieces to two rivals. The first man collapsed and died on the spot, unable to live with the humiliation of not being able to return a gift of like value. The other lived on for six months in misery and seclusion until he too died of shame.

Wasteful though the potlatch ceremony may have seemed to outsiders, at least it was an improvement on the bloody intertribal wars of earlier years. The Kwakiutls, once known for their relentless ferocity and skill in battle, described themselves in the days of potlatch as "fighting with wealth."

The custom may well have developed as a kind of famine relief system, through which, in lean years, tribes that were not so hard hit would give food and blankets to those in distress. The "haves" would gain prestige because of their generosity, and the "have-nots" receiving the gifts would lose status. But at least no one would starve.

DIAMOND OF DOOM

A jewel that drove men mad

In the Smithsonian Institution in Washington, D.C., lies the priceless Hope Diamond. Its blue rays flicker from an ice-cool heart. It seems harmless. Yet this cold and brilliant gem has a history of such blood and passion that more than 20 deaths have been blamed on its impassive beauty.

For over three centuries Kings, paupers, thieves, and courtesans have looked upon its opulence—and been driven mad.

Its first victim, according to legend, was a Hindu priest who fell under its spell 500 years ago, soon after it was mined from the Kistna River in southwest India. He stole it from the forehead of an Indian temple idol. But he was caught and put to death by torture.

The diamond turned up in Europe in 1642 in the hands of a French trader-smuggler named Jean Baptiste Tafernier. He made enough money from selling it to buy himself a title and an estate. Tafernier's son got so deeply into debt through gambling that the trader was forced to sell all he had gained. Tafernier headed back to India to remake his fortune—and was torn to death by a pack of wild dogs.

The gem reappeared in the possession of the French King Louis XIV, who had it cut from its original 112.5 carats down to 67.5 carats. Nicolas Fouquet, a government official who borrowed it for a state ball, was convicted in 1665 of embezzlement and imprisoned for the rest of his life. Louis himself died a broken and detested man as his much vaunted Empire crumbled in a series of military catastrophes.

Ignorant of the evil that they had added to their crown jewels, three more of the French royal family were to die.

The Princess de Lamballe, who wore it regularly, was beaten to death by a mob. Louis XVI and his Queen, Marie Antoinette, who had inherited it, died on the guillotine.

Then, in 1792, while postrevolutionary Paris was still in turmoil, the diamond vanished again—for nearly 40 years. The gap left plenty of room for legends.

A French jeweler, Jacques Celot, is said to have gloated over its beauty—until he went insane and killed himself. A Russian prince, Ivan Kanitovski, gave it to his Parisian mistress, then shot her dead, and was later murdered himself. Even Catherine the Great of Russia is believed to have worn the stone before she died of apoplexy.

It was only rediscovered for certain after a Dutch diamond cutter sheared it down to its present weight of 44.5 carats—and committed suicide when his son stole it from him.

The jewel continued to bounce from hand to bloody hand across Europe—and to Henry Thomas Hope, a very wealthy Irish banker who bought it for just $150,000 and gave the diamond its modern name. His grandson later died penniless.

In 1908 the Turkish Sultan Abdul Hamid bought it for $400,000. He gave it to his wife Subaya, then stabbed her. A year later he lost his throne. The jinxed jewel moved on to the United States where it was bought for $154,000 by business tycoon Ned McLean in 1911.

Over the next 40 years his young son Vincent was run down by a car; McLean was financially ruined and died in a mental hospital; his daughter died in 1946 of a drug overdose; and his wife Evelyn became a morphine addict.

Only American jeweler Harry Winston, who bought the blue stone from the heirs of the McLean family, has escaped the rays of doom. He gave it away—to the Smithsonian.

MOUNTAIN OF LIGHT

The present Queen Mother's crown is at the Tower of London; in the lower cross—Koh-i-noor.

TWO legends enhance the luster of the Koh-i-noor diamond: that its owner will rule the world and that it must never be worn by a man.

Koh-i-noor means the "mountain of light." But in its time the stone has sparkled over avalanches of destruction that have wiped out two mighty Empires. It flashed among the possessions of the Mogul Emperor Mohammed as he fell to Nadir, the Shah of Persia—and saw its new owner die in a palace revolt in 1747.

One hundred years later it was the brightest jewel in the turban of the Sikh Empire when its male-dominated lands were taken over by the world-colonizing British—and their Queen Victoria. It has glittered since then over the heads of three Queens of England. No British King has ever worn it.

O-KEE-PA, THE TORTURE TEST

The savage ordeal that a warrior had to survive

Before a young man of the Mandan tribe of Indians could become a fully fledged warrior, he had to undergo one of the world's most painful initiation rituals.

Early in the last century the Mandans lived in earthen, dome-shaped huts and roamed the Missouri plains, hunting buffaloes. To become one of their warriors, a young brave had to survive the ordeal of O-Kee-Pa, a torture designed to test his endurance and his courage.

First, the young man had to go without food, drink, and sleep for four days and nights. Then, wearing ornate clothes and with his body painted, he entered a ceremonial hut.

The chief medicine man carved slices from the chest and shoulders of the warrior-to-be with a jagged knife and thrust wooden skewers through the bleeding flesh behind the muscles.

Stout thongs, secured to the rafters of the hut, were then tied to both ends of the skewers, and the initiate was hoisted from the floor. To increase the agony, heavy weights were attached to his legs, and he was twirled around and around until he fell unconscious.

When—and if—he recovered from this treatment, the young brave was given a hatchet, with which he had to chop off the little finger of his left hand.

In the final stage his stamina was tested by tying ropes to his wrists and making him run in a circle, like a horse being broken in, until he dropped unconscious from exhaustion. If he survived all this, he was then able to return to his family in triumph as a fully fledged warrior.

No one knows how many braves died undergoing O-Kee-Pa.

TEST BY TORTURE. *Suspended by skewers through the flesh, two young Mandan Indians undergo the test of fitness to become warriors.*

Indeed, the ritual might never have been recorded at all but for American artist George Catlin, who painted its brutal details.

In the end, however, bravery alone was not enough to save the Mandans. In the 1840's they were almost wiped out by an enemy too small to see—the terrible scourge of smallpox. And the few survivors joined other tribes.

WHEN THE COBRAS CALL A TRUCE

SNAKE WORSHIP still forms an important part of popular religion in many regions of India. One day in the year—around the beginning of August—is devoted to a "festival of the serpents," when, it is believed, cobras will not bite anyone. The festival, which is called Naga Panchami (the words mean "snake" and "fifth"), falls on the fifth day of the Hindu month of Shravan, which runs from early July to early August.

On that day live cobras, or their images, are worshiped. Sometimes the snakes are handled by devotees of the cult.

Snake worshipers also ritually feed sacred cobras reared in special shrines and even leave out milk as an offering to wild cobras in places frequented by them.

THE MAGIC OF MAKE-BELIEVE

What lies behind nursery characters like Humpty Dumpty?

In Anholt, the Danish island in the Kattegat, children sing what is to them a non-sense rhyme. But most English-speaking children would see some sense in it:

Jeck og Jill
Vent op de hill
Og Jell kom tombling efter.

The rhyme demonstrates the powerful oral tradition that lies behind the survival of nursery rhymes and Mother Goose songs.

For "Jack and Jill" was taken to the Danish island by British soldiers during the Napoleonic wars and, although meaningless to children there, survives as an amusing jumble of sounds.

Rhymes and superstitions

The origin of many nursery rhymes is obscure, but the majority can be traced at least as far back as the 17th century. Some are rooted in old superstitions. For example:

Jack be nimble,
Jack be quick,
Jack jump over
The candlestick.

Jumping over a lighted candle was an ancient method of telling fortunes in medieval England. If the candle stayed lit, good luck was forecast. If it went out, bad luck would follow.

Popular lullaby

Other popular verses are said to have been penned as virtuous advice. "Rock-a-bye baby," probably the best known lullaby in the United States and Great Britain, with its story of the child falling when the bough breaks, is an example. When it first appeared in a nursery-rhyme book in 1765, a footnote said: "This may serve as a warning to the Proud and Ambitious, who climb so high that they generally fall at last."

Other verses stem from such diverse sources as snatches from the poems of strolling players, old proverbs, and seemingly lighthearted references to unpleasant events of the past.

"Goosey, goosey, gander," for instance, refers to Cromwell's goosestepping soldiers hunting for Royalist fugitives after the English Civil War. Anti-Puritan suspects were thrown into jail. As the rhyme puts it:

There I met an old man
Who would not say his prayers,
So I took him by the left leg
And threw him down the stairs.

"Ring-a-ring o' roses" is thought to date back to the Great Plague. A rosy rash was a symptom of the plague. Similarly, a popular saying, "Cross my heart and hope to die, drop down dead if I tell a lie," has a sinister origin dating back to when perjury was a capital offense, particularly when committed under the sign of the cross.

Many rhymes have parallels in different countries—even though in translation they do not readily appear to have any relationship.

Thus, "Humpty Dumpty" appears in France as *"Boule, boule"*; in Denmark as *"Lille, trille"*; in Switzerland as *"Annebadadeli"*; as *"Hillerin-Lillerin"* in Finland; and in Germany as various forms, including *"Hümpelken-Pümpelken."*

"Humpty," who may be thousands of years old, originated as a riddle. Once, the rhyme ended with the question "Who was Humpty Dumpty?" The answer, of course, was "An egg." But since every child now knows he was an egg, the question has long since been dropped.

Counting the "little piggies"

As well as being a way of keeping children amused, some nursery rhymes were also an elementary means of teaching them. Such rhymes as "This little piggy went to market," recited while taking hold of a child's fingers or toes, one by one, are still used as early aids to counting.

Still others—"Eeny, meeny, miny, mo" and "Hickory, dickory, dock"—may have had somewhat sinister beginnings. Some scholars believe that both were part of the ancient Druids' method of seeking the will of the gods in choosing a victim for human sacrifice.

Another, simpler explanation is that "Eeny, meeny, miny, mo" is a corruption of the prehistoric Celts' way of counting "one, two, three, four." "Hickory, dickory, dock," similarly, may be derived from *"Hocera, cocera, dik,"* the old Celtic form of "eight, nine, ten."

The fact that the Celts were involved in Druidic practices—stamped out by the Romans in Britain during the first century A.D.—may mean that both explanations hold good.

Hickory Dickory Dock.

THE MOUSE RAN UP THE CLOCK. *Once, the rhyme may have chosen sacrificial victims.*

ed to: "Ena, mena, mona, mite," and in New York, 150 years ago, children would chant: "Ene, tene, mone, mei." Similarly, an American rhyme known as Indian counting went "Een, teen, tether, fether, fip."

Another elementary educational aid for remembering the number of days in the months through the rhyme "Thirty days hath September" dates back to 13th-century France.

Back to the knights

Many children's rhymes and chants use words that have long since passed from everyday use but still survive in playtime vocabulary. "Truce" words used in children's games can be traced back centuries to medieval times.

The term "barley," widely used in Wales, the Scottish borders, and northwestern England, dates back to the 14th century. It was used by knights offering their jousting opponents a few moments' rest between charges. In southern England truce words include "fains" or "fainites"—survivals of the medieval English expression "Fain I," or "I decline."

In the 18th century nursery rhymes began to appear in books for children, and eventually, a host of authors concentrated on writing original verses for youngsters.

Many of them, in addition to being amusing verses, contained veiled references to certain political events and figures. "Wee Willie Winkie," for example, was said to be a popular Jacobite nickname for King William III.

Forms of the rhymes were used by the shepherds of Cumberland and Westmorland, toting up their flocks, well into the 20th century.

In Wisconsin settlers' children kept up the counting rhyme, but it became slightly corrupt-

GRANDFATHER'S PRIVILEGE—GETTING DRUNK

THE CODEX MENDOZA is a collection of ancient Mexican manuscripts and drawings describing life in the 14th century. One of these drawings, reproduced here, depicts the drinking of what was known as the white wine of the earth, made from the sap of a plant found growing on a mountain—called the frothy mountain because the wine was effervescent. The potency of the brew apparently gave rise to a general ban on overindulgence, for the script explains that the man drinking was allowed to get merry "on account of his age and his having grandchildren."

A second look at long-cherished notions

Popular facts and fallacies

·

THIS SAUCER EARTH

Did moon walkers march across a studio floor?

When astronaut Neil Armstrong set foot on the moon for the first time, on July 20, 1969, it represented one of the most inspiring achievements in man's history to millions of people throughout the world. But to a small organization called the International Flat Earth Research Society, it was nothing more than a piece of cleverly stage-managed science-fiction trickery.

And Armstrong's historic words when stepping down from the *Eagle* module onto the dusty lunar surface about 240,000 miles from earth—"one small step for a man, one giant leap for mankind"—was a phrase that could have come only from the pen of a scriptwriter.

The evils of science

As for the pictures reputedly taken in space showing the earth to be a rotating sphere, well, they were just too ludicrous for words. The sun, say the Flat Earthers, circuits the earth instead of the earth revolving around the sun—a notion that most people take for granted.

The society, whose membership is currently estimated to be about 1,400, dismisses much of accepted modern thinking about the shape of the earth as sheer nonsense and is convinced that the entire human race is being subjected to the greatest hoax in history.

From its headquarters in Lancaster, California, the society wages a war of words through newsletters and pamphlets against the evils of science.

The society was founded about 1800 in Great Britain and the United States and, says its American president Charles Johnson, was descended from the Zetetic Society, which took its name from an ancient Greek philosophical school of skeptics. It survived under this name until 1956, when its general secretary, Samuel Shenton, of Kent, England, changed it to the present title.

The society's belief is this: that the earth is flat, with the land masses grouped around the central point of the North Pole.

The Antarctic region is not the compact island mass it is commonly believed to be but an impenetrable ice-cold girdle around the earth. The Flat Earthers argue that transantarctic expeditions have never happened. Explorers, misled by instrument faults, merely traveled an icy arc within the girdle.

Space is different, too

The organization also argues about the nature of space itself. The moon, it says, is a mere 32 miles in diameter, compared with the official 2,160 miles, and only about 3,000 miles away from the earth. The sun, slightly larger than the moon, is also only 3,000 miles from the earth and not 93 million miles, as people have been led to believe.

"Can you imagine what sort of summers we would have if the sun were as far away as scientists believe?" Shenton scoffed.

And as for stars, they are very small bodies a "few thousand miles apart!"

But if the earth is flat, as the society main-

314

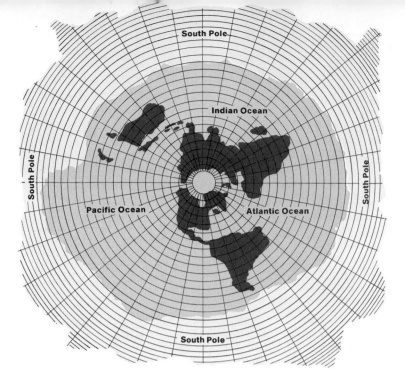

WORLD PLAN. *According to the Flat Earthers, the North Pole is the hub of the world, whose oceans are girdled by the South Polar regions. What lies beyond this icy barrier is somewhat vague.*

tains, the tricky question remains as to what lies on the other side. Shenton said that water is on the other side. But as to what lay beneath the waters, he confessed himself perplexed.

The society claims Biblical support for its beliefs, pointing out that Moses, in the first five books of the Old Testament, described the heaven above and the earth beneath and the water under the earth.

Shenton, who died some years ago, was convinced of the immobility and flatness of the earth. He once joked about the idea of setting up an international hauling company using balloons: if the earth were rotating, as he had been told, all he needed to do was to send up a balloon lifting the cargo, and, barring winds, it would stay still until the cargo's destination reached a point directly beneath it.

But this could happen only if the earth really was spinning—a belief that Shenton could not bring himself to share. Since the earth was in fact stationary, he reasoned, the launching site would stay just where it was—that is, underneath the balloon.

WORLD INSIDE THE WORLD

The new land where a man wanted to plant the American flag

If John Symmes' theory had been correct, the first men to reach the North Pole would have dropped into the earth through an opening in its crust and discovered a vast new country inside, rich in minerals and peopled by a strange race of men.

So strong was his conviction, and so many were persuaded by him, that his proposals for an expedition to the world within the earth got as far as the U.S. Congress. But the skeptical legislators would have nothing to do with the idea.

John Cleves Symmes, born in New Jersey in 1780, had a distinguished army career behind him, rising to the rank of captain, before he became passionately interested in astronomy.

The more he studied, the firmer grew his conviction that the earth was hollow.

This theory was not entirely new. It had been put forward in the past by such notable men as the English astronomer Edmond Halley, after whom Halley's Comet is named; Leonhard Euler, a Swiss mathematician; and Sir John Leslie, a Scottish scientist. Halley and Leslie suggested that there might be separate planets within our own.

Symmes agreed, but his "worlds within worlds" were concentric spheres, one inside the other but all open at the poles.

No one could prove that his theory was wrong, for at that time the polar regions were still unexplored.

Symmes cited as evidence of his theory the then unexplained northward migration of birds. They were, he believed, attracted to the source of warm ocean currents and an inner-earth sunshine—of which the northern lights are a reflection.

If birds could visit this inner world, Symmes declared, so could men. He wrote to scientific institutions all over the world: "I declare that the earth is hollow, habitable within, one with-in the other, and that it is open at the pole. . . . I pledge my life in support of this truth and am ready to explore the hollow if the world will support me in the undertaking."

When he failed to get U.S. backing, Symmes tried to join a Russian polar expedition but could not raise the fare to the departure port, St. Petersburg.

He died in 1829, still convinced that the earth was hollow.

MORE THAN A BODY CAN STAND

Myths about the human mind and body

People falling from a great height are dead before they hit the ground. Rather than be burned to death in his blazing shell-torn Lancaster on a bombing raid over Germany in 1944, Royal Air Force Gunnery Sergeant Nicholas Alkemade jumped from 18,000 feet without a parachute, calculating that this would be a quicker and less agonizing death.

Unbelievably, he suffered only slight injuries. The last part of his 122-mile-per-hour fall was broken by the branches of young pine trees, thick springy undergrowth, and finally deep snow. "It was rather like bouncing on a trampoline," he recalled.

Sergeant Alkemade's experience is a dramatic rebuttal of the idea that people falling from great heights are dead before they hit the ground. Asphyxia, brought about by the speed of the fall, and heart failure through shock were thought to occur long before the final impact.

The fallacy of this belief has been amply demonstrated by free-fall parachutists who regularly drop several miles before opening their parachutes. In 1960 Capt. Joseph Kittinger jumped from a balloon in the United States and fell 16 miles before opening his parachute. He landed conscious and unhurt.

Cold causes colds. The common cold is the world's most widespread illness—which is probably why there are more myths about it than any of the other plagues that flesh is heir to.

The most widespread fallacy of all is that colds are caused by cold. They are not. They are caused by viruses passed on from person to person. You catch a cold by coming into contact, directly or indirectly, with someone who already has one. If cold causes colds, it would be reasonable to expect the Eskimos to suffer from them permanently. But they do not. And in isolated arctic regions explorers have reported being free from colds until coming into contact again with infected people from the outside world by way of packages and mail dropped from airplanes.

During the First World War soldiers who spent long periods in the trenches, cold and wet, showed no increased tendency to catch colds.

In the Second World War prisoners at the notorious Auschwitz concentration camp, naked and starving, were astonished to find that they seldom had colds.

At the Common Cold Research Unit in England, volunteers took part in experiments in which they submitted to the discomforts of being cold and wet for long stretches of time. After taking hot baths, they put on bathing suits, allowed themselves to be doused with cold water, and then stood about dripping wet in drafty rooms. Some wore wet socks all day while others exercised in the rain until close to exhaustion. Not one of the volunteers came down with a cold unless a cold virus was actually dropped in his nose.

If, then, cold and wet have nothing to do with catching colds, why are they more prevalent in the winter? Despite the most painstaking research, no one has yet found the answer. One explanation offered by scientists is that people tend to stay together indoors more in cold weather than at other times, and this makes it easier for cold viruses to be passed on.

No one has yet found a cure for the cold.

There are drugs and pain suppressors such as aspirin, but all they do is relieve the symptoms.

Hair and nails continue to grow after death. Seven years after her death in 1862, the body of Elizabeth Siddal, wife of the painter-poet Dante Gabriel Rossetti, was exhumed from its grave in London for the recovery of a manuscript Rossetti had buried with her. According to legend, a witness described the awesome sight of the corpse with luxuriant red-gold hair practically filling the coffin.

If the hair was as remarkable as described, it must have been as it was when she died. Alternatively, the witness may have been grossly exaggerating. For hair does not grow after death. A certain amount of drying and shrinking of the skin takes place after death, and might reveal an extra fraction of an inch of hair—hardly enough to fill a coffin.

Hair and nails grow from the root by cell multiplication and are fed by the bloodstream. When death occurs, the heart stops, and the blood does not circulate. The nutriment supply to the cells ends, and they can no longer grow.

Hair can turn white overnight. It is sometimes said of a person who has suffered a terrible shock that "his hair turned white overnight," but no such cases have been verified. Gray hair (a mixture of dark and white) can seemingly turn white overnight, however, if the person develops an inflammatory condition of the scalp known as *alopecia areata:* the dark hair falls out suddenly, leaving the person with the more resistant white hair.

For those in good health the transition to white hair is usually slow. Hair normally grows about half an inch a month; so even if the hair began to lose pigmentation, it would take months for a full head of hair to change color.

A scratch from a rusty nail causes tetanus. Lockjaw, or tetanus, is an acute infectious disease caused by the toxin produced by a bacterium called *Clostridium tetani.* A scratch from a sterile piece of rusty metal cannot cause tetanus, because neither rust nor metal is poisonous.

On the other hand, a scratch from a *dirty* nail would be dangerous if there was any tetanus-producing organism present in the dirt. This would be especially true of a cut from a gardening implement that could have picked up such infections from the soil.

LUXURIANT HAIR. *Elizabeth Siddal's hair was said to have grown profusely after she died. But the claim is preposterous.*

Some people are double jointed. Stage contortionists, practitioners of advanced yoga, and others may appear to have unusual joints. The truth is that heredity and constant exercise have given the fibrous tissue binding their bones together more elasticity than most people's. No one has yet been born with truly double joints.

A drowning man surfaces three times. A drowning man, so it is said, comes up three times before sinking to his death. It is not necessarily true.

A person who panics in the water tends to sink and draw water into his lungs each time his head goes under. This may occur any number of times—or not at all—before he then dies from asphyxia.

A dying man sees all his life flash before him. Poets and novelists are largely to blame for the notion that a person's past life flashes through his mind in the moments before death. Of the many cases of people saved from what they believed to be certain death, some claim to have had flashbacks, but others claim they had no such experience.

An Englishman, A.R. Bayley, who was saved from drowning, wrote in 1916: "I remember thinking it was all up with me, but the events of my past life did not pass before me."

A pilot shot down in 1918 said after the crash: "I was sure I was going to be killed. I was just shaking my head, thinking of my girlfriend in England."

Only a sudden shock will cure hiccups. Thousands of remedies have been proposed for hiccups, each with its enthusiastic backers. Some seem to work, others do not. Research into known cases indicates that if a sufferer firmly believes a particular treatment will succeed, more often than not it does. So doctors have been led to the conclusion that the cure for hiccups is at least partly psychological.

One widely held belief is that a sharp fright will end a troublesome bout of hiccups, but many people prefer just waiting for them to go away as this "cure" is often worse than the ailment itself.

Between 1948 and 1956 Jack O'Leary, an American, reckoned he hiccuped 160 million times. He tried 60,000 remedies, all in vain. Finally, in desperation, he prayed to St. Jude, patron of hopeless causes. His hiccuping stopped.

Another victim was Heinz Isecke, a 55-year-old British plumber, who hiccuped for eight months after an operation in November 1973. Suggestions poured in to him from all over the world. He tried them all, without success. Doctors, alarmed by his failing strength, operated again. Still the hiccups went on.

Eventually, in despair, Heinz drank a "secret" herbal mixture sent by an anonymous donor. By the evening of that day his hiccups had gone. Was it the mixture, or his faith in it, that cured him? As yet, no one can say.

People who survived execution were automatically reprieved. Although there have been reprieves in cases where equipment failed or the victim recovered, there was never any law that made this obligatory, either in the United States or Great Britain.

Nevertheless, when the death sentence was lawful in many countries, there was a sense of humanity that sometimes resulted in mercy for criminals who survived execution attempts.

The most famous of all English cases was that of the murderer John Lee, still remembered as "the man they couldn't hang." Three times, as he stood on the scaffold in 1885, the trapdoor under his feet failed to open, although each time it had functioned perfectly during tests.

It was later thought that a warped board was responsible and that the weight of the prison chaplain—who was present only at executions and not at the tests—caused it to bend and jam the trap.

After the third unsuccessful attempt to hang him, Lee's sentence was commuted to life imprisonment on humanitarian grounds. He was later released and emigrated to the United States, where he died in 1933.

One of the earliest authenticated cases of a person being completely freed after "execution" is that of Ann Greene, sentenced to be hanged for infanticide in England in 1650. After hanging for half an hour, she revived as a surgeon was about to dissect her body. She recovered completely, married, and had three children.

In New South Wales in 1803, Joseph Samuels, still protesting his innocence on the scaffold, accused another man of the crime for which he was about to be hanged. Twice the rope broke, and once it stretched so that Samuels' feet touched the floor. The Governor reprieved him, and the man he had named was later hanged in his stead.

John Smith, sentenced for housebreaking in 1705, had been hanging in London for 15 minutes when a reprieve arrived, granted by Queen Anne. Smith was immediately cut down and revived. He was pardoned on the condition that he rejoin the army, and spent the rest of his life celebrated as "Half-Hanged Smith."

Thirty-five years later William Duell, an English rapist and murderer, was hanged but, like Ann Greene, recovered on the dissecting table. The death sentence was commuted, and he was transported overseas.

Another Englishman, Thomas Reynolds, who was hanged in 1736, was not so lucky. When men started to fasten down the lid of his coffin, he thrust it back and attempted to sit up. The astonished crowd tried to revive him fully with brandy, but he expired nevertheless.

Among the most curious of all cases of condemned people surviving their "executions" is that of Margaret Dickson, of Scotland. Customers at an inn, it is recorded, were "greatly scared" when they saw her climb out of her coffin on the way to be buried after her hanging in 1728. Under Scottish law at that time, since she had been officially executed, her husband was a widower. So, to legitimize their union, she was required to marry him again.

The Russian republic of Georgia has the world's oldest people. Centenarians, according to a U.N. estimate in 1972, numbered 25,000 throughout the world. According to the Soviet Union at that time, no fewer than 21,000 of them lived in Russia. If the Russians had not put their figure so high, it might have been accepted without a close examination. But statisticians who studied the data were suspicious.

The republic of Georgia, birthplace of Joseph Stalin, was particularly famed for the longevity of its inhabitants: 39 in every 100,000 of the population were said to be aged 100 or more. Then in 1961 the Russians claimed that, in the republic of Azerbaijan, the figure was 63 per 100,000. The same survey on which this claim was based discovered 592 people who had passed the age of 120. Occasional reports from the Caucasus region have spoken of inhabitants aged 150. One man who died in 1973 had given his age as 168.

All these claims have been subjected to close scrutiny, and the result is a good deal of skepticism.

First, although Russia claims to have several hundred citizens well over the age of 114, that is the top limit of any *confirmed* case of long life anywhere.

Second, wherever these self-styled centenarians exist in exceptionally large numbers, there are anomalies that the statisticians regard as suspicious—such as the fact that there are no correspondingly large numbers of people in their eighties and nineties. Why, they ask, the gap? If people born more than 100 years ago are living so long, why are those born only 70 or 80 years ago dying so young?

Doctors have strengthened these suspicions. Medical examination of the "grand old men" of 100 or more has suggested that many of them really are probably only in their seventies.

Many of these ancients are illiterate. They

WEAK CHINS—STRONG CHARACTERS

FOOLISH ARISTOCRATS are sometimes mocked as "chinless wonders," the idea being that strength or weakness of character is shown by the shape of a person's chin.

The notion has no basis in fact. Frederick the Great, Queen Victoria, Gen. James Wolfe (the conqueror of Quebec), the Brontë sisters—all had weak chins, but they were all strong characters.

The fallacy seems to have been fostered by the fondness of early fiction writers for typecasting their characters. A boxer, for instance, or a ruthless business tycoon, would have "a forceful, thrusting chin." A villain was branded by his low forehead and close-set eyes.

Criminologists say that there are no such things as "criminal features." The study of faces as reflectors of character is not a science at all, simply a superstition.

Frederick the Great, a King who earned his title without the aid of a "strong" chin.

Queen Victoria, a woman whose forceful personality did not show in her face.

Gen. James Wolfe, a war hero, but who would guess that from his picture?

have no idea of dates, and there are no records of their births. In the areas where they live, old men are venerated, so there is great prestige in being regarded as a patriarch. It has even been suggested that some of the less naive added years to their ages in 1914 to avoid military service in the armies of the Czar and have had to keep up the deception ever since.

Whatever the truth of the matter, the statisticians suspect that there are parts of the world where a man is not, as they say in the West, as old as he feels, but as old as he says he is.

Hairy men are stronger. Samson lost his strength when Delilah had his hair cut off. It made a good story, and the belief has persisted that a man's power and virility reside in his hair. But it is merely legend. Hair is already dead once it has emerged from the skin: It has nothing to contribute to the owner's strength.

It was not until well into this century that research dispelled many of the old fallacies connected with hair and baldness. What is now recognized as "male pattern baldness" depends on heredity, hormone production, and age.

About 1 man in 20 notices that his hairline is receding before his 21st birthday. Thirty-five percent have some baldness at the age of 35, 45 percent at the age of 45, and 55 percent at 55. Baldness tends to run in families.

SAMSON AND THE LION. *According to the Old Testament, Samson's strength lay in his hair.*

People who can be hypnotized are weak-minded. In fact, gullibility, intelligence, and education appear to be unrelated to a person's susceptibility to hypnosis. There is some evidence that very young people and well-adjusted people are more easily hypnotized than others.

Another mistaken belief is that a person can be hypnotized against his will. The subject's cooperation is usually required, although it is possible to be hypnotized unawares. It is improbable that a person under hypnosis can be persuaded to do anything strongly repugnant to him or foreign to his character.

Men have one rib fewer than women. In fact, men and women have precisely the same number of ribs—12. The fallacy probably arose from the account of the Creation given in Genesis 2:21–22. God was said to have taken a rib from Adam while he was asleep, and from that Eve was fashioned.

Male and female bones differ in size in most cases, but not in number. There are instances of deviation in the number of coccygeal, or tail, vertebrae; a person may have one fewer of these vertebrae because two of them have simply fused. But it has nothing to do with sex.

A woman's brain is smaller than a man's. Taking into account the proportionate sizes of the bodies, the weight of the brain in both sexes is about equal. Brain size varies only in proportion to body weight, stature, and age.

There is no evidence, moreover, that the size of the brain is related to the intelligence of its owner.

NO HAIR ON THEIR CHESTS. *But these Japanese wrestlers, at 400 pounds each, are not weaklings.*

HARD TO SWALLOW

Beliefs about food that are completely unfounded

Brown eggs are more nutritious. In many households in various parts of the United States, the whiteness of an eggshell is a sign of the egg's purity. Brown eggs are disdained. In Great Britain, however, brown eggs are preferred as being more wholesome. Naturally, farmers in both countries strive to produce more of whatever is in demand.

Both beliefs are myths. Eggs are not designed to be eaten by humans. They are to provide nourishment for the developing chick. The coloring of the shell, which is a late stage in the development of the egg, depends merely on the breed of the hen, and by the time the shell is formed, the nutritional value is established.

Brown bread is better than white. Nutritionally, there is often no difference between brown bread and white. White bread is simply made from flour from which the bran and outer coating of the wheat have been removed. Whole wheat contains the bran and wheat. Both contain the necessary vitamins, nutrients, minerals, and carbohydrates for adults and children.

There is a school of thought, however, that considers the roughage in whole-wheat bread beneficial to people with intestinal problems.

While all white flour sold in the United Kingdom must, by law, be enriched by nutrients, the standards vary from country to country. In the United States, where standards are high, 92 percent of white bread is enriched, while the content of riboflavin nutrient in Scandinavian countries is twice the required level of that in the United States.

Eating seeds causes appendicitis. Few medical reports have ever recorded the presence of seeds in appendixes that have been removed. But among the objects that have been found are gold tooth fillings, toothbrush bristles, and the end of a thermometer.

Never eat oysters unless there is an R in the month. It is sheer coincidence that the first four and last four months of the year contain R's, and it has long been said that only during these months is it safe to eat oysters. Before refrigeration the eating of oysters in the warmer summer months may have been risky. The chemical

THE OYSTERFEST. *Each year the mayor of Colchester, England, marks the opening of the local fishermen's oyster season—in September.*

composition of the oyster varies from season to season, especially during its spawning period in May and June. After spawning, it contains less glycogen and is paler and more watery. But it tastes much the same and is certainly not poisonous.

Eating fish is good for the brain. No particular food contributes specifically to the brain or any other part of the body. The tissues take what they require from the materials absorbed into the bloodstream during digestion. A balanced diet will satisfy all the requirements of the cells, although a lack of some types of food may result in deficiencies.

The belief that fish, in particular, is good for the brain, developed in the 19th century. The German philosopher and physician Friedrich Büchner (1824–99), on learning that the brain contained phosphorus, declared that "without phosphorus, there is no thought." The French chemist Jean Dumas (1800–84) confirmed that fish is a rich source of phosphorus. The Swiss naturalist Jean Louis Agassiz (1807–73) connected the two ideas and suggested that fish is good for the brain.

In fact, because of its abundance in the rocks and minerals of the earth, varying amounts of phosphorus are present in most foods.

It is easy to tell a mushroom from a poisonous fungus. There is no simple method of distinguishing between the two, because neither edible mushrooms nor poisonous fungi such as toadstools have any one common feature that is not found in the other.

The idea that mushrooms are edible if they are white, or have a ring at the foot of the stalk, for example, is a fallacy. The fungus *amanita virosa* has both these characteristics but is inedible. Nor is a mushroom that has turned a bluish color necessarily poisonous. The edible *boletus edulis,* when bruised, can turn dirty brown, light or deep blue, green, red, purple, violet, or even inky black. But it is still edible. The color changes simply mean that a fermentation process is taking place.

Smell is not a guideline, either. Some deadly poisonous fungi, such as the *amanita phalloides,* may smell quite pleasant. On the other hand, some unpleasant-looking fungi can be eaten with no ill effect.

Several "kitchen hints" about discovering whether fungi are safe to eat are also erroneous. One is the fallacy that edible mushrooms, unlike toadstools, can be peeled. The idea that soaking or cooking poisonous fungi in vinegar will make them edible is also false. It may neutralize poisonous or indigestible species slightly, but dangerous and deadly fungi are never truly safe to eat.

The best way to identify mushrooms and other fungi is by using one of the many illustrated guides available. But the ultimate rule should be: If in doubt, do not eat it.

Drinking seawater causes madness. There is nothing in seawater that specifically causes insanity, although it may contain harmful chemicals. But if seawater is drunk without any freshwater to dilute it, the concentration of salt will poison the kidneys and eventually cause death. Drinking small amounts to supplement freshwater is not harmful.

Canned foods become poisonous after opening. Whatever container food is in, it may become infected with germs and cause food poisoning if it is not in sterile conditions. But food in opened cans is no more susceptible than fresh, and there is nothing about the cans themselves that could cause poisoning. Food in damaged cans, however, may have become contaminated by germs entering through holes or cracks.

MANMADE MYTHS ABOUT NATURE

Can flying fish fly, and are gorillas really ferocious?

Flying fish fly. There are about 100 species of fish that fall within the general category popularly called flying fish. But none of them is capable of genuine flight.

These fish, which have enlarged pectoral fins that look like wings, can glide just above the surface of the water at about 10 miles an hour for up to 200 yards. They have even been known to land accidentally on the decks of passing boats. Their gliding is usually an effort to escape predators, particularly dolphins.

Moths eat clothes. The six species of moth that are responsible for damage to clothes and other materials do not eat at all. But they lay prodigious numbers of eggs from which larvae hatch,

and it is these that are the voracious devourers of wool, carpets, and upholstery.

There is no method of assessing just how much cloth an average moth larva might eat, since it depends on how long it spends in the larval stage. This in turn depends on such factors as the temperature and the availability of food.

Octopuses are extremely dangerous. The idea of octopuses holding divers in a viselike grip is largely fiction. Occasionally, swimmers are held by the suckers of an octopus' tentacles, but few cases have been reported of anyone coming to harm as a result. E. G. Boulenger, former director of the aquarium at the London Zoo,

IMPOSSIBLE DREAM. *The idea of an octopus holding a man, let alone a ship, in a viselike grip is largely fiction. The largest Alaskan species has a radial span of 32 feet. Most are smaller.*

says that a firm grip on an octopus' head and body is sufficient to induce the creature to relax its hold.

While the deep-sea octopus found off the Alaskan coast can grow up to 32 feet from the tip of one tentacle to another, most species are much smaller. One, found off the coast of Sri Lanka, is less than two inches across.

On the rare occasion when an octopus has bitten a swimmer, the usual result has been a slight swelling. But the venom of the blue-ringed octopus of the Pacific can be deadly.

Thunder turns milk sour. Thunder is a vibration of the air that cannot affect milk in any way. What does cause milk to turn sour during stormy weather, however, is the formation of bacteria that convert the sugar in milk into lactic acid. These bacteria thrive best in the humid weather that often accompanies thunderstorms in the summer. Milk is therefore far less likely to turn sour during winter thunderstorms.

Thrashing about in the water will frighten sharks away. Running down each side of a shark's body, from head to tail, are sensory systems by which it can detect vibrations in water over long distances. To a shark any

creature thrashing around in the water is either wounded or crippled in some way and is therefore likely to provide an easy meal.

Jacques-Yves Cousteau, the French underwater expert, says that wild splashing does not frighten away sharks. He says the best protection lies in easy movement, swimming slowly, and avoiding any abrupt change of position.

Sharks can also detect blood in the water a quarter of a mile or more away. While most fish have a keen sense of smell, the shark's is exceptional because a large proportion of its brain is concerned with this faculty. On either side of its snout it has two organs that are so sensitive that the shark can steer itself along a scent trail, making corrections in its course as it picks up weaker or stronger scents to the left or right, rather like an airplane following a radio signal. In this way the shark can "zero in" on wounded prey.

Catgut comes from cats. Catgut is made from the intestines of sheep, horses, and several other animals—but never cats. Nor is there any record of the material ever having been made from the entrails of cats.

The origin of the word is uncertain. It could be a contraction of "cattlegut" or may have arisen over confusion between "kit" and "kit-

323

DEAF TO MUSIC. *Snakes are charmed by the tap of the foot, the sway of the body and pipe—but not by the music that the snake charmer makes.*

ten"—a kit was a small violin that had catgut strings. The *Oxford English Dictionary* includes the story that it may originate from the "caterwauling" sound of a violin—though it does not guarantee the authenticity of the tale.

Snakes hypnotize their prey and can be charmed by music. While some animals may become curious or even freeze with fear when confronted by a snake, no zoologist seriously entertains the idea that the reptiles have any hypnotic powers. The courtship "dance," consisting of rhythmic swaying, of some snakes may have given rise to ideas of mesmerism.

Snake charming, on the other hand, is a form of hypnotism—of the snake. Snakes have extremely limited hearing and can only detect low-frequency sounds; so it is unlikely that they can respond to the music of a charmer's pipe. Cobras used by Hindu snake charmers respond to the tap of the charmer's foot, the beat of his stick on their basket, or the swaying of his body and pipe. Burmese snake charmers use rhythmic swaying movements to fascinate snakes, which will sway in a similar way, looking for a place to strike. In other parts of the world, charmers "talk" to their snakes, and the snakes respond to the vibrations they pick up through the ground.

But the swaying from side to side of a charmed snake is a physical necessity to keep the upper part of its body in the air. When it stops swaying, it is forced to slide back to the ground.

Rats desert sinking ships. Rats do not instinctively leave ships that are fated to sink but probably leave the bilges where they usually live if a ship springs a leak and starts to take in water.

Droves of rats scurrying out of a ship's hold in this way might well have made sailors suspicious of a vessel's seaworthiness. It is also possible that rats may be more sensitive than men to minor earth tremors or falls of plaster. For this reason an ancient belief that rats leave houses that are about to collapse might have substance. Rats were once believed to be useful in sensing impending cave-ins in coal mines.

Ostriches bury their heads in the sand. The most popular belief about ostriches is that they bury their heads in sand in the hope that their enemies will not notice them. But this, say naturalists, is almost certainly a myth.

Allan Pocock, a resident of the Oudtshoorn region of South Africa, where 200,000 ostriches were once reared for their feathers, noted that during the 80-odd years when records were kept, no one had reported a single case of an ostrich burying its head, or even apparently attempting to do so.

Ostriches may well listen intently for sound with their heads near the ground, and sometimes they even lower their heads to rest their neck muscles. They also poke their heads into bushes inquisitively—but they never bury them in sand. If they did, they would probably suffocate.

Gorillas are ferocious by nature. Belief in the ferocity of gorillas, probably engendered by their appearance, was universally established by the late 19th century and was perpetuated in drawings, paintings, and novels. But in their natural habitat both the lowland and mountain species of gorilla are relatively peaceable, despite their terrifying looks. The mountain type can grow to a height of six feet six inches—more than seven inches taller than the lowland variety. Other vital statistics include a chest measurement of 67 inches, 25-inch biceps, arms that can span 9 feet, and a weight of 700 pounds.

MOVIE MYTH. *The 1933 film* King Kong *helped to perpetuate the idea that gorillas are aggressive by nature. Zoologists say that in the wild they are shy, despite their appearance.*

The American naturalist George Schaller, who spent months observing gorillas in the wild, reported that they were extremely shy and that if a human encountered one and stood his ground the gorilla would usually go away.

In defense of their young, gorillas have been known to inflict terrible bites on humans; but there are no authenticated cases of their crushing people to death.

The 1933 film *King Kong,* based on a novel by Edgar Wallace in which a gigantic gorilla runs amok in New York, has contributed to the myth of the creature's aggressiveness.

Swans sing before dying. The belief that the usually voiceless swan sings beautifully before dying is an ancient piece of folklore beloved by poets and philosophers. The ancient Greeks thought that swans were creatures of Apollo, the god of music. According to Socrates in Plato's *Phaedo,* swans sing "not out of sorrow or distress, but because they are inspired of Apollo." Shakespeare refers to the "swan song" in his plays and poems, and the image is also used by Lord Byron in "Don Juan" and by Tennyson in "The Passing of Arthur."

A vaguely musical sound is produced by the whistling swan of Iceland, an accomplishment beyond the ability of all other species, whether on the point of death or not. The most common species in the Northern Hemisphere is

capable of no more than a violent hissing when it is angry or protecting its young—usually a prelude to attack. The absence of voice reflects its name—the mute swan.

SWAN SONG. *As a tribute to Apollo, swans are said to sing before dying. But the most common species in the Northern Hemisphere is mute.*

Mice love cheese more than any other food. Experiments by rodent controllers show that to guarantee catching a mouse cheese is not the best bait.

Edward Batzner, an American exterminator, uses lemon-flavored candy. This, he says, has the dual advantage of stickiness, which holds the mouse for the second it takes for the trap to

SWEET TOOTH. *An American extermination expert advocates candy, not cheese, as mouse bait.*

spring, and sweetness, which attracts the mouse more readily than cheese. It is equally fallacious to make similar presumptions about other animals: that all dogs prefer meat, for instance, or that all cats prefer fish. A creature's "preference" for a particular food is usually dictated by "conditioning," that is, what it has become used to eating. Thus, some cats prefer milk to water, and some dogs will eat only raw meat.

Camels carry water in their humps. The hump of the camel contains fat on which it can live for perhaps a week or 10 days if no other food is available. Undoubtedly, in digesting the fat, the animal does produce a certain amount of water, but it has no reservoir for liquids in its hump.

Porcupines and hedgehogs can shoot their quills. As a defense mechanism, the quills of the porcupine and hedgehog are highly effective. Apart from their obvious deterrent effect, they are frequently impregnated with dirt and bacteria and can cause serious infection. Also, the fact the quills are barbed makes it difficult for the victim to dislodge them.

But neither hedgehogs nor porcupines possess the necessary muscular mechanism to "shoot" their quills.

NATURAL ARCHER? *Neither porcupines nor hedgehogs can shoot their quills.*

GALLANTS, FIDDLERS, AND FAIRYTALES

The stories behind some long-loved fables

Nero fiddled while Rome burned. One of the most cherished legends of ancient Rome tells how the megalomaniac Emperor Nero was obsessed with the idea of building a magnificent new city as a permanent memorial to himself. Thwarted by the owners of family shrines that blocked the streets, he put Rome to the torch.

But there is no historical evidence that Nero had any part in starting the fire. Even more doubtful is the story's most famous detail—that Nero stood on top of a tower in the city and fiddled. The violin was not invented until the 16th century. However, other versions of the legend claim he played a lyre or a lute.

The historian Tacitus (ca. A.D. 55–117) wrote, only a few years after the fire, that Nero had been 50 miles away at his villa at Antium when the blaze started. Far from gloating over the inferno, Nero raced to the city and made frantic efforts to stop the blaze.

Whatever his motives, it was the only praiseworthy act of an otherwise deplorable life. Brought to power by his mother, Agrippina, as a boy of 17, he was hated by the people for having usurped the position of his half brother.

His private life was a scandal, even by Roman standards. What must have been even more painful was his insistence that everyone should attend performances of his plays and operas. Apparently, his lack of talent was equaled only by the awfulness of his voice.

Nero's cruelty toward Christians is legendary. They were an unpopular group, suspected of witchcraft, and they provided both Nero and Rome with a useful scapegoat for the fire. Hundreds were executed—though there is no record of them being thrown to the lions.

Finally, his cruelties and debaucheries sickened even his closest adherents. The Praetorian

RUINS OF ROME. *Emperor Nero was blamed for the fire that devastated Rome in A.D. 64, but according to the historian Tacitus, he was 50 miles away, at Antium, when the blaze started.*

Guard—the Emperor's private bodyguard—deserted him. Faced with inevitable deposition and execution, he committed suicide in the year A.D. 68.

Sir Walter Raleigh laid down his cloak for Elizabeth I. The handsome young gentleman stood amid the crowds as the Queen of England passed by with her retinue. When she was almost at his side, she paused. A mud puddle was in her path. The quick-witted gallant, a seaman named Walter Raleigh, immediately threw his cloak over the puddle. The Queen, impressed by his courtesy, stepped on it, smiling her gratitude for this expensive protection of the royal feet. This would seem to be a romantic and fateful meeting of two great figures of history—but it is untrue.

The story is believed to have been the invention of the historian Thomas Fuller (1608–61), who frequently added fictitious anecdotes to enliven dull facts. The tale was perpetuated by Sir Walter Scott in his novel *Kenilworth* (1821); Raleigh swears he will never brush the cloak "as long as it is in my possession," and the Queen, who appreciated a compliment, tells him to go to her wardrobe keeper with an order to give him "a suit, and that of the newest cut."

Raleigh is also said to have been the first man to bring potatoes to England, in 1586. However, there is no contemporary account of this. John Gerard, in his book *Herball* (1597), refers to a C. Clusius who had cultivated potatoes in Italy in 1585. The vegetable gained immediate popularity and was cultivated in most European countries during the following decade.

Similarly, Raleigh is usually credited, or blamed, for introducing tobacco into England

SUPREME GALLANTRY. *Sir Walter Raleigh's famous gesture was merely a romantic invention.*

on his return from the British colony of Virginia in 1586. A Frenchman had already introduced tobacco to France in 1559 or 1560. He was Jean Nicot, from whose name "nicotine" derived.

George Washington chopped down a cherry tree. At the age of six, the future first President of the United States stood accused of chopping down his father's favorite cherry tree. "I can't tell a lie," he admitted to his father. "I did cut it with my hatchet."

This irresistible mixture of boyish mischief and honesty has made the young Washington's confession one of the most famous "events" in American history. Here, surely, were the honest, forthright qualities of a great leader in the making.

Yet very little is known about Washington's childhood. In one of his first biographies—by a clergyman, Mason Locke Weems—Washington's entire early life occupies only a single page.

In the first edition of this *Life of George Washington,* published in 1800, the year after the President's death, no mention is made of the cherry-tree incident. It was later revised to include a number of new anecdotes, including young George's exploits with the hatchet.

Weems claimed that he heard the story from an anonymous "aged lady" who was once associated with the Washington household. But the author was known to have spent a great deal of time inventing "biographical anecdotes" for his books, lifting some of his stories from works about completely different people.

Later, he even admitted as much, although he did not say that the cherry-tree story was one of these. In his *Life of William Penn,* the founder of Pennsylvania, Weems made up the story of a treaty between the Indians and the settlers, complete with suitable quotations. But no such treaty existed.

Weems' biography of Washington ran to more than 70 editions during the 19th century, firmly establishing the cherry-tree story in American folklore. But no modern biographer accepts it as true, and some omit it altogether.

King Harold was shot in the eye by a Norman arrow. As the Battle of Hastings drew to a climax in 1066, the tall and powerful English King Harold stood his ground, surrounded by his bodyguards. Although his army had dwindled, the remainder continued to beat off one Norman assault after another. His adversary, William, Duke of Normandy, ordered his archers to fire into the air so that their arrows would fall into the densely packed knot of men around the King. A stray arrow pierced Harold's eye, and, as apparently depicted in the famous Bayeux Tapestry, he fell, and in the next charge he was slain by the Normans.

But according to the historian Lewis Thorpe, this account of Harold's death is not true. In his book *The Bayeaux Tapestry and the Norman Invasion,* Thorpe says that Harold was hacked to death by a Norman soldier, possibly one of four who attacked the King simultaneously.

The story of Harold's death may have be-

DID HE OR DIDN'T HE? *Artist Grant Wood's version of the Washington myth, with the first President's biographer, Mason Weems (right).*

DEATH OF A KING. *Was Harold mortally wounded by an arrow (left) or hacked down and killed by a Norman cavalryman (right)?*

328

"BRING YOUR PARASOL . . ."

Umbrellas began as parasols and were carried only by fashionable women at first.

In this illustration from an 1862 edition of Robinson Crusoe, *Crusoe has a parasol.*

In 1750 Jonas Hanway was the first man to adopt the umbrella, amid mockery.

UMBRELLAS were originally designed as sun shades and are depicted being used in this way in ancient Egyptian, Greek, and Byzantine art. They began to appear in Europe in the 16th century to keep off rain and were made with leather and oiled materials, rather than delicate silks.

At first, umbrellas were carried only by women, and it took the courage of a philanthropist, Jonas Hanway in 1750, to suffer jeers and catcalls in the streets of London before it became acceptable for men to carry umbrellas in public places.

come confused because at the place where the tapestry says, in Latin, *Harold rex interfectus est* ("Harold the King is killed"), there are two figures, either of which could be taken as Harold. One, on the left of a Norman horse, is standing, holding a shield and apparently trying to pluck an arrow from his eye. The other, falling, to the right of the horse, is being attacked by a Norman with a sword.

The arrow-in-the-eye story appears in 12th-century accounts of the battle by such historians as William of Malmesbury, Henry of Huntingdon, and Robert Wace. But Thorpe takes as a more acceptable account that of a Norman historian, Guy of Amiens, written in 1068, only two years after the battle, in a book called *Carmen de Hastingae Proelio (The Song of the Battle of Hastings).*

According to this account, William "called Eustace of Boulogne to his side and moved up to give all the relief that he possibly could to those who were being slaughtered by Harold."

In the attack Eustace was joined by Hugh de Montfort, Ivo (heir to Ponthieu), and Walter

Gifford the younger. "By the use which they made of their weapons," the Amiens version goes, "these four between them encompassed the king's death. With the point of his lance the first pierced Harold's shield and then penetrated his chest, drenching the ground with his blood. With his sword the second cut off his head. The third disemboweled him with his javelin. The fourth hacked at his leg and hurled it far away. Struck down in this way, his dead body lay on the ground."

Eve gave Adam an apple in the Garden of Eden. Though the apple has become the symbol of man's fall from grace, nowhere in the story of the temptation—recounted in Genesis 3—is there any mention of an apple. It is simply described as "the fruit of the tree which is in the midst of the garden," and it has been suggested that since Adam and Eve dressed themselves in figleaves after eating the fruit, the tree may well have been a fig.

The apple probably entered the story via Greek and Celtic mythology, in both of which the fruit belongs to love goddesses and symbolizes desire. When Aquila of Pontus translated the Song of Solomon from Hebrew into Greek in the second century A.D., he rendered "I raised thee up under the apple tree; there my mother brought thee forth" as "I raised thee up under the apple tree; there wast thou corrupted"—evidently taking the verse to refer to the forbidden tree. St. Jerome, translating the Old Testament into Latin, followed suit, and the idea has persisted ever since.

Thumbs down was the signal for death in the Roman arena. A painting by the French artist Jean Léon Gérôme (1824-1904), which was first exhibited in 1873 and became extremely popular in the form of engravings, showed a Roman Emperor giving the "thumbs-down" sign to a gladiator to kill his fallen opponent. Perhaps it was from this painting that the legend of the gesture arose, for so far as is known, the signal for death in the arena was apparently never indicated by the turning down of a thumb.

A 1693 translation of the *Satires* of Juvenal (A.D. 60–ca. 140) stated "where with thumbs bent back they popularly kill." Classical scholar John Mayor, in his 1853 edition of Juvenal's work, explained: "Those who wished the death of the conquered gladiator turned their thumbs toward their breasts, as a signal to his opponent to stab him; those who wished him to be spared

turned their thumbs downwards, as a signal for dropping the sword."

Roman Emperors would seek the guidance of spectators before giving the life-or-death signal to a victorious gladiator.

The *Latin Dictionary* of Lewis and Short (1880) gives, under the entry for *pollex* ("thumb"): "To close down the thumb (*premere*) was the sign of approbation; to extend it (*vertere, convertere, pollex infestus*) a sign of disapprobation."

Cinderella wore glass slippers. In the early French version of the popular children's fairy story, Cinderella wore *pantoufles de vair*—slippers of fur. But by the 14th century the word *vair* had gone out of use, and when the French author Charles Perrault (1628-1703) rewrote the story in 1697, he was unfamiliar with the word and took it to be *verre,* meaning "glass."

The popular Western version of the story is derived from Perrault's story, and so the glass slipper has passed into common retelling of the tale. The story of Cinderella is rooted in obscure folktales, and in the more than 500 versions that exist, the slipper invariably appears made of some rare or expensive material—of gold or silver, encrusted with jewels or pearls.

It is a folktale that occurs all over the world, not just in Europe. One of the earliest known versions is a Chinese story written in the ninth century A.D.

CANUTE ORDERED BACK THE SEA

IT IS NOT absolutely certain that the story of King Canute (A.D. 995-1035) ordering back the waves and being soaked ever occurred. And if it

According to one historian, Canute's seaside escapade was a demonstration of his great humility.

did, it seems, the tale may be misunderstood. The earliest version, contrary to popular supposition, does not make out the King as stupid but as a man of great humility.

A century or so after Canute's death, Henry of Huntingdon wrote, in his *Historia Anglorum,* that the King, angered by the flattery of his courtiers, who constantly told him he was capable of any achievement, arranged the seashore experiment. After ordering back the sea and getting his feet wet, Canute then said: "Let all men know how empty and worthless is the power of kings, for there is none worthy of the name, but He whom heaven, earth and sea obey by eternal laws." Afterward, according to Henry, Canute never again wore his crown. He hung it instead in Winchester Cathedral.

THEY NEVER SAID IT

Memorable, but misremembered phrases

Alas, poor Yorick, I knew him well—*attributed to Hamlet.*

This line is a distortion of the one in Shakespeare's *Hamlet,* act 5, scene 1, which reads: "Alas, poor Yorick. I knew him, Horatio."

Hamlet says the words to his friend Horatio after being handed the skull of Yorick, former court jester.

Tomorrow to fresh fields and pastures new—*attributed to John Milton.*

The saying, often used when embarking on some new venture or taking final leave of friends, is a misquotation of a line by the poet John Milton, with one word altered. In "Lycidas," published in 1638, Milton wrote:

At last he rose, and twitch'd his mantle blue;
Tomorrow to fresh woods, *and pastures new.*

In common usage, "fields" replaces "woods," probably because alliteration with the word "fresh" helps it to roll more easily off the tongue.

The English are a nation of shopkeepers—*attributed to Napoleon.*

The phrase is commonly attributed to Napoleon as a reflection of his contempt for the English as a nation of *petit bourgeois*—small businessmen.

But the phrase "nation of shopkeepers," or merchants, was already in print when Napoleon was a boy, and it was hardly his own creation. It was used in a political tract by the English economist Josiah Tucker in 1766, later by the Scottish economist Adam Smith in his *Wealth of Nations* (1776), and the same year in Philadelphia by Samuel Adams.

Later, when Napoleon was in exile, the phrase was attributed to him by two biographers. Napoleon's doctor, Barry O'Meara, in *Napoleon in Exile, or A Voice From St. Helena,* reported a conversation with the Emperor on February 17, 1817, in which he said of the English, "They are a nation of merchants."

It is clear from O'Meara's text that, while Napoleon agrees with the assessment, he is himself quoting the Corsican patriot Pasquale Paoli (1725–1807).

The journal of Gaspard Gougaud, who was also with Napoleon during his exile, certainly shows that the Emperor regarded the English as profit oriented.

But it was Adam Smith's book, which was well known to Napoleon, that said: "To found a great empire for the sole purpose of raising up a people of customers may at first sight appear a project fit only for a nation of shopkeepers."

Money is the root of all evil—*attributed to St. Paul.*

What St. Paul actually said was: "The *love* of money is the root of all evil"; he did not mean that money was evil in itself.

Let them eat cake—*attributed to Marie Antoinette.*

In October 1789 the poor women of Paris marched on the royal palace of Versailles in an attempt to force Louis XVI to create a new, fairer government. According to tradition, when his Queen, Marie Antoinette, heard the crowd outside and was told they were hungry and had no bread, she said: "*Qu'ils mangent de la brioche.*" This became popularly translated as "Let them eat cake."

The story was widely circulated at the time and after the Queen's execution. It was held to typify either her stupidity or her callous indifference to the sufferings of the poor. But there is no evidence that she ever made the remark.

The first reference to the phrase was in the 1760's—in Jean-Jacques Rousseau's *Confessions*—when Marie Antoinette was still a young girl.

Rousseau relates an anecdote about a "great princess," who, when told that the peasants had no bread, replied: "*Qu'ils mangent de la brioche.*" "*Brioche,*" a superior kind of bread, was the only kind the princess knew—so, in fact, the remark was kindly meant. It is possible that one of France's revolutionaries, who had read Rousseau, ascribed the remark to Marie Antoinette.

The Battle of Waterloo was won on the playing fields of Eton—*attributed to the Duke of Wellington.*

When the first Duke of Wellington was a boy at Eton, there were no playing fields and no organized team games, and as one of his descendants remarked, the first duke's career at the school was "short and inglorious." It is there-

EARLY CRICKET AT ETON. *The school had neither playing fields nor team games when the Duke of Wellington was a pupil there, so he is unlikely to have referred to them after his victory at Waterloo.*

fore highly improbable that he ever said this. It was first attributed to him in print by the French Count Charles de Montalembert in his *De l'Avenir Politique de l'Angleterre* (*England's Political Future*), which was published in 1855, three years after Wellington's death.

But there is no contemporary evidence that the duke made the statement, or even that he is likely to have done so, for he had no great affection either for his school or for the public-school spirit. It was only later that these were emphasized as the chief causes of England's military and colonial successes.

Up Guards and at'em—*attributed to the Duke of Wellington at Waterloo.*
It is doubtful whether Wellington ever used this phrase. One of his contemporaries, J.W. Croker, reported in 1884 that he had written to the duke asking if he really did give this command at the Battle of Waterloo. In an undated letter, the duke replied: "What I must have said and possibly did say was, 'Stand up, Guards,' and then gave the commanding officers the order to attack"—so repulsing the last attack of the French Imperial Guard.

Elementary, my dear Watson!—*attributed to Sherlock Holmes.*
The very phrase brings to mind Sir Arthur Conan Doyle's creation, Sherlock Holmes—most famous detective of all time. Yet nowhere in any of Conan Doyle's books does Holmes ever utter the oft-quoted words.

The closest Holmes comes to saying it is in the story *The Crooked Man,* published in the *Strand Magazine* in 1893 and included in *The Memoirs of Sherlock Holmes,* published in 1894.

In the story Dr. Watson, Holmes' former assistant, has married and no longer lives at Holmes' flat at 221B Baker Street, London. When Holmes calls on Watson to ask for his help in solving a mystery, he makes a few deductions about his old friend. He observes, for example, that Watson still smokes the same pipe tobacco—from the ash on his coat—and that he is very busy.

Watson asks how he knows this. Holmes says that Watson takes a hansom cab when he is busy and walks when he is not. Watson's boots are dusty enough to have been outdoors, but not dusty enough for him to have been walking. Therefore, Holmes says, he must have taken a hansom. Therefore, he must be busy.

"Excellent!" Watson says.

"Elementary," says Holmes.

Play it again, Sam—*attributed to Humphrey Bogart.*
Although this is one of the best known catchphrases associated with the tough-guy screen image of Humphrey Bogart, he never made the remark at all. The association arose from Bogart's 1942 film *Casablanca.* He played a

MELODY FOR SCREEN ROMANCE. *Humphrey Bogart and Ingrid Bergman starred in the film* Casablanca, *with Dooley Wilson as the club pianist who was asked to "Play it, Sam"—but not by Bogart.*

nightclub owner who was haunted by the song "As Time Goes By," because it reminded him of his love for the film's heroine, played by Ingrid Bergman.

In fact, it was Miss Bergman who said "Play it, Sam" to the club's pianist, overcoming his boss' injunction against the song. Bogart heard the tune and realized that his lost love had returned. His wrath for Sam was forgotten.

Come with me to the Casbah—*attributed to Charles Boyer.*

THE GREAT LOVER. *Boyer charms Hedy Lamarr in* Algiers . . . *without mentioning the Casbah.*

Charles Boyer built up a screen image that was to talkies what Rudolph Valentino had been to silent films. He was suave, handsome, and had a thrilling French accent. In his 1938 film *Algiers,* Boyer spent a lot of time in the Casbah of Algiers—but although his Gallic tones were

admirably suited to saying "Come with me to the Casbah," he never used the phrase.

By the time Boyer made the film he was a famous actor, much parodied and imitated as the archetypal French lover. It was probably through these imitations that the phrase came to be attributed to him.

You dirty rat—*attributed to James Cagney.*
Throughout three decades the name James Cagney personified gangster films. Cagney was the craggy-jawed, rasping hoodlum in the snap-brimmed felt hat. Yet he claims that he never said, in any of his films, "You dirty rat"—although the line is the one all impersonators use when they imitate the Cagney style.

TOUGH GUY. *James Cagney epitomized the screen gangster—but in none of his films did he use his impersonators' expression, "You dirty rat."*

333

Intriguing
and unsolved mysteries

•

NO ROOM IN THE ARK?

End of the dinosaur's 140-million-year dynasty

Dinosaurs dominated the earth's larger animals for 140 million years, spreading over the plains, the jungles, and the swamps. Then, approximately 65 million years ago—as far as modern man can make out—the dinosaurs suddenly died out. And no one really knows why.

It is one of the great unsolved mysteries of science. What makes it so baffling is that there was not just one kind of dinosaur but many genera and species.

Some were the sluggish monsters so often depicted by filmmakers, but others were quick-moving hunters.

Paleontologists—scientists who study extinct animal forms—used to suggest that dinosaurs were "stupid." But more recent study suggests they were no stupider than reptiles of our own day.

Hunters from space

Dinosaur remains have been found in many countries on most of the continents. Yet, until recently, scientists could see no reason why these animals should have completely disappeared. All that emerged was a mass of theories, some rather absurd . . .

Raids by hunters in flying saucers.

Lack of room in Noah's Ark.

Annihilation by cavemen (despite the fact that dinosaurs died out millions of years before the emergence of man).

Extraction of the moon from the Pacific Ocean, with cataclysmic consequences (if this ever

did happen, which most astronomers doubt, it would have been millions of years before the appearance of any advanced life forms on earth).

Lemminglike mass suicide by all the species in all those places at more or less the same time! Or even, as one researcher put it, *Paleoweltschmerz,* a superb term that suggests the dinosaurs became so disillusioned with their ancient world that they died of boredom.

Other theories seem more plausible—but only at first glance . . .

Disease and parasites: Again, it is unlikely that so many species in so many places could be affected by an epidemic.

Cosmic radiation: The theory is that, with the explosion of a supernova star in the galaxy, radiation on earth greatly increased, causing fatal mutations. But, if so, since mammals were also present, why should only one group of creatures be affected?

Starvation: Carnivorous dinosaurs may have become so efficient that they killed off all the plant-eating dinosaurs and then died of hunger. The converse, however, may be more likely—that as the plant eaters died out for other reasons, the flesh eaters would then also be doomed for lack of prey.

Inadequate construction: The idea that dinosaurs became too large for their environment gains some credence from the fact that in the fossil casts of some species it has been found that the pituitary gland, which controls growth, was excessively large. It may have become overactive through mutation and destroyed the dinosaurs by interfering with their metabolism. But some dinosaurs—the Hypsilophodon, for example—were no more than eight feet long. So why should such comparatively small creatures die out along with the large dinosaurs?

A dwindling brain: The only "evidence" concerns just one species, the "plated reptile," Triceratops, which had a great mantle around its neck. It was 25 feet long, weighed about 1¾ tons—and had a walnut-sized brain.

Egg-eating mammals: It is highly probable that other animals ate dinosaur eggs—but hardly

STARK RELIEF. *A dinosaur skeleton emerges as a paleontologist, working with great care, chisels sandstone away from a fossil at a site in Utah. This creature, a* Camarasaurus, *was 25 feet long.*

to the extent that the creature should become extinct. Several creatures today eat crocodile eggs, but crocodiles continue to exist.

Senility: The idea that dinosaurs suffered from a form of racial old age is hard to reconcile with the known fact that they were so profuse and so active.

In the last decade more sophisticated theories have evolved. Most of these are interlinked, and although the mystery may never be completely solved, bits of information begin to fit together like a huge biological jigsaw.

In 1972 a team from the University of Bonn discovered eight dinosaur eggs—two of them intact—in a rock wall near Corvières in the French Pyrenees.

These showed signs of a phenomenon known as eggshell thinning—which threatens many birds and reptiles today—and is known to be the result of hormone disturbances triggered by environmental stresses.

When this state occurs, the shells become so fragile that they break prematurely or else cannot provide sufficient calcium to feed the embryos within. Overcrowding is one of the environmental stresses known to produce this condition.

But the dinosaurs were probably already doomed, for overcrowding into a few places implies that enormous danger already threatened their environment.

Cool death

Their extinction occurred during the warm Cretaceous period. During this time large mountain ranges were formed. These would have had a gradual influence not only on the climate, bringing about less uniform temperatures, but on plantlife as well.

The variable weather undoubtedly killed off many dinosaurs and possibly caused overcrowding in warmer areas. But the great dinosaur killer—the major factor that wiped out the largest land animals that ever existed—may have been the innocent flowering of a few wild plants.

One recent theory, propounded in 1974 by Dr. Tony Swain of the Kew Botanical Gardens in London, hinges on the fact that dinosaurs, like most reptiles, probably had poor taste buds. Dr. Swain pointed out that dinosaurs had to eat great amounts of plants, mostly ferns. The hadrosaur, for example, is estimated to have eaten as much as 400 to 800 pounds of greenery a day.

Poison with no taste

When the first flowering plants appeared about 130 million years ago, some species developed chemical constructions that incorporated greater and greater amounts of alkaloids. Tests with modern-day reptiles indicate that the dinosaurs would probably have been unable to taste the alkaloids—and considering their enormous food intake, they might easily have poisoned themselves.

Swain points out that a common factor of dinosaur remains is that they are often found in contorted positions—rather like those of animals that have died from strychnine poison.

The alkaloid poisoning may also have been responsible for eggshell thinning, just as DDT is known to cause this phenomenon in birds.

With the dying out of the herbivorous dinosaurs, the days of their predators, the carnivorous dinosaurs, were also numbered. New players dominated the stage—the mammals, some of which are man's distant ancestors. For a time at least they would inherit the earth.

THE DINOSAUR LIVES?

DINOSAURS, generally regarded as extinct for 65 million years, may still be with us—in fact, may easily be seen by glancing out of almost any window. For two scientists claim that birds are descended from dinosaurs.

Robert T. Bakker, of Harvard University, and Peter Galton, of the University of Bridgeport, base their claim partly on the alleged similarities between the skeletons of the earliest bird known and one type of dinosaur. Most paleontologists consider that flying reptiles, birds, dinosaurs, and crocodilians evolved from the thecodontian, which lived 200 million years ago. Bakker and Galton cite the fact that the oldest bird remains are those of the archaeopteryx, which was the size of a crow and dates back only 140 million years—long after the first appearance of their supposed relative, the dinosaur.

REMAINS OF A MAMMOTH. *The body of this beast was found along the Beresovka River in 1902 after a big thaw, and more carcasses have been found in northern Siberia and Alaska.*

TEN-THOUSAND-YEAR-OLD STEAKS

The riddle of the mammoths that ate buttercups

A mammoth discovered half kneeling, half standing on a bank of the Beresovka River in Siberia perplexed scientists for many years; for the strangest thing of all about the frozen, well-preserved monster was that it had buttercups in its mouth. This odd fact, at first overlooked, was to provide a clue to a terrible moment in the earth's history.

Mammoths were long-tusked, hairy members of the elephant family, which roamed the world for half a million years and became extinct about 10,000 years ago. In the permanently frozen territories of northern Siberia, Alaska, and Canada, many of these ancient beasts can still be found, forever preserved like sides of beef in a freezer.

In spite of the thousands of years that have passed, the meat is still good enough to eat—according to those who have tried. Other long-extinct animals have also been found in the same deep-frozen condition, tumbled together in heaps of bones and mangled flesh.

Scientists had no difficulty in explaining this ancient tragedy. Huge herds of mammoths used to roam the tundra—the great arctic plains—feeding off the grasses, reeds, and other plants that still cover the land in summer. Every now and then one of them would get trapped in ice or would fall to its death down a crevasse in a glacier; there the carcass would freeze and be preserved, almost unchanged, through the ages.

The explanation was obvious; unfortunately, it was totally wrong.

Wrong theories

To begin with, the carcasses were found in the wrong places. Vast areas of the Arctic are covered with ice, but most of the tundra is composed of soil—sand, river silt, and loam—bound together by frozen water. And the frozen mammoths were discovered not in the ice but in the silt layers.

Moreover, during the relevant period, there were no glaciers in Siberia except in the upper reaches of the mountains where the mammoths did not graze.

A new theory was put forward: The mammoths had fallen into rivers and had been carried downstream to the estuaries, where they were buried in silt. But this did not fit either; the monsters were being found in the tundra between the river valleys. And they could not all have drowned, because many of the animals were still standing up.

Experts in the deep-freeze butchery trade were consulted. But instead of clearing up the mystery, they made it far more puzzling. It was not possible, they said, to deep-freeze a creature as large as a mammoth at the relatively moderate temperatures of arctic ice.

If meat is frozen slowly at freezing temperatures, crystals form in the cells of the flesh, bursting the cells and dehydrating the meat. This makes the meat unfit for consumption. No such process, the butchers added, could have produced the deep-frozen mammoth meat.

To satisfactorily freeze a side of beef takes 30 minutes at –40°F. To deep-freeze a huge living mammoth, insulated in thick fur, they estimated that stupendously cold temperatures of below –150°F would be required. Such temperatures have never been recorded—not even in the Arctic.

The evidence seems to show the absurdity of such a theory, particularly the evidence of the Beresovka mammoth. At the time of its death this beast had been eating sedges, grasses, and buttercups.

Suddenly frozen stiff

As many gardeners know, buttercups enjoy temperate conditions with alternating sun and rain.

Yet, apparently, at one moment the mammoth was munching away peacefully at the grass and buttercups growing lush in the sunshine of a temperate plain. The next—so the deep-freeze men insisted—it was subjected to cold so bitter that it was deep-frozen where it stood.

These were unalterable facts. The scientists had to explain how it could have happened, not only on the Beresovka but at many places all over northern Siberia and Alaska where mammoths were suddenly frozen stiff.

No known variation in climate can explain the sudden deep-freezing of so many great beasts so many thousands of miles apart. Only a sudden cataclysm of hitherto undreamed proportions could have been responsible.

The evidence suggests an earthquake and volcanic eruption more violent than any ever recorded in history.

The crust of the earth, which floats 20 to 60 miles thick over the molten interior of our planet, is known to be composed of several plates, pressed one against the other. Where two plates meet, under titanic thrusts from every side, volcanic eruptions and earthquakes may occur.

It is thought that the eruption that caused the death of the mammoths was the result of two plates grinding together and bursting open a vast seam deep within the earth's crust.

Cold unimaginable

In so violent an eruption, not only would fiery lava be spewed out from the interior of the earth but there would be a great discharge of volcanic gases.

If these gases were shot high enough into the upper atmosphere, they would be chilled to incredibly low temperatures. Then, in the upheaval, they would spiral toward the poles, eventually descending on the warm blanket of air beneath. Through this they would penetrate as violent gusts, cutting through the blanket at its thinnest spots and hurtling at incredible speeds down upon the earth.

The result in the localities where the gases struck would be unimaginably cold, sufficient to produce the –150°F temperatures postulated by the deep-freeze experts.

In Siberia the unsuspecting mammoth would have been grazing on the tundra when a cold so fierce descended on him that it immediately froze his lungs and literally turned his blood to ice.

In a few seconds he would have died; in a few hours he would be a solid statue, ready to sink into the earth over the years and be buried in the dusts of time.

Or perhaps the cold was accompanied by a wind so violent that every living creature—mammoths, tigers, lions, woolly rhinoceroses, bison, and beavers—would be hurled along in a maelstrom to the side of a hill, where they would be deposited in a frozen mass, to lie forever in a tangle of trees, boulders, and soil.

The picture is a terrible one, the more so since mankind has no guarantee that the cold wind will not happen again.

THE GIANTS OF EASTER ISLAND

Who carved the great stone heads—and why?

Dutch admiral Jakob Roggeveen had never seen anything like it in his life before—an uncharted island in the mid-South Pacific inhabited by what appeared to be 30-foot-tall giants. The giants seemed to be standing on huge walls that resembled the battlements of a gargantuan fortress.

As Roggeveen sailed his three ships closer, he was relieved to find that the giants were only statues and the men walking among them were of normal size. With a small landing party Roggeveen went ashore the next day to find that the "battlements" were only platforms for the statues. On each stood the bust of a man with long ears and a red headpiece.

The date was Easter Sunday 1722, and so Roggeveen named his discovery Easter Island. He then sailed away.

It was almost 50 years before Europeans landed again on Easter Island and another 100 years before serious explorations began.

By then, the statues were no longer erect as Roggeveen had seen them. During tribal wars most had been toppled from their platforms to the ground, where they remain to this day.

The giant statues proved to be carved from volcanic rock found in the dormant crater of Rano Raraku. More than 300 of them had been carved from the crater walls and lowered down its slope. They had somehow been maneuvered into upright positions on the platforms.

Inside the crater were some 400 uncompleted statues. Some had only a few chisel marks on them, while others were almost ready for transportation. Obsidian hatchets and chisels, abandoned by the ancient sculptors of the giant statues, were also found in the crater.

They had been left as though the craftsmen had intended to return some day but never did. Down the road leading from the crater were dozens of completed statues. They lay scattered every 50 yards for as far as the eye could see.

Several weighed up to 30 tons and stood 12 feet tall. One unfinished giant was 66 feet tall and weighed about 50 tons.

Long-eared people

Some of the statues were 10 miles from the crater, and to this day experts have still not worked out how the island's inhabitants trans-

THE ANCIENT GIANTS. *Scientists have asked for a long time how and why the huge stone sculptures came to be erected on Easter Island in the Pacific Ocean.*

ported the monuments or erected them on bases. Theories that logs were used as rollers were discounted, after tests showed that the Easter Island soil could not support trees of the size required for such an exercise. Another possibility considered was that vines woven into ropes were used to haul them. But this, too, was ruled out when it was proved that vine ropes could not stand the strain of pulling 30 tons.

Traces of ancient settlements indicated that Easter Island once supported from 2,000 to 5,000 people. Drawings that have been found show that they were probably divided into two classes. The "long-eared" people portrayed in the statues were probably the rulers—who used weights to stretch their earlobes—while the "short-eared" people were their subordinates.

Similar ear weights were used by the Incas of preconquest Peru. But the present inhabitants seem more closely akin to the Polynesians than to the people of South America. The vital key to Easter Island's mysteries could have been removed by a late-19th-century Peruvian slave trader who captured 1,000 natives, including the last King and "wise man" of the island.

No one knows exactly what happened to all the men who were carried off into bondage. Some may have returned, bringing disease with them that killed off the remainder of the population. With their disappearance may have gone the answers to questions of how a stone-age people created an army of monoliths.

THE GRAY-EYED INDIANS

How Raleigh's "lost colony" may have survived

Settlers driving inland along the Lumber River in North Carolina early in the 18th century were astonished to find a tribe of gray-eyed Indians whose native language was a kind of English!

They claimed that their ancestors could "talk in a book," which, the explorers understood, meant that they could read.

Today, the descendants of these mysterious people still live in Robeson County where they were discovered. Known as the Lumbee Indians, they have complexions ranging from dark to very fair. To this day blond hair and blue eyes are not uncommon.

No one knows the tribe's true heritage, but an intriguing theory has been pieced together over the years.

It is now thought that they may be the remnants of Sir Walter Raleigh's "lost colony" of Roanoke Island, from which all the English settlers disappeared in 1590. The Lumber River is about 200 miles from Roanoke.

When Elizabeth I granted a charter to Raleigh, two attempts were made at colonization. The first was abandoned in 1586 because of recurring Indian attacks and the shortage of supplies.

The party of more than 100 men and women, led by Gov. John White, who arrived in 1587, fared little better. Eventually, White decided to sail back to England with a skeleton crew of 15 to seek help and supplies. He left instructions that if the remaining colonists were forced to leave in his absence, they should inscribe their destination "in a conspicuous place."

Fortress ransacked

Because of the war between England and Spain, it was not until 1590 that White was able to return. A fortress had been built at Roanoke, but it had been ransacked and then abandoned; the settlers had vanished without a trace. Only one clue remained—the single word "Croatoan," carved into a post.

Historians still argue over its meaning. Some believed it was the name of an Indian tribe that attacked the settlement and killed the colonists.

But Croatoan was an island south of Roanoke, which the colonists knew was inhabited by the friendly Hatteras tribe. If the colonists had managed to reach this island and then had intermarried with the Hatteras, their descendants could be today's Lumbee Indians.

Governor White assumed the settlers had moved to Croatoan voluntarily, but, unable to search for them, he returned to England.

Now there is strong evidence to suggest that he was right. About 1650 many Hatteras Indians migrated to the mainland, settling in the Lumber River Valley. Of the 95 surnames of the "lost colonists" of Roanoke—names such as Sampson, Cooper, and Dare—no fewer than 41 can be found among the Lumbees.

"BEE IT KNOWNE VNTO ALL MEN." This brass plaque, apparently declaring Drake's annexation of "New Albion" in 1579, was found on a beach in California in 1936.

BRITISH CALIFORNIA

The plaque that establishes England's claim

One summer day in 1936, Beryle Shinn, a San Francisco store clerk, was picnicking on the shore north of the Golden Gate Bridge. Picking up a rock, he was mildly surprised to find that a dirty old brass plate lay beneath it.

Shinn took it home, thinking that it might come in handy for car repairs.

In the name of Her Majesty

He left the plate in his garage and forgot about it for eight months. Then coming across it again early in 1937, he cleaned it up with soap and water. It measured five inches by eight inches. It had a jagged hole at the bottom, and there was writing scratched on it. The word "Drake" could be faintly deciphered.

The discovery of that piece of brass was to start an international argument that involved American historians, metallurgists, scholars of Old English, and antiquarians. For on the plate were written the words of the formal annexation of California by Sir Francis Drake in 1579.

Shinn sent the plate to Dr. Herbert Bolton of the University of California, who carefully cleaned it and deciphered the inscription:

BEE IT KNOWNE VNTO ALL MEN
BY THESE PRESENTS
IVNE 17 1579
BY THE GRACE OF GOD AND IN THE NAME
OF HERR MAIESTY QVEEN ELIZABETH OF
ENGLAND AND HERR SVCCESSORS FOREVER
I TAKE POSSESSION OF THIS KINGDOME
WHOSE KING AND PEOPLE FREELY RESIGN
THEIR RIGHT AND TITLE IN THE WHOLE
LAND VNTO HERR MAIESTIES KEEPEING NOW
NAMED BY ME AND TO BEE KNOWNE VNTO
ALL MEN AS NOVA ALBION
FRANCIS DRAKE

Triumphantly, Dr. Bolton announced to a surprised California Historical Society: "Here it is. Recovered at last after a lapse of 357 years. Behold, Drake's plate—the plate of brass. California's choicest archeological treasure!"

Gods in California

But it was not as simple as that. The great argument was just beginning. It is known that Sir Francis Drake visited California in 1579 during his round-the-world voyage. He was being hunted by the Spaniards after sailing around the southern tip of South America.

Trying to escape pursuit by reaching the fabled Northwest Passage, which early navigators imagined would connect the Pacific with the Atlantic to the north of Canada, he landed in California, near what is now San Francisco. He and his crew were warmly received by the Indians. They thought the Englishmen were gods and offered them their entire country along the Californian seaboard.

According to reports of the voyage, Drake graciously accepted the offer, ordered a plate to be nailed to a post and set up on shore, and announced that the territory had now become a domain of Queen Elizabeth and would henceforth be known as New Albion.

Until Shinn's picnic nothing more had been seen or heard of the plaque. But now the whole academic world was agog. Some experts denounced the plaque as a forgery. They pointed out that contemporary reports stated that Drake had landed at a spot marked by "white bancks and cliffes." But there were none at the picnic spot.

Then the date on the plaque was hard to accept. The reports said that although Drake had landed on June 17, the Indians had not ceded the territory until June 26.

Science raises doubts

Analysis of the metal showed that the brass had a higher zinc content than was usual in the 16th century. And tests on the exterior of the metal showed it to have a high carbon content—as if fire had been used to hasten the aging process.

But the main attack came over the lettering and the words used. The letters were all Roman, used only by scholars in Elizabethan days, in preference to the commoner, ornamental Tudor lettering. Besides, the words had a suspicious conformity in a day when spelling varied from page to page. And the engraver had used the modern forms for words that in the 16th century were more often spelled "Yngland," "Kyng," "Quene," and "yt" ("it"). As a final objection they said the spelling "herr" (for "her") did not exist at that time.

However, Dr. Bolton was able to answer his critics point by point.

The Indians might well not have formally ceded the territory until June 26, but accounts of the voyage stated clearly that the plate was engraved on "the day and yeare of our arrival."

Moreover, the brass was now found by scientific analysis to be ancient and covered with a naturally acquired coating "formed over many years." Plant cells in the jagged hole were "undoubtedly mineralized," which could only have occurred if the plaque had been in the open air for a considerable period.

The report concluded: "Each individual groove of the lettering was examined under the microscope at magnifications of 50 to 200 diameters because, in the case of fraud, there is always the chance of finding a hidden area which would disclose a fresh, corrosion-free surface. . . . No indication or clue of artificial patination of any kind was found."

As for the lettering and the spelling, Dr. Bolton's supporters had answers to rebut the skeptics. Were there not scholars on board with Sir Francis, or at least books from which Roman script could be copied? Was it not reasonable for spelling to be uniform over so short a text? And were the "modern" spellings not current among Elizabethan variations?

Soon it was discovered that Drake had used the spelling "herr" in a prospectus for lands. The only criticism he was unable to refute was that Drake had landed near white banks and cliffs—until a surprising thing happened.

When the news of Shinn's find was published, a chauffeur named William Caldeira came forward. Four years previously, he stated, he had been waiting for his employer on the shore at Laguna Beach, when he had turned over a chunk of earth with his foot. Under it was a brass plate bearing what he thought was a Chinese inscription, although he had recognized the word "Drake" in English.

He, too, had kept the plaque for possible car repairs, but a few months later had thrown it away not far from where Beryle Shinn found it. Caldeira had found the plate at Drake's Bay—the spot traditionally accepted as the landing place—whose most outstanding features are tall, white cliffs. The plate was vindicated, and Britain's title deed to the state now rests in the University of California. So far, the British have generously refused to take up their option.

SLOW TRAIN TO IZMIR

The girl who vanished with the treasures of Dorak

Archeologist James Mellaart took little notice of the dark-haired girl sitting opposite him on the train from Istanbul—until a glance at the bracelet she was wearing told him it was thousands of years old and made of solid gold. That glance was to lead him to a hoard of priceless treasure—and a year-long battle to defend himself against a campaign of suspicion and calumny.

Was it all a hoax? Or was Mellaart the victim of a sinister plot to undermine his reputation? At the time he simply could not believe his good luck.

No archeologist could have ignored the bracelet. As the train trundled across Turkey he introduced himself. The girl told him the bracelet came from a collection at her home and agreed to let him examine the remainder.

By the time the train drew into Izmir, on Turkey's Aegean coast, that evening in 1958, Mellaart was burning with eagerness. So he paid little attention to the ferry and taxi route they took to the girl's home, where the collection was lifted piece by piece from its hiding place in a chest of drawers.

Mellaart was astounded. Here was a find comparable to the discovery of Tutankhamen's tomb. He asked if he could photograph it. The girl refused, but she said he could stay in the house while he made sketches.

Mellaart jumped at the chance. For days he worked without a break on the fabulous pieces, copying their intricate designs, taking rubbings of their hieroglyphs, noting every detail.

The girl, who said she was Greek, told him that the collection had been found during the Greek occupation after the First World War. It came from a secret excavation at a small lakeside village called Dorak.

Staggering evidence

To Mellaart the implications were staggering. For he knew that the pieces were 4,500-year-old bronze-age relics and that he had stumbled on the first evidence that a great seafaring city had flourished near Homer's Troy, ruled by a warrior caste and rivaling Troy itself in wealth and influence. It was an archeologist's dream. All the theories would now have to be reexamined.

Finally, late one night, he finished his work and left. It was the last time he saw the girl or the treasure. Mellaart realized only much later just how little he had discovered about the girl who was the key to his find. He could remember only that she spoke English with an American accent; she had given her address as 217 Kazim Direk Street; and her name was Anna Papastrati.

Mellaart's acceptance of this without checking up was his first dangerous mistake. Later, suspicious Turkish investigators said they could find no trace of anyone of that name; moreover, Kazim Direk Street simply did not exist.

His second mistake came when he reported to his chief at the British Institute of Archaeology in Ankara, Prof. Seton Lloyd. Mellaart, who was the assistant director, told Lloyd that he had found the treasure six years earlier and had only just received permission to publish his findings. It was a lie, invented for an entirely innocent reason. Mellaart had only been married for four years, and he did not want his wife to be embarrassed by gossip that he had spent several days in another woman's home.

The lost letter

Mellaart was to regret both mistakes during his long and bitter fight to vindicate himself against the accusations flung at him following the publication of his findings in the *Illustrated London News* in November 1959. He had written to the Turkish Department of Antiquities to warn them of the planned publication, but the letter had been mislaid.

When the article appeared, with Mellaart's drawings, Turkish officials were furious. They demanded to know where the treasure was, where it had been found, and why they had not been told. Thinking that a precious national treasure had been spirited away, they blamed Mellaart. Mellaart helped them all he could, but Anna—and the treasure—had vanished totally without a trace.

Smear campaign

There was no evidence to implicate Mellaart in any way with the disappearance of the treasure. Nevertheless, 2½ years later a smear campaign was launched, instigated by the Turkish newspaper *Milliyet*. The newspaper claimed that the date of the Dorak excavation was false; the finds, it said, had been made in the 1950's, when Mellaart and a mysterious woman had been seen near the site.

This was proved false. But the campaign of smears and cold-shoulder treatment went on. Though police inquiries had been dropped, Mellaart was banned from further work on a Turkish archeological site where he had already made several important discoveries.

Secret and influential enemies were busy in the background. But why should they try to discredit him by suggesting that his story was just an invention to further his career? Mellaart needed no publicity stunts to enhance his worldwide reputation as an archeologist.

And who was Anna? Was it sheer coincidence that she met Mellaart on the train that day? Or was she "planted" there by someone who knew that her bracelet could hardly fail to catch the archeologist's eye?

Art gang's dupe

One theory is that Mellaart was the bait in a cunning trap set by a smuggling gang who already had the Dorak treasure hidden away and ready for sale.

Such a gang would know that the value of their loot on the world black market would be enormously increased once it was pronounced genuine by an unsuspecting expert of Mellaart's repute.

The authoritative article in the *Illustrated London News* provided this stamp of authenticity that could be used by the smugglers. Were the pieces then quietly shipped away to secret buyers all over the world?

If that is what really happened, then the truth about Anna and the vanishing fortune may have been locked away forever—behind the doors of some of the world's wealthiest and most unscrupulous art dealers.

THE PITCHFORK MURDER

Was the harmless old villager a witch?

His two-pronged pitchfork was thrust through his neck, pinning him to the ground. His hedger's slash hook was embedded in his chest. The face of the dead old man was frozen in an expression of terror. This was how they found Charles Walton in 1945, victim of possibly the last ritualistic "witchcraft" murder in Britain.

Detective Superintendent Fabian—the famous "Fabian of Scotland Yard"—spent many months leading the investigation of the crime. But the mystery of who did it, and why, was never solved. It remains an enigma, horrific in its savagery and wrapped in an atmosphere of mystic fear.

Odd-job man

To all appearances Charles Walton was a harmless, endearing old man, such as one might meet in any English village that has not caught up to the pace of modern life. He lived with his niece in a thatched cottage in Warwickshire, earning enough to keep body and soul together by doing odd jobs around the farms.

He was not seen much in the local pubs, preferring to buy cider by the gallon and drink alone by his kitchen fireside. He was a man, as they say in the country, who "kept himself to himself."

But Walton, though not overfond of human companionship, was at home in the countryside alone with nature. He apparently spent many hours in the fields talking to the wild birds, and he believed that there was an understanding between them.

He did not much care for dogs, but in his back garden he bred toads. There was a local legend that he used to harness them to a miniature plow and follow them across the fields.

Whispering of witchcraft

It was a cold day in February when Charles Walton failed to return from his work in the fields, and searchers found his mutilated body under a willow tree. Donald McCormick, who wrote a book on the crime, claimed that he could make a good guess at who the killer was. So, too, could Fabian.

But no evidence could be produced to justify a prosecution. Only tales of Walton's communion with the birds, of his toad plow teams . . . and sinister whisperings that he was killed because he was a witch.

MARTYR OR MURDERER?

The hero who confessed to witchcraft

To the people of Brittany that September day in 1440 must have seemed like the end of the world. The magnificent, enormously wealthy Baron Gilles de Rais had been arrested and charged with sorcery, sacrilege, and the ritual murder of little children.

Even in the brilliant and extravagant court of 15th-century France, few careers had been so meteoric as that of Gilles. Heir to the greatest barony of Brittany, he had fought with Joan of Arc against England and was Marshal of France at the age of 24. So rich did he become that the number and splendor of his castles were second only to those of the King.

Then the blow fell. The prosecutors alleged that he maintained an Italian magician, Francesco Prelati, with whose assistance he had kidnapped and murdered more than 140 children. Their blood was alleged to have been used by Gilles, in fearsome potions, to gain magical power over his enemies.

On October 21 the marshal confessed to all the crimes with which he had been charged and explained that his motive was simply the gratification of his passions. "I tell you that there was no other motive. Have I not already told you enough to put 10,000 men to death?"

Gilles was hanged with his associates at Nantes before the end of October. Few people doubted his guilt; after all, surely no man, not even Gilles, could have achieved so much without some assistance from the Devil?

Monster or victim?

But the trial was held behind closed doors, and there were some disquieting doubts. Gilles' henchmen were certainly tortured, and the baron may have been subjected to the same treatment himself. Was he the victim of a conspiracy? If so, suspicion falls on John, Duke of Brittany, who stood to gain Gilles' lands.

Gilles was an easy target for accusations of sorcery, for he paid scant regard to conventional morality and interested himself in alchemy and astrology. Also, his gluttony, extravagance, and sexual activities were notorious. This is regrettable, perhaps, but not evidence that he was a murderer of children.

Why, then, if he was innocent, did he confess to such foul crimes? Perhaps he did con-

fess under torture. But there is a more likely explanation.

Gilles knew that once under the power of his enemies he was doomed, and since his life was forfeit in any case, his only concern should be for the eventual safety and welfare of his beloved family.

If Gilles denied the charges and was found guilty, his lands and wealth would be confiscated. But, if he confessed and died repentant, then the law provided that at least part of his estate would pass to his children.

And so it happened. Although Gilles' castles were granted to the Duke of Brittany, most of his wealth remained with his family who suffered no great disgrace. Some of them rose to high office in royal service—but none became so dangerously rich and powerful as Gilles himself.

ST. JOAN'S LIEUTENANT. *Gilles de Rais' supposed excesses earned him the title of "Bluebeard" and a shameful death.*

RICHARD III ON TRIAL

Was he really the "wickedest uncle in history"?

When the bones of two small boys were found beneath a staircase in the Tower of London in the late 17th century, it seemed to confirm the old story that Richard III, cruel, hunchbacked, and the wickedest uncle in history, had murdered his nephews. Not that most people needed convincing: Shakespeare's portrayal of Richard, crippled and twisted in body and mind, and his re-creation of the crime in the tower had already established the King's niche in the pantheon of villains.

Yet some historians believe that if Richard were brought to trial today, the prosecution would fail for lack of evidence. Indeed, what proof there was might point in another direction entirely.

When Edward IV died in 1483, his brother, Richard, was appointed Protector of the Realm and guardian of Edward's sons, the young King Edward V and his younger brother Richard, Duke of York.

While preparations began in London for Edward's coronation, Richard rode to Stony Stratford, near Northampton, and escorted the young King back to the Tower of London.

The younger nephew, Richard, had been taken by his mother for sanctuary in Westminster Abbey but soon joined his brother at the tower.

On one or two occasions the boys were seen playing together in the tower gardens. Then they disappeared forever from the public gaze. Sir Thomas More, in his biography of King Richard III, wrote that the King had the boys suffocated with a pillow. But More was writing from hearsay more than 30 years later.

There is not even any firm evidence that Richard stood to gain by the princes' murder. Only two months after their father's death it was being claimed by London preachers that the boys were illegitimate.

When Edward IV had married their mother, Elizabeth Woodville, in 1464, he had been betrothed to the daughter of the Earl of Shrewsbury. At the time such a formal betrothal was as binding as marriage itself, so technically the wedding was invalid—and Richard was the legitimate heir.

But if Richard did not murder the boys, who did, or who at least had sufficient motive? Many scholars believe the most likely suspect is Henry Tudor, who defeated Richard at the Battle of Bosworth Field in 1485 and became Henry VII.

Henry was the great-grandson of an illegitimate grandson of Edward III and had thus been excluded from the succession. He based his claim to the throne only on the right of conquest, and to make his position more secure, he married Elizabeth, sister of the princes in the tower.

He had Elizabeth declared legitimate, but in so doing, he restored the legitimacy of her brothers. If they were still alive, and Henry was to be King, he would have to dispose of them.

Nevertheless, there is no proof of Henry's guilt, any more than there is of Richard's. But Henry did not announce that the boys had been murdered by their uncle until July 16, 1486—nearly a year after Richard's death. As Henry had accused Richard of cruelty and tyranny immediately after he gained the throne, why did he not announce the murder then?

SLAUGHTER OF INNOCENTS. *A Victorian artist re-creates the popular notion of how the princes died in the Tower of London.*

THE MAN IN THE VELVET MASK

The prisoner the Sun King dared not kill

During the 60th year of Louis XIV's reign, in 1703, a mysterious man died in the Bastille. He had spent 34 years in prison, his face forever concealed from the world by a velvet mask.

A letter written by a French princess to a friend at the English court tells of the "ancient prisoner":

"For many years a man has lived, masked, in the Bastille and masked he has died. Two musketeers were always at his side to kill him if he unmasked. . . . There must, no doubt, have been some reason for this, as otherwise he was very well treated, well lodged and given all he wanted. . . . No one has ever been able to find out who he was."

The romantic novelist Alexandre Dumas *père* changed the nature of the mask in his book *The Man in the Iron Mask* and popularized the idea that the unidentified prisoner was either King Louis himself or a twin brother. But the known facts point to an even stranger explanation of the mystery.

Extraordinary precautions

From the moment he was arrested in the port city of Dunkirk in 1669, the prisoner was subjected to the most extraordinary security precautions. When he was sent to the prison of Pignerol, near Turin, which was then part of France, M. Saint-Mars, the governor of the prison, was given these instructions: "You are to threaten him with death if he ever opens his mouth to you on any subject other than his day-to-day needs."

Whenever Saint-Mars was transferred to another jail, his prisoner went with him, transported in a sedan chair sealed from curious eyes with wax paper. It is said that he almost died of the heat. In 1698 Saint-Mars took over as governor of the Bastille, and even then, nearly 30 years after the arrest, he was instructed to take all precautions to prevent the man from being recognized.

It appears that the mask was a precaution and not a punishment. Yet no one in the public eye was unaccounted for during the period, so why should such a precaution be necessary? The key to the riddle may well be that the prisoner bore a startling resemblance to a very important person—and that this close resemblance could have been very embarrassing.

One suggestion, put forward by the statesman and scholar Lord Quickswood, and one that fits all the known facts, is that the prisoner was the true father of Louis XIV.

During the 22 years of their marriage, Louis XIII and Anne of Austria had no children. Cardinal Richelieu was at that time the effective ruler of France, and it was in his interests that the King should have an heir, who could also be controlled by the Richelieu faction. For 14 years the King and Queen had lived apart. But Richelieu now managed to stage a formal reconciliation. And to the utter surprise of all France, the Queen gave birth to a son in 1638.

Since the royal couple had never had a child before, and cordially detested one another, it is not beyond the bounds of possibility that Richelieu persuaded the Queen to allow some handsome young nobleman to sire the child in her husband's stead. In Paris at the time there were many illegitimate sons of the promiscuous

ROMANTIC VERSION. *Such concepts of the mysterious prisoner were wrong. His mask was made of velvet, and he lived in style and comfort.*

Henry of Navarre—all half brothers of Louis XIII—so there would have been no necessity to search outside the royal Bourbon blood. Richelieu might easily have found a personable and willing young Bourbon and persuaded the Queen that there was no other way out of their dilemma.

Certainly, during the boy's childhood, it was said at court that the young Louis, strong and active, was totally unlike his father.

If the suggestion is true, the real father would probably have been sent abroad—possibly to the French colony of Canada. Eventually, he may have returned to France, imagining that the affair had been forgotten—or possibly hoping for a pension or other favors from his son, now the all-powerful Sun King.

The theory is that he resembled the King too closely, that his appearance would have been an embarrassment at court and a threat to the throne itself.

The obvious solution, to have him quietly murdered, would be out of the question. Louis was not overscrupulous, but even he would have balked at killing his own father. The alternative was total obscurity—a life that was comfortable yet utterly cut off from any human contact except that of his jailers.

He died as he lived, faceless and unknown, his anonymity preserved even to the grave. Like all who ended their lives in the Bastille, he was buried under a false name. The man who may have been the Sun King's father was listed on the records as Eustache Dauger, valet.

RIDDLE OF THE MONEY PIT

Fortune hunters swamped by ingenious engineering

For nearly 200 years, singly and in syndicates, men have been boring and tunneling on a small island off Nova Scotia in search of a fabulous treasure.

Vastly more treasure—nearly $1.5 million—has been poured into the search than has ever come out of it; for whoever dug the Money Pit on Oak Island was a brilliant engineer, who harnessed the sea to keep out trespassers.

The pit consists of a deep shaft, furnished with an ingenious arrangement of side tunnels that allow the sea to flood in whenever diggers plumb its depths. Many parties of hopeful searchers have retired, soaked and baffled.

The only finds so far have been: three links of a chain that may have been gold or copper (accounts vary); a tiny scrap of parchment showing two letters, V and I, written with a quill pen; and, found 90 feet down the shaft, a cipher stone with odd symbols, which were optimistically taken to mean "10 feet below $10 million are buried."

The hunt began in 1795, when 16-year-old Daniel McGinnis paddled over from the little Nova Scotian town of Chester to hunt game on uninhabited Oak Island. In a clearing at one end of the island, an old ship's tackle block hung from a tree over the center of a 12-foot-wide depression.

Undeterred by tales of hauntings and fired by legends of pirate treasure, he and two other boys started digging. They found a 13-foot-wide circular shaft dug through flinty clay, with thick oak platforms at 10, 20, and 30 feet. The work became harder and for various reasons—including the difficulty of getting help from superstitious townsfolk—was abandoned until 1804.

In that year a wealthy Nova Scotian named Simeon Lynds formed the first treasure company—and found the first and greatest obstacle to all further "open" explorations of the pit: water.

The diggers had broken through eight oak platforms, three of which were sealed with ship's putty and coconut fiber. The cipher stone was found at 90 feet, and when the hole had been dug only another 8 feet deeper, a crowbar hit something solid. Lynds was sure it was a treasure chest.

Next day he was mortified to discover that the pit was filled with 60 feet of water. Weeks of bailing with buckets and crude pumps failed to lower the level.

In 1805 Lynds' miners sank another shaft, close to and parallel with the pit, and at 110 feet they started burrowing toward the "treasure." They had to scramble for their lives when water suddenly burst into their shaft—and filled it to the same level as the water in the pit. The once-wealthy Simeon Lynds was now practically penniless.

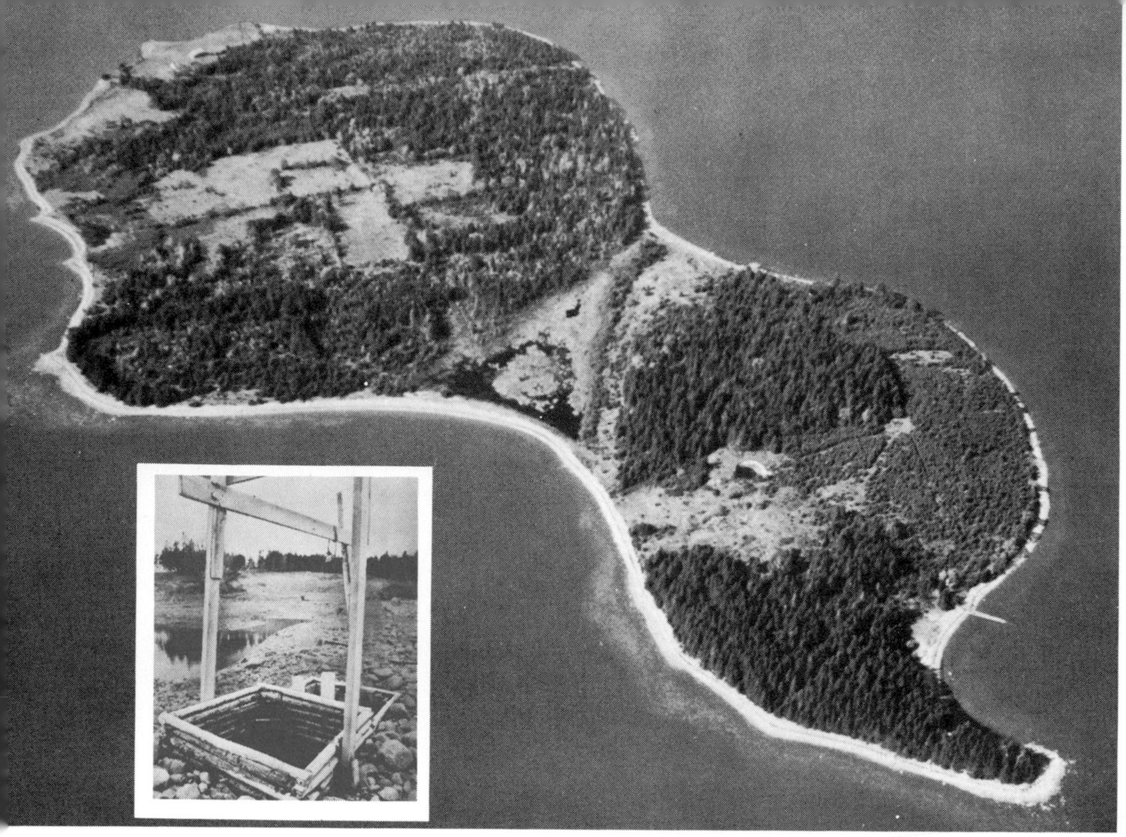

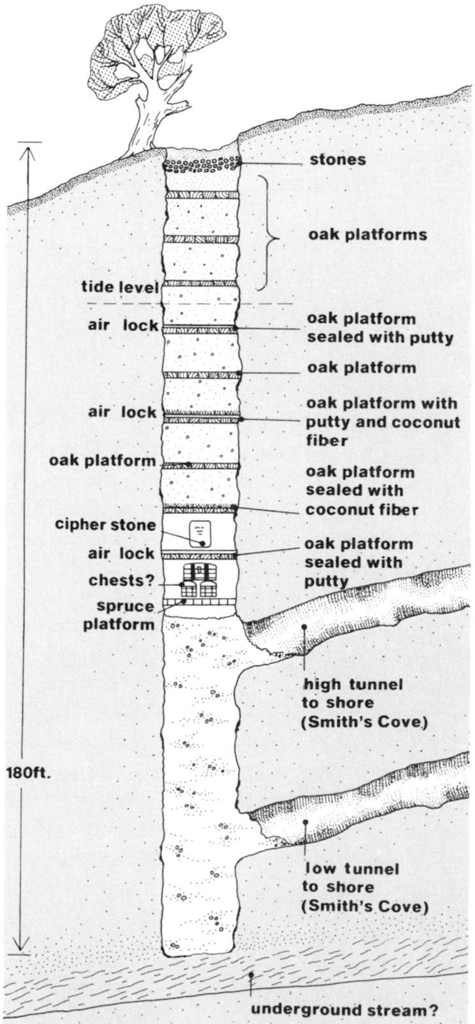
stones
oak platforms
tide level
air lock
oak platform sealed with putty
oak platform
air lock
oak platform with putty and coconut fiber
oak platform
oak platform sealed with coconut fiber
cipher stone
air lock
oak platform sealed with putty
chests?
spruce platform
high tunnel to shore (Smith's Cove)
180ft.
low tunnel to shore (Smith's Cove)
underground stream?

TRAIL OF MYSTERY. *For almost two centuries Oak Island (above) has tantalized fortune seekers. Beneath the shaft (inset), a deep pit (below left) is reputed to contain a legendary hoard of treasure.*

The original discoverer of the Money Pit, Daniel McGinnis, died. But in 1849 the two boys who had helped him with the first dig in 1795, John Smith and Anthony Vaughan, now in their seventies, tried again with the help of a syndicate from Truro, Nova Scotia.

Two or more chests

Their shafts, drillings, and pumpings seemed to confirm the existence of two or more chests that might contain treasure in some form; but their work weakened and undermined the pit itself and caused the bottom to collapse into what was thought to be a vast cavern—carrying down the chests and possibly breaking them up and dispersing the contents. But the Truro syndicate did discover why the pit flooded to a level that rose and fell with the tide.

A manmade tunnel, 111 feet down, connected with the sea. The tunnel was dynamited and blocked in 1893, but still the pit filled uncontrollably. A second tunnel, at 150 feet, was discovered in 1942.

There may be others. Nearly 200 years of drilling, digging, and pumping have so confused the area that the exact location of the original pit is not known.

There, for the moment, the matter rests. But the burning questions remain: Who buried what, and why? Early legends of Captain Kidd, perennial favorite of treasure seekers, may be safely dismissed. Whatever Kidd's skills as a seaman, he was quite incapable of executing so remarkable a piece of engineering. Obviously, the work had been carried out by a professional, backed by a team of skilled miners.

Rupert Furneaux, author of *The Money Pit Mystery*, has advanced the most plausible theory. Considering the state of the block and rope discovered in 1795, the pit could not have been dug much earlier than 1780, placing the operation in the middle of the Revolutionary War. In 1778 the British garrison in New York was threatened by Washington's army, and capitulation loomed. The Governor held the pay chests of all British forces in America, and it seems likely that, anxious for their safety, he ordered their concealment in a secret place. The unit entrusted with the task may well have been a detachment of the Royal Engineers stationed in Halifax, Nova Scotia. Furneaux argues that only a treasure of immense value—such as the pay chests—would call for so complex a hiding place as the Money Pit. And the only group in the area with the sufficient expertise was the British Royal Engineers.

The big problem is that there is no record of the British Army losing any great sums of money at the time—a scandal that would have led to the court-martial of the general concerned. This may mean that, when the danger was past, the chests were recovered, and the Money Pit is, in fact, empty.

WHAT HAPPENED TO THE ROMANOVS?

Someone died in the cellar . . . but was it the Czar?

The revolutionary Bolshevik government announced in Moscow at the end of July 1918 that Nicholas Romanov, once the Czar of all the Russias, had been executed for "innumerable foul crimes." The official statement said that the Czarina and her children had been moved to a secret place.

More than once the Bolsheviks changed their account of the execution, leaving a question mark hanging over the whole affair. Historians have no clear evidence to show if the Czar was put to death alone; if his entire family was shot with him; or if all the royal family—including Nicholas—was sent into secret exile.

Nicholas II was swept from power by the Russian Revolution in the early months of 1917. With Czarina Alexandra and his five children—Alexei, Olga, Maria, Tatiana, and Anastasia—he was imprisoned by the Bolsheviks in the Tsarskoye Selo Palace outside St. Petersburg (now Leningrad).

No chance of rescue

In August of that year they were moved to the small Siberian town of Tobolsk, a place so remote that there would be small chance of rescue by royalist sympathizers. Then, in 1918, they were moved again, this time to a house in the town of Ekaterinburg (now Sverdlovsk), situated near the Ural Mountains.

The people of Ekaterinburg were all Bolsheviks and were bitterly hostile toward the Czar and his family. Even so, czarists made several unsuccessful attempts to storm the house.

It was perhaps because the Czar might be liberated to lead the opposition forces that the Bolshevik government in Moscow may have decided to have him executed. Alternatively, they may have decided only to announce that he had been killed and then hide him.

Orders from Moscow

The announcement of July 1918 shocked the world, particularly western Europe, where the Romanovs had royal relatives.

But a few months later there was even more appalling news. The Bolsheviks said that the entire Romanov family had been executed by a firing squad on the night of July 19, 1918. According to this report, the orders came from Moscow, and the sentence was carried out under the command of a man named Yurovski, who fired the first shot in the massacre.

The Romanovs were given no warning. They were marched downstairs into the cellar, where they were invited to sit on a row of chairs. Yurovski's opening shot was followed by a volley from the Bolshevik guards, who were using new revolvers drawn from the local armory especially for their grim task.

IN CAPTIVITY IN SIBERIA. *One of the last photographs of the Czar shows him sitting on the roof of the prison in the remote town of Tobolsk with members of his family. At this time he had already abdicated.*

With the Romanovs was the imperial physician, Dr. Botkin, and three servants, who had all been ordered to stand alongside the royal family. When the shooting stopped, 11 bodies lay dead on the floor. The guards made doubly sure with bayonets and rifle butts.

In the early hours of the morning, the bodies were heaped onto a waiting truck and driven to the Four Brothers Mine, situated 14 miles from Ekaterinburg.

There they were doused in gasoline and burned. The charred remains were then thrown in a swamp, and the personal effects were soaked in acid and thrown down the mine shaft.

Four days later, on July 23, Ekaterinburg fell to the counterrevolutionary White Army. They found the cellars splashed with blood, but the walls had been partly washed, and there was no evidence to prove whether it had been royal blood or not.

The czarists' revenge

All the same, 28 local revolutionaries were later charged with having participated in the massacre of the royal family, and five of them were executed.

But the evidence was by no means conclusive, and to this day the Romanovs' fate remains shrouded in doubt. The only remains ever recovered from the mine shaft were teeth and glasses, later identified as belonging to Dr. Botkin, and shreds of clothing that might have been worn by the servants.

The Bolsheviks had one very good reason to keep the Czar alive. They had already made a treaty with Germany to allow him to leave Russia, unharmed, and the release of an irrelevant ex-Emperor would have gained sympathy for their cause in the West.

Unanswered question

The question still unanswered is: Who died in the cellar? Some people believe that the blood found by the White Army was that of Dr. Botkin and the servants only—who could have been executed to simulate the deaths of the Romanovs and remove all witnesses to their secret exile.

Rumors persist that Great Britain and the United States could have concluded an agreement with the revolutionaries. In 1919 an American secret agent published a book, *Rescuing the Czar,* in which he claimed to be the person responsible for taking the family through a secret tunnel into the British Consulate in Ekaterinburg before they were "spirited" out of Bolshevik Russia and eventually exiled to Tibet.

The book has never been accepted by any serious researcher or historian as a true account of what really happened to the Romanovs, for it presented little evidence to substantiate its claims.

But down through the years odd incidents have occurred that seem to suggest that the family might have survived.

When a memorial service was held for the Czar in London, George V refused to attend or send a royal representative. Could it be that the King knew the Czar was still alive? Even today the U.S. State Department is said to keep an open file on the Romanov family.

Polish spy's claim
In 1961 a Polish spy, Michal Goleniewski, defected and claimed that he was the Czar's son, Alexei. Three years later two women signed themselves by the names of two of the Czar's daughters—Olga and Tatiana—when they witnessed Goleniewski's marriage in New York. Long afterward Goleniewski continued to maintain that he was heir to the Russian throne. He said he had exposed some 200 Russian agents to the Americans because of his hatred for the Communist cause.

However, not even Michal Goleniewski could explain how he could be the hemophiliac son of the last Russian Czar, when he did not suffer from the "royal" disease.

Witnesses who really know what happened at Ekaterinburg—if any have survived—must now be growing old. It may well be that the secret of the Romanovs will go with them to their graves.

"I AM ANASTASIA"

Was the bedraggled near suicide a grand duchess?

Out of the mists that enshrouded the ultimate fate of the Romanovs, there emerged a whole host of pretenders. Some were cranks, genuinely believing themselves to be members of the Russian royal family; others, impostors hoping to establish some claim on the vast wealth of the Czar.

But the story of a teenage girl, dragged semiconscious from a canal in Berlin on February 17, 1920, had such a ring of truth about it that she was accepted by many leading Russian aristocrats in exile. She claimed to be the Grand Duchess Anastasia, youngest daughter of Czar Nicholas.

There was much at stake. A great deal of the immense Romanov fortune was reputed to have been smuggled out of Russia just before the Revolution and deposited in Western banks. Some estimates put the family's wealth in cash alone at $4 billion. Estates in Germany would add a great deal more.

Were the children spared?
According to the Bolshevik government's statement in July 1918, the Czar himself was executed, but the family was spared and sent to a secret place. If so, it was always possible that one or more of the children might turn up.

The girl dragged from the Berlin canal carried papers in the name of Anna Tschaikovski. But as soon as she regained her strength in the hospital, she claimed to be Anastasia and gave a detailed account of how she had managed to escape execution.

She said that she had been taken with the rest of the royal family for execution in the cellar at Ekaterinburg (now Sverdlovsk). She had been wounded in the shooting and had passed out. But she claimed that she regained consciousness to find herself hidden in a peasant's cart with two men and two women.

Smuggled to safety
The men were two of the Bolshevik guards, brothers named Tschaikovski, who had wanted no part in the killing. They told her that she had been left for dead on the cellar floor, but while they were carrying the bodies out of the cellar, they found that she was still breathing. So they had decided to smuggle her out of Russia to safety.

With money obtained by selling a pearl necklace and uncut emeralds sewn into her dress, Anastasia and her companions managed to reach the Rumanian Capital of Bucharest, where all three lived with relatives of the Tschaikovskis.

Anastasia, still too frightened of the Bolsheviks to emerge from hiding, married one of the brothers and had his child. But soon afterward her husband was seen on the streets by Bolshevik agents, recognized as a deserter, and assassinated. Anastasia suffered a breakdown, and the child was taken away to be adopted.

Her brother-in-law, Sergei Tschaikovski, decided to take her to Berlin, where she would perhaps be safer from the Bolsheviks. But on the day of their arrival after a fearful journey, Sergei disappeared. Anastasia was so exhausted and in such despair that she decided to end her life by jumping into the canal.

For the next 10 years she lodged claims for the return of her title and family fortune and made contacts with czarist sympathizers.

No trace was ever found of the Tschaikovski brothers or of her child. But Anastasia's knowledge of even the smallest details about the royal family's life won her many supporters in the West.

Denounced as an impostor

The Russian community in Berlin was divided. Many believed she was the grand duchess, while others denounced her as an impostor. Most of those who could have positively identified her were dead. Others stood to lose their shares of the Romanov fortune if her claim was proved to be true.

Pierre Gilliard, former French tutor of the family, was convinced that she was an impostor. He claimed that she did not understand Russian and crossed herself in the manner of a Roman Catholic, rather than in the fashion of the Russian Orthodox Church.

Grand Duke Cyril, the Czar's cousin and surviving head of the Romanovs, refused to grant her an audience or to have any further discussion on the subject.

Her supporters

Princess Irene of Prussia, the Czarina's sister, was sure that her forehead and eyes were those of Anastasia, but she had not seen the girl for more than 10 years.

Grand Duke Andrew, a cousin of the Czar, accepted her completely and said: "She is indeed the grand duchess."

Anastasia later claimed that her uncle, Grand Duke Ernest of Hesse, had made a visit to Russia from Germany in 1916—while the two countries were at war. He denied it and accused Anna of being a "blatant liar"—but in 1949 a former commander of a Russian Guards' regiment, Colonel Larski, swore under oath that Ernest was on a visit to Russia at the time Anastasia had claimed.

ANASTASIA. *This portrait of the grand duchess was taken before the Russian Revolution in 1917.*

In 1933 the Berlin Court granted a document of inheritance for the Czar's property in Germany to six surviving relatives—assuming Anastasia's death. The fight for Anastasia's recognition was renewed once more.

Anastasia underwent searching medical examination in the hospital, and X rays revealed serious head injuries that could have been caused by the butt of a gun. Bunions on her feet were in exactly the same place as those of the Czar's daughter. And a scar on her right shoulder, where a mole had been cauterized, was similar to one in Anastasia's medical records.

Hand crushed

Another small scar on the middle finger of her left hand was claimed to be the damage caused by a careless footman, who slammed the coach door on her hand as a child. Her opponents denied that this had ever happened, but a former lady-in-waiting corroborated her story.

In 1938 her lawyers brought an action to have the 1933 document canceled. The Second World War prevented it from being heard in court.

In May 1968 a court in Hamburg ruled against her—but speculation continues. Many people still believe that the Romanov story did not end in the cellar at Ekaterinburg.

353

"THE CROWN JEWELS ARE GONE!"

How Ireland's national treasure was stolen

The Star and Badge of the Order of St. Patrick—the Irish crown jewels—disappeared in July 1907. Suspicion and tragedy surrounded the men responsible for their safety; distinguished careers were ruined; and the jewels were never recovered.

The jewels—emeralds, rubies, and diamonds presented to the Irish nation by William IV in the 19th century—were kept in a safe in Dublin Castle's Bedford Tower. They were in the care of Sir Arthur Vicars, the Ulster king of arms, his nephew Pierce Mahoney, and two assistants, Francis Shackleton and Francis Bennett-Goldney.

On June 28, 1907, Vicars reported that his key to the tower's main door had vanished. Five days later a cleaning woman, Mrs. Farrell, found the main door unlocked when she arrived for work. Then, on July 6, she noticed something even stranger—the door to the strongroom where the jewels were kept had been left open overnight.

That afternoon a castle porter named Stivey entered Vicars' room while Vicars and Mahoney were examining the gold and enamel collar of the Order of St. Patrick. Vicars gave the porter a safe key and ordered him to put the collar with the jewels. Stivey soon returned with the alarming news that the safe was already open. Vicars made a swift inspection and cried, "My God, the crown jewels are gone!"

Police later found that the thief had spent at least 10 minutes carefully unscrewing the jewels from their seatings. Clearly, he must have been someone whose presence would not have aroused the castle staff's suspicions. Within a month a team of Scotland Yard detectives produced the name of their prime suspect, but the report was suppressed.

That autumn Edward VII demanded that all four men responsible for guarding the jewels should resign. Vicars was outraged and refused; he also boycotted a commission of inquiry set up the following January. But the commission censured him for negligence and ordered his dismissal as Ulster king of arms.

All the heralds met tragic ends. Bennett-Goldney died following a car accident, and Mahoney was killed while out shooting alone. Shackleton was jailed for defrauding an old woman; on his release from prison he vanished.

Vicars, too, died mysteriously. On April 14, 1921, his body was found in the garden of his home in County Kerry. It was riddled with bullets and bore a label saying, "Spy. Informers beware. IRA Never Forgets"—but the Irish Republican Army insisted that it was not involved. Most Irishmen believed Vicars to be an innocent man who had been badly treated.

No trace has ever been found of the stolen treasure, and it seems that the identity of the thief will remain shrouded in mystery.

STOLEN TREASURE. *The diamond St. Patrick Star (above), a gem-studded collar (left), and the St. Patrick Badge (right).*

PUZZLE OF THE "DEAD" PRINCE

Who was inside the Dauphin's coffin?

The heirs to the wealth of France's Bourbon royal family may be living in obscurity somewhere in the world, unaware of their claim to fame and fortune. For they would be the descendants of the Dauphin Louis Charles, son of Louis XVI and Marie Antoinette and heir to the throne, who "died" in 1795.

When his parents were executed in 1793, Louis Charles was put in prison to await the decision on his future. Seventeen months later it was declared that he had died at the age of 10.

Five people who inspected the body testified that it was the Dauphin—yet not one of them had ever seen the boy when alive. His sister, who was in the same prison, was not consulted.

When the funeral took place, many people wondered why so large a coffin was used for such a young child. Then, as evidence was pieced together, suspicions grew that a switch had taken place.

The changeling

A married couple who had been appointed jailers to the Dauphin gave up the job on January 19, 1794, when the boy was a robust, mischievous nine-year-old. About seven months later Gen. Paul Barras—soon to become dictator of France—visited the youngster and was confronted by a child who was obviously dangerously ill.

This astonishing change in the prisoner's health was explained 20 years later by the woman who had been his jailer. She told nuns nursing her in the hospital that she and her husband smuggled another boy into the jail and substituted him for the Dauphin the day they left. She would reveal nothing more, apart from asserting: "My little prince is not dead."

The woman's story was borne out to some extent by events that followed General Barras' visit to the prison. A new jailer was engaged, and he told the general that the child was an impostor. Barras immediately organized a nationwide search for the Dauphin.

Meanwhile, other government officials visited the prison. One is said to have concluded that the child was a deaf-mute; another described him as "the most pitiable creature I have ever seen."

A prominent banker named Petitival denounced the Dauphin's death certificate as a forgery. Less than a year later he and his whole family were murdered. When Barras reported to his government colleagues, he announced that everyone in the Petitival household had perished "except the child you know."

The doctors' verdict

From that it has been suggested that Barras' search for the Dauphin was successful and that the general's fellow ministers were aware that the boy was at Petitival's home.

Who, then, was the child who died in prison? When the body was exhumed in 1846, two doctors pronounced that it was a boy aged 15 or 16, rather than 10. In 1894 the bones were examined again, and it was agreed that the remains were those of a boy between 16 and 18. Whichever theory was correct, the child in the coffin could not have been the Dauphin.

After Napoleon's fall in 1815 the Bourbon monarchy was restored, to be plagued by a procession of "Dauphins." Twenty-seven men laid claim to the title. Most, however, were obvious charlatans.

Then, in 1833, Karl Wilhelm Naundorff appeared on the scene with very strong evidence to support his claim that he was the missing heir. He was recognized both by the Dauphin's nurse and by Louis XVI's Minister of Justice. The Dauphin's sister steadfastly refused to see Naundorff, although she was told that he bore a strong resemblance to members of her family. His adherents took her refusal as confirmation of his claim. It was known that she supported her uncle, Charles, as the rightful King.

One remarkable aspect of Naundorff's story was that it did not conform to the generally accepted theory that the Dauphin's jailers smuggled him to safety. He claimed instead that Barras had transferred him to another part of the prison and put the second boy in his place. Then, on the day the substitute died, the Dauphin was smuggled out and taken first to Italy, then to Prussia, where he took the name Naundorff. To push forward his claim to the title, Naundorff began a civil court action—and was promptly arrested and expelled from France. He went to London, where an attempt

A QUEEN AND HER CHILDREN. *Marie Antoinette nurses her son Louis Charles. On her left is the first Dauphin, Louis Joseph, who died in 1789, and on her right is Louis' sister, Madame Royale.*

was made on his life. Nine years later he died in Holland—and was described on the death certificate as "Louis Charles de Bourbon, aged 60, son of Louis XVI and Marie Antoinette."

To this day Naundorff's descendants pursue their claim in the French courts. But if he, too, was really an impostor, another possibility remains: Louis Charles may have lived the life of a commoner, unrecognized and perhaps unwilling to establish his identity. He may well have decided that being a royal heir was too dangerous in an era of revolution.

KASPAR HAUSER'S SECRET PAST

Was the boy who knew nothing heir to a dukedom?

On Whitmonday (the day after Pentecost) 1828, a strange boy of about 16 years of age suddenly appeared in Nuremberg. He was wearing rough peasant clothes, and all who met him thought him to be either drunk or an idiot. The newcomer carried a letter addressed to "The captain of the 4th Squadron of the 6th Regiment of Cavalry in Nuremberg."

A shoemaker took the boy to the captain's house where the lad repeatedly announced: "I want to be a soldier as my father was." When taken to the nearest police station, the boy answered every question put to him with, "I don't know." The mysterious youth seemed to have the mental age of a boy of three or four, but when handed paper and pencil, he was able to write the name Kaspar Hauser.

Kaspar was sent to a detention center for vagabonds while the unsigned letter he had been carrying was studied. It read in part: "Honored Captain, I send you a boy who is anxious to serve his King in the army. He was left at my house on October 7, 1812, and I am only a poor day laborer. I have 10 children of my own, and I have enough to do to bring them up. I have not let him out of the house since 1812. . . . If you do not want to keep him, you can kill him or hang him up the chimney."

Kaspar was taken into the home of the jailer, who observed many things about the boy. His new charge was well built but had feet as soft as a baby's. He had the smile of an innocent child but no other means of facial expression. When trying to walk, he stumbled about like a baby taking its first steps.

An amazing background

Kaspar quickly learned to talk in broken sentences. He could eat only bread and water; anything else made him sick. He showed no embarrassment when the jailer's wife bathed him and did not seem to appreciate the difference between men and women. The jailer concluded that the lad was no impostor and that some great mystery surrounded him.

Public interest in the mysterious foundling grew, and a young scholar, Dr. Daumer, supervised his education. Eventually, Kaspar was able to offer glimpses into his amazing past.

Kaspar claimed that before arriving in Nuremberg he had seen only one other human being in his life. For as long as he could remember he had lived in a cell six feet long, four feet wide, and only five feet high. He had always sat or lain down, having a straw bed to sleep on and a shirt and leather trousers to wear.

Each morning he found a jug of water and a piece of bread at his side. Occasionally, the water had a bitter taste and made him fall asleep; awakening, he would find that his clothes had been changed and his nails cut. There was never a light in his cell.

One day a man entered and showed him how to write Kaspar Hauser and to say, "I want to be a soldier as my father was." The man later lifted Kaspar onto his back and carried him outside where the light and open air made him faint. The next thing he remembered was finding himself wandering in Nuremberg.

Interest in the boy spread across Europe. He was visited by lawyers, doctors, and public officials who were convinced that he was somebody special.

Because of Kaspar's remarkable resemblance to them, his name was freely linked with the grand ducal family of Baden. In 1830, about the time of Kaspar's birth, the family had suffered the sudden deaths of two baby princes in the direct line of succession.

Soon after the death of the reigning grand duke in March 1830, the English Earl of Stanhope, who seems to have been a friend of the grand duke's successor, applied to become Kaspar's guardian. That application was granted.

Stanhope publicly stated that Kaspar was of Hungarian origin and had no connection with the family of Baden. He also desperately tried to persuade others to change their stories to say they had always thought he was an impostor. But Anselm Ritter von Feuerbach concluded that "the crime against Kaspar's liberty was not prompted by hatred or revenge, solely by selfish interest. Kaspar Hauser is the legitimate son of royal parents and was put out of the way to open the succession to other heirs."

When Von Feuerbach died suddenly in 1833, it was rumored that he had been poisoned after he found proof of Kaspar's royal origin. But none of that proof was ever produced.

Stabbed in the heart

Like everything else in his short life, Kaspar's ending was tragic and mysterious. One afternoon in 1833 he was lured to a park in Ansbach with the promise of information about his royal parentage. There he met a man who stabbed him in the heart. He managed to stagger home, but he died three days later.

It was reported that Grand Duchess Stephanie of Baden, Kaspar's reputed mother, wept bitterly when she learned of his death. Her husband, Karl, had been the last of the direct ducal line, and failure to produce an heir would leave the succession open to the children of the Countess of Hochberg.

There is a story that when Stephanie gave birth to her first child, the Countess of Hochberg smuggled the dead child of a peasant woman into the palace, switching it with the baby prince—Kaspar Hauser. The countess handed Kaspar to Major Hennenhofer, who placed the child in the care of a former soldier. Some say that when questioned, Hennenhofer confessed to having done this.

All the evidence, repeated attempts on Kaspar's life, the involvement of Stanhope, and the Baden family's efforts to hush up the matter seem to confirm the story.

But Kaspar Hauser's tale can never be proved, for, when Hennenhofer died, all his private papers were destroyed.

SPRING-HEELED JACK

Superman with eyes of a devil

Out of the mists of the night he came, a leaping, bounding superman who held a nation in a grip of terror for more than 60 years.

At first, he was just a rumor. Few took much notice when people crossing a common in southwest London first reported seeing an alarming figure that flew through the air in great leaps across their path. But the reports persisted, until they were terrifyingly confirmed a year later, in February 1838.

Jane Alsop was young and pretty. She lived with her two sisters and their father on a London back street. She had heard of the bogeyman called Spring-Heeled Jack. But she

LEAPING AWAY. *The descriptions of Spring-Heeled Jack varied little, although he was seen in many different areas.*

was too sensible to heed such tales.

One night there was a violent knocking at the door. Jane went to answer it. The man standing in the shadows near the front gate swung around. "I'm a police officer," he said. "For God's sake, bring me a light, for we have caught Spring-Heeled Jack in the lane."

"The stories were true after all," thought Jane excitedly, as she ran to fetch a candle. "I'll see him being arrested." She rushed back outside with the candle.

But as she gave it to the man at the gate, he grabbed her by the neck and pinned her head under his arm. Then he ripped at her dress and body. She screamed and tore herself away. He chased her, caught her by the hair, and clawed her face and neck. Her sister, hearing the screams, ran into the street and cried out for help. But before anyone could stop him, Jack soared away into the darkness.

Jane later described her inhuman attacker to police officials. "He was wearing a kind of helmet," she told them, "and a tight-fitting white costume like an oilskin. His face was hideous, his eyes were like balls of fire. His hands had great claws, and he vomited blue and white flames."

It was a description that was to be repeated over and over again in the following years. Always the leaps, the flames, and the eyes of hell were recounted.

Lucy Scales was 18 years old, the sister of a butcher. She had just left her brother's house one evening on her way home with her sister. As they walked along a lonely street, a tall, cloaked figure jumped out of the shadows. He spat blue flames at Lucy's face, blinding her.

During the 1850's and 1860's, Spring-Heeled Jack was sighted all over England, particularly in the Midlands.

In the 1870's army authorities set traps after scared sentries reported being terrified by a man who darted out of the darkness to slap their faces with an icy hand or sprang onto the roofs of their sentry boxes. Angry townspeople shot at him in the streets one night in 1877. Always, he laughed and melted away.

No one, even today, really has any idea who—or what—Spring-Heeled Jack was. For a while suspicion rested on the eccentric young Marquis of Waterford. But though the "mad marquis," as he was known, was one of the "wild ones" of Victorian society, he was never vicious.

Jack's eyes of hell were last seen in 1904 in Liverpool—66 years after the first sightings. There he started a panic one night by bounding up and down the streets—leaping from the cobblestones to rooftops and back. When some of the braver ones tried to corner him, he simply vanished into the darkness he came from—this time for good?

JACK THE RIPPER

The killer whose name became a legend

Five times the unobtrusive little man stepped out into the swirling night in London. Five times he talked to women of the streets. Each time the woman died, slashed in the style that was the bloody trademark of the man called Jack the Ripper.

Dozens of detectives—amateur and professional—have advanced theories as to who the little man was. No one has ever finally settled the question. His brutal crimes remain baffling, fascinating, and unsolved, nearly a century after he committed them.

Scene for crime

The East End of Victorian London was a festering sore on the face of England. Small houses huddled along the sides of streets that stank of refuse.

At night the alleys, yards, and corners were black caverns beyond the candlelit windows. Indoors, an overcrowded population fought for elbowroom in hovels. Outside, men, women, and children scratched a miserable and often criminal living in the streets. The only relief was oblivion, which could be found in a bottle of gin for a few pennies. For many women prostitution was the only means of making a living.

Jack the Ripper stepped into this caldron of human misery in the autumn of 1888. Fear and panic came with him.

First victim

Mary Ann Nicholls was down on her luck. At 42 she was getting too old to attract men. She could not even raise the four pennies demanded by roominghouses for a bed—the little money she possessed had already been spent on gin. When the man approached her in the narrow street, Mary saw only the chance to make

DON'T LOOK NOW. *A suspect is followed by a band of vigilantes during the Jack the Ripper terror that seized the East End of London during the late 1880's. The killer struck five times.*

enough to enjoy a good night's sleep. Even when he drew her back into the shadows, she was not alarmed. There were people just a few yards away.

By the time she realized anything was wrong, it was too late. The Ripper stepped behind her and put his hand over her mouth. Then he cut her throat. A trucker found her mutilated body in the early hours of Friday morning, August 31, 1888. The Ripper's reign of terror had begun.

He waited exactly seven days before he struck again. The victim was, as all of them were to be, a prostitute: 47-year-old Annie Chapman. Dark Annie, as she was known, was dying of consumption—a wasting disease of the lung—when the Ripper cut her down. Her body was found by a workman in a backyard. Her rings and a few coins had been laid out neatly at her feet, by the sickening remains of her corpse. She had been completely disemboweled.

Wild rumors

By now the area was aflame with rumors. One story had it that the killer carried his knives in a little black bag. Riots broke out as hysterical crowds chased anyone who carried such a bag. Vigilante groups were formed to patrol the streets. The police arrested dozens of innocent suspects.

But the Ripper had left no clues. All that police doctors could deduce was that he was left-handed and had some medical knowledge. The killings, said an inquest surgeon, had been "deftly and fairly skillfully" performed.

Solitary clue

On the night of September 30, the Ripper butchered two more women and left what may be the only direct clue of his grisly career. Long Liz Stride was found with blood still pouring from her throat. The body of Kate Eddowes—the most terribly mutilated of all—lay a few minutes' walk away.

From her hacked body a trail of blood led to a doorway, where someone had scrawled in chalk: "THE JEWES ARE NOT THE MEN TO BE BLAMED FOR NOTHING." Did it mean that the Ripper was a Jew out for revenge on a world that had persecuted him? Or was he a crazed judge who had become his own executioner? The real meaning of the message—whatever it was—could have been vital.

But it was never properly studied. For myste-riously, inexplicably, the head of the police, Sir Charles Warren, ordered it to be rubbed out.

The whole of London was gripped by the horror of the double murders. Rumors flew. The Ripper was a mad doctor, a Polish wild man, a Russian czarist secret agent trying to discredit the police, a Puritan obsessed by the city's vice. It was even suggested that Jack the Ripper was an insane midwife with a murder-ous hatred for prostitution. No one knew. The real Ripper remained at large. And on November 9 he struck again.

Final victim

The last person—apart from the killer—to see 25-year-old Mary Kelly alive was a passerby named George Hutchinson. She asked him for money to help pay the rent for her tiny room. Then he watched her move off to accost a small, well-dressed man with a fair mustache and a deerstalker hat. Her dismembered corpse was discovered the next morning in her room.

Mary was the Ripper's last victim. He never went back to his gruesome business. Detectives have tried to follow his trail ever since but with no conclusive results. Police files on the case have been locked away in Scotland Yard. They are not due to be released until 1992. And even then they may contain only more speculation.

For the Ripper left few tracks. Each time he killed, he simply vanished back into the seeth-ing crowds. How? If he was a poor man, how did he acquire the medical knowledge to carry out his fiendish surgery? If he was wealthy, why was he not noticed amidst the East End's abject poverty? And how could he have worked unno-ticed when surgeons of the time estimate that his terrible operations would have taken up to an hour to perform? The questions are still unanswered. The police closed their file on the case a few months after Mary Kelly's death. And although others have raked over the trail since then, their conclusions have always been guesswork.

The most likely theory of the Ripper's identi-ty seems to be that put forward by author and broadcaster Daniel Farson. He based his re-search on the notes of Sir Melville Macnaghten, who joined Scotland Yard the year after the killings and became head of the Criminal Inves-tigation Department in 1903. According to Macnaghten, police had concentrated on three suspects: a homicidal Russian doctor named Michael Ostrog; a woman-hating Polish Jew named Kosmanski; and a depraved lawyer named Montague John Druitt. In the end they decided Druitt was the killer.

Farson, after years of research into Druitt's family, agrees. He says that Druitt's family believed him to be the Ripper; and he points out that his cousin, Dr. Lionel Druitt, had an office only a 10-minute walk from the farthest of the murder sites. Druitt's mother, Farson adds, was insane, and Druitt may have feared he was going mad as well.

Druitt was never arrested. He disappeared soon after the last murder. His body was found floating in the Thames seven weeks later—on December 31, 1888.

Did Druitt commit suicide? Or could he, too, have been a murder victim? If Druitt really was the butcher, it would have been poetic justice.

Only one man ever knew the truth of it all— Jack the Ripper himself. But whoever he was, his dreadful secret has been buried forever.

LONG AT THE FAIR

Did the young English girl book in alone?

Paris in 1889, the year of the Great Exhibition, was packed with businessmen, buyers, and tourists. Most hotels were fully booked.

In May an English mother and her daughter arrived in the city from Marseilles, where they had disembarked from India. They had booked two single rooms at one of the most famous hotels in Paris.

They signed their names in the register and were taken up to their rooms. The mother was placed in room 342, a luxurious room with heavy curtains of plum-colored velvet, rose-covered wallpaper, a high-backed sofa, an oval satinwood table, and an ormolu clock.

Almost immediately, however, the older woman fell ill and went to bed. The hotel doctor who was called examined her and put some questions to her daughter. He and the hotel manager then conferred excitedly in a corner of the room. Though the girl did not speak French, she was able to understand the instructions slowly spelled out to her by the doctor. Her mother was seriously ill and required a particular medicine available only at the doctor's office on the other side of Paris. As he himself could not leave the patient, he asked the girl to go in his carriage.

The girl set out at what proved to be an exasperatingly slow pace. After an agonizing wait at the office and an equally slow journey back, she arrived with the medicine. Four hours had passed.

Jumping from the carriage, she rushed into the foyer. "*Comment va ma mère?*" she asked the manager. He stared blankly at her. "To whom do you refer, Mademoiselle?" he asked. Taken aback, she stammered an explanation of her delay. "But, Mademoiselle, I know nothing of your mother. You arrived here alone."

Distraught, the girl protested: "But we registered here less than six hours ago. Look in the book." The manager produced the register and ran his finger down the page. Halfway down was the girl's signature, but immediately above it, where her mother had signed, was the name of a stranger. "We both signed," the girl insisted, "and my mother was given room 342. She is there now. Please take me to her at once."

The manager assured her that the room was occupied by a French family, but they went upstairs. Room 342 was empty save for the personal belongings of strangers. There were no plum-colored curtains, no rose-covered wallpaper, no high-backed sofa, and no ormolu clock.

Downstairs again she encountered the hotel doctor and asked him about her mother's fate. He, too, denied ever having met her before and swore he had never attended her mother.

The girl reported the story to the British Ambassador, who would not believe her; nor would the police or newspapers. Eventually, she returned to England, where she was committed to an insane asylum.

One explanation of this strange story is that the mother had contracted plague in India. The doctor, having recognized the symptoms, had conspired with the hotel manager to conceal the news, which would certainly have wrecked the Great Exhibition. But could room 342 have been redecorated in four hours? What happened to the mother's body? The mysteries remain.

"REMEMBER THE MAINE." *The blowing up of the U.S. battleship* Maine *at the Havana harbor in 1898 resulted in 260 deaths and U.S. entry into the Spanish-American War. The actual cause of the explosion was never established.*

AN UNSOLVED MYSTERY THAT LED TO WAR

Did sabotage or an accident cause the sinking of the Maine?

For almost a month—from December 15, 1897, to January 12, 1898—Capt. Charles D. Sigsbee and the 24-gun battleship, the U.S.S. *Maine*, had waited in Key West, Florida, for the code words, "two dollars" (to be repeated once), from Gen. Fitzhugh Lee, American consul in Havana, Cuba, 90 miles away. The message would signify that American lives and property were threatened in the Cuban revolution against Spanish rule and that U.S. military assistance was needed.

On the mainland other Americans waited, hoping for an excuse for the United States to intervene in the revolution. Encouraged by the lurid yellow journalism, especially of two New York newspapers, the *World* and the *Journal*, Americans sympathized with the Cuban patriots for humanitarian and economic reasons.

When Lee's message finally came, it was a false alarm, rescinded before the ship could get under way. About two weeks later President William McKinley ordered the *Maine* to steam into the Havana harbor on an official courtesy call. The *Maine* dropped anchor off Cuba on January 25 as the United States concentrated its warships in Key West, ready for battle.

The days passed without anti-American demonstrations. Then on February 9 American relations with Spain worsened when William Randolph Hearst's *Journal* published a stolen private letter written by the Spanish minister in Washington to a friend in Cuba. In blunt language the Spaniard called President McKinley crude and weak. Spain, eager to avoid hostilities, recalled the minister immediately.

Six days later at 9:40 p.m. all but four of the *Maine*'s crew of 26 officers and 328 men were aboard for the night. Captain Sigsbee sat in his cabin, finishing a letter to his wife, when the first of two explosions knocked him to the floor. Ashore, General Lee, who had been writing a dispatch to Washington about the minister's letter, rushed to his window to see the *Maine* in flames and its stern sinking.

As the 6,682-ton vessel sank and its ammunition exploded in the water, Spanish officers in small craft helped save American lives. The extent, but not the cause, of the disaster was soon apparent. The explosion had occurred directly under the sleeping quarters of the crew. Two officers and 250 men were killed instantly. Eight men were fatally injured. As a heavy rain began to fall, Captain Sigsbee was the last man to leave the sinking ship.

Sigsbee's first wire after being rescued urged Americans to withhold judgment until a complete investigation could be made, but the U.S. press and public reacted with immediate anger and rage. "Remember the *Maine*" buttons were sold. Newspapers urged the United States into war with a reluctant Spain. Hearst's *Journal* sold more than a million copies for the first time on February 17 because of its *Maine* coverage.

As Hearst sent a team of newsmen into Cuba, his newspaper announced its own investigation of the disaster. Joseph Pulitzer's *World* chartered a tugboat and hired divers to explore the wreckage but was denied permission to investigate. The *Journal* claimed, "The warship *Maine* was split in two by an enemy's secret infernal machine," while the *World* headlined, "The *Maine* explosion was caused by a bomb" and "Suspicion of torpedo."

The Hearst newspapers blamed Spain for the destruction of the *Maine*, but General Lee thought it was accidental. Many Navy Department officials suggested spontaneous combustion in the coal bunkers as the cause and pointed to similar incidents on other U.S. ships. Various theories were advanced: The ship had drifted into a mine; a device had been brought aboard by a visitor in Havana or placed in the coal bins in Key West; or gunpowder had been packed incorrectly.

Spanish officials declared the explosions had been internal and accidental. They ordered an immediate investigation to prove the claim and interviewed the first witnesses within an hour after the disaster. On February 20 a Spanish court announced it could find no evidence suggesting an external cause. Refusing a Spanish offer for a joint investigation, the United States conducted its own inquiry, interviewed 78 witnesses in 22 days, and concluded late in March that explosions in two or more forward magazines had been caused by a submarine mine. No blame was assigned.

On April 11, President McKinley asked Congress to intervene militarily in Cuba. Two weeks later there began what Theodore Roosevelt described as "a splendid little war," which ended in a U.S. victory by August 12. As a result of the war, Spain was driven out of the Western Hemisphere and the Philippines.

But the mystery of the *Maine* grew. In 1911, when the ship was raised from the Havana harbor, another inquiry was made into the cause of the explosions. The second U.S. investigation agreed that the cause had been external but suspected a different detonation point. In 1912, before the bottom of the ship could be studied, the ship was towed out to sea and, after a ceremonial burial with full military honors, disappeared beneath the waves.

THE JUDGE'S STRANGE DISAPPEARANCE

How can a prominent person vanish without a trace?

On the evening of August 6, 1930, a tall, heavy-set man wearing a double-breasted brown suit, gray spats, and a high collar walked out of a New York City restaurant, waved goodby to two friends, stepped into a taxi—and was never seen or heard from again. The man was Joseph Force Crater, a 41-year-old justice of the New York State Supreme Court. How was it possible for such a prominent person to vanish without a trace from the face of the earth?

The question has puzzled millions of people for nearly half a century. Not a year goes by without the New York Police Department's getting tips from callers who claim they have seen the missing judge. Yet despite these reports and a massive search, Judge Crater remains America's most famous missing person.

An odd aspect of the case is that so much is known about Judge Crater and his life until his disappearance. He was impressive in both physical structure and dapper dress. Although he stood six feet tall and weighed 180 pounds, he walked with short, mincing steps. His face was fleshy, and his iron-gray hair was parted neatly in the middle.

Judge Crater's career was notably successful. A native of Easton, Pennsylvania, he was graduated from Lafayette College and the Columbia University Law School. In 1913 he began to practice law in New York. Ambitious and hard working, he entered politics and soon became president of a Democratic Party club in Manhattan. His law practice flourished, and because of his close ties with the city's Democratic leadership at Tammany Hall, he was appointed to the New York Supreme Court in April 1930.

Crater's private life was apparently just as successful. In 1916 he was retained as a lawyer in a divorce action by a woman named Stella Wheeler, and the next year, after Mrs. Wheeler's divorce became final, Crater married his client. They appeared to be a devoted couple.

In the summer of 1930, Judge Crater and his wife were vacationing at their cottage in Belgrade Lakes, Maine. On August 3 he received a telephone call from New York and told his wife that he had to go to the city for a few days; he did not explain why. The following day he arrived at his Fifth Avenue apartment, but he seems to have done nothing extraordinary that day or the next. On the morning of August 6, however, he spent two hours going through his files in his courthouse chambers, and he had his assistant, Joseph Mara, cash two checks for him amounting to $5,150. At noon he and Mara carried two locked briefcases to his apartment, where he dismissed Mara for the day.

The same evening Judge Crater went to a Broadway ticket agency and bought one ticket for that night's performance of a new comedy, *Dancing Partners*, at the Belasco Theater. He then went to Billy Haas' chophouse on West 45th Street, where he encountered two friends, a fellow lawyer and a showgirl, and joined them for dinner. The lawyer later testified that Crater had been amiable and had given no sign that anything was troubling him. It was 9:10 p.m., well after the play's curtain time, when the judge said goodby to his friends in front of the restaurant and hailed a cruising taxi.

Ironically, there was no immediate reaction to Judge Crater's disappearance. When he had not returned to Maine after 10 days, Mrs. Crater inquired of her husband's whereabouts among his friends in New York. She was told that everything was all right, that the judge would eventually show up. Only when he failed to appear at the opening of the courts on August 25 did his fellow justices become alarmed and conduct a private search, which revealed nothing. It was not until September 3 that the police were notified; the following day the disappearance finally became front-page news. The police found that the judge's safe-deposit box was empty and that the two briefcases in his study were missing. They received thousands of false reports from people claiming to have seen him.

A grand jury began to investigate the case in October, called 95 witnesses, amassed 975 pages of testimony, and concluded: "The evidence is insufficient to warrant any expression of opinion as to whether Crater is alive or dead, or as to whether he has absented himself voluntarily, or is a sufferer from disease in the nature of amnesia, or is the victim of a crime."

In January 1931 Mrs. Crater returned to their New York apartment and found in a bureau drawer several checks, stocks and bonds, three life insurance policies, and a note from Judge Crater himself. The note listed his financial assets and concluded with but one point of personal information: "I am very whary [weary], Joe."

Why did he disappear?

Many theories have been advanced to explain Judge Crater's disappearance. Mrs. Crater and his close friends believed that he was the victim of foul play. She stated that her husband was murdered "because of a sinister something that was connected with politics." Mrs. Crater obliquely linked her husband's murder with his possible failure to pay all of a year's judicial salary to Tammany Hall in return for his nomination to the bench. She also indicated that his disappearance might have been connected with his judicial role as receiver for a hotel property in Manhattan that had been bought by a corporation for only $75,000 and was sold to the city for $2.85 million. Mrs. Crater discounted theories that her husband had deliberately disappeared, saying that "Joe Crater would not run away from anybody but would meet his problems directly, whatever they were."

In 1937 she sued three insurance companies for double indemnity on her husband's life insurance policies. In the court action her lawyer, Emil K. Ellis, also advanced the murder theory, but for different reasons. He claimed that Judge Crater had been blackmailed by a Broadway showgirl and had withdrawn the $5,150 to pay her off. When she had demanded more money and Crater had refused to pay it, a gangster friend of the showgirl had killed him, perhaps accidentally. Ellis' evidence was insufficient to impress the court, however, and double indemnity was denied.

Judge Crater was declared legally dead on June 6, 1939, but reports of his reappearance still pop up. The police investigation has not been officially closed. Nearly half a century after his disappearance, Judge Crater is still missing!

MINE OF SOLID GOLD NUGGETS

It protected its riches with violent death

Somewhere in the mountains of Arizona there is reputed to be a gold mine so rich that if the walls are tapped with a hammer, nuggets of gold come tumbling down.

But the fabled mine has guarded its treasure well. Death and disaster have struck down many who sought to despoil it. And for the past 50 years it has been lost.

The Dutchmen's mine

It is known locally as the Dutchmen's mine because two of the many 19th-century claimants were thought to be prospectors from Holland, although, in fact, they were Germans.

The discovery of the mine is lost in legend. It is thought that the Apache Indians showed it to the first Spanish monks reaching Arizona from the colonies in Mexico.

Tales were rife of a mine where gold could be shoveled out of the earth in spadefuls; and it is likely that expeditions traveled north to search for this Eldorado—but it is not known with what success.

The mine is first mentioned in Spanish registers as included in a grant made in 1748 by Ferdinand VI of Spain. He gave 3,750 square miles of what is now Arizona to Don Miguel Peralta.

The Peralta heirs are supposed to have made several trips to the mine from their homes in Mexico for the next 100 years. Then, according to later claimants, an Enrico Peralta took an expedition to Arizona in 1864.

Apaches on warpath

By this time the Apaches were no longer friendly. Enrico's party was ambushed, and all, save one man, were killed during a three-day running battle. The survivor reached Mexico with a map of the area showing the mine.

There was another European discoverer. He was Dr. Abraham Thorne, who lived in Arizona and was on friendly terms with the Indians. In 1870 the Apaches offered to show him a place where he could pick up gold. The only condition was that he should be blindfolded during the journey of 20 miles.

When the blindfold was taken away, Dr. Thorne saw he was in a canyon. A mile or so to the south was a sharp pinnacle of rock. There was no sign of a mine, but at the base of one of the canyon's walls was a pile of almost pure gold. He picked up as much as he could carry and was led to his home. He sold the gold for $6,000.

A year later the "Dutchmen" came on the scene. They were two German adventurers, Jacob Waltz and Jacob Weiser, who said they had rescued a man named Don Miguel Peralta from a brawl in the Mexican town of Arizpe.

Share of profits

This second Don Miguel was Enrico's son, and he told his rescuers of the family mine. The two Jacobs agreed to go with him to Arizona for a share of the profits. According to stories later told independently by Waltz and Weiser, they found the mine with the aid of the Peralta family map, and the three men picked up $60,000 worth of gold. Don Miguel sold the map and the title to the mine to the Germans for their half of the proceeds.

Soon afterward Dr. Thorne returned to the area with a group of friends. But this time the Apaches attacked and killed them all.

The "Dutchmen" return

In 1879 the Germans, using Don Miguel's map, returned to the canyon alone and shot dead a couple of Mexicans they found working the mine.

Before his death 12 years later, Waltz described the terrain. "It was such rough country that you could be right in the mine without seeing it," he said. The mine was a large pit, shaped like a funnel. Enrico had cut a tunnel into the hillside to the bottom of the pit.

The Germans continued to work the mine, but then disaster struck. Waltz came back to their camp one evening to find Weiser had disappeared. On the ground were a blood-stained shirt and Apache arrows.

Soldiers shot dead

During 1880 and 1881 the mine was twice found by chance. The first discoverers were two young soldiers who appeared in the town of Pinal with their saddlebags full of gold. They said that the ore came from a funnel-shaped mine in a canyon near a sharp pinnacle of rock.

They set off to return to the mine. A search party found them shot dead. Then, in 1882, the Apaches decided that they must hide the mine. Through the white man's lust for gold it had brought only death and violence.

An Indian known as Apache Jack later told of the tribe's decision. The squaws were set to work filling in the pit. Then rocks were shifted around to disguise the area. Soon afterward, Providence lent a hand. An earthquake further rearranged the landmarks.

Eight years later Jacob Waltz died, and with him went the secret of the mine's location.

Documents forged

Prospectors continued to search for the Dutchmen's mine, but in 1895 an event occurred that further confused the whole issue. A man named James Addison Reavis was convicted by a court at Santa Fe, Arizona, of forging the ancient documents giving a fictitious Don Miguel Peralta the land grant. The court case revealed that Reavis had traveled to Mexico and Spain to insert his forgeries into registers. He topped off his work by marrying a Mexican girl who was alleged to be an heir of the Peralta family.

It is likely that Reavis based his forgeries on fact. There is strong circumstantial evidence that a Mexican family named Peralta did own a mine in Arizona and that members of the family made forays into Arizona to collect ore. It also seems likely that Weiser and Waltz were given, or stole, a map of the area.

And there have been two confirmations of the story in this century.

Ingots in the grass

In 1912 prospectors found gold ingots in the long grass at the spot where Enrico Peralta is alleged to have fought the Indians in 1864. And, nearby, there are the remains of camps and evidence that trees were cut down for pitprops. In this area is a sharp rock pinnacle now known as Weaver's Needle.

In 1931 a man named Adolph Ruth told his friends that he had acquired a map from someone named Peralta and went off into the mountains. A few weeks later his decapitated body was found.

In his jacket was a piece of paper with "About 200 feet across from cave" written on it. Underneath was the Latin tag *"Veni, Vidi, Vici"* ("I came, I saw, I conquered").

Since then, although the area has been carefully prospected many times, there has been no further sign of the fabulous Dutchmen's mine.

THE BURNING OF THE REICHSTAG

An excuse for Hitler to destroy the Communists

Marius van der Lubbe, a 24-year-old Dutchman, was executed on January 10, 1934, for arson. His crime: starting a fire that gutted the Reichstag, the German Parliament building in Berlin.

But was Van der Lubbe, a Nazi hater and Communist, truly guilty? Or was he a scapegoat of Adolf Hitler and his Nazi henchmen? And were other conspirators involved?

The blaze was a turning point in German history, for it enabled Hitler to seize power.

It was first spotted by a theological student, Hans Flotter, who was walking past the southwest corner of the building shortly after 9 p.m. on February 27, 1933. Flotter, hearing the sound of glass breaking, looked up to see a man with something burning in his hand, on a first-floor balcony.

He ran off and alerted a police sergeant, who dashed to the front of the building. There the policeman fired his revolver at a man who appeared to be carrying a burning torch, rushing from window to window on the first floor.

By 9:40 p.m. some 60 fire pumps were on the scene. The building's Assembly Hall was a wall of flames, and other parts of the building were ablaze.

In the Bismarck Hall a policeman arrested at gunpoint a man, bathed in sweat and naked to the waist. His passport bore the name of Marius van der Lubbe. Asked why he did it, he told the arresting officers: "As a protest." He confessed to having tried unsuccessfully to set fire to three other public buildings.

The political effect of the fire was tremendous. It elevated Hitler, who had at the time been Chancellor of Germany for only 27 days, to Führer of the Third Reich. When told by Hermann Goering of the fire and the arrest of Van der Lubbe, Hitler is reported to have said:

THE REICHSTAG BLAZES. *The fire in Berlin on the night of February 27, 1933, was a landmark in Adolf Hitler's dramatic rise to power.*

MARIUS VAN DER LUBBE. *He was executed for starting the fire, but was he just a scapegoat for the Nazis? Some historians think so.*

"It is a sign from heaven. This is the beginning of the Communist rising."

Absolute power

"Every Communist official must be shot. All Communist Deputies must be hanged this very night. There must be no mercy."

The Nazis needed to turn the German people against the Communists. For although the Nazis had the largest party in Parliament, the leftwing blocked their way to absolute power.

Overnight 5,000 Communists were rounded up, and four party leaders were charged with complicity in the act of arson.

In a general election called for March 5, 1933, the Nazis still did not gain the two-thirds majority they needed to have overall rule. They had only 44 percent of the vote.

But in the absence of the Communist Deputies, who were barred from attending, Hitler got Parliament to pass an enabling act, handing over all powers to his Cabinet.

Experts from the Berlin fire brigade were of the opinion that the fire could not have been the work of a single arsonist, that he must have needed about six or seven accomplices. Yet a trial in Leipzig acquitted four of Van der Lubbe's supposed fellow accomplices.

Although Hitler blamed the fire on the Communists, and the feebleminded Van der Lubbe paid with his life, the rest of the world had little doubt that the Nazis themselves had planned the blaze.

The Communists, in a brilliant stroke of counterpropaganda, suggested that Goering and a group of accomplices went along an underground passage to the Reichstag, started the fire, and left by the way they had come. At the Nuremberg trials after the Second World War, Gen. Franz Halder, Chief of the German Staff, recalled that Goering had boasted in 1942: "The only one who really knows about the Reichstag is me, because I set it on fire."

The final twist

Goering denied having made the remark, but as everyone knew, the Nazis were masters of the doublecross. The final twist came years after the war, when modern research pointed to the conclusion that there had been a triplecross—and the Nazis were its victims.

Van der Lubbe, it seems, started the fire entirely on his own, using four packets of firelighters and a box of matches, and Goering's men at worst exploited it by hampering the fire services.

MYSTERY OF THE "MARY CELESTE"

The ship that sailed itself

The *Dei Gratia*, a bark sailing from New York to Gibraltar, was fast approaching the strange two-masted square-rigger. The ship's course was unsteady, as though it were being crewed by drunks. When the wind veered, it shifted aimlessly.

The captain of the *Dei Gratia* could see no one at the helm. He ran up a signal, but there was no answer.

As the bark closed in, a boat was lowered, and the captain, the second mate, and two other men pulled toward the oddly silent ship. Then, as they rowed closer, they saw its name painted clearly across the stern—*Mary Celeste*.

The captain and the mate clambered aboard. It was 3 o'clock on the afternoon of December 5, 1872.

What the two men found sparked off a mystery that has bobbed tantalizingly beyond explanation for more than a century. For when they reached the deck, no crew member came forward to meet them. They searched the ship from stem to stern, but the vessel was deserted. The *Mary Celeste* was sailing itself—alone across the wide Atlantic.

The ship was in first-class condition. Hull, masts, and sails were all sound. The cargo—barrels of alcohol—was still lashed in place in the hold. There was plenty of food and water.

Captain's last breakfast

In the fo'c'sle the crew's sea chests and clothing lay dry and undisturbed. Some razors lying about were still unrusted. In the galley pots containing the remnants of a meal hung over a dead fire.

The table in the captain's cabin had been laid for breakfast, though it looked as though the meal had been abandoned halfway through. There was porridge on one of the plates, and the top of a boiled egg had been sliced off. Next to one plate was an open bottle of cough medicine. The cork still lay beside it.

On the other side of the cabin was a smaller table with a sewing machine, and on it was a child's nightgown.

Nearby were bottles of oil, cotton, and a thimble, and against the wall there was a collection of books and a reed organ in a rosewood case.

Everything was undamaged and in its proper place, as though the entire crew had made a sudden and collective decision to hurl themselves overboard together. Whatever had occurred could not have been very long before, because the food would have rotted and the metal would have tarnished in the sea air.

The mate's cabin was the same—perfectly in order. On the desk lay a piece of paper with an unfinished calculation written on it. He, too, it seemed, had been interrupted. Gold lockets, jewelry, and money were still locked in the ship's safe. All that was missing was the ship's chronometer.

Was it mutiny?

The *Dei Gratia*'s captain suspected mutiny. But if there had been a mutiny, how had the crew escaped? The *Mary Celeste*'s lifeboat still hung on its davits. So they must either have been taken off by a passing ship or jumped over the side.

The captain and mate of the *Dei Gratia* did find some clues—of a sort. In one cabin there was a cutlass, smeared with what seemed to be blood—though this was later derided at the official inquiry. They found similar stains on the starboard deck rail, near a cut that looked as though it had been made by an ax. On each side of the bows, a strip of wood six feet long by one inch wide had been recently cut from the outer planks. There was no obvious reason why this should have been done.

When he examined the ship's log, the captain of the *Dei Gratia* found that the last entry was on November 24. That would have been 10 days earlier, when the *Mary Celeste* had been passing north of St. Mary's Island in the Azores —more than 400 miles west of where it was found.

If it had been abandoned soon after that entry, the ship must have drifted unmanned and unsteered for a week and a half. Yet this could not have been.

The *Mary Celeste* was found with its sails set to catch the wind coming over the starboard quarter: In other words, it was sailing on the starboard tack. The *Dei Gratia* had been following a similar course just behind. But throughout the 400 miles from the Azores, the *Dei*

Gratia had been obliged to sail on the port tack.

It seems impossible that the *Mary Celeste* could have reached the spot it did with its yards and sails set to starboard. Someone must have been working the ship for at least several days after the final log entry. But who? Or what?

The investigation by the British Admiralty's Gibraltar office did nothing to answer the questions. The inquiry discovered that the *Mary Celeste* was listed on the 1871 American Lloyd's Register as a New York-based brigantine of 206 tons and that one of the barrels of alcohol had been tampered with. They found, too, that besides the chronometer, the sextant and cargo documents were missing.

They also found that 10 people had sailed aboard the *Mary Celeste*—Captain Briggs, seven crewmen, and the captain's wife and young daughter. None of them was ever seen again.

Official explanation

The explanation that seemed most reasonable at the time was the official one put out by the British and American authorities. This suggested that the crew had got at the alcohol, murdered the captain and his family, and then somehow escaped to another vessel. But the story does not really stand up. There were no visible signs of a struggle on board, and if the crew had escaped, some of them would surely have turned up later.

Dozens of theories were put forward. Had the vessel been attacked by an octopus or some other monster that had somehow or other managed to extract the crew without damaging the ship itself? Or could the ship have encountered a mysterious island, newly risen from the deep? Might the crew have gone ashore, but then, being unable to regain the ship, have drowned as the island descended once more into the Atlantic? Marginally less bizarre was the notion that every soul on board had been sucked off the decks by a sudden whirlwind or waterspout.

The Fosdyk papers

A far more remarkable solution was advanced in 1913, 40 years after the event, in an article in the *Strand* magazine in London. It was written by a schoolmaster named Howard Linford, who told the story of some papers left him by one of his employees, a well-educated and much-traveled man named Abel Fosdyk.

The dead man's papers contained notes that explained not only the fate of the crew but also the curious marks cut into the bows of the *Mary Celeste*.

Fosdyk claimed that he had been a secret passenger on the ship's last voyage—and the only survivor of the tragedy that overtook it. He was, the papers revealed, a close friend of Captain Briggs. Briggs had agreed to give him secret passage because Fosdyk—for some undisclosed reason—had to leave America in a hurry.

During the voyage Briggs had the ship's carpenter build a special deck in the bow for his small daughter. It was the supporting struts for this deck that were slotted into the cuts in the bow planks.

One day Briggs had a lengthy argument with the mate about how well a man could swim with his clothes on. To prove his point, Briggs leaped into the water and started swimming around the ship. Two men followed while the rest of the crew watched from the deck.

Suddenly, one of the sailors swimming around the bow gave a yell of agony. Everyone, including the captain's wife and child, crowded onto the newly built deck—which promptly collapsed under their combined weight. All were flung into the sea, where, according to Fosdyk, they were devoured by the sharks that had attacked the first seaman.

The one that got away

Only Fosdyk survived, and he, unable to regain the ship, clung to the shattered decking as the *Mary Celeste* drifted away. He floated for days until he was washed up half dead on the northwest coast of Africa. The Fosdyk papers tell a neat tale. But they offer no solution to the mystery of how the ship got to where it was found. And they are wrong on details that should not have escaped an educated man.

Fosdyk says the *Mary Celeste* weighed 600 tons. In fact, the ship weighed a third of that. Fosdyk also says that the crewmen were English, when, in fact, they were mostly Dutch. And most of all, it seems highly improbable that anyone would go swimming around a ship that, according to the *Dei Gratia* evidence, must have been making several knots at the time.

Bizarre as it is, no better explanation than Fosdyk's has so far emerged. And after more than 100 years, it is unlikely to do so. The enigma of the ship that sailed itself seems destined to puzzle us forever.

THE VANISHING SPY DIVER

What really happened to Buster Crabb?

Comdr. Lionel Crabb, Britain's foremost underwater expert in the postwar years, booked into a hotel in Portsmouth on April 17, 1956, with Bernard Sydney Smith, an agent of the British Special Intelligence Service (SIS). On the following day the Russian cruiser *Ordzhonikidze*, accompanied by two destroyers, anchored in the Portsmouth harbor. It was carrying Soviet Premier Nikolai Bulganin and the country's Communist Party First Secretary Nikita Khrushchev on a state visit to Britain.

Downing Street had issued a directive that no attempts were to be made to spy on the Russian visitors. Yet, while Bulganin and Khrushchev were in London, Buster Crabb—on the instigation of the SIS man—secretly made a series of dives in the harbor to inspect the hull of the Russian warship.

Under the ship

He began the operation with test dives on the day the cruiser docked. Then, shortly after dawn on April 19, Crabb entered the harbor again and emerged to report that he had been under the ship but was having trouble with the breathing apparatus of his frogman's suit. The equipment was Royal Naval issue, considered dangerous for use below 33 feet, and Crabb explained that he had had to surface to clear the system of poisonous excess carbon dioxide.

He then made another dive—and Smith never saw him again.

The cruiser and its two attendant destroyers sailed for home on April 29, and the following day the Admiralty issued a statement saying that Crabb was presumed dead "as a result of trials with certain underwater apparatus." According to the official announcement, Crabb was lost in the vicinity of the Russian ships on April 20.

Diplomatic notes passed between the Soviet Embassy and the British government, the British emphasizing that Crabb had been operating without government permission having been granted.

When John Dugdale, a Member of Parliament, asked in the House of Commons for more information, he was told by the Prime Minister, Sir Anthony Eden, that it would "not be in the public interest" to disclose the circumstances in which Crabb was presumed to have died.

He added that because "what was done was done without the authority or knowledge of Her Majesty's Ministers," disciplinary action was being taken.

This was all very well, but what had happened to Crabb?

Being a civilian, he was in death disowned by those in whose service he had died—if, indeed, he had died at all.

Had he been killed by some top-secret underwater protective device? Had Russian frogmen done it? Had the Russians captured him and taken him back to the Soviet Union?

To reach any conclusions it is necessary to look at Crabb's background and discover what sort of man he was. He started his career during the Second World War as a bomb- and mine-disposal expert with the Royal Navy. Although an indifferent surface swimmer, he was a skilled and daring skindiver and an acknowledged expert at his craft.

Awards for bravery

During the war he dealt with Italian underwater saboteurs off Gibraltar. After this he helped combat terrorists attempting to sabotage ships in the Mediterranean. He won the George Medal and was made an Officer of the Order of the British Empire.

He retired in early 1956. The end of his service career seems to have taken much of the old spirit out of him, for he became bored and even talked to friends of suicide. Crabb had also become a heavy drinker who tended to be talkative about his undercover exploits. It is known that he was drinking the night before he left the hotel for his last dive.

He was an eccentric, who enjoyed wearing his rubber wet suits under his street clothes and even in bed.

Why should the SIS hire such a man for their delicate mission?

An answer to that is that they needed a civilian, for a serving officer would be much more difficult to explain away in the event of failure. Crabb was an expert diver at a time when skindiving was not a popular pastime. He was experienced in what the SIS wanted—and

he would be easy to persuade, for he needed the money desperately.

None of this could, of course, be verified, for Smith, the intelligence agent, was spirited away from prying questioners immediately after the failure, along with the page in the hotel register that he and Crabb signed.

More than a year later, on June 9, 1957, the body of a man in a rubber suit was found by fishermen in a harbor a few miles east of Portsmouth. Conveniently, it had no head or hands.

The body had a scar on one leg, similar to one on Crabb's leg; the wet suit was of the

UNDERWATER SPY.
Buster Crabb vanished when he dived near the three Russian warships. Was he killed or captured on that ill-fated mission at Portsmouth?

Italian make that Crabb favored; and the corpse had hammertoes, like Crabb, although seemingly less distorted than his had been.

There were no positive identification factors—skull, teeth, or fingerprints—but the coroner declared himself "quite satisfied" that it was Crabb's body.

Far from ending the case, the inquest verdict fanned interest in it, and speculation once again became intense.

At this time, strange and disturbing stories began to reach Britain, allegedly from Russian sources.

A West German newspaper carried a story claiming that a Russian naval officer had said Crabb was a Soviet prisoner.

Join or be shot?

He was alleged to be in a Moscow prison, where he was considering the alternative of either being shot as a spy or joining the Russian Navy. He was said to have decided on the latter course—on condition that he never had to undertake missions against a British ship.

Another rumor, this time credited to Russian officers in Berlin, said that Crabb had been held underwater by a powerful magnetic device under the Russian cruiser and had drowned.

Yet another suggestion was that Crabb was killed by a limpet mine planted on the ship by a fanatic Russian émigré group. It had blown up as he bravely tried to carry away the device and to disarm it.

But the rumor that gained most credence was that the British war hero had joined the Russians, in spite of his pronounced right-wing views in political matters.

This rumor gained strength from an unexpected source outside Great Britain.

Photographic evidence

A Russian military magazine that reached the West carried a picture of a group of Soviet naval officers, one of whom was a Lt. Lvev Lvovich Korablov, reportedly an instructor in underwater operations.

Although the photograph was rather blurred, Korablov was identified as Crabb by the missing frogman's ex-wife Margaret and one of his colleagues from wartime days.

Crabb's supposed reappearance in Russia was backed up by another report: that sailors from the *Ordzhonikidze* had described how the ship's hospital was sealed off during the return journey from Britain, with an unknown and heavily guarded patient inside.

If Crabb is alive in the Soviet Union, it is difficult to understand why the Russians have never attempted to make any propaganda capital out of it.

If Korablov is Crabb, whose body was washed up in that harbor? This is a question that is never likely to be answered satisfactorily.

Faked body theory

Those who believe Crabb is alive suggest that a suitable body was procured by the Russians, given a leg scar, matured for a suitable period in seawater, then "planted"—minus head and hands.

Another, somewhat melodramatic, theory is that the SIS itself disposed of the unfortunate Crabb when they realized that the Prime Minister's wrath would descend on them if the mission went ahead as planned.

Finally, the simplest and likeliest explanation is that Comdr. Lionel Crabb drowned because his equipment was faulty.

LOST GOLD REEF OF THE AUSTRALIAN DESERT

FAR OUT beyond the Petermann Range in the burning desert of central Australia lies the gold reef of Harold Bell Lasseter.

Lasseter, a stocky bushman, claimed to have found the reef in 1897, but it took him 14 years to raise funds for an expedition. That first trek was so hazardous that it was abandoned. It was not until 1930 that he was able to finance a second party to dig out the riches he had seen.

One by one, the gold hunters fell victim to the desert until Lasseter, alone except for two camels, was left to proceed to his goal. He became sand blinded, and his body was found later in a cave—dead from starvation.

But his legend, and the legend of his reef, lives on—glinting and tempting in the sun beyond the Petermann Mountains.

THREE WISE MEN AND A STAR

The horoscope that changed the world

The Star of Bethlehem, said by the New Testament to have guided the three Magi to the birthplace of Christ, has puzzled scholars for centuries. What kind of phenomenon could, as described by Matthew, have appeared in the East and moved before the wise men, "till it came to rest over the place where the child was"?

One popular theory is that Halley's Comet, seen in the Holy Land around the time of Christ's birth, might have been taken as an omen by the Magi. But there are several objections to this idea that are difficult to overcome.

The comet is now known to have appeared over the Middle East in 12 B.C., showing up at latitude 31° N., almost the precise latitude of Bethlehem.

Report to Herod

Having come from the East and "seen" the star, Matthew says, the Magi reported to Herod, who asked them to find the child, and: "When they had heard the king, they went their way; and, lo, the star, which they had seen in the East, went before them, till it came to rest over the place where the child was." Why then, according to Matthew, would Herod have had to *ask* where the child was?

And, of course, Halley's Comet, or any other comet for that matter, would have been seen with equal brightness everywhere; and it would not have behaved in this way—moving on ahead, then hovering over one spot.

In any case, Christ is believed to have been born at the time of the Romans' Imperial Census, which, according to most historians, was in 4 B.C. There are no records of any comets being seen anywhere in the world that year.

Another theory about the Star of Bethlehem is that it might have been a nova or a supernova, exploding stars that are bright enough to remain visible for some time. There is no evidence that a supernova was seen at the time of Christ's birth, but ancient Chinese records indicate that a nova was possibly present.

Certainly, if such a spectacular heavenly display had occurred, not only would other contemporary chroniclers and figures have seen it—including Herod—but the Romans and Chinese would undoubtedly have recorded it.

Was it a large meteor, or meteors, streaking across the sky perhaps? This is improbable, because meteors are visible only for seconds and are certainly incapable of hovering or even appearing to do so.

A more probable theory, and one that is gaining ground in theological circles, is that the Magi were astrologers and had calculated that a particular star was in the ascendant, or rising in the East, and foretold the birth of a Messiah.

The Dead Sea Scrolls—a collection of ancient writings belonging to a little-known religious group and first discovered in caves by the northwest edge of the Dead Sea in 1947—give this theory some substance. Among the fragments of the scrolls is a document giving the signs of the zodiac and another outlining the influence of the stars and planets on those born in various segments of the zodiac.

The scrolls also refer to a teacher of righteousness, or prince of light, who has been identified by some scholars with both John the Baptist and Jesus.

It could be, therefore, that contemporary astrologers were watching the heavens and trying to calculate the necessary planetary conjunctions they believed would herald the birth of a Messiah.

Cardinal's theory

The late Jesuit scholar Cardinal Danielou accepted the theory that the star was one in a messianic horoscope.

Danielou considered the Magi's statement, "We have seen His star in the East," to be an allusion to a star at its rising, or in the ascendant—the most important factor in casting any horoscope.

He wrote: "In those Jewish circles of the day in which astrology was widespread and the Messiah hoped for, there was speculation as to the star under which He would be born. It becomes clear that once the combination foretold in one of those horoscopes actually took place, people would believe that the Messiah was born and would start to look for His birthplace."

This is perhaps what the Magi, or astrologers, were doing when they visited Herod.

Footsteps into the unknown

•

THE FLYING DUTCHMAN

Legend of a ship that never reached port

A burnished haze of heat hung over the blue waters of False Bay, a seaside playground on the tip of South Africa. It was a blazingly hot day in March 1939, and on the sun-bleached sands of Glencairn beach some 60 people relaxed beside the warm waters of the Indian Ocean.

Suddenly, out of the haze sailed a fine full-rigged East Indiaman such as had not been seen in the waters off the cape for several centuries. Those who noticed it called out to others, and soon everyone on the beach stood in an excited group, chattering at the edge of the sea.

Vanished without trace

According to a newspaper report published on the following day, the ship "with all her sails drawing well, although there was not a breath of wind at the time, appeared to be standing toward Muizenberg."

The *British South Africa Annual* of 1939 reported: "With uncanny volition the ship sailed steadily on as the Glencairn beachfolk, shaken from their lethargy, stood about keenly discussing the whys and wherefores of the vessel which seemed to be bent on self-destruction somewhere on the sands of Strandfontein. Just as the excitement reached its climax, however, the mystery ship vanished into thin air as strangely as it had come."

In the days following the appearance of the phantom ship, several theories were advanced. One was that the watchers at Glencairn had seen a mirage and that the mystery ship was, by

some accident of light refraction, the image of a ship sailing several hundred miles away.

But, as those who had sighted the ship pointed out, the broad, squat hull and high poop, and even the rigging, were unlike those of any modern sailing ship. It was unmistakably a 17th-century merchantman.

Helene Tydell was among the crowd of witnesses on the beach that day. "Let the skeptics say what they will, that ship was none other than the *Flying Dutchman*," she said.

Well-known legend

Even before it inspired Wagner to write his opera, *Der Fliegende Holländer*, the Flying Dutchman legend had been known to many generations of sailors around the world. Old records show that in 1680 a Dutch East Indiaman captained by Hendrik Vanderdecken sailed from Amsterdam for the Dutch East Indies settlement at Batavia. Vanderdecken, a man of fearless and adventurous disposition, apparently had few scruples and an unsavory reputation. But he was a skilled seaman, and the owners had few qualms about giving him command of the vessel, in spite of his boasts in the waterfront wineshops that he would return with a fortune.

All seems to have gone well with Vanderdecken and his crew as they sailed south through sunny tropical seas, but near the Cape of Good Hope a sudden tropical gale tore the sails to shreds and wrecked the rudder. As days stretched into weeks, the vessel was tossed about off the cape, unable to make headway against the battering force of a southeasterly gale.

According to legend, Vanderdecken became increasingly furious as every trick of navigation and seamanship he tried failed to bring him around the cape.

Cursed the Almighty

Taking advantage of Vanderdecken's frenzied state of mind, the Devil suggested to him in a dream that he should defy the Almighty's attempt to stop him from rounding the cape. In a rage the Dutch sea captain took up the challenge:

With frantic mien the appalling oath he took,
And loudly cried above the tempest's din:
"My destined course and resolute career
The power of God I thus defy to stay
Nor shall the Fiend of Hell awake my fear
Though I should cruise until the Judgment Day."

Who first quoted the captain's words is not known. But retribution came swiftly as the angel of the Lord commanded that Vanderdecken should roam the seas forever "until the trump of God shall rend the sky."

The ship would eventually founder, and the crew would die, but Vanderdecken must keep his vigil until doomsday.

Vanderdecken and his ship never reached Batavia. Since 1680 there have been countless sightings of his ship reported. Any ship that sights the phantom is said soon to encounter bad luck.

This was the case in the 1880's when the future George V, then a midshipman on HMS *Bacchante*, saw the phantom ship and a figure in ancient dress on her poop as the *Bacchante* sailed 50 miles off the cape. The next day a member of the crew fell from the rigging and was killed.

The last recorded cape sighting was in September 1942, when four people sitting on their balcony in Cape Town saw the ghostly East Indiaman sail into Table Bay and disappear behind Robben Island.

Scientific view

Scientists continue to insist that what they, George V, and the people of Glencairn beach saw were mirages and that other ships have been sighted in that way. A mail ship of Britain's Pacific and Oriental line bound for India was once spotted at Aden. The ship's log showed later that she was at least 200 miles away at the time.

But science has not explained the constant similarities of detail given by those who have seen the East Indiaman—or the fact that ships of her type last sailed more than 200 years ago.

SHIP OF ILL OMEN. *Long before it inspired Wagner to write his opera,* Der Fliegende Holländer, *the Flying Dutchman legend was known to generations of sailors as a portent of disaster.*

THE ANGELS OF MONS

Did a phantom army save the British from certain death?

A month after the bitterly fought Battle of Mons in the First World War, a report appeared in the London *Evening News* that caused a sensation at the time and has created controversy ever since.

The report, by a Welsh-born journalist and author, Arthur Machen, told how the tiny British Expeditionary Force (BEF), outnumbered by three to one, was apparently saved by heavenly reinforcements. The Angel, or Angels, of Mons (accounts varied between one and a platoon) suddenly stood between them and the Germans. Understandably, the enemy fell back in confusion.

The battle took place on August 26, 1914, and when the report appeared in September, most of the survivors were still in France. In May of the following year, a clergyman's daughter anonymously published in a parish magazine what she claimed was a sworn statement by a British officer.

In it the officer said that while his company was in retreat from Mons, a unit of German cavalry came rapidly after them. They made for a place where the company might stand and fight—but the Germans got there first.

Expecting almost certain death, the British turned and saw to their astonishment a troop of angels between them and the enemy. The German horses were terrified and stampeded in all directions.

An army chaplain, the Rev. C. M. Chavasse, recorded that he had heard similar accounts from a brigadier general and two of his officers.

A lieutenant colonel described how, during the retreat, his battalion was escorted for 20 minutes by a squadron of phantom cavalry.

From the German side came an account that their men refused to charge a point where the British line was broken because of the presence of a large number of troops. According to Allied records, there was not a single British soldier in the area.

An imaginative writer

What is notable about all the Mons reports is that not one of them is firsthand. In each case the officers from whom the reports originated wished to remain anonymous, feeling that they might be accused of having an overactive imagination—a possible hindrance to promotion.

Years later Machen, himself a writer of stories of horror and the supernatural, and a onetime member of the mystical society known as the Hermetic Order of the Golden Dawn, admitted that his original account had been no more than a piece of imaginative writing.

So the mystery becomes even more compelling. Despite the denial scores of returning soldiers did reminisce about the strange events at Mons, and investigators did come to believe that something supernatural had indeed taken place.

Did the returning soldiers seize upon and support a story that appealed to them?

Or did something—a mirage, perhaps—happen that made both the British and the Germans believe that they had seen a spectral army of angels?

Whatever the explanation, the British did achieve something like a miracle. Despite overwhelming odds and heavy casualties, the retreat was successfully accomplished, and the BEF remained an effective fighting force.

RIDERS IN THE SKY. *The legend of the angels that saved the British Army in retreat became so popular that a waltz was written on the theme.*

WHEN THE DEVIL WALKED IN DEVON

What else could leave a 100-mile trail of hoofprints?

All over southern England, the winter of 1854–55 was the coldest in living memory. Overnight, on February 9, there had been a severe frost, and two inches of snow blanketed the county of Devon. The Exe River was frozen over, and birds were trapped where they had stood on the ice.

When dawn came, the snow lay white, smooth, and even, marked only by bird and animal tracks and, across about 100 miles of the county, a trail of mysterious footprints. They zigzagged through five parishes, across gardens, over rooftops, haystacks, walls, and in and out of barns.

They were 4 inches long, 2¾ inches wide, and 8 inches apart, and appeared to have been made by a creature with cloven hooves, walking upright on two legs.

To the country people of the area, there was no doubt about the cause of the footprints. They had been made by the cloven hooves of the Devil.

Hooves of fire

The weird prints began in the middle of a garden in the parish of Totnes and ended as mysteriously as they had started, in a field at Littleham. In one village they led into a shed and out at the other side. Whatever made them had gone through a six-inch-diameter hole.

In another village the creature appeared to have crawled through a drainpipe, leaving tracks at both ends.

In some places the marks seemed to have been made by fiery hooves in the hard-frozen snow or, as at Woodbury, by a hot iron outside the door of the church.

Hundreds of people saw the prints, and scores of letters to newspapers debated what could have caused them.

Near the village of Dawlish the trail led into dense bracken and undergrowth. When dogs were brought in to flush out the thicket, they are said to have retreated, howling dismally.

Many theories

The naturalist Sir Richard Owen, in a letter to *The Illustrated London News,* suggested the prints were those of a badger. He pointed out that the badger places its hind feet in the marks left by its forefeet. Although it hibernates, it sometimes ventures out in search of food.

Other suggestions included a fox, an otter, cranes, wild cats, a donkey, or a pony with a broken shoe. One amateur naturalist even suggested that the prints resembled those of a kangaroo and that the animal might have escaped from a traveling menagerie, then returned to its cage without anyone noticing its absence.

Rats, rabbits, squirrels, and toads were also suggested as possible culprits.

A vicar, the Rev. Henry Fudsen, gave a sermon in which he declared the prints to be the paw marks of several cats.

One group of villagers, believing there might be a wild beast at large, set out with pitchforks and bludgeons to track it down, but without success.

But local people were not convinced. Many refused to go out after sunset, and children hid in closets and cupboards, terrified by the fireside gossip they had heard: that the Devil had walked in Devon that winter night.

THE ILLUSTRATED LONDON NEWS

FOOT-MARKS ON THE SNOW, IN DEVON.

(*From a Correspondent.*)

As many of your readers have perused, I have no doubt, with much interest, the paragraph which appeared in several of the papers of last week, relative to the mysterious foot-marks left upon the snow during the night of Thursday, the 8th, in the parishes of Exmouth, Lympstone, and Woodbury, as also in Dawlish, Torquay, Totnes, and other places on the other side of the estuary of the Exe, in the county of Devon, extending over a tract of country of thirty or forty miles, or probably more; and as the paragraph I allude to does not fully detail the mysterious affair, it may probably be interesting to many to have a more particular account—which I think this unusual occurrence well deserves.

The marks which appeared on the snow (which lay very thinly on the ground at the time), and which were seen on the Friday morning, to all appearance were the perfect impression of a donkey's hoof—the length 4 inches by 2¾ inches; but, instead of progressing as that animal would have done (or indeed as any other would have done), feet right and left, it appeared that foot had followed foot, in *a single line;* the distance from each tread being eight inches, or rather more—the foot-marks in every parish being exactly the same size, and the steps the same length. This mysterious visitor generally only passed *once* down or across each garden or courtyard, and did so in nearly all the houses in many parts of the several towns above mentioned, as also in the farms scattered about; this regular track passing in some instances over the roofs of houses, and hayricks, and very high walls (one fourteen feet), without displacing the snow on either side or altering the distance between the feet, and passing on as if the wall had not been any impediment. The gardens with high fences or walls, and gates locked, were equally visited as those open and unprotected. Now, when we consider the distance that must have been gone over to have left these marks—I may say in almost every garden, on door-steps, through the extensive woods of Luscombe, upon commons, in inclosures and farms—the

TRACKING THE DEVIL. *The mysterious hoofprints across 100 miles of Devon drew a great deal of correspondence (above) in the newspapers.*

VOICE IN THE NIGHT

For 400 years she has mourned her children

At the stroke of midnight an eerie cry that has echoed through more than four centuries is said to be heard in the heart of Mexico City.

The mournful voice is that of a grief-stricken woman, who wails: "Oh, my children, my pitiful, wretched children."

She is La Llorona, the Wailing Woman. Wearing a torn and blood-stained gown, she haunts the night, wailing her grief.

According to Mexican legend, dating back to 1550, the voice belongs to Doña Luisa de Olveros, a Spanish Indian of outstanding beauty, who took as her lover a nobleman, Don Nuño de Montesclaros. She bore him two children, loved him deeply, and prayed for the day when she would become his bride.

But Don Nuño did not return her feelings, and, once his passion had died, he neglected her.

Lonely and puzzled, Luisa finally decided one night to walk to the palatial home of the wealthy and influential Montesclaros family in the hope of seeing her lover and begging him to come back.

She found him—but to her horror he was in the center of a lavish party, celebrating his marriage that day to a Spanish noblewoman.

Luisa rushed to him in tears, but he pushed her away, coldly telling her that because of her Indian blood she was unacceptable and could never have become his wife.

Hysterical, she ran home to her children and killed them with a small dagger that had been a present from her lover. Covered with her children's blood, she fled from the house and dashed screaming through the streets, until she was arrested and thrown into prison. She was convicted of sorcery.

Doña Luisa de Olveros was publicly hanged in Mexico City, and as a final humiliation, her body was left swinging in "public mockery" for six hours. Every night since then, her ghostly cries have rung out and will continue to, so the legend says, until the end of time.

FISHER'S REVENGE

The murderer was caught by his victim's ghost

On a dark winter's evening in 1826, James Farley, a highly respected farmer of Campbelltown, New South Wales, was walking near a house belonging to a man named Frederick Fisher. There he saw a figure sitting on a railing and pointing to a spot in Fisher's paddock. So sinister was the figure that Farley fled, convinced he had seen a ghost.

Fisher was a paroled convict who had become a prosperous farmer. Some time before, when he had been imprisoned for debt, he had transferred his assets to a friend, another ex-convict, named George Worrall, in order to prevent them from being seized by his creditors. After six months in prison he had returned unexpectedly.

On June 26, 1826, some months before Farley saw the ghost, Fisher had been observed leaving a Campbelltown pub after a long drinking session and had not been seen since. Worrall circulated the perfectly reasonable story that Fisher had returned to England on the ship *Lady Vincent*. But three months after Fisher's disappearance the authorities became suspicious and inserted a notice in the *Sydney Gazette* that offered a reward of $100 for the discovery of Fisher's body.

Worrall was questioned by the police because he had been seen wearing trousers known to have belonged to Fisher. He accused four other men of murdering his friend, saying that he had seen them do it. This unlikely tale deepened official suspicion, and Worrall was arrested.

It was at this point that Farley saw the ghost. On Farley's insistence a Constable Newland went to the paddock with an aborigine tracker. He found traces of human blood on a rail and, at the spot that the ghost had indicated, discovered Fisher's savagely battered body in a shallow marshy grave.

Worrall was convicted of the murder and, before his execution, admitted that he had killed Fisher, but he said the blow was accidental.

BARNEY DUFFY'S CURSE

Two soldiers ignored it . . . and died

Barney Duffy was a giant of a man. He towered over the two young soldiers, uttering a terrible curse: "Take me or report me, ye red-coated, lily-livered lice! Aye! And then I'll hang—but hear me curse on ye! So surely as ye do this, before me corpse has hung a week on King's Town gallows, ye'll meet a violent death, the pair of ye!"

Duffy, an Irishman, had been imprisoned by the British on Norfolk Island, in the Pacific Ocean, about 900 miles northeast of Sydney, Australia. The island is one of the most beautiful in the world, but its past is a long tale of blood.

Scores of its present residents claim they have seen ghosts: ghosts of the descendants of the *Bounty* mutineers, who outgrew tiny Pitcairn Island and moved to Norfolk in the 19th century, and ghosts of rebellious Irish convicts, hanged there after the British authorities shipped them from Botany Bay.

The convict's life was a continuous night-mare. Men got 50 lashes for possessing tobacco or singing. They ate with their fingers and drank water from buckets. Those sentenced to hang thanked God for deliverance, while the remainder prayed not for freedom but for death.

Barney Duffy escaped from this hell and hid in a hollow pine in the thick rain forest. He emerged at night to raid the vegetable gardens of the settlement. His beard and hair were long and matted, and he had just a few rags to cover himself, when the two soldiers, who were out fishing, discovered him.

They shrugged off his curse and pushed him back to the settlement with their muskets. Duffy was hanged, and two days later the soldiers went to fish at the same spot near the hollow pine. Shortly after, a foot patrol found their bodies, battered and broken, drifting in the tide nearby.

To this day Norfolk Island maps show Barney Duffy Gully, where two soldiers ignored Barney Duffy's curse and paid with their lives.

WHOSE IMAGE?

Photographic evidence of Christ's death

In a reliquary in the chapel of the dukes of Savoy at Turin Cathedral lies a piece of cloth, measuring 14 feet 5 inches by 3 feet 8 inches, which faintly bears the back and front images of a man.

Approximately four times a century the cloth is put on display, and thousands of pilgrims flock to see it. They believe that they are gazing on the features of Jesus Christ.

The Holy Shroud of Turin is one of the most closely guarded and controversial Christian relics in the world. If it is genuine, it is certainly the most precious.

It is believed to be the linen in which Christ's body was placed in the tomb, after His crucifixion. His image appears to have imprinted itself on the cloth, as if it were a photographic plate.

Whether the shroud is genuinely that of Christ or not, it has been the subject of many investigations, which have uncovered some amazing facts and posed intriguing questions.

The shroud is believed to have been kept in hiding for three centuries during the early Christian persecutions. Later, it was acquired by the Byzantine rulers of Constantinople, where it remained until the city fell in 1204.

It was taken by Crusaders to Besançon Cathedral, in the French province of Doubs, where it narrowly escaped being destroyed by fire in 1349.

Finally, the shroud was presented to the dukes of Savoy in 1432. After being slightly damaged in another fire, this time at the ducal palace, it was removed to the cathedral at Turin, where the dukes had another residence. It has been kept there since 1578.

The first photographs

In 1898, Secondo Pia, an archeological photographer, took the first pictures of the shroud and found to his astonishment that his negative plates gave a much clearer image of the figure than the image that appeared to be on the cloth.

IS THIS THE FACE OF CHRIST? *The image captured in the age-old piece of cloth treasured at Turin Cathedral is certainly remarkable. Is it also a photographic record of Christ's death?*

Dr. Yves Delage, a distinguished French physician, began an investigation into the relic and presented his findings to the French Academy of Sciences in 1902.

His colleague, Paul Vignon, suggested that the stains on the shroud were caused by perspiration and spices, with which the cloth was impregnated.

Dr. Delage reported that the image was a perfectly detailed portrayal of the body of a man who had undergone a brutal series of tortures, culminating in the agony of crucifixion.

The face bore the marks of several blows; the nose was injured; there was severe bruising and swelling of the right cheek; the right eyelid was sharply contracted; and bloodstains on the forehead and back of the head indicated that the skin had been punctured by some kind of sharp instrument.

The whole body, with the exception of the face, hands, and feet, was covered with marks that suggested scourging by a two-thonged lash, studded with balls of lead or bone, and administered by two people. These marks were particularly severe on the chest and abdomen. The shoulders had wounds that would be likely after the man had carried a heavy object. Both knees were cut, as if from heavy falls. There were bloodstained wounds, which could have been caused by nails, in both wrists and feet.

Wrist wounds

The wrist wounds were just behind the heel of the hand. A large wound on the right side, between the fifth and sixth ribs, was clear, and there was a corresponding stain of blood and a colorless liquid, possibly fluid from a pierced lung.

The body had been sprinkled with powdered aloes. Traces of this remained, but contrary to Jewish custom, the body apparently had not been washed or anointed—perhaps indicative of a hasty burial.

Dr. Delage summed up by saying: "On the one hand, we have the shroud, probably impregnated with aloes, which brings us to the East, outside Egypt, and a crucified man who has been scourged. On the other, we have an account, pertaining to history, legend, and tradition, showing Christ undergoing in Judaea the same treatment as we decipher on the body whose image is on the shroud."

His report sparked off a controversy that has never really died down. Critics claim the shroud is a fake, the work of an extremely clever artist.

But Dr. Delage pointed out that the shroud bore no apparent traces of pigment. As it had been authenticated since the 14th century, if the image was a fake there must have existed an unknown artist "capable of executing a work hardly within the power of the greatest Renaissance painters."

He also said that it seemed impossible for anyone to paint a negative image with such accuracy. Why, he asked, should anyone go to such lengths? And particularly in a time when photography was an art yet undreamed of?

In 1931 another photographer, Guiseppe Enrie, was commissioned to take pictures of the shroud. After studying his plates, which were far superior to those of 1898, he declared: "The imprint is not the work of an artist. The biggest enlargements establish that there is no trace of any dye whatsoever on the fabric."

X-ray examination

Conventions were formed in Germany and Italy, and the members made a deep study of the shroud and its religious implications. In 1959 the German convention petitioned Pope John XXIII to allow a small portion of the shroud to be removed for chemical and microscopic examination, X rays, infrared and ultraviolet rays, and dating by the radiocarbon process.

The appeal was dismissed by Cardinal Maurilio Fossati, Archbishop of Turin. No reason was given.

Kurt Berna, a German writer who had made a study of the shroud, points out that if the shroud is that of Christ, the bloodstains indicate that His heart was still beating *after He was taken down from the Cross.* If His heart had stopped beating, the wounds would have ceased to bleed, and any blood outside the body would have quickly congealed, long before it was wrapped in its shroud.

This proposition has enormous religious implications for Christians and Jews, whose Old Testament prophesied that the Messiah would die on the Cross.

Berna says that Christ was not killed by the crucifixion, nor by the spear thrust into His side. He claims that photographic reconstruction shows that a lance thrust into the body as indicated on the shroud would not have pierced the heart.

And he believes that Jesus might merely have lost consciousness and stopped breathing because of the torture inflicted upon Him, loss of blood, or the fumes of the vinegar offered to Him by a Roman centurion.

Revived by cold

Believing Him to be dead, the executioners allowed Him to be removed and placed in a tomb.

It is there, Berna suggests, that aloes and ointments, and the cold atmosphere, might have revived Him, allowing Him to appear alive to the disciples before the Ascension.

Berna also makes much of the fact that the nail wounds on the shroud image are through the wrists. He says that this lends authenticity to the shroud, because if, as popularly believed, nails had been driven through the palms, they would have been torn out because of the weight of the body.

Other medical experts, who have examined photographs of the shroud, have noted the muscular deformities on the image, which, they say, are consistent with the effects of the crucifixion.

Dr. David Willis, an English police surgeon, noted that the thumbs of the image were sharply retracted—the exact result of having nails driven through the median nerve that runs down the center of the wrist.

Those who are convinced of the shroud's authenticity point out that anatomical details such as these are not likely to be reproduced by an artist. They ask: Could even a Michelangelo depict with such fine accuracy a body that had gone through such agony and distortion?

Only when the Turin authorities allow a full scientific analysis can the many mysteries be solved.

THE WOMAN WITH WILLPOWER

An amazing case of mind over matter

The young female soldier in the Russian Red Army was bored. A frontline fighter at 14, she had been wounded by a German shell fragment just as the Second World War was nearing its end, and recovery was proving a long business.

"I was very angry and upset one day," Ninel Kulagina later recalled. "I was walking toward a cupboard, when suddenly a jug moved to the edge of the shelf, fell, and smashed to bits."

Other, similar things happened—lights went on and off, doors opened and closed, and dishes moved on tables, all with no visible human intervention. At first Ninel thought of poltergeists—the mischievous spirits that plague human beings. But she sensed that the force moving the objects came from inside her.

She practiced concentrating and learned how to focus her power. One of the first scientists to take an interest in her was Edward Naumov. He scattered a box of matches on a bench, and she clasped her hands over them, shaking with the strain. Suddenly, all the matches moved in a body to the edge of the bench, then fell one by one to the floor.

Many more tests followed, and more than 60 films were made of Ninel in action. In perhaps the most notable test that was filmed, a raw egg was broken into a glass tank filled with saline solution. By intense concentration she separated the white from the yolk and moved the two apart—though she was standing several feet from the tank at the time.

Instruments connected to Ninel showed that she was under considerable emotional and mental stress.

Dr. Genady Sergeyev, who conducted the experiment, also measured the electrostatic field around Ninel. At the moment that she started to separate the yolk and the white, the field began to pulse at the rate of four cycles a second.

Dr. Sergeyev deduced that these vibrations acted like magnetic waves.

"The moment these magnetic vibrations, or waves, occur, they cause the object she focuses on, even if it is something nonmagnetic, to act as if magnetized," he stated publicly. "It causes the object to be attracted to her or repelled by her."

THE MIRACULOUS MONK

An Italian padre who could be seen in two places at once

Gen. Luigi Cadorna, Chief of the Italian General Staff, was in despair after a crushing defeat of his armies by the Germans in Slovenia in November 1917.

He sat in his tent holding his service revolver and contemplating suicide. Suddenly, a monk appeared and admonished him: "Don't be so stupid!"—then vanished entirely.

Years after the First World War, the general visited the church of San Giovanni Rotondo at Foggia in central Italy. He saw a monk, whom he recognized as the one who had appeared in his tent. As the monk passed, he told the general, "You had a lucky escape, my friend."

The monk was Padre Pio, a humble peasant priest who has since become famous as a worker of miracles, as a clairvoyant, stigmatic, and, since his death in 1968, a possible but controversial choice for canonization.

What makes the story of the general so remarkable is that, for the duration of the war, Padre Pio never left his friary at Foggia.

Born in the village of Pietrelcina, near Benevento, in 1887, the son of a poor farmer, Padre Pio entered a Capuchin monastery at the age of 15. For several years he quietly studied and did his duties with his fellow novices.

Then, on September 20, 1915, he complained of pains in his hands, feet, and right side. Doctors could find no physical explanation. On September 20, 1918, while praying at the altar of the church at Foggia, he collapsed in agony. Fellow monks found him unconscious and bleeding from his hands, feet, and side—wounds closely corresponding to those suffered by Christ on the Cross. Padre Pio was examined by doctors, but none could give a satisfactory explanation for his injuries.

Such wounds, called stigmata, have appeared, apparently involuntarily, on a number of people during the Christian era and have been accepted by devout persons as marks of sanctity.

The most common manifestations are bleeding from the hands and feet and from the right or left side. Bruises on the shoulders represent the agony of carrying the Cross, while bleeding from the brow closely resembles the injuries inflicted by the crown of thorns.

Other stigmatics have felt the chafing of the ropes that bound Christ to the Cross, while others have been scarred by the welts of the scourge.

Medical theories

Doctors have long ago dismissed the idea that stigmata arise from any physical cause. They, and theologians, have observed that most stigmatics are people given to brooding intensely upon the sufferings of Christ. And the most common explanation is that autosuggestion is involved.

The Roman Catholic Church has put forward several possible causes for stigmata: divine revelation; diabolic intervention to confuse believers; and conscious or unconscious suggestion. None can be proved.

Whatever the cause in Padre Pio's case, he carried on his duties and became famous throughout the Catholic world as a kind and gentle confessor.

Avoided publicity

Never did he try to capitalize on the strange phenomenon of his stigmata, and he always tried to avoid publicity or any hint of notoriety—even to the extent of covering his hands in public. Nevertheless, money was sent to him and his monastery from all over the world. In 1956 a hospital that cost nearly $5 million, and completely paid for out of donations, was opened at Foggia.

Padre Pio's home village of Pietrelcina also began to prosper as pilgrims flocked to his birthplace.

Twice he was suspended from his duties by the Vatican to which his fame was an embarrassment, particularly because of the money sent to him. Eventually, the padre was absolved from his vows of poverty, provided that all money sent to him was willed to the Holy See. Meanwhile, the padre's fame for his clairvoy-

THE MARK OF CHRIST. *This rare photograph of Padre Pio clearly shows the stigmata on his right hand.*

ance and other powers continued to spread throughout the world.

On January 20, 1936, three men visiting the convent were approached by Padre Pio, who said: "Please pray with me for a soul who is soon to appear before the tribunal of God."

They obeyed and were then told by the priest that they had been praying for King George V of England, who had died at the time they were praying.

In the 1920's a Monsignor Damiani, of Salto, in Uruguay, met Padre Pio and was so impressed that he vowed he wanted to die in the priest's presence.

Padre Pio told him: "You will die in your native land—but do not be afraid." Consoled, Damiani returned to Uruguay.

A deathbed mystery

Then, in 1942, the Archbishop of Montevideo was awakened late at night by a Capuchin monk, who urged him to go to the bedside of Damiani.

When he got there, Damiani was dead. But by the bed was a slip of paper on which was written: "Padre Pio came."

It was not until 1949 that the archbishop met Padre Pio—and recognized him as the Capuchin who had summoned him to Damiani's bedside.

When he died, on September 28, 1968, Padre Pio's followers began to demand that he be canonized—demands not yet acceded to.

GHOST ON THE PROW

Dead or alive, he could not leave his ship

A German U-boat drifting aimlessly off Ireland was a target too good to miss in July 1918. The American submarine that spotted her was maneuvering for the attack when a huge explosion seized the U-boat and sent her to the bottom with all hands.

What caused that explosion will never be known, but for the U-65 it was the final blow in a series of disasters.

For she was a jinxed ship. Even before she had left the shipyard at Bruges, Belgium, two years earlier, she had already claimed one life. A shipyard worker was killed when hit by a girder that was being lowered into place for the hull. On her first sea trials the engine room filled with fumes, and three men suffocated.

As it was wartime, news of the deaths was kept within the German Admiralty. More trials with a group of sister ships were without incident, at first—until the captain of the U-65 ordered her first dive.

The captain sent a sailor forward for a routine inspection of the hatches. The sea was calm, and there was very little wind; but instead of making the inspection, inexplicably, he stepped overboard and was swept away in the backwash.

The silent crew gazed nervously at each other as the captain closed hatches to dive. He gave the order to level off at 30 feet, but the U-65 continued down until it struck the seabed, where it refused to budge. For 12 hours it lay there as the water seeped in. And for the second time it began to fill with battery fumes. Then, once again, for some unexplained reason, it lifted from the bottom and rose to the surface.

After an overhaul back in Bruges, the U-65

was passed fit for service, and refueling and arming began. During this operation a torpedo warhead exploded and brought the death toll to 11. One victim was the second lieutenant.

As the U-65 was towed into drydock, a hysterical crewman swore he saw the dead second lieutenant standing, arms folded, on the prow of the ship. Before it sailed for duty again, another seaman had deserted after reporting that he, too, had seen the dead officer.

Repaired, the U-65 sailed for the Dover Straits, and during its tour of duty reports of more sightings of the second lieutenant did little to increase morale. The duty officer was found trembling on the bridge after he saw the ghost and watched as the figure faded from sight.

The members of the crew were all thankful when their ship returned to base, although it was under aerial attack. As the captain walked down the gangplank, he was struck and killed by a splinter from a bomb.

The Imperial Navy took the case so seriously that they had the U-65 exorcised by a priest. But, on the next tour of duty, a gunner went mad, the chief engineer broke his leg, and there was a suicide.

On the morning of July 10, 1918, the ship was spotted drifting off the Cape Clear coast of southwest Ireland by an American submarine.

When the submarine's captain looked through his periscope, he was puzzled by a lone figure, standing with arms crossed on the prow of the ship. Then came the shattering explosion, which ripped the U-65 from stem to stern.

Loyal even in death, the second lieutenant had stayed with his comrades to the end.

BATTLE TRAPPED IN TIME?

The women who heard a battle nine years late

Just before dawn on August 19, 1942, Canadian and British troops attacked the German-held port of Dieppe in Normandy, in a large-scale coastal raid. It was an action from which the Allies learned much—but at a terrible cost. Of the 6,086 men engaged (some 5,000 were Canadians), 3,623 were casualties.

Almost nine years later, on August 4, 1951, two English women on vacation near Dieppe were awakened by the sound of gunfire. What happened in the next three hours was like listening to a battle that had become trapped in time. The women heard an uncannily accurate repetition of events of nine years before. Their account of the savage battle for Dieppe was confirmed from military records.

The two women, who were sisters-in-law, were staying at Puys, a seaside village near Dieppe, which had been one of three landing points for the assault.

Below is shown how the two women's description of what happened on August 4, 1951, compares with the official Allied records.

No one else in the area heard anything unusual. Although the women had read accounts of the battle, the British Society for Psychical Research investigated the incident in 1952 and declared that it was satisfied that "the experience must be rated as a genuine psychic experience."

About 4 a.m.—The women hear men's cries "as if above a storm," with distinct sounds of gunfire and dive-bombing steadily becoming louder.	*3:47 a.m.—Allied assault vessels exchanged fire with German ships. Troops manning beach defenses were probably shouting to each other.*
4:50—Abrupt silence.	*4:50—Zero hour for troop landings at Puys, but the operation was running 17 minutes behind schedule, and firing may have stopped at this point.*
5:07—Waves of loud noise—mainly dive-bombers—but some faint cries in the background.	*5:07—Landing craft beached at Puys under heavy fire; then destroyers bombarded Dieppe with shells while aircraft attacked seafront buildings.*
5:40—Silence again.	*5:40—Naval bombardment stopped.*
5:50—Sound of aircraft in large numbers, with fainter background noises.	*5:50—Allied air reinforcements arrived and encountered German aircraft.*
6:00—All noise died away. 6:25—More cries, gradually becoming fainter. 6:55—Uninterrupted silence.	*8:30—Attack repulsed with appalling Canadian casualties. Survivors surrendered.*

SYMBOLS OF DEFEAT. *The burning wrecks of a Canadian landing craft and tank on a Dieppe beach record the disastrous landing in 1942 some two years before the invasion of France. Allied casualties were 59.5 percent.*

LIFE AFTER DEATH? *About 70 years after being declared dead, Dorothy Eady was still living in the ruins of the Egyptian temple built by Seti I for the god Osiris.*

PRIESTESS OF THE NILE

The reincarnation of a little girl who "died" in a fall

On the banks of the Nile near an ancient temple built to the god Osiris by Pharaoh Seti I lives an elderly English-woman. Dorothy Eady, who "died" when she was three years old, is deeply convinced that she has been reborn as an Egyptian priestess.

Dorothy was born in 1903 into a wealthy London family. But in later life she called herself Um Seti, believing herself to be the reincarnation of a woman who served at King Seti's court. Her strange journey into the distant past, which she described in 1973, began when as a child she fell down a stairway and was declared dead by the family doctor. When the doctor returned with a nurse to lay out the body, he found the little girl very much alive and well.

Soon afterward, Dorothy took to hiding under tables and behind furniture. She bewildered her parents with demands to be "taken home." One day the family visited the British Museum, and in the Egyptian galleries Dorothy ran wild.

For no apparent reason she began kissing the feet of statues, clinging to mummy cases, and screaming, in a voice that her mother recalled as sounding "strange and old," that she wanted to be left with "my people."

On another occasion Dorothy was shown a photograph of the temple built by Seti I. She immediately told her father that the temple was her "real" home—a conviction she never lost.

Dorothy claimed that she had known Seti and that he was a kindly man. As her convictions grew, Dorothy began to learn how to read hieroglyphics at the British Museum. She astounded her teacher with her ability to learn the symbols and explained she was not learning a new language, only relearning a language she had forgotten.

In 1930 Dorothy married an Egyptian and went to live in Egypt. They named their only child, a boy, Seti, and Dorothy called herself Um Seti—mother of Seti.

For 20 years she worked as an archeological research assistant. In 1952 she made her first pilgrimage to Abydos, the site of Seti's temple and the tomb of Osiris.

A "homecoming"

She was quite unable to read modern Egyptian, but when her train stopped near a range of limestone hills, she knew she had arrived at the right place. Dorothy described her first sighting of the temple as a "homecoming." In 1954 she returned to Abydos to live out her life. She helped with the upkeep of the temple and prayed daily to Osiris—which made her his sole living devotee.

By 1973 she had even obtained permission from the temple curators that when she died she would be buried in the grounds of the temple she called home.

But belief in reincarnation is by no means unique. Many people at some time have the feeling they have done something or been somewhere in a previous life, but they cannot explain how or when.

In 1956, during a two-hour sitting with Welsh hypnotherapist Arnall Bloxham, a teenage English girl named Ann Ockenden suddenly began talking of a previous life as a man in a land where people were decorated with scars and animal teeth.

Reborn after three centuries

Another of Bloxham's clients claimed she was the daughter of Charles I and Queen Henrietta Maria. Although this anonymous woman had not studied history, she was able to give accurate details of the court of French King Louis XIV, where she and her "brother," Charles II, lived in exile.

Arthur Guirdham, an English psychiatrist, has recorded the story of a woman he calls Mrs. Smith. From her teens Mrs. Smith had recurrent dreams of a former life as the wife of a 13th-century French Cathar preacher. The Cathars were a heretical Christian sect that soon became the subject of much persecution by the Inquisition. History records that most of the Cathar preachers and followers were killed in a massacre. And Mrs. Smith's most fearsome nightmare was that of being burned to death at the stake.

Mrs. Smith knew nothing of the Cathars, but in 1944 she described the clothes they wore. She described them as green or blue robes—which they were.

INNER FIRES

Strange cases of human incendiary bombs

On an October evening in the late 1950's, a pretty 19-year-old secretary, dancing with her boyfriend in a London discotheque, suddenly burst into flames.

As though driven by an inner storm, fire burst furiously from her back and chest, enveloping her head and igniting her hair. In seconds she was a human torch, and before her horrified companion and other people on the floor could

beat out the flames, she died from first-degree burns.

With his burned hands swathed in bandages, her boyfriend testified at the inquest: "I saw no one smoking on the dance floor. There were no candles on the tables, and I did not see her dress catch fire from anything. I know it sounds incredible, but it appeared to me that the flames burst outward, as if they originated within her body." Other witnesses agreed with him, and the mystified coroner's verdict was eventually "death by misadventure, caused by a fire of unknown origin."

Rare, but real

Such terrifying cases of what seems to be spontaneous human combustion are fortunately rare—but they have been reported throughout history. In southeastern England, in the 17th century, an elderly woman was found burned to death in her cottage. But though the heat must have been intense, nothing else in the cottage—not so much as the bedclothes on which she lay—was even scorched.

"No man knoweth what this doth portend," said one observer; he then hinted darkly at divine retribution, though for what he did not say.

More recently, an English building contractor was driving past one of his construction sites and waved through the car window; a moment later he simply burst into flames. Similarly, another Englishman was found totally incinerated in the cab of his truck.

The London *Daily Telegraph* reported: "Police witnesses testified they had found the petrol tank full and unharmed by fire, the doors of the cab opened easily, but the interior was 'a veritable furnace.' The coroner's jury declared they were unable to determine how the accident occurred."

Reynold's News, a few years later, recorded the tragic death of a London man who, while walking along the street, "appeared to explode. His clothes burned fiercely, his hair was burned off, and the rubber-soled boots melted on his feet."

Costly damage

Not always, it appears, are these human incendiary bombs only self-destructive.

The late Prof. Robin Beach, of the Brooklyn (New York) Polytechnic Institute, founder of the electrical consultant agency Robin Beach Engineers Associated, believed that these unfortunate people are inadvertently responsible for fire damage costing millions of dollars each year. One of his clients was an Ohio factory owner whose plant was suddenly bedeviled with as many as eight small fires in one day.

One of Professor Beach's solutions was to persuade each of the factory's employees in turn to step onto a metal plate while holding an electrode; at the same time he took readings from an electrostatic voltmeter.

One of the workers was a young woman recently employed; when she stepped onto the metal plate, the meter showed a tremendous jump. She registered 30,000 volts of electrostatic electricity and a resistance of 500,000 ohms. Wisely, Professor Beach recommended that she be transferred to some part of the factory where she would not come in contact with combustible materials.

The professor, an authority on explosions and static electricity, explained that under certain conditions—walking on carpets during dry winter weather, for example—almost anyone can build up an electrostatic charge of several thousand volts. Hence the shock we sometimes experience when touching a car door or other metal surface. Usually, the electricity is harmlessly discharged through the ends of the hair; however, the professor maintained, there are some people—maybe one in 100,000—whose abnormally dry skin permits them to generate an excessive charge.

Danger to others

People carrying static charges may be highly dangerous. They may, for example, be the detonators that touch off explosions in hospital operating rooms whose atmosphere contains a mixture of anesthetic vapor and air. In 1964 it was estimated that such explosions result annually in approximately 1,000 deaths. The accumulation of static electricity from the clothing of hospital personnel was judged to be a hazardous factor.

In addition, the professor is convinced that workers in ordnance factories and petroleum refineries should be tested to discover whether they have the type of skin that retains electric charges more persistently than others.

He quoted an instance in which a man proved to be a hazard to himself: "In one case I investigated, a driver decided to see if the battery of his car needed filling with water. It was a dry, cold fall day, and the man walked a short distance on a concrete driveway, raised the hood of his car, and unscrewed the caps of the battery. There was an immediate explosion as he touched off the hydrogen gas escaping from the battery of the recently parked car. He was severely injured."

But while Professor Beach's ingenious theories may well account for many mysterious fires and explosions hitherto ascribed to arson or sabotage, a strong element of mystery remains.

Against natural law

Did the unfortunate girl on the dance floor really burst into flames from "within," as her companion testified? Electrical engineers have pointed out that no known form of electrostatic discharge could possibly have such an effect. The fate of the old woman in her cottage, and that of the truck driver, are also in flat contradiction of natural law; both bodies were utterly consumed by fire, yet their inflammable surroundings were completely undamaged by the flames that had engulfed them.

Are there then human beings who possess complex physiological constitutions and who are electrodynamic beings so charged with energy that they may be potential victims of spontaneous combustion—or even human bombs?

THE ELUSIVE BRIDEY MURPHY

A case of reincarnation . . . or a total recall of childhood?

When a Colorado businessman and amateur hypnotist put a local housewife into a trance, it sparked off some startling revelations—and launched a search for a woman who had supposedly died almost a century earlier.

The housewife was called Ruth Simmons (her real name has never been revealed), of Pueblo, Colorado, and, speaking as "Bridey Murphy," in 1952, she told the story of her childhood, marriage, death, and funeral in 19th-century Ireland—and her rebirth in the United States 59 years later.

The hypnotist was Morey Bernstein, who wrote the bestselling book on the case, *The Search for Bridey Murphy*, which was published in 1956.

Bernstein used a technique called hypnotic regression, during which the subject is gradually taken back to childhood. He then attempted to take Ruth back one step further, before birth, and suddenly was astonished to find he was listening to Bridey Murphy.

The rambling tale began in 1806 when Bridey was eight years old and living in a house in Cork. She was the daughter of Duncan Murphy, a lawyer, and his wife Kathleen. At the age of 17 she married lawyer Sean Brian McCarthy and moved to Belfast.

Saw her own funeral

Bridey told of a fall that caused her death—and of watching her own funeral, describing the tombstone and the state of being in life after death. It was, she recalled, a feeling of neither pain nor happiness. Somehow, she was reborn in the United States, although Bridey was not clear how this event had happened.

Ruth Simmons herself was born in the Midwest in 1923, had never been to Ireland, and did not speak with even the slightest hint of an Irish accent.

The "facts" related by Bridey were not fully checked before the publication of Bernstein's book. However, once the book had become a bestseller, almost every detail was checked by reporters who were sent to Ireland to track down the background of this elusive woman.

No official records

It was then that the first doubts about the "reincarnation" began to appear.

Bridey gave her birthday as December 20, 1798, in Cork, and the year of her death as 1864. There was no official record of either event, nor was there any record of a wooden house, called the Meadows, in which she said she lived. Indeed, most houses in Ireland are built of brick or stone.

She pronounced her husband's name as "Seean" but said it could also be "Shawn." Sean is pronounced "Shawn" in Ireland. Brian, which is what Bridey preferred to call her husband, was the middle name of the man to whom Ruth Simmons was married.

But some of the details did tally. For instance, her descriptions of the Antrim coastline were accurate. So, too, was her account of a journey from Belfast to Cork. She said she went to St. Theresa's Church. There is one where she said it was—but it was not built until 1911.

The young Bridey shopped for provisions with a grocer named Farr. It was discovered that such a shop had existed.

Despite the holes in Bridey's story, it was still a remarkably detailed account of life in 19th-century Ireland—information unlikely to have come the way of Ruth Simmons.

The case was studied by psychiatrists and psychologists, who had used hypnosis in treatment for many years.

Many subjects in deep hypnosis are highly suggestible and will act on the slightest hint given to them, seeking to supply the answer they subconsciously believe the hypnotist wishes to hear.

Such hypnosis is largely a matter of releasing relevant details from the brain's incredible store of information. For instance, the subject can speak in a foreign language not used since childhood and in which he would not be able to converse in normal conscious life.

Not telling the truth

A subject can even quote verbatim from a long-forgotten childhood book. However, someone under hypnosis is not automatically telling the truth, even if that person is seeking to give a satisfactory response. Bernstein admitted that, while she was under hypnosis, he did tell Ruth Simmons what he wanted and that it was then that she became Bridey Murphy.

The experts who examined the case of Ruth Simmons came to the conclusion that the best way to arrive at the truth was not to check back to Ireland but to go back to her own childhood and her relationship with her parents.

The book stated that Ruth Simmons was brought up by a Norwegian uncle and his German-Scottish-Irish wife.

True enough, but it did not say that her actual parents were both part-Irish and that she had lived with them until she had reached the age of three.

Scientists are satisfied that anything Bridey Murphy said can be explained as a memory of Ruth's long-forgotten childhood. And they believe that the riddle would be unraveled if Ruth would allow her own infancy to be examined under hypnosis.

GHOST FACES ON THE KITCHEN FLOOR

AN ELDERLY WOMAN and her infant grandchild were sitting in the kitchen of their village home when suddenly the child cried out excitedly. The innocent eyes of the child had seen nothing more than a diverting new game; but it was a "game" that terrified the old woman and developed into a mystery for which scientists, despite every test, have as yet been unable to find any natural explanation.

It happened in the village of Bélmez, not far from the city of Córdoba in southern Spain, on a hot morning in August 1971.

Wider and wider

What the child had seen was a human face that had spontaneously imprinted itself on the pink floor tiles—a face with troubled features, infinitely sad. No recognizable pigment of any kind had formed the image, and when the family tried to rub it out, they were horrified to find that the eyes only opened wider and the expression grew even more sorrowful.

Alarmed and bewildered, the owner of the house tore up the floor and replaced the sinister tiles with concrete. But three weeks later a second face emerged, this time with even more clearly defined features.

The affair had taken a turn far beyond the grasp of the simple village folk, and now the local authorities became involved. They ordered a section of the floor where the faces had appeared to be cut away, and an official inquiry began. Workmen dug the floor up, uncovering the remains of a medieval cemetery.

Meanwhile, a third apparition took place, then a fourth, then a series of faces all together. The kitchen was locked and sealed. Four more faces, including that of a woman, appeared just as mysteriously in another part of the house. But they were the last: The phenomenon melted away as inexplicably as it had begun.

All this time the curious apparitions had attracted many kinds of experts to the house. Even the most cynical of them were unable to prove that the images were the work of a human hand. Their puzzlement was enhanced by the evidence of ultrasensitive microphones planted in the house.

Strange languages

These microphones had recorded sounds not audible to the ear—voices speaking strange languages, agonized moans matching the torment in the eyes of the faces on the floor.

No one yet has come forward with a really satisfying explanation for the Faces of Bélmez. All the experts have been able to suggest is that the house was once the scene of some tragic and terrible incident, perhaps connected with some form of medieval witchcraft.

THE CARBON-COPY SCHOOLMARM

Her "double" caused no end of trouble

People who protest that they cannot be in two places at once might ponder the strange case of Madame Sage. She was a schoolteacher, and her method of overcoming the difficulty was to have a double—or so it was said.

When she was working at a girls' school in Livonia, Russia, in 1845, it was remarked that there appeared to be really *two* Madame Sages. One, for instance, would be sitting facing her class while the other was writing on the blackboard. Two pupils once saw her sitting indoors and at the same time picking flowers outside.

The mysterious duplicates were noted not only by her possibly overimaginative pupils. A friend was reading one day to the schoolmistress, who was in bed with a cold, while a facsimile apparently walked around the room.

After 18 months or so the gossip became too much for the school governors, who demanded to know what was going on. Yes, she told them, it was quite true. She could project an image of herself by willpower. The trick, she had found, was a great aid in maintaining discipline: She could keep an eye on her class when her back was turned.

But the governors were not amused. She was fired—not, she confessed, for the first time.

There is no record of the teacher-in-duplicate's first name. She was always referred to just as Madame Sage—whether because she was a married woman or because she was a "schoolmarm" is not recorded.

A pity: Her husband, if any, could have written a fascinating memoir of his life with the two Madame Sages.

These are just two of the mysterious Faces of Bélmez—the one on the left is probably that of a woman. These and other human faces began to appear on the kitchen-floor tiles of a cottage in Spain in 1971. Despite a most exhaustive scientific inquiry no one has ever been able to supply a completely satisfactory natural explanation.

THE MAN WITH TWO LIVES

Gestures, handwriting, and memories all differed

A man named A. J. Brown rented a store-room on East Main Street in Norris-town, Pennsylvania, at the beginning of February 1887. He lived in the rear half and traded in the front, selling candy, stationery, and several other inexpensive items.

On Sunday, March 13, Brown went to the local Methodist Church, then retired to bed as usual.

At five the next morning he was awakened by what he thought was the sound of a pistol firing. He opened his eyes but could make no sense of his surroundings.

He felt weak, as though he had been drugged, and recognized nothing out of the window of the room.

For some two hours, in mounting distress, he lay and tried to remember how he, Ansel Bourne, came to be in this strange room.

Finally, he opened the door to see the owner of the house, a Mr. Earle.

"Where am I?" he asked his astonished landlord. "You're all right, Mr. Brown," was the reply.

"But my name isn't Brown," said Bourne.

The landlord told him which town he was in, and the date, the 14th.

"Does time run backward here?" he asked. "When I left home, it was the 17th."

"The 17th of what?" asked Earle.

"Of January."

"It's the 14th of March."

Last recollection

Earle called a doctor, and Bourne insisted the last things he remembered were the wagons on Broad Street in Providence, Rhode Island, after he had left a nephew's shop, now two months and several hundred miles away.

The nephew was contacted and came to get him. His family, who had reported him miss-ing, asked him about his strange experience, but he could remember nothing of it. He could not imagine why he, a carpenter, preacher, and farmer, should go into a business he knew nothing about and had no interest in.

Three years later, Prof. William James, of Harvard, heard of the case and examined Bourne. Under hypnosis Bourne said his name was Albert John Brown and detailed his jour-ney to Pennsylvania on January 17, 1887. He remembered setting up a small store a couple of weeks later, but he was confused and remem-bered little clearly about his life before the move to Pennsylvania.

He knew he had suffered in his life and that his wife had died in 1881—as Bourne's wife had. His memory of events after March 13 was clouded.

Facial expressions

Professor James established that the personal-ities of Bourne and Brown were distinct and quite different, each with his own gestures, facial expressions, and handwriting. As hypno-sis progressed, the personality of A. J. Brown faded away, never to return.

It was the second tribulation that Bourne had faced. The first came on October 28, 1857, when he went for a walk near his home in Westerly, Rhode Island, and the idea came into his head that he ought to go to church, al-though he had earlier drifted away from the Baptist Church. But he said to himself he would rather be struck deaf and dumb than go to church.

Struck blind

A few moments later he felt dizzy and sat down by the roadside as, it seemed to him, a powerful hand drew something over his head, face, and body, and all power of sight, hearing, and speech went from him. He was convinced God had granted his wish and blinded him as well.

His sight returned after a day, and on No-vember 11 he had friends carry him into a local chapel, where he proclaimed his conversion. The following Sunday he stood in the middle of the congregation, held up his hands to heaven, and instantly regained his hearing and speech. This experience led to his becoming a preacher—a calling he followed for many years.

After his wife died, when he was in his middle fifties, he resumed his trade as a carpen-ter, began farming, and by 1887 had saved enough to buy some land. He drew $551 from the bank and went to visit his nephew in Providence. How he was transformed to A. J. Brown is not known. But with the $551 he set himself up in business in Norristown.

NOVELS WRITTEN FROM THE GRAVE

The woman whose books were "ghosted"

Mrs. J. H. Curran, of St. Louis, Missouri, was no scholar. She had little knowledge of history, only a slight interest in books, and even less idea of the intricacies of language history.

Yet from her poured a stream of writings that astonished the most eminent academics on both sides of the Atlantic.

Mrs. Curran, despite a dislike for spiritualism and mediums, was persuaded to take part in a seance.

Enter Patience Worth

On July 8, 1913, her hand on the Ouija board traced out the name Patience Worth. From that time onward, Mrs. Curran and Patience Worth —whoever she was—became good and inseparable friends.

Through the writings or speech of Mrs. Curran, when in a trance, Patience Worth first told of her birth in Dorset, England, in the 17th century. She detailed the emigration of her parents to America and her eventual death at the hands of an Indian war party.

Then, in frequent sittings over a number of years, Patience Worth dictated a set of historical novels in a variety of literary styles. They ranged from *The Sorry Tale*, set in the time of Christ, to *Hope Trueblood*, a novel of the 19th century.

Critical acclaim

Hope Trueblood received wide acclaim from the critics. The correspondent of *The Athenaeum*, who was unaware of the way in which the book was written, wrote enthusiastically of "Definite and clear-cut characterization, good dialogue and arresting runs of expression, deep but restrained feeling."

Mrs. Curran could write two or more novels simultaneously as they were "dictated" by Patience Worth. She would write a chapter on one book, then do the same with a totally different subject, and always continue the first book without losing the theme.

Nor was she limited to novels. She could write poems and reply in period prose to various subjects put to her. It was that remarkable knowledge of language and style that led to her most highly acclaimed work, *Telka*, a novel of medieval England, written in the English of the time, which Mrs. Curran had never studied.

The intelligence and wit of Patience Worth continued to astonish psychologists. But to Mrs. Curran she was just a wonderful friend who told fascinating stories of days long ago.

TRAVELER IN TIME. *Mrs. J. H. Curran had seances with a 17th-century girl and produced some remarkable novels.*

HANGED—BECAUSE OF A STRANGER'S DREAM

WHEN SHAUN COTT disappeared from his home in New South Wales during the last century, it was assumed he had joined the gold rush—until a newcomer to the area had a vivid dream that led the police to dig up part of the farm where Cott had worked. They found his body, with his skull battered in. Cott's employer was hanged for the murder—discovered through the dream of a stranger.

THE CROSS CORRESPONDENCES

Did three men make contact from beyond the grave?

Thousands of miles apart, five women, none of whom knew each other, sat down and tried to communicate with the dead. The method they chose was automatic writing, by which the medium, in a state of trance, is apparently able to write down messages from the other world.

At first, the messages each received appeared garbled, often meaningless. But when compared later, the scripts appeared to provide links with three dead men.

All three had been founders of the British Society for Psychical Research: Henry Sidgwick, Frederic Myers, and Edmund Gurney. All were dead by 1901 when three women, completely independent of each other, began their experiments.

In England, Mrs. A. W. Verrall, a classical scholar at Cambridge University, who had known the three men, received fragments of messages purportedly from Myers.

Later, in the United States, Leonora Piper began to receive similar messages signed "Myers." In India, Alice Fleming, a sister of the author Rudyard Kipling, began to receive messages, as did her daughter Helen. Back in England a Mrs. Willett also found herself scribbling down messages from people she had never heard of.

Over the next 30 years some 3,000 messages—which became known as the cross correspondences—were produced, and their contents were carefully investigated and annotated by the society.

A collective consciousness

From the different women there emerged a complex pattern of fragmentary messages, largely based upon classical literature. Apart from Mrs. Verrall none of the others had much knowledge of, nor interest in, the classics.

The dead men, on the other hand, had all been classical scholars.

The scientists, scholars, and businessmen who examined the scripts found in them a sense of purpose that seemed to be the product of a collective conscious mind.

It was considered impossible that the writers had collaborated in such a complex hoax. If there had been any unconscious telepathic communication, it contained a fantastically complicated series of classical cross-references that only Mrs. Verrall was capable of understanding.

In 1903 Mrs. Holland (nee Helen Fleming) produced a script saying that "F" (Frederic Myers) wished to speak to some old friends. The message went on to describe Mrs. Verrall, of whom Mrs. Holland had never heard.

It ended: "It is like entrusting a message on which infinite importance depends, to a sleeping person—get a proof—try for a proof if you feel this is a waste of time without. Send this to Mrs. Verrall, 5 Selwyn Gardens, Cambridge."

Obscure references

Despite Mrs. Holland's ignorance of Mrs. Verrall's existence, the address was correct. Mrs. Holland, in fact, sent the script to the Society for Psychical Research, which then began to link up all the scripts.

Eventually, an American researcher, G. B. Dorr, devised a test. He asked "Myers," through Mrs. Piper, what the word "lethe" meant to him. The responses were so detailed and included such obscure references that only the most dedicated classicist could have discovered their origin and relevance. The answers were well outside Mrs. Piper's experience.

Some time later, in England, the physicist Sir Oliver Lodge, also a psychical researcher, put the same question to Mrs. Willett, who was unaware of the American test. As well as responding with the same classical allusions, her automatic script spelled out "Dorr"—the name of the American investigator.

Mrs. Fleming's scripts in India often contained frustrated and anguished passages, which seemed to indicate the sender's desperate desire to communicate.

Behind frosted glass

Through her "Myers" wrote: "The nearest simile I can find to express the difficulties of sending a message is that I appear to be standing behind a sheet of frosted glass—which blurs sight and deadens sound—dictating feebly to a reluctant and obtuse secretary. A feeling of terrible impotence burdens me."

Later, "Myers" wrote: "Yet another attempt to run the blockade—to strive to get a message through. How can I make you docile enough . . . how can I convince them?"

Mrs. Piper in the United States and Mrs. Willett in England received similar messages.

Mrs. Willett's scripts suggested that she try to make mental conversation with the three men. She developed this technique so that a second person could hold conversations, through her, with Myers, Gurney, and Sidgwick.

Topics of discussion went far beyond Mrs. Willett's normal interests and her intellectual capacity.

"Sidgwick" spoke with Lord Balfour, brother of the Prime Minister, about three conflicting theories on the relation of mind and body. "Gurney" spoke of the origins of the human soul.

Discussion of the scripts continued for many years, and no one has yet been able to explain satisfactorily how the communications came about.

Many theories have been advanced, from the continued existence of personalities beyond death to the notion of a psychic plane in which ideas alone survive, waiting to be picked up by anyone sensitive enough to receive them. But when the women died, their correspondents spoke no more.

A GHOST'S CHANGE OF ADDRESS

For almost a century she mourned her lost love

Rosina Despard was getting ready for bed at her father's house in Cheltenham, Gloucestershire, England. As she undressed, she thought she heard her mother's footsteps near the door.

But when she opened it, the corridor outside was empty. She looked along the passage, and there, standing silently at the head of the stairs, she saw a woman in a long, black dress, holding a handkerchief to her face. After a few seconds the woman descended the stairs, Rosina's candle went out, and she saw no more.

That was in June 1882. During the next seven years the phantom in black was seen quite frequently by various members of the Despard household, who appear to have accepted it almost as one of the family. On one occasion Rosina watched it for half an hour, then, touched by the figure's obvious distress, tried to speak to it. She received no reply, and it vanished, its head pathetically bowed.

Dinner at the Despards could be an unnerving affair, due to the figure's ability of appearing to one or two people in the room while remaining invisible to the others. Sometimes it would suddenly stand between two guests who, oblivious of its presence, would go on gaily chatting. Try as they might, Rosina and her father—to whom the phantom most frequently appeared—were unable to prevent a certain flagging in their own conversations.

All these appearances were carefully recorded by Rosina, who also tried to discover the ghost's identity. The most likely candidate seems to have been Imogen Swinhoe, who had been the mistress of a previous occupant of the house. Expelled by her lover after a quarrel, she had died elsewhere in poverty and misery in 1878.

The appearances seem to have ceased in 1889, possibly after an exorcism requested by Despard. Though the case aroused considerable interest at the time and was carefully investigated by the Society for Psychical Research, lack of further evidence caused it to fade from the public mind until even Cheltenham had forgotten the story.

After 69 years

Then, in 1958, the most extraordinary thing happened. A man living in a home a few houses down the street from the building once owned by the Despards woke up one night to see a woman silhouetted against his bedroom window. She was dressed in late Victorian costume, her head was bowed, and she appeared to be sobbing quietly into a handkerchief held to her face. When the man cried out in alarm, she vanished.

The man had never heard of the ghost and had little interest in the supernatural. This lack was amply compensated during the next few years by the woman in black. Often she would be seen flitting down the staircase or wandering through the rooms, weeping piteously into her handkerchief. Obviously, time had not assuaged her grief; but why she should have changed residences remains a mystery.

DANTE'S GHOST LED THE SEARCH

How the missing parts of The Divine Comedy *were recovered*

When Dante Alighieri died in 1321, parts of the manuscript of his masterpiece, *The Divine Comedy*, were missing. For months his sons, Jacopo and Pietro, unsuccessfully searched the house and all their father's papers.

They had given up hope when Jacopo dreamed he saw his father dressed in white, bathed in ethereal light. He asked the vision if the poem had been completed. Dante nodded and showed Jacopo a secret place in his chamber.

With a lawyer friend of Dante's as a witness, Jacopo went to the place indicated in the dream. There was a small blind fixed to the wall. Lifting it, they found a small window.

Inside were some papers covered with mold. Carefully, they lifted them out, brushed off the mold, read the words of Dante—and *The Divine Comedy* was complete. But for a ghostly vision in a dream, one of the world's greatest poems would have remained unfinished.

14TH-CENTURY GENIUS. *But for his son's dream, Dante's masterpiece would be incomplete.*

MRS. WILMOT CROSSES THE SEA

Apparition seen by a husband and his cabin companion

Bound from Liverpool to New York in 1863, the *City of Limerick* ran into a fierce North Atlantic storm. It raged for more than a week, and at home fears grew for the lives of those on board.

At last the storm began to abate, and Mr. Wilmot, one of the passengers, was able to enjoy a night's sleep. He dreamed that he saw his wife, wearing her nightclothes, entering his stateroom. She hesitated at first when she realized that it was a shared cabin and that another man was staring at her from the bunk set above and slightly back from her husband's. Then she went to her husband's bedside, kissed him, and left quietly.

Wilmot awoke to find the man above staring down at him. The man, a Mr. Tait, was shocked that Wilmot should have had a lady visit him in such a way. He described Mrs. Wilmot's actions as they had occurred in Wilmot's dream.

When Wilmot eventually arrived home, his wife surprised him by asking if he'd had a visit from her the week before. She described how at the height of her anxiety, at four o'clock one morning, she had felt she was going out to find him.

The wife's dream

She had crossed the dark, heaving sea and come to a steamship. Going aboard, she walked down belowdecks at the stern of the ship and found her husband's stateroom.

"Tell me," she asked him, "do they ever have staterooms like the one I saw, where the upper berth extends farther back from the lower one? A man was in the upper berth, looking right at me, and for a moment I was afraid to go in, but soon I went up to the side of your berth, bent down and kissed you, and embraced you, and then went away."

MUSIC FROM THE IMMORTALS

Beethoven and Bach dictated works to a London widow

When Igor Stravinsky appeared to Rosemary Brown 14 months after his death and dictated 60 lines of music, she was not surprised. For he was, she said, the 20th dead composer or author to use her extraordinary talent.

Rosemary was only seven years old when she was introduced to the world of dead musicians. A spirit with long white hair and a flowing black cassock appeared and told her he was a composer and would make her a famous musician one day. Rosemary did not know who he was until, about 10 years later, she saw a picture of Franz Liszt.

Rosemary's mother and grandmother were psychic, and she herself displayed psychic powers at an early age. She told her parents of events before her birth, and when asked how she could know, she replied that her "visitors" had told her.

Liszt, however, was not among them. He did not reappear until 1964, by which time Rosemary had married and brought up two children.

Living in a Victorian terraced house in London, she was now a seemingly unexceptional middle-aged widow.

Before 1964 she had paid little attention to music and had had little instruction in it. After the war she had bought a secondhand piano and taken lessons for a year. But a neighbor, once a church organist, was not impressed. "She could just about struggle through a hymn," he said.

Then in 1964 Liszt renewed contact, and original compositions began flooding in from great musicians of the past. Mrs. Brown transcribed pieces from Beethoven, Bach, Chopin, Schubert, Rachmaninoff, and, of course, Liszt himself.

These included a 40-page Schubert sonata, a Fantaisie Impromptu in three movements by Chopin, 12 songs by Schubert, and 2 sonatas by Beethoven, as well as his 10th and 11th Symphonies, both of them unfinished.

Each composer had his own way of dictating to Mrs. Brown. Liszt controlled her hands for a few bars at a time, and then she wrote down the

THE MELODIES LINGER ON. *Rosemary Brown is shown working on the scores she said were dictated to her by dead composers. Behind her are the opening bars of a piece "sung" to her by Schubert.*

notes. Others, like Chopin, told her the notes and pushed her hands onto the right keys.

Schubert tried to sing his compositions to her, "but he hasn't got a very good voice." Beethoven and Bach simply dictated the notes—a method she disliked since she had no idea of what the finished product would sound like.

They all spoke to Rosemary in English, which did not surprise her. "Why shouldn't they have gone on learning on the other side?" she asked. But when agitated, they were liable to relapse into their native tongues. "*Mein Gott!*" Beethoven exclaimed when they were hard at work and the doorbell rang.

What the critics said

The opinions of musical critics were varied on the merit of Rosemary's transcriptions. But most agreed that in their style they bore a great resemblance to the composers' published works.

Forgeries and imitations have frequently been made in the past, but considerable musical knowledge is required for this. Rosemary's

FRANZ LISZT. *It was Franz Liszt's visit to Rosemary Brown in 1964 that started her transcribing the works of great composers, long since dead.*

musical knowledge was such that she was unable to play many of the pieces dictated to her, although she became more proficient at the piano under instruction from Brahms. He drilled her in finger exercises, while Rachmaninoff and Liszt attended to her style.

Rosemary was thoroughly investigated by musicians and psychologists. None could find any way in which she could be cheating, and all who met her were said to dismiss the idea after only a few minutes.

How she did it

Maurice Barbanell, editor of the London-based *Psychic News*, said: "She appears to be a medium who is both clairvoyant and clairaudient. It is comparable to what hundreds of other mediums have done—the only difference is that you have some famous composers involved."

Other explanations were put forward. One was that composers had left behind them unknown, written music and that Rosemary was able to read these sheets, unwittingly using a form of telepathy.

Another suggestion was that she picked up music from people around her by telepathy. However, she did not spend her time in the company of musicians who might be composing works in the manner of Bach and Brahms.

Of the music itself, Richard Rodney Bennett, the British composer, said: "A lot of people can improvise, but you couldn't fake music like. this without years of training. I couldn't have faked some of the Beethoven myself."

What musicians felt

Hephzibah Menuhin, the concert pianist and sister of Yehudi, was also impressed. She insisted: "There is no question but that she is a very sincere woman. The music is absolutely in the style of these composers."

Alan Rich, the music critic of *New York* magazine, took a different line. Having heard a privately issued record of piano pieces by the spirits of Bach, Beethoven, Chopin, Debussy, Liszt, and Schubert, Rich concluded that they were just substandard reworkings of some of their better known compositions and were not original at all.

However, the record contained only the simpler pieces. Richard Rodney Bennett found other compositions to be subtler and far more complex.

GIRL WHO FETCHED THE DOCTOR

She begged help for her mother—a month after her own death

Dr. S. Weir Mitchell, an eminent 19th-century nerve specialist in Philadelphia, fell asleep in his chair one winter evening after an exhausting day in surgery.

Awakened by the ringing of his doorbell, he found a thin, shivering girl on the doorstep, pulling a threadbare shawl around her shoulders. She begged him to come and treat her mother who, she explained, was desperately ill.

The doctor followed her through the snowy streets to an old tenement, where the girl led him upstairs.

There, the doctor found a sick woman, whom he recognized as a former servant of his household. He diagnosed her condition as pneumonia and sent for the medicines she needed. Mitchell then made the woman as comfortable as he could—and congratulated her on having such a dutiful daughter.

Daughter was dead

To this the old woman looked up with surprise and then said: "My daughter died a month ago. Her shoes and shawl are there in that little cupboard."

The doctor looked and found the same shawl as that which had been draped over the shoulders of the pathetic girl who rang his doorbell. It was folded and dry, and it could not possibly have been worn outdoors that same night.

The girl who had showed him in was nowhere to be found.

THE SHATTERED DREAM OF XANADU

Insensitive behavior of the person from Porlock

Samuel Taylor Coleridge's famous poem "Kubla Khan" has been surrounded by mystery ever since it was first published in 1816, nearly 20 years after the poet had written it and at a time when he was short of money.

Coleridge explained that the 54 lines were a mere fragment of a glorious vision inspired by an opium dream. The dream had been shattered by an interruption, and the rest of the poem had been lost forever.

It came to him while he was staying at a lonely farmhouse, recuperating from an illness. He had taken two grains of opium for medicinal purposes. (He was, in fact, an addict.) On awakening, he began to put down the poem in an ecstasy of inspiration.

When he got to:

For he on honey dew has fed,
And drunk the milk of Paradise,

he was interrupted by an insurance salesman from a nearby town. Desperately, he tried to get rid of the man, but somehow he was detained for an hour, talking mundane finance.

Try as he might, Coleridge could never recapture his vision of the legendary world of Xanadu. All that was left was the first fragment of "Kubla Khan," which for 20 years he did not consider worth publishing.

PARADISE LOST. *Coleridge's drug-induced dream vanished when he was interrupted by an insurance salesman.*

MESSAGE ACROSS THE SEA

A dream that sent a ship on a life-saving mission

The captain of a ship crossing the Atlantic Ocean to Newfoundland in 1828 glanced through the open door of a cabin adjoining his own and saw a man who was standing in the shadows. He had never seen him before.

He was not one of the crew, and no passengers were being carried on that voyage. Certain that he had trapped a stowaway, the captain burst into the cabin; but as he did so, the figure disappeared from sight.

All the evidence that remained was a scrawled message on the cabin wall: "Steer to the northwest."

The captain was considerably shaken but at the same time so impressed by the stranger's message that he altered course according to the scribbled instructions.

After a few hours his vessel came across a foundering ship. The only person aboard was the man whom the captain had encountered in the cabin of his own ship. He said that he had just awakened from a deep sleep during which he had dreamed that he was about to be rescued.

THE NIGHTMARE OF BORODINO

The countess who dreamed that her husband died in battle

As Napoleon's armies advanced into Russia in 1812, the wife of a Russian general, Count Toutschkoff, had a dream. She saw herself in a room at an inn in a town that she did not know.

Into the room came her father, holding her small son by the hand. Sorrowfully, he told her that her husband had been killed by the French. "Your happiness is at an end," he said. "He has fallen. He has fallen at Borodino."

Twice more the dream came to her, and in the end she told her husband. Together they searched maps, but they could not find a mention of Borodino anywhere. On September 7, 1812, however, the retreating Russian armies turned and defied the French—at a village called Borodino. They were defeated.

Countess Toutschkoff and her family stayed at an inn only a few miles from the battlefront, while her husband commanded the reserves. The next morning her father entered the room, holding her small son by the hand.

"He has fallen," he stammered. "He has fallen at Borodino."

PREPARING FOR AN EXPENSIVE BATTLE. *Officers of the French cavalry prepare for the next round in the Battle of Borodino, which was to cost more than 30,000 French and 45,000 Russian lives.*

A VISION OF VICTORY AT SEA

Two weeks before battle a Pope thanked God for success

The treasurer's voice droned on as he went through the accounts of the papal states. Suddenly, Pope Pius V stood up, opened a window, and stared out. After a few moments he relaxed and turned back to his senior Vatican officials with eyes shining.

"Leave all this for now," he said, waving toward the ledgers and financial statements strewn about the table. "We must go and give thanks to God. Victory has gone to the Christian fleet."

The businesslike treasurer made a note of the strange incident in the minutes of the meeting. It happened, he wrote, just before 5 p.m. on October 7, 1571.

Exactly a fortnight later, on October 21, a messenger galloped into Rome from Venice with news of a historic naval victory.

A Christian fleet, under Don John of Austria, had trounced the Turkish fleet at Lepanto. According to the official report, it had become clear that victory was theirs just before 5 p.m. on October 7.

POPE WITH A MESSAGE. *During the battle depicted at the top of this engraving, Pius V prayed for a Christian victory.*

A GHOSTLY WARNING

The ugly man who saved a lord's life

In the 1880's, Lord Dufferin, the British Ambassador in Paris, was vacationing at a friend's country home in Ireland. One night he awoke suddenly, unaccountably startled from a deep sleep.

Getting up and going to the window, Lord Dufferin looked out on the lawn to see, in the moonlight, a hunched figure staggering under the weight of a coffinlike object. Dufferin went outside and called to him: "What have you got there?"

The man lifted his head from beneath his burden, and Lord Dufferin saw a wizened, ugly face that utterly repelled him. When Lord Dufferin asked the man where he was taking the coffin, the figure disappeared.

The next morning he told the experience to his host, who was at a loss to explain the strange apparition.

A few years later, in the 1890's, Lord Dufferin was back in Paris to attend an international diplomatic reception at the Grand Hotel. Just as he and his private secretary were about to enter the elevator, Dufferin recoiled and refused to step inside. The elevator operator was the same ugly little man he had seen before.

The elevator ascended, without Lord Dufferin and his secretary. The Ambassador went to the reception desk to ask who the strange man was.

As the elevator reached the fifth floor, its cable snapped, and with a resounding crash, it plunged to the bottom of the shaft, killing all the occupants.

The accident was reported in the newspapers and recorded by the British Society for Psychical Research, but the Ambassador was unable to discover the identity of the elevator operator who turned out to be his savior. Neither the management of the hotel nor the accident investigators could find any record of the man's name or background.

LITERARY GHOSTS

Did Washington Irving haunt the library?

It is altogether fitting that the literary giant who wrote one of the first American ghost stories should himself be the subject of a ghost story. Washington Irving, who pioneered the American short story by writing about a headless horseman in *The Legend of Sleepy Hollow*, reportedly made a ghostly appearance himself.

As you may recall, Irving's Sleepy Hollow legend describes a ghostly rider who pursues the hapless country bumpkin Ichabod Crane and throws a large, round object at him. Convinced that the object was the horseman's head, the terrified Ichabod fled the scene. The story's conclusion in which the villagers find a smashed pumpkin at the site implies that the whole thing was a prank. Dashing Brom Bones had frightened poor Ichabod in order to discourage him from pursuing the lovely Katrina van Tassel, whom Brom then marries.

The ghost of the story's impish author is said to have appeared in a far less dramatic fashion.

LIBRARY SPIRIT. *Fun-loving author Washington Irving reportedly haunted the library where he wrote one of America's early ghost stories.*

In fact, Washington Irving's first reported appearance as a ghost turned out to be a case of mistaken identity. It happened shortly after the famous author's death in 1859.

Dr. J. G. Cogswell was working alone at New York's Astor Library late one evening when he was startled to see a man reading a book near the shelves in the main gallery. As he was walking over to inquire how the man had entered the locked building, the figure put a book back on the shelf and disappeared. The puzzled Cogswell thought that the browsing ghost resembled his late friend Washington Irving, who had helped to found the Astor Library and often used its facilities.

Some time later Cogswell again saw the same visitor while working late at the library. This time he tiptoed sufficiently close to the ghostly figure to identify it not as Irving but as a doctor friend who had died a few weeks before. When Cogswell reported what he had seen to the library trustees, they advised him to go to the country for a rest.

Shortly thereafter, Irving's nephew, Pierre Irving, visited the Astor Library. He told staff member Frank H. Norton that the ghost of his uncle had appeared at the Irving home, Sunnyside, in Tarrytown, New York.

Pierre said that he and his two daughters were sitting in the front room when an apparition suddenly walked through the parlor and entered the library, where Irving had done his writing. "Why, there's Uncle!" one of the girls exclaimed. They rushed into the library but found the room empty.

Neither Pierre Irving nor Frank Norton speculated on whether Irving's ghost had appeared at his own library in order to complete the writing of an unfinished story. Yet is it not more likely that the ghost would appear at his own library, rather than at the Astor Library?

Appearances by the Astor Library ghost were reported by New York newspapers in the 1860's, and the story of Washington Irving's ghost was recounted by Norton in a letter to *The Nation* magazine in 1911.

Although Irving himself did not believe in ghosts, it is certain that the fun-loving author would have liked the idea of haunting his own library.

THE END OF HMS "VICTORIA." *A photograph, taken from HMS* Collingwood, *shows the* Victoria *sliding bow first beneath the sea. To the left is HMS* Nile, *which rescued survivors.*

THE LAST VOYAGE HOME

He died at sea—yet guests spoke to him in London

At precisely 3:34 p.m. on June 22, 1893, the Royal Navy flagship *Victoria* was rammed and later sank. She went down off the Mediterranean port of Tripoli; many lives were lost, including that of her commander—Admiral Sir George Tryon.

A naval board of inquiry heard that the *Victoria* was rammed by another ship in the same squadron—the *Camperdown*—during a difficult maneuver ordered by Sir George. The maneuver meant that two columns of ships, including the *Victoria* and *Camperdown*, turned inward toward each other. Only when Sir George saw that a collision was imminent did he order the *Victoria* "full astern."

No one knows what made Sir George, an experienced sailor, order such a disastrous maneuver. But as his ship went down, survivors heard him say: "It is all my fault."

At the time of the collision, Lady Tryon was giving a party in her home at Eaton Square in London. Shortly after 3:30, guests saw the unmistakable figure of the admiral stride across the drawing room.

When the guests politely remarked that it was nice that Sir George could be present, Lady Tryon, who had not seen the figure, told them that her husband was with his ship. Some of the guests later claimed to have spoken to the figure and were perfectly certain that he was Sir George.

The admiral was never seen again, and the mystery remains unsolved. Perhaps, knowing that he was about to die, Sir George turned his thoughts to his wife and home, somehow projecting a fleeting image of himself in the drawing room.

ADMIRAL ON THE BRIDGE. *A contemporary engraving shows Admiral Sir George Tryon going down with his ship, HMS* Victoria.

PREMATURE FLIGHT. *It is now thought that the 777-foot R101 was launched too soon. It had not been sufficiently tested when it set off on a nonstop flight to India, which the British government hoped would coincide with a Commonwealth conference on transport.*

MEN WHO FELT THEY WERE DOOMED

The chilling story behind Britain's airship disaster

On October 4, 1930, the pride of British aeronautical engineering, the R101 airship, left England on its maiden, nonstop voyage to India. The weather was not good. As the R101 crossed the channel, it was tossed and buffeted by ever stronger gusts of wind. Visibility was reduced to nil, and the airship, traveling at about 1,000 feet, bucked in unintentional swoops, losing 200 to 300 feet at a time, which the crew regained only with the utmost difficulty. At 2:05 a.m. the following morning the cigar-shaped vessel crashed at the edge of a woods near Beauvais in northern France and burst into flames.

Only six of her crew and passengers, who were all accommodated in a gondolalike compartment slung under the airship's belly, escaped. Forty-eight other people died.

The 5½ million cubic feet of hydrogen that had lifted the 777-foot-long ship contributed to the inferno that sent flames shooting 300 feet into the air.

Forecasts of disaster

The disaster gave rise to much speculation, many inquiries, and eventually an official report. But in addition to these aspects of the tragedy, a more chilling side emerged.

Investigators discovered that five years earlier, while the airship was still in its design stage,

WRECKAGE OF A DREAM. *The pride of British aviation, the R101 had been equipped with all the passenger amenities of an ocean liner. When it crashed in a woods near Beauvais in France, 48 people died, and airship development was interrupted temporarily.*

Sir Sefton Brancker, director of civil aviation, had consulted an astrologer. He had been told that there was nothing to be seen in his life after six years. Together with Lord Thomson, the Secretary of State for Air, Sir Sefton was killed.

They heard how, when one of the riggers who flew in the airship, Walter Radcliffe, left home on the morning of October 4, his young son began to cry: "I haven't got a daddy."

Radcliffe did return home once more that day after checking some of the girders, but he left again to go on the flight and was killed.

The captain's wife knew

When a friend went to the home of the R101's captain, Flight Lieutenant Carmichael "Bird" Irwin, to inform his wife of his death, Mrs. Irwin said: "It's all right. You needn't worry. I know. You see, Bird is Irish, and I'm Scottish. We both knew he wasn't coming back again."

Even stranger was the fact that at the exact time of the crash, the switchboard operator at the Cardington base heard a click on the telephone line connected to Irwin's office. A duty officer went to investigate and found the office empty.

Most puzzling of all, however, was the report of a seance held in London three days after the tragedy. The medium, Eileen Garrett, in a trance, spoke in a man's voice and mentioned the name Irwin.

The voice listed technical defects in the airship that were not known publicly until the following year when the results of the official inquiry were published.

Three weeks later Mrs. Garrett is reported to have received more messages from Irwin and others who died.

One of the voices was said to have been that of Sir Sefton.

THE "UNSINKABLE." *When the liner* Titanic *left Southampton on her maiden voyage in 1912, a novel and a short story had both foretold her fate with uncanny accuracy. But the tragedy helped to save a later ship—a tramp steamer bound for Canada from England in 1935.*

THE FICTION THAT CAME TRUE

Strange case of the two Titanics

A floating palace sailed from Southampton in 1898 on her maiden voyage. It was the biggest and grandest liner ever built, and rich passengers savored its luxury as they journeyed to the United States. But the ship never reached its destination: Its hull was ripped open by an iceberg, and it sank with heavy loss of life.

That liner existed only on paper, in the imagination of a novelist named Morgan Robertson. The name he gave to his fictional ship was *Titan,* and the book's title was *Futility.*

Both the fiction and the futility were to turn into terrifying fact. Fourteen years later a real luxury liner set out on a similar maiden voyage. It too was laden with rich passengers. It too rammed an iceberg and sank; and, as in Robertson's novel, the loss of life was fearful because there were not enough lifeboats. It was the night of April 14, 1912. The ship was the RMS *Titanic.*

Passenger's preview of doom

In many other ways than the similarity of their names the *Titan* of Robertson's novel was a near duplicate of the real *Titanic.* They were roughly the same size, had the same speed and

the same carrying capacity of about 3,000 people. Both were "unsinkable." And both sank in exactly the same spot in the North Atlantic.

But the strange coincidences do not end there. The famous journalist W. T. Stead published, in 1892, a short story that proved to be a preview of the *Titanic* disaster. Stead was a Spiritualist: He was also one of the 1,513 people who died when the *Titanic* went down.

Backward recollection

Neither Robertson's horror novel nor Stead's prophetic story served as a warning to the *Titanic*'s captain in 1912. But a recollection of that appalling tragedy did save another ship in similar circumstances 23 years later.

A young seaman named William Reeves was standing watch in the bow of a tramp steamer, Canada-bound from England in 1935. It was April—the month of the iceberg disasters, real and fictional—and young Reeves had brooded deeply on them. His watch was due to end at midnight. This, he knew, was the time the *Titanic* had hit the iceberg. Then, as now, the sea had been calm.

These thoughts took shape and swelled into omens in the seaman's mind as he stood his

EYEWITNESS. *As the* Titanic *sank, these sketches were made from an overturned lifeboat by John B. Thayer. No other survivor spoke of the ship breaking in half, however. Having torn a 300-foot gash in her side, she went down in 2 hours and 40 minutes, taking 1,513 people with her.*

lonely watch. His tired, bloodshot eyes strained ahead for any sign of danger, but there was nothing to be seen; nothing but a horizonless, impenetrable gloom. He was scared to shout an alarm, fearing his shipmates' ridicule. But he also was scared not to do so.

Then, suddenly, he remembered the exact date of the *Titanic* accident—April 14, 1912. The coincidence was terrifying—it was the day he had been born. He shouted out a danger

warning, and the helmsman rang the signal: engines full astern. The ship churned to a halt—just yards from a huge iceberg that towered menacingly out of the night.

More deadly icebergs crowded in around the tramp steamer, and it took nine days for ice-breakers from Newfoundland to smash a way clear.

The name of the ship that nearly shared the *Titanic*'s fate was, ironically, the *Titanian*.

CROSSWORD STARTED A SPY SCARE

Clues led to vital secrets of D-day invasion

Solutions to the popular crossword puzzle in the *Daily Telegraph* gave a headache to security officers who were responsible for guarding the secrets of the planned Allied invasion of Europe in June 1944.

Members of MI-5, Britain's counterespionage service, noticed that some of the clues appeared to give away code names invented to cloak the mightiest seaborne attack of all time.

The answer to the clue "one of the U.S." turned out to be, for instance, "Utah," and another, "Omaha"—beaches on which the American armies were to land. Another answer was "mulberry," the floating harbors that would accommodate supply ships. "Neptune" was the naval support. Most suspicious of all,

there was a clue about "some bigwig" that produced the answer "overlord," the code word for the entire operation.

MI-5 was in a flap. Was the *Telegraph* crossword being used to tip off the Germans? Two officers were sent to Leatherhead, in Surrey, to find out. There they interviewed the compiler of the puzzles, Leonard Dawe, a teacher.

Why, they demanded, had he chosen these five words for his solutions? Why not? replied Dawe. Was there any law against choosing whatever words he liked?

Dawe's patent honesty convinced MI-5. He had no knowledge of the coming invasion.

His crossword solutions were just another of life's astonishing coincidences.

407

LINCOLN'S DREAM

The President foresaw his own death

People who claim their dreams come true are seldom taken seriously. Even President Abraham Lincoln, when he experienced precognition in 1865, was not immediately believed by his associates.

Lincoln recounted his dream to a close friend, Ward Hill Lamon, who wrote down the President's words that same evening.

"About ten days ago I retired very late. . . . I soon began to dream. There seemed to be a deathlike stillness about me. Then I heard subdued sobs, as if a number of people were weeping. I thought I left my bed and wandered downstairs.

"There, the silence was broken by the same pitiful sobbing, but the mourners were invisible. I went from room to room. No living person was in sight, but the same mournful sounds of distress met me as I passed along. . . . I was puzzled and alarmed. . . . Determined to find the cause of a state of things so mysterious and so shocking, I kept on until I arrived at the East Room. . . . There I met a sickening surprise. Before me was a catafalque, on which rested a corpse wrapped in funeral vestments. Around it were stationed soldiers who were acting as guards; and there was a throng of people, some gazing mournfully upon the corpse, whose face was covered, others weeping pitifully.

" 'Who is dead in the White House?' I demanded of one of the soldiers. 'The President,' was his answer. 'He was killed by an assassin.' "

A few days after that account, on April 14, Lincoln was shot by John Wilkes Booth at Ford's Theater in Washington. His body was taken to lie in state in the East Room of the White House.

DEATHS OF THE PRESIDENTS

How fate linked the destinies of Lincoln and Kennedy

The assassinations of Presidents Abraham Lincoln and John Fitzgerald Kennedy are linked together by an amazing series of coincidences.

Abraham Lincoln was first elected to Congress in 1846. John Kennedy followed exactly 100 years later.

Lincoln was elected as the 16th President of the United States on November 6, 1860. Kennedy was elected to be the Republic's 35th President on November 8, 1960.

After their deaths they were both succeeded by southerners named Johnson. Andrew Johnson was born in 1808, and Lyndon Johnson in 1908.

John Wilkes Booth, the man who killed Lincoln, was born in 1838, while Lee Harvey Oswald, Kennedy's killer, was born 101 years later. Both men were southerners, and both were themselves shot before they could come to trial.

Booth committed his crime in a theater and then ran to a barn. Oswald pulled the trigger on Kennedy from the window of a warehouse—and ran to a theater.

Both had forebodings

On the day he was assassinated, Lincoln told a guard, William H. Crook: "I believe there are men who want to take my life. . . . And I have no doubt they will do it. . . . If it is to be done, it is impossible to prevent it."

And Kennedy unsuspectingly told his wife, Jackie, and his personal adviser Ken O'Donnell: "If somebody wants to shoot me from a window with a rifle, nobody can stop it, so why worry about it?"

He happened to say this on November 22, 1963. Kennedy was shot a few hours after making this statement.

Lincoln and Kennedy were both historic civil rights campaigners, and both were shot on a Friday, in the back of the head. Their wives were with them.

Lincoln was shot in Ford's Theater. Kennedy was shot in an automobile made by the Ford Motor Company—a Lincoln.

One final, unhappy coincidence is that Kennedy had a secretary named Evelyn Lincoln, who reportedly advised him against going to Dallas.

THE WITCH DOCTOR'S CURSE

When a judge was sentenced in his own court

Witchcraft and magic still play a significant part in the lives of many tribal Africans, even some of those who have now settled in urban communities. They still believe that a curse, particularly a death curse, can be broken only by the invocation of stronger spirits and the help of an even stronger witch doctor.

Anthropologists insist that the curse merely creates a death wish that the victim fulfills. However, there are instances in which white people, who are not usually psychologically affected by witchcraft or magic, have been the victims of such curses.

There have been two spectacular cases in Rhodesia in the last 33 years.

Witch doctor's medicine

A witch doctor appeared before the Salisbury High Court in 1949 and was imprisoned for two years for illegally practicing his craft. The old man simply shrugged his shoulders, fatalistically accepting his punishment. But he burst into a furious temper when the judge ordered that all his charms and medicines should be destroyed.

He screamed a curse that lions would return to the streets of the city. By 1949 Salisbury was an established, modern, sophisticated city, and lions had not been seen in its streets for 50 years.

However, three weeks later a pride of lions, an adult male and female and three almost fully grown cubs, strolled nonchalantly across a street just two miles from the city center.

Pets slaughtered

A few days later they attacked a tame goat in the garden of a house one mile away, under the horrified gaze of the family on the veranda.

The chain of events went on, with dogs and cattle being slaughtered. A hunt was launched; poison was put down—all without success. After a week of siege, the lions moved away and were next seen in Mazoe, 16 miles away, causing havoc at a gold mine.

The lions made two kills at a farm, in spite of two hunters who sat up all night waiting for them. All the hunters bagged that night was a pedigreed bull that had wandered over to investigate the bleats of a goat staked out as lion bait.

After this the lions were never seen again.

Seven years before, Adrian Brooks had an encounter with witchcraft. He was an enthusiastic young man who had been assigned to the Government Administrative Office at Kasama in Northern Rhodesia (now Zambia).

Superstitious tribesmen

This was the small administrative headquarters of the deeply superstitious Wemba tribe. For the tribesmen a spirit lurks behind every tree, and there is an occult reason for even the most everyday happening.

Brooks was district officer at Kasama and quickly settled into the routine. He was a keen amateur photographer and spent his free time looking for unusual subjects, pictures of which he might be able to sell to magazines and newspapers.

After three months he learned from a tribesman of the Wembas' sacred burial ground of the paramount chiefs. It was located in a secret place, which had never been visited by a white man.

The burial ritual has been handed down over the centuries. The chief's body is placed in a royal hut and watched over until the flesh has rotted from the bones. The skeleton is then buried in a sitting position, with its hand sticking out of the ground, held upright by a forked stick, so that passersby can shake hands with the dead chief.

Deadly picture

The sacred grove is guarded by two elderly witch doctors. In spite of their vehement protests, Brooks walked in and started taking photographs with an air of nonchalance that further angered the guardians of the grove. When he left, they warned him that he had angered the spirits and would soon be dead.

Brooks was not at all worried, and when he got back to Kasama, he joked about the curse with a macabre relish.

Three days later he was standing outside his office building when the flagpole crashed down and killed him.

The official report stated that termites had been eating the base of the pole, and it had fallen just as Brooks paused below it.

THE MOST HAUNTED HOUSE? *For the better part of a century, Borley Rectory, Essex, England, was allegedly bedeviled by a phantom nun, a headless coachman, and showers of stones that came from nowhere.*

ENGLAND'S MOST HAUNTED HOUSE

Monastic chants, strange scribbling, and a slap on the face

Borley Rectory was a damp, rambling Victorian building on the north bank of the Stour River in Essex. It was the most haunted house in England.

For more than a century there were sightings of phantom coaches, a nun, and a headless man. There were poltergeists throwing things about, mysterious footsteps, objects appearing and disappearing, bells ringing, writing on walls, and, from the Borley church nearby, weird monastic chantings and organ music.

WALL MESSAGES. *The first may mean "Marianne get help. (To die unrep) entant bothers me." The capitals are Mrs. Foyster's replies.*

The rectory was built in 1863 for the Rev. Henry Dawson Ellis Bull, on the reputed site of a medieval monastery. As soon as he, his wife, and their 14 children moved in, the happenings started. Footsteps and taps were heard in the night. Bells rang, and voices whispered.

One daughter was awakened by a slap in the face; another saw the dark figure of an old man in a tall hat by her bed. One frequent visitor saw a nun several times. No one was harmed, but the experiences were unnerving.

The vicar's son, Harry Bull, took over the rectory in 1892 and stayed until 1927. In that period a headless man was seen in the bushes; a phantom coach appeared; a cook reported that a locked door was open every morning; and four of Bull's sisters together saw a young nun who disappeared without a trace.

In 1929 poltergeists, the mischievous spirits that toss things about, were recorded at Borley for the first time. Among the objects that appeared inexplicably were pebbles, keys, and medals, one with the head of St. Ignatius engraved on it and the word "Roma" beneath a design of two human figures.

Between 1930 and 1935 the rectory was in the hands of the Rev. Lionel Algernon Foyster, his wife Marianne, and their daughter Adelaide. Messages were scribbled on walls and scraps of paper; footsteps were heard. A voice called out Marianne's name, and an invisible assailant attacked her, the first recorded time that someone was harmed. There were also strange smells, especially of lavender. Many of the scribblings on the wall were illegible, but one appeared to say "Marianne get help."

Edwin Whitehouse, who later became a Benedictine monk, visited the rectory with his aunt and uncle during 1931. On one occasion a fire started in the baseboard of an unused room. As the flames were put out, a flint the size of a hen's egg fell to the floor. Later, while the vicar conducted a service of exorcism in his room, Edwin and his aunt were hit by falling stones.

The experts move in

In 1937 Harry Price, founder of Britain's National Laboratory of Psychical Research, advertised in *The Times* for people of leisure and intelligence who were intrepid, critical, and unbiased, to join a group of observers. From more than 200 people who applied, he chose 40.

Ellice Howe, an Oxford graduate, saw objects move. Others reported unexplained noises. Comdr. A. B. Campbell, of the BBC "Brains Trust" team, was hit by a piece of soap in a sealed room. Dr. C. E. M. Joad, the philosopher, another member of the team, reported that a thermometer recorded a sudden and inexplicable drop of 10 degrees.

The rectory was damaged by fire in 1939. On the night of the fire, two mysterious figures were seen leaving the building—although the only person known to have been in it was the new owner, a Captain Gregson. Several people saw the figure of a young girl at an upstairs window.

But still the phenomena continued. A chauffeur, Herbert Mayes, heard the thunder of hooves approach and pass him close to the rectory when there was nothing to be seen.

During the wartime blackout air-raid wardens were summoned many times to deal with lights seen in the windows.

In 1943 the site was excavated. At a depth of three or four feet, workers found fragments of a woman's skull and pendants bearing religious symbols.

As late as 1961 torches, car headlights, and camera flashes all failed during an investigation of the site.

Other researchers into Borley Rectory have learned at seances that, in the 17th century, a young French nun, Marie Lairre, was induced to leave her convent at Le Havre to marry one of the Waldegraves of Borley, a landed family. They were told that she was strangled by her fiance on May 17, 1667, in a building standing on the rectory site.

Her body, according to the spirit messages, was buried in the cellar.

ODD BEHAVIOR OF POLTERGEISTS
Why should they prefer the company of youngsters?

A curious conclusion has been reached by researchers investigating poltergeists, the spirits that traditionally cause "bumps in the night." It seems that they prefer to operate when young children or teenagers are present.

Their name is a combination of the German words *Polter* ("noise or racket") and *Geist* ("spirit"). They are reputed to send objects flying across rooms, shatter pottery, and make weird noises after dark.

In November 1967 a German lawyer, Herr Adam, was practicing in the Bavarian town of Rosenheim, when all sorts of inexplicable happenings occurred.

Herr Adam was a respected member of the community with little knowledge of the super-

natural. Suddenly, light bulbs in his office began to shatter, lampshades fell off, and all four telephone lines rang without reason.

Baffled, he called in technical experts who installed a recording device to check the electricity supply. At times it showed such surges in the current that the needle ripped the graph paper—but not once did the power overload blow a fuse.

So Herr Adam had recourse to Prof. Hans Bender, an expert in parapsychology, specializing in telepathy, clairvoyance, and extrasensory perception. Bender set traps to see if the incidents were the work of a hoaxer, but all proved negative.

After interviewing all available witnesses, he suggested that the events might have been connected with poltergeists, and attention focused on Herr Adam's clerk, a 19-year-old girl named Anne-Marie. A check on dates showed that the events began about the same time that Anne-Marie began working in the office. They stopped while she was away briefly and resumed upon her return. When Herr Adam, with this knowledge, said to her, "Now all we need is for the pictures on the wall to move," the pictures indeed did just that.

Anne-Marie was tested by doctors and psychologists who found nothing unusual. Attempts to induce psychokinesis, the ability to move objects by concentration, all proved futile. All that is known for certain is that the events ceased when Anne-Marie left the office and took another job. It was reported that the disruptions continued at her next office but only in a minor way.

Another poltergeist case began on February 3, 1958, in the house of James Herrmann, in Seaford, New York, near New York City. There were two children in the Herrmann family—Lucille, aged 13, and James, 12.

Holy water spilled

The phenomena began when a bottle of holy water with a screw cap became unstoppered and the contents spilled out on a bedroom floor. In the bathroom a similarly capped bottle of shampoo also spilled, as did a bottle of medicine and other bottles in the kitchen and basement.

While brushing his teeth in the bathroom, Herrmann clearly saw a bottle of medicine slide 18 inches across a level ledge and smash into the basin. No human hand had been near the bottle, and there was nothing in the bathroom that could have propelled it.

Something weird

A skeptical but polite police officer, James Hughes, was called to the house, and he interviewed the family. While he sat with them in the living room, more bottles began to pop their caps. Hughes returned to his police station with the report that "something weird" was happening at the Herrmanns', and a detective, Joseph Tozzi, joined the case.

Even today, says Tozzi, he does not believe in the supernatural, but he can offer no explanation for what he saw.

On one occasion he was at the house when a porcelain figure flew across the dining room and smashed against a desk.

The strain proved too much for the Herrmanns, and they went to stay with relatives, taking the two children with them. Nothing happened while they were away, but on the night of their return a glass bowl flew into the air and smashed.

Neither the Rosenheim nor the Seaford events can be explained. They are just part of the unfathomable that makes human lives more fascinating.

COFFINS THAT KEPT MOVING

The tomb mystery scared Barbados 150 years ago

In the 18th century the Walronds, a wealthy family of planters, built a rock-hewn tomb at Christ Church, Barbados. It was sealed with a massive marble door, making it more a fortress than a tomb.

One family member to be interred there was Thomasina Goddard, in 1807. A year later the vault was taken over by the Chase family—also slave-owning planters—who used it to bury two daughters in 1808 and 1812.

When the tomb was opened again in 1812 to receive the body of their father, Thomas Chase, the girls' lead coffins had been stood on end upside down. There was no sign of a break-in.

Nor was there in 1816, when the tomb was again opened for the body of a male relative.

But the Chase coffins had again been wildly disarranged.

That of Thomas, which had taken eight men to carry, was leaning upright against a wall of the vault.

By the time of the next funeral, eight weeks later, word of the strange tomb had spread, and a huge crowd turned up for the ceremony. They were not disappointed. Although the tomb was sealed, the four Chase coffins inside were once more in disarray.

The Governor of Barbados, Lord Combermere, stepped in. In 1819 he supervised the orderly restacking of the coffins and had seals put around the door slab. The following year, after reports of noises, he revisited the site.

NO PEACE FOR THE DEAD. *On the several occasions that this tomb in Barbados was opened to put in another coffin, those already inside had been disturbed. The cause remains a mystery.*

His seals were intact. But the lead coffins were in their customary jumbled confusion. Only the crumbling, wooden coffin of Mrs. Goddard still lay peacefully in its corner.

No explanation seemed to fit the case. Negro slaves could not have moved the coffins in revenge without leaving some trace. There was no indication of flooding. And earthquakes would hardly have shaken one tomb without disturbing others in the surrounding area.

Sir Arthur Conan Doyle, creator of Sherlock Holmes, suggested that supernatural forces had moved the coffins to protest their lead construction, which prevented the speedy decay of the bodies inside. He thought these forces might have been strengthened by the fact that Thomas Chase and one of his daughters had committed suicide.

Whatever the reason, the moving coffins caused such concern that the tomb was immediately emptied of all its occupants.

It remains empty to this day, except for the litter, blown in by the wind through the gaps in the bars of the door.

URI GELLER'S PERPLEXING POWER

Spoons bent under the forces of his will?

Uri Geller, a soft-spoken Israeli, caused a stir in the scientific world of the 1970's by what appeared to be remarkable mental powers.

He seemed to bend a variety of metal objects, including forks, spoons, and keys, by just stroking them or on occasion merely concentrating on them. He apparently made watches stop or go, caused the watch hands to bend or twist, and sometimes break off completely, by nothing more than passing his hands over them.

Geller, who became a household word in his native country, the United States, and Great Britain, could not explain his "powers." He said: "I just feel it must come from some external source. . . . Perhaps everybody has got this within them, but it requires a certain power

to trigger it off. I am sure, though, the power must come from an intelligent form of energy."

He was born in Tel Aviv in 1946, and even at the age of three he knew he could "do things," including reading people's minds. In 1969 he demonstrated his powers before an audience at school.

After this first public performance he was asked to appear all over Israel. Some of his critics said he was no more than a brilliant conjurer, but even the most skeptical had to admit that he could perform the most astounding and amazing feats.

In Germany, in 1972, he snapped the handles off spoons and left knives and forks slowly bending as he walked away. Watches stopped, started, and broke in his presence, and keys

413

bent. Even more impressive, he drove a car while he was blindfolded, through the crowded streets of Munich. Geller's fame spread.

At the instigation of Andrija Puharich, a physician and research scientist, Geller went to the United States to demonstrate his abilities under scientific observation.

Scientists mystified

In late 1972 and again in 1973 the Stanford Research Institute in Menlo Park, California, conducted various experiments to test Geller. He was asked to pick out from 10 small metal cylinders the one that contained a metal ball. Concentrating and passing his hands over them, he picked out the correct cylinder. Geller was also asked to duplicate drawings hidden from view. In one case he drew a cluster of round shapes—the test picture showed a bunch of grapes, and he had drawn the same number of round objects as there were grapes in the picture.

In tests of telepathic power and clairvoyance Geller seemed to do quite well. But scientists were even more interested in his apparent demonstrations of psychokinesis—the power of the mind to move or bend physical objects. But at Stanford Geller failed to achieve any such feat that could be absolutely authenticated.

Geller, who objected to the monitoring devices at Stanford, said that he was interested in performing to "sympathetic" audiences. He claimed he needed the energy of others to generate his mental forces efficiently.

Influence on TV

That energy must have been forthcoming the night Geller appeared on British television in 1973. For after performing his feats before scientists and a studio audience, hundreds of people phoned to say that metal objects in their homes had bent and broken while Geller was on TV, and that old, stopped watches had started ticking!

Physicist John Taylor, professor at King's College in London, became one of Uri's supporters and declared that Geller "appears to have posed a serious challenge for modern scientists."

But the famous magician, "The Amazing (James) Randi," called Geller a fake and pointed out that things became "Gellerized" only when the attention of the audience was distracted.

Taylor and E. Balanovski conducted a three-year investigation of various "paranormal" phenomena, including psychokinesis, believing that if it occurred, it must be by electromagnetic emanation (EM). But not even a trace of abnormal EM radiation was detected by the sensors attached to their subjects. In November 1978 the two scientists reported that the bending of metal by mind power and other such feats were scientifically impossible.

It has been reported that Geller uses a confederate for some of his telepathic feats, that he treats cutlery sometimes with corrosive chemicals, that he switches items by sleight of hand, and that he uses gimmicks. He has been found using a palmed magnet to alter the time on a watch. It has also been observed that he is a master at the "psychological misdirection" of his audience.

Geller may be part fraud, but is he all fraud? Only three months after the Taylor-Balanovski report, physicist Helmut Schmidt startled the American Physical Society with his own qualified conclusion that there *is* statistical evidence for psychokinesis.

SURGEON WITH A KITCHEN KNIFE

Brazil's country bumpkin who healed tens of thousands

The surgeon was an illiterate Brazilian peasant. His only surgical instrument was an old kitchen knife. The operation, for the removal of a cataract from an eye, was painless and completely successful. It was another miracle cure performed by Zé Arigó—"Joe From-the-Sticks."

Born in the Brazilian town of Congonhas do Campo, in the state of Minas Gerais, Zé was one of a family of 10 children. His real name was José Pedro de Freitas, but he was nicknamed Arigó because he never lost his peasant accent and rough, country-bumpkin manners.

Bitter poverty

In his boyhood Zé knew the taste of poverty—made more bitter by the knowledge that the family had seen better days; his grandfather had been a prosperous landowner and mine-owner, but the family business went to pieces after his father inherited his share of the family fortune.

"I used to sleep on piles of banana leaves or against the leather of a packsaddle," Zé Arigó once told a reporter. "But that was when the pumas weren't nosing about; for then I used to sleep in the forks of trees, with my arms round the trunk just like a monkey, and trembling with fear.

"I looked after cattle, led a troop of donkeys or an oxcart. I only left my father's house to get married. I was 21, and all I had in this world was a cheap three-piece striped suit."

But he did have a mystical talent that became more evident as he grew older. At first, his nights were tortured by a mysterious voice and strange visions of a man in a medical gown, wreathed in mist, consulting other doctors and carrying out interminable operations.

Eventually, in 1955, the spirit announced itself as "Dr. Fritz," a German surgeon who died in the First World War. From that moment Zé was transformed into a great healer.

Every day up to 1,500 people would flock to his office, a small room with a rough table and chair. They came from all parts of Brazil looking for miraculous cures—and Zé provided them. The blind regained their sight; the lame threw away their crutches.

Doctors baffled

Thousands were treated, and not one died or had his or her condition worsened because of Zé's ministrations. Doctors from Rio de Janeiro, São Paulo University, and Minas Gerais Medical Academy watched him at work. They were baffled by his methods, but all agreed that they were successful.

Zé's routine never varied. Rising at 6 a.m., he would go to the Jesus of Nazareth Spiritualist Center, where his patients awaited him. He would ask them to leave the waiting room for a few moments.

When they returned, they found the country bumpkin turned into a professional man. He would then explain that he performed as agent for the spirit of Adolpho Fritz and that he himself was not the healer.

All he asked his patients was their name and address. He did not inquire about their symptoms—indeed, he stopped them if they started to elaborate on what was troubling them. "I know that already," he would say. He was invariably right.

One of God's remedies

On one occasion when a journalist, Rosinha Sarda, was present, a young man came to him. Zé told him: "I am not going to prescribe any human remedies. Your own doctor has already done so. Instead, I am going to give you one of God's remedies."

He wrote on his prescription pad: "Every day on waking and at six in the evening, pray. On going to bed, read a chapter of the Bible." When the young man had gone, he said: "He has not long for this world. He has advanced cancer and does not know it." Rosinha Sarda checked soon after and found the young man had died.

Twice Zé was prosecuted by the local medical association and found guilty of being a "charlatan," but no one was able to show he was guilty of anything other than practicing medicine without a license.

After the first conviction he was pardoned; the second time he served eight months in prison.

Not a single patient out of all the thousands he had treated would go into the witness box against him.

They and other well-wishers sent him a total of $840,000, but he sent it all back—"Dr. Fritz" would never accept a fee.

Zé Arigó was killed in a car accident on January 11, 1971, on his way to his property, where he loved to tend his roses. Two weeks before the accident he had said: "I am afraid that my mission on earth is finished. I will leave soon."

MAKING A DEADLY POINT

MANY AUSTRALIAN aborigines still believe that they can kill an enemy by pointing a human or kangaroo bone at him, while singing a death chant. They think that this will implant an invisible splinter of bone in the victim's body, although he might be far away. Often the enemy dies from sheer terror. His only hope is that a magician will go through the motions of removing the invisible bone.

Dismissed as travelers' tales—but were they true?

Legendary
lands and beasts

.

THE LETTUCE-EATING DRAGON

An image that varied between East and West

In the West the dragon—spiky-tailed, scaly, and breathing fire—represents evil. But in Far Eastern philosophy dragons were largely benevolent creatures, though they also symbolized rain, mist, and wind.

Every river and stream in Korea had its own dragon. In northern and central China dragons were rain gods, moistening the rice paddies and forming clouds with their breath. Two fought in a pool in Liang, in 503 B.C., and spat out fog that blanketed the entire landscape.

From ancient times floods, tempests, and thunderstorms were supposedly caused by dragons fighting in the air or on the rivers. Beauti-ful pebbles lying by mountain brooks were thought of as dragons' eggs, which split open in thunderstorms, releasing the young into the sky. Dragons raised whirlwinds on land and waterspouts at sea. As they left their smoking burrows in the ground and climbed through the air, the pressure of their feet on the clouds brought rain.

Chinese dragons came in different colors: black for destruction and the thunder dragon of the imperial household, yellow for luck, and azure to announce the birth of great men. (On the night Confucius was born, two azure drag-ons came to his mother's house.)

SCALE DRAWING. *This tapestry from a Polish castle is a fine example of the Renaissance conception of a dragon. In the West all dragons were bad; in the East a good dragon could be man's best friend.*

They could also change their shapes. They could glow in the dark, become invisible at will, shrivel to the size of caterpillars, or expand until the skies and the land were blotted out. They rested at the bottom of the sea in pearl palaces and spoke in pleasant voices like tinkling copper trinkets.

Dragon bones, a popular feature of Chinese traditional medicine, were almost certainly fossils of prehistoric animals, and most pharmacies stocked them in ground or powdered form.

Sparring partners for heroes

In the West man-eating dragons often guarded treasure at the bottom of the sea or underground. They flew at night, spitting fire or poison, as a warning of war or other disasters.

The story of the dragon slayer has many gory variations. The crowning achievement of nearly every ancient hero—Siegfried, Beowulf, St. George, St. Michael, Tristan, and Merlin—was to kill a wicked dragon.

Legends abounded. Blacksmith John Smith fed milk to one greedy monster in England. It drank the milk and lay down in the sun with its scales ruffled up—and the burly blacksmith cut off its head.

Nearby, a dragon slayer fed his enemy a poisoned pudding so big it had to be transported on a cart. The dragon gulped it down—cart, horses, pudding, and all.

In most of the legends dragons dine off maidens, but the early-17th-century writer Edward Topsell, in his *History of Foure-Footed Beastes,* gives them a more wholesome diet: "They greatlie preserve their health (as Aristotle affirmeth) by eating of wild Lettice, for that they make them to vomit, and cast fooreth of theyr stomacke whatsoever meate offendeth them, and they are most speciallie offended by eating Apples, for theyr bodies are much subject to be filled with winde, and therefore they never eate Apples, but first they eate wild Lettice."

Alarming as they seemed to be, there were friendly dragons. The Roman writer Pliny the Elder mentions a man named Thoas of Arcadia, who was saved from a robbers' attack by his pet dragon.

Dragon legends were common to so many lands that the question arises: What were they? Artists' impressions are extraordinarily close to science's careful reconstruction of dinosaurs.

A remarkable guess

Dinosaurs vanished from the earth 70 million years ago, and man's immediate ancestors did not appear until a few million years ago. So the dragon legends cannot be a folk memory of the time when monsters ruled the planet. The likeliest origin of the legend is that ancient man, coming across the fossilized bones of dinosaurs, decided that they must belong to some gigantic, terrifying, lizardlike creature. The remarkable thing is how close to the truth they were.

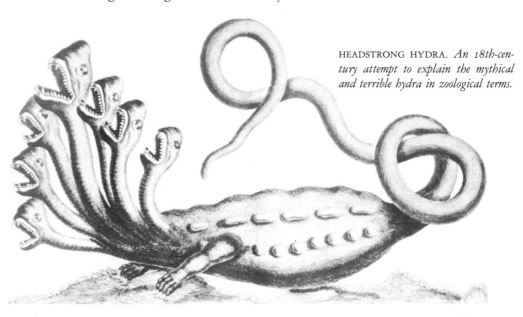

HEADSTRONG HYDRA. *An 18th-century attempt to explain the mythical and terrible hydra in zoological terms.*

PHOENIX : BIRD OF IMMORTALITY

Rebirth in a funeral pyre of wild cinnamon

The phoenix, most beautiful of fabulous creatures, symbolized hope and the continuity of life after death.

Clad in feathers of red and gold, the color of the rising sun, it had a melodious voice that became mournful with approaching death. Other creatures were then so overcome by its beauty and sadness that they themselves fell dead.

According to legend, only one phoenix could live at a time. The Greek poet Hesiod, writing in the eighth century B.C., said that the phoenix lived nine times the lifespan of the long-living raven. Other estimates went up to 97,200 years.

When the bird felt death approaching, it built itself a pyre of wild cinnamon and died in the flames. But from the ashes there then arose a new phoenix, which tenderly encased its parent's remains in an egg of myrrh and flew with them to the Egyptian city of Heliopolis, where it laid them on the Altar of the Sun.

These ashes were said to have the power of bringing a dead man back to life. The profligate Roman Emperor Elagabalus (A.D. 205–22) decided to eat phoenix meat in order to achieve immortality. He dined off a bird of paradise, sent in place of a phoenix, but the substitute did not work. He was then murdered shortly afterward.

Scholars now think that the germ of the legend came from the Orient and was adopted by the sun-worshiping priests of Heliopolis as an allegory of the sun's daily setting and rebirth.

Like all great myths, it stirs deep chords in man. In Christian art the resurrected phoenix became a popular symbol of Christ risen from the grave.

Strangely, its name may come from a misunderstanding by Herodotus, the Greek historian of the fifth century B.C. In his account of the bird he may have mistakenly given it the name "phoenix" because of the palm tree (Greek: *phoinix*) on which it was customarily pictured sitting in those days.

LIFE FROM FIRE. *As flames bear away the spirit of one phoenix, another rises from the ashes.*

BEAUTIFUL SEA MAIDENS

Mermaids had long tresses and fishtails but no souls

The mermaid caught in Belfast Lough in Northern Ireland in A.D. 558 had an unusual past. Three hundred years earlier she had been a little girl named Liban, whose family died in a flood. She lived for a year beneath the waves, gradually being transformed into a mermaid.

The mermaid eventually gave herself away by singing beneath the waves. She was overheard, and a party of men rowed into the lake and caught her in a net. They called her Murgen, which means "sea born," and displayed her in a tank of water for everyone to see. She was baptized, and when she died, she was called St. Murgen. Many miracles were attributed to her.

In 1403 another mermaid was stranded on mud flats in the Netherlands. According to a 17th-century historian, she was befriended by village women who "cleansed her of the sea-mosse, which did stick about her." She never learned to speak but lived for 15 years and was given a Christian burial in the local churchyard.

The beautiful mermaid of the Holy Island of Iona (off Scotland) daily visited an unknown saint who lived there. She was in love with him and wanted the soul that mermaids lack.

The saint told her that to gain a soul she must renounce the sea. This was impossible, so she left in despair and never returned. But her tears remained and formed the gray-green pebbles that are found only on the island.

Mermaids appear in the oldest legends of some of the world's most ancient cultures. The Philistines and the Babylonians of Biblical times worshiped fishtailed gods. Mermaids appear on Phoenician and Corinthian coins. Alexander the Great, it was said, had several adventures with beautiful sea maidens, visiting the bottom of the sea in a glass globe. The Roman writer Pliny recounts how an officer of Augustus Caesar saw many mermaids "cast upon the sands and lying dead" on a beach in faraway Gaul.

In folk tradition mermaid stories are often pathetic. The mermaids are lonely, occasionally taking human form for a night to join in village fun. Sometimes a man will seize their magic cap or belt, preventing their return to the sea, often with disastrous consequences.

Marriages with humans are seldom happy, although some coastal people, notably in northwestern Scotland and southeastern England, claimed they had mermaids for ancestors.

In the Middle Ages distinguished French

SAILOR'S TRAP. *A mermaid in an 18th-century woodcut combs her tresses to lure sailors.*

families tampered with their pedigrees to claim ancestry from the mermaid Mélusine, wife of Raymonde, a relative of the Count of Poitiers.

Their love story had a typically tragic ending. A condition of the marriage was that Raymonde should leave Mélusine alone on Saturdays. For years they lived happily together. But one Saturday, egged on by family gossip, he peeped at his wife through the bathroom key-

THE LITTLE MERMAID. *The statue that sits at the entrance of the Copenhagen harbor, as a memorial to Hans Christian Andersen's fairytale, was made by the Danish sculptor Edvard Eriksen. It is felt to symbolize the port's seafaring tradition.*

hole. She was sitting in the bath, partially transformed, with a fish's tail.

Mélusine cried out in dismay and fled through the window. Raymonde never saw her again, though she would return at night to suckle her babies. Nurses saw a gleaming figure with a blue and white scaly tail hovering over the cradles.

Sailors returning from far-off lands and seas often told of seeing mermaids and "sea wives." A detailed description of a "see wyf" found in the East Indies appears in a lavishly illustrated work on marine life in the Indian seas, published in Amsterdam in 1718. It reads: "Zee wyf. A monster resembling a siren, caught near the island of Borneo in the Department of Amboina. It was 59 inches long and in proportion as an eel. It lived on land, in a vat full of water, during four days seven hours. From time to time, it uttered little cries like those of a mouse. It would not eat, though it was offered small fish, shells, crabs, lobsters, etc."

The multicolored mermaid

The creature had seaweed-colored hair, olive-tinted skin, and olive webbing between the fingers. Around its waist was an orange fringe of hair bordered with blue. Its fins were green, and it had a gray face. A delicate row of pink hairs ran along the tail.

An African who posed as a mermaid had a more serious purpose—to save his life. King Chen, a 14th-century ruler of Benin (now part of Nigeria), became paralyzed in his legs—and tribal custom demanded that Kings who grew old and sickly should be put to death.

But the wily King Chen claimed he was the reincarnation of a sea god and had legs like a mud fish. This gave him an excuse not to walk and to hide his legs from his subjects' view.

There is a statue of him in this form in the British Museum.

A profitable myth

Perhaps no one found the mermaid myth more profitable than the enterprising London taxidermist who in the 1830's manufactured a hideous creature he said was half-fish, half-human. It was displayed in a London hall and sold to two Italian brothers for about $50,000. A naturalist of the time complained that the creature was a monkey stitched onto the skin of a fish.

This monkey and fish combination was also the basis of a flourishing trade in mermaids by which 19th-century Japanese fishermen supplemented their incomes. Many specimens found their way to Europe to be exhibited in traveling circuses and fairs.

Origins of the legend

The mermaid legend almost certainly goes back to the fishtailed gods of early civilizations. But probably it owes most to those creatures of the sea that seem almost human.

In tropical waters sea mammals, such as the dugong and the manatee, rise up in the water as they suckle their young—perhaps this is the origin of a constant theme of the mermaid nursing her child.

In colder regions there are the seals that love to bask on the rocks uttering strange cries.

Credulity, wishful thinking, mistaken identity—whatever the origins, the mermaid myth dies hard. In 1961 the Manx (Isle of Man) Tourist Board offered a prize to anyone who could bring in a mermaid from the sea—alive, of course.

WORM THAT TERRORIZED DURHAM

PEOPLE in Durham (England) still sing of the *worm*—Old English for "dragon"—which terrorized the county in the Middle Ages. It all began when the young heir to Lambton Castle went fishing on a Sunday. He caught an eellike creature, which he threw down a well.

In the well the *worm* grew to an enormous size, and when the young knight went off on a crusade, it broke out and devoured men and beasts. Every night it would sleep while wound three times around Lambton Hill, now called Worm Hill.

Young Lambton managed to slay the dragon on his return from the crusade, but only by promising a witch he would kill the first creature he met after his victory. Unfortunately, it was his father who was first on the scene. Young Lambton refused to kill him, and, because of this, the Lambton family was put under the witch's curse—a curse said to be effective still.

THE ISLAND-SIZED KRAKEN

Nightmare of fishermen in the northern seas

The fishermen's nets were stretched almost to the breaking point. Something was making the water teem with shoals of fish. The men worked feverishly, knowing that the invisible creature terrifying the fish could at any moment rise from the sea and swallow their ship whole. Or it might choose to pluck them one by one from the deck.

They knew it was the kraken, the biggest of the giant sea monsters.

Many such stories abound in Norway's literature, for legend has it that fishermen over the centuries have been terrorized by the sudden appearance and disappearance of the leviathan.

The back of a fully grown kraken was about 1½ miles long. With its bumpy spine and tentacles floating like strands of seaweed, it was often mistaken for a good-sized island.

Several writers have described the kraken, kraxen, or sea korven.

Bishop Pontoppidan, of Bergen, Norway, wrote in 1755 that floating islands that appeared and disappeared suddenly in the northern seas were certainly krakens.

The Bishop of Midaros found a kraken on the shore. Thinking it to be a rock, he set up an altar on its back and celebrated Mass. The creature waited respectfully until the bishop had finished and then quietly slipped into the sea and vanished. Modern skeptics tend to dismiss the kraken, saying that witnesses had probably been confused by sightings of giant squids. But in the vast depths of the sea, who knows? Perhaps as the poet Tennyson wrote:

Below the thunders of the upper deep;
Far, far beneath in the abysmal sea
His ancient, dreamless, uninvaded sleep
The kraken sleepeth. . . .

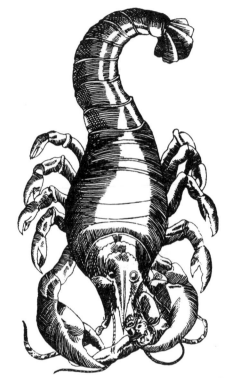

NORWEGIAN SEA DRAGON. *A kraken is shown about to devour a terrified human victim.*

GIANT SNAKE OF THE DEEP

"A great head and neck rose out of the water"

Tales of gigantic monsters lurking deep below the waves have been passed down by successive generations of fishermen and sailors in almost every country in the world. But no monster has been better authenticated than the giant sea serpent that is said to have its lair off the east coast of Brazil.

One of the most reliable accounts of its appearance came in 1905 when two members of the British Royal Zoological Society were traveling on the steamship *Valhalla* off Brazil.

The two men—Meade-Waldo and Michael Nicholl—were on deck when they saw what at first appeared to be a rock. Waldo later wrote: "I looked and immediately saw a large fin or frill sticking out of the water, dark seaweed-brown in color, somewhat crinkled at the edge.

"It was apparently about 6 feet in length and projected from 18 inches to 2 feet from the water. I could see under the water, to the rear of the frill, the shape of a considerable body. A great head and neck rose out of the water in

A SEA SERPENT. *This animal with hairy neck and undulating coils, by a 19th-century artist, closely resembles modern ideas—and even photographs—of the Loch Ness Monster.*

front of the frill. The neck appeared about the thickness of a man's body. The head had a very turtlelike appearance, as had also the eye. I could see the line of the mouth, but we were sailing pretty fast and quickly drew away from the object. It moved its neck from side to side in a peculiar manner; the color of the head and neck was dark brown above and whitish below."

Commotion in the water

The monster seems to have made another appearance within 14 hours, for Nicholl reported "a great commotion in the water." The first and third mates of the *Valhalla* also saw it.

Nicholl wrote: "At first they thought it was a rock awash about 100 to 150 yards away, but they soon made out that it was something moving and going slightly faster than the ship, which was at that time going about 8½ knots. One of the crew who was on lookout saw it too. Although there was a bright moon at the time, they could not make out anything of the creature itself, owing to the amount of wash it was making; but they say that from the commotion in the water it looked as if a submarine was going along just below the surface."

The monster disappeared after several minutes. John Lockhart, who in 1924 wrote about the sightings in *Mysteries of the Sea,* commented:

"Most of the witnesses agree on certain outstanding features: It is a long serpentine creature; it has a series of humps; its head is rather like a horse's; its color is dark on top and light below; it moves by undulations up and down; it appears during the summer months." But Lockhart added: "It is harmless, for it never actually attacked anybody."

The *Valhalla* account tied in with previous sightings made centuries earlier—also describing a long serpentine animal, which snaked through the sea.

In the fourth century B.C. Aristotle wrote of large serpents off Libya: "Mariners sailing along the coast have told how they have seen the bones of many oxen, which, it was apparent to them, had been devoured by serpents. And as their ships sailed on, the serpents came to attack them, some of them throwing themselves on a trireme and capsizing it."

The serpent as weather prophet

In 1555 the Archbishop of Uppsala in Sweden, Olaus Magnus, described a sea serpent measuring 200 feet long and 20 feet thick. It had hair hanging from its neck and sharp scales.

A Norwegian missionary named Hans Egede wrote of a "terrible sea monster" he saw in 1734 near Greenland. "It had a long, sharp snout, and blew like a whale, had broad, large flippers, and the body, as it were, covered with a hard skin, and it was very wrinkled and uneven on its skin; moreover, on the lower part it was formed like a snake, and when it went under the water again, it cast itself backward, and in doing so it raised its tail above the water, a whole ship-length from its body. That evening we had very bad weather."

Reports of sea serpents in the 19th century were centered on "the animal of Stronsa" in the Orkneys in 1808. The carcass of a monster was seen by fishermen, and experts inspected the body. Some said that the animal was unknown to science; others said that the remains were those of a basking shark. For years controversy raged, but learned opinion finally agreed that the carcass was indeed that of a basking shark.

The most famous sea serpent "spotting" was in 1848 by the captain and crew of HMS *Daedalus* off the African coast in the Atlantic. Capt. Peter M'Quhae reported that he saw an enormous serpent. "Its head and shoulders kept about four feet constantly above the surface of the sea. It had no fins, but something like a mane of a horse, or rather a bunch of seaweed, washed about its back," said the captain. Zoologists were not convinced that the legendary serpent had been sighted and explained the "monster" away as a species of seal or a squid.

But while some zoologists dismiss the sea serpent as folklore, others maintain that somewhere in the world's oceans there may exist at least one such creature—perhaps the last remaining descendant of the gigantic animals that ruled the earth before man appeared.

STORM RAISER IN MONK'S ROBES

SEAGOING men as far apart as Scandinavia and the Orient once told stories of a strange creature that could raise storms. They called it the sea monk or sea bishop. The sea monk of Norway was a small and normally harmless animal, despite its frightening appearance. It got its name from its monk's cowl and tonsured head. It had fins for arms and a human face, although of a crude kind. The Far Eastern variety is sometimes referred to as the sea bonze. (A bonze is a Buddhist monk.) Sailors feared it, for, as well as causing storms, it sometimes attacked their junks and capsized them. Sailors performed a ritual dance whenever a sea monk threatened. On every junk there was at least one deckhand who was specially trained to ward off the creature by waving a stick decked in red streamers. It has been suggested that the sea monk was conjured up by imaginative seamen who had glimpsed skates or rays. Their underside, with strangely shaped gills and mouth, bears a faint resemblance to a deformed human face.

The sea bishop was one of several creatures conjured up by seamen—possibly after glimpsing the strange underside of skates or rays.

The sea monk was frightening to look at but rather inoffensive. Sailors believed its one fault was a tendency to raise storms.

DOES THE CAMERA LIE? *This photograph, taken in 1972, seems to show the Loch Ness Monster heading toward the right with its hump protruding well above the surface.*

THE CAMERA-SHY MONSTER

Not even TV could solve the 1,400-year-old enigma of Loch Ness

Loch Ness, in Scotland, is the reputed home of a monster that has been chronicled, with varying degrees of credibility, over the past 1,400 years. The loch is the largest mass of freshwater in Britain and perhaps the most sinister, even when the sun shines on its murky, peat-stained waters.

Those waters are so deep—more than 900 feet in parts—that they would engulf most of the world's tallest buildings.

Some of the stories about the Loch Ness Monster appear equally tall. The earliest of

them goes back to about A.D. 565, when the monster was said to have been sighted by Columba, the Irish saint. According to his biographer, St. Adamnan, writing a century later, a disciple of Columba was swimming across the mile-wide loch to fetch a boat for his master from the opposite shore, when the monster suddenly rose to the surface "with a great roar and open mouth."

The onlookers, converts and heathen alike, were, according to Adamnan, "stricken with a very great terror." But St. Columba, making the

THE FIRST PHOTOGRAPH. *This picture of Nessie was taken in 1933 by a London surgeon on vacation.*

EARLY RISER. *A monsterlike object was photographed by torchlight on the loch one dawn in May 1960.*

may have had some kind of connection with the spate of sightings reported around that time. There were frequent explosions as engineers blasted a path for the road.

Did the noise disturb the monster from the depths of the loch? Or was it just that, with the coming of the road, new vistas were opened up, enabling tourists to see, for the first time in centuries, something that had always been living in the water?

Whatever the answer, that first photograph was published in the London *Daily Mail* and provoked an argument that was to rage for years.

Skeptics claim that it portrays either a mass of decaying vegetable matter lifted to the surface by trapped gases or the tip of the tail of a diving otter photographed out of scale.

On the other hand, true believers in the monster say that the picture tallies with the description given by many people who claim to have seen the creature and that, in any case, an eminent surgeon would hardly be likely to risk his reputation for a hoax.

The last argument may indicate a touching faith in the medical profession. All the same, many people who are convinced that they have seen the monster belong to groups normally considered to be truthful witnesses: schoolmasters, naval officers, Benedictine monks, one Nobel prizewinner, two town clerks, and many dour Scottish professional men—none of whom are inclined by nature to risk ridicule or to court publicity for its own sake.

Surprised forestry worker

While naturalists and zoologists tended to steer clear of the argument, bolder spirits pressed on with the search for more evidence. Sometimes this appeared to those who were not looking specifically for such evidence—such as Lachlan Stuart, a forestry worker who lived beside the loch. In 1951, when he went out one morning at 6:30 to milk his cows, he noticed a disturbance on the water, and three humps appeared, moving in line toward the shore.

Stuart ran back to the house, grabbed his small box camera, and brought a family friend to back up the evidence of his own eyes. He managed to take one picture before the monster (if such it was) vanished, and the camera shutter jammed.

Stuart's picture, taken from a range of 60 yards, got wide publicity, as the surgeon's had

sign of the cross and invoking the Almighty, is said to have repelled the monster with the words: "Think not to go further, nor touch thou that man. Quick, go back. . . ." The beast obeyed and has never hurt anyone since.

Adamnan's account may have been a powerful argument for the efficacy of prayer, but it was somewhat vague as a portrait of the monster. Indeed, no clear picture of it emerged until 14 centuries—and innumerable sightings—later. Then in 1933, a London surgeon, driving past the loch on vacation, secured the first photograph of a monster—or what was claimed to be one. It showed a long neck, arched over the water from a thick body, and was taken, according to the surgeon, from a distance of 200 to 300 yards, near Invermoriston.

At that point the road runs 200 feet above the loch. The road was then newly built, which

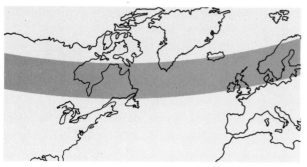

MONSTER BELT. *Lake monsters are said to live within a wide belt across the world.*

18 years before. But most people remained skeptical of this and all of the other photographic evidence.

The first moving pictures of something that might have been "Nessie," as the monster was now affectionately known, came in 1960. The cameraman was Tim Dinsdale, an aviation engineer, who was so convinced of his film's authenticity that he gave up his career to live in a small boat on the loch, in full-time pursuit of the elusive monster.

Dinsdale's enthusiasm fired others and helped to pave the way for a more scientific approach to the question of whether the monster really exists. In 1961 the Loch Ness Phenomena Investigation Bureau was formed, at the instigation of two naturalists and David James, a Member of Parliament who became the bureau's organizer.

He collated, checked, and published all the reports of sightings and enlisted students and other volunteers to man, during the summer months, the 36-inch cameras set up at strategic points around the 24-mile loch.

The range of one camera overlapped the next, so that observation was complete—as well as continuous. But the evidence they yielded has been inconclusive. So has that of British and Japanese television crews, who hoped to record the monster's activities with the aid of the most modern scientific equipment.

One such expedition, in 1969, deployed the Vickers' submersible *Pisces,* with low-light-level underwater cameras, closed-circuit TV, and video-tape recording machines. There was also a one-man American submarine, the *Viperfish,* and a team of sonar experts. Elevated cameras constantly covered the surface during the day, and a "night-sight" camera was used for ship patrols after dark.

More bizarre items of equipment included a noise-making machine, lent by the Royal Navy, with which it was hoped to disturb the monster. In addition, an evil-smelling bait of suitably monstrous proportions was dangled in the loch. The bait weighed 50 pounds and was compounded of dried animal blood, snake hormone, and other fearsome ingredients, which it was hoped might have some appeal to "Nessie."

But the beast remained coy as ever. No sight or sound of her appeared on either camera or sonar gear, and this particular expedition's sole contribution to the world's knowledge of "Nessie" and her habitat came from the submersible *Pisces.* Diving off Castle Urquhart, its crew took a sounding that showed the loch to be 950 feet deep at that point—200 feet deeper than was supposed. The *Pisces,* on this dive, also found a vast underwater cavern.

Lair discovered?

The monster's lair? Maybe—but of the monster, no sign. The expedition left, with its leader lamenting that it was the "end of a legend."

Others continued the search, especially the Phenomena Investigation Bureau, whose organizer maintained his belief in the existence of some unidentified creature in the loch.

But what sort of creature? David James offered five possibilities: a mammal, such as a long-necked seal; a salamander or other long-tailed amphibian; a fish, possibly a giant eel; a mollusk, like a huge marine slug; or one of the plesiosaur family, a species of fish-eating reptiles that has been officially extinct for 70 million years. Those who support the plesiosaur theory point out that the coelacanth fish was supposedly extinct—until one was caught in the Indian Ocean off South Africa in 1938.

They also contemplate the possibility that a family of creatures was left stranded in what became Loch Ness at the end of the last ice age. That was 10,000 to 15,000 years ago, and the reasoning is this: As the icecap retreated, sea levels in the Northern Hemisphere must have been raised considerably by the melting ice. Numerous glens and valleys became flooded and were transformed into fiords. Is it not feasible, these theorists ask, that some plesiosaurs, feeding at the headwaters of a fiord, were swept along with the floodwaters into the newly formed loch, where they have lived ever since, almost unnoticed.

Eel or slug, seal or plesiosaur, the Loch Ness

Monster is not unique. Reports of similar creatures have come from other lochs.

Some are just as fearsome as the one St. Columba encountered. An early Scottish historian, Hector Boece, wrote in 1527 of the creature that emerged from Gairloch in Ross and Cromarty: "a terrible beast as big as a greyhound, [that] struck down great trees and slew three men with three strokes of his tail."

Loch Morar is the traditional lair of a monster, known locally as Mhorag. Descriptions of it vary: "about the size of an Indian elephant"; "about 30 feet long with four humps"; "about 20 feet long, with snakelike head and four legs."

In Ireland, too, lake monsters are an accepted part of local zoology—and mythology. Similar shadowy creatures have been reported in the Scandinavian countries, in Iceland, and across the Atlantic—but still in roughly the same latitude—in British Columbia.

There, on the Pacific slopes of the Rocky Mountains, lies Lake Okanagan, a sheet of water thrown up by the retreating ice age and inhabited (it is said) by a water demon named Ogopogo. The Indians, who appeased the demon with ritual offerings of livestock, called it Naitaka and left crude drawings of the creature on stone. These show a long-necked animal remarkably like the photographs and descriptions of "Nessie."

Reported sightings of Ogopogo are no more conclusive than those of "Nessie" but are enough to prompt the question: Is there a "monster belt" across the Northern Hemisphere, where supposedly extinct creatures can be found?

THE GREEDY GULO

ONE OF the most useful of mythical beasts was the gulo of northern Sweden, which looked like a big dog with a cat's face (inset). According to Olaus Magnus, Archbishop of Uppsala in 1555, the Swedes used its thick, brown hair to make caps, its guts for strings for musical instruments, its hooves to cure vertigo and earache. But, he said, the gulo had one fault—a voracious appetite. "He devours so much that, finding a straight [narrow] passage between trees, he passes between them that he may discharge his body by violence." The myth may have been based on the gluttonous wolverine (photograph).

THE TENDER TRAP. *The only way to capture a unicorn—according to medieval scholars—was to use a virgin as bait. Her purity induced the beast to lay its head on her lap.*

DEADLY ENEMY OF THE ROYAL LION

A unicorn could impale three elephants on its horn

On the royal arms of Great Britain the lion and the unicorn have been together since Scotland and England were first united under James I in 1603. Before that the English shield was supported by a lion and a dragon. The unicorn came from Scotland, whose coat of arms was supported by two of those noble beasts.

To bring the lion and the unicorn together at all was taking a risk, for though the medieval heyday of unicorn spotting was past, the beasts were still considered to be deadly enemies. One 17th-century author has a lively description of their battles: "Wherefore as soon as ever a Lion seeth a Unicorn, he runneth to a tree for succour, that so when the Unicorn maketh force at him, he may not only avoid his horn but also destroy him; for the Unicorn in the swiftness of his course runneth against a tree wherein his sharp horn sticketh fast." He added cheerfully: "Then the Lion seeth the Unicorn fastened by the horn, without any danger at all he falleth on him and killeth him."

Other ancient writers also mentioned some of the unicorn's problems. For instance, it was credited with such remarkable strength that it could impale and carry away three elephants on its horn. However, it was unable to shake them off and usually died either from starvation or from the stench as the elephants rotted. Uni-

corn hunters had to go to the mountains or deserts to find their quarry, and an encounter with the beast might daunt the stoutest heart: "There was nothing more horrible than the voice or braying of it, for the voice is strained above measure." Also, it "biteth like a lion and kicketh like a horse"—and had no fear of iron weapons.

The unicorn was very bad tempered with its own kind, even with the females, "except when it burneth in lust for procreation." But with other animals it was "sociable, delighting in their company."

Antidote to poison

Unicorn leather boots were believed to ensure sound legs and protection from plague, and a paste of egg yolk and unicorn liver was said to heal leprosy. But of all its admirable parts, the most useful was the horn. If a man drank from one, it would relieve epilepsy and stomach troubles. Moreover, it could neutralize poison. If a serpent's venom had spoiled a drinking hole, the unicorn only needed to stir it with his horn to make the water pure again.

During the Renaissance, when assassination by poison was a daily hazard, cups made of "unicorn horn"—probably narwhal or rhinoceros tusk—were used as a protection against deadly drinks, for the horn was supposed to sweat and change color in the presence of poison. Venomous insects would not dare to cross a line marked out with it, and poisonous plants or animals anywhere near it would burst and die.

Needless to say, a horn with such properties was enormously expensive. The German traveler Paul Hentzner claimed that he saw one among Queen Elizabeth's crown jewels in 1598, which was valued at $500,000.

Frauds were common when such profits were to be made. A Venetian recipe for fake unicorn horns was "compounded with lime and sope and peradventure with earth or some stone."

There was only one way to tame a unicorn. Isidore of Seville described it in the early seventh century. A maid had to get the unicorn to lay its head on her lap. Then, said Isidore, he "leaveth all his fireness and sleepeth in that wise." Sadly, Isidore went on, the trusting beast is then "slain with darts of hunters."

Did unicorns ever exist? Possibly they were a confused blend of several animals, garbled together in travelers' tales. A Greek, Ctesias, who described one in 400 B.C., probably saw a rhinoceros. The rhinoceros horn was an ancient Chinese cure for poison.

It might also have been an oryx—a large, long-horned antelope—seen in profile with one horn broken off. And Queen Elizabeth's valuable horn was almost certainly the tusk of a narwhal, a small whale that grows one tooth to a great length, which is twisted spirally and pointed like the legendary unicorn's horn.

MONSTER FROM THE AUSTRALIAN SWAMPS

ABORIGINES sitting around campfires in the Australian outback still tell tales of the bunyip—the monster from the swamps that terrified both aborigines and many early settlers.

Pioneers believed the bunyip was a creature "terrible in appearance, with a voracious appetite for human flesh. Its booming voice in the night filled their minds with fear." For them it was a living fossil, a huge water beast that had survived from prehistoric times by lurking in deep swamps, lakes, and lagoons.

To the aborigines it was a creature of many different shapes: a bullock with a long maned neck, a head like that of an emu, and a body covered with fur or feathers. It was often depicted in their drawings as having a horselike tail, flippers, and the tusks of a walrus.

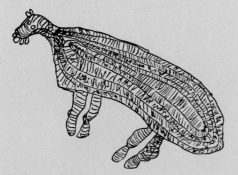

The horror of the Australian swamps is credited with widely different forms. One aboriginal artist drew this nightmare beast.

Aborigines also believed in a monstrous snake called Myndie or Mindi, which would extend its body for 10 miles to devour people who broke tribal laws or wandered beyond their totem boundaries—the tribal areas that they believed were protected by their gods.

But early settlers also believed in the bunyip of the swamps, and some claimed to have seen it. In 1886 horsemen fording a river near present-day Canberra (Australia) saw a whitish creature about the size of a dog, with "the face of a child," and threw stones at it. A similar beast, in New South Wales, disappeared with a grunting noise into a lagoon when it was fired on.

Sadly, however, the bunyip appears to be just a legend.

Though the Maoris of New Zealand had never heard of the bunyip they did have an equivalent—the taniwha, a giant man-eating monster, which took the form of a lizard, snake, or fish. It lived everywhere—in springs, rivers, lakes, caves, and mountains. The beast had supernatural powers. It could fly through the air and transform itself into other creatures.

The origins of the taniwha legends are obscure, and no white man has ever claimed to have seen one. But it has been suggested that the taniwha represents some folk memory of the man-eating crocodiles of the western Pacific region. There, the word for crocodile is *Moko-tolo*, and the Maoris use the same word, *moko*, for all lizards and for the taniwha.

GUARDIAN OF THE TREASURE

Only one man braved the great snake's cavern

Somewhere in the Richtersveld, an area of scrubland in South Africa, is a legendary cavern crammed with diamonds. There is only one problem: The cavern is guarded by the Grootslang, or Great Snake of the Orange River, a fearsome 40-foot-long serpent with enormous gems in its eye sockets.

Guides are reluctant to take expeditions to the cavern, which is known as the Wonder Hole or Bottomless Pit. Only one man, a tough prospector, is said to have tried to explore the hole. He used a winch and cable to reach a ledge far below. Tunnels led off the ledge, and there was a strong smell of sulfur. He dropped his electric torch when bats flew in his face and was hauled back to the surface; he did not try again.

Some travelers claim to have seen the Grootslang, and reports of it have appeared in South African newspapers. Witnesses confirm the beast's length as 40 feet and tell of 3-foot-wide tracks along the Orange River. Prospectors once followed the track for miles before it disappeared into the river. Natives say the Grootslang is a spirit snake, and anyone who encounters it is overcome by a sense of evil.

Does a giant snake live in the Orange River country? If so, it could only be a python, and although it is not impossible that one of these reptiles might attain a length of 40 feet, it is unlikely. The longest African python reliably recorded was 32 feet, but this was a freak.

Pythons 25 feet long have been shot in the area, and one of these, if seen up close, would be sufficiently alarming to make exaggeration understandable. However, the natives maintain that there is only one Grootslang.

WHEN YOUR HOME IS POSSESSED BY FOXES

PEOPLE who suddenly start to overeat, talk gibberish, and fret about whether their faces are getting longer may be possessed by goblin foxes. At least that is the widely believed Japanese theory. Stories of these goblin foxes are popular throughout Japan, and there are even present-day reports of people being "possessed," or taken over, by them. Families in some rural areas are said to keep foxes for practicing sorcery against other members of the community.

In 1963 the priest of a temple near Tottori described how to identify families keeping foxes. "It is easy," he said. "You can see the foxes sitting in rows along the eaves, shading their eyes with their paws, or playing together in front of the house."

People buying a fox owner's property inherit the stigma of being involved in such fearful behavior, and purchasers are hard to find even when prices have tumbled to rockbottom.

The treatment for possession is a drastic one. Within living memory a woman was treated by having all her nourishment stopped, pepper sprinkled in her eyes, nose, and mouth, a rubdown with red-hot sticks, and holes bored in her breast and abdomen. Whether the treatment was successful is not known, because the patient died within three days.

A Japanese print shows ghostly foxes joining in a spiritualists' session of table turning with cheerful gusto and abandon.

MAN'S BEST FRIENDS

A nation that even looked like dogs

Many dog owners are proud of their pets' pedigree. But the Koniagas, a tribe of North American Indians, trace their own pedigree back to a dog. And the legend of a breed of men with dogs' heads is a recurring one in many different civilizations.

One of the best accounts is in the medieval writings of Sir John Mandeville. "Men go by the sea ocean, by many isles, unto an isle that is clept [called] Nacumera, that is a good isle and fair.

"And it is in compass about, more than a thousand miles. And all the men and women of that isle have hounds' heads, and they be clept *Cynocephales* [Greek for 'dog heads']."

Marco Polo said these people lived in the Andaman Islands in the Bay of Bengal, but the whole idea of dog-men probably grew out of early sightings of baboons, which have projecting, doglike muzzles.

Pictures of St. Christopher in Eastern art sometimes show him with a dog's head. According to legend, he was unusually handsome, and, because he was constantly pestered by women, he prayed to be given a dog's head as protection. It is possible that the tale originated in early Christian times, when the Egyptian cult of the dog-headed god Anubis may have been confused with stories of St. Christopher.

CANONIZED CANINE. *A Byzantine painted icon of St. Christopher shows how pre-Christian gods were assimilated into the new faith as saints.*

KALLIKANTZAROI

The Greeks have a word for unpleasant goblins

It used to be a serious matter for a Greek couple to have a child born at Christmas. Although Christmas was a happy time, it meant that the baby had been conceived on March 25—the feast of the Annunciation, when the angel told Mary she would bear Jesus.

Great care was needed to stop such a baby from turning into a Kallikantzaros, or goblin. It was believed that the baby should be strapped up with garlic or have its toenails singed to prevent the transformation.

These goblins are singularly unpleasant. Some are so tall that their loins are level with the rooftops. They have big heads and, in general, are black and hairy, with bloodshot eyes and long curved nails. Fortunately, they are occupied for most of the year hacking away with axes at the tree that holds up the world. But each year, just as they are about to chop the tree down, the birthday of Christ comes around again, and the tree miraculously renews itself.

The goblins get into a terrible rage and rush above ground to create havoc for the 12 days of Christmas. During the day they hide in damp, dirty places, making their meals off snakes and worms. But once it is dark, they emerge to swarm down chimneys and wreck houses, tearing to pieces anyone they meet. To stop them, Greeks hang a pig's jaw in the house or throw a shoe on the fire—the smell puts them off.

431

VAMPIRES GALORE!

Cause and cure varied from country to country

Travelers who visited remote parts of Transylvania in the 16th century returned with strange and horrifying tales of creatures that were neither living nor dead . . . creatures that left their haunts at night and feasted on human blood.

These monsters went by various names: *vurculac, wampyr* . . . and vampire. Although similar creatures are recorded in Greek, Roman, and Hebrew mythology, the story of the vampire stems almost entirely from eastern Europe: from the Carpathian Mountains, Transylvania and Wallachia, and other areas in the Balkans.

Two concepts lie at the root of the vampire myth: first, that an evil spirit can take over a corpse and use it for its own malevolent purposes; second, that the soul of a person considered too wicked to be allowed into the realm of the dead can continue to inhabit his own body—in the guise of a vampire.

The mythology of the vampire is remarkably detailed—and specific. The Transylvanian species, for instance, is said to be recognizable by its gaunt appearance and pale complexion.

It is said to have full, red lips and pointed canine teeth; gleaming eyes with a hypnotic gaze; long, sharp fingernails; eyebrows that meet; and hair on the palms of its hands.

Its breath is said to be foul, and its diet of blood endows it with superhuman strength, despite its cadaverous, emaciated appearance.

In addition to these characteristics, some European vampires are said to have red hair and a harelip. The Russian vampire—according to legend—has a purple face and is believed to have been, in human form, one who rebelled against the church or was perhaps a witch.

The vampire stories abound with a wealth of detail. Vampires found in Bulgaria had only one nostril; the Bavarian variety slept with its left eye open and its thumbs linked—and was held responsible for cattle plague.

The Moravian vampire was addicted to throwing off its shroud—and attacking its victims in the nude. Albanian vampires wore high-heeled shoes, and the Brazilian type had feet that were plush covered, which presumably indicated a velvet tread.

The Chinese vampire, according to its chroniclers, drew its strength from the light of the moon; the American species—from the Rocky Mountains—was said to suck the blood from its victims' ears through its nose; and the Mexican vampire was recognizable by its fleshless skull.

Accounts of the vampire's powers vary from country to country. But the monster has been

THE VEGETABLE LAMB OF TARTARY

HALF PLANT, half animal, the Vegetable Lamb of Tartary stems from the Middle Ages—a traveler's tale from the Far East. Its full name: *Planta Tartarica Barometz*—the word "barometz" being the Tartar name for "lamb."

The fruit of this animal-tree was cotton, but European travelers, who knew nothing of cotton at that time, took it for wool—a fabric they did know.

Wool, they reasoned, came from sheep. So arose the legend of the Vegetable Lamb of Tartary. The cotton was considered to be the fleece of lambs that grew from the tree and were attached to it by their navels.

It was said that the plant bent to let the lambs graze and that when they had eaten all the grass around, the lambs and the plant died.

credited with the ability to assume a variety of animal shapes, such as those of bats and wolves, and with the power to control all the creatures of the night.

Methods of combating vampires seem to be as numerous as the species themselves. Some Rumanians believe that the best day to tackle a vampire is Saturday, which is the one day when it is powerless to leave its grave. What is the method of disposal? Pour a basin of boiling water into a hole near the grave. Such a hole, Rumanians believe, is a sure sign that the occupant of the grave is a vampire.

Chalk and holy water

Others claim that vampires can be discouraged by sprinkling chalk and holy water, but those in favor of more direct methods prefer to drive a wooden or iron stake through the creature's heart as it rests by day in its grave. To make absolutely sure, cut off the vampire's head with a sexton's spade and fill the mouth with garlic.

The rays of the sun are said to be fatal to a vampire, and a crucifix is also held to be a powerful deterrent.

In eastern Europe the search for a vampire's grave involved a ritual in which a virgin boy, riding a black virgin stallion, was led through a churchyard. The tomb where the stallion first halted was presumed to be that of the vampire.

The vampire's origins varied considerably from country to country. In Rumanian tradition, if a vampire stares at a pregnant woman, there is a strong chance that her child will become a vampire—one of the so-called undead. So will a corpse over which a cat has jumped or a dead person with a wound that has not been scalded with hot water.

But by far the most common method of joining the clan is to become a vampire's victim. Once the nocturnal visitor has drained the blood of its human prey, the victim dies and, in turn, is condemned to walk the night as one of the undead.

In Serbia, in 1727, it was reported that a peasant, Arnold Paole, had fallen from a cart and broken his neck. From then on, his neighbors declared that Paole entered houses in the village at night and that those people he visited always died. Paole's body was exhumed, and his shroud was found to be saturated with blood. The corpse was burned by the villagers, and Paole's ashes were scattered.

By the late 18th century the vampire was an

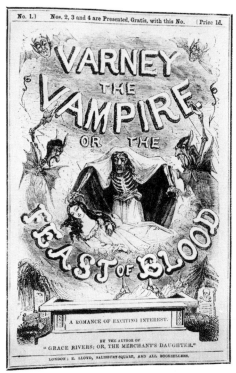

EARLY-VICTORIAN VAMPIRE. *Fifty years before Dracula was written, a vampire named Varney left its imprint on British bookshelves.*

ideal character for stories set in mist-shrouded castles. In the early 1800's the vampire made its first appearance on the stage. Writers such as Alexandre Dumas churned out blood-curdling plays about the exploits of these creatures.

Bram Stoker's classic

In 1897 Bram Stoker, a relatively unknown Irish writer, published *Dracula,* which became the undisputed classic of vampire stories. Inevitably, Hollywood made a movie of the novel. First of the U.S. vampire thrillers, the 1931 film starred Bela Lugosi as the bloodthirsty count, and millions watched in terror as the fearsome prince of the undead accomplished his fiendish deeds. Hollywood responded to popular demand with as many variations on the vampire theme as the imagination allows—among them, *The Mark of the Vampire, Son of Dracula* (starring Lon Chaney, Jr.), *House of Frankenstein* (with John Carradine as Dracula and Boris Karloff as the monster), and *Brides of Dracula.* Often repeated on television, the films have ensured immortality to Dracula and his fellow vampires.

BIG BAD WEREWOLVES

Even a King could come under suspicion

Even he who is pure of heart
And says his prayers by night
May become a wolf when the wolfbane blooms
And the moon is full and bright.

So runs an ancient rhyme describing the risk run even by good and honest people of becoming werewolves.

What the vampires are to Transylvania, the werewolves are to northern and western Europe. The werewolf legends may have sprung from myths of the Norse gods who were said to change into animal forms, such as the bear and the wolf.

Later, during the 16th-century witch hunts, the idea developed that a witch could change into a wolf, so it was grafted onto the list of creatures—toads, cats, and hares—whose form witches were said to assume.

In its human form it is not easy to distinguish a werewolf from a vampire, since they share many characteristics. These include eyebrows that meet, clawlike fingernails, small ears that may be slightly pointed, and hair growing on the palms. But there is one slight difference: A werewolf's third finger on each hand is supposed to be as long as, or longer than, the second finger.

Transformed, the creature appears either as an extra-large wolf, moving on all fours, or as an extremely hairy biped, retaining recognizable, although particularly repulsive, human facial features and clawed hands.

In either of these shapes, it tears out the throats of its victims and devours the flesh raw.

Internal hair

In Italy it was believed that some werewolves grew hair internally, and in 1541 at least one suspect died under the scalpels of his examiners.

WORRIED MAN. *A 15th-century German print shows a werewolf attacking its victim. The recurring legends seem to have sprung from the myths of the Norse gods who changed themselves into animals.*

England's unpopular King John, who reigned from 1199 to 1216, was said to have been a werewolf. A Norman chronicle describes how monks, hearing sounds from his grave, dug him up and took his body out of consecrated ground:

"Thus the ill presage of his surname Lackland was completely realized, for he lost in his lifetime almost all the domains under his suzerainty, and even after death he could not keep peaceful possession of his tomb."

There are many ways in which a man may become a werewolf. A medieval churchman, Gervase of Tilbury, said that stripping naked and rolling in the sand under a full moon was an effective method. But in Italian folklore, being conceived at the time of a new moon or sleeping outdoors under a full moon on a Friday is enough to create a vampire.

In Ireland, St. Patrick is said to have cursed an entire clan who displeased him by their lack of faith and turned them into werewolves.

Some European legends say that drinking from a stream from which a wolf has drunk, being bitten by a rabid wolf, or eating the wolfbane plant will cause the transformation.

The methods used to deal with werewolves are equally varied. French-Canadian lore advocates an exorcism by speaking the name of Christ or calling the werewolf three times by its true Christian name.

In France it was said that the *loupgarou,* as the werewolf was known, could be defeated by taking three drops of blood from the creature during its wolf period.

But by far the best known method of freeing a human from the curse of the werewolf is to shoot the creature with a silver bullet, preferably consecrated silver, such as a crucifix from a church.

Practically every nation has its lore of werecreatures. In Africa some primitive people believe in men who become wereleopards; in Asia the weretiger is feared by the superstitious; and Scandinavians believed in people who hunted as bears.

Strangely, some of these weird stories may be founded on fact. Odd cases, fortunately rare, have been reported of people who believed they were animals and who attempted to drink blood and eat raw flesh; this condition is known as zoanthropic paranoia.

WEREWOLVES GATHERING. *This 19th-century print shows the werewolves of Normandy, in France. They were believed to steal into cemeteries and dig up corpses to devour.*

THE BEAST OF GÉVAUDAN

FROM 1764 to 1767 an unknown monster terrorized shepherds and shepherdesses who worked in the fields near the Auvergne Mountains in France. Known as the Beast of Gévaudan, the creature was held responsible for the savage deaths of 40 people and vicious attacks on more than 110. Local people claimed that the creature was red, covered with scales, and had a mouth the size of a lion's. It could run at tremendous speed and evade any trap or hunter. In 1767 a large wolf was killed, and the attacks ceased. But no one is certain whether some other beast—or human—was responsible.

STRANGE GIANT. *This shy creature hurried away when rancher Roger Patterson started to film it near Eureka, California, in 1967. Is Patterson's film genuine? Was it the legendary Bigfoot he saw?*

HUNTING THE YETI

Mountain men give it many names

In every mountain range in the world live people who tell stories of a strange, shambling, manlike creature; of footprints too large to belong to any human; of isolated communities living in fear of a monster that goes by many names.

In the Himalayas he is called the yeti. Elsewhere in Asia, from the Gobi Desert in the north to Assam in the south, he goes by the names of Meti, Shookpa, Migo, or Kang-Mi. To people living in remote, wooded parts of the northwestern United States, he is Bigfoot. In the foothills of the Canadian Rockies he is known as the Sasquatch.

Whatever the name, the description is roughly the same: height, up to 10 feet; weight, about 300 pounds; appearance, hairy and apelike, but walks upright on two legs; species, unknown.

Seen in 1832

In one form or another, yetis have been in and out of the public eye since 1832, when Nepal's first British Resident, B.H. Hodson, described a hitherto unknown creature that "moved erectly, was covered in long, dark hair, and had no tail."

But it was not until 1951, when the British mountaineer Eric Shipton published a series of photographs (taken in the Gauri Sankar range of the Himalayas) of humanoid footprints, 13 inches long and 8 inches wide, that the yeti, or Abominable Snowman, became an international household name.

Too large for a bear

Shipton said the tracks were too large to have been made by a bear and too fresh to have been enlarged by melting.

"What really made my flesh creep," he added, "was that where we had to jump crevasses you could see clearly where the creature had dug its toes in."

Yeti hunting became a popular pastime. Sherpas were happy to relate stories of these giant creatures of the mountains, and monasteries in many parts of the Himalayas turned up bones, skins, and scalps allegedly of yetis.

A conical scalp found in a village in Nepal was triumphantly displayed in the West. But it was analyzed as skin and hair similar to that of a Nepalese goat.

No one has ever managed to capture a yeti, but the clues continue to accumulate year after year:

In 1948 a Norwegian uranium prospector, Jan Frostis, claimed he was attacked and his shoulder badly mauled by one of two yetis he encountered near Zemu Gap, in Sikkim.

A fragment of skin, the joint of an index finger, and a thumb from a mummified hand were found in Nepal, in the 1950's. It was thought by some zoologists and anthropologists to be "almost human" and "similar in some respect to that of Neanderthal man."

Thomas Slick, a Texas oilman who cosponsored a 1957 yeti hunt, was told by scores of Nepalese villagers that yetis had battered to death at least five people in the preceding four years.

An expedition sponsored by the London *Daily Mail* found footprints and droppings, which, when analyzed, were found to indicate the diet of a creature that, like man, lived on part animal, part vegetable matter.

Prehistoric ape theory

One theory about yetis is that they could be descendants of *Gigantopithecus,* which includes the giant ape, remains of which were found by Dutch paleontologist Ralph von Koenigswald. In the 1930's Von Koenigswald found teeth in various parts of Asia that could have belonged to an ape between 11 and 13 feet tall.

It has been argued that if giant apes such as these could not compete for survival with man in the forests, they may have taken to remote, mountainous regions to avoid annihilation.

Skeptics have pointed out that such "clues" as teeth could be left by bears, langur monkeys, Himalayan foxes, gray wolves, or snow leopards. Others have suggested that yetis are hallucinations caused by lack of oxygen at high altitudes.

But not all the evidence has been satisfactorily dismissed, nor have the skeptics been able to explain the sightings of similar creatures in the northwestern United States.

Literally hundreds of sighting reports have poured into Canadian newspapers and broadcasting stations. In 1973 a Canadian publishing company offered a $100,000 reward to anyone who could bring in a Sasquatch alive.

In 1967 rancher Roger Patterson, of Yakima, Washington, shot 29 feet of 16-millimeter film of a tall hairy creature, walking upright across a creek 125 yards away, near Eureka, California. He got a blurred, brief sequence of the animal—a female with pendulous breasts—taking long strides, swinging her arms, and turning briefly to look at the camera, before disappearing into the woods.

Trail of river slime

Recently, Bigfoot, as Californians call the creature, seems to have put in appearances in southern Illinois. From Murphysboro, a small community on the banks of the Big Muddy River, came several reports of a huge apelike creature.

At midnight on June 25, 1973, a couple sitting in a parked car heard weird shrieks from a nearby woods. Lumbering toward them was an eight-foot figure, covered in light-colored hair and matted with mud. The couple drove off and reported the incident to the police.

Other sightings of what became known as the Murphysboro Mud Monster followed. Two teenagers said it smelled of foul river slime.

Workers on a nearby fairground said that they saw the monster gazing at some tethered ponies.

Police chief Toby Berger ordered a search, but all that was found was a trail of crushed grass, broken trees, and gobs of black slime.

Tony Stevens, editor of *The Southern Illinoisan,* said: "This is no hoax. This is hunting country, and anyone who goes around in an animal costume is going to get his butt shot off."

The mystery remains, from the Himalayas to the Rockies, from the Gobi Desert to southern Illinois. There have also been reports of apelike, hairy men in regions of Africa and South America.

The ancient legend

The legend of wild half-men is universal, reaching from the satyrs and centaurs of Greek mythology to Tarzan and similar heroes of modern fiction.

Harlan Sorkin, an expert in yeti lore from St. Louis, Missouri, believes that the creature is the result of a gene deviation in a species of large ape.

He comments: "The gorilla was not discovered until the early 1800's. Can you imagine what people thought when they first saw it?"

DROWNED CITIES

The sea takes revenge for royal crimes

Seas around Britain have drowned at least three flourishing kingdoms, according to legend. One was Tyno Helig, which is said to have stretched northward from Gwynedd, under what is now Conway Bay.

Tyno Helig was apparently destroyed in the sixth century A.D. as a divine retribution for the sins of its rulers, who lived in Llys Helig Palace, two miles out in the sea as measured from the present Welsh coastline.

One version of the legend says that it was the crimes of King Helig ap Glannawg that brought disaster to his land. The sea swept in, drowning everyone except the King and his sons, who were spared to lead better lives.

For centuries people living on that part of the Welsh coast insisted that the ruins of the palace could be seen beneath the sea at low tide. However, in 1939 an underwater investigation proved that the "ruins"—covering five acres—were a natural rock formation, which had been submerged during the iron age.

Victim to human failings

A similar investigation in Cardigan Bay destroyed part of the legend of another "lost" land—the Lowland Hundred. This, too, was said to have perished through human failings. The story of the Lowland Hundred may well be a localized version of the Tyno Helig legend.

According to tradition, the Lowland Hundred was a fertile and prosperous territory, 40 miles long and 20 miles wide, connecting what is now Bardsey Island with the present coast. It was defended from the sea by a system of embankments and sluices.

The main city was Caer Gwyddno, where the lord of the territory, Gwyddno Garanhir, held court in the early sixth century.

It was there that a great feast was held one night—and during the festivities the sluice gates were opened either through carelessness or as a drunken prank. The whole land was drowned, along with all but a few inhabitants.

Seven miles west of Land's End a group of rocks called the Seven Stones is referred to by some Cornish fisherman as "The Town." It is said to be the site of the Capital of Lyonesse, a flourishing kingdom that, according to legend, once connected Cornwall with the Scilly Isles. Lyonesse—called Lethowstow in Cornish—had many prosperous villages and no fewer than 140 churches.

One man escaped

The sea apparently began encroaching on Lyonesse at an alarming rate some time in the fifth century A.D., yet only a man named Trevellyan realized the potential danger. He sent his family to Cornwall for safety. Soon afterward the land was swallowed up by the Atlantic, but Trevellyan reached Cornwall on horseback—the sole survivor of the catastrophe.

In the 16th century there were reports of fishermen hauling up window frames and other parts of buildings near the Seven Stones, which gave rise to the belief that Lyonesse's Capital lay there.

Although Lyonesse, Tyno Helig, and the Lowland Hundred belong to mythology, parts of all three areas were inhabited at one time. Traces of human occupation have been found on submerged salt flats between the Scilly Isles and off the coasts of Cornwall and Wales.

The people who lived there would have been gradually driven farther inland, and their accounts of abandoned hamlets being engulfed by waves were, perhaps, embellished by the fertile imagination of their descendants.

HORSE REMEMBERED. *The coat of arms of the Trevellyan family depicts the white horse on which their ancestor escaped from Lyonesse.*

LOST CONTINENTS

Which one was the Garden of Eden?

Stories of lost continents and cities have stirred men's minds for centuries. To this day the search goes on for the island of Atlantis, which was supposedly destroyed by earthquakes and tidal waves in the 15th century B.C. But if the legend is to be believed, two vastly bigger civilizations have vanished without a trace—also victims of natural disasters. They are the continents of Lemuria and Mu, each one credited with being the original Garden of Eden.

The theory that Lemuria once covered a huge area of what is now the Indian Ocean gained scholarly support in the mid-19th century, to explain similarities in animal and plant life on continents separated by thousands of miles of sea. The British zoologist P. L. Sclater coined the name Lemuria from the lemur family of animals, which are found in Africa, southern India, and Malaya. He claimed that the lemurs must have been split up when the sea swamped their central homeland—an area that presumably stretched from the Malagasy Republic across the south coast of Asia to the Malay Archipelago.

Fossil links

This theory was backed up by the finding of similar animal fossils in the South African province of Natal and southern India. Nineteenth-century evolutionists, such as England's Thomas Huxley, expressed their belief in Lemuria, and the German biologist Ernst Haeckel went a step further by suggesting that the vanished continent had been "the probable cradle of the human race." From this developed the idea that the continent of Lemuria was Eden.

The lost continent of Mu was supposed to have been situated in the Pacific. According to Col. James Churchward, the Anglo-American who first told the world of Mu in 1870, this continent was 5,000 miles long and 3,000 miles wide, with its center just south of the Equator.

Ancient language

Churchward claimed to have learned about Mu in India during the famine of 1866. He described how a Hindu priest taught him an ancient language, Naacal, which was apparently the original tongue of all mankind. The colonel was then able to decipher the story of Mu on ancient stone tablets hidden in the priest's temple.

The tablet revealed that man first appeared in Mu 2 million years ago, and a sophisticated race of 64 million people had evolved. Then the continent was completely destroyed in a single volcanic eruption. But there were some survivors, and from them sprang all the world's present races.

Both Lemuria and Mu may well have existed, for earthquakes, floods, and volcanic eruptions have changed the face of the earth many times. Certainly continents thousands of miles apart were once joined together, which accounts for plants and animals of the same species being found in different parts of the world. It is now known that this is due to continental drift—masses of land moving away from each other. But the continents drifted apart long before man first appeared on the earth several million years ago.

BUSHMAN'S PARADISE

THE BUSHMEN of South Africa's Kalahari Desert are poor by the world's standards, but there is a legend that they know of a secret oasis, hidden among the Kalahari's burning dunes, where huge diamonds lie on the ground in enormous quantities. There is a story that only one white man, a soldier lost from his patrol in the desert, has ever seen the fabulous oasis. He was captured and taken there by Bushmen, the primitive tribesmen who inhabit the Kalahari. But he escaped and raised money for an expedition to make his fortune.

He was found dead weeks later with a Bushman's arrow through his heart. In his pocket, according to the story, were several rough diamonds and a map showing the route to the Bushman's paradise. No one knows what became of the map, but some believe the diamond oasis still awaits discovery.

WHO IS THE MAN IN THE MOON?

CHILDREN OF THE Western World have translated the markings on the moon as a human face that they have dubbed half-seriously the Man in the Moon.

According to a German tale, he is an old man who offended God by cutting sticks on a Sunday and was swept up to eternal imprisonment on the moon. Another story labels him as a Christmas Eve cabbage thief, who on each anniversary reveals his bundle of cabbage to the world.

A Puritan yarn claims that he is being punished for using brambles and thorns to block the path to church. One of the many punishments that tradition has heaped upon Judas Iscariot is that of being imprisoned upon the moon. To the Masai of Kenya, the markings show a woman's face with swollen lips and a missing eye. These injuries were inflicted in a quarrel, by her husband, the sun.

The Chinese tell gentler tales. They see the Man in the Moon as a toad, a rabbit pounding rice, or an old man who binds married couples with a silken cord.

THE KINGDOM OF PRESTER JOHN

Somewhere was a country where poverty and vice were unknown

Early in this century Portuguese missionaries in Ethiopia reported finding ancient Christian banners and swords that had been handed down from generation to generation with the story that they had once belonged to a godlike Christian King.

Could this King have been the legendary Prester John? For centuries stories persisted of a fabulously wealthy priest-king and his mysterious land in the East, where peace and justice reigned and poverty and vice were unknown.

It was also a land of marvels. In the Middle Ages a traveler wrote: "In one region grows no poisonous herb, nor does the querulous frog ever quack in it; no scorpion exists, nor does the serpent glide amongst the grass."

Getting there was a frightening ordeal. In the desert were wild men "hideous to look on; for they be horned, and they speak nought, but they grunt, as pigs." Then came vicious pygmies, giants, and finally a race "who feed on the flesh of men and of prematurely born animals, and never fear death.

"When any of these people die, their friends and relations eat him ravenously, for they regard it as a main duty to munch human flesh. We lead them at our pleasure against our foes, and neither man nor beast is left undevoured. When all our foes are eaten, then we return with our hosts home again."

Prester John's palace was built of crystal and roofed with precious gems. A magic mirror gave him a warning of any plotting that was being done in the realm.

Fountain of youth

The King slept on a bed of sapphires. His robes were made of salamander wool and cleaned in fire. Dragons were saddled and ridden through the air. The fountain of youth was available to all, and the King himself was 562 years old.

Prester John, whose name meant John the Priest, was said to be leader of the Nestorians, an early Christian sect, and descended from one of the three Kings who visited the infant Jesus.

The stories about him seem to have been started by Bishop Hugh of Gebal (presently Lebanon) in 1145. Christians of the Nestorian sect played some part in the conquests of the Mongol conqueror Yeh-lu Ta-shih, and the bishop may have deliberately confused the reports to make it seem that the conquerors were Christian.

Then, in 1165, a forged letter circulated throughout the courts of Europe. Several copies of the letter exist, one in the British Museum. It purports to have been written by Prester John himself.

Addressed to the Byzantine Emperor Manuel, it refers to Prester John as ruler of India and "Lord of Lords."

In 1177 Pope Alexander III sent a letter to "John the Illustrious and Magnificent King of the Indies." It gave Prester John permission to build a shrine in Rome, thus uniting the Christian Church.

Nothing more was heard of the legend until 1221, when information reached Rome from a

CHRISTIAN KING. *The Portuguese cartographer Diogo Homem's atlas of 1558 shows Prester John presiding over his kingdom. For centuries travelers sought this land of milk and honey.*

prominent churchman, the Bishop of Acre. He shed new light on the mystery by reporting that King David of India was alleged to be a grandson of John. This David was probably none other than Genghis Khan.

About 1300 the elusive empire was placed in China. Marco Polo and Giovanni da Montecorvino reported that a prince "6th in descent from Prester John" ruled a territory west of Peking.

After the middle of the 14th century, the search was directed toward Abyssinia, now Ethiopia, and Prester John was believed to be its Christian ruler.

Some modern scholars have suggested that "John" is merely an incorrect rendering of "Zan," the royal title of Ethiopia. The country has been Christian since the fourth century. About 1270 the present royal line was founded, claiming its descent from King Solomon and the Queen of Sheba.

BLACK STUMP AND CROOKED MICK

"BEYOND THE BLACK STUMP." To many Australians this phrase conjures up a land where the improbable becomes likely and reality shades into fantasy.

There may never have been an actual black stump to mark the border of the wild outback, even though some people say it stood between Gunbar and Crow's Nest Tank in New South Wales.

Beyond it lies the Speewah, a mythical sheep station of enormous size. The wandering sheep shearers of the 1870's and 1880's told of mighty deeds done on the Speewah, especially by Crooked Mick.

Mick was the mythical shearer who worked at such a clip that his shears ran hot and had to be stood in the water pot to cool. He ate two sheep at each meal. When he was fencing, he used an ax in each hand. He dug holes for posts with a shovel in one hand and a crowbar in the other to save time.

THE FORTUNATE ISLES

The dream lands to the west

Men have always dreamed of earthly paradises: places of great peace and beauty, where there is no war or poverty and there is justice for everyone; islands where there is permanent respite from the cares of the world.

Despite the efforts of the medieval church to discourage such popular mythology, belief in some kind of western paradise was still widespread among people at all levels of society. The Celts, in particular, believed in the Isles of the Dead—another world where men's immortal souls could find eternal peace.

Poets and minstrels spread their versions of these imaginary lands, and strange flotsam from far across the seas that washed up on the western coasts of Europe may have helped to make the dream appear more real.

From the ancient Greeks to the Celts and Anglo-Saxons, these earthly paradises, generally thought of as islands somewhere in the west, beyond the setting sun, were known variously as Meropis, Ogygia, the Fortunate Isles, the Garden of the Hesperides, and Avalon. To the Scottish and Irish Celts in particular, it was known as Tir nan Og—the Land of Youth.

When the legendary King Arthur, who is believed to have reigned over the Britons before the Saxon conquest, was about to die, he was reputedly carried off in a barge to the Isle of Avalon, the Celtic Isle of the Blessed.

Glastonbury, in England, is often associated with the Isle of Avalon and with the stories of Arthur's passing.

In 1190 what were believed to be the remains of Arthur and Queen Guinevere were found in the ancient cemetery of Glastonbury Abbey. They were put in the abbey church, in a tomb that was rediscovered in 1931.

Arthur's court

Glastonbury Tor, a curious conical hill set in rich meadows, was surrounded by swamps and marshes around A.D. 500, the assumed time of Arthur, and is probably what was thought to be the Isle of Avalon.

Camelot was Arthur's legendary court, and speculation has placed it at several different sites in Britain.

In *Morte d'Arthur,* Sir Thomas Malory sug-

gests Camelot was at Winchester; but other suggestions, based on local folklore, have placed Camelot at Colchester, for which the Roman name was Camulodunum, or near Tintagel, in Cornwall, where the River Camel and the market town of Camelford are situated.

Cadbury Castle

But the most popular site, backed to a certain extent by archeological evidence, is Cadbury Castle, in Somerset. The castle—the remains of a fortified hill—is near the village of Queen Camel. John Leland, an antiquarian of Henry VIII's reign, wrote that local people often referred to the hill on which the fort was found as "Camalat."

It has also been claimed that the nearby Cam River was the scene of King Arthur's last battle, Camlann, which is referred to in *Historia Britonum,* written by the ninth-century British historian Nennius.

It is said that farm laborers once unearthed a large number of skeletons in a mass grave west

of Cadbury Castle, as if a battle had once taken place there.

The legend of Arthur being only wounded in the battle, eventually recovering, and returning to rule in a golden age has a parallel in another medieval myth of the land of Ogygia.

Plutarch (A.D. 46–120), the Greek writer-philosopher, wrote that Ogygia was in the west, a place of enchanting beauty beneath the setting sun.

There, it is said, sleeps Cronus, the Greek Titan god, who castrated his father, Uranus, and devoured most of his children for fear of being usurped. Like Arthur, Cronus would one day awaken to rule in a golden age.

Ancient Greek poetry says that Ogygia is a land where youth reigns, a land of plenty where the golden age lasts forever.

Glass palace

There, a glass palace floats to receive the souls of the blessed. Youths and maidens are said to dance on soft, dewy grass. Trees are laden with apples, and cows can fill ponds at one milking.

Stories of a distant island paradise became so popular in medieval Europe that it became the subject of burlesque and, in France, was nick-named "Cockaigne," or "land of cakes."

A 13th-century English poem describes Cock-aigne as being west of Spain, while a French one said roast geese go down the streets of Cock-aigne and there is a fountain of youth there.

But despite the fun poking, the myth of a happy western land held its own in the popular imagination among medieval peoples. Germans called it Engel-land (since England lay to the west), and Slav people dreamed of an apple-orchard paradise in a far-distant western land.

The Irish and Scottish Celts believed that Tir nan Og was a city of palaces, located either somewhere beneath the Atlantic or at the bottom of an unknown lake.

This creation was also adopted into the mythology of the Norse people who invaded Ireland and took back legends to their home-lands. They called it Ireland hit Mikla (Greater Ireland) and believed it lay west of the Ireland they knew.

WAS THIS CAMELOT? *Rising out of green English fields, the ancient fortified hill of Cadbury Castle is backed by both local legend and modern archeology as the seat of King Arthur's legendary court.*

THERE IS A HAPPY LAND

Age-old ideas of life after death

The twin concepts of heaven and hell have fascinated man since his earliest days. Cultures all over the world have shared a common belief in the promise of eternal peace and happiness for those who have lived virtuously—and the awful threat of eternal agony for those who have transgressed.

The classic vision of heaven and hell in modern times has tended to become a cliche, and few clergymen now subscribe to the picture of angels, harps, and halos, or to the alternative fate of an underground inferno.

However, they believe in the life hereafter, although no one can possibly know exactly what this entails. Men's dreams of what lay beyond the grave were often a reflection of earthly desires. Desert peoples envisaged cool fountains; Viking warriors, the company of heroes.

Garden of Eden

The word "paradise" was originally Persian, and was later borrowed by the Greeks; it means literally "the land of the blessed." It denoted the enclosed pleasure gardens of the Persian Kings, and the name was adopted for the Garden of Eden.

Later, New Testament writers applied it to heaven, the celestial abode of the blessed Christian dead. In most mythologies and religions, this is located somewhere in the sky.

The Indian Vedic religion placed it in the outer sky, a realm of light. This paradise, too, was an enhancement of the individual's earthly lot, with "music, sexual fulfillment, no pain, and no care."

The dwelling of angels

Hinduism also has its paradise up above the clouds, while Buddhism has a graded series in a vague, nonastronomical heaven in the sky.

Christianity borrowed from both Hebrew and Greek religions. From Judaism came that region of the sky where God and his angels dwelt. From Greece came the spiritual journeyings.

The idea of seven heavens—the seventh and last being the ultimate in joy—is also Greek. Elysium was the home of the blessed of Greek mythology—hence, the Elysian fields of the poets. According to Homer, the most famous

CHINESE VIEW. *The souls of the just were allowed to enter the dwelling place of the immortals as a reward for having lived a good life. This design appears on an 18th-century porcelain dish.*

MEDIEVAL CONCEPT. *This detail from the painting "The Seven Deadly Sins," by the Dutch artist Hieronymus Bosch, shows an early medieval concept of heaven and the seat of judgment.*

GRADES OF HEAVEN. *Mahayana Buddhism teaches about a series of graded paradises, but its followers aim at release from personality, not enjoyment in paradise.*

PATHS TO HEAVEN AND TO HELL. *Many 19th-century American Christians had a clear idea of the ways to everlasting life or damnation.*

of the poets of ancient Greece, these fields lay "at the world's end." Other Greeks were more precise about their location—they were out over the Atlantic, where "the bounteous earth beareth honey-sweet fruit, fresh thrice a year."

Scandinavia's vision of Valhalla, the Viking's version of heaven, was slightly less restful, as Wagner's mighty operas depicted. Valhalla was the hall of the slain in Nordic mythology. The great palace of Asgard was said to have 450 gates so wide that 800 slain warriors could enter abreast. Inside, the god Odin feasted with the heroes brought to Valhalla by the Valkyries, his handmaidens. They rode resplendent into battle to select those of the dead worthy of dining with Odin. There was obviously no peace even for the brave, for once the dead were in Valhalla, they had to fight all day. But those who fell in battle were always restored in good time for the evening feast with their warlike god.

Ancient Chinese philosophy gave a gentle interpretation of the natural order thousands of years before Christ.

Many different heavens evolved where the dead journeyed to live together in happiness. The most important were the Isles of the Blest, in the Eastern Sea, and the Western Paradise, in the Turkestan Mountains.

The universe contained two interacting forces, the yang and the yin. Yang was the positive, or masculine, force—it was warm, active, hard, bright, procreative, and steadfast.

Negative qualities

Yin was negative, or feminine—and was represented as wet, cold, passive, soft, mysterious, dim, and changeable.

Their eternal intercourse brought into being heaven, which was predominantly yang, and earth, which was predominantly yin. While the dualism of other philosophies—such as good and evil—are always in conflict, yang and yin were invariably in accord.

Taoism is at the root of Chinese philosophy. It is a "way" or a "road," and understanding of Tao is the very secret of life. The unity of

JUDGMENT DAY. *A Japanese view of the fate of sinners is illustrated below.*

FROZEN HELL. *Dante imagined hell to be a frozen lake where all feelings died.*

heaven and earth is possible only when Tao is allowed to take its natural course. In time Taoism took on occult and magical overtones and became a dreamland ruled by a fairy queen.

Islam, youngest of the great religions, is also the simplest, revering a single supreme God, known as Allah. The word "Islam" itself means "submission"—to God's will. The word "Moslem" means "he who submits." Islamic belief is that God spoke through Mohammed, the prophet of Allah.

Mohammed himself set down the first units of the Koran, the Islamic "Bible," although whether it was completed in his lifetime is not known. The Koran vividly described the delights of heaven. It offers gardens, fountains, wine, and lovely virgins. Those who enter are at last allowed to drink the wine they were forbidden on earth.

Buddhists do not share the common belief in paradise. They—and all living things—are bound instead to countless cycles of birth, death, and rebirth.

Buddhism, which is the religion of followers of Gautama Buddha, sprang up in northern India in the sixth century B.C. and seeks to show man the way to deliverance from the pain of life. Only when a man surmounts his cravings and physical desires can he turn to the basic Buddhist concept of Nirvana—a state in which total peace is attained.

In early China, Japan, and Tibet, however, one sect of Buddhists believed in "The Great Western Paradise." This is described in an ancient text that has survived as "a place surrounded by radiant beams and brilliant jewels of untold price. . . .Buddha sits on his lotus seat like a gold mountain in the midst of all the glories, surrounded by his saints."

Threat of brimstone

Hell can be many things, but traditionally it has been portrayed through the ages of Judaism and Christianity as the grisly and terrifying means of keeping prospective sinners in line. This was the threat of certain eternal damnation, prefer-

WINGED DEMONS. *The damned, tormented by the winged demons of hell, are shown in a detail from Signorelli's "Last Judgment." It is based on Dante's journey through the nine circles of hell.*

ably in flames, and much ingenuity was used to depict doom and torture as a cogent reason for avoiding atheism, immorality, and crime.

A more modern view of hell would be Sartre's vision in his play *Huis Clos,* translated "Closed Circle," in which hell was quite simply two women and a man locked forever in a small room.

However, the early Christians totally accepted the threat of brimstone, which would account for the popularity of the *Apocalypse of Peter* in the second century A.D.

It says: "And some were there hanging by their tongues; and these were they that blasphemed the way of righteousness, and under them was laid fire flaming and tormenting them. . . .And in another place were gravelstones sharper than swords or any spit, heated with fire, and men and women clad in filthy rags rolled upon them in torment. . . .Beside them shall be girls clad in darkness for a garment, and they shall be sore chastised, and their flesh shall be torn in pieces. These are they that kept not their virginity until they were given in marriage."

Homer depicted for the Greeks a dreary darkness to which all, or very nearly all, the dead must go. This was the home of Hades, the god of death, ruling, as the *Iliad* put it, "hateful chambers of decay that fill the gods themselves with horror."

The Styx, an Arcadian stream, became the main river of the underworld. The dead were ferried across it by Charon, whose toll was a coin placed in the mouth or hand of the corpse.

For Islam, too, the picture was gloomy. Hell featured "coverings of fire . . . pestilential winds . . . scalding water."

DAY OF WRATH. *The 15th-century German artist Stephan Lochner depicts the terrors and joys of Judgment Day. Demons devour the damned while angels usher the blessed into paradise.*

PART

4

Tricksters who rocked and shocked the world

Hoaxes, frauds and forgeries

•

BUNGA-BUNGA

The supreme prank of a great practical joker

It was an awesome display of Great Britain's seapower. Line upon line of battleships and cruisers of the Home and Atlantic Fleets lay at anchor across the wide sweep of Weymouth Bay in Dorsetshire. In their midst loomed the vast bulk of the HMS *Dreadnought*, the Royal Navy's mightiest battleship.

On this February day in 1910 she was gay with flags and bunting in honor of a visit by a group of Abyssinian princes, accompanied by a high-ranking Foreign Office representative and an interpreter.

Protocol was strictly observed. The visitors were piped aboard and welcomed by officers in cocked hats and full dress, and naval ingenuity quickly overcame naval ignorance of the flag and national anthem of Abyssinia. The standard of Zanzibar was run up instead, while the Royal Marine Band played Zanzibar's national anthem. The guests were too polite to comment on this. In fact, they were full of admiration for everything they saw and occasionally threw up their arms and shouted "Bunga-bunga" in delight at the marvels of modern naval architecture. Only one thing looked as if it might mar the highly successful visit. The admiral refused to provide prayer mats for the party's sunset devotions. Embarrassment was avoided by not sounding the sunset bugle call, thus abolishing sunset for that day.

At the end of the visit crowds milled around the train at Weymouth station as the guests waited to make their return journey to London. It was noted that the chief prince had his face turned away as he waved his last farewell from the window of the train. This was because he had just sneezed and had blown away half of his mustache.

That sneeze almost gave away one of the most audacious hoaxes planned and executed by William Horace de Vere Cole, the greatest practical joker of his time.

The "princes" who trod the decks in flowing costumes were: Anthony Buxton, well known as a public school and university cricketer; Duncan Grant, an artist; Guy Ridley, a judge's son; Virginia Woolf, the novelist, who played a slender prince; and her brother, Adrian, who posed as the party's German interpreter. Herbert Cholmondeley, the man from the Foreign Office, was Cole himself.

Cole, a wealthy man-about-town, had a lively, creative mind and great planning ability. He exploited these gifts in the execution of his outrageous hoaxes, which sent Europe into gales of laughter.

When planning the *Dreadnought* affair, he decided that it would be impossible for the princes to learn Abyssinian. So he ordered visiting cards to be printed in Swahili and instructed his fellow hoaxers to make up a language of their own as they went along.

Cole persuaded Willy Clarkson, actress Sarah Bernhardt's makeup man, to disguise the party. Willy warned him, however, that any eating by the hoaxers would ruin the makeup—a warning that caused some complications later.

On the morning of the visit Cole donned his

THE ABYSSINIAN "PRINCES." *This is one of the photographs that William Horace de Vere Cole sent to newspapers to show the group of Abyssinian "princes" who paid a ceremonial visit to the* Dreadnought. *All Europe rocked with laughter at the navy's discomfiture.*

morning dress and went to the railroad station, announcing himself as Herbert Cholmondeley of the Foreign Office. He demanded a special train to take the princes to Weymouth, and an official committee to see them off.

The stationmaster protested at the short notice but agreed to add a special coach to a scheduled train. Then he put on his top hat, collected an honor guard of ticket inspectors, and greeted the dusky princes on a hastily laid red carpet.

Meanwhile, another conspirator sent a telegram in the name of the Foreign Office to the admiral of the fleet, ordering him to set up facilities for the distinguished visitors.

The admiral was annoyed by this interruption to the fleet's routine, but everything went well until tea was served in the *Dreadnought's* wardroom.

The man from the Foreign Office partook hungrily, and so too did the German interpreter. But the princes, aware of the precarious state of their makeup, refused to eat even one slice of cake.

When officers questioned Cole about the princes' lack of appetite, he explained that the Abyssinians were strict about having only two meals a day and that they had already had their quota.

The crisis was only just over when a more alarming threat to the hoaxers arose. The chief staff officer, who knew nothing about the visit, suddenly walked into the wardroom and was startled to hear the heavy German accent of the interpreter.

Cole was appalled, for the staff officer was related to Virginia Woolf and himself, and knew them both well. But he need not have worried; the officer was far too concerned that a possible German spy had been able to inspect all the secrets of the mighty *Dreadnought*.

He was about to tell the admiral of his disquiet, when Cole hastily gathered the party together and announced they would have to leave for their sunset prayers ashore.

Cole still had a few refinements to add. On the train back to London he explained to the dining-car waiters that, according to Abyssinian custom, the princes could receive food only from people wearing gray kid gloves. When the train stopped at Reading, a man was sent off to buy the gloves to serve the visitors properly.

451

THE MEDICINE MAN

His success as a surgeon led to his downfall

Everybody wants to be somebody. But Ferdinand Waldo Demara went a stage further. He wanted to be almost everybody. Demara, one of the great impostors of all time, successfully posed as a theologian, psychologist, doctor of philosophy, prison officer, teacher, and surgeon.

In 1941, after deserting from both the U.S. Army and Navy, he used the name of Dr. Robert Linton French, a doctor of philosophy, and joined a Trappist monastery in Kentucky. He introduced himself as a man who was sick of war and wanted only the peace of a religious order.

Demara submitted to all the disciplines except frugality. He began to steal food and then, by happy chance, was sent to work in the vineyards where he and another monk consumed grapes and let their vows of silence go by default.

Unfortunately, their sins found them out. The other brother confessed and remained in the monastery, but Demara decided he had had enough and left.

Exposed by brilliance

Unlike most impostors, whose deceptions are exposed by flaws in their schemes, Demara's downfall came about as a result of his brilliance.

This was in 1952, when he was in the middle of his most spectacular escapade. Demara had used the credentials of a doctor friend to get a commission as a surgeon-lieutenant in the Royal Canadian Navy during the Korean War.

He had met the doctor, Joseph C. Cyr, while posing as a physician turned theology student in New Brunswick. Young Dr. Cyr wanted an American medical license in Maine, so that he could practice in both Canada and the United States. Demara offered to present the doctor's papers to the Maine medical board. Instead, he used the papers to get himself accepted in the navy as Dr. Cyr.

His first task as medical officer on board HMCS *Cayuga* was to pull a tooth from the captain, Comdr. James Plomer. Demara, who had never pulled a tooth before, sat up all night reading a book on dentistry. In the morning he gave the captain a shot of novocaine and deftly removed the tooth.

From then on he revealed an amazing talent for medicine and surgery. His first serious case came when three wounded South Korean soldiers were brought on board. One had a bullet lodged near his heart. Before the eyes of many of the crew Demara went to work as if he had been a surgeon for years. Twelve hours later the soldier was able to leave the ship. A week later the *Cayuga* was again in the area, and Demara went ashore to find that his patient was making good progress.

While ashore, Demara was shocked by the lack of medical care and facilities, so he set up a clinic. Without any assistance he performed operations and amputations daily.

Portrait of a hero

Unfortunately for him, one of the *Cayuga*'s officers handled the navy's public relations in the Far East. This was a story not to be missed. The officer prepared a press and radio release that described the achievements of the heroic young doctor.

Less than a week after the story appeared in

THE DAY THE CHANNEL CAUGHT FIRE

BY THE end of September 1940 everyone in Britain had heard the story. The Germans had attempted to invade, and as a result, the entire English Channel was choked with charred German corpses. Waiting until the last possible moment, the defenders had, at the touch of a button, flooded the coastal waters with gasoline and set the sea ablaze. Doubters who wondered if there was sufficient fuel in all Britain for such a task were ignored. Everyone knew someone who had actually seen the bodies. To this day no one knows how the story began. The Germans never attempted an invasion, and though the British experimented with submerged oil pipes as a means of defense, the idea was quietly abandoned. Yet even now many people remember the day when the channel was set on fire.

American and Canadian newspapers, Demara was called to the captain's cabin. In embarrassed tones Captain Plomer said that he had received a message saying: "We have information that Joseph C. Cyr, surgeon-lieutenant o-17669, is an impostor. Remove from active duty immediately, repeat immediately. Conduct investigation and report facts to Chief of Naval Staff, Ottawa."

The story had been published in Canada where it was read to Dr. Cyr. He identified the navy's brilliant surgeon as the man he had known and admired as Dr. Cecil B. Hamann. To make matters worse, the real Dr. Hamann, who lived in Kentucky, said Demara sounded like the man who had been expelled from St. Louis University for cheating.

Demara was returned to Canada to face a naval inquiry board. He was discharged with all the pay due to him and told to leave the country.

That was by no means the end of Demara's escapades. Soon after leaving Canada, he sold his story to a magazine, then drifted from town to town until, in Houston, Texas, he read a recruiting advertisement for the prison service. He applied for a job as a prison officer under the name of Ben W. Jones and used a number of his earlier aliases as references.

As usual, he found that he had a flair for the job. He organized writing classes and sports days for the inmates.

His work quickly brought him to the attention of the director of the Texas Prison System, O. B. Ellis, who asked him to try out his progressive ideas at Huntsville Prison, which housed the state's toughest criminals.

Demara threw himself wholeheartedly into his new role, organizing classes, arranging movie showings, and establishing a helpful routine for the prisoners.

At the height of Demara's success disaster struck. One day a prisoner was reading a magazine when he discovered that Ben W. Jones was Ferdinand Waldo Demara, alias Joseph C. Cyr, alias Cecil B. Hamann and others.

Ellis called a meeting of prison officials to confront Demara. They showed him the magazine, and Demara flatly denied that he was the man in the article. He accused the officials of taking a prisoner's word against his and challenged anybody who disbelieved him to a duel. But Demara did not bluster for long. He packed his bags and left.

Ellis, like most of Demara's employers, has admitted that if Demara could return with genuine credentials and his past wiped out he would take him back. "He was one of the best prospects ever to serve in the prison service," he said.

Why did a man with such undoubted talents not study for genuine qualifications? When this question was once put to Demara, he replied cheerily: "Rascality, pure rascality."

In the end he became an ordained minister of the church. At last the great impostor had an identity of his own.

VICTIMS OF ARROGANCE

The Prussian officer was an odd type—but orders were orders

The elderly Prussian captain marched smartly up to a platoon of soldiers on a Berlin street and began to bark orders imperiously. He stopped a bus bound for the outlying Köpenick district and hustled the men aboard.

There, he marched them briskly to the office of Köpenick's mayor and snapped: "You are under arrest!"

Intimidated by the overbearing, authoritative manner of the officer, the mayor managed to ask, timidly: "Where is your warrant?"

"My warrant," roared the captain, "is the men I command."

The mayor, himself a reserve officer, wondered why the captain wore his cap badge upside down and was so old. But he kept his curiosity to himself.

And now the money
The captain then ordered the borough treasurer to hand over all the cash in the treasury—4,000 marks, worth about $2,000 today—and issued an "official" receipt.

The mayor, his wife, the treasurer, and the deputy mayor were then marched outside the town hall and held under guard. The captain ordered the men to stay at their posts for half an hour—and marched away with the money.

The captain was, in fact, Wilhelm Voigt, a

STRANGE PROCESSION. *Cobbler and ex-convict Wilhelm Voigt marched his commandeered platoon to the town hall of Köpenick. His haul was only $2,000.*

THE CARTOONIST'S VIEW. *Voigt's mocking of the Prussians' deep respect for uniforms was eagerly seized upon by contemporary cartoonists.*

cobbler and ex-convict, who had exploited the Prussian awe of uniformed authority to rob Köpenick of its petty cash in October 1906.

Ten days later, when the police arrived at Voigt's attic home, they found the uniform wrapped in a bundle. Voigt did not resist arrest but asked only to be allowed to finish his breakfast.

Voigt, who explained that he had learned to mimic the speech and mannerisms of Prussian officers while mending their boots as an apprentice in Tilsit, was imprisoned for four years.

His exploit had attracted great public sympathy and affection, however, and he was pardoned by the Kaiser after serving half his sentence. Voigt retired in comfort to Luxembourg on a life pension, given to him by a rich Berlin dowager who had been impressed by his sheer audacity. The moral seems to be that crime sometimes does pay—if done with style.

DOWNFALL OF GOOD OLD STAN

The hoaxer who made the mistake of playing straight

Stanley Clifford Weyman was known as a pleasant fellow, a smooth talker with an ability to influence people. "Good old Stan" is how he is remembered by most of those who knew him.

Good old Stan, alias Stephen Weinberg, posed, among other things, as the U.S. consul in Morocco, Peruvian ambassador to the United States, Rumanian consul general in New York, Serbian military attaché in Washington, and a State Department protocol expert. In 1948 he was released from prison after serving a seven-year sentence for organizing schemes for dodging the U.S. Armed Forces draft.

Pretending to be a former journalist, he got a job as a news agency reporter at the United Nations in New York. Every day he broadcast reports on the United Nations for a small radio station and once a week brought international celebrities to the microphone.

He told members of the Thailand delegation that he worked with the U.S. Office of Strategic Services in their country during the war—though, in fact, he spent most of the war in jail.

The Thais were impressed and asked him to become their press officer, a post carrying diplomatic status. After years of diplomatic self-appointment it seemed a dream come true for Weinberg.

He wrote to the U.S. State Department in 1951, asking if his American citizenship would be affected if he took the post. That led to his undoing. The department checked on his past —and his whole list of deceptions was revealed.

Weinberg could not take the diplomatic job, and to add to his misery, the news agency fired him. Good old Stan's one attempt to play it straight had led him to disaster.

RISE OF MARVIN HEWITT

The "academic" who wrote his own references

Given the right references and enough self-confidence, it is possible to go far in the academic world. Marvin Hewitt had both, for he wrote the references himself. Though he had left school at 17 without completing his studies, he posed as a doctor of philosophy in physics and lectured at several U.S. universities for eight years.

Hewitt had an obsession for mathematics, but his family did not have enough money to send him to college. On leaving school he worked in factories for six years, before he saw an advertisement for a schoolteacher. He described himself as a university graduate and taught for a term. But he was more ambitious.

In 1945 he took a name from a university staff list and used it to become an aerodynamicist at an aircraft factory. But the name he chose was so well known that he knew it would only be a matter of time before he was found out.

Hewitt moved to the Philadelphia College of Pharmacy and Science, where he taught physics as Julius Ashkin, of Columbia University.

The following year he went to a teachers' college in Minnesota, where he impressed the college president with his impeccable—although imaginative—references. Here, he made something of an academic name for himself. This was unfortunate, because the real Julius Ashkin wrote to him gently suggesting that the masquerade should end.

Other names, other titles

Hewitt was not a man to give up easily. He successively became George Hewitt, "formerly research director of the Radio Corporation of America," Clifford Berry, Ph. D., and Kenneth Yates, Ph.D. Once again his obsession for taking other people's names and fictionalizing his accomplishments betrayed him. Somebody discovered that the real Kenneth Yates was working for an oil company.

This time the newspapers picked up the story, and the publicity was so extensive that Marvin Hewitt had no alternative but to find work outside the academic world.

THE GREATEST LIAR ON EARTH

THE STORY by Louis de Rougement of "30 years among the cannibals of Australia" caused a sensation. Scientific societies invited him to give lectures on his experiences, and a waxworks model of him was placed in Madame Tussaud's in London. In 1898 De Rougement described in the magazine *Wide World* how, after being shipwrecked off the northwestern coast of Australia, he had taken part in cannibal feasts, built a house of pearl shells, sent off fleets of pelicans carrying messages in six languages, and ridden on 600-pound turtles. He also claimed to have cured himself of fever by sleeping in the body of a dead buffalo. When exposed as a fraud, the unabashed Louis cashed in again by giving lectures in South Africa, describing himself as "The Greatest Liar on Earth."

THE TICHBORNE CLAIMANT

A race horse that changed into a cart horse

For 11 years the Dowager Lady Tichborne had waited for her son to return from the dead. Now the miracle had happened. In her hands she held a letter that seemed to justify the waiting and her faith.

The letter from Australia appeared to be from her long-lost son, Sir Roger Charles Doughty Tichborne, heir to the Tichborne estates in Hampshire, England, and descendant of a family dating back 200 years before the Norman Conquest. Though the handwriting was crude and the language smacked more of London's East End and the Australian bush than the drawing room, Lady Tichborne was pathetically eager to be convinced that the letter came from Sir Roger.

She had last seen him in March 1854, after he had resigned his commission as an officer of the Sixth Dragoons. A love affair with his cousin Katherine had broken up, and he decided to set off on a long tour of South America and Mexico to get her completely out of his mind.

By the following month he had reached Rio de Janeiro, which he left aboard the *Bella* of Liverpool. The ship was never seen again. As the months wore on, all hope of survivors disappeared. The letters Roger had asked to be directed to Kingston, Jamaica, remained uncollected. Eventually, Lloyd's of London wrote off the *Bella* as lost and settled insurance claims.

Roger's French-born mother, Henriette, refused to abandon hope and after the death of her husband, Sir James, clung even more to the conviction that her son was still alive.

She placed advertisements in several newspapers in South America and Australia, offering

THE CLAIMANT. *Arthur Orton weighed 330 pounds when he first claimed to be Sir Roger Tichborne in 1866. He had wavy fair hair and no tattoo marks. He could not speak French.*

THE HEIR. *Sir Roger Tichborne weighed under 125 pounds before he disappeared at sea in 1854. He had straight dark hair and a tattoo on his left arm. He spoke French fluently.*

a reward for information. One of them was seen by Arthur Orton. The youngest of 12 children, he had been forced to leave his overcrowded home in London's East End and go to sea. In 1849 he deserted his ship in Valparaiso and some time later returned to England, using the name Joseph M. Orton. In 1852 he departed again, this time for Australia.

There he was alleged to have been a member of a horse-stealing gang. He next turned up as a cattle slaughterer in Wagga Wagga, and it was there in 1865 that he read Lady Tichborne's advertisement and began his long deception.

Orton was about to file a bankruptcy petition when he confessed to his lawyer that he had property in England. He also hinted that he had been shipwrecked. The lawyer, who had also seen the advertisement, was interested.

After Orton was seen carving the initials "RCT" on trees, posts, and even on his pipe, it was hardly surprising that his lawyer should ask him: "Are you Roger Tichborne?" The impostor allowed himself to be persuaded to write to Lady Tichborne about his "inheritance."

Deeply involved

Orton was by now far too deeply involved to back out as he had already raised about £20,000 on the strength of his "expectations." In 1866 he and his family set sail for England.

Soon after he arrived, he traveled to Hampshire and quietly tried to familiarize himself with his "home" surroundings and at the same time enlist the support of the Tichborne locals.

But he met with little success. The village blacksmith dismissed Orton's suggestion that he was Sir Roger: "If you are, you've changed from a race horse to a cart horse!"

Sir Roger had weighed under 125 pounds, had a long, sallow face with straight dark hair, and had a tattoo on his left arm. Orton weighed 330 pounds and had a large, round face and wavy fair hair. He had no tattoo. In spite of this glaring disparity, Orton decided to meet Lady Tichborne. She was then living in Paris, and eventually, it was there, in Orton's hotel bedroom, that their meeting took place on a January afternoon. Orton said he was ill, and the room was kept darkened.

He spoke to her of his grandfather, whom the real Roger had never seen, wrongly said he had served in the ranks of the army, and referred to his school, Stonyhurst, as Winchester.

His blunders were glaring and, to anyone but

a grief-stricken and self-deluding old woman, completely damning. But without hesitation she accepted him as her son. "He confuses everything as in a dream," she fondly observed.

The rest of the family, their friends, and servants refused to have anything to do with him, but this did not deter Orton. He began a legal action, claiming the Tichborne estates, worth between £20,000 and £25,000, from the trustees of the infant Sir Alfred Tichborne, posthumous son of Roger's younger brother. Before the case got to court, his case was drastically weakened by the sudden death of Lady Tichborne.

While he awaited the court hearing, Orton engaged as servants two men who had been in Roger's regiment. With their help he memorized many details of regimental life so well that 30 of the dead man's brother officers were willing to swear that he was Sir Roger despite his extraordinary change in appearance.

He produced more than 100 witnesses who testified that he was the real Sir Roger. None was really close to the family, but they made a powerful showing against the 17 who spoke against him.

Inevitably, it was his rough way of speaking that condemned him. "I would have won if only I could have kept my mouth shut," he said later.

The case went on for 102 days and cost the Tichborne family £90,000. After losing the action, Orton was charged with perjury. He was jailed for 14 years.

Loyal supporters

Amazingly, the discredited Orton still had supporters. Dr. Kenealy, the lawyer who defended him, tried to turn the case into a national issue, and his vehement defense led to his being disbarred for unprofessional conduct.

Orton completed 10 years of his 14-year sentence and, after his release, arranged a tour of public meetings in a vain attempt to regain sympathy. He also worked at a music hall and later in a saloon and a tobacconist's shop. With poverty facing him, he sold his "confession" to the newspaper *People* for £3,000. But he still died penniless.

Even in death, Orton was able to inspire the belief of one unknown person, for there is an inscription on his grave: "Sir Roger Charles Doughty Tichborne; born 5 January 1829; died 1 April 1898."

THE NECKLACE OF FATE

A jewel that led to revolution

The most brazen confidence trick in history had its beginnings in 1772, when Mme. du Barry, mistress of the aging Louis XV, demanded that her doting royal lover buy her the most expensive diamond necklace in the world.

Louis could refuse her nothing and commissioned Boehmer, the court jeweler, to search Europe for the finest diamonds in existence. Boehmer was delighted. He bought some 600 stones and strung them together in a necklace whose price of 2 million livres (about $7 million by today's reckoning) was almost as breathtaking as its vulgarity.

Proudly, Boehmer awaited the summons to Versailles; but, unfortunately, the King fell victim to a smallpox epidemic and died. Ruin stared the jeweler in the face. Neither the new King, Louis XVI, nor his 20-year-old Queen, Marie Antoinette, had any use for a necklace "like a scarf."

For years Boehmer besieged the palace. Each time the Queen gave birth to a child, he would hurry to Versailles, hoping that she would change her mind and buy the necklace for the christening. But she never did.

The cardinal and the adventuress

Marie Antoinette's distaste for the necklace was exceeded only by her loathing for Cardinal de Rohan, who during her girlhood had been French Ambassador to the court of her mother, the Empress of Austria. Indeed, the objects of her dislike had much in common; to the Queen both were worldly, pretentious, and immoral. De Rohan's affairs were notorious throughout Europe. A courtier as well as a prince of the church, he had amassed a fortune in bribes, much of which he spent on his mistresses. He was well aware that the Queen despised him, and more than anything else he wanted to ingratiate himself with her.

It is at this point that Jeanne de la Motte, self-styled countess, enters the story. She was born Jeanne de Saint-Remy and was apparently a genuine descendant of the Valois, the old royal family of France. Her husband, De la Motte, was a penniless army officer, who on the strength of his wife's royal blood awarded himself the title of count.

It was said of Jeanne that she could charm people into believing anything, and she used all her wiles to convince Cardinal de Rohan that she had such influence with the Queen that she could restore him to royal favor. Jeanne's gentle persuasion extended over several months. With the aid of a forger she produced a number of letters, apparently in the Queen's handwriting, proving that Marie Antoinette's heart had softened toward the cardinal.

Then she brought out her master stroke. She found a girl who somewhat resembled the Queen and arranged that the cardinal should meet her late one night in a dark grove on the grounds of Versailles.

All De Rohan could see was a silhouette of the same height and build as the Queen, and as he knelt in adoration, she pressed a rose into his hand and flitted away into the darkness.

The cardinal was overjoyed. Not only had the Queen forgiven him but she was apparently in love with him as well. So when he received a

HOAXER'S VICTIM. *Marie Antoinette, born Maria Antionetta, daughter of the Empress Maria Theresa of Austria, was despised by the Paris mob even before the scandal of the necklace and the supposed love affair with the cardinal. She was guillotined in 1793.*

note from her beseeching him to buy the necklace on her behalf, he was delighted to comply. Naturally, the transaction would be secret, and the only go-between permitted would be the Queen's dearest and most trusted friend, the Countess de la Motte.

So the cardinal bought the necklace and passed it on to Jeanne, whose husband promptly carried it off to London. There it was broken up and the stones sold to several Bond Street jewelers. Wisely, the "count" remained in England, but Jeanne continued to live in Paris, where, with the money her husband sent her, she bought a house and carriages and entertained her lovers in grand style.

Outraged Queen

It took about six months before the cardinal summoned sufficient courage to ask the Queen why she did not wear the necklace. Marie Antoinette was outraged and, instead of hushing the matter up, demanded that it should be put before Parliament. Jeanne was arrested, found guilty, branded with a V for *voleuse* ("thief"), and thrown into prison.

The court rocked with laughter, but the scandal took the French people by storm. Marie Antoinette was already unpopular, and the mob was entirely prepared to believe that the cardinal was her lover who had bought her fabulous presents while Frenchmen starved. Riots broke out, and Jeanne, who was considered to be an innocent scapegoat, mysteriously vanished from prison, probably with the aid of revolutionaries. She fled to England, where she wrote to the newspapers protesting her innocence and insisting on the Queen's guilt.

Gunpowder of revolution

Undoubtedly, the necklace affair was one of the sparks that touched off the gunpowder of revolution. In 1793, when Marie Antoinette was on trial for her life, she was asked about her connection with Jeanne de la Motte; her protests that she had never met her were howled down. The Queen, who was already unpopular, was guillotined.

There were no means of confirmation one way or the other, for Jeanne had died two years earlier, having jumped from the window of her lodgings off the Edgware Road in London in an attempt to avoid her many creditors.

SPARK OF REVOLUTION. *Six hundred of the finest diamonds were used to create the world's most expensive necklace for Mme. du Barry, mistress of Louis XV. Yet no one ever wore it; after it was stolen, the necklace was broken up, and the stones were sold in London.*

THE END OF THE AFFAIR. *From a Paris window the artist Jacques Louis David made this sketch of the doomed Queen Marie Antoinette on her way to the guillotine. At her trial she was accused of being Cardinal de Rohan's mistress and of conspiring with him to steal the necklace. Both charges were probably untrue, but it made little difference; the mob was determined to have her head.*

THE PROTOCOLS OF ZION

The most damaging fraud in history

One summer day in 1903 the citizens of the Russian capital of St. Petersburg were startled by the news in their morning paper. It claimed to have unmasked a sinister plot by a small group of men to seize power and rule the world by force. Cities were to be bombed and opponents wiped out by injecting them with dreadful diseases. The myth of the great Jewish conspiracy—the "Protocols of the Elders of Zion"—had been born.

The item in the St. Petersburg newspaper had been entitled: "A Program for World Conquest by the Jews. Minutes of a Meeting of the Elders of Zion." The editor of the paper, a well-known anti-Semite, did not reveal the source of his information but claimed that it was a translation of a document originally written in French.

The forgery professed to be a series of lectures in which a member of a secret Jewish society outlined its plot to achieve world domination. This ambitious plot was said to be well under way.

The rot spreads

In the early stages the liberal democracies of Europe were to be undermined and Christian morality discredited by propaganda. Jewish businessmen would stir industrial unrest by keeping prices high. And then, when the Gentile society collapsed, the bombs and germs would be thrown into battle.

So widely accepted did this nonsense become that in 1905, just two years after the "Protocols" were published, the Metropolitan of Moscow ordered them to be quoted in every church in the city, as a warning to the faithful.

But it was after the First World War that the "Protocols" really spread. In Britain *The Times* commented on them, though it also published a refutation. In Germany a translation appeared in 1920 and rapidly sold 100,000 copies.

Henry Ford helped spread the readership of the "Protocols" during the 1920's by reprinting parts of them, along with other anti-Semitic items, in his newspaper, the Dearborn *Indepen-*

PROLOGUE TO MURDER. *The belief, based on a forgery, in a global Jewish plot spread in the 1920's and 1930's. This Spanish pamphlet is typical.*

CZAR'S MAN IN PARIS. *Pyotr Ivanovich Rachkovsky, head of the Russian secret service abroad, was the most likely author of the forgery.*

dent. He later apologized and proclaimed his friendship with the Jewish people.

Who was the forger who created this evil hoax? There are two main suspects. Ilya Tsion, an elderly Russian political journalist living in Paris at the time, may have done it to discredit political opponents. Tsion was an extreme reactionary, and some of the views in the "Protocols" were very close to his own. He may have written them as a means of impressing the Czar with the danger of the liberals.

A far more likely candidate, however, is Pyotr Ivanovich Rachkovsky, head of the czarist secret service abroad. Rachkovsky was the author of several anti-Semitic tracts and certainly believed in the existence of a worldwide Jewish conspiracy, particularly directed at Russia. He had many enemies, and some passages in the "Protocols" may be oblique references to them. One enemy, a Russian Jewish official in Paris called Efron, was even mentioned by name.

Rachkovsky had his headquarters in Paris for 18 years, until he was recalled in 1902. And when a Russian official arrived to close up the Paris office after the Revolution of 1917, one of Rachkovsky's former aides admitted that the "Protocols" had been forged in Paris. And the man who gave the order for the forgery? Pyotr Ivanovich Rachkovsky.

THE DOCUMENT THAT SPLIT THE CHURCH
Strange case of the Donation of Constantine

For 600 years Popes of the Church of Rome used the Donation of Constantine (*Constitutum Constantini*) to support their claim to be the rulers of Christendom.

Constantine was the first Roman Emperor to be converted to Christianity. He was said to have made the gift of half his Empire, in A.D. 315, in gratitude for his religious conversion and for his miraculous cure from leprosy. The Donation—the document that recorded the gift—gave to the See of Rome spiritual authority over all the churches of the earth and temporal authority over Rome, all Italy, and the Western World. Those who tried to overthrow it would "be burned in the lower hell and shall perish with the devil and all the impious."

The 3,000-word Donation first became known in the ninth century, and it was a powerful weapon in the dispute between the Eastern and Western churches. This quarrel culminated in the separation of the Eastern Orthodox Church and the Church of Rome in 1054.

No fewer than 10 popes cited the document, and its authenticity remained almost unquestioned until the 15th century. Then, Nicholas of Cusa (1401–64), the greatest ecclesiastical scholar of his age, pointed out that Bishop Eusebius of Caesarea, Constantine's contemporary and biographer, had not mentioned the Emperor's gift.

Now the document is almost universally regarded as a forgery, probably made in Rome in about A.D. 760. And the forgery was not even particularly clever. For example, it gives the Roman See authority over Constantinople before that city had been founded!

Small wonder that the French philosopher Voltaire described it as "the boldest and most magnificent forgery which deceived the world for centuries."

GUARD OF DISHONOR
The agony of Captain Dreyfus

There was a spy in the French Army, and Capt. Alfred Dreyfus was the perfect suspect. A hard-working and conscientious man, he aroused jealousy in his fellow officers because of his ability. And in the anti-Semitic mood of the times, the fact that he was both rich and a Jew ensured his unpopularity.

He was arrested in 1894 after a letter addressed to the German military attaché in Paris, Col. Max von Schwartzkoppen, fell into the hands of the French General Staff. The letter listed a number of military secrets that the author offered for sale.

The General Staff, aware that a traitor was

461

SPY TRIAL. *Capt. Alfred Dreyfus leaving the court-martial building at Rennes, France, after the first day's hearing. He was charged with spying for Germany.*

passing secrets to the Germans, needed a scapegoat. On the evidence available, they decided that he must be a junior gunnery officer who had served in several camps before joining the General Staff. Dreyfus filled all these requirements, and because his handwriting also resembled that in the letter, he was arrested.

Yet, at his court-martial, it seemed that the prosecution had little enough to go on. Dreyfus had a first-class military record, and handwriting experts doubted whether he *had* written the incriminating letter.

Just when it seemed that the court had no choice but to acquit Dreyfus, Comdr. Hubert Joseph Henry, the intelligence officer who had conducted the preliminary inquiry, intervened. A sealed packet was shown to the judges.

Inside that packet were documents that put Dreyfus' guilt beyond doubt—especially an "intercepted" letter from the Italian military attaché, Panizzardi, to his German counterpart, Von Schwartzkoppen. It referred to the French traitor as "that dirty dog, D."

Dreyfus was found guilty and sentenced to imprisonment for life on Devil's Island.

Proof was a forgery

Yet the truth was that Commander Henry, convinced of Dreyfus' guilt, had written the Panizzardi letter himself.

Only two years after the court-martial, it became apparent to the General Staff that French military secrets were still being passed to the Germans. The Dreyfus file was reopened, and the new investigating officer, Colonel Picquart, began to have grave misgivings.

Picquart's probings, however, worried senior officers, who thought the honor and reputation of the army to be more important than the fate of one Jewish officer. So Picquart was sent to Tunisia—while Henry tried to cover up his own guilt by removing some of the Dreyfus papers and tampering with the Panizzardi letter.

That proved his undoing—for Picquart had already had the documents photographed. The forgery came to light, and Henry himself was arrested and charged. He confessed and a few days afterward committed suicide in prison. The real spy in the French War Office, a Franco-Hungarian officer named Ferdinand Walsin Esterhazy, fled to London.

That was four years after the arrest of Dreyfus. Another eight years passed before Dreyfus' innocence was established—in 1906.

The highest court of appeal in France, the Cour de Cassation, annulled the conviction against Dreyfus. He was reinstated and decorated with the Legion of Honor. In the First World War he was recalled to active service. He died in Paris in 1935, at the age of 76.

462

MAJOR WILLIAM MARTIN, ROYAL MARINE

The dead man who won a battle

The Briton who lies in a Spanish cemetery may have done little enough for his country in his lifetime. Yet, in death, this pneumonia victim of the damp English autumn fooled Nazi intelligence and helped to save thousands of lives.

In 1942, as the North African campaign drew to a close, it became obvious to the Germans that the next objective of the Allies would be Sicily. Therefore, it was a matter of desperate urgency to convince them that they were wrong.

A solution was put forward by Royal Naval Intelligence. They suggested that a body, ostensibly that of a courier killed in a plane crash, carrying misleading but apparently top-secret papers, should be allowed to drift ashore on the coast of neutral Spain. Almost certainly, German agents would get a glimpse of the papers.

The first task was to find a corpse whose cause of death could be taken as drowning. The pneumonia victim's body was obtained in return for a promise that his true identity would never be revealed.

He was "reborn" as Maj. William Martin, Royal Marine. Among the papers he carried was a letter from the Vice Chief of the Imperial General Staff to General Alexander, commanding the 18th Army Group in Africa. It explained why he could not have his own way and that the invasion target was not Sicily but somewhere else in the western Mediterranean.

Major Martin also carried a message from Lord Mountbatten to Admiral of the Fleet, Sir Andrew Cunningham. An apparently indiscreet sentence was included, hinting that Sardinia was the proposed invasion area: "He might bring some sardines with him—they are on points [rationed] here!"

The major sailed on his first and last assignment on April 19, 1943, hidden in the torpedo compartment of HM Submarine *Seraph*.

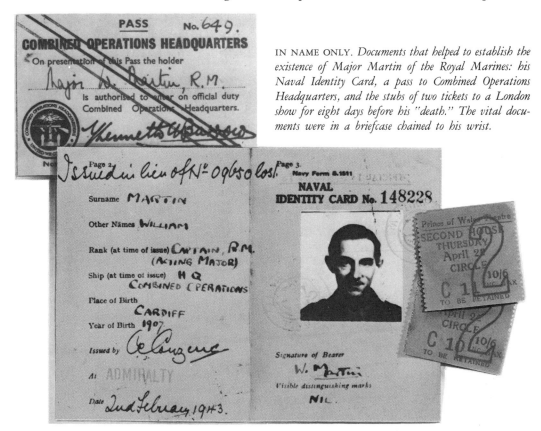

IN NAME ONLY. *Documents that helped to establish the existence of Major Martin of the Royal Marines: his Naval Identity Card, a pass to Combined Operations Headquarters, and the stubs of two tickets to a London show for eight days before his "death." The vital documents were in a briefcase chained to his wrist.*

Eleven nights later the body was lowered over the side. At dawn the following morning the tide washed it toward Huelva, where it was discovered by a fisherman. The Spanish authorities informed the British vice consul, and Major Martin was buried with full military honors. But there was no word of the documents.

An alarmed formal demand was made to Spain, and the papers were eventually returned on May 13. Scientific tests proved that the envelopes had been opened, but it was not until after the war that Major Martin's contribution was fully realized. Even Hitler had concluded that the attack would be directed mainly against Sardinia.

The German High Command scattered its forces and left gaps in its defense lines that the Allies were able to exploit. The invasion of Sicily was opposed by an Italian force and only two German divisions. As a result, Allied losses on the beaches were reduced, and the invasion was successful.

SHIP OF PREY

The windjammer that went to war

To anyone who went aboard the *Maletta* in Hamburg in 1916, she appeared to be a normal three-masted windjammer of about 1,500 tons. Stacks of timber lined the decks, stamped with the names of Norwegian lumberyards.

The crew's clothing, aged and worn, bore Norwegian labels. Pictures of the King and Queen of Norway hung on the saloon and cabin walls. And among the crew's effects were family snapshots of hometowns and villages and letters from relatives in Norway. Even the captain's underwear was embroidered: "Captain Knudsen of the *Maletta*."

But behind the elaborate facade lay one of the most daring wartime ploys of all time. The *Maletta*, alias the *Walter,* alias the *Hero*, was, in fact, the *Seeadler* (*Sea Eagle*), a warship of the Imperial German Navy.

Its mission: to run the British blockade in the North Sea, head south through the Atlantic, and attack Allied shipping in the Pacific. For during the First World War the Germans were convinced the only way to beat the British was by cutting their trade routes. Warships proved too expensive, so merchant ships were armed and set against merchant ships.

These commerce raiders achieved successes, but British surveillance was constantly improving, and by 1916 the blockade was highly effective.

Then the German Admiralty realized they had a near-perfect secret weapon in their possession: a sailing ship, the *Pass of Balmaha*, built in Glasgow in 1888 and captured by a U-boat in 1915. The innocent-looking vessel was fitted with auxiliary engines and two 4.2-inch guns, concealed by foldaway railings, and renamed the *Seeadler*. She was given a largely Norwegian-speaking German crew of 57 men and 6 officers, and put under the command of Count Felix von Luckner.

The deck of the wardroom was mounted on a hydraulic lift so that, at the touch of a button, the officers could disappear to the deck below and attempt to retake the ship should she be boarded and captured. The ship was riddled with secret passages and compartments, including quarters for prisoners.

Von Luckner, meanwhile, took a job as a longshoreman in Copenhagen, where a Norwegian ship called the *Maletta* was unloading a cargo of wheat. He studied the vessel, a three-master like the *Seeadler*, and managed to steal the ship's log.

The *Seeadler* was now renamed the *Maletta*. Her forged papers even included a letter from a British naval officer warning of the dangers of German raiders. If the *Seeadler* was boarded, seaman Hugo Schmidt was to play Jeanette, Captain Knudsen's wife—wearing powder, wig, and padding.

On December 23, 1916, the *Seeadler* ran the British blockade and a hurricane-force gale without incident. South of Iceland she was boarded and given clearance by a British inspection party—then sailed into the Atlantic.

First strike

On January 9 the *Seeadler* made her first strike. The target was a British freighter, the 3,628-ton *Gladys Royal*, taking coal to Buenos Aires.

Norwegian flags flying, the *Seeadler* moved in, using auxiliary engines to increase maneu-

THE "SEA EAGLE" UNDER SAIL. *Despite her innocent appearance she was a warship of the Imperial German Navy, fitted with 4.2-inch guns and auxiliary engines. Belowdecks she was riddled with secret passages.*

ADVENTURER. *Von Luckner masqueraded as a Norwegian.*

THE END OF A RAIDER. *The Seeadler lies dismasted and smashed on a reef on the Pacific island of Mopihaa in 1917 after being hit by a freak wave.*

verability. Deception was necessary until the last instant before attack—to prevent the possibility of a detailed radio message being sent by the victim. As the British ship came within range, Von Luckner gave the order.

Down came the Norwegian flag, and up went the black, white, and red ensign of the Imperial German Navy. The breakaway railing on the port side went clattering to the deck, and the 4.2-inch gun slid out. A shell was fired across the bows of the *Gladys Royal*, and Von Luckner sent a prize crew aboard.

At dusk, when Von Luckner considered it safe to do so, the 26-man crew of the *Gladys Royal* was moved to the sailing ship. The *Gladys Royal* was then sunk with explosive charges.

The next day the *Seeadler* brought her complement of prisoners to 50, capturing and scuttling the *Lundy Island*, a 3,095-ton steam freighter from northern England.

From January 21 to March 21, the *Seeadler* captured and sank 10 more vessels; about 40,000 tons of Allied shipping had been destroyed.

Eventually, the *Seeadler* could hold no more prisoners. Von Luckner decided to transfer all his captives to a French sailing ship, the *Cambronne*, while he headed for the Pacific.

The *Cambronne* reached Rio and, as Von Luckner had anticipated, alerted the British. Cruisers were sent after the *Seeadler*. But even then it was not the British Navy that ended the *Seeadler*'s career.

In August 1917 Von Luckner stopped at the island of Mopihaa, in the Pacific, to take on rations. While he and the crew were ashore, a freak wave swept in and wrecked the *Seeadler* on the island's reefs.

Von Luckner refused to accept defeat. He set off with a party of five in one of the *Seeadler*'s 18-foot motor cutters to try to capture another ship. After a long and arduous journey, the mission ended at last when the Germans were captured in the Fiji Islands by the crew of a British steamer.

FORCES' FAVORITES

How to kill an enemy with kindness

The radio station of the German forces, Gustav Siegfried Eins—GSI—had a special appeal to the nation's soldiers during the Second World War. As well as its excellent news coverage and highly popular disc-jockey programs, the station also mounted its own outspoken crusades on behalf of the ordinary soldier. The troops quickly discovered they could learn a great deal from these broadcasts by reading between the lines and making logical interpretations of the information.

There was the time, for example, when GSI launched a bitter condemnation of profiteering "while our brave troops are freezing to death in Russia." To soldiers who dreaded being sent to Russia, the profiteering was unimportant; what mattered was the official confirmation of winter conditions on the eastern front.

Again, the station inspired more disquiet than admiration when it praised the skill of doctors at camps housing civilians bombed out of German cities. Dedicated work had reduced the cholera and typhus death rate to an average of only 60 a week, the troops were told.

Too much patriotism

The outspokenness that made Gustav Siegfried Eins so popular was adopted by two later stations—Atlantiksender and Soldatensender Calais—broadcasting to German forces in occupied Europe. However, their patriotism sometimes tended to create troublesome problems for commanders.

One topic that regularly aroused the wrath of the broadcasters was desertion. They deplored in detail the methods used by disillusioned soldiers to enter neutral countries when they were on the run.

Nevertheless, there was sympathy for listeners with genuine reasons for wanting to leave their posts. Bulletins kept them informed of the extent of Allied raids on Germany, and men with families in the bombed cities were advised how to apply for compassionate leave.

The information contained in the broadcasts was always confirmed by the forces' newspaper, *News for the Troops*, delivered to the front by air.

Truth and falsehood

These services for the German soldier were not provided by the Wehrmacht, however. Radio stations and newspaper were both the brainchildren of Allied Intelligence. The radio stations, based in England, were so powerful that they drowned out real forces' broadcasts. They owed their success as propaganda instruments to a careful blending of truth and falsehood, which was used to play upon the anxieties of soldiers far from home.

News for the Troops, which closely resembled a real German forces' paper, was dropped each night by British aircraft. It, too, followed a similar policy of interlarding truth with fiction.

Joseph Goebbels, head of the German propaganda machine, admitted that the fake information service gave him a lot to worry about. But as one propagandist to another, he paid the supreme compliment. The service's hints on sabotage, desertion, and dodging extremely dangerous combat duty were translated into English and dropped by the Germans behind the British and American lines.

THE FORGER WHO HAD TO PROVE IT

IT WAS most embarrassing for Parisian Jean de Sperati. The French customs had intercepted a consignment of postage stamps he was sending to a Lisbon dealer and accused him of evading export duties. At his trial in 1942 Dr. Edmond Locard, the country's leading criminologist, gave evidence that the stamps were extremely rare and suggested a value of 223,400 francs (about $60,000). Only De Sperati knew that the stamps were worthless forgeries he had printed himself. To avoid being convicted, he had to prove the stamps were counterfeit and so not subject to tax. He confessed that he had been a successful stamp forger for more than 30 years. On this occasion he was acquitted, but in 1952 he was sentenced to two years in jail for fraud. His advanced age, however, saved him from serving the sentence. Ironically, collectors now prize his forgeries and pay high prices for them.

THE MONEYMAKERS

Prisoners who produced £150 million in cash

A few days after the German surrender in 1945, a truck loaded with British money worth £21 million was handed over to U.S. counterespionage officers. More notes were reported floating in the Enns River in Austria.

A Bank of England official flew to Frankfurt to examine them and pieced together the amazing story of Operation Bernhard, a gigantic Nazi hoax that almost wrecked Britain's already strained wartime economy.

For almost two years during the war an alarming number of near-perfect forgeries, in batches of £100,000, had appeared in London from Zurich, Lisbon, Stockholm, and other neutral cities. The bank believed a gang was responsible, but the capture in Edinburgh of a German spy carrying some of the finest forgeries ever seen convinced the experts that they were up against the German government.

A break in the case

Until the truckload of notes the bank had no lead, but now the German officer in charge of the truck said that he had been given the money by an SS man near Redl Zipf, Austria. There, in a mountain tunnel, officials found presses and machinery—but no plates, paper, or records.

Operation Bernhard, named after Maj. Bernhard Kruger who directed it, was the brainchild of gestapo chief Heinrich Himmler. The aim was to break Britain's economy, but Reichsbank civil servants, fearing the British would retaliate similarly, rebelled at the idea of forgery.

So Kruger recruited engravers and printers from concentration camps. They were promised preferential treatment, sworn to secrecy, and put to work making phony money at Sachsenhausen Camp near Berlin.

Plates were made, and the Bank of England's paper was reproduced. The first batch of forged notes was sent to gestapo agents in neutral countries. Most banks accepted them.

When the tide of battle turned against Germany, Himmler decided to wind up the operation, but Kruger persuaded him to move it into the Alps. He argued that the forgers could provide escaping Nazis with forged money and documents.

By the time the move was completed, the Allies were closing in. The plates were destroyed, but the forgers could not bring themselves to dispose of Kruger's hoard of notes. It was these that were found in the trucks, on their way to be buried for later recovery.

The Bank of England calculated that Kruger's operation had produced almost 9 million notes—about £150 million. For a time some were found on the black market, but no one ever found Maj. Bernhard Kruger.

THE SECRET OF DR. JAMES BARRY

DR. JAMES BARRY, a retired army surgeon, died in London on July 25, 1865, at the age of 73. Throughout his long and distinguished career, spent mainly in the West Indies, South Africa, and India, he had been a popular and efficient officer. In his younger days his dashing good looks had gained him the reputation of being something of a lady's man, and on one occasion it was said he had quarreled with a brother officer over a woman and fought a duel with him.

It was only at his death that the amazing truth about Dr. Barry was discovered.

Dr. Barry was a woman. Not only that, a postmortem examination revealed that, at some time in her youth, Dr. Barry had given birth to a child.

To this day the true identity of Dr. Barry remains a mystery. In 1808, at the age of 16, she had been accepted as a medical student at Edinburgh University in the name of James Barry. Even in her student days, apparently, no one had suspected that Barry was a girl.

It seems possible that, disillusioned by being jilted early in her life, she decided to spend the rest of her days as a man.

What happened to the child is another secret that she took with her to the tomb, which was inscribed with the name she had borne through most of her life—Dr. James Barry.

THE ACADEMIC HOAXER

He caused the repainting of a submarine fleet

Reginald Jones, a professor of natural philosophy at Aberdeen University and scientific adviser to successive British governments, is one of the world's most successful practical jokers. His feats range from persuading a distinguished academic to drop his telephone into a bucket of water to tricking German bombers onto a wrong flight path.

When Jones was a research fellow at Oxford in the 1930's, he telephoned an eminent doctor of philosophy several times and hung up as soon as he got an answer. Then he called again, pretending to be a telephone engineer reporting a fault on the line. When the victim agreed that there must be one, Jones suggested that "a leak to earth" was the cause. His victim cooperated in all sorts of suggested remedies—from tapping the phone with his fountain pen to standing on one leg and hitting the receiver with a rubber eraser. Finally, Jones talked the man into lowering the phone into a bucket of water.

Professor Jones' jokes are never malicious and have sometimes been of value to his country. When he worked for Air Ministry Intelligence during the Second World War, he discovered that the Germans were using directional beams from the Continent to guide their bombers onto British targets.

A less original scientist would have jammed the beams, but Jones had one signal duplicated and sent out from London. The result was that the German planes went off course and dropped their bombs onto empty fields.

Another of Jones' wartime hoaxes concerned a navigational device called H2S, which helped Allied bombers seek out U-boats. The Germans realized that the RAF had something new, but Jones put them off the scent. He "invented" an infrared beam to locate submarines and made sure that news of it was fed to the enemy. The entire U-boat fleet was repainted to counteract the nonexistent rays.

THE CARDIFF GIANT

The petrified man who hoaxed a nation

On October 16, 1869, two handymen were digging a well at William C. Newell's farm near Cardiff, New York, a village 12 miles south of Syracuse. They had dug down three feet when their shovels hit a large stone shaped like a human foot. Excitedly uncovering the rest of the obstruction, the diggers discovered to their amazement (or at least so they said) a gypsum statue of a reclining man. It measured 10 feet 4 inches from head to toe. The giant's face bore the hint of a smile.

"It's a big Injun!" one of the diggers shouted. The two men had unearthed the Cardiff Giant.

Word about the stone fossil, or "petrified man," spread quickly, and crowds of the curious soon gathered at the Newell farm. Some onlookers repeated the local Indian legend that a race of stone men had once lived in the valley; others recalled the "giants in the earth" mentioned in the Old Testament.

Farmer Newell recovered from his supposed surprise sufficiently to raise a tent over the pit within two days and to begin selling tickets of admission at 50 cents each. The stone giant drew hundreds of paying visitors on weekdays and as many as 2,500 on Sundays, all of whom were asking, "What is it?"

The "petrified man" theory soon had its supporters and detractors. A local science lecturer named Dr. John F. Boynton pointed out that human flesh could not petrify and declared that the gigantic figure was a statue carved about 250 years ago by a Jesuit priest. A geologist, James Hall, agreed that the statue was of some antiquity. Other experts upheld the petrification theory, pointing out that the giant had thousands of tiny holes in its stone skin that resembled human pores.

The public apparently decided that the Cardiff Giant, regardless of whether it was a man or a statue, was well worth seeing. Newell cashed in on the fantastic discovery by selling a three-fourths interest in the giant to a group of local businessmen for $30,000. On November 5 they shipped the giant to Syracuse for exhibition and arranged a tour of eastern cities.

A REAL PETRIFIED MAN?
The famed Cardiff Giant rests in peace after having fooled many so-called experts more than 100 years ago. The 10-foot gypsum statue is still on view, at the Farmers' Museum in Cooperstown, New York.

By this time doubts had been raised about the figure's authenticity. The New York *Herald* was the first to call it an outright hoax, claiming—erroneously—that the statue had been carved but a year earlier by a Canadian sculptor. Yale paleontologist Othniel C. Marsh inspected the Cardiff Giant and denounced it as "a most decided humbug" of recent origin. Even Dr. Boynton, after a second inspection, decided that the statue was less than a year old.

The whole fabric of deception began to come apart with the disclosure that William Newell had paid a sizable sum of money to his brother-in-law George Hull, a Binghamton cigar manufacturer. People in Cardiff now remembered that Hull had delivered a large, heavy, iron box to Newell's farm in November 1868. Subsequent inquiries revealed that Hull had previously bought a block of gypsum weighing more than 3,000 pounds from a quarry in Fort Dodge, Iowa. Two Chicago stonecutters confessed that they had carved a giant statue to Hull's specifications, including the puncturing of tiny holes with a mallet head of steel needles.

Faced with this evidence, Hull admitted in early December 1869 that he had manufactured the statue, and with Newell's connivance he had buried it for nearly a year to give it the appearance of antiquity. His expenses in perpetrating the hoax totaled $2,600.

Ironically, the confession added to the publicity for the Cardiff Giant and increased Hull's considerable profits from the venture. Beginning in late December, the statue was exhibited for two months to large crowds in New York City. Showman P. T. Barnum, whose offer to lease the giant for $60,000 had been refused, built a wooden replica of it—a fake that drew even better than the real one because of Barnum's deft promotion.

In February 1870 the statue was moved to Boston, where it continued to attract crowds, but a tour of smaller cities in New England proved unsuccessful.

After gathering dust in storage for 30 years, the Cardiff Giant was revived for showing at state fairs and carnivals. It exchanged hands several times and in 1948 was settled permanently at the Farmers' Museum in Cooperstown, New York. There the stone giant is exhibited under an open shed in a reconstructed village much like the old Cardiff.

Its creator, George Hull, died in obscurity in 1898, but he probably took great satisfaction in the fact that he had perpetrated a classic American hoax.

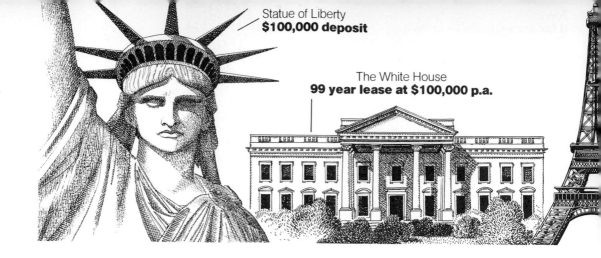

Statue of Liberty
$100,000 deposit

The White House
99 year lease at $100,000 p.a.

EVERYTHING HAS ITS PRICE

For sale—Big Ben and the Statue of Liberty

Arthur Furguson was a Scotsman with phenomenal selling ability, though, like many another genius, he was unaware of the fact until one blinding moment when opportunity and inspiration combined. Furguson's moment occurred in Trafalgar Square one summer morning in the 1920's. The source of his inspiration was a rich American from Iowa, whom Ferguson discovered gazing reverently at Nelson's Column.

Furguson appointed himself as a temporary guide to the square. The statue on the column was, he explained, that of Admiral Lord Nelson, England's greatest hero. Such a shame, he mused. The place would not be the same without it. But Britain's debts were soaring, and it had to go—column, statue, lions, and fountains.

The American was sympathetic and asked the price. A mere £6,000 (about $30,000), sighed Furguson. Of course, it would have to be the right buyer—someone who would appreciate these great monuments of Britain's former glory.

By an odd coincidence, it was Furguson himself who had been entrusted with the sad task of making the sale, which had to be kept secret.

The American begged Furguson to help him buy the monument, and at last he consented to telephone his superiors for instructions. He returned within minutes. It was agreed. Britain was prepared to accept a check right away and complete the whole deal without further delay. Ever eager to help, Furguson gave his client the name and address of a reliable firm that would dismantle the square ready for shipping.

The American handed him a check, the receipt was presented, and the men parted company. Furguson immediately cashed the check while his customer got in touch with the contractors. They were reluctant to accept the job and told him why. But it was not until Scotland Yard assured him he had been duped that the buyer was convinced.

That summer in London was a happy one for Arthur Furguson. The police, however, were not so pleased; one American complained that he had paid £1,000 for Big Ben, while another bewailed the fact that he had made a £2,000 down payment on Buckingham Palace and had been unable to complete the purchase.

It all led Furguson to the conclusion that since Americans had been his best customers, he should continue his operations in their country.

Westward ho!

In 1925 he went to Washington, D.C., where he leased the White House to a cattle rancher for 99 years at the giveaway price of $100,000 a year—the first year's rental payable in advance.

Furguson's nest egg was now sufficiently large for him to begin considering retirement. But vanity would not allow him to slip quietly from the scene without some grand finale.

He found his ideal victim—a man from Sydney, Australia—and Furguson soared to new heights of inventiveness. The New York harbor was to be widened, and the Statue of Liberty was in the way. Mere sentimental attachment could not be allowed to impede the march of progress, and the government was prepared to sell the monument to anyone willing to pay for having it taken away.

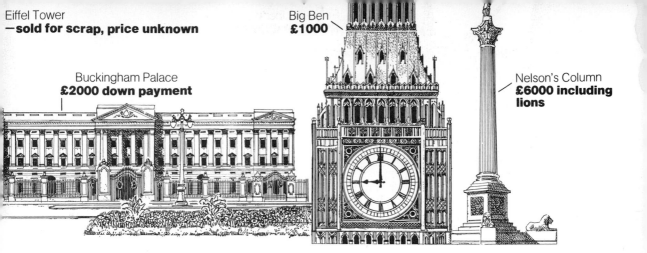

Eiffel Tower
—sold for scrap, price unknown

Buckingham Palace
£2000 down payment

Big Ben
£1000

Nelson's Column
£6000 including lions

The Australian spent the next few days trying to raise the $100,000 deposit from Sydney. Furguson never left his side, keeping him well away from anyone to whom he might be tempted to boast of the bargain he had made. But as a souvenir of the deal, Furguson kindly allowed himself to be photographed arm in arm with the buyer in front of the Statue of Liberty.

There was a delay in getting the money through, and Furguson grew impatient—and the Australian suspicious. Finally, the buyer took the photograph to the police. Here was the break the police wanted. They knew about the supersalesman of great monuments, but until then he had always managed to escape them.

The Australian led them straight to the hapless Furguson, who was promptly arrested. He was jailed for five years, a small price to pay for the fortune he had made. He was released in 1930 and moved to Los Angeles, where he lived in luxury—paid for by a string of new confidence tricks—until his death in 1938.

THE MAN WHO SOLD THE EIFFEL TOWER

It seemed the chance of the century

Count Victor Lustig, a high official in the ministry responsible for public buildings, explained to the five Paris businessmen in his office that the Eiffel Tower was to be scrapped. The costs of its maintenance were enormous, and its preservation was no longer considered practical. The tower would amount to at least 7,000 tons of high-grade iron, and the five men—scrap-metal merchants —were invited to submit sealed bids.

The bids arrived promptly, and the following day André Poisson, a self-made man of substance, was informed that his offer had been accepted.

Within a week Poisson had raised the money, and the final meeting was arranged. But why, he asked, were such important negotiations being carried out in a hotel and not at the ministry?

The count ordered his American secretary, Dan Collins, from the room and explained: "The life of a government official is not easy. We must entertain, dress in fashion—yet all on pitifully small salaries. In letting a government contract, it is customary for the official in charge to receive. . . ." Poisson understood at once; obviously such a suggestion, however delicately put, could not be made within the ministry's walls. He willingly handed over his certified check, together with a wallet bulging with banknotes, and left, triumphantly clutching the deed of sale.

Within an hour the check was cashed—Lustig never revealed how much he had made— and he and Collins were sitting grinning at each other in a first-class compartment on the Vienna express.

Lustig, born in Bohemia, the son of a highly respected citizen, and Collins, a smalltime American crook, stayed in one of Vienna's best hotels for a month, studying the Paris newspapers. But there was no report of the swindle.

The buyer, too embarrassed to report the hoax, had left the field clear for Lustig and Collins to sell the tower again. They did, but this time the victim went to the police. Lustig and Collins were never caught, but the publicity almost certainly prevented a third sale.

EVEN CRIME IS COMPUTERIZED

Tricksters with ultramodern tools

For nontechnical people, the computer is an incomprehensible mystery. But with its help experts have committed some highly successful frauds. Computers can be valuable and obedient accomplices.

An employee of a large bank in Minneapolis ordered the bank's computer to ignore all the checks he drew on his own account. His fraud was discovered when the computer broke down and the bank was forced to revert to human accounting.

A Boston bank employee replaced the blank deposit slips on the bank's counters with forms bearing his own account number. Ignoring the name and address on the form, the computer credited all these deposits to the employee's account.

A dime here, a dime there

Another bank employee had programed the bank's computer to shave 10 cents off every account and add it to the last account on the books. Since customers' names were listed alphabetically, he then opened an account under an assumed name beginning with Z. All went well until a Mr. Zydel opened an account. He noticed that his balance kept inexplicably increasing. Being an honest man, he reported this, and inquiries exposed the fraud.

A large catering firm in London received a series of bills from a company for supplies of smoked salmon and shellfish. The food never arrived, but the computer had paid £50,000 before a clerk noticed the unusual account number and checked to see that all was well. The thieves—one man in each of the companies—had programed the computer to accept bills and make payments. Had they used an existing account number with a false name and address they might have avoided discovery.

Perhaps the most successful computer crime arose after a big chemical combine, with its headquarters in London, decided to control the accounting for its three major divisions by means of a central computer system. The computer revealed that one division was selling chemicals to another division at the full market price, although the buying department should have been claiming a 40 percent discount for bulk buying.

Profits for a middleman

With this information the chief programer and the head of the buying department set up a fictitious subsidiary. This new branch bought all the chemicals at full discount and on extended credit terms. They then resold the supplies to the parent company at full price and on immediate-payment terms and made a profit of £150,000 in 2½ years.

Soon the two men were supplying 50 outside customers as well.

By the time the subsidiary was unmasked, it was undercutting the combine so efficiently that the executives who had originated the idea were employed as fee-earning consultants to advise on the running of the once fraudulent operation.

THE BEST LAID PLANS . . .

THE DREAM of every gambler is to know the result of a horserace before it starts. Politician Horatio Bottomley, himself a racehorse owner, hit on an audacious scheme to make this dream come true shortly before the First World War. The plan was simple: Not only would he back every horse in a particular race, he would also own every horse and make sure that they finished in the right order.

Bottomley chose Belgium for his "coup" because racing rules there were not as strict as in Britain. He engaged six English jockeys to ride his team of horses at Blankenberge, a seaside town where the racecourse veered alongside the shore and sand dunes sometimes obscured the horses.

The jockeys were given strict instructions—and Bottomley's associates in England laid heavy bets on the exact finishing order. But disaster struck midway through the race when a thick sea mist swept over the course and the jockeys got hopelessly out of touch with one another. They crossed the finishing line in a jumble—and Bottomley's "coup" cost him a fortune.

MADAME HUMBERT'S HALFPENNY

The story of an elusive inheritance

Thérèse Humbert, daughter-in-law of the French Minister of Justice, was a beautiful woman, famed as much for the extravagance of her spending as for the parties that made her the most successful hostess in Paris. In eight weeks in 1897 she spent $5,000 on flowers, and $20,000 was by no means too much for her to pay for gowns in a season.

Born Thérèse Aurignac, the daughter of a hard-drinking peasant from the village of Bauzelles, near Toulouse, she later married the son of the mayor of Toulouse, much to the consternation of his parents. Shortly afterward, Madame Humbert claimed she had inherited a vast fortune in unusual circumstances.

In 1879, while sitting on a suburban train, she reported, she heard groans from the next compartment. While the train was still moving, she climbed along the outside of the carriage and found Robert Henry Crawford, an American, suffering a heart attack. She made him comfortable and administered smelling salts. Crawford, sure that she had saved his life, took her name and address.

The grateful American

Two years later Thérèse received a letter from Crawford's lawyers in New York, enclosing a copy of his will in which she was named as a beneficiary. The other heirs were Thérèse's younger sister, Marie, and Crawford's two American nephews, Robert and Henry. Under the will Henry Crawford was to marry Marie when she left school to keep the fortune in the family. Until the wedding Thérèse was to guard the inheritance in a safe.

Raising a loan with the inheritance as security, Thérèse and her husband Frederic moved into a luxurious mansion on the Avenue de la Grande Armée in Paris. To repay her loans, Thérèse Humbert raised larger loans at higher rates of interest.

In 1883 a newspaper article was published that cast doubt on the existence of the Crawford fortune. But Thérèse's father-in-law, by this time Minister of Justice, had himself publicly discussed the inheritance, so the newspaper account was not given much credence.

Shortly after the publication of the article, Thérèse announced that she had quarreled with the Crawford family, who had started a lawsuit to force her to lodge the fortune with Credit Lyonnais. She eventually won the case and considerable public sympathy, the final judgment stating that the locked safe should remain in her keeping.

But after a casual conversation with Jules Bizat, a high official of the Bank of France, Thérèse found herself once again in trouble. Bizat asked Thérèse how the inheritance was invested. She replied that it was in government securities. Bizat checked with the bank to find out whether the securities had been cashed to collect the interest due. None had been cashed.

Confidence shattered

Thérèse Humbert then floated an insurance scheme called the Rente Viagère, which was so attractive that investors flocked to deposit great amounts of money every day. Thérèse promptly withdrew the money to pay for her loans and buy enough government securities to allay the fears of her anxious creditors. But the confidence of the creditors was finally shattered when they calculated that the lawsuits with the Crawfords would have taken most of the inheritance, leaving too little to cover her costs.

The newspaper *Le Matin* again took up the story and called, in a series of scathing articles, for the opening of the safe. In 1902 Madame Humbert's creditors sued her, and the court ordered the safe to be opened.

Inside, they found a brick and an English halfpenny. Thérèse Humbert's story had been a hoax. The Crawfords had never existed. Accomplices—her brothers—had brought the lawsuit and posed as the Americans.

But by this time, Thérèse and her family had disappeared. Detectives searched the world, and, finally, they were found and arrested in Madrid in December 1902.

Returned to Paris for trial, Thérèse was imprisoned for five years. Her two brothers were sentenced to two and three years respectively. Frederic had died some years earlier, and the Minister of Justice and Marie had been innocent dupes.

The empty safe went on display for a year in a store window on the Rue Blanche in Paris. The 20-year swindle was over.

THE ANCESTRESS OF MAN

Whose skull at Piltdown?

From the moment that Charles Darwin published his *Descent of Man,* in 1871, the entire scientific world was intrigued by the search for the "missing link" that would prove his theory. Darwin argued powerfully that men and apes were descended from a common ancestor. If so, said his critics, then why had no fossils of this creature ever been found? Because, replied his supporters, men simply have not looked hard enough.

It took years of searching, but in 1912 the Darwinites were triumphant. From a gravel pit near Piltdown Common, in East Sussex, England, were unearthed fragments of bone and teeth from a creature that seemed to be half man and half ape, and roamed the earth half a million years ago.

Respected lawyer

The discoverer was Charles Dawson, a highly respected lawyer, amateur geologist, and fossil hunter. Dawson sent the first of his Piltdown finds—prehistoric flint tools, fossilized teeth, and a fragment of an unusually thick human skull—to his contact at the British Museum, the paleontologist Dr. Arthur Smith Woodward. And so excited was Woodward that he wasted little time in traveling down to Sussex to join Dawson at the gravel pit. It was the beginning of one of the most successful partnerships in the history of excavation.

When, near to where the skull had lain, Dawson discovered the jaw of an ape, he and Woodward could hardly contain their excitement. For the teeth were worn in a way that, it seemed, could only be produced by the rotary action of a human jaw. Here were all the requirements for a missing link—a creature with the brain of a man and the ability to use tools, but with the appearance of an ape.

Painstaking reconstruction

With painstaking care the experts reconstructed Piltdown man's life story. He should, as it happened, have been called Piltdown woman, for the remains were those of a female—and, moreover, a dumb one; there was no ridge on the skull to anchor the speech muscles. From the way the teeth were worn, observed Dr. Woodward, she must have been a vegetarian.

The idea of a nontalking female was irresistible to a suffragette-conscious public. The *Daily Express* said: "She could not cook. She could not talk. She could not wash. She could not light a fire."

That sort of ridicule meant little to Dawson, for he was about to receive one of the highest honors in science. Dr. Woodward, with the authority of the British Museum, decided to name Piltdown man after its discoverer. It went into the records—and posterity—as *Eoanthropus dawsoni,* Dawson's Dawn man.

And still Dawson's luck held. Teeth, bones, and tools turned up at the gravel pit for the next three years, and in 1915 Dawson found the stained teeth and skull fragments of a second Piltdown man in a field two miles from the pit.

Dawson died in 1916, at the age of 52, and the finds ceased, although Woodward continued digging until his own death many years later.

But rumbles of dissent began as early as 1913, when David Waterston, professor of anatomy

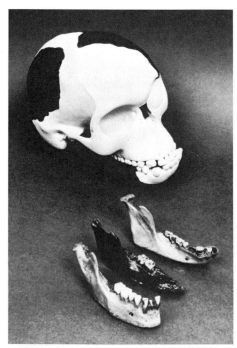

MONKEY BUSINESS. *A reconstruction of the skull of Dawn man shows the stained jaw compared with those of an ape (top) and man.*

at King's College, claimed that the Piltdown jaw was practically identical with that of a chimpanzee.

In addition, there was a disturbing story about the visitor who one day had walked into Dawson's office without knocking and found him busy staining bones in a crucible. But most experts agreed that the skull and jaw belonged together, and the fragments were jealously guarded from doubters who would have scraped and examined them carefully.

Fluoride and the tooth test

It was not until 1949 that a young geologist at the British Museum, Dr. Kenneth Oakley, was allowed to take minute samples from the bones and date them by a new chemical test. When bones lie buried, they absorb fluoride from water in the ground, and the amount absorbed is a good indication of how long they have been buried.

Dr. Oakley's tests showed that the skull and jawbone were a mere 50,000 years old. The idea of a missing link alive at the same time as the far more advanced Neanderthal man raised nagging doubts.

One person who did something about those doubts was Dr. J. S. Weiner, an anthropologist at Oxford University. He tried to isolate all the factors that made Piltdown man so unlikely: a thick human skull and human teeth (which were worn flat as if they had been filed) in an apelike jaw. That was the answer!

Taking a chimpanzee tooth, Weiner filed and stained it, producing almost an exact replica of a Piltdown tooth. Dr. Oakley helped him with further tests on the Piltdown fragments in 1953, and results proved conclusively that although the skull was a genuine fossil, the jaw was a cunningly stained fake. It belonged to a modern orangutan, and the teeth had been filed down before staining.

The hoaxer has never been positively identified, but everything points to Dawson. He had access to fossils and enough knowledge of anatomy and chemistry to fake and stain the fragments found at Piltdown. There were no further discoveries after his death. And Dawson was the only man in the entire hoax with anything to gain. He did not need money, but Piltdown man brought something that he valued far more—fame.

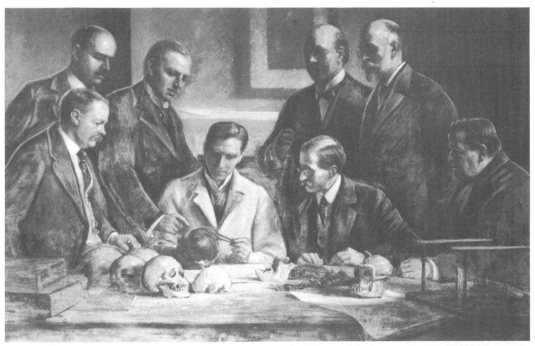

PALEONTOLOGICAL LEG PULL. *A group of experts examine the "historical find." Dawson stands third from right, and on his left is Dr. Arthur Smith Woodward of the British Museum, who followed up the find. The group portrait was made in 1915 to mark the occasion.*

THE BOY WHO WROTE SHAKESPEARE

"When this solemn mockery is o'er"

Drury Lane Theatre was packed to capacity on the night of April 2, 1796. Every available seat in the theater had been booked, and those who had paid for boxes, only to find the seats allocated several times over, scrambled over the lowest tier to fight for a place.

John Kemble, a renowned actor, was creating the role of Vortigern in a newly discovered play by William Shakespeare, *Vortigern and Rowena*, the love story of Vortigern, King of the Britons, and Rowena, daughter of Hengest, leader of the Saxon invaders of Britain in 450.

The whole event, sensational as it was, would have been acknowledged as all the more extraordinary had the public then known that Shakespeare's play was, in fact, the work of 17-year-old William Henry Ireland.

Young Ireland, son of a London book engraver, was taken to Stratford-on-Avon during his early teens. Greatly moved by this visit to Shakespeare's birthplace, he began his first few simple forgeries. On blank sheets of paper taken from Elizabethan folios, using ink artificially aged, he started with the bard's autograph on a lease. He explained to his delighted father that a wealthy man he had met, knowing of the boy's interest in old papers, had given him documents handed down by his ancestors.

Encouraged by success

Encouraged by that success, in 1795 Ireland produced an original manuscript of *King Lear* and parts of *Hamlet*, both forged in Elizabethan handwriting. Experts and critics alike were willing to testify to the genuineness of the documents. Kneeling before them, James Boswell, biographer of Samuel Johnson, said: "I now kiss the invaluable relics of our bard, and thanks to God that I have lived to see them."

When the idea of an entirely new play dawned on Ireland, he tried for several days to think of a suitable subject. Then, as he later described it, "a large drawing executed by Mr. S. Ireland [his father], representing Rowena in the act of presenting wine to Vortigern, which hung over the chimney-piece in Mr. Ireland's study, suddenly attracted my attention."

Rashly, the boy mentioned that he had discovered the play before even a line had been written, and from then on his father persistently asked to see it.

Ireland was so ignorant about the length and form of a Shakespearean play that he chose one at random and counted the lines. He did not name the play that he used as a model, but it was unfortunate for him that it was unusually long, 2,800 lines in all. In two months he produced a play of identical length, claiming that he had copied it from the original.

Dramatist Richard Sheridan read the play and said: "There are certainly some bold ideas, but they are crude and undigested. It is very odd: One would be led to think that Shakespeare must have been very young when he wrote the play. As to the doubting whether it be really his or not, who can possibly look at the papers, and not believe them ancient?"

Although Sheridan questioned the play's quality, he did not doubt its authenticity and bought it for about £300 and a share of the profits from its production on the stage.

The leading actor, John Kemble, suspected that the play was a fraud and tried unsuccessfully to have it staged on April Fool's night. He did, finally, manage to have a play entitled *The Lie of the Day* included on the bill.

On the first night Kemble was delivering a solemn monologue to Death:

And with rude laughter and fantastic tricks
Thou clapp'st thy rattling fingers to thy sides.

Then Kemble paused and spoke the next line in a "sepulchral tone of voice":

And when this solemn mockery is o'er. . . .

The audience got the point. Reporting on the evening later, Ireland said there was a howl from the pit that lasted 10 minutes. At last it died down, and Kemble once more took the center of the stage. Before ending the speech he repeated that line "with a solemn grimace."

The game was up for Ireland. The doubters came forward, and Edmund Malone, a renowned Shakespearean expert, denounced *Vortigern* as a fraud. The run at Drury Lane was abruptly finished after the first night.

His father was blamed for the forgeries, and Ireland confessed. But many people felt he was trying to protect his father, and Mr. Ireland

Copye of mye Letter too hys grace offe Southampton

Mye Lorde

Youre devotedlye and withe due respecte

Wm Shakspeare

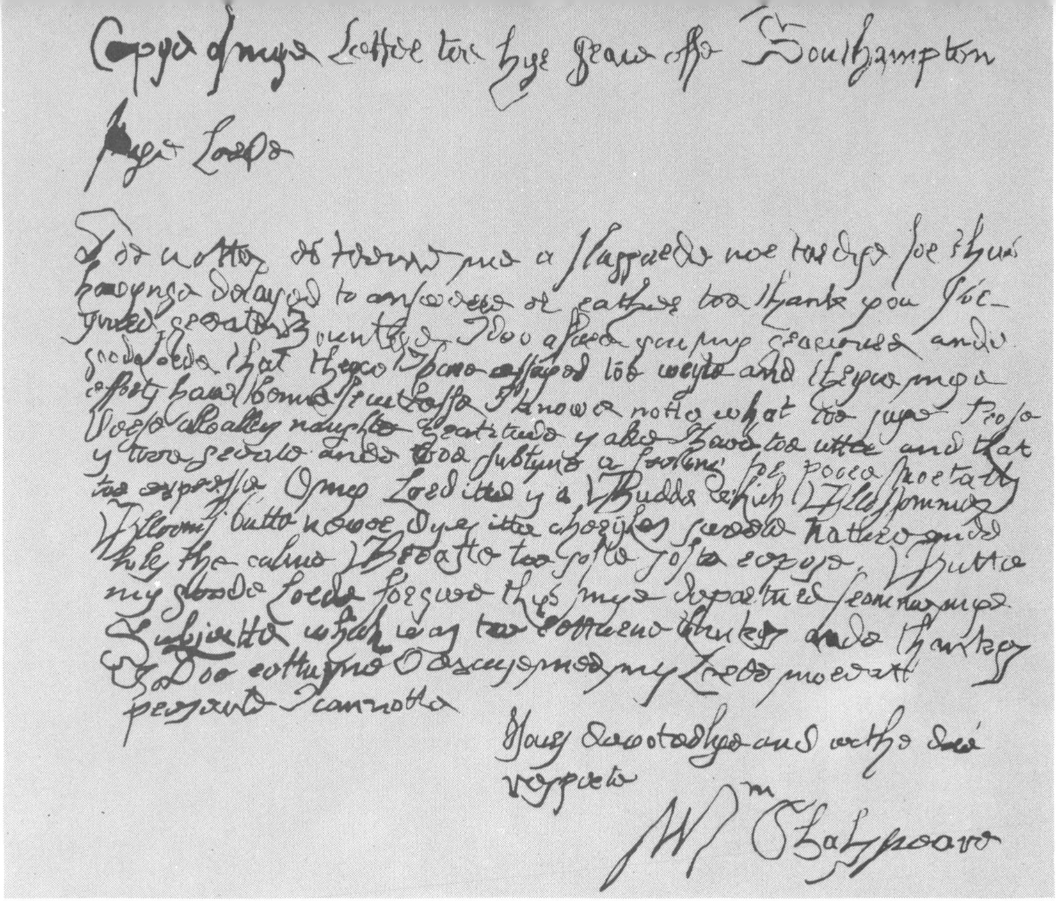

THANK-YOU NOTE FROM THE BARD. *One of Ireland's most famous forgeries was the letter shown here, apparently a copy of a note that William Shakespeare had written to the Earl of Southampton thanking him for his valuable and highly valued patronage of the playwright.*

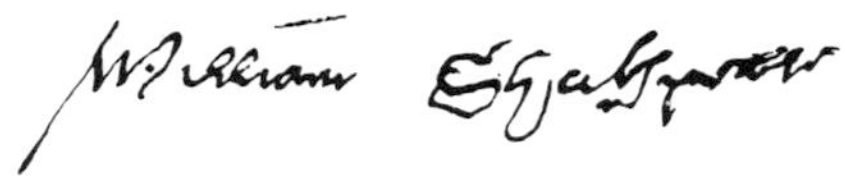

Shakespeare's real signature on a document.

himself believed that William had made a false confession to shield some unknown culprit.

The boy stuck to his previous plan of writing Shakespearean plays covering every reign from William the Conqueror to Elizabeth I. But his *Henry II* aroused no interest. He wrote several novels and poetry under his own name before he died in 1835. But only his forged Shakespearean plays are remembered and are now on display in the British Museum.

THE LOUVRE'S GOLDEN FORGERY

Ancient tiara was only one year old

For seven years a priceless gold tiara held a prominent place in the Louvre. It had been found on the site of the town of Olbia, in southern Russia, and was inscribed in Greek: "The Senate and People of Olbia to the Great Invincible Saitaphernes." The Louvre paid 200,000 francs (about $40,000) for the tiara—and it went on display on April 1, 1896. It was in a remarkable state of preservation for an object believed to be 2,200 years old. And so it should have been—it had been made only a few months earlier.

In 1895 Schapschelle Hochmann, a Rumanian wheat dealer, commissioned a goldsmith, Israel Rouchomovsky, to make a gold tiara in antique style. Hochmann paid Rouchomovsky 2,000 rubles (about $10,000) for the work, took the tiara, and carefully battered it to simulate age.

The tiara might still be on display had not a Montmartre painter, known as Elina, falsely claimed to have created it. A friend of Rouchomovsky who had seen the goldsmith fashioning the tiara would not allow an unknown artist to steal the glory, so he exposed the fraud.

ETRUSCAN WITHOUT A THUMB

Italian gang made three mistakes in their forgery

The giant clay figure of an Etruscan warrior was more than seven feet tall and weighed more than 1,000 pounds. It almost filled the room in which it had been created by three Italian sculptors.

Glaze and coloring were added to the figure, and the scaffolding surrounding it gently removed. Then the workmen stood back, admired their work—and pushed it over, smashing it on the floor.

Their next move was even stranger. They began to piece the fragments together again. The end result, with its cracks and scratches, was an Etruscan statue, which the Metropolitan Museum of Art in New York bought in 1921 for $40,000, then a fabulous sum.

Late discovery

And it was not until 40 years later that the museum learned it had been hoaxed by forgers. The forging ring, a family affair, was begun by the brothers Pio and Alfonso Riccardi and three of their six sons.

The Etruscans were a highly civilized people living in middle Italy, who were eventually conquered by the Romans and absorbed by Rome. Their numerous relics, still being found today, are highly prized by museums and private collectors.

It was Pio's eldest son, Riccardo, who planned the giant statue, which became known as the "Big Warrior"—and it was not the first masterpiece to be created by the team. They began their career when Roman art dealer Domenico Fuschini hired them, first to forge fragments of Etruscan pottery and later complete vases.

Two-horse chariot

Having mastered the technique, the team then produced their first major forgery—a complete bronze chariot. In December 1908 the British Museum was told that a *biga*—a two-horse chariot—had been found on an Etruscan site near Orvieto, Italy. After its supposed burial for

THE "OLD WARRIOR." *Fashioned after ancient models, the forgery is now listed in the Metropolitan Museum as "20th-century A.D. in style of 5th-century B.C. Etruscan work." The severed thumb can clearly be seen.*

2,500 years, it needed cleaning—and the museum was told the work was being carried out by the Riccardis.

The museum bought the chariot from Fuschini and officially announced its acquisition in 1912. The same year the Riccardis moved their business from the outskirts of Rome to Orvieto. Pio died soon afterward.

But the Riccardis—helped by a master sculptor named Alfredo Fioravanti—were quickly back at work, this time on a statue called the "Old Warrior." The figure, which stands 6 feet 7½ inches high, wears a plumed helmet, a breastplate, and armor on its calves. It is naked from breastplate to knees, and the right arm and left thumb are missing. The forgers had argued about the positioning of the right arm so much that, in the end, they discarded it.

Two sales to the Metropolitan

Once completed, the statue was sold to the Metropolitan Museum, which also acquired the gang's next major forgery—a piece called the "Colossal Head," which was four feet seven inches high from the neck to the top of its helmet. Experts who examined it later thought it formed part of a statue 23 feet high. The price for both was only a few hundred dollars.

The next forgery was the "Big Warrior"—which was the last to be completed by the gang. Riccardo Riccardi was killed when he was thrown from a horse before the statue was completed. After the figure had been sold to the Metropolitan Museum, the gang split up and ceased operating as a team.

The museum put the three pieces on exhibit in February 1933. Many Italian experts doubted their authenticity, but it was not until 1937, when the museum published a paper about them, that the conflict came into the open.

Even so, it was not until 22 years later that the museum began an inquiry into the allegations. After exhaustive tests it was found that the glaze on the three pieces contained manganese—a coloring agent unknown in the Etruscan era, which flourished about 800 B.C.

But the museum authorities were still not convinced they had been hoaxed. The proof they sought came a year later, from experts who examined genuine Etruscan artifacts. They found that the Etruscans always made and "baked" their pottery in one piece and that to do so vents were always left in statues to allow proper airing when they were in the kiln.

The Riccardis had made their statues in sections and had not left any vents—a mistake that showed the statues to be clever fakes.

But it was left to Alfredo Fioravanti, the man who had helped make the statues, to put the issue beyond doubt. On January 5, 1961, the craftsman, who was then 75, went to the American consul in Rome and signed a complete confession.

And to prove he was telling the truth, he took from his pocket the missing left thumb of the "Old Warrior"—a souvenir he had kept.

CASE OF THE HUMBLE COUNTERFEITER

The Secret Service was baffled by phony one-dollar bills

In November 1938 the U.S. Secret Service, which is responsible for enforcing the laws against counterfeiting money, began investigating a case that soon baffled its agents. A bank teller in New York City had detected a one-dollar counterfeit bill, and within a month 40 more of the phony bills were turned up. The Secret Service was used to dealing with clever, greedy men who counterfeited money in larger denominations and circulated the bills in huge quantities. In this case, however, the number of detected bogus bills amounted to only 585 by the end of a year. Who ever heard of a counterfeiter who was content to earn less than two dollars a day?

The Secret Service was also puzzled by the ineptitude of the counterfeiter. The fake bills were printed on cheap paper, the numerals and letters were botched, the retouched portrait of George Washington was murky—and after a time even his name was misspelled as "Wahsington." Such a poorly made product was laughable, but New York storekeepers seldom inspected bills of low denominations. Most of the counterfeit money was caught by experienced bank tellers.

The case of the humble, inept counterfeiter entered official Secret Service files as No. 880, and agents assigned to the case began to refer to the unknown counterfeiter as "Old Eight-

Eighty." After five years the Secret Service had collected 2,840 of Old Eight-Eighty's dollar bills, had informed 10,000 New York storekeepers how to detect the forgeries, and had distributed 200,000 circulars describing the fake bills. But Old Eight-Eighty continued to pass his fraudulent money for more than nine years before he was apprehended—and only then as the result of a fluke.

Children's aid

In January 1948 seven boys playing in a vacant lot on Manhattan's West Side found an assortment of junk that included two zinc engraving plates and about 30 dollar bills. They thought they had found stage money. The father of one of the boys turned in some of the bills to the police, who in turn called in the Secret Service. Three agents investigated and found that the plates and money had been thrown into the lot by firemen while putting out a recent blaze in a top-floor apartment of an adjoining tenement. The agents went to the apartment and found more bills, a small printing press, and Old Eight-Eighty himself.

His name was Edward Mueller. He was a 73-year-old widower who, with his blue eyes, toothless grin, white hair, and matching mustache, looked innocuous and amiable. He cheerfully admitted that he had made and passed counterfeit dollar bills for nine years, at the rate of 10 to 12 a week, to supply his modest needs. His wife had died in 1937, his son and daughter had married and moved away, and he had given up his job as a building superintendent to collect junk in the streets with a pushcart. He had cooked his own meals, washed his own laundry, walked his own dog—and, when he had needed cash, he had made his own money!

"They were only just one-dollar bills," he explained happily. "I never gave more than one of them to any one person, so nobody ever lost more than the one dollar."

Edward Mueller considered himself to be an honest man and was genuinely surprised to be arrested by the sympathetic agents. In September 1948 he pleaded guilty before a federal district judge but, in view of his advanced age, served only four months of a year's prison sentence. Before going to jail, Old Eight-Eighty had to pay a nominal fine—of a dollar, a genuine one.

PRIDE GOES BEFORE A FRAUD

Medieval frescoes painted by a modern master

On September 2, 1951, Dietrich Fey, head of a firm of art restorers, proudly escorted the West German Chancellor, Konrad Adenauer, around the newly restored frescoes of the Marienkirche (the Evangelical Lutheran Church of St. Mary), in the Baltic port of Lübeck. It was the church's 700th anniversary. Christians and art lovers throughout Germany celebrated the event, and the government issued 2 million postage stamps depicting the "medieval" frescoes.

The following year when Lothar Malskat, an unknown artist from Königsberg and a member of Fey's team, suddenly announced that the frescoes were entirely his own invention, nobody believed him. Enraged by this slur on his artistic integrity, Malskat instructed his lawyer to file charges against himself and Fey. During their trial the story emerged.

When the Marienkirche was damaged by an incendiary bomb explosion in 1942, the peeling whitewash uncovered huge figures of saints on the walls of the nave. The bomb destroyed the roof, and by the time it was replaced, the frescoes had suffered from years of exposure, and only faint traces of the paintings remained.

The West German Association for the Preservation of Ancient Monuments gave about $50,000 toward the cost of restoration, and despite the provincial curate's warning that Fey was untrustworthy, he was given the contract. Fey and Malskat worked behind closed doors.

At their trial Malskat produced a film, revealing that the walls were almost bare when work was started. The frescoes had been done completely from Malskat's imagination.

Some of the figures were inspired by photographs of Marlene Dietrich and by Malskat's sister Frieda. Also depicted were Rasputin, the "mad monk" of the Czar's court, and Genghis Khan, the Mongol "scourge of God"—both wearing halos.

The reason for Malskat's seemingly unnecessary confession was simple: It was pride. Mals-

kat was furious that Fey should receive the glory that belonged to him. Also, Fey became steadily richer, while Malskat's demands for a half share in the profits from this and other forgeries were met with blank refusals.

Fey was sentenced to 20 months' imprisonment, while Malskat received only 18 months.

But financially, Malskat was still the loser, although later he did get an honest job.

He was commissioned to do imitation 14th-century decorations for a restaurant in Stockholm and continued to paint in the Gothic, Romantic, and Byzantine styles, of which he was master.

"MONA LISAS" TO ORDER

The day Leonardo's masterpiece was stolen

In 1911 no fewer than six Americans each paid $300,000 for the "Mona Lisa," and every one became the proud possessor of nothing more than a clever fake. All six paintings were the work of the master forger Yves Chaudron. What made the buyers believe they had the real thing was the fact that the "Mona Lisa" had been stolen that year from the Louvre in Paris.

It was the culmination of a series of art forgeries that had begun at the turn of the century, all perpetrated by the self-styled Marquis Eduardo de Valfierno and his accomplice, Chaudron. Valfierno had started his career by selling fake old masters to rich Argentinian widows. He offered them as memorial bequests that the widows could place in churches.

Chaudron, a former picture restorer, specialized in copies of paintings by the Spanish artist, Bartolomé Estéban Murillo.

When the pair had saturated Argentina with fake Murillos, they moved to Mexico City where Valfierno's sales technique was perfected.

First, Valfierno would sneak Chaudron's copy of a painting into the back of the frame of the original. Then, a prospective buyer would be taken to the gallery, shown the painting, and, while no one was looking, urged to mark the back of the picture.

In this way, he was told, he would be sure that the painting eventually delivered to him was the one he had seen hanging. In fact, he would have marked the back of the copy.

Valfierno also had a series of faked newspaper clippings reporting the theft of various paintings, which he would send to his clients. The fact that the original was still hanging in the gallery he would explain away, by saying that the authorities had put up a copy.

How much Valfierno made in this way is not clear, but it enabled the pair to depart for Paris.

Using the same techniques, Valfierno went to work on selling paintings "stolen" from the Louvre. This time he would supply clients with forged documents on Louvre stationery, including a confidential report that a masterpiece had been stolen and a copy substituted.

After three years Valfierno, Chaudron, and three confidence men with whom they had teamed convinced an American that they could steal the "Mona Lisa" for him—and delivered to him one of Chaudron's copies.

ENIGMA VARIATION. *Confusion over the subject of the Louvre's portrait is complicated by the similarity of Mona Lisa del Giocondo's name to the nickname of Medici's mistress, "La Gioconda."*

This particular triumph made the gang so self-confident that they decided to sell a whole series of "Mona Lisas"—and to steal the original.

Valfierno recruited Vincenzo Perugia, an Italian who had worked as a glazier on a protective glass box for the "Mona Lisa." He knew exactly how the painting was hung.

On Monday, August 21, 1911, a day when the gallery was closed for cleaning, Perugia and two accomplices dressed as workmen. After spending the previous night hiding in a store-room, they walked casually to the Salon Carré, took the 18-pound portrait, and walked out.

Over the next few months six U.S. buyers each surrendered $300,000, convinced they had the original.

But the gang did not make any money from the masterpiece itself. Perugia stole it from them and, in November 1913, offered to sell it to a Florentine art dealer. The dealer became suspicious, Perugia was caught and jailed, and the painting was returned to the Louvre.

THE OTHER "MONA LISA"

A woman whose nickname was "Smiler"

The face of the "Mona Lisa" smiles mysteriously down, not only from the wall of the Louvre in Paris but also from the wall of an apartment in London. The latter is not a reproduction, says its custodian Dr. Henry Pulitzer, but another version by Leonardo da Vinci and his studio. While there are more than 60 alleged "Mona Lisas" cataloged throughout the world, Dr. Pulitzer—inventor, scientist, and art connoisseur—is convinced of the authenticity of his own painting.

Leonardo, he points out, habitually did two or more versions of his portraits. The original sitter was Mona Lisa del Giocondo, wife of a Florentine nobleman. At the time she was mourning the death of her baby daughter and wore a transparent veil during the sittings.

Leonardo spent four years on the portrait and eventually left it with the Giocondos. Then, shortly before he went to France, at the invitation of Francis I, Guiliano de Medici asked him to paint a portrait of his current mistress, Costanza d'Avalos. Coincidentally, Costanza not only resembled Mona Lisa slightly but also was nicknamed "La Gioconda"—which means, approximately, "Smiler."

PORTRAIT OF A PORTRAIT. *This sketch, by Raphael, was made while Leonardo was still working on his masterpiece. Several features, such as the two columns, are similar to the painting (below) kept by Dr. Henry Pulitzer in London.*

NUDE GIOCONDA. *There are more than 60 alleged "Mona Lisas" on catalog. This seminude portrait, "La Belle Gabrielle," is in the collection of Lord Spencer of Northamptonshire, England, and is attributed to the school of Da Vinci.*

LONDON'S "MONA LISA." *This version bears fingerprints that match up with those on other authenticated paintings by Leonardo. It is thought to be of Mona Lisa del Giocondo, while the Louvre version is of Costanza d'Avalos, "La Gioconda."*

Leonardo adapted his alternative version of Mona Lisa del Giocondo's portrait, turning the face into that of Costanza.

But no sooner had he completed the work

than Medici dropped his mistress in favor of a profitable marriage and so did not buy the picture.

It was this second portrait, Dr. Pulitzer says, that Leonardo took with him, along with all his other unsold works, to France. It is this version—of Costanza—Dr. Pulitzer maintains, that graces the walls of the Louvre.

The first painting

The other portrait—of Giocondo's wife, who was 19 years younger than "La Gioconda"—stayed with the Florentine family until it eventually found its way to England and was bought early this century by William Blaker, an art connoisseur and curator of the Holburne of Menstrie Museum of Art, Bath, England, and more recently by a Swiss syndicate of which Dr. Pulitzer is a member.

Dr. Pulitzer has had the painting examined by microscopic photography techniques and says that fingerprints on the canvas match up with those on other authenticated works of Leonardo.

Another indication of the painting's authenticity is a sketch by Raphael, made while Leonardo was still working on the portrait in his studio. Raphael's sketch shows features, including two columns in the background, that are on the painting in London but not on the version in the Louvre.

Also, the younger girl in the London portrait is wearing a fine, transparent veil of mourning.

REVENGE OF AN UNDERRATED ARTIST
How Van Meegeren ruined his critics' reputations

Crowds flocked to Rotterdam's Boymans Museum in 1937 to see its latest exhibit—"Christ and the Disciples at Emmaus"—painted by Jan Vermeer, the 17th-century Dutch master.

This was an important discovery. At that time only 36 other works by Vermeer were known. Dr. Abraham Bredius, a renowned art authority and the man credited with its discovery, basked in the glory of his greatest moment.

Only one other man in the excited throng matched his happiness. He was Hans van Meegeren, and he alone could truly appreciate the subtlety of the painting's color and composition—because he had painted the picture himself. This was Van Meegeren's special moment, a time to savor his revenge on the so-called experts and critics whom he considered beneath contempt.

His hostility dated back to his early days when, as a highly promising painter in his own right, he had refused to bribe a corrupt critic to obtain a favorable review. Later, his work was savaged by the man, and Van Meegeren was ignored by the critics in general.

In May 1945, after the fall of Nazi Germany, Hermann Goering's priceless collection of looted art treasures was found at Berchtesgaden and hidden in a salt mine near Königsee. There were 1,200 paintings, among them "Woman

FORGER'S MASTERPIECE. *Hans van Meegeren passed off "Christ and the Disciples at Emmaus" as a Vermeer. He had spent four years learning how to age paintings artificially.*

Taken in Adultery," signed by Vermeer. What distinguished it was the fact that it was one of the few paintings that Goering had not stolen. Someone in Amsterdam had sold it to Goering's agent for about $500,000.

The Dutch police followed an intricate trail that led them to Van Meegeren, then a wealthy nightclub owner. His money had come from selling his collection of six Vermeers—five to Dutch museums, the sixth to Goering. Van Meegeren told police that he bought the painting from an Italian family and had sold it in good faith.

The skeptical authorities were unimpressed. Van Meegeren was arrested, and after three weeks in custody, under constant interrogation, and with the threat of execution for collaborating with the Germans, he cracked.

"Fools," he yelled. "You are like the rest of them. I sold no Vermeer to the Germans—only a Van Meegeren, painted to look like a Vermeer. I have not collaborated with the Germans, I have duped them." More was to come.

He confessed to forging 14 Dutch masterpieces by Frans Hals, Pieter de Hooch, and Vermeer, including "Christ and the Disciples at Emmaus." This sensation was enough to shake the reputation of Bredius and all the other connoisseurs, as Van Meegeren intended.

The experts called him a liar. They could do little else, for his confessions threatened them with professional ruin. "Prove your wild tale," they challenged. "Paint Emmaus again."

Van Meegeren went one better and offered to paint a "brandnew Vermeer." And so he embarked on what was to be his last picture, "Young Christ Teaching in the Temple." He worked under the ever-present eyes of a panel of official witnesses. He was allowed his usual arsenal of chemicals to reproduce the pigments of Vermeer's day, but his work was so impressive that he did not even need to finish it. The collaboration charge against him was dropped.

However, he was brought to trial in 1947, accused of forging signatures. His forgeries hung on the courtroom walls, and after a one-day trial Van Meegeren was found guilty. Two weeks later the judge sentenced him to one year in prison, but before he could begin his term, he had a heart attack. Six weeks later Van Meegeren died, at the age of 58.

An ironical touch to the affair was that Van Meegeren, the master forger, had himself been duped by a master criminal. Goering paid him for his forged Vermeer with forged banknotes.

As a youth the artist had boasted that his work was destined to adorn the walls of Holland's greatest museums and galleries, and, indeed, for a time, they did. In his own way he had proved himself the equal of the old masters.

Eccentrics and prophecies

•

THE SPENDTHRIFT SQUIRE

He bombarded his friends with bundles of money

Guests had already gathered for dinner when the host made his entrance—riding on a bear. Even they were startled, although they had learned to expect eccentricities from the celebrated John Mytton, a hard-hunting English squire.

But their amusement turned to alarm when Mytton spurred his steed and was bitten in the leg—a typical ending to one of his escapades.

On one occasion he drove his gig at high speed into a rabbit warren to see if the vehicle would overturn. It did. In the further pursuit of knowledge, he determined to prove that a horse and carriage are unable to jump a closed tollgate. He was correct.

Sport and drink—he got through about eight bottles of port a day and a large amount of brandy—were the twin passions of his life. He would hunt wearing the thinnest of clothes, or none at all, in the coldest weather.

Mytton was much admired for his generosity. He would toss bundles of notes to his friends and servants, or hurl the money into a hedge. His father had left him £60,000 in cash and an income of about £10,000 a year; but he dissipated the fortune in less than 15 years.

It was a wonder it had lasted so long. In 1834 he died in the debtors' prison of the King's Bench; he was 37. His body was returned to his old family home, Halston Hall in Shropshire, and there, in the presence of 3,000 friends and hunting companions, he was laid to rest.

BEAR-BACK RIDER. *Guests leap for safety as their host, John Mytton, rides in to dinner on a ferocious bear. However, it was the prankster and not his victims who came off worst.*

STRANGE COMPANY. *Lord Bridgewater astonished Paris by giving dinner parties for dogs. But though he was an animal lover, he also liked to shoot captive game birds in his garden.*

DINNER WITH THE EARL

His guests were dogs, dressed as men and women

The French were not surprised that the milord living in Paris was unusually fond of animals. They expected such bizarre conduct of an Englishman. But they raised their eyebrows a little when they heard he gave dinner parties for dogs dressed in the height of fashion, even down to fancy miniature shoes.

Nor did it accord with their ideas of English sportsmanship that Francis Henry Egerton, eighth Earl of Bridgewater, should keep partridges and pigeons with clipped wings in his garden to shoot because of his failing eyesight.

Strangely, this odd nobleman was an extremely learned scholar, a connoisseur and patron of the arts, and a fellow of the Royal Society. He was the donor of the important Egerton Manuscripts to the British Museum.

Yet this was the eccentric who wore each pair of his shoes once only and then had them arranged in rows so that he could measure the passing of time. And to return a book he had borrowed, he would send a sumptuous carriage attended by four liveried footmen.

He never married, and with his death in 1829, the title became extinct.

COUNTRY CAPERS. *An engraving published in 1840 showing Jemmy in his carriage with an odometer on the axle; hunting on the bull Jupiter; out shooting with dog and pig; and Jupiter in a bullfight.*

TWELVE MAIDS ALL IN A ROW

Jemmy wanted his funeral to be a happy occasion

Guests at parties 200 years ago in Rawcliffe, Yorkshire, England, were often unnerved when they realized that their drinks were being served from the host's favorite coffin. But usually they got used to the idea and moved on to inspect his second-best coffin.

This had folding doors and a window and stood on its end. When visitors climbed into it, the doors closed automatically and could not be opened from the inside. Men had to pay a penny to be released, and women had to surrender one of their garters.

The man who devised this odd hospitality was James, or "Jemmy," Hirst, who had the reputation of being the most eccentric man in England. His fame reached London, and King George III commanded him to attend court. Jemmy did not hurry off immediately; he informed His Majesty that he was very busy teaching an otter to swim but would call on him in due course.

Arriving in style

When he did arrive, it was in great style. His wickerwork carriage was painted like a rainbow, and he wore a lamb-skin cap, nine feet in circumference, an otter-skin coat lined with red flannel, a waistcoat of drake's feathers, patchwork breeches, red and white striped stockings, and shoes with huge silver buckles.

The King was delighted with Jemmy and restocked the wine cabinet in his carriage from the royal cellars.

Jemmy, who was born in 1738, gave early signs of his love of the bizarre. He rode his teacher's pig and trained it to jump low hurdles. But his tricks led to his expulsion from school, and he was apprenticed to a tanner. He fell in love with his teacher's daughter and was brokenhearted when she died.

He returned to his father's farm where he saddled a bull named Jupiter and from that day forward rarely rode a horse. He rode Jupiter to hounds and generally wore the same kind of clothes as those in which he visited the King.

But for all his eccentricities, he was a shrewd businessman and quickly built up a fortune dealing in farm produce.

The wickerwork carriage that he designed was originally pulled by Jupiter, but he had it extended for sleeping in. It was then pulled by two mules.

On one occasion, however, he had sails rigged on the carriage and "sailed" into Pontefract, where a sudden gust blew him and the carriage into a clothier's window. He also fitted the wheels with an odometer he invented, a clocklike device that rang a bell once a mile.

Before he died, at the age of 91, he left instructions that his coffin should be carried by 12 old maids, to the accompaniment of a fiddler and bagpiper.

Sadly, only two women could be found who would swear on oath to their maidenly status; the vicar banned the fiddler; and the piper was allowed to play only solemn music.

MANUFACTURER OF MONSTERS

The man who improved on nature

Pope Pius VII was extremely annoyed. Some young mischievous Englishman had climbed St. Peter's in Rome and left his gloves on top of the lightning conductor. They must be removed at once. But who would dare to carry out His Holiness' wishes? Sadly, only that same young man had the courage. So Charles Waterton, a good Roman Catholic, penitently reclimbed St. Peter's and brought down his own gloves.

That was in 1817 when Waterton was 25, and this was the first time he caught the public eye. He then went traveling in the West Indies and North and South America, observing wildlife, collecting birds, and eventually writing a bestselling book on his travels in Latin America and the natural history of the region, on which he became the acknowledged expert.

Again, he showed his physical courage. In South America, Waterton caught an alligator by riding on its back and seizing its front legs. Helpless in this judo hold, the animal was dragged ashore. Later he cut its throat and skinned it.

As an experiment, on one of his expeditions, he tried to get a vampire bat to bite his big toe by sleeping with his foot dangling out of his hammock. However, the bat then ignored him, choosing instead to bite his native servant.

When he returned to his home in Yorkshire, he built a nine-foot-high wall encircling three miles of his estate, making it one of the world's first wildlife sanctuaries.

His interests as a naturalist had made him an accomplished taxidermist, and he built up a whole museum of stuffed birds and animals.

Not content with nature

But he was not content with animals as nature had created them. He took different parts of birds and animals and amalgamated them into his own monsters. In the case of his celebrated "Nondescript," he contorted the face of a red howler monkey, convincing many people that he had stuffed a human head.

To many of these homemade monsters he gave the names of some well-known Protestant personalities.

But this was not his only eccentricity. One of his favorite pranks was to hide under a hall table until a guest had put down his coat, then leap out to bite the astonished visitor.

After the death of his wife he slept on the bare floor with a block of wood for a pillow. He rose at 3 a.m. each day and spent the time before breakfast at 8 a.m. reading and praying.

Then he would spend the rest of the day studying wildlife. When he was over 80—he lived to 83—he would shin up trees to examine birds' nests. He scrambled up "like an adolescent gorilla," according to a contemporary.

A flying machine

One of the eccentric squire's projects was the construction of a flying machine. It took a great deal of persuasion by his friends and servants before he gave up the idea of testing the machine by leaping from an outhouse roof.

It was this kind of unusual activity that brought about his death in 1865. He fell while carrying a huge log and died of his injuries 10 days later. He was buried with great ceremony, and a fleet of funeral boats escorted his body across the lake on his estate.

His valuable natural history collection was presented to a college.

CHARLES WATERTON IN 1834. *Despite appearances, he was a forerunner of the wildlife preservation societies of today.*

DINING IN STYLE. *The dining room of "The Breakers," the Vanderbilts' Newport mansion, rises two stories.*

THE LIFE OF LUXURY

Or how to dispose of excess wealth

HIS-AND-HER BARGAIN. *From the famed Neiman-Marcus department store's Christmas catalog, an $18,700 submarine for two.*

According to the late socialite-author Lucius Beebe, "American people are a spending people," to whom "a rich man is the noblest handiwork of God."

If we don't have the means for lavish spending ourselves, we relish the extravagances of those who do: cigarettes wrapped in $100 bills, birthday parties for diamond-collared poodles, a hotel ballroom transformed for a night into a replica of the Belmont racetrack.

The mold for the life of luxury, U.S. style, was cast in the post-Civil War years by the Vanderbilts, Carnegies, Astors, Rockefellers, and other members of the $50 million club.

Mansions, estates, resorts

Sumptuous city mansions, styled after European chateaus (from which entire rooms were often imported), were crammed with many Old World masterpieces, while some secluded estates sported million-dollar gardens.

The wealthy also brought their opulent life-styles to a succession of fashionable resorts—a "cottage" at Newport, Rhode Island, such as Cornelius Vanderbilt's "The Breakers," might have 70 rooms.

COMFORT AFLOAT. *Majestic in full sail, the 316-foot* Sea Cloud *cost heiress Marjorie M. Post untold millions in the 1930's. The sailing yacht required a crew of 50, and its rigging alone was worth several million dollars. It now belongs to a member of the multimillionaire Mellon family.*

Yachts and railroad cars

Oceangoing yachts such as the *Sea Cloud*, which cost tens of thousands of dollars yearly to maintain, remained beyond the means of even most of the superrich.

Private railroad cars were more easily attainable, for they could be rented as well as bought. Invariably plush and brocaded, the cars were tailored to their owners' personal notions of necessary comforts: a wine cellar, a sunken bathtub, a barber's chair, and even that hallmark of opulence and culture, a pipe organ. Lucius Beebe's own private car was a comparatively modest affair.

Today's millionaires are more circumspect in their spending, by and large. Corporate ostentation, such as the lavish executive living quarters in New York's newest Fifth Avenue "mansion," Olympic Towers, must substitute for the former splendors of bygone days.

There are some compensations, however. Anyone with a modest credit rating can be included in the mailing list for the Neiman-Marcus department store's sales catalogs—and dream of his-and-her submarines or more conventional luxuries. The submarine, after all, costs but $18,700 and has sufficient space for a couple and their guests.

MANSION ON RAILS. *Lucius Beebe (left) poses in his own custom-built private railroad car—a hallmark of wealth from the 1880's up to the Second World War.*

THE ELEPHANT THAT WAS FORGOTTEN

LITTLE SURVIVES of the work of the 18th-century French architect Charles Ribart, which is a pity because, in an age when the fashion was for grandeur, he was an architect with a sense of fun. In 1758 Ribart planned an amazing addition to the Champs Elysées in Paris, to be constructed where the Arc de Triomphe now stands. It was a building on three levels, in the shape of an elephant, and with entry through a spiral staircase in the elephant's underbelly. The building was to have some form of air-conditioning and furniture that folded into the walls. The drainage system was incorporated in the elephant's trunk. But the French government was not amused and turned the plan down.

THE HERMIT WHO BECAME LONELY

LIKE several other 18th-century English gentlemen, the Hon. Charles Hamilton felt that the landscaping of his estate would be incomplete without the melancholy presence of a hermit. So he built a suitable retreat among the gnarled roots of trees and advertised that the successful applicant would be given a Bible, spectacles, food and water, a mat, and a robe. He must not cut his hair, beard, or nails, nor speak to anyone for seven years, at the end of which time he would be given £700. But the man who got the job lasted only three weeks. He explained that he was lonely.

LUDWIG THE CASTLE BUILDER

The simple pleasures of a mad King

The groom at the royal riding school did not question the King's wishes. If his royal master chose to ride around and around the riding school from 8 p.m. to 3 a.m., it was his duty to follow, changing the horses from time to time. And he enjoyed the pleasant stop for a picnic supper. The King was known for his generosity to servants who pleased him, and the loyal groom was rewarded with a gold watch for attending His Majesty on this so-called gallop "from Munich to Innsbruck."

For the royal horseman was Ludwig II, the "mad" King of Bavaria, and imaginary journeys calculated on the distance around the riding school were one of his simple pleasures. The inconvenient hour was dictated by the fact that Ludwig had chosen to reverse night and day.

And yet the start of his reign had seemed promising after he succeeded to the throne upon the death of his father, Maximilian II, on March 10, 1864.

Agreed, the family background was slightly odd. His grandfather, Ludwig I, had fallen in love with a "Spanish" dancer, Lola Montez—in reality the Irish Eliza Gilbert—when he was 60, and squandered the national treasury on her. And there was his aunt, Princess Alexandra, a talented woman whose excessive concern for her health was based on the impression that she had swallowed a grand piano made of glass.

But the handsome 18-year-old monarch had captured the imagination of the Bavarians and immediately showed signs of wishing to be a conscientious ruler. However, he had heard Wagner's *Lohengrin* at the age of 15 and had been entranced by the whole Wagnerian world of Germanic legend.

At the time of Ludwig's accession, Wagner had gone into hiding to escape his many creditors. The King sent his secretary to find him, and on May 3 Wagner was finally run to ground. The secretary delivered the King's message. Wagner was to go at once to Munich where all his debts would be paid, and he would be provided with everything that he needed so that he could continue his life's work without interruption or worry.

Thus began a deep friendship, in which Ludwig idolized the composer. He reveled in his company and threw himself into his artistic enterprises. But Wagner's extravagance was also of regal proportions. There were mutterings in Bavaria about how much his genius was costing. On one occasion Wagner sent his mistress to draw one of the King's payments from the bank. It was paid in sacks of small

NEUSCHWANSTEIN CASTLE. *One of King Ludwig's most extravagant follies, the fairytale palace perched on a hilltop has become a great attraction for tourists in Bavaria.*

coins so the lady had to convey it conspicuously in two cabs—whether the bank did this deliberately to stir up feeling against Wagner is not known.

But the composer also began to dabble in politics, and it was put to Ludwig that he must choose between his private friendship and his public duty. Sadly, he decided he must accept his royal responsibilities, and he asked Wagner to leave Munich. His devotion to the composer continued, however, until Wagner's death.

A sofa for a sentry

So far, the King was showing few signs of eccentricity—though there were odd incidents like sending out a sofa to one of the palace sentries when he thought he looked tired. He tried to take an interest in affairs of state and even became engaged to his cousin, Sophie, although women did not attract him. In fact, he did not go through with the marriage.

It was about this time that he turned to the passion for which he is best remembered—the building of his castles. His mother, Queen Marie, had recorded that as a child he had loved playing with bricks and showed an aptitude for construction.

In 1868 he wrote to Wagner: "I propose to rebuild the ancient castle ruins of Vorderhohenschwangau, near the Pollat Falls, in the genuine style of the old German knights' castles, and I must tell you how excited I am at the idea of living there." It would, he said, be in the spirit of *Tannhäuser* and *Lohengrin*.

And so it began. This was to be Neuschwanstein, his fairytale castle perched on a giddy mountain pinnacle. But there was also the baroque splendor of Linderhof and the opulence of Herrenchiemsee, a replica of Versailles. The King retreated into the dream world of his castles far from affairs of state.

He no longer contented himself with jaunts around the riding school but on winter nights went on wild drives through the mountains in a golden rococo sleigh, attended by coachmen, outriders, and lackeys who were obliged to dress in the style of Louis XIV.

His lack of attention to affairs of state and boundless extravagance could not go on forever. In June 1886 his uncle and heir, Prince Luitpold, had him declared insane and succeeded him as regent.

But the story was to end in mystery as well as tragedy. Ludwig was confined at Schloss Berg, outside Munich, on June 12, and the following day he set out on a walk with Dr. Bernhard von Gudden, his personal physician. When they failed to return, a search party was sent out, and the two bodies were found floating in shallow water about 20 yards from the bank. Many theories of murder, suicide, and accident have been put forward, but no one has proved conclusively how Ludwig's bizarre life came to its tragic end.

ANNA'S ICE PALACE

Chilly rebuff for an erring courtier

Anna Ivanovna, Empress of all the Russias, was a coldhearted woman. So it was not wholly inappropriate that she should build a palace completely of ice.

It was 1740, and Europe was in the grip of the worst winter in 30 years. The Seine, Rhine, Danube, and Thames froze solid for months, and wine turned to ice in the glass even before roaring fires.

The design was entrusted to architect Peter Eropkin, who had just completed a plan for the rebuilding of St. Petersburg. Hundreds of serfs and artisans were put to work on the project.

The palace, 80 feet long, 33 feet high, and 23 feet deep, was designed in the classical style. The ice used was carefully chosen for its transparency, and each block was measured with a compass and rule before being cut and lifted into position. The blocks were joined with water, which instantly froze, so that, in effect, the edifice became one single chunk of ice.

Ice trees were sculpted, some as tall as the palace; others were dwarf orange trees bearing ice fruit. Ice birds sitting in the trees were painted in their natural colors. Ice statues stood in niches, and windows were glazed with ice.

In the bedchamber was an elaborate, curtained four-poster, with mattress, quilt, two pillows, and two nightcaps all carved out of ice. There was even a meticulously carved model clock as well as all the other usual furnishings that one would expect.

The most striking feature on the grounds was a life-size ice elephant ridden by an iceman in Persian costume. From the elephant's trunk a 24-foot spout of water jetted during the day. At night gasoline was used so that the animal spouted flame. A trumpeter concealed inside its body simulated roars.

There were also six cannons and two mortars made of solid ice. The amount of gunpowder they could withstand was calculated carefully, and they were fired many times without damage either to themselves or the crowd.

The only thing not made of ice was a wooden fence around the palace to keep the public at bay. For this was not an extravagant but harmless folly for their amusement. The ice palace had been designed as a cruel jest.

Prince Michael Alexievich Golitsyn had angered the Empress by marrying, without her permission, an Italian Roman Catholic, who died soon after the wedding. Anna made him court jester as a token of her displeasure.

This was not enough, however. She also ordained that he should remarry, and the Empress herself chose the bride—a particularly ugly Kalmuk serving woman. And the ice palace was for their honeymoon. The unhappy couple was paraded in a cage on the back of an elephant, leading a procession of the grotesque human beings Anna had gathered about her

and an array of animals including bears and pigs. Then they were bedded down publicly in the icy bedchamber.

The ending of the story was not too unhappy, however. With the spring the ice palace melted into the river, and the Empress died later that year. Prince Michael and his Kalmuk bride found they got on well together and lived happily ever after.

COOL RECEPTION. *A contemporary engraving shows the drawing room of Anna's ice palace.*

COLD COMFORT. *Anna Ivanovna, the capricious Empress of Russia, ordered a prince who had incurred her displeasure to marry an ugly serving wench and built an ice palace for their wedding night.*

THE FOLLY OF RICHES

The rise and fall of Fonthill Abbey

Put enormous wealth into the hands of an eccentric and allow him to indulge himself, and the results are likely to be prodigious—and foolish. So it was with William Beckford, who constructed England's biggest and most extravagant folly.

In 1770, at the age of 10, he inherited about £1 million in cash, land, and houses in England and sugar plantations in Jamaica with thousands of slaves. His income was £100,000 a year—a fabulous sum in the 18th century.

Beckford was brought up like a prince, studying music with Mozart and architecture with Sir William Cozens, designer of London's Somerset House. At the age of 21, Beckford justified his expensive education by writing *Vathek,* a romantic novel, which later earned praise from Byron. He is said to have written it in French in three days and two nights.

For a time Beckford was a Member of Parliament but spent most of his time on a grand tour of Europe, accompanied by a retinue of servants, including his own musicians.

Then, in 1794, he set about the fulfillment of his greatest ambition—the building of a Gothic "abbey" at his Fonthill estate in Wiltshire.

Beckford's approach to the project was distinctly odd. To begin with, he built a 12-foot-high wall around the entire estate to keep out prying eyes. Behind the wall he lived in seclusion, seldom admitting visitors. But each evening he would order dinner for 12 and sit at table alone, eating only a single dish. If Beckford decided to take a morning stroll through the woods, he expected the villagers to work all night cutting down trees to clear his path.

Lofty disregard

Fonthill Abbey was built with the same lofty disregard for expense. Hundreds of builders were kept at work day and night, and an additional 400 men were diverted from working on St. George's Chapel in Windsor, in order to complete Beckford's project.

If only he had left them alone to get on with the job, he might have had better results. But

WILLIAM BECKFORD'S IMPRACTICAL FANTASY. *The lofty halls and soaring towers of Fonthill Abbey were in keeping with the romantic idealism of the day. But high towers call for firm foundations, which it did not have.*

he would insist on directing the work. His notions of management were more generous than practical. Each day the builders were given an ever-increasing liquor ration as an incentive to finish on time; as a result, the workers were generally drunk and incapable.

Then he ordered a 400-foot wooden tower to be built so that he could see its effect. He did not like it and had it pulled down.

Little chance

But the project had little chance from the start. Beckford was so impatient that he could not wait for proper foundations to be dug. Instead, the abbey was built on those laid for a small summer house.

Beckford vowed to eat Christmas dinner cooked in the abbey's kitchens. And so he did, though they collapsed as soon as the meal was over. The main tower also fell down in 1800.

In the words of a contemporary, Fonthill Abbey was "a desert of magnificence, a glittering waste of laborious idleness, a cathedral turned into a toy shop."

In 1822 Beckford came to the edge of ruin when he lost two of his Jamaican estates in a legal action and was forced to sell his dream house.

It was perhaps as well. Soon after the new tenant moved in, the main tower fell down again. Not surprisingly, little of Fonthill Abbey remains today.

THE OTHER MAN IN AN IRON MASK

Only war could break his resolve

Could a man walk around the world without showing his face? It was one of those idle questions that arose when members of London's National Sporting Club were gathered together after a good lunch in 1907. John Pierpont Morgan, the American millionaire, and the sporting peer, Lord Lonsdale, were arguing. Lonsdale said it could be done; Morgan said it could not.

The argument resulted in a wager equivalent to $100,000, and all that was needed was someone to attempt the feat. In that same company was Harry Bensley, a 31-year-old playboy with an annual income of £5,000 from investments in Russia. He wanted to get away from the tedium of club life—and offered his services.

A stiff set of rules was drawn up, the main one being that, like the character in Alexandre Dumas' novel, *The Man in the Iron Mask*, Bensley would wear an iron mask at all times. In addition he would push a baby carriage, set out with £1 in his pocket, and take nothing but a change of underwear.

He had to pass through a specified number of British towns and 125 towns in 18 other countries. He also had to find a wife on his journey, who was not to see his face; and to finance himself, he would sell picture postcards. To ensure that he kept to the rules, a paid escort was to accompany him.

Harry set out on January 1, 1908. Wearing a 4½-pound iron helmet and pushing a 200-pound spindly-wheeled baby carriage, he left Trafalgar Square amid cheering crowds.

At Newmarket Races he met Edward VII, and sold him a postcard for £5. The amused King asked for his autograph, but this would have revealed his identity, known only to his backers, so Harry had to refuse.

At Bexleyheath, Kent, a zealous policeman arrested him for selling postcards without a license. Harry appeared in court wearing his mask, and the angry magistrate ordered him to remove it. But when the wager was explained to him, the magistrate allowed Harry to be charged as "the man in the iron mask," and only fined him a small amount of money.

Harry Bensley spent six years pushing his carriage across 12 countries, passing through New York, Montreal, and Sydney. Two hundred offers of marriage poured in, some from titled ladies, but Harry declined them all.

In August 1914 he arrived in Genoa, Italy, with only six more countries to visit. But the First World War had broken out, and as a patriotic young man he felt he had to join the British forces. The bet was called off. Harry was given a consolation prize that amounted to $20,000, which he gave to charity.

He was one of the lucky ones who survived the war, but in 1917 his fortunes suffered a blow. His investments were lost in the Russian Revolution, and he was penniless. He died in 1956, in a one-room apartment in Brighton.

ELAGABALUS THE HORRIBLE
An Emperor to whom rule was a joke

No one dared refuse an invitation to dine with the Roman Emperor Elagabalus. But the best they could hope for was a thoroughly unpleasant evening—and the worst, a particularly nasty death.

For the young Emperor devoted his short

ELAGABALUS OF ROME. *He served his dinner guests glass, and died by order of his grandmother.*

reign to playing elaborate practical jokes on some of his unfortunate subjects.

One of his greatest joys was to invite the seven fattest men in Rome to dinner. They were seated on air cushions that slaves then punctured, sending the fat men sprawling on the floor. Other guests would be served with artificial food made of glass, marble, or ivory. Etiquette compelled them to eat it.

When real food was served, guests were likely to find spiders in the aspic or lions' dung in the pastry. Anyone who dined too well and fell asleep might wake up in a room filled with lions, leopards, and bears. If he survived the shock, he found that the animals were tame.

Elagabalus, who reigned from A.D. 218 to 222, was fond of animals, and often his chariot was pulled by dogs, stags, lions, or tigers. But he was equally likely to arrive at a state function in a wheelbarrow pulled by naked women.

Often he would order his slaves to gather spiders' webs, frogs, scorpions, or poisonous snakes that he would send to his courtiers as gifts. On one occasion he had the seemingly pleasant idea of showering his dinner guests with rose petals. He used so many that some of them suffocated.

The state coffers were emptied by his extravagances. He would order a magnificent bath to be built, use it once, then have it demolished.

But Rome did not approve of his high living—nor did it share his sense of humor. Finally, his own Praetorian guard murdered him on the orders of his grandmother, and his body was bundled into the Tiber. He was just 18 years old.

THE WORLD OF DADAISM
Eccentricity as a way of life

During the First World War a number of writers, artists, and musicians banded together in a movement whose object was the destruction of the middle-class values that they believed had led Europe into war.

The movement was called dadaism, and deliberate eccentricity was the lifestyle of its members. Bourgeois standards were toppled in

a campaign of insults waged against anyone not prepared to adopt their ways. The principal weapons in the battle were bizarre sculptures, paintings, and verse that bewildered and offended much of the public.

The movement began in Zurich during 1916 with the foundation of the Cabaret Voltaire in a popular bar. It was a nightly "happening" of

498

gibberish recitals, punctuated by bells, drum-rolls, and shouts.

Dadaism evolved through confusion and contradiction of established beliefs. Even the name is obscure. A Frenchman named Jean (Hans) Arp said: "I declare that Tristan Tzara found the word on February 9, 1916 at 6 p.m. I was present with my 12 children when Tzara uttered this word which filled us with justified enthusiasm. I am convinced that this word is of no importance and that only imbeciles and Spanish professors can take an interest in dates."

"Imbeciles" was one of the kinder words used by the staid Swiss press in describing Russian-born poet Tzara and his fellow "artiste," the German Hugo Ball. Prancing about on stage clad in a blue cardboard cylinder and red collar, Ball was the first person known to use the flashing red lights so popular in present-day discotheques. But as suddenly as he had appeared, Ball opted out of the avant-garde and retreated to a semimonastic life.

Spanning the Atlantic

Meanwhile, dadaism swept the world. In New York the movement was led by the writer Fabian Lloyd, who for reasons best known to himself adopted the name of Arthur Cravan. Earlier in Paris, Lloyd had startled society women attending an art lecture by taking off most of his clothes in what may have been one of the first "streaks." What happened to Lloyd is not known. He left Mexico in an attempt to sail a small boat to Buenos Aires and was never seen again.

A painter named Marcel Duchamp took over from Lloyd as leader of the movement. Duchamp's object was to shake off artistic convention in a deliberate "antiart" campaign, which included a version of the "Mona Lisa" with a mustache. Another of his works was a bicycle wheel attached to a stool and a snow shovel entitled "In Advance of the Broken Arm." Duchamp's masterpiece, "The Great Glass,"

took him eight years to assemble. It was an abstract made of paint, wire, varnish, and New York dust, held between sheets of glass. On the way to a Brooklyn exhibition in 1923 the glass broke, but the undaunted Marcel Duchamp announced the work as "The Last Refinement" and showed it anyway.

Everything he did was intended to be a rejection of art. Ironically, his works now fetch enormous prices.

End of dadaism

During the mid-1920's, the dadaist movement gradually dwindled out. The grand finale came in Paris with an all-out brawl as rival factions clashed. The dadaists felt they had made their point and left the future for the world to decide.

AN EARLY DADA. *Hugo Ball, wearing his gaily colored cardboard suit, appeared on stage at the Swiss Cabaret Voltaire.*

NAME YOUR POISON

GUSTAV III of Sweden believed that coffee was poison. To prove his theory, he sentenced a murderer to drink coffee every day until he died. To provide comparison, another murderer was pardoned on condition that he drink tea every day. Two doctors were appointed to supervise the experiment and see who died first. The doctors were the first to die. Then the King was murdered in 1792. Finally, after many years, one of the criminals died—at the age of 83. He was the tea drinker.

"AGAIN I DIE!" *One of Robert Coates' postures that reduced his audiences to helpless laughter. Overelaborate costumes detracted nothing from the awfulness of his acting.*

HAM CAN BE JAM

Success comes to the world's worst actor

So bad an actor was Robert Coates that he became a star of London in the early 19th century. People traveled from far away to see if he really was as bad as they had heard. He did not disappoint them. His incompetence amounted almost to dramatic genius.

In one play, where Coates had to die, he drew a silk handkerchief from his pocket, spread it carefully on the stage, and then laid his elaborate headdress upon it so that he might expire in style. This so enchanted the audience that they demanded encores and had him die several times over.

Coates was born on the West Indian island of Antigua in 1772, the son of a rich merchant and plantation owner. But it was in England, where he was brought up, that he acquired a passion for the theater. For years he wore a bejeweled Romeo costume without ever getting an invitation to play the part.

Finally, his opportunity arrived, and on February 9, 1810, he made his first stage appearance—as Romeo. His debut was in Bath, England, then a center of the rich and fashionable world.

His acting was so appalling that he became an overnight hit.

Before long he had moved on to still greater success in London. There he rewrote Shakespeare, ad-libbed outrageously, and addressed the audience in the middle of scenes, often threatening to cross the footlights and fight those who laughed too loudly.

But the laugh was really on the audience. Coates continually played to packed houses, which included such personalities as the Prince Regent. He became so prosperous that he could flaunt himself in a carriage shaped like a kettledrum, painted in brilliant colors and drawn by two white horses. On its side was emblazoned a heraldic cock with his motto: "While I live I'll crow."

And so he did to a robust 75, when he came to a dramatic end. Crossing a London street to retrieve his opera glasses from a theater, he was struck by a passing cab and died soon afterward.

COALS TO NEWCASTLE

Strange business deals led to a stranger home life

Although he was born too early to sell refrigerators to Eskimos, Timothy Dexter did manage to sell coals to Newcastle—and show a handsome profit from the deal.

He was born into a poor family in 1747 and apprenticed to the leather trade. In Newburyport, Massachusetts, he first showed his financial acumen by marrying a widow with some property and going into business himself. But it was at the end of the War of Independence that he demonstrated the flair that was to make him a brilliantly successful entrepreneur.

He bought up a large amount of Continental currency, which, due to the dearth of trade during the war, was almost valueless in America. Several years later it almost regained its prewar value, and he found himself in possession of a fortune. With it he bought ships and began his series of trading coups.

Dexter conceived what seemed to be the crazy idea of selling 40,000 warming pans to the sweltering islands of the West Indies. People thought he was throwing away his money, but in fact the pans fetched high prices for cooking and as ladles in the molasses industry.

He even got a good price for a consignment of mittens sent to the West Indies, for another trader bought them for reexport to Russia. Dexter had similar luck when he sent coal to Newcastle. Somebody pulled his leg by saying there was a huge market for coal there. But when Dexter fell for this and sent off several ships full of Virginian coal, he had the astonishing good fortune to land it in Newcastle during a miners' strike. As a result his cargoes were snapped up.

Rejected by polite society because of his lowly birth and *nouveau riche* ways, he decided to call himself Lord Timothy Dexter and establish his own court in a sumptuous mansion. Besides his nagging wife, crazy daughter, and alcoholic son, his "courtiers" included a fortuneteller, a six foot seven inch tall idiot whom he called the dwarf, and a poet laureate appointed by himself. This "laureate" was Jonathan Plummer, a former fishmonger and purveyor of pornography, whom he dressed in cocked hat and silver-buckled shoes.

Within the mansion he built up a collection of hundreds of watches and clocks. Then he set about turning the grounds into an outdoor museum by employing a ship's carver to make 40 life-sized wooden figures of such famous characters as William Pitt, Lord Nelson, Benjamin Franklin, George Washington—and himself.

Visitors to the collection would also view the tomb that he had built for himself, containing a magnificently decorated coffin and, among other funeral accoutrements, a speaking trumpet, a set of pipes with tobacco, and, of course, a box of fireworks.

In later life Dexter wrote a booklet called *A Pickle for the Knowing Ones; or Plain Truths in a Homespun Dress.* Published in 1802, it was distributed free, but so popular did it become that copies changed hands at high prices. It ran to eight editions.

Its main claim to fame—and it has been praised by such eminent critics as Oliver Wendell Holmes—is that it contained no punctuation whatsoever, although it was interspersed with numerous capital letters, mostly in the wrong places. It related Dexter's experiences and attacked politicians and the clergy.

The book suggested that what the United States needed was an Emperor; and that Americans need look no further than Lord Timothy Dexter of Newburyport.

LORD TIMOTHY. *In his garden he erected statues of the world's most famous men—including Lord Timothy Dexter.*

THE EMPEROR WHO HURT NOBODY

Norton I ruled San Francisco with a gentle hand

The editor of the *San Francisco Bulletin* was the first to hear about it. The down-and-out in the cast-off army colonel's blue and gold uniform told him quite simply: "I am the Emperor of the United States." The editor was amused and agreed to print his visitor's first proclamation on the front page. So began the fabulous 20-year reign of Joshua Abraham Norton.

Norton was born in London in 1819 and, two years later, moved with his family to South Africa where his father, a farmer and ship's chandler, helped to pioneer Grahamstown. When his father died in 1848, Norton sold everything and went to Brazil. Meanwhile, gold had been discovered in California.

In November 1849 Norton arrived in San Francisco with $40,000. He decided there was more money to be made in the booming city itself than in panning for gold. He opened a general store and dabbled in real estate.

By 1853 he had piled up $250,000. But he got greedy. He decided to corner rice, buying up every cargo. The price soared from 4 to 32 cents a pound, but he still refused to sell. Without warning a fleet of ships arrived from South America laden with rice, and the market collapsed. Norton was ruined. Two years later he was bankrupt.

He still was when he issued his first proclamation in September 1859. A week later a second decree said that because of corruption in high places Congress was abolished. Henceforth, he would rule in person.

San Francisco was delighted. Norton had become the city's favorite "character."

When Washington ignored his second decree, Emperor Norton ordered the commander in chief of the U.S. Army to "proceed with a suitable force and clear the Halls of Congress."

All states of the Union were ordered to send delegates to San Francisco's Music Hall to pay homage and "make such changes as are necessary in the law."

This was soon followed by a declaration that, because the Mexicans were obviously unable to manage their own affairs, the Emperor had assumed the role of "Protector of Mexico."

In a drab roominghouse, with pictures of Napoleon and Queen Victoria on the wall, Emperor Norton held court. In the afternoons he sauntered through the streets with two mongrel dogs at his heels, gravely acknowledging the bows of his subjects, inspecting drains, and checking streetcar timetables. He attended a different church every Sunday.

Theaters reserved a special seat for him, and the audience would rise in respectful silence when he made his entry. Once an overzealous young policeman arrested him for vagrancy, and the whole city reacted angrily. The chief of police personally released the Emperor Norton with profuse apologies.

When the Civil War broke out in 1861, he followed the course of the fighting with "deep concern." He summoned President Lincoln and Jefferson Davis, President of the Confederacy, to San Francisco so that he could mediate, but neither of them turned up.

All this time Norton was being kept by the citizens of San Francisco. He was given free board, free meals, and free travel. He once "abolished" the Central Pacific Railroad for refusing him a free meal in the dining car and was only appeased by a gold pass for life.

But he was always short of ready cash so he introduced a system of taxation: 25 to 50 cents a week for shopkeepers and $3 a week for banks. San Franciscans laughed—but most paid up.

When his uniform grew faded and shabby, Norton decided that he should issue a proclamation: "Know ye . . . that we, Norton the First, have divers complaints from our liege subjects . . . that our imperial wardrobe is a national disgrace." The next day the city council voted funds for a new outfit.

The people of San Francisco were loyal and true subjects. When he died on January 8, 1880, 10,000 citizens filed past his coffin in two days.

In 1934 a marble slab was placed on his grave in Woodlawn Cemetery with the simple inscription: "Norton I, Emperor of the United States and Protector of Mexico, Joshua A. Norton, 1819–1880."

The real explanation of the attraction that Joshua Norton held appeared in his obituary in a San Francisco paper: "The Emperor Norton killed nobody, robbed nobody and deprived nobody of his country—which is more than can be said for most fellows in his trade."

Norton I.
Emperor U.S.
& Protector of
Mexico.
19th Day of
June 1879.

An Edict.

His Imperial Majesty, Norton I., has issued the following edict to Hall McAllister, Esq.:

H. McALLISTER, ESQ.—You are hereby commanded to apply to the United States Supreme Court for a Writ of Error, so that we can legally proceed to the capitol, at Sacramento, and *burn up* the new Constitution.

Given under our hand and seal, this twenty-second day of May, A. D., 1879.   NORTON I. [SEAL.]

Dei Gratia Emperor of the United States, and Protector of Mexico.

THE EMPEROR'S NEW CLOTHES. *When Norton issued edicts such as the one shown above, they delighted San Francisco. And his appeal for a new "imperial wardrobe" was heavily subscribed.*

A HEARTY APPETITE

Dr. Buckland ate anything—including royal relics

Crocodile with orange juice was the unusual breakfast often served at the home of gourmet extraordinaire Francis Buckland, who, as was well known, would eat anything.

Buckland, a 19th-century British surgeon and naturalist, was a founding member of the Society for the Acclimatization of Animals in

BUCKLAND AT HOME. *Caged monkeys were his company. When he went to college at Oxford, he kept a menagerie in his room—including a tame bear.*

the United Kingdom—an organization devoted to increasing the nation's food supplies by breeding anything from kangaroos to bison in the fields of England.

In 1862 Buckland was responsible for the society's annual dinner. It was a rare feast with a menu that catered to the most jaded of appetites. There was kangaroo meat from Australia and Southeast Asian trepang sea slug. The slug looked so repulsive that only a few diners were able even to sample it. On another occasion

Buckland complained that it was a pity earwigs were so "horribly bitter."

But despite this gastronomic setback, he persevered in his crusade. From mouse on toast—served to his fellow students at Oxford—he graduated to the "delights" of boiled elephant's trunk, rhinoceros pie, and a whole roast ostrich. The ostrich apparently gave the eminent zoologist Sir Richard Owen a severe case of indigestion, though Sir Richard's wife described it as tasting "very much like coarse turkey."

Another of Buckland's failures was broiled porpoise head. He said he could not stop it tasting like an oil-lamp wick. But he considered some of his food-pioneering work so successful that he offered the recipes to the public in a magazine. Slug soup and garden snails were but two of his unsavory suggestions.

Buckland's worst dishes included stewed moles and bluebottles—even he admitted he could not eat those.

He had a passion for the unusual and exotic in anything. His collection of curiosities included Ben Jonson's heel bone, a piece of skin from a frozen Siberian mammoth, and a lock of hair from the head of Henry IV.

In 1878 he was given a four-poster bed that had once belonged to the 18th-century surgeon John Hunter. Hunter had been a lifelong hero of Buckland's, so he promptly cut the bed up and made it into the chair that now stands in London's Royal College of Surgeons' museum.

Buckland also took a deep interest in royalty. During a meal with a friend he once confided: "I have eaten many strange things in my lifetime, but never before have I eaten the heart of a King." On the plate was the heart of Louis XIV, which had been plundered from the royal tomb during the French Revolution.

STRACHEY'S TIMELY RETURN

WILLIAM STRACHEY lived most of his life ahead of time—six hours ahead, in fact. After five years in India he returned home to England and decided not to go back. While in India, Strachey decided the only accurate clocks were in Calcutta. For the rest of his life he lived by Calcutta time, which was six hours ahead of Greenwich. He spent 56 years rising in the middle of the night and going to bed as other Englishmen were taking afternoon tea.

THE GOVERNOR WORE GOWNS

The Queen's representative who went too far

The elaborately dressed aristocrat who opened the New York Assembly in 1702 on behalf of Queen Anne was fittingly regal. Spectators gasped at the extravagant hooped gown, the elegant headdress, and fan. For dressed in the finest ladies' fashion of the day was none other than Lord Cornbury—governor-general of the colony.

When other officials at the ceremony com-

But the most remarkable of the peer's foibles was his frequent habit of dressing up as a woman. Some of his closest acquaintances claimed that he was fulfilling a mysterious vow by wearing only female clothing for a month each year. Others suggested that the real reason was his conviction that he resembled the monarch. The most widely accepted explanation was that when the Queen ordered him to represent

DRESSED AS A MAN. *Lord Cornbury, Queen Anne's cousin, preferred to represent his monarch by wearing queenly attire in public.*

QUEEN ANNE'S REPRESENTATIVE. *Some people thought that Cornbury (above) interpreted his appointment too literally.*

plained that the Queen's representative had made them a laughingstock, he said: "You are all very stupid people not to see the propriety of it all. In this place, and on this occasion, I represent a woman, and in all respects I ought to represent her as faithfully as I can."

Lord Cornbury was credited by some of his contemporaries with doing more to harm British rule in America than any other official.

He was awarded the posts of captain-general and governor-general of New York and New Jersey solely because he was the Queen's cousin.

He was hopelessly inefficient as an administrator, and while he spent money lavishly, he was so stingy in regard to his wife that she was forced to steal.

her in America, he took her literally. A woman who knew him in New York said: "He was a large man, seen frequently at night on the streets wearing a hoop skirt and headdress."

One man wrote of Lord Cornbury: "He is a spendthrift, a grafter, a bigoted oppressor and a drunken, vain fool." Another writer was to report: "He is a frivolous spendthrift, an impudent cheat and a detestable bigot."

In 1708 Lord Cornbury was removed from office and put in prison in New York because of his debts. The following year he was able to free himself and return to England.

But his talents were recognized in the end. In 1711 he was made a member of Her Majesty's Privy Council.

THE CURIOUS CURES OF DR. GRAHAM

Magnetic treatment for impotence at £500 a night

In 1781 childless London couples were invited to cure their unfortunate state by spending a night together in the Celestial Bed—for fees of up to £500.

The proprietor of this remarkable device was Dr. John Graham, an Edinburgh, Scotland, physician, who had created a fashionable cult of cures by magnetism and electricity.

His bizarre treatments became the rage of fashionable London, and he opened a Temple of Health in the Royal Terrace of the Adelphi. There, attended by Negro servants, he administered special baths, sat his gullible patients on "magnetic thrones," or gave them mild shocks in an electric chair.

At the Temple of Health his chief assistant was none other than the beautiful Emma Hart, who later became Lady Hamilton and Lord Nelson's mistress. Dressed in scanty robes, she entertained the patients as "The Rosy Goddess of Health."

Of all Graham's equipment the Celestial Bed was the most splendid. An ornate couch standing on eight brass pillars, it owed its curative powers, he said in his advertisements, to "about 15 cwt of compound magnets . . . continually pouring forth in an everlasting circle."

The treatment does not appear to have worked, for he was obliged to return to Edinburgh, where he was sent to prison as a lunatic.

DOCTOR OF FASHION. *A contemporary engraving shows Dr. Graham in a foppish suit of white linen.*

REMEDY FOR CHILDLESSNESS. *The scantily clad Rosy Goddess of Health reclines on Graham's Celestial Bed.*

BRIDES BY MAIL ORDER

How New England girls were brought to the West

An advertisement in 1865 in the Seattle *Puget Sound Herald* brought a wistful flutter to many a rough, tough heart. In those days Seattle was a pioneer town on the barely settled Pacific coast, and almost all its inhabitants were single men. The advertisement proposed a meeting to devise ways of persuading young ladies to move out West. Lonely bachelors packed the meeting.

A few days later another advertisement appeared: "I, Asa Mercer, of Seattle, Washington Territory, hereby agree to bring a suitable wife of good moral character and reputation from the East to Seattle on or before September, 1865, for each of the parties whose signatures are hereunto attached; they first paying me the sum of $300, with which to pay the passage of said ladies from the East and to compensate me for my trouble."

By the time Mercer left on his mission of matrimony, he had the signatures on 500 firm orders. But as the weeks went by, the customers became restive. Mercer was meeting with resistance from the staid New Englanders, who knew little of the West except that it was populated by roughnecks.

Nevertheless, he was a persuasive man, and one after another girls came forward to volunteer. Of course, they did not admit to seeking husbands but claimed they just wanted to visit the West out of feminine curiosity.

The long journey by land and sea was not easy in those days. And in San Francisco the crew had to fight a battle to prevent the boatload of girls from being hauled off by the local males. When they arrived in Seattle, the town had spruced itself up as never before. The men were shaved, the taverns closed, the buildings newly whitewashed.

Within a week the first wedding took place, and soon every mail-order bride was married—including one who became Mrs. Asa Mercer.

THE LADY WAS A CHAMP

John L. Sullivan ruled the ring until he met Hessie's haymaker

John L. Sullivan, the "Boston Strong Boy," held the world heavyweight boxing crown from 1882 to 1892. During that time he was knocked out only once—by a woman.

Mrs. Hessie Donahue was a big, handsome woman, married to Charles Converse, who ran a school for boxers in Worcester, Massachusetts. In 1892 Sullivan was touring theaters, boxing with several sparring partners, and he invited Charles Converse to join his company.

Converse agreed, and as an extra attraction Hessie was invited to spar with Sullivan. Hessie was well acquainted with the sport, for she had watched the boxers at her husband's school.

Hessie and Sullivan worked out an act. Sullivan would claim that he could lick any man in the house and offer a reward to anyone beating him.

Having disposed of his challengers, usually with one punch, he would announce that he had been challenged by a woman, whereupon Hessie would enter the ring wearing boxing gloves and clad attractively in blouse, skirt, bloomers, and long stockings.

One night in the third round Sullivan caught Hessie with a hard blow to the face. Seething with anger, she lashed out with a right to the jaw—and the world champion hit the canvas, where he stayed for a full minute.

The incident created a sensation, and although Hessie's punch had been a fluke, it was decided to keep the knockout in the act. Sullivan would hit Hessie all around the ring for three rounds, and at the end of the third round she would produce her knockout punch. The referee would pronounce her the new champion, then Sullivan would bounce up laughing.

The act continued for several months and always got a big laugh.

But on September 7, 1892, John L. entered the prizefighting ring in earnest, to defend his title against James J. Corbett—"Gentleman Jim." After 21 grueling rounds Sullivan was knocked out—for the first time in his career by a man.

HESSIE DONAHUE. *Who would suspect that this dear old lady once lost her temper and floored the great John L. Sullivan in the third round?*

THE HUMAN FLY
George Polley hit the heights

Many thousands of New Yorkers craned their necks to look up at the Woolworth Building—in 1920 the tallest in the world—where the tiny figure of a man was inching his way to the top.

He reached the 30th floor, and had 27 more floors to go, when a policeman stuck his head out of a window.

WHOOPS! *Part of George Polley's act was to pretend to slip. Here he is seen in midair, dropping from one ledge to another. Polley climbed 2,000 buildings without a fall.*

George Gibson Polley was promptly arrested—for climbing a building without an official permit!

Polley scaled 2,000 buildings in the United States, without ever slipping or falling. He became known as the Human Fly and was often hired by store owners as part of their opening ceremony. He was able to command a fee of $200—in those days a princely sum.

His career started when he was a boy playing baseball in Richmond, Virginia. George hit a fly ball onto the roof of a six-story building. As it was the only ball they had, he climbed up to fetch it.

In 1910 his family moved to Chicago, and George got a job as a newspaper boy. One day he saw an expensive suit in a store window.

"I'd stand on my head on top of this building for a suit like that," he declared.

The store owner laughed. "If you did that, I would give you the suit," he said. George got his suit, and the episode attracted so much attention that a local theater offered him a booking. He climbed buildings to attract crowds to the show.

The Human Fly performed his feats all over the United States. In Boston he climbed 500 feet up the Custom House; in Hartford he scaled three buildings in one day; and in Providence he wore a blindfold to shin up a flagpole.

His daredevil stunts were always backed up by sound, commonsense safety precautions, and he carefully inspected every building before a climb.

George Gibson Polley's career came to an abrupt end at the early age of 29, however. He died, not from a fall, but from a fatal brain tumor.

SAM, SAM, THE PHARMACY'S MAN

IF SAMUEL JESSOP were alive today, he might possibly bankrupt any medical insurance company. Born in 1752, Jessop was the hypochondriac to end them all. A rich English farmer, he was unmarried and had no relatives. Jessop devoted his latter years to protecting his "delicate" health, dosing himself with remedies of all kinds. From 1795 to 1816 he swallowed 226,934 pills—an average of 10,806 a year, or about 29 every day—and consumed no less than 40,000 bottles of medicine. In spite of this massive medical intake, or, some might say, perhaps even because of it, Samuel Jessop survived until the ripe old age of 65.

THE STONY-HEARTED SCULPTOR

Joseph Nollekens, the popular miser

Misers are often lonely and obscure men whose wealth is revealed only after their death. Joseph Nollekens, however, was a popular sculptor with many friends and was known to possess a large fortune. Yet he lived the life of a pauper.

Born in Soho, London, in 1737, he worked in Rome repairing antique statues, which he then sold as perfect. He added to his income by smuggling stockings, gloves, and lace inside hollow busts. His appearance was always ragged, and his table manners were appalling.

Nollekens rose to be one of the most admired sculptors of his day. On his return to England he produced busts of George III, William Pitt, Samuel Johnson, and the Duke of Wellington. His austerity extended into his professional life, and he would deliberately model a bust with the head looking over the shoulder, so that he could use pieces of marble rejected by other sculptors as too small.

At home he would sit in the dark, and if guests came, he would light a small fire—and quickly put it out when they left.

When dining at the Royal Academy he would stuff his pockets with pepper and salt from the table.

A FRIEND AT COURT. *Joseph Nollekens poses with one of his most famous and successful works, the bust of George III.*

Mrs. Nollekens was just as stingy. She kept her servants on low pay and haggled with shopkeepers over the most trivial items. She once traded in the handle of an old mop when buying a new one.

Joseph Nollekens died in 1823. He left a fortune of £200,000—about $1 million.

A WOMAN OF MEANS

Hetty Green, the "Witch of Wall Street"

Hetty Green was one of America's richest women—and she was also one of the most miserly.

She was the wealthiest member of the Quaker Howland family, whose fortune was made in the whaling industry.

Although she inherited $833,332 from her father, plus $4 million in property and investments, she tried hard to add her Aunt Sylvia's fortune as well. She failed, after contesting the will with an apparently forged document.

With shrewd investments and incredible stinginess, she built herself up as a formidable operator who became known as the Queen of Wall Street. Some rival investors, jealous of her success, substituted "witch" for "queen." But there was nothing occult or magical about

Hetty Green's financial achievements—just plain tightfistedness!

She took it to amazing lengths, living in cheap boardinghouses, wearing ancient, tattered, and faded clothes, and riding around town in a carriage that had once been used as a henhouse.

Hetty begrudged even the expense of an office. Instead, she conducted her daily business sitting on the floor of her bank, surrounded by cheap trunks and suitcases full of her many documents.

This little eccentricity was benignly overlooked by the bank—a tolerance no doubt influenced by the fact that their valued client kept a current balance of more than $2 million.

She became obsessed with the delusion that

she was marked down to be kidnapped or killed, and she went to ridiculous lengths to throw off her imaginary would-be attackers. Her routes were always circuitous, and she would double back on her tracks and even hide in doorways to evade the fortune hunters she was sure were always following her.

Hetty was also convinced that her father and aunt had been poisoned by their enemies.

Surprisingly, in view of her extreme stinginess, she was always remembered with great affection by her many friends.

However, she was not above criticizing her friends for what she believed were totally unjustifiable extravagances. And it was one such incident that killed her.

The Countess Leary, one of her closest associates, was staying with her in 1916 when one of the servants lost patience and turned on Hetty for criticizing the countess' spending.

Such insolence was unheard of and was too much for poor Hetty. She suffered an apoplectic fit and died. Her estate was estimated at about $100 million.

LUCK OF THE DRAW

A Californian's remarkably accurate election predictions

Four weeks before the U.S. Presidential election of 1956, a California paint manufacturer, Jack Swimmer, wrote down his predictions of the votes that would be cast for Gen. Dwight D. Eisenhower.

In Los Angeles County, 1,218,462.

In California, 2,875,637.

In the whole country, 33,974,241.

He also wrote a check for $5,000 and deposited both documents with a charity commissioner clerk in Los Angeles.

Sealed in a safe

The clerk, Gordon Nesvig, sealed Swimmer's predictions in a brass container, put that in a wooden box, and deposited the box in the safe of the sheriff, and a guard was kept to ensure fair play.

After the election newspapermen were called to the sheriff's office, and the paper was taken out. Swimmer's predictions were 100 percent accurate . . . down to the last digit.

He had offered the $5,000 to charity if he had been wrong, but he was so delighted with his success that he handed over the money anyway.

Swimmer refused to reveal the secret of his success. It may have been an incredibly lucky guess, but previously he had predicted the 1952 election results and the scores in a baseball World Series.

PROPHETS WHO COULD NOT WAIT

A 2,000-SEAT amphitheater, costing $100,000, was built overlooking the Sydney harbor in Australia, in 1925. Members of the Order of the Star of the East, led by Hindu mystic Krishnamurti, believed that Christ would return to earth and walk across the Pacific Ocean to the amphitheater. When He did not arrive by 1929, however, the group dissolved.

EUROPE'S GREATEST PROPHET

The uncanny words of Nostradamus

In the autumn of 1939, when Adolf Hitler was in the midst of unleashing war on the world, the wife of his Minister of Propaganda, Joseph Goebbels, drew attention to a remarkable set of prophecies that had been made 400 years earlier.

Written by a Frenchman named Nostradamus, they seemed to predict the rise of Hitler, and even came near to mentioning him by name, when they referred to a German leader called Hister.

Unfortunately for Hitler, even the most skilled interpretation of the prophecies could not predict success for the Third Reich—so the Propaganda Ministry composed fake verses. In 1940 the Luftwaffe dropped thousands of "Nostradamus leaflets" over France and Belgium, announcing that Germany would be victorious and prophesying that southeastern France would be spared in the conflict. The aim was to ensure that refugees would not choke the roads leading to Paris and the channel ports.

In retaliation British Intelligence also made up "Nostradamus writings," but these, of course, predicted an outright Allied victory over the Axis.

A revolutionary doctor

Michel de Nostredame—who later latinized his name to Nostradamus—was born in 1503 in St. Rémy de Provence, France. His family was Jewish but converted to Christianity, and the young Michel was brought up as a Catholic. He was a brilliant student, who first became famous as a skilled physician dealing with plague victims. Many of his successes in this field were undoubtedly due to his refusal to bleed patients —a revolutionary concept in the early 16th century.

He was ahead of his time in other ways too. Nostradamus proclaimed that the earth circles the sun, 100 years before Galileo's findings.

His prophetic gifts came to light in 1555 when he published the first of 10 books, all simply entitled *Centuries*. Each volume contained 100 predictions, all of which were written in verse form.

Nostradamus never made any secret of his technique for looking into the future. He placed a bowl of water on a brass tripod and gazed into it, in much the same way as a fortune-teller intently studies a crystal ball.

But occasionally his predictions came to him in spontaneous flashes of intuition. One day, when he was a young man and traveling in Italy, he fell on his knees before a passing monk named Felice Peretti. To the astonishment of the monk and onlookers alike, Nostradamus declared: "I kneel before His Holiness." In 1585 the monk became Pope Sixtus V.

And once when visited by Catherine de Medici, he was intrigued by a boy in her entourage, proclaiming that he would one day be King of France. The boy was Henry of Navarre who became Henry IV.

Exhumation foretold

On another occasion a French nobleman tried to confound Nostradamus' prophetic powers. He asked him to predict the fate of two suckling pigs he had in his yard. The answer was that the nobleman would eat the black one, and a wolf the white one. The nobleman instantly ordered the white one to be killed for dinner that night. When dining later with Nostradamus, he was amazed when told that a tame wolf cub had carried off the meat of the white pig and that he was, after all, eating the black one.

Before he died in 1566, the prophet had a date engraved on a small metal plate, instructing that this should be placed with him in his coffin. In 1700 the coffin was taken from the grave, where it had lain for 134 years, and was moved to a more prominent site. The plate was resting on the prophet's skeleton. It bore the date 1700.

To avoid being accused of witchcraft by the Inquisition, Nostradamus confused the dating of his predictions and wrote in a bewildering mixture of anagrams, symbols, Old French, Latin, and other languages.

This deliberate confusion has led to some curious and widely varied interpretations of his prophecies. Even so, many of his predictions are uncannily close to the facts—enough to justify his reputation as the greatest prophet Europe has ever produced.

On the following pages his prophecies have been translated into modern English, but the names are in the original spelling.

511

HENRY II OF FRANCE

Before it became tragically true, no one at the French court dared mention Nostradamus' notorious prediction, of how King Henry would die:

The young lion will overcome the elder
In a field of combat in a single fight.
He will pierce his eyes in their golden cage,
Two wounds in one, then dies a cruel death.

This was fulfilled four years later in 1559 when Henry, one of whose heraldic emblems was a lion, had a friendly joust with a young officer named Montgomery, captain of the French King's Scottish Guard. Montgomery's lance accidentally pierced the visor of Henry's gilt helmet, wounding him in the eye and throat. The King died after 10 days of agony.

Nostradamus' successful prediction was a particularly cruel blow for Henry's widow, Catherine de Medici. She believed in the prophet implicitly and had become his patron. In gratitude, Nostradamus once created "visions" of all France's future monarchs in a mirror at the palace. This was probably a trick using reflections of accomplices in an adjoining room, but the superstitious Catherine was deeply impressed, and her patronage for the prophet was ensured.

With his own prospects guaranteed, Nostradamus was able to carry on with his serious work of foretelling future events for all mankind on a grand scale.

Henry II was the subject of an early example of Nostradamus' uncanny prophetic skill.

LOUIS XVI

The unsuccessful flight of Louis XVI and Marie Antoinette to Varennes, France, in 1791 was graphically described in these words:

By night will come through the forest of Reines
Two partners by roundabout way;
The Queen, the white stone,
The monk-king dressed in gray at Varennes,
The elected Capet causes tempest, fire
  and bloody slicing.

The royal couple fled by night through the forest, having escaped from the Queen's apartments. They lost their way and chose a bad route. The white stone is thought to refer to the diamond necklace affair that ruined the Queen's reputation, but she was also in the habit of wearing white dresses.

The monk-king could be an allusion to the King's one-time impotence. It is known that at the time of his capture he was wearing gray clothes.

He was a member of the Capet royal line, and though he was not directly responsible for the guillotine executions ("bloody slicing"), he was a cause of the revolution and the terror that followed.

Louis XVI's arrest at Varennes was foreseen in nearly all of its details by the prophet.

NAPOLEON

The prophet foresaw the rise of Napoleon, whom he described as the first anti-Christ (the second was Hitler, and a third has apparently yet to appear). Of Napoleon's rise to power and years as Emperor, he wrote:

An Emperor will be born near Italy,
Who will cost the Empire very dearly.

Napoleon certainly cost France dearly in both manpower and political strength.

English King Charles I was executed in 1649 at the hands of the Roundheads.

CHARLES I

Nostradamus made several predictions about Charles I of Great Britain, of which the most comprehensive covers Charles, Archbishop Laud, and Cromwell:

> *The unworthy man is chased from the*
> *English kingdom.*
> *The counselor through anger will be burnt.*
> *His followers will stoop to such depths*
> *That the Pretender will almost be received.*

Charles' irresponsibility lost him his kingdom. His counselor, Archbishop Laud, was burnt in 1645. The followers who stooped so low were the Scots who sold the King back to Parliament in 1646, and the Pretender is presumably Oliver Cromwell, the Lord Protector of England from 1653 to 1658, who was almost accepted as King by the English people.

Nostradamus' most accurate prediction regarding Charles was:

> *The Parliament of London will put their King to*
> *death. . . . He will die because of the shaven heads*
> *in council.*

Clearly, the prophet was referring to the Roundheads. Their leader Cromwell has been described as "more like a butcher than an English King."

THE GREAT FIRE AND THE PLAGUE

Nostradamus rarely gave precise dates, but the Great Fire of London was an exception. He was very precise when he wrote:

> *The blood of the just will be demanded of London*
> *Burnt by fire in three times twenty plus six.*

The disaster occurred in 1666, and Nostradamus adopted the Italian habit of leaving out the first two digits in the date.

This is how he prophesied the Great Plague that ravaged London in 1665—retribution, he suggested, for the murder of Charles I:

> *The Great Plague of that maritime city*
> *Shall not cease till death is avenged*
> *By the blood of the just taken and*
> * condemned through innocence*
> *And the great dame outraged by feigning saints.*

The "feigning saints" appear to be the Puritans, and the "great dame" is thought to be St. Paul's Cathedral, destroyed in the fire.

The Great Fire of London was more devastating than the German blitz in the Second World War.

Nostradamus also made this prediction of Napoleon's fate:

> *The great Empire will soon be exchanged*
> * for a small place,*
> *Which will soon begin to grow.*
> *A small place of tiny area in the middle of which*
> *He will come to lay down his scepter.*

Napoleon was exiled to the small island of Elba but escaped for 100 days, then relinquished all power for exile on tiny St. Helena.

NAPOLEON, *Emperor turned exile.*

LOUIS PASTEUR

Nostradamus' remarkable prophecies sometimes predicted both a name and a date:

Pasteur will be celebrated as a godlike figure.
This is when the moon completes her great cycle.

Pasteur made a vital contribution to medical science when he founded the Pasteur Institute in 1889. The lunar cycle about the earth takes 19 years to complete; one such cycle was completed in 1889.

Louis Pasteur pioneered the use of inoculation to fight disease.

The Duke and Duchess of Windsor lived in exile after his abdication.

EDWARD VIII

Nostradamus foresaw the abdication of Edward VIII, caused by his love for the divorced American Wallis Simpson. He wrote:

For not wanting to consent to the divorce,
Which afterwards will be recognized as unworthy,
The King of the islands will be forced to flee
And one put in his place who has no sign of kingship.

Because he insisted on marrying Mrs. Simpson, Edward VIII was forced to abdicate the British throne in 1936. Mrs. Simpson was considered "unworthy" to be Queen by many. George VI, who had no training or experience in kingship, ascended the throne in his elder brother's stead.

GENERAL FRANCO

In describing the Spanish Civil War (1936–39) Nostradamus names the main leaders of the Fascist forces, Primo de Rivera and Franco, who later served as dictator of Spain. The last line refers to Franco's temporary exile when he was not allowed to cross the Mediterranean Sea to enter Spain:

From Castille, Franco will bring out the assembly.
The ambassadors will not agree and cause a schism.
The people of Rivera will be in the crowd,
And the great man will be denied entry to the gulf.

General Franco's role in the Spanish Civil War was predicted by Nostradamus, who not only referred to him by name but forecast his temporary exile.

ADOLF HITLER

Nostradamus produced several extraordinarily accurate predictions about the Nazi leader. One verse sums up Hitler's life and even predicts the fact that his death in Berlin in 1945 would never be satisfactorily confirmed:

Near the Rhine from the Austrian mountains
Will be born a great man of the people, come too
late.
A man who will defend Poland and Hungary
And whose fate will never be certain.

Another verse describes the early years of the Second World War when the German armies swept across the Rhine into France. Though most of Europe was allied against him ("the greater part of the battlefield"), Hitler, or Hister, was for a time only too successful:

Beasts wild with hunger will cross the rivers,
The greater part of the battlefield will be
against Hister.

The prophet also warned of "weapons heard in the skies" and "machines of flying fire"—references to aircraft, bombing, and the early V-weapons.

Adolf Hitler was foreseen by Nostradamus as the second anti-Christ.

Nostradamus vividly described what a wartime pilot would look like in an oxygen mask, helmet, and goggles: "Half pig, half man when battles are fought in the skies."

HIROSHIMA

The nuclear bombs dropped on Hiroshima and Nagasaki in 1945 were forecast:

Near the harbor and in two cities will be two
scourges the like of which have never been seen.
The explosions were horrors never seen before.

The Nagasaki bombing, one of "two scourges the like of which have never been seen."

ABOUT THE FUTURE

Nostradamus refers to a third war during this century in the Northern Hemisphere after two great powers align themselves against the East:

When those of the Northern Pole are
united together
In the East will be great fear and dread. . . .
One day the two great leaders will be friends;
Their great power will be seen to grow.
The New Land will be at the height of its power:
To the man of blood the number is reported.

The man of blood is identified elsewhere as being the world's third anti-Christ who will emerge in Asia. The "new land" was a common term used by Nostradamus to refer to what we now call America.

Thus, Nostradamus seems to be suggesting that a war will occur between China and a Russo-American alliance.

The prophet even gives a precise date for when the conflict will come—"when the cycle of the centuries is renewed." Nostradamus writes the following:

In the year 1999 and seven months
From the sky will come the great King of terror . . .

WORLD WITHOUT END

Thousands believed when William Miller predicted Armageddon

On April 3, 1843, thousands of people assembled on hilltops in New England to await the end of the world. They were disappointed, but despite this setback they never lost their faith in the man who had predicted the cataclysm—William Miller, a farmer and former deist who believed the second coming of Jesus to be imminent.

Having studied the prophetic Books of Daniel and Revelation, Miller issued his first warnings in 1831. He became a preacher and traveled widely.

DAY OF ATONEMENT. *Some of William Miller's followers dressed in shrouds and waited in graveyards when he predicted the end of the world.*

His predictions of the approaching doomsday were reinforced by shooting stars in 1833, halos around the sun, and a spectacular comet in 1843.

Then the New York *Herald* ran Miller's story that the world would be destroyed by fire on April 3.

A few followers were reported to have murdered their relatives and committed suicide, believing that the dead would be first through heaven's gate.

In Westford, Massachusetts, a villager blew a large horn, and the Millerites cried, "Hallelujah, the time has come!" The horn blower jested: "You fools, go dig your potatoes! Angel Gabriel won't dig 'em for you!"

Undaunted, Miller revised the date to sometime before March 22, 1844, and once more the Millerites believed. Some families dressed in shrouds and waited for the end in graveyards.

Several Millerites sold all they possessed—although it is not recorded what they planned to do with the money.

On March 22, 1844, Miller admitted that he had made a miscalculation and set October 22 as the date of Armageddon. One farmer took his cows, dressed in white robes. "It's a long trip," he said. "The kids will want milk."

At last, on October 23, the Millerites began to doubt their leader. Stunned and shaken by disappointment, Miller refrained from further predictions and soon retired from preaching.

But thousands of people adhered to his teachings about the second coming of Christ, even though they rejected his date-setting predictions. Eventually, they and other Protestants formed a separate Adventist Church.

THE PROPHET WHO FORESAW HIS KILLER'S DOOM

A 16TH-CENTURY Scottish mystic known as the Brahan Seer prophesied many events, but when he told the Countess of Seaforth that her husband had a mistress in Paris, the countess ordered that the seer should be boiled in tar. He then prophesied doom for his executioners—that the last of the house would be deaf and dumb, and the inheritor would be "a white-hooded lassie who would kill her sister." In 1815 Francis Mackenzie, last of the line, died after an illness that made him deaf and dumb. His eldest daughter, wearing white in mourning for her husband, inherited the estate. Later, when she was driving a carriage, her sister was thrown out of the vehicle and was killed—thus fulfilling the prophecies of the Brahan Seer.

SHOT IN THE DARK

John Williams dreamed of the Premier's death in advance

Engineers and bankers are two groups of people unlikely to suffer from flights of fancy. John Williams was both a mining engineer and a banker, yet on the night of May 2 or 3, 1812, he had one of the most remarkable precognitions ever recorded. The details of the scene in which a British Prime Minister was assassinated were portrayed in a dream.

He told his dream to a writer, John Abercrombie, who recorded it in 1834 as follows: "Mr. Williams was in the House of Commons, where he saw a small man in a blue coat and white waistcoat. Then, as he watched, a man in a brown coat with metal buttons drew a pistol from his coat. He fired at the small man who fell, blood pouring from a wound a little below the left breast. Mr. Williams heard clearly the report of the pistol, saw blood fly out and stain the waistcoat, saw the color of the man's face change."

The assassin was seized, and when Williams, in his dream, asked who had been shot, he was told "the Chancellor." At that time Spencer Perceval was both the Prime Minister and Chancellor of the Exchequer. Williams had the dream twice more the same night.

During the next week he told several people of his experience—among them his brother, his

MURDER IN THE LOBBY. *John Williams foresaw the assassination of Prime Minister Spencer Perceval almost exactly as it happened in London in 1812.*

partner, and two of the prominent men in his hometown of Falmouth, Cornwall.

On May 11, precisely as Williams had foretold in his dream, Perceval was shot dead in the lobby of the House of Commons by John Bellingham. Every detail of the dream was verified by witnesses, right down to the appearance of the murderer and victim.

John Williams' experience was described in *The Times* five days after the murder took place.

JEANE DIXON PREDICTS

Death of "a blue-eyed Democrat"

Clairvoyants—those people who claim knowledge denied to the rest of mankind—seem to predict bad news rather than good.

Mrs. Jeane Dixon was the first person to warn friends of President Kennedy that he was in danger. And she repeated the warning frequently. In 1952, 11 years before his death, she foresaw that "a blue-eyed Democrat" would become President in 1960—and that he would be assassinated.

On the day in 1963 when Kennedy was shot, she told friends at lunch: "Something dreadful is going to happen to the President today."

Jeane also predicted the deaths of President

Roosevelt in 1945, of Mahatma Gandhi in 1948, and of Martin Luther King in 1968.

When she met Churchill in Washington in 1945, she told him he would be out of office after the war but would be back in power by 1952. Both predictions were correct—as were her forecasts of race riots in American cities in 1963–64 and of Russian pioneering in space.

Jeane foresees a world holocaust for the 1980's and the rise of a powerful world leader born in the Middle East in 1962. She also said that peace would come only in 1999. Similar predictions were made four centuries earlier by Nostradamus, who foresaw a great war coming in 1999.

VISIONS OF DEATH

The seer who sealed his own fate

Writer Jacques Cazotte was greeted with incredulity when he told guests at a Paris dinner party in 1788 what fates would befall them in the revolution that would shortly overwhelm France. "You don't have to be a prophet to foresee a revolution today," someone scoffed. Most of the writers and courtiers present agreed to this.

There was a cry of protest when Cazotte went on to assert that the King would be executed—and so would several ladies at the party.

He was even more specific. Looking gravely at Nicolas Chamfort, a celebrated playwright who had risen from humble origins, he said to him: "You will cut your veins with a razor 22 times—but you will not die until some months later."

To the Marquis de Condorcet, a philosopher-mathematician married to one of France's most beautiful women, he announced: "You will die on the floor of a prison cell, having taken poison to cheat the executioner."

Perhaps the most surprising prediction was reserved for critic and playwright Jean de la Harpe, a well-known atheist. Cazotte forecast that the revolution would make him a devout Christian.

Chamfort worked for the revolution in its early days but later criticized its excesses. In 1793, faced with the threat of imprisonment, he tried—but failed—to kill himself by slashing his wrists. He died a few months later.

Condorcet was elected to the Revolutionary Assembly and for a while was its secretary. But when he opposed the Reign of Terror, he was outlawed. Two days after being imprisoned, in 1794, he was found dead on the floor of his cell. He had cheated the executioner, just as Cazotte had foretold.

La Harpe, too, was thrown into prison. There he reconsidered his spiritual state and became an ardent Catholic.

As for Cazotte, his visionary powers brought him little happiness. For they enabled him to foresee the exact manner of his own death—arrest, release, rearrest, and the guillotine.

PROPHECY OF CAZOTTE. *He became a legend by foretelling uncannily his guests' fate in the French Revolution.*

HOUSE OF BLOOD

"GOD will give him blood to drink!" With this curse on the man who secured his conviction for witchcraft, Matthew Maule went to the gallows nearly 300 years ago in the Massachusetts village of Salem. Maule, a poor Puritan, owned a fine freshwater spring; Gilbert Pyncheon, a rich merchant, coveted the site and engineered Maule's trial on a false charge. Then he acquired the land and built a grand house later called the House of Seven Gables, which still stands. But on the very night of the housewarming Gilbert Pyncheon was found dead of a hemorrhage. The people of Salem remembered Maule's curse—and shivered.

THE PROWLING FOXES

Death warnings of Europe's ancient families

The annals of European nobility abound in weird tales of supernatural portents, some of which have survived to this day. Among them is the sinister legend of the foxes of Gormanston.

Whenever a Lord of Gormanston is about to die, Gormanston Castle in County Meath, Ireland, is surrounded by foxes. All the local people know the legend, whose origins stretch back into the remote past.

On the day of the 12th viscount's death in February 1860, a local hunt returned without having sighted a fox all day. A laborer told them: "All the foxes have gone to see the old lord die."

In September 1876 Lady Gormanston saw a pack of foxes prowling by the castle gate. Her husband, the 13th viscount, died that night. At the funeral a few days later foxes followed the coffin to the graveside.

When the 14th viscount died in 1907, a pack of foxes prowled all night outside the chapel where his body lay in state, despite attempts to drive them away.

The Arundells of Wardour, in Wiltshire, also possessed private harbingers of doom. Immediately before the death of one of the family, two spectral owls could be seen perched on the battlements of Wardour Castle. Perhaps the owls will never appear again—the last Lord Arundell died in 1944, and the title became extinct.

A floating trunk

In 1586 the English antiquarian William Camden recorded the omen of the Breretons of Cheshire. He said: "I have heard it affirmed many times that for some days before the death of a Brereton heir, the trunk of a tree has been seen floating in the lake adjoining their mansion." Curiously, this omen appeared only on the death of an heir—never when the master himself died.

Some ghostly portents are believed to be the specters of long-dead members of the family. The famous White Lady of the Prussian Hohenzollerns, for instance, is thought to be the ghost of Countess Agnes of Orlamunde, who was walled up alive for infanticide. Another tale says she is the Princess Bertha von Rosenburg. But whoever she may be, her appearance always foretells the death of a Hohenzollern.

Frederick William IV of Prussia, who fashioned a great European nation out of his small German state, went mad in 1861 after a horrifying appearance.

Headless pallbearers

A sentry at the castle gate saw the White Lady leading four headless pallbearers carrying a coffin. They glided silently into the castle and reappeared a few seconds later bearing a body in royal robes. The corpse was headless—but where the head should have been, there lay a crown.

The King never recovered and died early the next year. The death of his father, Frederick William III, had been foretold by her appearance; and an ancestor, the Margrave of Bayreuth, had seen the White Lady just before his horse threw him to his death in 1678.

The royal family of Bavaria shared a death warning with the ducal family of Hesse. This was the Black Lady of Darmstadt, who is generally thought to be the ghost of a long-dead grand duchess. In 1850 she was seen at Archaffenburg as the Grand Duke of Hesse-Darmstadt was taking tea with his parents. Within days his mother died of cholera. In 1854, at Pillnitz Castle on the banks of the Elbe, the Queen of Saxony saw her dressed in black mourning clothes and hovering near a chair. The Queen's anguished attendants were certain that their mistress' death was imminent; but they were wrong. Next day the news reached them that the King of Saxony had died in Dresden.

Haunted Borgias

The bloodthirsty Borgias were said to have been a haunted family—perhaps not without justice. The best known incident happened to Pope Alexander VI, the ruthless Rodrigo Borgia. A cardinal, on entering the papal apartments one night in 1503, found the Pope lying on a spectral bier and lit by a ghostly light.

Terrified, he made the sign of the cross, and the vision faded. But before midnight the Pope had died.

THE TRIBE THAT DIED

When a prophecy was political

Superstition, a blind faith in witchcraft, total economic dependence on cattle, and a constant fear of the white man's encroachment were the elements that ruled the lives of South Africa's native peoples in the 19th century.

All four were tragically intertwined in the strange story of Nongqause, the 14-year-old Xhosa girl who saw a vision and all but destroyed her nation.

One of the largest Bantu tribes, that of the Xhosa (numbering many thousands), was involved for decades in disputes over land, cattle, and labor with the frontiersmen who pushed relentlessly inland to set up farms and townships.

An uneasy border between the Xhosas and the white man had been established in 1778 along the Fish River, bounding the Ciskei and Transkei territories in the east of Cape Province.

There followed a century of unrest, cattle stealing, and frontier disputes with the white farmers. Drought reduced the size of the Xhosa herds, and those cattle that remained were in poor condition—because, they thought, of the spells cast by English witch doctors.

Tribal elders and chiefs were as deeply under the influence of the witch doctors as the people they ruled. In 1819, for example, Chief Ndlambe was persuaded to attack the whites at Grahamstown—because witch doctor Makana assured him that his medicine would render the white man's bullets harmless. One thousand Xhosas died in the battle.

It was against this background of fear and superstition that in May 1856, Nongqause, niece of the witch doctor Umhlakaza, claimed to have had her vision. At this time she is thought to have been about 14 years old.

Ancestral messages

She went to the river near her village to fetch water, she said, and there she met five strong black men—messengers from the spirits of her ancestors. The spirits, they said, grieved at the decline of the Xhosa nation and were resolved to appear among their people. They would be an invincible army that would drive out the white man and restore the Xhosas to their former glory.

But before this help was given, the ancestors required proof of the Xhosas' unquestioning obedience. They must kill all their cattle, destroy all their grain, and abandon all cultivation of the land.

They were to build new barns for the fat, healthy cattle that would come from the ancestral abodes, and dig vast grain pits to take the overflowing crop that the spirits would bring with them.

Only when those instructions had been carried out would the ancestors return. They would be preceded by a frightful whirlwind that would sweep the unbelievers, and anyone who had not obeyed their orders, into the sea.

Chief persuaded

Nongqause's uncle persuaded Chief Kreli that the young prophetess' vision was a genuine message from the tribal ancestors. Kreli ordered the immediate destruction of crops and the slaughtering of cattle.

When a few doubters refused to obey, Nongqause received another message. While she was standing by the river, the ground rumbled beneath her feet—the mutterings of the discontented ancestors, her uncle explained. People from all over the tribal lands flocked to Nongqause's village to gaze into the swampy pool that was believed to be the gateway to the ancestral abode. They saw the horns of oxen and heard the bellowing of cattle impatient to rise.

Others reported that they had seen the dead Xhosa heroes rise from the Indian Ocean, some on horseback, some on foot, passing in front of them, then disappearing.

For 10 months there was no farming. The believers destroyed their crops and killed their cattle. Thousands of Xhosas died of starvation.

Despite the warnings of the British commissioner Charles Browntree that Nongqause's prophecies would never come true, the tribe refused to till the land and carried on with the slaughter of cattle.

Then at last Nongqause named the date when the ancestors would return—February 18, 1857. The sun would rise blood red and stand still in the sky. Then it would move around and set again in the east. Whirlwinds and hurricanes would sweep the earth, scattering the whites and the nonbelievers among the Xhosas into the sea.

On the eve of the great day, the Xhosas decked themselves in beads and painted their bodies. Those who still had strength danced through the night. Others sat, hungry and patient.

The sun rose and made its slow passage through the hot February sky—only to set in the west. It left behind the bitterness and disappointment of a starving people.

The desperate tribe ate roots, berries, even the bark and gum of the mimosa tree. They gnawed the bones and hide of their long-slaughtered cattle and poured into the mission stations and larger villages, looking for help.

Umhlakaza, the witch doctor uncle, hid from his disillusioned people. His ambition to incite them to rise in a frenzy of hunger against the whites had failed, and he died of starvation.

Nongqause was arrested and sent to a farm in the Eastern Province, where she died in 1898—surely the most tragic single figure in the history of southern Africa.

And her people? More than 20,000 had died of starvation, and of the 43,000 remaining, some 30,000 were saved only by taking work on the white man's farms.

VEHICLE VISIONS

Cars and planes were just a matter of time

Andrew Jackson Davis, the son of a poor, drunken shoemaker, had virtually no education and was forced by poverty into a lifetime of menial work. Yet, from his visionary mother he inherited a clairvoyant talent that marks him out as an outstanding soothsayer. He foretold the coming of both the airplane and the car.

Some time before 1842, his family settled in Poughkeepsie, New York, and it was there he met William Levingston, a journeyman tailor and amateur mesmerist. Levingston recognized Davis' rare clairvoyant abilities and promoted him initially as a traveling faith healer.

Davis gave more than 150 lectures in Manhattan, most of them in a state of trance, and wrote a number of books. He made prophetic statements that achieved a startling degree of accuracy and detail.

Cars in the sky

He is said to have predicted prefabricated concrete buildings, and in his book *The Penetralia,* published in 1856, he wrote of "aerial cars . . . which will move through the sky from country to country."

He predicted the internal combustion engine and the automobile in the same book: ". . . carriages and traveling saloons on country roads—sans horses, sans steam, sans any visible power, moving with greater speed and safety than at present. Carriages will be moved by a strange and beautiful and simple admixture of aqueous and atmospheric gases—so easily condensed, so simply ignited and so imparted by a machine somewhat resembling our engines as to be entirely concealed and manageable between the forward wheels. These vehicles will prevent any embarrassments now experienced by persons living in thinly populated territories. The first requisite for these land-locomotives will be good roads, upon which, with your engines, without your horses, you may travel with great rapidity."

CLAIRVOYANT. *Andrew Jackson Davis predicted airplanes and cars in a book that was published in 1856.*

The unconscious heritage shared by us all

Curious and bizarre beginnings

•

SPEAKING VOLUMES IN SILENCE

Sign language—from the aborigines to aviation

Before the development of even the most elementary vocal language, primitive man was forced to use a combination of basic noises and simple, evocative signs to communicate with his fellow men. In much the same way that animals convey basic emotions such as anger, fear, aggression, and contentment, early man used facial expressions and bodily gestures to supplement his limited repertoire of grunts, roars, and growls.

But sign language, which began as an aid to communication, has survived the evolution of complex languages. It is still found around the world today among primitive peoples, like the aborigines of Australia, and in modern society, as an extra mode of conveying moods, feelings, and commands. However, while many gestures are almost universal, others have totally different—and sometimes opposite—meanings in different countries.

PRIMITIVE TALK

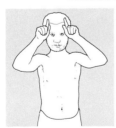

Forefingers at the brow is a way of saying "cattle."

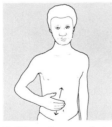

Rubbing the stomach is aboriginal for "good."

TWO WAYS TO SAY GOODBY

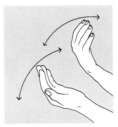

In the East beckoning says "goodby."

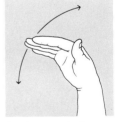

In other countries the wave is standard.

AGREEING TO DIFFER

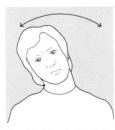

Headshaking is "yes" in Mediterranean lands.

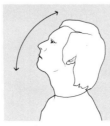

Elsewhere the nod is the sign of agreement.

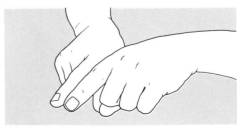

The Arabs place their forefingers together like this when they want to agree or say "yes."

INDIAN SIGN LANGUAGE

By clasping both hands together, Indians give the sign for "peace."

The word "bowl" is conveyed by cupping the hands in a bowl shape.

A snap of the index finger forward from this position means "speak."

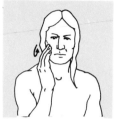

A gesture similar to a woman's rouging her cheek means "red."

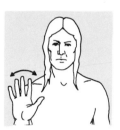

Rotating the hand at shoulder level indicates a question follows.

"Friend": The fingers are raised from this position to the face.

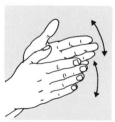

Chopping the hands up and down past each other means "to work."

Fists held together in front of the chest signifies "soldier."

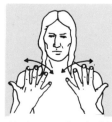

Moving apart hands with open fingers: "people."

Fingers form an open circle to signify "sun."

AT THE GAMING TABLES

When a croupier crosses his fingers, he wants to be relieved from his post.

Pointing to the thumb is a sign that a player be allowed to go on.

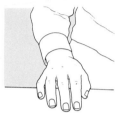

Anxious croupiers call for help like this.

Cheats are signaled by fingertips on the table.

BROADCASTING TALK

A producer or director points to the performer to start a program.

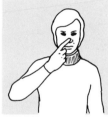

This gesture indicates that the program is on time.

A circular motion with one's forefinger means "speed up the pace."

Crossing the forefingers is a sign there is half a minute left.

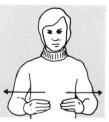

This hand motion means "slow down the pace."

Finger across the throat means "cut."

SEMAPHORE ON THE LANDING STRIP

On an airstrip this means a "turn to the right."

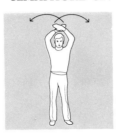

Repeated crossing of hands signals "stop."

Right arm circling means "start engine."

Arms swinging outward says "chocks away."

LANGUAGE OF THE DEAF

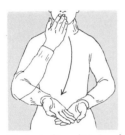

To the deaf "good" is signed as shown above.

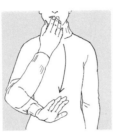

For the word "bad" the hand is turned palm down.

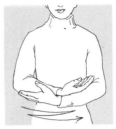

"Baby" is indicated by a rocking motion of the arms.

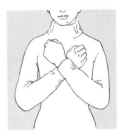

Closed fists crossed over the heart expresses "love."

THE LANGUAGE DETECTIVES

How they found the tribe that gave us words

Tracing missing persons can take much patient detective work. But a special kind of "private eye" can trace the missing ancestors of whole peoples by studying the clues buried in words.

These philologists, as the language detectives are called, have traced the word trail back from peoples in Europe, India, South Africa, the Americas, and the Pacific islands to a tiny, nameless, and forgotten tribe that roamed central Eurasia 5,000 to 6,000 years ago, before the dawn of written history.

Word clues

For a long time scholars puzzled over the striking similarity of words in different languages. In Dutch, *vader*; in Latin, *pater*; in Old Irish, *athir*; in Persian, *pidar*; in the Sanskrit of distant India, *pitr*. These words all sounded alike and meant the same thing—"father."

How did it happen that widely separated peoples used such closely related sound symbols? The problem baffled linguists for years,

the more so because "father" was but one of a host of such coincidences. Toward the end of the 18th century it dawned on scholars that perhaps all these words stemmed from some common language.

The language law

At last a brilliant German, Jacob Grimm—joint collector with his brother Wilhelm of *Grimm's Fairy Tales*—and other scholars of his time worked out a "law" of language changes. Their discoveries showed that the changes that take place as a language develops and spreads are regular and consistent enough to permit enlightening comparisons between languages and to allow the earlier stages of these languages to be reconstructed.

Once the pattern of change was clear, scholars could see that the many words for "father" all pointed back to an original, *pater*. Also, "water" in English, *wasser* in German, *hydor* in Greek, *voda* in Russian (vodka is "little water"), *udan* in Sanskrit, and even *watar* in the language of King David's captain, Uriah the Hittite—all could have come only from an original *wodor*. Using the law, they could trace the origin of countless words.

Philologists have evolved an entire ancient vocabulary. They labeled this early speech "Indo-European" because it had Indic and European branches. There is a Latin branch, from which stems Italian, Spanish, Portuguese, French, and Rumanian. There is a Germanic branch, which includes English, German, Danish, Dutch, Swedish, and Norwegian. The Celtic branch includes Welsh, Irish, and Breton. The Slavic includes Russian, Polish, Czech, Bulgar, and Serb.

In addition, Indo-European languages include Lithuanian, Persian, Greek, Armenian, and a score of dialects in India that have sprung from ancient Sanskrit.

What tribe first spoke that mother tongue that hatched this brood of cousin languages? Today we know a good deal about these dawn people, even though archeologists have uncovered not a single crumbling wall nor any pottery that we can be sure was theirs.

How they lived

Our speech ancestors had domesticated the "cow," *gwou*, which gave them "milk," *melg*. From this strain they also bred "oxen", *uksen*, which were joined together by a "yoke," *yug*. They also knew sheep (their *owa* became English "ewe"), which must have been tame, for from their "fleece," *pleus*, they got "wool," *wlana*, which they had learned to "weave," *webh*, into cloth and then "sew," *siw*, into garments.

We might think of these ancestors as only wandering nomads had we not found their word for "plow," which was *ara*. Because of Latin *arare* ("to plow"), we speak in English of land that is arable—capable of cultivation.

What did they plant? Their word *grano* gives English "grain." One kind of *grano* may have been light in color, for their word for "white," *kweit*, coming down through Old Germanic *hweits*, gave us the English "wheat."

These speech ancestors of ours ground their grain in a "mill," *mel*, added "water," *wodor*, and "yeast," *yes*, to make a "dough," *dheigh*, which they would "bake," *bhog*, in an "oven," *uqno*, to make "bread," *pa* (Latin *panis*, hence English "pantry," the place where bread is kept).

All this we know from those old root words, which have come down to us in a score of languages. So have their numerals, which were: 1, *oinos;* 2, *duo;* 3, *treies;* 4, *qetwer;* 5, *penqe;* 6, *sweks;* 7, *septn;* 8, *okto;* 9, *newn;* 10, *dekm.*

Where they lived

Where did these ancestors live? Since all Indo-European languages lack a common word for lion, tiger, elephant, or camel, the homeland could not have been far south.

Their old word *sneighw* (English "snow," Russian *sneig*, Greek *nipha*, Welsh *nyf*, Latin *nix*, French *neige*) might even push this homeland far northward.

Wild animals they knew were the "snake," *serp*, the "beaver," *bhebhru*, the bear, the goose, the rabbit, and the duck. They had a word for a "small stream," *strew*, and another for a "little pond," which came down into English as "marsh," "mire," and "moor," and into Latin as *mare*—hence English "mariner" and "maritime." But of vast salt oceans they probably knew nothing. When, fanning out, migrating branches of the tribe met the thunder of ocean surf, each gave this new marvel a separate name.

Of trees they knew the birch and the beech, and because, much later, the writings of northern Europe were scratched on smooth boards of "beech," *bok*, we get the English word "book."

All these animals and trees are natives of the temperate zone. Many other signs point to one possible location in central Europe. But gradually, pushed by overpopulation or invaders, the Indo-Europeans began to move.

Their wanderings lasted thousands of years and led them far afield. One branch was to push Slavic up to the polar sea, another was to bring Latin down to the Mediterranean, while still others were to carry Celtic into what is today Great Britain and France, and Germanic down to the right bank of the Rhine and up into the far northlands of Scandinavia.

On their wanderings they must have pondered the origins of things, for the English word "God" has its roots in *ghutom*, meaning "the Being that is worshiped." To them, as to us, the syllable *sac* meant "sacred"; and from *prek* ("praying") down through Latin *precari* ("to pray") comes our word "prayer."

The ideas enshrined in these words are not the least of the inheritance from that long-forgotten tribe—an inheritance more ancient than the walls of Troy and probably more enduring than the pyramids.

WORDS! WORDS! WORDS!

And the remarkable stories behind them

Assassin. For 200 years a murderous sect of religious fanatics terrorized the Middle East, using the town of Alamut, in South Persia, as their base. They killed under the influence of drugs and became notorious through their Arabic name of *Hashshishin* ("users of hashish"). The sect was wiped out by the Mongols in the 13th century, but the Anglicized version of the name lives on.

Berserk. Vikings and other Norse warriors of the 8th to 11th centuries sometimes used an extraordinary weapon: sheer rage. Gripped by an inexplicable fury, they roared and howled, bit their shields, and charged forward, killing anyone in their path. People who fled from these wild, fur-cloaked hordes described the warriors as "berserk" (Norse for "clad in bearskin"). This rage, which may have been induced by drugs extracted from herbs, was thought to make the "berserkers" invincible.

Blurb. When the publishers of American comic author Gelett Burgess wanted to promote one of his books by giving away copies at a booksellers' dinner in 1906, they commissioned Burgess to produce a special cover. He wrote a brief and nonsensical text under a picture of a beautiful model whom he named Miss Belinda Blurb. Burgess later wrote a dictionary of made-up words—for example, *agowilt* ("fear"); *looblum* ("flattery"); *pooje* ("embarrass"); and *yab* ("fanatic"). But blurb—meaning the fulsome praise on the cover of a book—was the only one to survive for any length of time.

Book. Northern Europeans scratched their early writings on thin beech-wood boards, bound into bundles, and it is from the old Teutonic word *bok*, meaning "beech," that the modern word is derived.

Booze. The Dutch had a word for drinking to excess—*buizen*. By the 16th century *buizing* had been adopted in English, and over the years the word became completely Anglicized as slang for alcoholic drink.

Boudoir. Any well-bred young lady in the Middle Ages was sent to her room to get over the sulks. The word comes from the French *bouder*, "to pout." So it is a pouting room.

Boycott. During Ireland's agrarian troubles in the 19th century, Capt. Charles Cunningham Boycott was agent for Lord Earne's estates in County Mayo. When, in 1879, landlords tried to impose harsh levies on their tenants, the Irish radical leader Charles Parnell urged tenants to isolate the greedy owners like lepers of old. Boycott was the campaign's first victim. Laborers refused to work for him, postmen would not deliver his mail, and traders imposed such a successful ban on dealings with the Boycott

BOYCOTT BOYCOTTED. *Defeated by the Irish peasantry who refused to work for him, Captain Boycott is given military protection as he begins his journey to enforced retirement in England.*

family that provisions had to be brought in by steamer. After a year the Boycotts were forced to flee to England. The captain died there in 1897. But the year under siege had established his name firmly in the language.

Bunkum. Felix Walker was determined to prove himself an active Congressman after the electors of Buncombe County in North Carolina sent him to Washington in 1820. On one occasion he made a rambling irrelevant speech just as Congress was about to vote on a slavery issue. When colleagues asked him later why he had delayed matters, he replied: "I was not speaking to the House but to Buncombe." From that moment Buncombe became associated with absurd remarks. The spelling was changed when the English novelist Charles Kingsley first used it in a book in 1857.

Canard. Belgian journalist Egide Cornelissen reported in the early 19th century on a macabre experiment he had carried out with 20 ducks. He said he had roasted one duck and fed it to the other 19, then fed one of the 19 to the other 18, and so on until he had only one left—a duck that had eaten 19 of its fellow creatures. The story was printed widely in Europe and America, and when Cornelissen admitted that he had made it all up, a rueful world adopted *canard*, the French word for "duck," as the term for any preposterous hoax.

Candidate. When a Roman politician went campaigning, he wore an immaculate white toga to make a good impression on the voters. The Latin *candidatus*, meaning a person dressed in white, later became synonymous with someone seeking public office.

Carnival. The Italians coined the word *carnivale* to describe the week of feasting that preceded Lent, when Christians were forbidden to eat meat. The word comes from the Latin *carnem levare* ("to remove meat").

Chauffeur. In the days of steam-driven cars, the men employed to drive them also had to keep the boiler alight. So, today, hired drivers are still called by the French word for "stoker."

Checkmate. Like the game of chess, the word for the winning move comes from Persia. The Persian phrase *Shah mat* means "The king is dead."

Clue. The hero Theseus used a ball of thread to find his way out of the labyrinth after he killed the Minotaur of Crete in the old Greek legend. And after the story was told in medieval England—where the word for a ball of thread was "clew"—a guide to the solution of any problem became known as a "clew" or "clue."

Coach. Large horse-drawn carriages first appeared in the 15th century in the Kocs region of Hungary. They were known as *Kocsi szeker*—literally, a Kocs cart. By the 16th century similar carriages were being built in England, with the name Kocs amended to coach.

Codswallop. English owes this word for nonsense to an American called Hiram Codd who, in the 1870's, invented a gastight bottle to keep the fizz in lemonade. Since "wallop" is a slang term for beer, and beer was never kept in a Codd bottle, "Cod's wallop" was a drink that was worthless, compared with beer.

Deliberate. The word meant originally to "weigh in the balance" from the Latin *libra*, meaning "scales." So someone who makes a decision after careful thought is said to be acting "deliberately." From the same root comes the abbreviation for a pound weight, lb.

Derrick. Of all the stories about the origin of this word, the oddest is the one that dates it to the late 16th century, during England's wars with Spain. It seems that 24 soldiers from the English fleet were condemned to death for looting in a raid on Cadiz. Since no one was keen to carry out the sentence, one of the 24, a man called Derrick, was pardoned in return for hanging the other 23. Later he became hang-

HOORAY! HOORAY! *Dixie, the popular term for the Confederate states, was derived from this 10 (dix) dollar bill issued in the 1850's by a bank in Louisiana.*

man at London's Tyburn prison and gained accidental immortality from the dockyard crane that looks like one of his gallows.

Dixieland. America suffered such a flood of paper money prior to the Civil War that banknotes were suspect. But notes from Louisiana bearing the name of the Citizens' Bank and Trust Company of New Orleans were trusted throughout the nation. They were printed in a

THE WORKING DOLLAR. *The first one-dollar bill was issued by the United States government in 1862.*

BRILLIANT "DUNCE." *The followers of John Duns Scotus (1265–1308) were derisively labeled "dunsers."*

mixture of English and French, and the popular $10 bill carried the French word *dix* on the back. Louisiana became famous as "the land of Dixes" or "Dixies," meaning solid currency.

Dollar. Silver coins used in 16th-century Europe were minted in Joachimsthal, a region of Bohemia. They were known as *Joachimsthaler*, which was later abbreviated to *thaler*, or dollar. The dollar sign ($) is thought to be derived from the symbol of Philip V of Spain—a ribbon winding between the two Pillars of Hercules, Gibraltar and Ceuta. Dollars became America's official currency in 1792.

Doughboy. Originally, doughboys were small, round dough cakes served to American sailors aboard ship. But from the late 1840's the term came to be applied to American soldiers, because the large brass buttons on their uniforms resembled the cakes.

Dunce. By a curious twist of fate one of the most brilliant thinkers of the Middle Ages, John Duns Scotus, gave his name to fools. His teachings were dismissed after his death in 1308, and during the Renaissance scholars at Oxford, Paris, and Cologne who supported his ideas were contemptuously dubbed Dunsers.

Eavesdrop. Before roof guttering was invented, houses in medieval England used to have very wide eaves so that rain cascading off their thatched roofs did not soak into the foundations. People who lurked near doors and windows to overhear conversations had to stand in this "eavesdrop" space to be close enough to listen. These listeners were therefore condemned as eavesdroppers.

Farce. Originally, "farcing" was the padding in clothing or the stuffing in a chicken. Then in the Middle Ages, when mystery plays—early dramas based on religious stories—were performed, it became the custom for English actors to liven up their lines by "farcing," or padding, them with topical asides and jokes. The ad-libbing became so popular that by the late 17th century comic padding had expanded into a dramatic form in its own right. The earlier meaning survives in forcemeat, so called because it is "forced," or stuffed.

Fees. These would be decidedly inconvenient if they were still paid with their literal meaning. The word comes from the Old English *feoh*, meaning "cattle," which were bartered for other goods before money was developed.

Fiasco. Venetian glassmakers in the 15th century used only perfectly flawless material for their prized articles. If any glass showed a fault, it was set aside to be made into a small flask—*fiasco*.

Fireman. The first firemen did not stop fires. They started them. It was the fireman's hazardous job in a coal mine to go first into the pit each morning. Wrapped in wet rags, he carried a candle on a long stick to ignite any "firedamp"—an explosive mixture of methane and air—that had seeped out of the seam during the night. Because the fires he started in this way made the pit safe for his fellow workmen, the name was eventually applied to anyone who saved people from blazes.

Foolscap. Before the Commonwealth was set up in England after the 17th-century Civil War, the King licensed papermaking, and every sheet bore the royal cipher as a watermark. The Republican leader, Oliver Cromwell, with characteristic contempt for the trappings of royalty, abolished this and substituted a watermark of his own showing a "fool's cap."

Gazette. Countless newspapers bear this title, which is thought to derive from the Italian *gazetta*, a small coin that was the price of a government newspaper published in Venice around 1536. Alternatively, the word may come from *gazza*, Italian for "gossip."

Gerrymander. Elbridge Gerry, who became Democratic Vice President of America in 1812, was accused during his governorship of Massachusetts of juggling the electoral boundaries to beat a Republican rival at the polls. One observer said of the twisting boundaries: "They look like a salamander." Another critic retorted: "Gerrymander, rather," and the word stuck for political manipulation.

GI. In the Second World War every piece of equipment used by American soldiers was stamped GI for "Government Issue." It was only a matter of time before the men applied the initials to themselves.

Handicap. Two men who wanted to barter possessions of unequal value in medieval England sometimes played a game known as hand in cap. They found someone to act as umpire. Then all three put a token sum of money into a cap. The umpire was asked to decide which of the two possessions being bartered was less valuable and how much money should be added to it to make the exchange fair.

When the umpire announced his decision, the two men put their hands in their pockets. If both took out money, it was a sign that they accepted the umpire's verdict, and the deal went through, with the umpire taking the forfeit money in the cap. If only one took out money, he took the forfeit money, but the possessions were not exchanged. And if neither did, the deal was abandoned, and the umpire took the forfeit.

By the 17th century the hand in cap system was being used in racing to decide which horses should carry extra weight to make a race fair, and eventually the word came to mean anything that acts to someone's disadvantage.

Hitchhike. This term is said to have originated in America in the 19th century to describe how two men could travel with only one horse. One man rode ahead an allotted distance, then hitched the horse to a tree, and continued on foot. When the second man reached the horse, he rode it until he overtook his companion, and so the sequence went on.

Hoodlum. This term for a criminal is said to have been coined around 1870 by a San Fran-

cisco newspaper reporter who was looking for a word to describe young ruffians. He took a local gang leader's name and reversed it from Muldoon to Noodlum—but his writing was so bad that the typesetter thought it was Hoodlum, and this was the word that stuck.

Hooligan. The Houlihans were a rowdy Irish family living in South London in the 1890's. They became notorious for their wildness, and their name—mispronounced as stories about them spread—became part of the language.

Jargon. Scientists who baffle laymen with the specialized language of their subject might feel less smug if they knew that the term comes from the Old French *gargon*—describing the twittering noise that birds make.

Jeep. In 1937 the American cartoonist E. C. Segar introduced a creature called Eugene the Jeep into his popular Popeye cartoon strip. Jeeps, according to the strip, were tough little animals who lived on orchids and could become invisible. When, a few years later, the Willys company of Ohio won a U.S. Army transport contract with a powerful open-topped four-seater vehicle that was just 11 feet long and could go anywhere, soldiers gave the rugged little machine the same name.

Juggernaut. Once a year a 45-foot-high statue of a Hindu god is paraded through the streets of Puri in northeastern India on a huge wagon pulled by hundreds of devotees. In the past, it is said, pilgrims threw themselves to their deaths beneath the wagon's massive wheels. When

POPEYE'S PAL. *Jeep, part dog and wholly fantasy, gave his name to the tough little general-purpose vehicle of the Second World War. The car's achievements became as legendary as its namesake's.*

RELENTLESS LORD. *The 45-foot effigy crushed everything—including voluntary victims.*

reports of the ancient custom reached Europe in the 14th century, the Westernized version of the local name for the god—*Jagannath*, which means "lord of the world"—came to mean a relentless force that crushed everything in its path. More recently, it has been applied to the giant trucks on modern roads.

Jumbo. The word used for anything of great size comes from an African elephant of the same name that was a star attraction in the Paris and then the London Zoos in the mid-19th century. Jumbo, whose shoulders towered 10 feet 9 inches high, was eventually sold to the American showman P. T. Barnum and died in 1885 after being struck by a train during a tour of Canada.

Love. This word for a zero score in tennis comes from the French *l'oeuf*, meaning "egg." In France *l'oeuf* became slang for zero because of its shape.

Namby-pamby. The British poet Ambrose Philips wrote such insipid little verses for children in the 18th century that this play on his Christian name has become the derogatory term for anything affectedly pretty and coy. The expression was coined in 1726 by dramatist Henry Carey, who scoffed at Philips' nursery poems with the words:

So the nurses get by heart,
Namby Pamby's little rhymes.

Nickname. The "nick" part of this word comes from the early English *eke*, meaning "also." So an extra name was known as an "eke-name," later slurred so that it became a "nickname."

Pagan. To start with, this meant the same as "peasant," from the French word *pays* meaning "country." But as towns grew up, their haughty inhabitants gave "pagan" its present meaning of uncivilized or godless.

Pamphlet. A Latin poem called *Pamphilus* proved so popular in the 12th century that numerous copies were produced. The title is Greek for "Loved by All." Thin paper-covered books were later dubbed pamphilets, shortened over the years to pamphlets.

Pedigree. In Old French *pied de grue* meant "foot of a crane," and the term came to be applied to family backgrounds because the arrow-shaped marks linking generations on a genealogical table look rather like the footprints of birds.

Perfume. This was the name given at one time to a disinfectant, hence the link with the word "fumigate." The Romans combined the Latin *per* ("through") with *fumus* ("smoke") to describe a smell drifting through the air like smoke.

Quaker. The religious sect called originally the Children of Light, and now known as the Society of Friends, is said to have acquired this nickname because members quaked with religious fervor at its emotional prayer meetings.

Another version of the origin of "Quaker" concerns the sect's founder, the 17th-century English preacher George Fox, who was regarded with open hostility by the authorities of his time. Once, in October 1650, Fox was hauled into court on a charge of preaching illegally. The defiant Fox thundered from the dock that it was not he, but the judge, who had the most to fear. "Tremble at the word of the Lord," he urged. Instead, the judge, Gervase Bennet, sneered that the only "quaker" in court was Fox himself, and the nickname stuck.

Quarantine. Sick people bored by a spell in an isolation ward may like to console themselves with the thought that originally quarantine meant being shut away for a full 40 days (from the Middle Latin *quarantena*). By the end of 40 days people who had been exposed to a disease were either dead, recovered, or presumed to be no longer contagious.

Quiz. In about 1780, so the story goes, a Dublin theater manager named Daly made a bet that within 24 hours he could introduce a new word into the English language. He spent a whole night chalking the letters *QUIZ* on walls throughout the city, and the next day the strange word was on everyone's lips—yet nobody knew what it meant. Thus it became a byword for a jokey puzzle. Later it came to mean a set of puzzling questions or, as a verb, to interrogate someone.

Robot. The Czech dramatist Karel Capek invented this word in a play about mechanical men. The play was called *R.U.R.*, which stood for Rossum's Universal Robots, and the term entered the English language when it was translated in 1923. Capek made up the word by shortening the Czech term for "slave," *robotnik*.

School. Children toiling at their lessons may be surprised to learn that this word comes from the Greek *schole*, meaning "leisure." The Greeks saw learning as a purely leisure-time activity.

Serendipity. The origin of this term, which means finding one thing while looking for another, can be traced right to the day. In 1722 a fairytale called *The Travels and Adventures of Three Princes of Serendip* was translated into English. In the story the heroes from Serendip—the old name for Ceylon, now known as Sri Lanka—constantly made discoveries by accident. The English writer Horace Walpole was delighted with the tale, and in a letter written on January 28, 1754, he coined the word.

Silhouette. When Étienne de Silhouette became France's Finance Minister in the mid-18th century, his cheese-paring economies over court salaries proved so unpopular that within a year he was replaced. Silhouette retired and practiced his stinginess at home by using cheap black paper cutouts in place of conventional decorations. And he raised extra money by making portraits with the same technique. In 1759 the idea was taken up at an exhibition in Paris. Soon, black profile "portraits" became a craze that spread to England—perpetuating the name of the tightfisted M. de Silhouette.

Silly. This word comes from the German *selig*, meaning "holy." But over the years it came to mean innocent, rustic, plain, simple, simple hearted, frail, weak, and finally foolish.

CUTOUT. *When deposed Finance Minister Étienne de Silhouette (1709–67) fell on hard times, he made extra money by the portraiture style named after him.*

Sirloin. There is a persistent story that James I of England was so delighted with a certain cut of beef that he knighted it, giving rise to the term "Sir Loin." In fact, the word is just a misspelling of the Old French *surloigne*, meaning "top of the loin."

Spinster. Girls awaiting marriage would at one time spin threads to make household linen for their trousseau. It was said rather unkindly of the ones who never got husbands that they kept spinning and waiting all their lives.

Teetotal. The most interesting story to explain this word concerns a reformed 19th-century drunkard named Dicky Turner, who proclaimed in a stuttering voice at an English temperance meeting: "Nothing less than t-t-t-total abstinence will do."

A more likely derivation is from a New York temperance society which demanded that members who signed the pledge against drinking alcohol should write the letter T by their names to indicate total abstinence. They were known as T-totals.

Thug. In the early days of British rule in India—and long, long before—thousands of travelers died at the hands of the Thags, members of a macabre religious cult. The victims were strangled in a ritual form of murder called *Thagi*, then their bones were broken to make burial easier in small graves. By the mid-19th century a British campaign led by Sir William Sleeman had virtually wiped out the cult, but the Anglicized name lives on, as a description of a violent criminal.

Tip. Customers at 18th-century English coffee-houses were invited to drop coins into staff collection boxes bearing the words "To Insure Promptness." Later, only the three initials were used—and the name for a gratuity was born.

Tommy. British soldiers have been known—to friends and foes—as Tommies ever since they were issued a Soldier's Account Book after the Battle of Waterloo in 1815. The book explained how they could collect their pay, and with each copy was a sample form filled out in the name of Thomas Atkins. The account book has long been superseded, but the imaginary soldier's name has stuck.

Treacle. This term has its roots in the Greek for "wild animal," *ther*. From that word came *theriake*, meaning the "antidote to an animal's bite." This became "treacle" in English to describe the balm that was put on a wound. It came to mean a sugary syrup because sugar was widely used in medicine.

Trivial. In ancient Rome serious business was carried out at the Forum, the main marketplace. But gossipers gathered at a crossroads—the *Tri-Via* ("three streets")—and the name was initially intended to describe the idle stories they exchanged there.

Tycoon. One of Comdr. Matthew Perry's souvenirs from the American expedition to Japan in 1854 was this term for a business magnate. It is an Anglicized spelling of the Japanese *taikun*, which was derived from the Chinese words *ta*, meaning "great," and *kiun*, meaning "prince."

Walnut. The name is probably derived from the Old English *wealh*, meaning "foreign," to distinguish it from the native hazelnut. *Wealh* usually signified a Roman or Celtic foreigner, and the words Wales and Welsh come from the same root.

Wedding. Cynics who suggest that the risks of marriage are equivalent to a lottery can point to the fact that "to wed" originally meant "to wager." In Old English "weddian" meant to pledge money in a bet—or to pledge yourself in marriage.

EASTERN VIEW. *Commodore Perry, seen here through Japanese eyes, gave us the word "tycoon."*

WHAT'S IN A PHRASE?

The meanings and origins of popular sayings

Blueblooded. The expression is derived from the Spanish *sangre azul*, used by aristocratic families of Castile to describe themselves as being uncontaminated by Moorish or Jewish blood. It probably originated because the veins of people with fair complexions would appear blue.

By hook or by crook. The metaphor has been credited with many different origins, but it is most probably derived from the feudal custom of lords allowing their tenants to gather as much wood from their lord's land as they could rake up from the undergrowth with a hook or pull down from the trees with a shepherd's crook.

It is easier for a camel to go through the eye of a needle than for a rich man to enter into the kingdom of God. Some scholars have claimed this memorable Biblical quotation to be a mistranslation because a few secondary Greek and Armenian versions refer to a rope, not a camel. But proverbs in the Talmud and the Koran allude to a large animal (elephant or camel) passing through a needle's eye—which suggests that Jesus may have used the word "camel" for purposes of emphasis.

Catherine wheel. The firework was named after St. Catherine, whose symbol was the wheel. According to legend, she was martyred by being tied to a spiked wheel and rolled down a hill. The spinning wheel then became the motif of institutions that were named after her, such as St. Catherine's College, Cambridge, England.

Double Dutch. This expression is used by English-speaking people to describe something that to them is unintelligible. "It's all Greek to me" is another way of putting it. Other nations have similar forms. The French and Greeks say, "It's Chinese to me," while Polish people say, "I'm listening to a Turkish sermon." The Finns speak of "Pig German." The Germans, on the other hand, use the word *kauderwelsch*, which is the same as saying, "These are Bohemian villages to me."

Hip, hip, hooray! Crusaders in the Middle Ages used a version of this whoop of triumph. "Hip" is thought to be a corruption of "Hep"—from the initials of the Crusader battle slogan *Hierosolyma est perdita*, meaning "Jerusalem is fallen."

ST. CATHERINE. *A spiked wheel—the instrument on which she was martyred—became her symbol.*

"Hooray" could be from the Slavonic *Hu-raj!*—
"To Paradise!"—the cry with which they pursued their non-Christian victims to their deaths.

Humble pie. Medieval lords and ladies always feasted on the better parts of the animals that their hunters brought home. However, their servants had to make do with the "umbles," or offal. Because it was a poor man's dish, "umble pie" came to be misdescribed as "humble pie"—the meal for those who are forced to make do with second or third best because they dare not claim the lion's share.

The gods. The term was first used in London's Drury Lane Theatre where, around the early 19th century, the ceiling was decorated with paintings of classical gods and goddesses.

Kilroy was here. The slogan that came to be chalked up on walls throughout the world in the Second World War was originally the "signature" used by James J. Kilroy, a shipyard inspector in Quincy, Massachusetts, to indicate that he had passed a piece of equipment as satisfactory. It found its way to many American war zones, and the frequent appearance of Kilroy's signature everywhere tickled the soldiers' imagination so much that it was counterfeited almost everywhere there was something to write with and a surface to scribble on.

A similar character of obscure origin, known as Chad, appeared in Britain in the early postwar years—accompanied by phrases such as Wot no butter, eggs, milk?—as a lighthearted protest against food shortages and rationing.

Lumber room. The Lombard family were more than just bankers in medieval England. Until Elizabethan times they also had a monopoly on pawnbroking. So goods in pawn became known as Lombard goods. Eventually, the term was widened to include all articles stored away, and storerooms anywhere became known as "Lombard," or "Lumber," rooms.

Lynch law. During the American Revolution, when the work of the courts was disrupted, a public-spirited justice of the peace called Charles Lynch took charge of law and order by presiding over an unofficial court in Bedford County, Virginia. Except in one case of conspiracy, for which he imposed the death penalty, the most severe sentences he handed out were fines and whippings. In 1782 the state government decided that Lynch's sentencing of the conspirators had been justified because of the imminent danger to the state during the war and exonerated him. He died in 1796.

But a century later his reputation for mercy was forgotten, and all that was remembered was that he had meted out unofficial justice. So his name came to be used to describe the justices of vicious mob "courts" that executed nearly 5,000 people in the United States between 1882 and 1962.

Men of straw. This expression, nowadays applied to people of no substance, or of dubious trustworthiness, was originally used to describe professional perjurers. These were men who would hang around outside law courts in Paris and London in medieval times and could be hired to give false evidence. They identified themselves by a straw—the badge of their profession—sticking out of their shoes.

Not an iota of difference. The expression stems from a religious controversy in the Byzantine Empire. There were two religious factions—the orthodox Catholics, who believed that God the Father incorporated God the Son, and the Arians, who believed that God the Father and God the Son were alike but not the same being. In the original Greek the idea of God the Father and the Son together is *Homo-ousion* and the idea of God the Father and God the Son as separate is *Homoi-ousion*. The only difference between the two phrases is the Greek letter *iōta*. In A.D. 325 the Arian doctrine was declared heretical.

P's and Q's. This is believed to stem from the days when alehouse keepers used to chalk up customers' debts on the wall—the number of pints owed for under the letter P, the quarts in the Q column. There are, however, other explanations for the saying. One is that children, or printers' apprentices, were told to be careful in distinguishing between the back-to-front forms of "p" and "q". Another suggests that dancing masters in the time of Louis XIV would tell pupils to mind their "p's" (meaning *pieds*, "feet") and "q's" (*queues*, "wigs"), which might fall off when they bent low in a formal bow.

Queer Street. The description began as Query Street, from the habit English shopkeepers had of putting a question mark in their books against the name of a customer whose credit was shaky. The customer was said to be in Query (later Queer) Street until he had paid his debts.

Robbing Peter to pay Paul. A common fable about this phrase is that it refers to the fact that in 1550 many of the estates of St. Peter's, Westminster, England, were appropriated to

LYNCH LAW. *"Courts" that executed nearly 5,000 people in the United States from 1882 to 1962 were named after Charles Lynch, who took the law into his hands during the American Revolution.*

pay for the repairs of St. Paul's Cathedral. But it seems the phrase was common long before this. In 1380 the preacher John Wyclif is reported to have said: "How should God approve that you rob Peter, and give this robbery to Paul in the name of Christ?"

Show a leg. Some sailors took their wives to sea in Lord Nelson's day. When the bosun went around the crew's quarters in the morning, he would tell any reluctant risers to "show a leg." If the limb was a woman's, she was allowed to sleep on.

Showing the white feather. A gamecock with a white feather in its tail was taken by fanciers as a sign of inferior breeding and lack of courage. The symbol was later used to denote cowardice.

Not to be sneezed at. During the 17th century snuff takers learned to control their sneezing and reserve it as a sign of boredom or disapproval. Anything that merited their favor, therefore, was deemed "not to be sneezed at."

Selling down the river. This dramatic way of expressing the idea of being badly let down came into use during slavery days in the United

States. Colonists in the northern states would be offered high prices for their domestic slaves by plantation owners in the South when slave ships from Africa were delayed and labor was scarce. A slave who was sold in this way, usually sailing down the Mississippi, could expect a much harsher way of life, much suffering, and perhaps an early death at the hands of tougher taskmasters.

Tell it to the marines. The diarist Samuel Pepys claimed that Charles II first used this phrase when a colonel of the marines told him he had seen a flying fish. It was a tall story, the King explained, but he would be prepared to believe it if the much-traveled marines believed it.

He'll never set the Thames on fire. The origin of the phrase is believed to refer, not to the river, but to a piece of flour-mill equipment called a temse. When flour was sifted through this sieve by hand, it was sometimes said that a man worked so hard the friction made the wood smolder. A slow worker, therefore, would never set the temse on fire.

The cold shoulder. This term for a polite snub came into use in medieval France. A chateau guest who was served a cold shoulder of beef or mutton instead of hot meat was intended to take it as a gentle hint that he had overstayed his welcome.

To knuckle under. There are two possible derivations of the phrase, which means to concede defeat. One is the medieval form of submission, bending the knee—then called a knuckle. The other derivation is a player's old custom of rapping the underside of a table to admit defeat in a game.

To truckle under. This expression, meaning to adopt an inferior or subordinate posture, comes from the truckle, or trundle, bed—a contraption rather like a wheelbarrow, which noblemen had carted around with them in the days when travelers could not always count on comfortable night quarters. The master slept on the truckle bed, and his servant slept under it.

Touch and go. One of the many common expressions that come from the English seafaring tradition. Many a ship would "touch" bottom in shoal water and "go" when the tide floated her off—a narrow escape from the possible disaster of a shipwreck.

White elephant. Because albino elephants are so rare, custom at the court of the King of Siam used to decree that they be given nothing but the best by their owners. So whenever a courtier angered him badly, the King used to announce that he was planning, as a mark of his special regard, to present the man with one of his own royal white elephants. The courtier then had to choose between insulting the King by refusing the gift or being ruined by the expense of keeping it. Mostly, the luckless courtiers decamped in a hurry—as the King had hoped. The phrase was brought into the English language by travelers to Siam who had witnessed the court custom. It now means any useless and burdensome gift.

THE NUMBERS GAME

How a King invented the yard by rule of thumb

In a world where nature creates nothing to a standard size, man since the earliest times has used his own body as the basis for measurement. Over the centuries he evolved rules of thumb—and of arm and foot—to give himself units of length.

Cubit for Noah's ark

The cubit, the measure that Noah used in building his ark, was originally the length from elbow to middle fingertip, about 18 inches. It was divided by the ancient Egyptians into fingers and palms. Four finger widths, or digits, made a palm, and six palms made a cubit. Later, about 4,000 years ago, the Egyptians added a seventh palm, and the royal cubit, as it was known, became standardized at approximately 21 inches.

The inch first represented the width of a man's thumb, but it was standardized in classic Rome as one-twelfth of a foot. In 1305 Edward I of England defined the yard of three 12-inch feet and decreed that the inch should be equal to three grains of dry barley laid end to end. The barleycorn unit of measurement is still used by shoemakers.

It is said that in the 16th century King Henry VIII used his thumb to redefine the yard. According to tradition, Henry fixed the yard as the distance from the tip of his own nose to the tip of his thumb at the end of his outstretched arm.

The foot, as its name suggests, was once the distance from the heel to the tip of the big toe. It too was standardized in ancient Egypt as two-thirds of a short (six-palm) cubit. It came to be used to measure an acre, thanks again to Edward I. Before Edward's time an acre was the amount of land a yoke of oxen could plow in a day. But since this could vary enormously, Edward pegged an acre at 40 rods by 4 rods—each rod being 16½ feet long—a measurement that has survived unchanged to this day.

The metric method

The first and only system based on logic, rather than physical accident, was worked out during the French Revolution, as part of a general reaction against the iron hand of tradition. The metric system of weights and measures was the creation of 12 scientists, appointed for the job by the French National Assembly in 1791.

The scientists decided to find some fundamental length in the natural world—to be called a meter, after the Greek *metron*, meaning "measure"—and to make it the basis of a system on multiples of 10.

The length they picked was the circumference of the earth measured on a line through the poles. The scientists measured a quarter of that circumference on a meridian through Paris and, to give themselves a convenient-sized unit, called it 10 million meters or 10,000 kilometers. So the meter, which is slightly longer than a yard, was fixed as 1/40,000,000 of the earth's circumference through the poles. Today, however, it is defined in terms of wavelengths of light.

Marking time

In Britain and the American colonies, September 3, 1752, never happened. Nor did the 10 days that should have followed it. For in that year Britain adopted the Gregorian calendar, and to get back in step meant "losing" 11 days. The decision caused riots at the time because people thought that the government had stolen 11 days of their lives.

Most early calendars were based on the moon, which takes roughly 29½ days to circle the earth. The ancient Babylonian calendar, adopted by the Hebrews, was entirely lunar-based, with 12 months of alternately 29 and 30 days and thus a 354-day year.

But this calendar rapidly got ahead of the seasons, so it was adjusted to keep it roughly in step with the solar year. The Babylonians observed that 235 lunar months coincided with a cycle of 19 solar years. So around 380 B.C. they decided that 7 of every 19 years should have 13 months instead of 12. The Jewish calendar still follows this lunar-solar arrangement, but the Muslim calendar remains lunar-based, with regressive months.

There were many attempts to devise a calendar that approximated the actual time it takes the earth to circle the sun—365 days, 5 hours, 48 minutes, 46 seconds—without losing the 12-month lunar year.

The ancient Egyptians had nearly succeeded, with a 365-day civil calendar. But it was apparently overlooked by the rest of the world until Julius Caesar adopted and modified it as the official calendar of Rome. His reformed calendar commenced January 1, 46 B.C.

Caesar's "leap" forward

Caesar was also the first to introduce the idea of a four-year leap year (with a 30-day February) to make up for the extra fraction of a day over 365 that the earth takes to complete its annual cycle.

Caesar's Julian calendar lasted well. It was much more accurate than its predecessors. But

EIGHT MINUTES SAVED THE DAY

THE RAILROADS and a court case helped to sound the death knell of local timekeeping in Britain.

On November 24, 1858, at 10:06 a.m. by Dorset clocks, a Dorchester judge ruled against a man involved in a land battle because he was late for the 10 a.m. hearing.

Two minutes later the man arrived and claimed that he was on time—by the station clock in his hometown of Carlisle in Cumberland.

The case had to be retried, and in 1880 Parliament ended the confusion by ordering the whole country to set its clocks by Greenwich Mean Time.

it was still 0.0078 days too long. And 1,500 years later the accumulated error had added up to 10 full days.

At this time Pope Gregory XIII established the calendar used in the West today. In 1582 he solved the problem of the 10 extra days—by simply omitting them. He decreed that in that year only, October 4 was to be followed by October 15. The reason why England and her colonies had to lose 11 rather than 10 days was that they did not adopt the Gregorian calendar until 170 years later, by which time it was another complete day ahead of the real year.

Gregory rings the changes

Gregory's calendar was a reformed version of the Julian one. Gregory rearranged the lengths of the months into their modern versions and, more important, devised a way of overcoming the slight inaccuracy in the Julian calendar. He decreed that in order to qualify as a leap year, a century year (100, 1500, and so on) had to be divisible not just by four but by 400. That is why the years 1700, 1800, and 1900 were not leap years, but 2000 will be.

The 10-day week

Weeks have always been an odd time out in mankind's measurement of the passing of the seasons. Days are related to the spin of the earth, months to the phases of the moon, and years to the earth's slow journey around the sun. But weeks have been as varied as the people who used them. The ancient Egyptians and Greeks split their month into three 10-day weeks, while some West African tribes used a 4-day week, and the ancient Assyrians arranged their lives around a 6-day cycle.

The seven-day week, which is now standard throughout the world, seems to have originated with the Babylonians about 4,000 years ago; its days were named for the seven planets known at that time. Various countries have tried to change the habit, but always they have been defeated by the force of custom. In 1792 the French introduced a decimal 10-day week to go with their new metric system, but it was soon abolished by Napoleon. Russian efforts to start a five-day week in 1929 and a six-day week in 1932 failed because people ignored them.

The first clockwatchers

Dividing a day into 24 hours is another man-made notion. The Sumerians divided their day into six watches (three day and three night), and the Babylonians divided it into 12 equal periods. It was probably the Egyptians who first picked a 24-hour day to mark their priestly ceremonies. They chose 24 because stargazers noticed that the night was marked off by the consecutive rising of 12 bright stars. Bent on symmetry, they divided the day to match.

Then about 1400 B.C. the Egyptian Pharaoh Amenophis decided that he needed a better way to tell the time at night. He had his chief engineer build a water clock. Shadow clocks—primitive sundials—gave the approximate time during daylight. The water clock worked by allowing water to trickle slowly out of a carefully graded bowl. By dipping his fingers in and feeling how many of the bowl's ridged markings were above the waterline, Amenophis could then tell roughly how long it was until sunrise.

The idea was developed by Greeks and Romans, whose water clocks (called *clepsydras*) were able to measure fractions of hours.

A degree of luck

Of the three major temperature scales in use today, two got their figures by sheer luck. Only the third, centigrade, was deliberately arranged to divide the temperature between the freezing and boiling points of water into 100 equal parts.

The first thermoscope, having no scale, was invented by the Italian scientist Galileo. He had noticed that when alcohol was heated in a very narrow glass tube, it expanded and rose in the tube in proportion to the increase in temperature. A century or so later Gabriel D. Fahrenheit, a German physicist in Amsterdam, developed a temperature scale for a mercury thermometer.

He took as zero the lowest temperature he could produce—with a mixture of ice and ordinary salt—and planned originally to fix the blood temperature of a healthy man at 12°. But he found he needed a more finely graded scale, so he divided the interval into 96 parts instead of 12, with 96° for blood temperature.

Using this scale, Fahrenheit found that pure water froze at 32°, and boiled at 212°. Later adjustments established 98.6° as normal blood temperature.

In 1730 the French physicist René de Réaumur tried to develop a centigrade thermometer, using a solution of alcohol and water instead of mercury. He decided that logically zero ought to be the freezing point of water. So he marked that and scaled his thermometer so that one degree equaled 1/1,000 part of the fluid's volume at the freezing level.

Unfortunately, the solution boiled at the 80° mark, wrongly taken by others as the boiling point of water.

The centigrade scale was developed a dozen years later by the Swede, Anders Celsius. It now has zero as the freezing point of water and 100° as its boiling point. This scale has generally superseded the others.

Counting sheep

As soon as man the hunter became man the herdsman he began to need a way of keeping track of his flocks—hence numbers. Since fingers were the obvious thing to count on, most early men used 10 as their basic number. But there are primitive tribes who to this day use totally different systems. Some have no bigger numbers than six, so that any larger total has to be written as multiples of six plus whatever the remainder. The Western figure 15, for instance, would in such a system be written as 23, meaning $(2 \times 6) + 3$.

Some of the earliest written numbers were chisel-shaped marks scratched on clay tablets by Mesopotamian scribes around 5,000 years ago.

Some 3,000 years later the Romans were still using the clumsy letter system of numbering (I, II, III, IV, V . . . X . . . L . . . C . . . D . . . M), which expressed big numbers as a row of smaller numbers added together. For instance, DCCLXVI meant the numbers 500 + 100 + 100 + 50 + 10 + 5 + 1 = 766.

Arabic numerals, similar to the ones used in the West today, were only developed fully in the ninth century A.D. Fewer figures are needed than in the Roman system because the positions of the figures themselves determine their values. In the number 234, for instance, the figures 2, 3, and 4 are not added together as in the Roman system to give the total value. Instead, each is multiplied by 100, 10, or 1 depending on its position.

Without the zero, however, this simple positional way of writing numbers was impossible. And the Arabs owe that invention to an unknown Indo-Chinese mathematician who, in A.D. 683, hit on the idea of putting a dot for blank spaces when he was jotting down the numbers from his abacus. The dot was changed to a zero in Europe, becoming standard in modern mathematics.

Proof spirit

Spirits—vodka, whisky, gin, and so on—are composed of alcohol, water, and flavoring substances. Before the 18th century distillers had a simple method of determining a spirit's strength; equal quantities of spirit and gunpowder were mixed and a flame applied. If the mixture failed to burn, the spirit was too weak, and if it flashed, too strong. Only if the mixture burned evenly with a clear blue flame was the spirit said to have been "proved." In 1803 an exciseman, Bartholomew Sikes, invented a hydrometer, which measured the specific gravities of alcohol and water mixtures, a device that is still used to this day.

"Proof" is an arbitrary measure of the proportion of alcohol to water and varies from country to country.

In the United States 100 proof means 50 percent alcohol (with a specific gravity of .7939 at 60° F) and 50 percent water.

In Great Britain the proportion is 57.1 percent alcohol to 42.9 percent water. Because this is a stronger drink, British liquors are usually made at less than 100 proof.

WHY "ALL THE REST HAVE 31 . . ."

"THIRTY DAYS hath September, April, June, and November," runs the children's mnemonic, "all the rest have 31, except February, which has 28." The reason months have different numbers is that when the Romans under Julius Caesar invented the Julian calendar they decided to give months with special religious significance 31 days and the ones of lesser importance 30 days. Thus January, named after the god Janus, March, after Mars, and July, in honor of Caesar himself, are among the months with 31 days. Caesar's successor, Augustus, named August after himself and, naturally, gave it 31 days. In order to do so, he borrowed a day from February and reduced the length of that month to 28 days. Then, to avoid a succession of three long months, Augustus made September and November 30-day months and lengthened the alternate months of October and December to 31 days.

Beer. In one form or another beer has been brewed from various grains and plants for as long as historical records go back. And as early as 3400 B.C. a tax on barley wine, one of the most popular beers, was levied in the ancient Egyptian city of Memphis, on the Nile. The

BEER HARVEST. *Made from fermented malt, beer is flavored by hops (seen being harvested here).*

Romans picked up the knowledge of brewing from the Greeks, and Caesar's legions, whose main drink was beer, spread it throughout all the lands they conquered. It is made by fermenting malt, flavored with hops or other bitters.

Chicken Marengo. After a successful encounter with the Austrians at the Battle of Marengo in Piedmont, Italy, in 1800, a hungry Napoleon demanded a meal. The army's supply train had not caught up with the frontline troops, so a foraging party was sent out to find the Emperor some food. Their "bag"—a small hen, three eggs, four tomatoes, and six crayfish—was cooked in a little garlic and oil and served with bread and a nip of brandy. So pleased was he with the result that Napoleon ordered the meal to be served after every battle. And today the original recipe is enjoyed, unchanged, in many parts of the world.

Coca-Cola. This world-famous soft drink originated in the back kitchen of a chemist's shop in Atlanta, Georgia, in 1886. The chemist, John Pemberton—known as Dr. Pemberton, because of his fondness for making up remedial concoc-

tions—had been trying to find the recipe for a pleasant soft drink, and at last he was satisfied. He sold the rights four years before his death. Within 40 years Coca-Cola had become a name known the world over. The name comes from *coca*, a South American shrub, and *cola*, an extract from the kola nut. The exact recipe is a closely guarded secret.

Cocktail. Among the many stories concerning the origin of this name for a mixture of alcoholic drinks, the most interesting is that it was first drunk as a toast in the days of cockfighting to the cock that had the most tail feathers left after a battle. Another theory is that it was named after a *coquetier*, a type of cup in which it was served during the early French colonization of New Orleans. Yet another alternative says it stems from *cokale*, a fiery brew once used in England to keep fighting cocks on their mettle.

But it most likely originated in 1776 at an Elmsford, New York, barroom that was decorated with tail feathers. A drunk ordered a glass of "those cocktails," and a barmaid smartly poured him a mixed drink with a feather stuck in it.

Doughnuts. The world-famous cakes that are simply a sugar-coated ring of fried dough with a hole in the center were "invented" by a New England schoolboy. Young Hanson Gregory, tired of having to eat his mother's cakes that always seemed too heavy in the middle, persuaded her to remove the center before frying the dough. His idea worked, quickly caught on in the neighborhood, and eventually spread to become a favorite coffee-break snack in many parts of the world.

Granny Smith. The apple that has become internationally popular was named after Maria Ann Smith, who emigrated to Sydney, Australia, from England with her family in 1839. By budding and grafting on some seedlings, which had sprung up in her garden, she developed a strain so superior to anything known in Australia that cases stamped "Apples from Mrs. Smith" became eagerly sought in the markets. Their fame spread, and soon professional fruit farmers were producing them as Granny Smiths.

Grog. This was the name given to a mixture of rum and water, which was a daily issue in the

COCKFIGHTING. *Did the popular idea of mixing a cocktail derive from this savage old sport?*

British Navy for 200 years. It is derived from the nickname of Adm. Edward Vernon, known as Old Grog because he used to wear a cloak of coarse cloth, or grogram. In 1740 he attempted to stamp out drunkenness in the navy by ordering that the sailors' daily issue of a half-pint of neat rum should be diluted and served in two installments, with six hours between. The ration was abolished in 1970 as being out of keeping with the modern, highly technical—and sober—navy.

Ice-cream sundae. It was forbidden to sell ice cream with soda on the Sabbath in the puritanical town of Evanston, Illinois, in the late 19th century. But some confectioners got around the ban on soda by serving ice cream with syrup instead. The confection became known as a Sunday, although the final "y" was changed to "e" to overcome religious objections.

Peach Melba. The French chef Auguste Escoffier was an ardent admirer of Dame Nellie Melba, the famous Australian soprano, but was too shy to send her flowers. When she dined alone at London's Savoy Hotel at the turn of the century, however, he concocted a special dessert for the singer. It consisted of a peach,

DAME NELLIE MELBA. *It was after the famous soprano that the dessert Peach Melba was named by a French chef in London.*

541

poached in vanilla syrup, in a dish of vanilla ice cream, covered with crushed raspberries. When she said how much she enjoyed it and asked its name, M. Escoffier said he would be honored if he could call it Peach Melba. The idea became the rage of London and eventually a popular dessert all over the world.

Sandwiches. The Fourth Earl of Sandwich (1718–92) was such a compulsive gambler that he did not want to take time away from the card table to eat a cooked meal. Instead, he chose to have pieces of cooked meat served between two pieces of bread during his games. Although the snack now bears his name in recognition of the fashion he set, it is thought that the idea of eating meat in this way was introduced to Britain by Rome's conquering legions.

Spam. In Britain, Spam was first eaten as a wartime substitute for fresh meat. But it had been sold since 1936 in Minnesota, where a $100 prize was offered for the best name. The winning entry was the word derived from the main ingredient: SPiced hAM.

Tea. Although popularly thought of as an "English" beverage, tea was fashionable in Holland by 1640, about 12 years before it appeared in Britain. The Dutch established plantations in Java in 1606 and by 1610 began to import tea to Europe. Forty years later they took it to America. The first tea to reach England was a small amount found on a captured Dutch ship in 1652. It was another eight years before it was first publicly sold in London, despite outraged protests by preachers and writers that it was "inimical to health, morals, and public order." It was at first considered an aphrodisiac, and

HEAVY GAMBLER, LIGHT SNACK. *Portrait of the Fourth Earl of Sandwich.*

"IMMORAL" TEA. *Tea, grown and dried in the Far East, outraged many English preachers.*

WINE: MAN'S ANCIENT COMFORT

WINEMAKING can be traced back to the ancient civilizations of the Near East. An early reference occurs in the Old Testament book of Genesis, which says that Noah "planted a vineyard; and he drank of the wine, and became drunk."

This fresco from an Egyptian tomb shows how wine was made in ancient Egypt.

542

people not only brewed it but ate the leaves on bread and butter.

The people of Eire are the world's greatest tea drinkers today: 7.76 pounds (about 1,200 cups) per head was the average consumption in 1973.

The practice of tea drinking is worldwide, but the way in which it is drunk varies. In Tibet, for example, the traditional method is to stir boiled tea with a rancid yak butter until it is like a thick soup. The Tibetans, moreover, do not use tea leaves. They buy their tea from China in bricks compressed with rice flour and flake pieces off when they are needed.

Toasts. The custom of drinking to a person's honor is so-called because in Elizabethan times pieces of toast were often put in celebration drinks.

Tomato. The word began in Mexico as *tamatl*, entered Spanish as *tomate* and Italian as *pomo d'ore* ("golden apple"). In the 16th century the French mistakenly presumed that the fruit was an aphrodisiac and named it *pomme d'amour* ("love apple"). Despite this reputation, it was grown chiefly as a decoration until the 1830's.

Whisky. The earliest written record of whisky—a spirit liquor distilled from malted barley—is in Scotland, dated 1494. But the process of distillation was known in Britain from at least the 10th century and may have been brought to the British Isles by Arab traders seeking tin. There is evidence that the ancient Egyptians knew how to distill spirits from grain. The name "alcohol" is derived from the Arabic *al-koh'l*, meaning "powdered antimony." It came into use in English to mean any fine powder or extract, including that used in spirits.

But the word "whisky" is from the Gaelic *uisge beatha*, meaning "water of life," a name used by many other nations to describe various alcoholic drinks—*eau de vie* in French, *akvavit* in Swedish, and *aqua vitae* in Latin.

Worcestershire sauce. This internationally famous food dressing was concocted almost by accident. When Lord Sandys returned to England about 1835, after a period of colonial service in Bengal, he brought with him a recipe for an Indian sauce. He asked two chemists, John W. Lea and William Perrins, of Worcester, to make it up for him. The two men also made a quantity for themselves but found it so unpalatable that they stored the jars away and forgot about them for a time. Later, they found the sauce in their cellars and tasted it again. It had matured and was delicious. Lea and Perrins got permission to market it and called it Worcestershire sauce.

The sauce that was almost lost is still made from the same recipe today. The ingredients are stored in wooden hogshead barrels to mature for several months—up to 1,000 barrels, each containing 54 gallons at any one time. Once a week they are rolled over to blend the ingredients; then the liquid is refined and bottled.

An ancient Persian legend of how wine was discovered is perhaps the most interesting. Prince Jemshed ordered a number of goatskin bags to be labeled "poison" after the grape juice in them, which was fermenting, had given him a stomachache. His favorite wife, having lost his attention, decided to kill herself by drinking from the bags. But by that time the wine had matured, and she became gay and vivacious again—and won back the favor of her wandering husband. Wine was introduced into northern Europe about 600 B.C. but was always "still" after maturing because it was brewed in open vessels. Originally, bottles were stopped with wool dipped in oil and wax, but in the late 17th century corks were introduced by a Benedictine monk, Dom Perignon. This leak-proof stopper allowed the secondary fermentation of champagne-type wine and put the bubbles into "bubbly."

WHAT'S IN A NAME?

How kindergarten, Kodak, and Christmas trees happened

Ampersand. The symbol "&" is one of the few survivors of Roman shorthand. A merging of the letters "e" and "t" (*et* is the Latin word for "and"), it first appeared in A.D. 79. It is used to represent "and" in many languages.

Blotting paper. Sand was used to mop up damp ink until early in the 19th century, when blotting paper as we know it was discovered by accident by a papermill worker in England. He forgot to size some writing paper (by treating it with a glutinous wash to give it a finished surface), and it was thought that the batch was spoiled. The millowner thought he might as well use up the paper as scrap and tried writing on a sheet. The ink from his pen was simply absorbed—giving him the idea for blotting paper.

Christmas trees. The 16th-century Protestant reformer Martin Luther is one of the first persons recorded as having had a candlelit tree in his home at Christmas. His purpose was to simulate a bright starlit sky.

Tree worship, however, has its roots much deeper in German history. In pagan times trees were regarded as fertility symbols because their leaves sprout after winter. This probably led directly to the tree becoming a symbol of the feast of Christ's birth. The familiar conifer was probably chosen because it is green at the right time, and its shape resembles a church steeple.

Cigar bands. In Cuba, in the days of the Spanish Empire, it was fashionable for rich and titled women to smoke cigars. They started the custom of wrapping narrow paper bands around the cigars to protect their fingers from nicotine stains.

Cigarettes. A group of Turkish soldiers is said to have invented cigarettes while defending the city of Acre from Napoleon in 1799. When their hookah (a water-cooled communal smoking pipe) was destroyed by cannon fire, they rolled tobacco in touch papers used for firing their guns.

Kindergarten. Memories of an unhappy childhood inspired Frederick Froebel to establish a "small child occupation institute" (*Kleinkindbeschäftigungsinstitut*) in Blankenburg, Germany, in 1837. Later he decided that "kindergarten" ("children's garden") was a happier-sounding name for his schools, where children of four and five could enjoy themselves playing in the sun or listening to poetry and stories. After 14 years the authorities closed the schools because of the "dangerous freedom" of Froebel's ideas. But the schools caught on rapidly in the United States.

Kodak. Cameras were big and cumbersome until George Eastman, an American inventor, marketed the first handy Kodak camera in 1888. He chose the name Kodak because it was "short, vigorous, could not be misspelt and, to satisfy trademark laws, meant nothing."

Madame Tussaud's. When the Bastille was stormed in 1789, young Marie Grosholtz, already famous in Paris for her wax portraits, was summoned to mold the likenesses of the prisoners whom the revolutionaries had released. As she descended to the dungeons, the story goes, her foot slipped, and she was saved from falling by a young man, Maximilien Robespierre. Only a few years later she was to hold his severed head in her lap while she created his death mask, for inclusion in her wax museum in Paris.

In the same way she modeled the heads of hundreds who perished on the guillotine.

Marie Grosholtz became rich, and in 1795 she married an engineer named Tussaud. But the marriage was not a success, and in 1802 she sailed for England, taking most of her wax collection with her.

She toured Britain successfully for 30 years with her portraits of royalty and famous personalities, and then she opened a museum on London's Baker Street in 1834. She died in 1850 at the age of 88.

Matches. John Walker, an English chemist, hit on the idea of matches when he discovered that friction ignited a mixture of potassium chloride and antimony sulfide. He sold his first box in 1827 but never bothered to take out a patent. A small piece of sandpaper to strike the matches on was given free with each box.

Paper money. The world's first banknotes were used in China in the ninth century because copper was scarce and not enough coins could be minted. The first paper money to be circulated in Europe was issued by the Bank of Sweden in 1661, though this was also a temporary measure.

In 1694 the Bank of England was founded

CANDID KODAK. *The first box camera and celluloid roll film were both invented by George Eastman in 1888 and 1889. The entire camera had to be returned to the manufacturers for reloading.*

and began to issue promissory notes, originally handwritten but later printed. These quickly became a universally acceptable form of exchange and were the first true banknotes.

The first paper money in America was issued by Massachusetts Colony in 1690, in denominations from two shillings to five pounds. The United States government first issued paper money in 1862.

Queen Mary. The liner *Queen Mary*, launched in 1934, got her name through a misunderstanding. The Cunard Line had decided to call her *Queen Victoria*. The company chairman went to see George V and told him they wanted to name their new ship after one of England's most noble Queens.

Before he could finish, the King interrupted: "Oh, Her Majesty will be so pleased." So *Queen Mary* it had to be.

Red Square. The famous square in Moscow got its name not from the 1917 revolution but from a Russian word, *krasnaya*, which means "red and beautiful." It has been Red Square since the Middle Ages.

Rubber boots. Centuries ago Indians living in the Amazon basin used rubber in a way that oddly anticipated the Wellington boot. They would dip molds of their feet and legs in latex, the raw liquid from the rubber plant. After the latex dried, the result was a tight-fitting "boot," which protected the skin against thorns and insect bites.

The original Wellington boots were made from leather. They were named after the Duke of Wellington who, along with some other officers, wore them at the Battle of Waterloo. The first reference to the boots came in a play written by the English dramatist William Moncrieff, in 1817. The first rubber Wellingtons appeared in shops in 1851, a year before the duke died.

Safety glass. Thousands of road-crash survivors owe their lives to a trivial accident in a Paris laboratory in 1904. For the idea of safety glass came to a French scientist named Benedictus when he knocked an empty bottle off a shelf. The bottle was smashed, but to his surprise it had kept its shape. Benedictus noted that the

FROM SMALL BEGINNINGS . . .

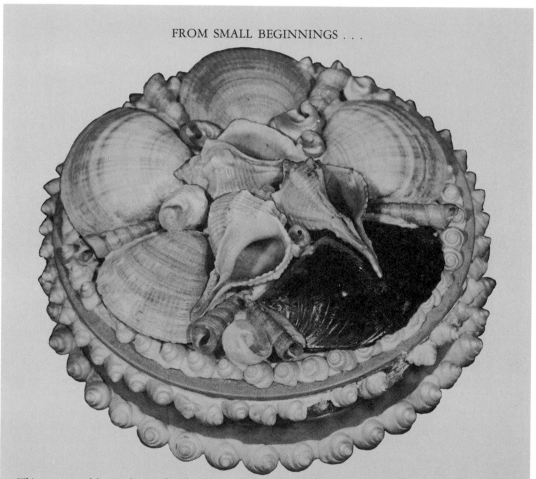

This ornamental box is decorated with tropical shells of the kind imported into Britain by shopkeeper Marcus Samuel. He also imported oil—and his interests eventually merged into the Shell combine.

SHELL, the giant oil combine, was named by one of its founders, Marcus Samuel. He ran a business in London, known as the Shell Shop, because of its brisk trade in boxes fancifully decorated with seaside shells. Another side of his business was transporting oil. It was the merging of this firm with other companies in 1897 that created the mighty Shell concern. Its familiar symbol of a scallop shell on the fuel pumps was retained as a reminder of the company's beginnings.

glass had contained a collodion solution. The solvent had evaporated, leaving on the inside of the bottle a cellulose skin that had held the glass splinters together.

Saluting. Roman soldiers may well have invented the military salute to show that they did not conceal a weapon in the right hand. The Roman salute—a raised arm, hand slightly to the left and palm opened away from the face—may be seen on the statue of Emperor Marcus Aurelius in Rome.

Historians believe that the modern form of salute may have originated with soldiers in armor raising their visors to show their faces to a friend or superior. A British tradition, sometimes discounted, holds that saluting began at a naval tournament that was attended by Queen Elizabeth I to celebrate the defeat of the Spanish Armada in 1588. The officer in charge ordered that "on account of the dazzling loveliness of Her Majesty, all seamen, upon receiving their prizes, should shield their eyes with their right hand."

Scotch tape. Scotch tape was developed for paint sprayers in the United States in 1925 as the answer to the problem of masking separate color areas. The sprayers called it Scotch because at first there were complaints that the makers were being overeconomical in the use of adhesive, for the tape would not stick properly to the surface.

Scotland Yard. The medieval Kings of Scotland stayed in a residence on a site at Whitehall when they visited London. The area was divided into portions, or yards, and the residence came to be known as Great Scotland Yard. The first Metropolitan Police headquarters, established in 1842, backed onto the site and was soon nicknamed Scotland Yard.

When the Metropolitan Police moved their offices to the Thames Embankment in 1890, the new building—originally designed as the National Opera House—was named New Scotland Yard, but it gradually came to be called just Scotland Yard. The next move was in 1967, to a tower block a quarter of a mile away in Victoria Street. It, too, has been named New Scotland Yard. The Embankment building, however, survives—but only as a departmental offshoot.

Shorthand. Several forms of shorthand were tried out by the ancient Greeks and Romans. The inventor of the first important system was Marcus Tiro in Rome in 63 B.C. It was made up of more than 5,000 symbols and was in use for 600 years. The system was rediscovered by German scholars in the late 15th century and provoked a new interest in the subject. It is thought that the shorthand was used to record the speeches of Martin Luther.

In Britain nearly 500 methods of shorthand have been published since the 17th century. Samuel Pepys, in writing his famous diary, used a method he had invented himself. In the mid-18th century Thomas Gurney became the first official shorthand writer at the Old Bailey Courts of Justice in London. His Gurney system was in use well into the present century, gradually being superseded by a method that had been invented in 1837 by Englishman Isaac Pitman.

The Pitman method employs 26 strokes and their derivations to represent consonants, and a range of dots and dashes to represent vowels and diphthongs.

The fastest-ever Pitman speed—350 words a minute—was achieved by Nathan Behrin in New York in December 1922. The fastest user of Pitman's rival—the Gregg system—was Englishman Leslie Bear, who served as an editor of the official Parliamentary report, *Hansard*, until 1972.

The two systems have millions of users throughout the world.

In the United States 90 percent of secretaries use Gregg; in Great Britain 80 percent use Pitman.

Silk. China has been producing silk for well

HAIL, CAESAR! *This statue of Emperor Marcus Aurelius in Rome demonstrates what was probably the ancestor of all military salutes.*

THE FIRST WILLOWS. *An 18th-century drawing of Alexander Pope's house flanked by weeping willows, including the one grown from a Turkish basket. It may be the ancestor of many weeping willows in the United States and Britain.*

over 4,000 years. The discovery of how to rear the worms on mulberry trees, reel the thread, and weave the cloth is credited to an Emperor's wife, Lady Hsi-ling-shi, who was worshiped as the Goddess of Silk.

The cultivation of the silkworm was introduced into Constantinople by Emperor Justinian in the sixth century, and the silk industry had spread throughout Europe by the 17th century.

The first silk mill in the United States was constructed at Mansfield, Connecticut, in 1810.

Starlings. A serious environmental problem in America owes its origin to a quotation from Shakespeare's *Henry IV*, which runs: "I'll have a starling that shall be taught to speak nothing but 'Mortimer.'"

A wealthy New Yorker named Eugene Schieffelin, whose two consuming passions were Shakespeare and birds, decided in 1890 to introduce into America every bird mentioned in the great dramatist's plays. Most of them died—but not 40 pairs of starlings. They bred so prolifically that they became pests and remain so in most cities today.

Table knives. Diners ate with pointed daggers until the 17th century, when the French Cardinal Richelieu was so upset by courtiers using them as toothpicks that he ordered the ends to be rounded.

Vaseline. Petroleum jelly, as Vaseline was first called, was developed by a London-born chemist, Robert Chesebrough, while visiting the Pennsylvania oilfields in 1859. He noticed that workers soothed cuts and burns with a colorless residue that collected on the pump rods of drilling rigs. He took supplies of this "rod wax" with him to New York and refined it into the petroleum jelly we know today. Chesebrough, who lived to the age of 96, claimed that he swallowed a spoonful of Vaseline every day.

Weeping willows. Many weeping willows in the United States and Great Britain may be descended from a Turkish basket sent to Lady Suffolk in England early in the 18th century. The poet Alexander Pope was present when the basket, containing figs, arrived. He had one of the withes from the basket planted in his garden by the Thames River, where it grew into a fine weeping-willow tree. Years later a British officer took a twig from the tree before leaving for the American colonies. It was planted in Abingdon, Virginia, and became the ancestor of thousands, perhaps even millions, of trees.

548

FRANKENSTEIN'S MAKER

The monster born in a dream

Outside the gloomy Swiss château the night was wild, split by storms. Inside, by a flickering fire, an 18-year-old girl listened to her husband talk about the evolutionary theories of Erasmus Darwin. Later the same night she was awakened by a nightmare so vivid that she dared not sleep again.

At dawn she began to write it down. "By the glimmer of the half-extinguished light, I saw the dull yellow eye of the creature open; it breathed hard, and a convulsive motion agitated its limbs." This was the birth of Frankenstein's monster.

The year was 1816; the girl was Mary Shelley, wife of the English poet; and the place was the Swiss home of Lord Byron. The friends had agreed before retiring that each should write a ghost story. But only Mary had true inspiration.

Two years later her dream was published as *Frankenstein*, a horrifying novel about a medical student who builds a living body from parts of corpses.

Mary's creation, however, was not the first example of an artificial man.

According to historical legend, the medieval German theologian Albertus Magnus built a robot that answered questions. And in 1580 Rabbi Löw of Prague made a giant human figure from river mud and, according to legend, brought it to life by magic—the golem of Jewish mythology.

The 16th-century Swiss alchemist Paracelsus was also rumored to have devised a formula for creating life.

Mary Shelley used these themes to develop her masterpiece.

ROBINSON CRUSOE, SCOTTISH PIRATE

DANIEL DEFOE'S *Robinson Crusoe* might never have been written without an argument Alexander Selkirk had aboard a Scottish privateer one night in 1704. Selkirk was the ship's first mate on an expedition to the South Seas, and in the heat of the dispute with the captain, he demanded to be put ashore. He was—on the uninhabited island of Juan Fernandez, off the coast of Chile. Nobody knows now what the row was about. But it led to Selkirk living on the island for nearly 4½ years, until he was rescued in 1709 and taken back to England. As a journalist, Defoe heard about Selkirk and used the pirate's story as the basis of his own tale—about a pious man marooned for 24 years.

The castaway pirate Alexander Selkirk dances with a goat in this romantic 18th-century picture. His story made front-page news in British papers when he was rescued in 1709.

BULL'S-EYE. *William Tell takes aim at the apple on his son's head. Beyond them stands the Austrian tyrant Gessler. But it seems that they existed only in the imagination of a 16th-century writer.*

WILLIAM TELL

Real-life hero or a writer's creation?

The order was clear and humiliating. Every Swiss citizen had to bow before the Austrian tyrant's hat, stuck on a post in the village square. One man only was brave enough to refuse to bow: the marksman William Tell.

The tyrant, Hermann Gessler, made Tell the victim of a savage jest. He could have his freedom if he shot an apple from the head of his son Walter. If he missed or refused, he would be executed.

Outside the village of Altdorf, Tell faced his son. One deadly bolt lay on his crossbow. Another jutted from his belt. He fired—and the apple split in two. Why, asked Gessler, had he taken the second bolt from his quiver?

"It was for your heart if the first had harmed so much as a hair of my son's head," replied Tell. Gessler yelled to his soldiers, "Take him to the castle." Tell was bundled into a boat with

Gessler, and his guards took him across Lake Uri to Gessler's grim fortress.

On the way a storm blew up. The guards freed Tell so that he could guide them to shore. He did—then leaped out and pushed the boat back into the lake.

Gessler's men were swept to their deaths, but the tyrant himself struggled back to shore. Tell was waiting with his second bolt. He fired— and Switzerland was free of the Austrian yoke.

William Tell's story was first told in the Swiss chronicles of Aegidius Tschudi, a 16th-century writer, about 200 years after Tell was supposed to have lived. But there is no contemporary evidence that Tell or Gessler existed.

It seems that Tschudi's account is a Swiss embellishment of an 11th-century legend, for stories of expert archers occur all over northern Europe. Tschudi only added details—and made Tell the Swiss folklore hero he is today.

550

THE TRUE TRAVIATA

Verdi's opera was inspired by a courtesan

Operas are often based on classical legends. But Verdi's *La Traviata* owes its existence to a real-life Parisian street waif and the talent of Alexandre Dumas, son of the man who wrote *The Three Musketeers*.

The girl was Rose Alphonsine Plessis, who was born in 1824 in the village of Nonant, near Normandy, France. At the age of 15, Rose ran away from home. She arrived penniless in Paris and, being faced with starvation, turned to prostitution.

By the time she was 18, Rose had changed her name to Marie Duplessis so that she could not be traced by her family and was a famous courtesan. She lived on the fashionable Boulevard de la Madeleine and was visited by many wealthy men such as Count de Stackelberg, former Russian Ambassador to Vienna.

Introduction to Dumas

Dumas first saw Marie stepping out of a carriage in the Place de la Bourse. He was captivated by her beauty, and when he saw her again, in a box at the Théâtre des Variétés, he managed to arrange an introduction.

The meeting started a strange romance, which survived her marriage to another man and lasted until her death. Marie, who was racked by chronic tuberculosis, told Dumas: "You will have a sorry mistress, a woman who is nervous, ill, sad, and gay with a gaiety sadder than grief, a woman who spits blood and spends 100,000 francs a year. All the young lovers I have had have very soon left me." But the young writer, who was utterly in love, ignored her warnings.

As her illness grew worse, Dumas bankrupted himself to pay for doctors. Even when she married an old flame, Vicomte de Perregaux, he remained faithful. None of it made any difference. On February 3, 1847, she died. She was 23 years old. Covered with camellias, her favorite flowers, her coffin was lowered into the earth of the cemetery in Montmartre.

Dumas began *La Dame aux Camélias* soon after Marie's death. He rewrote the novel later as a play, which in 1853 supplied the inspiration for Verdi's opera, giving Marie a musical immortality she would have considered no more than her due.

CRUSHED EXPECTATIONS

Dickens and the jilted Australian bride

A jilted bride 11,000 miles away may have given Charles Dickens the idea for one of his famous characters—Miss Havisham, the aged recluse of *Great Expectations*.

In 1856 Eliza Emily Donnithorne, of Sydney, Australia, was left standing at the altar on her wedding day. She was so heartbroken by the experience that she became a hermit in her own home. From that day until her death, 30 years later, she never went out again.

The door of the room in which the wedding celebrations were to have been held was locked. The decorations and the wedding breakfast inside rotted untouched on the tables.

Fictional lady

In Charles Dickens' novel Miss Havisham lives and dies in an almost identical way. This is how Pip, the young hero of *Great Expectations*, describes his first meeting with the formidable old lady:

"I saw that the bride within the bridal dress had withered like the dress, and like the flowers, and had no brightness left but the brightness of her sunken eyes. I saw that the dress had been put upon the rounded figure of a young woman, and that the figure upon which it now hung loose, had shrunk to skin and bone."

There is no conclusive evidence that Dickens based Miss Havisham on Miss Donnithorne. But through his contacts with travelers and journalists he would have been among the first in England to hear of the recluse on the other side of the world.

The novel was completed in 1861, just five years after Miss Donnithorne's fiance disappeared. It enshrined her loneliness and misery forever.

DEACON BRODIE'S SECRET LIFE

The man who was Jekyll and Hyde

William Brodie was a well-respected man in Edinburgh in the mid-18th century. In a straitlaced city, he shone as a model of civic sobriety. The son of a prosperous cabinetmaker, he was a deacon of the masons' guild, and a city councillor.

But the deacon was also the model for one of English literature's most horrifying characters, Robert Louis Stevenson's schizophrenic scientist, Dr. Jekyll. For Brodie, like the gentle doctor, had a secret life behind his mask of virtue. By day he was a businessman. By night he was a gambler and a vicious thief.

No one knew his secrets, not even his two mistresses, who had his five children. They did not even know about each other.

Brodie was 27 when he turned to crime. In August 1768 he made copies of the keys to a city bank and robbed it of £800 (about $4,000). But though he went on to burgle scores of buildings over the following 18 years, no hint of suspicion ever fell on him.

Getaway and capture

The beginning of the end came in 1786, when he joined forces with three petty thieves. To-gether, they planned Brodie's most daring raid—on the headquarters of the Scottish Customs and Excise. The gang was surprised by an employee, and though Brodie got away, one of the thieves, John Brown, turned king's evidence to escape deportation for other crimes he had committed in England.

Brodie fled to Amsterdam, hoping to escape to America. But on the eve of his departure, the police caught up with him. Brodie was extradited and put on trial in Edinburgh.

The evidence was damning; the police found the proof of his double identity: false keys, pistols, and a burglar's black suit. Brodie was condemned to death. But on the night before his execution, he wired his clothes from neck to ankle to lessen the jerk of the rope and lodged a silver tube in his throat to cheat the noose.

Neither trick worked. On October 1, 1788, he died on the Edinburgh gallows.

Nearly a century later Robert Louis Stevenson and William Henley wrote a play based on Brodie's exploits. *Deacon Brodie, or The Double Life*, was first produced at the Prince's Theatre, London, in 1884. In the play the burglar explains the freedom he finds in his nocturnal life of crime.

Two years later Stevenson turned the theme into *The Strange Case of Dr. Jekyll and Mr. Hyde*, his memorable short story about the darker side of man.

In the story Dr. Jekyll discovers, through experiments with a drug, that "man is not truly one, but truly two," and describes how "I learned to recognize the thorough and primitive duality of man."

He explains his fascination with the experiment: "If each, I told myself, could but be housed in separate identities, life would be relieved of all that was unbearable; the unjust might go his way, delivered from the aspirations and remorse of his more upright twin; and the just could walk steadfastly and securely on his upward path, doing the good things in which he found his pleasure, and no longer exposed to disgrace and penitence by the hands of this extraneous evil."

In this way Stevenson explained the way in which the evil inherent in man took its hold on the good Deacon Brodie.

DOUBLE TROUBLE. *Deacon Brodie with the dice and cards that led to his downfall.*

AMERICA'S UNCLE SAM

The legend on a barrel of meat

Samuel and Ebenezer Wilson boasted that their meat-packing company was the best in New York State because it could butcher and pack 150 head of cattle a day.

So when the United States and Britain went to war with each other in 1812, the confident brothers went after—and won—a contract to supply the troops with barrels of beef and pork.

Samuel Wilson was delighted. He was a jovial, popular man who stood out in any crowd with his mane of gray hair and his high top hat, and he was known to everyone as Uncle Sam. He was always happy to let visitors wander around his factory in Troy to see what he was doing for the boys at the front.

Then, one day, one of the visitors noticed that each barrel was stamped with the initials E.A.–U.S. (standing for the government contractor Elbert Anderson and United States), and asked a worker what the letters meant. "I don't know," said the man, "unless it means Elbert Anderson and Uncle Sam."

It was one of those jokes that stuck. The visitors and employees spread it around. Cartoonists picked up the idea in the 1830's and, though Sam himself died in 1854, Congress eventually gave him a permanent niche in the nation's heart. In 1961 they passed a resolution formally recognizing Samuel Wilson as the symbol of the United States of America.

Unlike his American counterpart, Britain's plump and cheery mascot, John Bull, had no

WHIP-ROUND. *A raffish Uncle Sam guards the nation's wealth in an English cartoon of 1886. In real life Samuel Wilson was clean shaven.*

real-life model. He made his first appearance in a somewhat heavy-handed political satire by John Arbuthnot, which was published in 1712 under the title *Law Is a Bottomless Pit.*

In the book, which became known later as *The History of John Bull,* he is an Englishman, Lewis Baboon is a Frenchman, and Nicholas Frog a Dutchman. But only John Bull won the hearts of the historians, commentators, and cartoonists who have immortalized him.

HOW LITTLE JACK HORNER BECAME A BIG OWNER

ACCORDING to legend, the original Horner was steward to Richard Whiting, the last of the abbots of Glastonbury. In the 1530's, the time of the Dissolution of the Monasteries, it is said that the abbot, hoping to placate Henry VIII, sent His Majesty an enormous Christmas pie containing the deeds of 12 manors. The task of carrying the pie to London was entrusted to Horner, who managed to open the pie and extract the deeds of the Manor of Mells in Somerset—presumably the "plum" referred to in the rhyme.

Certainly, one Thomas Horner did assume ownership of Mells, but both his descendants and the present owner of the house, the Earl of Oxford and Asquith, claim that the rhyme is a slander. Horner, they say, bought the manor from the King; his name was Tom and not Jack; and there is evidence that the rhyme existed before the Tudors.

THE INCREDIBLE DR. BELL

The man who was Sherlock Holmes

One evening, about the turn of the century, after a weekend shoot in Scotland, a dozen guests sat around a dinner table discussing famous unsolved crimes. One guest, Dr. Joseph Bell, had the others wide eyed with his deductive acrobatics. He was an eminent surgeon whose classroom wizardry influenced five decades of Edinburgh University students, including Conan Doyle, Robert Louis Stevenson, and James M. Barrie.

"Most people see but do not observe," he said. "Glance at a man and you find his nationality written on his face, his means of livelihood on his hands, and the rest of his story in his gait, mannerisms, watch-chain ornaments, and the lint adhering to his clothes.

"A patient walked into the room where I was instructing some medical students. 'Gentlemen,' I said, 'this man has been a soldier in a Highland regiment, and probably a bandsman.' I pointed out the swagger in his walk, suggestive of the Highland piper; his shortness told me that if he had been a soldier it was probably as a bandsman. But the man insisted that he was a shoemaker and, furthermore, that he had never been in the army.

"I asked him to remove his shirt, whereupon I could see a little blue D branded on his skin. That was how they used to mark army deserters during the Crimean War. He finally confessed having played in the band of a Highland regiment. It was really elementary, gentlemen."

Someone remarked: "Dr. Bell might almost be Sherlock Holmes." To which Dr. Bell snapped, "My dear sir, I am Sherlock Holmes."

Dr. Bell was, indeed—as Arthur Conan Doyle admitted in his autobiography.

Important trifles

Sherlock Holmes' rules for deduction and analysis merely echoed the real-life gospel of Dr. Bell. "I always impressed upon my students the vast importance of little distinctions, the endless significance of trifles," Dr. Bell once said.

"Nearly every handicraft, for example, writes its sign manual. The scars of the miner differ from those of the quarryman. The carpenter's callosities are not those of the mason. The soldier and sailor differ in gait. And with a woman, especially, the observant doctor can often tell exactly what part of her body she is going to talk about."

SUPERSLEUTHS. *On the right, Conan Doyle's creation, Sherlock Holmes. Behind, Dr. Joseph Bell, the university lecturer used by Conan Doyle as the model for his famous detective. The author once told an interviewer that Bell's powers of observation were so acute that he could diagnose a patient's illness and give details of his past life before the man had even opened his mouth. He taught his students the "vast importance of little distinctions, the endless significance of trifles."*

Dr. Bell believed that the development of observation was a necessity to doctors and detectives, but that every man can transform his world from one of monotony into one of excitement and adventure by developing the faculty.

One afternoon Dr. Bell was at his desk in Edinburgh's Royal Infirmary when someone knocked. "Come in," he called. A man entered. Dr. Bell stared at him. "Why are you worried?"

"How do you know I am worried?"

"The four knocks. Unworried people content themselves with two, or at the most three."

The man was worried.

Conan Doyle himself told of one example of Dr. Bell's skill. In silence Dr. Bell studied an outpatient, then spoke.

"Well, you've served in the army, in a Highland regiment, and you're not long discharged."

"Aye, sir."

"You were a noncom officer, stationed at Barbados?"

"Aye, sir."

Dr. Bell turned to his students. "You see, gentlemen, he was a respectful man but did not remove his hat. They do not in the army, but he would have learned civilian ways had he been long discharged. He has an air of authority, and he is obviously Scottish. As to Barbados, his complaint is elephantiasis, which indicates the West Indies." Conan Doyle was sufficiently impressed by this incident to reproduce it closely in his Holmes story *The Greek Interpreter.*

Doyle graduated from Edinburgh University in 1881. He put up his oculist's plate and waited for patients. Six years later he was still waiting. Desperate for any kind of income, he turned to writing. After one false start, and under the influence of Émile Gaboriau and Edgar Allan Poe, he decided in 1887 to try a detective story. And for it he wanted a new kind of detective.

"I thought of my old teacher, Joe Bell," Doyle recalled in his autobiography. "If he were a detective, he would surely reduce this fascinating but unorganized business to something nearer an exact science. It is all very well to say that a man is clever, but the reader wants to see examples of it—such as Bell gave us every day. The idea amused me. What should I call the fellow?"

He called him Sherlock Holmes, after a cricketing acquaintance and the American jurist Oliver Wendell Holmes.

COUNT DRACULA

Was the fanged demon based on a human tyrant?

Count Dracula, the Transylvanian vampire, has haunted the imagination of the world for fewer than 100 years. But the bloodsucking creatures of which he has become the horrible chief have lurked in the legends of Europe since the ninth century.

The fanged noble came out of the shadows in 1897—in the pages of the Irish author Bram Stoker's novel *Dracula.* And it seems that Stoker partly based his diabolical character on a real Rumanian tyrant, Vlad V. For Vlad, nicknamed the Impaler, was also known as *Draculaea,* the Rumanian word for "son of the Devil."

Vlad ruled Wallachia, now part of Rumania, from 1456 to 1462. In those six years he is said to have executed 40,000 people by impaling them on long stakes. No one was immune from his brutal whim: captives in his wars with Turkish invaders, noble hangers-on in his own court, even priests and holy men who were usually revered.

He was well known, too, for his directness in diplomacy. On one occasion he nailed the slipper of the Turkish Ambassador to his skull and sent him back to Constantinople in a litter, thus expressing his contempt for all Turks.

Stake through the heart

Stoker, who never visited Transylvania but researched his novels in the British Museum, knew the vampire legends and knew that to kill an "undead" body a stake had to be driven through its heart. It seems that Vlad's habit, which Stoker heard about from a Hungarian historian, pierced the author's imagination and vibrated a chord that has quivered the nerves of readers ever since.

Stoker may have been further inspired by another bloody noble—the Hungarian Countess Elizabeth Bathory. She was the wife of Gen. Ferencz Nadasdy and lived at Csejthe Castle in the dark Carpathian Mountains.

BLOOD AND THUNDER. *Actor Christopher Lee is another in a long line of film Count Draculas. Author Bram Stoker (inset), who created Dracula, was once manager to actor Henry Irving.*

While her husband was away on his numerous military campaigns, the beautiful countess gathered around her a sinister band of witches, sorcerers, and alchemists who indulged her in her belief that drinking and bathing in the blood of young girls would preserve her beauty.

In the dead of night the countess and her henchmen would crisscross the countryside in a black coach hunting for girls. Any they found were kidnapped and driven back to the castle.

There, the girls were tortured and hung on chains while their blood was drained to fill the countess' bath.

News of her reign of terror finally reached the ears of Hungarian King Matthias II. When his men searched the castle, they found scores of bodies hanging from chains in the dungeons.

Entombed alive

At her trial in 1611, the countess was convicted of murdering some 50 girls. Her accomplices were beheaded or burned at the stake. But Countess Elizabeth Bathory herself escaped execution because of her noble birth. Instead, she was condemned to a living death—walled up in a tiny room in the castle of doom and kept alive only by scraps of food pushed through a small slit. She died four years later, still in her tomb.

There is a spine-tingling echo of the countess' fate in Stoker's short story called *Dracula's Guest.* In the story a man journeying to Castle Dracula and seeking shelter from a storm in a cemetery finds the tomb of a noblewoman—with an iron stake driven into her coffin.

The "vampire" children

Like many stories that have been absorbed into folklore, the vampire legend has some medically factual backing. During the late Middle Ages, interbreeding among eastern European nobles led to various genetic disorders, including a rare disease known as erythropoietic protoporphyria. The disease itself was not diagnosed until the 19th century, but from records of the time doctors are now convinced that many so-called vampires were in fact victims of this disease. Since sufferers rarely lived long, most would have been children.

The disorder makes the body produce too much porphyrin—a substance basic to red blood cells. This results in redness of the skin, eyes, and teeth, a receding upper lip, and cracks in the skin that bleed when exposed to light.

Doctors of the time could treat the condition only by locking the patients away during the day and by encouraging them to drink blood to replace what they lost by bleeding. But rumors of these nocturnal blood drinkers could have led to a spate of vampire stories in the region—and encouraged Stoker to set Castle Dracula in the strange eastern European land of Transylvania.

MANTLE MAKETH MAN

The checkered pedigree of fashion

Bathing suits owe their existence to George Stephenson, the pioneer of the railway age.

Annual seaside holidays were made possible by the coming of the railroad, for coastal towns were quick to point out the therapeutic advantages of saltwater bathing, hitherto regarded as the province of eccentrics.

There were no swimming suits at that time. Men and women disported themselves in the surf naked—though on separate beaches. Victorian rectitude began a long, hard struggle to restore the proprieties.

Between 1855 and 1865 *The Times* of London extensively covered the scandal of naked bathing. For instance, a Dr. J. Henry Bennett returned from a holiday in Biarritz aglow with enthusiasm for a French innovation. He wrote to *The Lancet:* "Both ladies and gentlemen wear what is called a Bathing Costume. With the ladies, it consists of woolen drawers, and a black blouse descending below the knees and fastened by a leather girdle. The gentlemen wear a kind of striped sailor's costume."

The answer had been found, and swimming was to remain relatively respectable until the advent of the bikini—so devastating in its effect on the fashion scene that it was named after an atomic explosion on Bikini Atoll in the Pacific.

While the controversial bikini is a fairly recent means of attracting attention, a woman's hair has always been regarded as one of her most exciting features. Until very recently women were required to wear hats in church, in obedience to a medieval ecclesiastical ruling forbidding them to expose their hair lest the thoughts of men be distracted from higher things.

The terrifying topper

Male headgear, too, has had its brushes with authority. In 1797, when James Hetherington gave the top hat its first public airing in London, an immense crowd collected around its embarrassed inventor. So intense was the crush that several women fainted. Dogs barked, children screamed, and a boy had his arm broken.

Hetherington was arrested and charged with a breach of the peace, having "appeared on the public highway wearing upon his head a tall

BEACH BELLES. *By the 1860's girls wore bathing suits of modern serge. Earlier belles either wore nothing at all or plunged into the water wearing vast canvas smocks.*

structure of shining luster and calculated to disturb timid people." The innovating Hetherington was bound over to keep the peace in his own recognizance of $2,500.

That other badge of Victorian gentility, the bowler, arrived about 50 years later. Apparently, there was no comparable flutter when William Coke, a Londoner, produced his notion of a more practical headgear for riding.

Coke envisaged a low-crowned hat of hard felt, firmly reinforced, and submitted some sketches to the hatting firm of Lock's of St. James's. They in turn submitted the problem to a manufacturing house whose owner was a man called Beaulieu—from whose name (pronounced in French "Bowl-yer") the name of the hat is derived.

Lock's, however, piqued at the idea of publicizing a mere subcontractor, refers to the bowler to this day as a "coke" or "hard felt." In the United States it is called a derby, because Lord Derby was the first to popularize the hat here.

Coke's innovation in male headgear is only one of the fashions whose origins may be traced back to man's long association with the horse.

Man and horse

For example, the most formal evening wear, the tails suit, was the hacking jacket of some 175 years ago. The front was cut away so that the knees of the wearer should not become entangled while his feet were in the stirrups. The stripes down the sides of the trousers are all that remain of a fly down the legs, which allowed them to be closely buttoned in the manner of breeches. The tails are divided to fall comfortably on each side of the horse.

Though the horse has been eclipsed as a means of transport, its influence lingers still. Cross pockets—pockets placed at the front of the trousers—were admirably suited to the horseman but were abandoned in favor of side pockets as man took to the automobile. Then, as trousers became tighter, the cross pocket made a triumphant return. Convenience yielded to fashion.

Many aspects of male attire are leftovers from early fashions. The buttons on the cuff, which once closed the wristband against inclement weather, are useless nowadays, yet few tailors omit them. A really first-class suit is still identified by the fact that it not only has buttons on the cuff but also has real buttonholes into which they are fastened. Curiously, buttons were worn for nearly 4,000 years simply as decorations and had no functional use until well into the late Middle Ages.

A man's jacket always buttons left over right so that the flap of loose material will not impede the swift drawing of a long-vanished sword. It is said that the woman's jacket fastens

TAILS FOR ALL SEASONS. *In the back of the modern tailcoat are two buttons—reminders of the days when the tails were buttoned back to facilitate a gentleman's ascent to the saddle.*

IRON CHANCELLOR. *Prince von Bismarck wears a tunic from which lapels derived.*

INFORMAL HUSSAR. *Tunic undone, Marshal von Mackensen shows his lapels.*

right over left in order to facilitate breast feeding, while the child is supported by the stronger right arm. Lapels almost certainly evolved from the wrap-over standup collar style of Prussian military uniforms. When the wearer was off duty, he would unbutton the confining tunic across the chest and at the throat. The fronts would then fold back in two triangles of material cut in almost exactly the same way as the present-day collar and lapels.

One of the buttons, incidentally, is still retained in some jackets at the top of the lapel, together with a small flap of cloth. In more elegant days this used to house the bouton-niere—a small posy of flowers.

Many dress innovations evolve from practical adaptations of an earlier age. Trouser turnups, for example, evolved initially out of the habit of turning up one's trousers to avoid contact with the mud of Victorian and Edwardian streets.

But because a gentleman was never at par-ticular pains to look after his clothes—he had servants to do it for him—the habit was consid-ered rather vulgar. *The People*, of September 23, 1894, quotes an American observer: "I have never seen men of fashion in London turn up their trousers under any circumstances. In wet weather they take cabs, but to appear on Rotten Row in the season with his trousers turned up would be justly considered a serious breach of decorum."

Only after the First World War, when the Prince of Wales turned up his trouser bottoms, were gentlemen persuaded to follow suit.

His Royal Highness was probably responsi-ble for more innovations in dress than any other

personage in the last 50 years. He is credited, among other things, with popularizing suede shoes, Fair Isle sweaters, midnight-blue dinner jackets, wide shirt collars, and, of course, the revolutionary Windsor knot in the tie.

COLORFUL PRINCE. *Among the many fashions popularized by the Prince of Wales (later Duke of Windsor) was the Fair Isle sweater.*

But even these notable achievements pale beside those of his grandfather, Edward VII, whose improvisations include pressing the trousers down the front and back of the leg instead of down the sides; the wearing of white waistcoats and stiff dickey shirts in the evening; and the introduction of the homburg hat to Britain. He is also held responsible for the curious habit of leaving the bottom waistcoat button undone. Apparently, his waistline advanced too rapidly for his tailor to keep up with it.

But despite his fondness for his own inventions, he frowned on any member of his circle who attempted experiments of his own. When Lord Harris had the temerity to appear in the Royal Enclosure at Ascot wearing a somewhat cheerful tweed suit, the King looked him over with a baleful eye. "Mornin', Harris," observed His Majesty coldly. "Goin' rattin'?"

A good deal of fashion comes from following the examples of famous people. The long coat, it is said, was first worn by Louis XIV to conceal his bandy legs—whereupon even straight-legged courtiers followed his example.

Sartorial immortality

On the other hand, some men have achieved immortality by having garments named after them. The raglan sleeve, for instance, is named after Lord Raglan, the Crimean War field marshal. The sleeve, which slants up the shoulder to the neck, was the result of his thoughtfulness in clothing his soldiers in sacks as an extra layer of clothing against the savage Russian winter. A hole for the head and a slightly caped effect gave the lead for the innovation.

The cardigan came from another Crimean warrior, the Seventh Earl of Cardigan, who led the charge of the Light Brigade.

The blazer, surprisingly enough, is not so called because it is a blaze of riotous color but because the captain of HMS *Blazer* decked his crew out in a brass-buttoned striped livery in the 1840's before there was an official naval uniform.

Many fashions, of course, are the result of slow evolution through the centuries. Originally, the tie was simply a drawstring at the neck of the shirt, while the shirt itself was underwear and not supposed to be seen at all. But garments tend to work outward, as in the case of the halter, which is, after all, no more than a visible brassiere.

MERRY MONARCH. *Edward VII (1841–1910) is seen here wearing a homburg hat and double-breasted coat—both his own innovations.*

The loose cloth once worn about the neck evolved into a collar and was later elaborated into the cravat—named after the Croatian Guards at the court of Louis XIV who popularized the style. In the 18th and early 19th centuries, the cloth was wound several times around the neck and tied in a flouncing bow. In the bow tie it has been simplified to a pair of short, hanging folds.

Hats also reflect this evolutionary process. Hatters continue to tuck a tiny, brightly colored feather into the hatband of soft felt hats—a reminder of the days when hats were decorated with plumes. The band itself is all that remains of a ribbon that allowed the hat to be adjusted to the head size of the wearer.

Travelers and empire builders have made several contributions to our wardrobes. Pajamas were adapted from the normal day wear of northern India, though their name is derived

ROYAL GRACE. *In this portrait of 1682, the Duke of Bourgogne, son of the Dauphin, is wearing a cravat, named after the Croatian Guards.*

from that of the full, baggy trousers worn by ladies in Persian harems. The so-called safari-style jacket is an adaptation of the bush shirt, long favored by old Africa hands, which was in itself a version of the belted tweed Norfolk jacket introduced by Victorian explorers.

HM's stockings

King Henry VIII started a fashion and an industry when he pulled on a pair of hand-knitted stockings imported from Spain in 1547.

In 1600, when Sir Walter Raleigh was Governor of Jersey, he sent Queen Elizabeth a pair of machine-knit "Jersey Stockes," which so delighted her that she granted Jersey a license to trade freely in knitted articles.

Apart from the obvious connection of Jersey with knitted sweaters, it is interesting to note that the Elizabethans used the word "stockes" when referring both to stockings and the wood-

en leg halters used to imprison criminals for minor offenses.

Despite the efforts of the immortal Jeeves, the effect of servants upon fashion has been mainly a negative one. Living in close proximity with the gentry, they either adapted their styles by taking over the hand-me-downs of their employers or had the fashions forced upon them. This is especially true of formal dress; and so great is the gentleman's terror of being mistaken for a butler or footman that the moment servants are attired in something approaching his own dress, then that particular fashion is dead.

Tails doomed

The rise and fall of the evening dress tailcoat is an excellent example of this process. Though it is still worn on occasions hallowed by tradition—the opera, formal dinners, and the like— it was doomed as general evening wear as soon as it was seen on the backs of waiters.

It was this factor more than any other that helped to popularize the dinner jacket—a garment of truly international ancestry. It began in mid-19th-century Europe as the smoking jacket, which gentlemen wore at informal evening activities. Then, in 1886, Griswold Lorillard electrified American society by appearing at the Autumn Ball of the Tuxedo Park Club near New York City in a short jacket with satin lapels.

Le smoking

And so the tuxedo was born, though France still knows it as *le smoking* and Great Britain calls it the dinner jacket.

Despite its adoption by orchestras in the 1920's and 1930's it managed to survive. The musicians wore white or colored jackets; only the customers wore black.

It was the inclusion of breeches and stockings in servants' livery that eventually excluded them from the gentleman's wardrobe, though they were a long time dying. In the 1820's the Duke of Wellington was refused admission to his club because he arrived wearing trousers instead of breeches.

During the same period students at Oxford and Cambridge Universities were marked "absent" if they appeared wearing trousers.

As the 20th century progresses, so the number of dress taboos decreases. The dictators of fashion are no longer royalty and aristocrats— but pop stars and actors.

SONG AND DANCE

The men who wrote the world's favorites

Rock of Ages. The Rev. Augustus Montague Toplady was taking a stroll in Somerset, England, when a violent storm forced him to take shelter in the cleft of a large rock. The date is not known, but it was some time between 1762 and 1775.

While taking shelter from that storm, Toplady, then a curate in Somerset, composed the words and music of one of the best known of all hymns, "Rock of Ages, Cleft for Me." Anxious to get the words on paper, he is said to have written the verse on the only piece of paper on his person—a playing card.

Home Sweet Home. The words of this most sentimental of all Victorian ballads were written by an American, John Howard Payne, who had no home.

He wrote "Home Sweet Home" in the 1820's to the music of an Englishman, Henry Rowley Bishop. As late as 1851, Payne wrote to a friend: "It is strange that it should have been my lot to cause so many to boast of the delights of home when I never had a home of my own and never expect to." However, later he did find a roof over his head when he became American consul in Tunis.

Bishop was a well-known London conductor and the first musician ever to be knighted. When "Home Sweet Home" was first heard, he was accused of stealing the tune from Sicilian sources. But eventually it was acknowledged that he had composed the tune himself as a national anthem for Sicily in his opera *Clari, or the Maid of Milan*.

Colonel Bogey. This stirring marching tune—it was the song used in the movie *Bridge on the River Kwai*—owes its origin to a British Army officer who was playing golf on an English course in 1913.

Maj. F. J. Ricketts, who was bandmaster of the Argyll and Sutherland Highlanders, happened to be on the fairway when a colonel wanted to drive off from the tee. Instead of shouting "Fore!" the colonel whistled two warning notes at the major. They stuck in Ricketts' head, and later he wrote them down as the first two notes of a new march.

He called it "Colonel Bogey" in memory of the whistler. In American golfing terms "bogey" refers to a hole scored in one over par, par being the number of strokes a good player should require to hole the ball.

Major Ricketts, who composed 17 other marches, wrote under the name of Kenneth Alford. No words were officially put to his tune, but in both World Wars anonymous British barracks poets wrote bawdy lyrics that were sung with gusto.

Major Ricketts became director of music of the Royal Marines in 1926. He died in 1944, knowing that his march had inspired two generations of soldiers.

Paul Jones. It is generally agreed that the Paul Jones, the "change-your-partners" dance, is named after John Paul Jones, the American naval commander. But there are several theories about why this brilliant, dashing sailor should be linked with the ballroom.

John Paul Jones, who was born in Scotland in 1747, saw service with both the American and the Russian Navies. He became known as "the sailor England feared."

Some say that the men in the dance change partners in the way that Jones abandoned his own ship to go to seize another that lay grappled alongside. Others believe that the dance got its name because Jones was a notoriously fickle lover.

The Tarantella. A strange sickness kept striking the southern Italian port of Taranto. It was said to be caused by the bite of the tarantula spider, and the only cure was to dance madly and sweat

DULCE DOMUM. *Victorians decorated their walls with the title of Payne's sentimental song.*

out the spider's poison. Fortunately, Taranto had a special wild dance to work the cure. Called the tarantella, it caught the imagination of many composers by its frenzied, death-cheating rhythm.

But doctors, who investigated the disease of tarantism and its cure, found little proof that people suffered from spider bites or that the dance was much of an antidote if they did. They came to the conclusion that tarantism was a myth.

Historians now believe that, in the pre-Christian era, Taranto was a cult center for the rites of the Greek god Dionysus—the Roman Bacchus. These rites always included drunken, licentious festivities and frenzied dancing.

Naturally, the Christian Church expressly forbade the cult of Dionysus and its feasts. But

DANSE MACABRE. *People of Taranto, Italy, believed that the tarantella cured them from the bite of the tarantula (inset). Probably the dance survived from Bacchanalian rites.*

in Taranto the dancing was so popular that it was maintained, though ostensibly for another and more respectable purpose—as a medical treatment. It has survived as a folk dance.

The Marseillaise. Ironically, the stirring French national anthem has twice been banned because of its revolutionary connections—and the man who commissioned it, himself an aristocrat, ended on the guillotine.

It was written in Strasbourg, the French city on the Rhine, in the desperate year of 1792. Three years after the storming of the Bastille, France was still in the throes of revolution, and Austria had declared war on her. The mayor of Strasbourg called for a rousing marching song in order to fire the revolutionary troops with enthusiasm.

In the city's garrison was a captain of engineers, Claude Joseph Rouget de Lisle, who answered the appeal by composing in one night what he called "War Song for the Army of the Rhine." On the way to Paris volunteers from Marseilles sang the anthem with such gusto that the Parisians attributed it to them and it became known as "La Marseillaise."

A decree of July 14, 1795, confirmed Rouget de Lisle's song as the French national anthem, but it was outlawed because of its rabble-rousing nature when Napoleon came to power, and it remained banned until the July revolution of 1830. Banned again by Napoleon III, it was not restored as the country's national anthem until 1879.

P. F. Dietrich, meanwhile, the wealthy mayor of Strasbourg who commissioned the song, had, like so many other aristocrats, gone to the guillotine.

The Star-Spangled Banner. The melody of the American national anthem was written by an Englishman—and was not officially adopted by the United States until 117 years after the words had been composed.

In 1814 America was at war with Britain—the only war the two countries fought since the American Revolution. As the British were shelling Fort McHenry, near Baltimore, a young American, Francis Scott Key, went to ask them to release a friend who had been taken prisoner some time before. A naval commander agreed to his friend's release but kept both men in protective custody until the attack was over.

Throughout the bombardment the Stars and Stripes fluttered over the fort, and in the end the British had to admit failure.

Key, his heart aglow with patriotic fervor as he gazed upon the scene, set about writing a poem on the back of an envelope:

> *Oh, say can you see by the dawn's early light*
> *What so proudly we hail'd at the twilight's last gleaming,*
> *Whose broad stripes and bright stars through the perilous fight*
> *O'er the ramparts we watch'd were so gallantly streaming?*

While writing his lyrics, Key had had the tune in mind—a melody used at hymn meetings. Ironically, it had been written in England by John Stafford Smith (1750-1836) as an anthem for a London social club.

It was not until 1931 that an act of Congress adopted Key's song as the official American national anthem.

There's a Long, Long Trail a-Winding. For the American and British troops slogging through the mud and dust in the First World War, the long, long trail they sang about was right before their eyes. And the land of their dreams that it led to was across the seas in Britain and the United States. But when Alonzo Elliott, a student at Yale University, wrote the song, he was thinking not about the trenches of Flanders but about Napoleon's retreat from Moscow.

Elliott wrote the music in 1913 and tried to sell it in America but could arouse no interest among music publishers. When he went to England in 1914 to complete his studies at Cambridge, the song was snapped up. It sold 4 million copies and was even more popular in the United States than in Britain.

With the many thousands of dollars the song brought him, Elliott studied how to write operas. In 1952 his song "There's a Long, Long Trail a-Winding" was used by 20th Century-Fox in the movie *What Price Glory?*

Tipperary. The song, which all over the world is associated with the British Tommy marching off to the First World War, was written as the result of a bet in a pub at Stalybridge, Cheshire, England, in 1912.

Jack Judge, who wrote the words, and his musical friend Harry J. Williams were challenged by a group of actors to write a song and perform it in the same day.

They did. Within 24 hours "It's a Long, Long Way to Tipperary" was complete, and Judge had sung it himself at the Stalybridge Grand Theatre.

PART
5

The world of tomorrow 566

The world of tomorrow

•

SLOWING DOWN THE AGING PROCESS

Can science help man to grow old more slowly?

Aging begins at the moment we are born. The long process of running down and wearing out reduces the body's capacity to cope with illness, shock, and damage, so that even the most athletic must yield to the weight and toll of our years.

Some parts of the body, such as the brain and the muscles, develop and, barring accidents, gradually wear out. Others, such as skin cells and blood corpuscles, are renewed regularly every day, even up to the end of life, in a constant program of replacement.

But something seems to go wrong with the copying mechanism with age. The skin loses its elasticity, nerve cells lose their sensitivity, and the body as a whole becomes less resistant to disease and less able to adjust to strain or injury. Some cells may even become such poor copies of their active predecessors that the body may reject them.

Delaying this process is a matter of deep concern to most of us, and some researchers believe that by ensuring that, through injections, older people maintain the same hormone levels as younger people, cell replacement can carry on almost indefinitely.

Others have submitted the notion that the replacement system breaks down because of chemical reactions. In an attempt to reverse this process, rats and mice have been fed with massive doses of chemicals that reduce the oxygen content of the blood, while others have been given doses of DDT to stimulate the liver.

In some cases it appeared that aging processes were slowed down, although the precise reasons for this are not yet clear.

But the most promising method of retarding age is through diet. Laboratory animals given a balanced diet containing all the essential ingredients, but with the calorie intake reduced to only three-fifths the normal level, have shown a lifespan two-fifths longer than normal.

All the normal deteriorations in vigor and age-related complaints also occurred some 40 percent later than usual. The effect is to stretch the whole aging process.

In theory, then, the lives of humans might be made nearly half as long again. Reports of individuals in the Soviet Caucasus who have led unusually active lives well into their second hundred years appear to bear out the theory. All that is needed, it seems, is the perseverance to stick to the recommended diet for long enough. The main problem so far has been that the doctor could see whether the diet worked only when a patient eventually died after a lifetime following it—by which time the physician might well be dead, too.

But new ways are being found for measuring aging rates more quickly. By such methods as checking skin elasticity and the sharpness of a patient's hearing, it should soon be possible to check the diet against results in a matter of only a few years. Before long, therefore, the choice may be up to the individual—unrestricted eating or a longer, more active life.

THE ADVENT OF SUPERSOUND

Bringing "earsight" to the blind

Blind people usually possess one advantage over other people who *can* see: Their sense of hearing is far more acute. Sounds that most others would miss can carry a great deal of information to a sightless person. For instance, teams of blind children can enjoy fast-moving games of soccer with a bell inside the ball and a new hand-held ultrasonic device to guide them. And that sound-location system could help to build up an even more complete sound picture of a blind person's surroundings.

Bats, whose sight is poor, use a sound-location system to help them avoid obstacles in the dark. They send out pulses of sound waves, pitched at 50,000 cycles per second, far above the limits of the human ear, which can hear sounds up to frequencies of about 20,000 cycles per second. As the echoes bounce back off such obstacles as trees and walls, the bats are able to take appropriate action.

The first steps to help blind people to see with sound are based on exactly the same principle. The sound is emitted by an ultrasonic torch, shaped like a double-barreled version of an ordinary flashlight. It works in a similar way to a sonar unit on a warship or submarine.

The unit's transmitter sends out pulses of ultrasonic waves at the same frequency as the bat, and the receiver picks up the returning echoes. Because these are still above the frequency at which the human ear can pick them up, the echoes are filtered through circuits that turn them into clearly audible "bleeps" before passing them into headphones.

This means that a person holding the torch can point it ahead of him and "scan" the area for obstacles over a range of about 25 feet. If there are no return echoes coming through the headphones, then there is nothing in the way.

If echoes *do* come back, then the closer the obstruction, the faster the succession of bleeps, and the deeper the pitch of each. With practice the torch could help a blind person to lead a more normal life—without needing someone to guide him. Experienced operators of the torch system claim they can distinguish grass from bushes, trees, posts, and curbstones.

Hearing with spectacles

But before blind people can be helped to feel really independent, the system needs to be more streamlined. At present, the experimental ultrasonic torch requires a shoulder bag to carry the battery cables for the power supplies and earphones, in addition to the torch itself. But miniaturization of electronic equipment is

"SEEING" WITH SONAR. *Prototype demonstration of the ultrasonic transmitter that, by means of sound waves, may enable the blind to locate the exact position of obstacles up to 25 feet away.*

making such rapid progress that it should not be long before the whole setup can be reproduced in a form small enough to fit into a pair of spectacles.

The transmitter and power supplies, with all the circuitry, would be packed into the bridge-piece above the nose. The sending and receiving sensors would be in the "lenses." And the filtered bleeps would come through the ear-pieces, as with hearing-aid spectacles. This would mean that scanning one's surroundings would become instinctive. The wearer would face in the direction he wanted to check and lift or lower his head just as a sighted person would.

THE CHANGING FACE OF MAN

How man may become an eggheaded cyborg in a million years

In science fiction the man of the future is often depicted as a weird and, to present-day eyes, repulsive monster. He may be a bald, eggheaded creature of superior intellect. He may be tall, with firm muscles, but covered in scales and with webbed hands and feet. He may be part human, part machine with replaceable, artificial limbs and organs, and immense strength—a combination known as a cyborg.

Oddly enough, these characteristics may be a description of what could happen to man in the next million years.

The already-established medical practice of transplanting living organs and tissue to replace damaged parts is a pointer to future development. Although still in its infancy, the technique of spare-part surgery could save millions of lives in tomorrow's world.

Today, man has the necessary surgical skills to carry out operations to replace almost every organ and limb in the body. All that surgeons now need to overcome is the rejection of "foreign" tissue by the body of the recipient.

Rejection is basically caused by the body's own defenses. White blood cells and antibodies attack and digest foreign cells in the body. So far, surgeons have tried to overcome this by using drugs that suppress these defense mechanisms. But this method can lower the body's resistance to infection, which in turn can lead to death.

Just as somebody needing a blood transfusion can accept it only from a donor whose blood group is compatible with his own, so there are compatible and incompatible tissue groups. Researchers are trying to improve the methods of matching types of tissue to prevent rejection without impairing a patient's resistance to infection. In the United States attempts are being made to perfect a synthetic

NEW PARTS FOR OLD. *Future man will prolong life and activity and maintain appearance by replacing defunct organs with transplants or synthetic spare parts. Some are already here. Others are the possibilities envisaged.*

1. *Liver*
2. *Heart*
3. *Lungs*
4. *Kidney*
5. *Pancreas*
6. *Metal or bone skull plate*
7. *Wig to cover surgery scars*
8. *Silicone skull plug*
9. *Artificial acrylic cornea*
10. *Silicone, acrylic, or glass eye*
11. *Contact lenses*
12. *Spectacles*
13. *False teeth*
14. *Silicone ear*
15. *Silicone chin*
16. *Plastic or silver windpipe*
17. *Hearing aid*
18. *Tube to drain water from brain*
19. *Rubber larynx*
20. *Battery-powered pacemaker*
21. *Metal upper arm*
22. *Plastic, fiber, or metal heart valves*
23. *Silicone breast implant*
24. *Arteries of concertina-pleated Dacron*
25. *Woven artificial vein*
26. *Metal elbow joint*
27. *Cap and hinge for elbow*
28. *Fiber patch for abdomen wall*
29. *Metal hip joint*
30. *Articulated artificial limbs*
31. *Silicone or acrylic testicles*
32. *Metal thigh support*
33. *Metal finger joints*
34. *Metal knee joint*
35. *Metal knee plate*
36. *Metal shinbone*

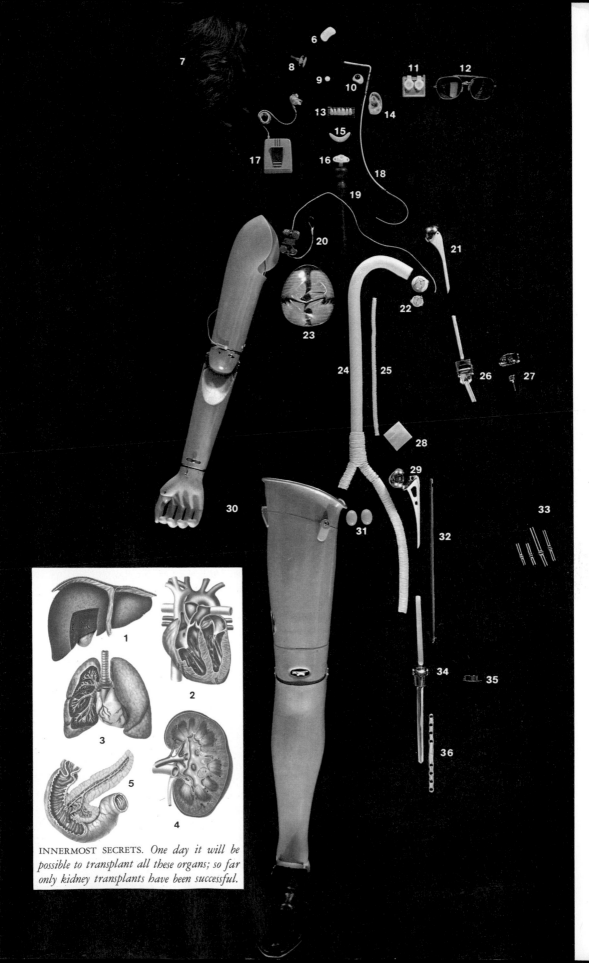

INNERMOST SECRETS. *One day it will be possible to transplant all these organs; so far only kidney transplants have been successful.*

blood that will not react to "alien" matter. Already the University of Cincinnati medical center has used a synthetic blood, made of inert, inorganic oxygen solvents, to keep rats alive.

Side by side with the transplant of living tissue, the development of manmade spare parts is progressing. But here too there are many complicated problems to be overcome.

Miniature powerpacks to drive artificial limbs, for example, are often too short-lived or too heavy. Materials that are acceptable to the human body, and at the same time totally reliable, are difficult to come by. And often, motors cannot respond as sensitively as the signals given out by muscles.

But all these problems are regarded by researchers as temporary. They could be solved virtually overnight as breakthroughs occur in materials' technology.

Already, experts in cybernetics—the science of feedback systems that are required for working artificial limbs—are developing ways of improving the sensitivity of manmade extensions to the human body.

While it is at present considered unlikely that such sensations as touch, temperature, pressure, and pain could ever be fed directly into the nervous system from an artificial sensor, there are other ways of passing on to the brain "information" about the outside world. Vibrations, sound tones, lights, or mild electric currents, for example, could be used as codes to inform the wearer of an artificial limb about the temperature and texture of objects around him.

But what about the long-term future of man? By studying man's adaptation to his environment over the last few million years, scientists can project some idea of future changes in man's appearance and capabilities.

From the squat, but upright, *Australophithecus* creature of about 5 million years ago, to *Homo erectus* of 500,000 years ago, man has evolved through variants of *Homo sapiens*, such as Neanderthal man of 70,000 years ago, to his modern form, *Homo sapiens sapiens*.

An American anthropologist, Harry L. Shapiro, has studied these physical trends and believes that future man, or *Homo futurus*, may be taller, have a dome-shaped, almost hairless head, an improved, slightly larger brain, and possibly lose his little toe. This new-look man, already envisaged in science fiction, should be around in about 500,000 years, according to Dr. Shapiro.

On the other hand, a Russian scientist, A. P. Bystrov, believes that man's evolution stopped long ago. He does not believe that *Homo futurus* will be any different from *Homo sapiens sapiens*. Bystrov's belief is supported by experts in the anthropology department of the Natural History Museum in London. They say there is little sign that *Homo sapiens sapiens* has shown much biological change since the last ice age.

Other scientists, concerned about overpopulation, envisage an offshoot of future man called *Homo aquaticus*, or water man. As earth's resources on land become depleted, it is thought that man could adapt to a marine environment, farming and mining the great floors of the ocean.

The adaptability of man is pointed to by Francisco Figueroa, of the University of Manila, who, in 1965, claimed he had found a 12-year-old "sea boy," who spent more time in the sea than on the Pacific island where he lived. He was an astonishing swimmer, weighed 168 pounds, but had only limited powers of speech. Without the benefit of a racing-dive start or flip-over turn in a swimming pool, the boy was said to be able to do 100 meters in only a few seconds more than the 51-second world record.

But before man could seriously contemplate living in the sea, he would require an artificial assist to his breathing capabilities. Dr. Johannes Kylstra, an American physiologist, has been experimenting with a liquid breathing system that he hopes will enable man to live and breathe underwater. He believes that a lung filled with water instead of air would be able to withstand the higher pressure of the outside water because liquids are virtually incompressible. Water would take the place of nitrogen or any of the other gases used in deep-diving mixtures as a carrier for oxygen.

Dr. Kylstra experimented with mice immersed in containers filled with saltwater through which he bubbled high-pressure oxygen. The animals managed to live in the containers for 18 hours without putting their heads above water. Dr. Kylstra claimed that the essential breathing mechanism of the mice's lungs was not impaired and that they took oxygen from water as easily as from air.

An American scientist, Dr. Walter Robb, has developed another technique designed to facilitate underwater life for man. He constructed a bubble made of fine, silicone rubber membrane, 1/1,000-inch thick, supported by a mesh-covered steel frame, that would provide an air supply direct from seawater. The membrane can allow gas, but not water, to pass through it. Such a membrane, with seawater flowing past it, would extract oxygen if the pressure on the inside were less than the oxygen pressure in the surrounding water. Dr. Robb claims that animals have lived inside such a membrane for extended periods.

Over thousands of years living underwater, man's body might eventually adjust to a new environment, so that he would ultimately need no artificial equipment at all to survive.

But, despite his adaptability, it is unlikely that man—without artificial aids—will ever develop into a superman.

While it may appear that men are growing stronger and more resilient, as new athletic records are broken from year to year, there are limits to the capabilities of the human frame. The main limitation is in man's ability to supply the oxygen required to renew the high-energy chemicals used in exercise. Calculations have been made of how long a physical effort can be sustained once the limit has been reached, and this has led to the prediction that no one is likely to run a mile in less than 3 minutes 45 seconds. The barrier of the four-minute mile seems to have been largely psychological, though credit for breaking it must also be given to modern training methods.

All the same, superman will remain in the realms of science fiction. But supercyborg—man raised to incredible strength and endurance through artificial limbs and organs—could very well be the form of future man.

OUTLOOK SUNNY

How man may overcome the energy crisis

Archimedes built a giant solar reflector, generally known as his "burning mirror," to concentrate the sun's rays on Roman warships and set them afire. Primitive tribes channeled ocean water into shallow pans, so that it would evaporate in the sun leaving its salt behind. We use oil to generate heat and electricity, and are in effect burning concentrated aeons of sunlight, for oil is nothing more than the product of centuries of plant and animal life, impacted under the earth. The sun, in fact, provides the basic source for almost all the energy on earth.

But the notion of trapping and storing the heat of the sun for conversion into heat, steam, or electricity is relatively new. And for Americans accustomed to creating energy from coal or oil, solar energy—cheap, nonpolluting, and ever-renewable—seems like a fairytale solution to the energy crisis. Nevertheless, solar enthusiasts believe that we are already well on the way to a functioning solar technology; and with concentrated, well-funded research, within a decade, the United States could have a solar industry that would supply a good proportion of our power needs.

Solar power

The term "solar power" covers a number of different and seemingly unrelated methods of creating energy. Wind energy, solar heating and cooling, bioconversion (transforming plantlife into fuel), ocean thermal technology, the transmutation of light into electricity are all energy systems that are powered by the sun. With the exception of solar heating and cooling, they are in the beginning stages of development—which means that even when theory proves out in practice, the costs are still too high for large-scale use. Tomorrow, or next year, the story may be very different.

Spotted here and there throughout the United States—especially in parts of the South and Southwest—are houses that seem completely conventional, except that their roofs are covered on the sunny side with large, flat panels. Called solar collectors, these panels are usually made of piping mounted on a flat, dark-painted surface and enclosed between two sheets of glass or plastic. Water or some other liquid is run through the pipes. Heated by the sun, the liquid can reach temperatures of $130°F$ or more. The hot water is piped to an insulated storage unit, and its heat is circulated via fans. The heat can also be used for cooling, by powering refrigerators and air-conditioners.

Solar collectors can heat, cool, and produce hot water for an entire house, if there is abundant sunlight and a source of electricity to power a fan and pump. In cold and cloudy climates, however, today's solar technology can provide only a portion of the heating needed.

Still, the future for solar power looks so promising that, in 1975 alone, the U.S. government appropriated $50 million to finance research. Large school buildings as far north as Minneapolis and Boston have been fitted with solar collectors. Blueprints for business buildings more and more include a solar plant as part of the heating and cooling system. And experts predict that by 1985 a billion-dollar solar-energy industry will provide 1 percent of the nation's total energy output—and substantially more as the century draws to a close.

Clean energy

At Odeillo in the French Pyrenees, a huge concave mirror gathers up and concentrates sunlight, generating temperatures of up to 7,000°F—hot enough to melt a crucible of steel. Since the sun is a completely clean source of energy—there are no polluting by-products, such as smoke or smog—the Odeillo crucible can manufacture rare alloys and pure single crystals, which must be produced under contamination-free conditions. A solar furnace, like the one at Odeillo, could be used to focus the sun's heat on a huge boiler, which would make steam to turn electricity-producing turbines. If some 10,000 square miles of Arizona desert were covered with mirrors and the necessary turbines and boilers, it is estimated that more than twice the electricity generated today in the United States could be produced.

Although few would relish the thought of a mirror-covered desert, the potential for solar power production in North America's hot regions is enormous. It is possible, for instance, to grow crops not for food but for fuel. Plant matter can be put under pressure to remove its water and the edible protein it contains; the remaining material, mostly cellulose, can be burned to produce heat or electricity. (In St. Louis an electric company burns shredded solid wastes together with coal and expects soon to be able to consume most of the solid wastes in the metropolitan area—thus simultaneously producing power and eliminating garbage.)

Plant materials heated in a vacuum give off gas and oil. For example, when the algae that grow in sewage are allowed to ferment in an airless environment, they produce methane, a fuel used to power engines and turn turbines.

Wind, another creation of the sun's rays,

offers still another energy-producing possibility. Wind generators, already in use today, can create enough electricity to power a house. Technologists foresee armies of huge windmills in windswept areas like the Great Plains or

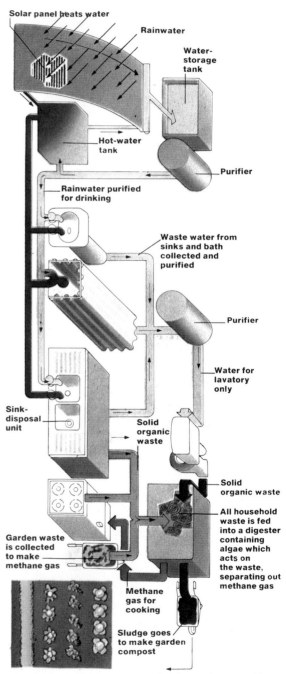

WASTE NOT, WANT NOT. *The future house's self-contained system (above) provides everything from water to gas for cooking.*

anchored off the northeastern U.S. coast, producing one-fourth of the nation's electricity.

A large proportion of the sun's heat is absorbed and stored in the surface layers of tropical oceans, while their deeper layers remain cold. It is possible to exploit the temperature difference to make electricity, using a turbine powered by a fluid—ammonia, for instance—which expands and becomes a gas when warmed by the surface water and condenses

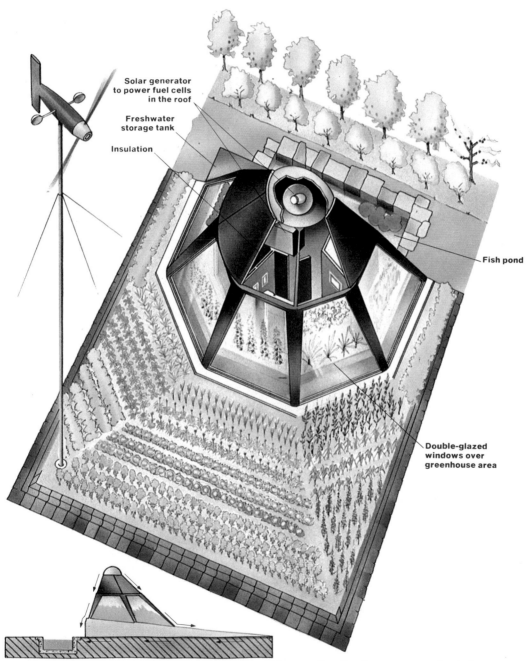

Solar generator to power fuel cells in the roof

Freshwater storage tank

Insulation

Fish pond

Double-glazed windows over greenhouse area

POWER FROM THE SUN. *The solar house of the future would be virtually self-sufficient. An outside wind generator would provide all the household power needed, stored in batteries in the basement. The sun would contribute energy for heating and growing greenhouse vegetables.*

back to a fluid when it meets the colder water pumped up from the ocean depths. Researchers in the field of ocean-thermal technology believe that we could have the first ocean-based power plant functioning in the Gulf Stream near Florida within eight years. By the turn of the century fleets of these plants could be producing about 4 percent of the nation's total energy.

Solar cells

All these techniques use sun power as a catalyst to create energy. It is also possible to convert sunlight directly into electricity. The solar cells used as energy generators in space satellites function as "photochemical reactors": When light strikes them, an electric current is created that can be used immediately or stored in batteries. The material used in the newest solar cells is silicon, which will last almost forever. But constructing a silicon cell is so expensive that mass production is virtually ruled out at present. (It would cost some $300,000 to power a house with the kind of silicon cells used in spacecraft.) However, a new technique for producing the cells in the form of a hair-fine ribbon promises to lower costs enough so that, if today's research is successful, electric plants using solar cells could be operating by 1985.

Another far-out possibility for solar-cell energy is the building of six-mile-long solar panels to orbit around the earth and beam the power they generate back to land on microwaves. But the technology and tools for space construction are still relatively primitive. The giant solar panel will have to wait until our space science is considerably more advanced.

The Geysers

In the search for alternative sources of energy, the use of geothermal heat is a possibility with almost as many variations as solar energy now seems to offer. Where easily accessible, the heat, steam, and hot water trapped in the earth, often under tremendous pressures, are already utilized for heating and energy production. The world's largest geothermal power plant, the Geysers, 90 miles north of San Francisco, uses the steam created naturally by a "hot spot" in the earth's crust. Tapping the steam, however, requires drilling, often to depths of two miles or more. The process is difficult and, because of the pressures involved, often dangerous.

The Geysers is one of the few "dry steam" facilities in the world. More common are plants that use wet steam—a mixture of steam and hot water. (Old Faithful, at Yellowstone National Park, is a wet steam geyser.) Power production from wet steam is more complicated because the water, often heavy with dissolved minerals, must be removed before the steam can be used. But steam fields are tapped today for heating homes in Iceland, Siberia, and in Oregon and

TURNING SUNLIGHT INTO ENERGY

THE FIRST solar furnace was built in the 18th century by the French chemist Antoine Lavoisier. He used two converging lenses to focus the sun's rays and produce high temperatures that melted iron and platinum.

Using the same principle, French engineers constructed a more complex solar furnace at Odeillo-Font-Romeu in 1970. The site is nearly a mile high in the eastern Pyrenees Mountains and is favored with 170 to 180 sunny days a year. The furnace has 63 large mirror panels that track the sun and reflect the light onto a reflector made up of 9,500 small mirrors. The curved reflector focuses the sun's rays onto a target area to produce thermal power up to 1,000 kilowatts, at a maximum temperature of about 7,000°F.

The Odeillo solar furnace has been used to melt metals and ceramics at high temperatures. Because the solar operation is pollution-free, the energy produced can be employed for contamination-free preparation of high-purity oxides such as alumina and lime. It is also used for pilot studies of simpler industrial furnaces and solar conversion systems.

Odeillo has shown that solar furnaces can now be used on a large scale to fire ordinary materials such as bricks and cement. And its experiments indicate that solar furnaces of the future can produce varying amounts of electrical energy—from a few hundred to millions of kilowatts—thus replacing diesel or thermal power stations. This bodes well for those developing countries where sunshine is plentiful but power sources are rare or nonexistent.

Idaho in the United States. The U.S. Geological Survey has identified a geothermal belt that runs through almost 2 million acres in the western states and Alaska. Here, where molten rock from the earth's interior has forced its way into the crust, forming the hot spots that create the heat and steam, are the potential future sites for more power plants—when our technology is finally capable of taming the earth's immense interior pressures.

Whether we utilize the sun, or tap the earth's heat, or both, depends largely on the research being done today. Although the funds appropriated by Congress seem paltry, compared with the funding for nuclear research (some $350 million earmarked for alternative energy programs versus almost $2 billion for nuclear research), the success stories continue to mount up.

Alternative sources of energy—not fossil fuel, which is a diminishing resource; nor nuclear power, which is potentially hazardous; but self-renewing, nonpolluting, cheap, and limitless solar or geothermal energy—may offer the brightest hope for the world's power systems of the future.

SALVATION FROM THE SEA

The oceans may become earth's larder

One of the greatest challenges facing mankind is feeding the world's ever-growing population. Vast new food sources must be found, for by the year 2000 there will probably be 7 billion people in the world, compared with 3.6 billion in 1970.

The sea is likely to provide much of the extra food. Oceans occupy 70 percent of the earth's surface area, yet so far their food potential has been exploited only in a haphazard way.

British marine zoologist Sir Alister Hardy forecasts that new techniques will allow divers to weed out unwanted fish that compete with edible breeds for food, paving the way for undersea "cowboys" to stage gigantic fish roundups in submarine "tractors."

In Britain popular fish, such as plaice, sole, and turbot, are already being bred on experimental fish farms at the Suffolk port of Lowestoft. Trout and carp are being produced in huge numbers from freshwater hatcheries at other centers. Similar farms operate in the U.S.

The oyster—cultivated long before the Christian era by the Chinese and Romans—is being turned rapidly into a thriving product of intensive farming. It is bred in brackish, shallow estuaries after starfish, oyster drills (snails), and other natural enemies have been eliminated from the area. In Japan oysters are cultivated in hanging farms (consisting of oyster shells attached to rods suspended from cast and spun concrete floats), which preserve them from predators lurking on the ocean bed.

In the Far East hopes for vastly increased fish harvests are pinned on the mackerellike Asian milkfish, whose larvae are collected from beaches in Taiwan, Indonesia, and the Philippines, then cultivated in manmade ponds.

But perhaps the most ambitious fish-farming project is envisaged by the Mexican government, which hopes to convert its huge coastal lagoons into the world's biggest fish farms, producing millions of tons annually.

Ocean fish farming will have its own inverted form of irrigation. Nuclear-powered blowers in the icy depths of the seabed will force up nutrition into the poorer surface layers. Chemi-

FOOD FOR MILLIONS. *The fastest growing known plant, the giant kelp, grows to a length of 200 feet, at a rate of 1½ feet a day.*

cal nutrients will also be introduced to the fish ranch, while giant mirrors on the surface will trap the sun's rays to encourage the growth of algae. The ranch hands themselves will have sea jeeps, miniature submarines, and remote underwater televisions to supervise operations.

By the end of the century it is likely that every possible fish product will be utilized. The Canadian government helped to set up a plant in Nova Scotia to convert waste from fish-processing factories into a near-tasteless powder containing 95 percent high-grade protein. The process is so cheap that it costs little more than $2 to provide a year's protein supply for an adult. And the powder can be processed further to look and taste like fish again.

Plant farming in the sea also offers the prospect of rich new food supplies. In most ocean areas light does not penetrate below about 160 feet, and plants cannot grow in darkness. But the black depths contain enough fertilizing materials from decayed animal and vegetable matter to support plantlife on land for centuries.

Biologists hope to find a way of lifting these fertilizers to within about 20 feet of the surface and so convert ocean "deserts" into flourishing areas of life. The number of fish would then increase dramatically.

Seaweed—a traditional food in Wales—is now used to a limited extent elsewhere as a processed-food additive. In Japan it is harvested and put into mincemeat.

But the most promising crop is the fastest growing plant on earth—the giant kelp. Off California it grows 200 feet long and up to 3 feet across at the base, with fronds extending at the rate of 1½ feet a day. This towering underwater plant stores mineral nutrients, such as iodine and potassium. So far, it has been used only in cattle food, but in the future it could become an important food source for man.

FARMING FISH. *In this fish farm biotrons in fish hives (lower left) contain spawn, which is carried by divers to hatcheries (left background), where the eggs are fertilized and then piped into corrals and reared under mesh at a depth of no more than 100 feet. A feeding device (center foreground) sends synthetic food on currents into the corrals. The fully grown fish are transported in tube-shaped containers by crane to waiting ships. Fish can also be raised in pens made of residue gases bubbling up from perforated pipes on the seabed (left rear).*

BLACK GOLD FROM THE SEA

Present-day oil rigs, although considered a marvel of modern technology, are actually inefficient and dangerous. In the future oil may be drilled and refined on the seabed. Storms, the chief hazard of surface rigs, will be avoided, while the crews, working four- or five-hour shifts, will live in undersea houses, breathing gases at the same pressure as the water outside. Slow depressurization to prevent the bends—killer of many divers in the past—will therefore be unnecessary until immediately prior to surfacing.

ALTHOUGH OCEANOGRAPHY, as a science, came into being more than 100 years ago, men have obtained most of their knowledge of the sea through instruments carried on ships. Few pioneer investigators have ventured down to the bottom of the ocean to explore its vast mineral resources. The new era of ocean studies may see men working on the ocean bed, with the aid of aqualungs, bathyscaphes, and undersea houses. Oil may be drilled on the ocean bed rather than from the surface. Balloon-shaped balls (above) hold the drills in place, while the crude oil is stored in containers (left) and pumped into a refinery (foreground), and then sent to the surface by pumps on the seabed (background left), or carried by giant underwater plastic tanks (center background), towed by submarines.

IRRIGATION FROM ICEBERGS

Turning mountains of polar ice into a freshwater supply

By the end of this century, giant tugs may be plying the South Atlantic, towing icebergs seven miles long to water the green fields of the Sahara.

More than three-quarters of the world's freshwater is locked up in the icecaps of the Arctic and Antarctica. These icecaps are created from snow that has fallen for the past 50,000 years or more. Thus they contain no trapped particles of salt, as sea ice does.

If only a fraction of this pure water could be transported to where it is needed, the parched areas of the world might be transformed into crop-bearing prairies.

Moreover, the water is ready packaged in an easily transportable form. Along the edges of the icecaps, icebergs are constantly breaking off, pushed by the pressure behind them. In the North Atlantic about 16,000 icebergs, some many miles long, are "calved" each year, mostly from the enormous glaciers along the shores of Greenland.

They slowly float away, their drift dictated by ocean currents, gradually melting in the sea. The closer they approach the warm waters of the Gulf Stream, the faster they disappear.

Many icebergs are too small to be towed very far without disintegrating. But some Antarctic monsters are as big as the Isle of Man; and one sighted in 1956 was more than 200 miles long and 60 miles broad. It covered an area of 12,000 square miles—bigger than Belgium.

It would be impossible, using any known technique, to tow an iceberg of this size. But engineers think it feasible to cope with one up to 7 miles long by 1½ miles wide. A tug as big as a supertanker could tow such an iceberg at a rate of about 20 miles a day.

An iceberg of this manageable size would contain more than 250,000 million cubic feet of water—as much as flows over Niagara Falls in two months. Such quantities would be sufficient to turn parts of the world's most forbidding deserts into rich farmland.

The Sahara, the Yuma desert of California, the Atacama of Chile, the dry wastes of Arabia and Western Australia all have the advantage of lying close to the sea. They are therefore open to irrigation without the prohibitive cost of long-distance pipelines.

Some of the ice would obviously melt during the voyage, particularly if it had to be made through tropical seas. But the melting would not be so great as might be deduced from observation of small icebergs, which last only a short time.

The bigger the berg, the smaller its outer surface in proportion to each ton of ice it contains. So, pound for pound, less heat gets into the big berg through its exposed surfaces from the sun, the atmosphere, and the sea.

The same principle can be seen in children's snowmen left in the garden after a thaw. The little snowman disappears in a few hours; the really big one sometimes takes weeks to melt.

Even with the giant tug envisaged, a seven-mile-long iceberg would perhaps require a voyage of 6 to 12 months from polar region to desert. But it should not be beyond the bounds of technology in the coming decades to improve this performance. And in many regions ocean currents could be used in the same way that airliner pilots utilize the 100- to 200-mile-per-hour jetstreams 10 miles above the earth to increase speed and cut down on fuel.

Irrigation system

Once the big iceberg reached its destination, there would be no need for expensive docking installations. The iceberg would simply be left near the shore to melt into the sea. Because freshwater is less dense than seawater, the melted ice would lie uncontaminated on the surface, while the displaced saltwater would sink.

The fresh surface water could easily be pumped ashore and into the irrigation pipeline system.

Greenland's icy mountain would have come at last to India's coral strand.

MAKING THE DESERT BLOSSOM

Can the Sahara again become the fertile plain it once was?

The arid moonscape of the Sahara covers millions of square miles of lifeless sand and rock, upon which the sun glares without respite. Except at oases, not a blade of grass or a drop of water relieves the monotony.

A man stranded there without shelter would die of heatstroke and dehydration within 48 hours. The superheated bone-dry atmosphere extracts the moisture from the body like blotting paper. Here and there, on the fringes of the wilderness, small numbers of nomads manage to scratch a precarious living, depending for their survival on animals, which crop the few pathetic strands of vegetation.

Yet fossils and cave paintings on the Tassili plateau indicate that thousands of years ago the Sahara was covered with luxuriant vegetation. And etched into this now dry and barren world are the traces of huge river systems and plentiful oases, which once supported numerous flourishing communities.

An American research team has put forward a theory as to why the land became a desert. They believe that goats, herded for centuries by every community of desert dwellers, devastated all the region's foliage, leaving the land exposed to soil erosion.

The source of the Sahara's problems is the

MAN'S BATTLE AGAINST THE DESERT. *Despite erosion and lack of moisture, experiments with plants and patterning prove that desert cultivation may be possible.*

soil itself. The lack of trees means there is no shade to prevent the sun burning off the surface water. The earth dries up, and the scant plant-life dies.

Unhelpful rains

As the ground itself grows hotter and hotter, the few rain showers that do fall sink uselessly into it, washing away the salts and trace elements, which could make it fertile, until only rocks and sand are left. In time the sand becomes so hot that many of the showers that leave the clouds never even reach the ground but evaporate on the way down.

So poor is the sand at retaining heat that the desert grows bitterly cold at night. The droppings of the nomadic herdsmen's animals become prized as fuel, and even that meager fertilizer is not returned to the land.

Yet the same sun that causes the Sahara's problems is the world's most powerful source of energy. But day after day it is squandered in heating up more than 3 million square miles of desert to temperatures of more than 130°F.

Focusing and concentrating this awesome power to create still hotter temperatures may seem the last way to improve conditions, yet this could be the first small step in making the desert bloom again.

Free electricity

Scientists in Spain and the Sahara have already used the sun's rays to generate virtually free electricity in huge quantities. This power can then be used to drive pumps and drilling machines to tap the vast reserves of water that have filtered down through the sands of the desert. Over the centuries these have formed enormous natural reservoirs thousands of feet under the arid surface.

Some deep wells have already been established for supplying the oil-prospecting teams at work in the desert. One drill, more than a mile down, produced a fountain of pure ice-cold water at the rate of 80 gallons a second in the parched heart of the Sahara.

Energy from the solar furnace can also be used to help with the "fixing" of nitrogen from the air to produce nitrogen-based fertilizers on an immense scale—food that could begin to put nourishment back into the sand.

Harnessed rays

In the short term even more use can be made of the sun by harnessing its ultraviolet rays. For example, they can be used to refine heavy oil into high-grade fuels, and at nominal cost they can speed up production of insecticides to clear the scourge of malaria from existing oases and village wells.

But the greatest use of the sun's radiation is to stimulate the growth of algae, the simple microscopic plants that thrive in the most hostile conditions. By exposing a mixture of raw chemicals to the sun's rays, man can obtain a burgeoning crop of algae, an adequate source of food for humans and animals alike in the parched desert. In the long term—given chemi-

HOPE FOR THE FUTURE. *While no trees have yet been grown to maturity in desert conditions, researchers hope they can be made to thrive.*

PUTTING DOWN ROOTS. *Trees will be vital in the cultivation of desert. Their shade would cool the earth and let rainfall be held in the soil.*

cal fertilizers, water, and power—men could begin to re-create the old fertile world that vanished thousands of years ago.

First they could lay a carpet of tarmac of any size and cover it with a layer of moisture-absorbing material. On top would go a thick layer of artificial soil, built up from dry desert sand, mixed according to a precise formula with all the minerals and elements present in normally fertile soil.

Reclaiming the soil

The results of experiments on these lines are astonishing. The combination of ample water, bright sunshine, and the right proportion of chemicals produces a rich harvest. Experimental farms on the fringe of the Sahara and Negev deserts are producing acres of corn and wheat, beans and peas, maize, onions, and barley.

The base layers of tarmac and moss capture the water and hold it at a depth where the plants' roots can easily reach it to drink their fill. Even the occasional showers that still fall right in the stony heart of the desert are put to good use instead of being left to evaporate or sink into the sand.

But this type of farming, however encouraging, is only a temporary victory. The new face for the desert will be assured only when trees can be grown successfully. There are two major obstacles: Trees require more complex conditions than crops in which to flourish, and they take longer to grow. While no trees have yet been grown to maturity in the desert, except at oases, researchers are hopeful that this will be possible over wide areas of the Sahara that are now all but useless to man.

Shade for the desert

Groves of fruit trees established on a large scale will then provide the shade that the desert so desperately needs. Gradually, the ground temperature will begin to drop, and rain will reach the earth and do its job properly. More trees will thrive, and the desert will grow progressively cooler and more fertile. There is no reason why the process should not work on a small scale at first. Then, as the fertile areas extend, their effect on the rest of the desert will multiply, until eventually the whole Sahara may be transformed into the rich, fertile area it once was. And all, ironically, thanks to the sun, which contributed to the desert's becoming a barren waste to begin with.

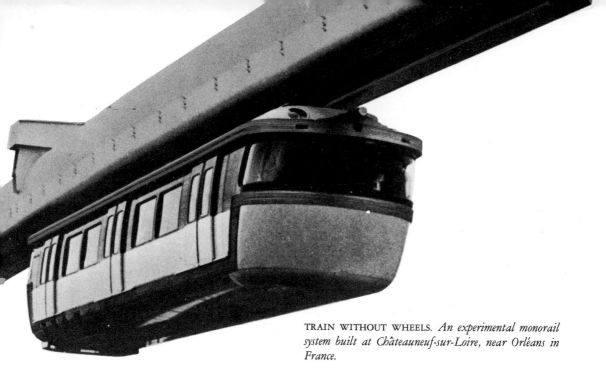

TRAIN WITHOUT WHEELS. *An experimental monorail system built at Châteauneuf-sur-Loire, near Orléans in France.*

WILL THE WHEEL SOON BE OBSOLETE?

Man's first great invention is reaching the end of the road

One of the most crucial steps on early man's long road to civilization was the invention of the wheel. Yet it looks as if the day of the wheel is over. Already, the wheel is running into problems as a means of transporting people and goods.

It was the airplane that signaled the beginning of the end for the wheel. Once an aircraft takes off, its wheels are useless and have to be folded away into the wings or fuselage so that they do not cause wasteful drag.

Now it is possible to take off without wheels. The development of directional jet nozzles, such as those on the Hawker Siddeley Harrier, is giving birth to a whole new generation of aircraft that can hover and land and take off vertically, like helicopters.

Many helicopters have landing skids in place of wheels. Unlike wheeled aircraft, they can touch down safely on almost any surface—sand, snow, ice, swamp, water, and rough or uneven ground. Even on paved runways the comfort is greater and the wear and tear much less. Tomorrow's vertical takeoff airliners and private planes are likely to adopt the same techniques.

The wheel is becoming a prisoner of its own disadvantages, even for transport that stays on the ground. The designers of high-speed train projects for intercity travel are anticipating problems with vibration, lubrication, and com-plicated suspension systems, all because the wheels have to be kept in contact with the rails.

The most likely future development seems to be Hovercraft suspension combined with power supplied by a linear motor—roughly like a normal electric motor slit down one side and then stretched out flat, parallel to the rails. This would eliminate wheels altogether, and with them all the present complex difficulties of wear and tear, vibration, and metal fatigue.

Punishing tests

Hoverpower provides its own cushioning effect. When engineers tested a hover-suspension system, they hammered it with punishing vibrations equivalent to those caused by two-inch bumps to a train traveling at 300 miles an hour. Yet the only movement that would have been transmitted to passengers in the coach was less than a quarter of an inch. Conventional wheels turning at these speeds would create vortices, or whirling pockets of air, under the train, causing drag and absorbing much of the power.

There are other advantages of hover suspension. Steel wheels on steel rails weaken and break up through metal stress at very high speeds. Wheel bearings can break, and there is always the possibility of derailment at full speed. Stopping a high-speed train running at maximum speed by normal braking multiplies the stresses several times over, and an emergency stop to avoid an accident might easily cause a far worse calamity should the suspension give way under the strain.

Letting air carry the weight instead of wheels—with no axle boxes to overheat or springs to break—avoids all these problems. Stopping ceases to be a strain—a linear motor can be put into full reverse power at the touch of a switch. This gives a powerful braking force with no dangers of slip, wheel locking, or vibration, because it acts on the main structure of the train and not through its wheels.

German engineers are designing an electromagnetic suspension system to drive the train, as well as carry it. British Rail also has investigated the possibilities of linear, motor-driven, high-speed passenger service.

The Council of Europe decided several years ago that, in its view, the future would be wheelless. After studying rival systems, the council opted for a 4,000-mile hover-train network covering the Continent—linking Brussels, Luxembourg, and Geneva with Paris, Hamburg, Milan, and France's channel ports.

The council decided that city-center routes for hover-train tracks would cause far less pollution and disruption than urban motorways of similar capacity.

The 500-mile-an-hour shuttle
The United States gravity-vacuum shuttle project is even more futuristic. This proposes an underground, 500-mile-an-hour intercity train, closely tailored to fit into a tunnel and driven by suction from powerful pumps with a steep downward gradient out of each station. The same force in reverse would bring it smoothly to a halt.

At such speeds wheels would be useless. The coach, cushioned upon and surrounded by a layer of air, would be between the walls of the tunnel—rather like the old-fashioned department-store vacuum system for transporting bills.

Space travel demands far higher speeds, and space vehicles are almost totally without wheels. The powerful rocket motors that make space flight possible are relatively simple, without the compressors and turbines of the jet engine. Long-distance spacecraft for exploring the farthest reaches of the solar system will have no landing and takeoff problems anyway; they will be assembled in orbit outside the atmosphere of the earth. This will save having to cater to the enormous stresses of taking off and landing under earth's gravity.

Relatively cheap space shuttles, combinations of rocket and glider, that can land on retractable legs or skids will fly between the spacecraft and the planet to be explored.

Last stronghold
Even the transporting of freight may eventually dispense with wheels. Hovercraft engineers are experimenting with bases supported on air cushions. With all the weight carried by the suspension, one man could push heavy objects around on such floating trolleys, even over bumpy surfaces, and place them exactly where they were required. A similar type of vehicle, already in existence, is the hover lawnmower.

For carrying small objects in bulk over long distances—like parcels through the mail, for example—there is no good reason why pipes could not carry these goods suspended in liquid. One such pipeline could carry a succession of different consignments, and branch pipelines and crossfeed pipes could allow door-to-door service, all without a wheel having to turn.

But one of the main developments in tomorrow's transport may hark back to the past—to the giant airships that vanished from the skies after the Hindenburg exploded and burned in 1937. The trip from Britain to Australia would take less than a week. And the ships could be fueled with cheap natural gas.

The last stronghold of the wheel may well be cars and trucks on which industry depends so heavily. Yet in more than half the world, road transport is still a relative rarity, because of the difficulty and expense of building highway networks. The hover car or hover truck, able to drive at will over sand, swamp, or grassland, is far more practical.

Even private transport must change eventually. As hoverpower grows cheaper and more efficient, wheel-less private cars will be able to leave roads and take to the countryside or water—provided man has devised adequate hover traffic controls.

The U.S. Army has experimented with personal, strap-on jet packs and one-man helicopters for lifting soldiers into battle. Civilian equivalents would give man a mobility never dreamed of.

The wheel may be reaching the end of its long road at last.

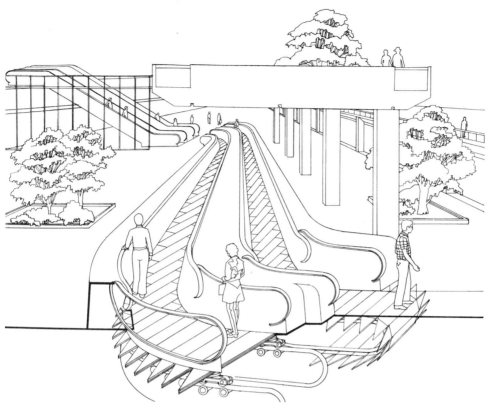

MOVING PAVEMENTS. *Cities of the future may well build 10-mile-per-hour integrators to swiftly carry people to work and shop without the misery of the rush-hour jams.*

A STEP AHEAD

Conveyor-belt pavements to beat the rush hour

Pedestrians in the cities of the future may speed through the streets at up to 10 miles an hour—just by standing still. For a network of moving pavements could slash traveling time in city centers and, by cutting out the necessity for buses and cars, end rush-hour jams forever.

Moving walkways, such as airport ramps, have been known for years, of course. But city authorities have fought shy of them because they are too slow for long-distance travel.

Now, however, Switzerland's Battelle Research Center, working with the Dunlop tire firm, has invented an accelerating device that makes high-speed moving pavements a practical proposition. Their invention means that pedestrians will be able to step on and off a high-speed network as easily as they now step onto an ordinary escalator.

The device, called an integrator, looks like a flat escalator. But at one end it moves at only 1.5 miles an hour—a comfortable speed for a pedestrian to step onto. At the other it can be traveling at up to 10 miles an hour—a little slower than the track record for the mile. At the fast end pedestrians could step across to a main pavement going at the same speed alongside. This main pavement, which could be covered to keep out bad weather, would link up with other pavements to give access to any destination on the future city network. And, unlike the present buses and subways, there would be no waiting lines.

As a pedestrian was approaching his destination, he would step onto a reversed version of the integrator; the pace would be gradually slackened, and he would be carried comfortably and slowly back to firm ground.

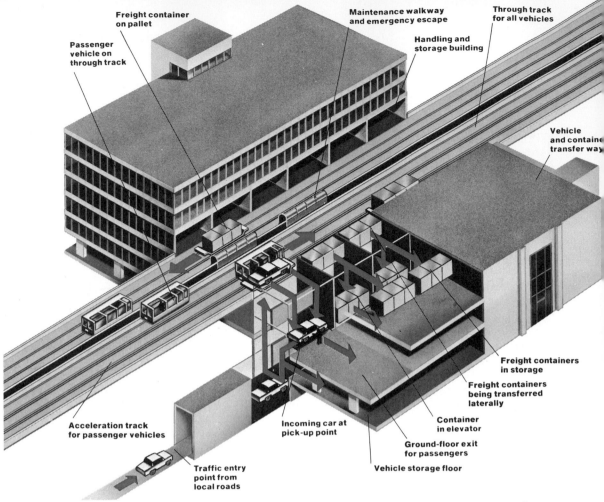

Freight container
on pallet

Passenger
vehicle on
through track

Maintenance walkway
and emergency escape

Through track
for all vehicles

Handling and
storage building

Vehicle
and container
transfer way

Acceleration track
for passenger vehicles

Incoming car at
pick-up point

Freight containers
in storage

Freight containers
being transferred
laterally

Container
in elevator

Ground-floor exit
for passengers

Vehicle storage floor

Traffic entry
point from
local roads

DREAMWAY. *This PAT system, designed for Puerto Rico, envisages an overhead motorway. In most metropolitan areas, however, it would be more convenient to have the garage space underground.*

ON THE RIGHT TRACK

Robot trucks could end road chaos

In a few decades the strain and tedium of highway driving could be a thing of the past—thanks to an American system of high-speed robot trucks called PAT. The system has been designed to combine the advantages of cars and trains; drivers using it will be able to sit back and relax, while the trucks whisk them toward their destination at a high speed—whatever the weather or the traffic.

PAT, standing for Palletized Automatic Transportation, was born at the Massachusetts Institute of Technology in 1968. It may be the key to faster, and safer, intercity travel.

The system could work like this. Drivers would take their cars or trucks, in the normal way, to the nearest interchange. There they would find an underground storage building or garage with a subway entrance from street level. To join the PAT system, the driver merely loads his vehicle onto a pallet that is waiting underground. An elevator will then transfer both the driver and his vehicle to ground level. There, the driver and his friends will board one of the PAT passenger vehicles while his car travels separately on a nearby pallet. Mounted on the passenger trucks will be a dial, and, by using this, he will be able to dial the nearest junction to his destination. Each vehicle will move at a precise two miles a minute until its dialed exit is reached, when, together with its pallet, it will be smoothly shunted off. Then the motorist will disembark, and, taking the elevator to the underground storage park, he will rejoin his car for the last stage of his journey.

AT THE SPEED OF THOUGHT

Pilots may soon be able to fly simply by thinking

The split-second decisions that a modern jet pilot has to make may soon involve linking up the pilot's brain with the mechanics of his aircraft—via a computer. When the electrical output of his brain is interfaced directly to a computer system connected to an aircraft's controls, vital seconds could be saved when they matter most. The pilot would have only to think of an action, and his decision would be transmitted to the plane's control system immediately.

The idea is presently a fanciful extrapolation from a research program now in progress under support from the Advanced Research Projects Agency of the U. S. Department of Defense. Electrodes positioned in a pilot's helmet would pick up and relay impulses to the computer, which would instantly feed back information, such as altitude, airspeed, or engine temperature, on a screen in front of the pilot. The pilot would have to learn a code system, possibly in terms of colors, to trigger the correct impulses that would signal to the computer what information was required. In this way a pilot would save time and prevent errors caused by having to search through a cockpit of crowded dials, and more of his attention could be kept on the essential duty of controlling his aircraft.

The computer could also monitor pilot response to warning signals, determining not only if a stimulus had been perceived but also whether its significance was understood.

For military purposes the brain-wave signals could be utilized by a computer connected to the firing circuits of a fighter plane's armaments. At a simple thought missiles could be launched, bombs dropped, or other decisions executed at the exact instant they are made.

Once missiles were on their way, the computer could make any last-second adjustments to ensure they were on target.

If research now under way is successful, it is anticipated that a wealth of other applications will suggest themselves.

ENIGMA OF THE UFO

Are they alien visitors, hallucinations, or natural phenomena?

To many people unidentified flying objects are a harmless hoax. Yet they have been seen and photographed by astronauts, airline pilots, policemen, astronomers, housewives, meteorologists, and farmers.

The big mystery, which has remained unsolved since the popular term "flying saucers" was first coined in 1947, is: What are they, and where do they come from?

All kinds of explanations have been put forward to account for the worldwide sightings of disks, egg shapes, spheres, and other oddly formed aerial objects.

They have been explained away as unusual cloud formations, fireballs, meteorites, weather balloons, optical illusions, hallucinations, or simply fabrications engineered by publicity-seeking cranks.

But not every reported case can be dismissed in this way. The most logical attitude toward UFO's is that man is faced with a series of strange, at times inexplicable phenomena.

The attitude of ufologists—students of UFO's—goes a step further. They usually claim that the earth is under surveillance by alien intelligences.

Tomorrow, perhaps, the truth will emerge. Meanwhile, mankind is left with a mass of evidence that ranges from impartial, level-headed accounts to the totally implausible.

The first saucers

The flying saucer story began on June 24, 1947, when a private pilot, Kenneth Arnold, who was taking part in a search for a missing transport aircraft, saw nine disk-shaped objects flying over Mount Rainier, Washington.

He described the objects as "flying like a saucer would if you skipped it across the water." Arnold's veracity and professional reputation were beyond question, and his account of the incident was accepted by the authorities. Newspapers picked up the story and labeled the objects "flying saucers."

Since then, there have been waves of reports of sightings. Even the House of Representatives' Committee on Science and Astronautics has held special hearings to take evidence from witnesses.

One of the most spectacular recent reports came from a *Gemini 4* astronaut, James McDivitt, in June 1965. In orbit, about 90 miles above the earth, McDivitt saw a cylindrical object, apparently with arms sticking out of it, which he took to be another spacecraft with antennae. It appeared to be in free-drifting flight over the Pacific, somewhat higher than the *Gemini* capsule. McDivitt took one still photograph and some movie film.

He observed that the object was nearby and moving in a path toward his own spacecraft, but closing in fast. McDivitt and his fellow astronaut, Edward White, were hastily preparing to take evasive action when the UFO disappeared from view.

After splashdown the film was taken away, and McDivitt did not see it again for several days. When he did inspect the film, the object was "hazily" outlined against the sky. But he remained unalterably convinced it was a positive identification.

Originally, McDivitt thought he had seen some unmanned satellite. The official view was that he had spotted the unmanned photographic satellite *Pegasus*. But that was 1,200 miles away at the time.

However extraordinary their content, such reports have been given serious consideration.

LANDING BY SAUCER. *An engineer photographed an alleged UFO in July 1951 in Italy's Bernina Alps. The saucer-shaped object landed, a figure emerged, reentered, then took off again (below).*

As highly trained observers, astronauts are unlikely to give way to speculation or imagination.

Capt. Ed Mitchell, the sixth man to walk on the moon, told a press conference in 1974: "I am completely convinced that *some* UFO sightings are real. The question isn't where the UFO's are from. The question is what are they."

UFO's in orbit

A total of about 26 astronauts have reported seeing UFO's while in orbit. The first sighting was in 1962, and later reports include those made by men aboard *Skylabs 1, 2,* and *3.* NASA (the National Aeronautics and Space Administration) takes the phenomenon seriously and checks into every sighting and analyzes all photographs.

UFO SIGHTING. *This object was seen near the hamlet of Areal, in central Brazil.*

During their stint of duty in *Skylab* 2, astronauts Jack Lousma, Owen Garriott, and Alan Bean watched and photographed a red UFO for 10 minutes. They were then 270 miles above the earth. They said the object rotated every 10 seconds and was 30 to 50 miles away in an orbit very close to their own.

In a prepared statement, put before the Committee on Science and Astronautics of the House of Representatives in 1968, Prof. James E. McDonald, a physicist from the University of Arizona, said: "My own present opinion, based on two years of careful study, is that UFO's are probably extraterrestrial devices engaged in something that might very tentatively be termed 'surveillance.'"

An "occupant sighting" was reported on April 24, 1964, in Socorro, New Mexico. State policeman Lonnie Zamora gave up chasing a speeding motorist to chase a UFO instead, when he saw one apparently coming in to land about a mile away.

Zamora reported that he found it outside the town, a bright, metallic oval, the size of an upturned car. Standing beside it, he said, were two humanoid figures, about the size of 10-year-old children.

As he called headquarters to report, the figures retreated inside, and the object took off.

On July 1 the following year, a French lavender grower in the Provence village of Valensole saw what he thought were youths trying to steal his valuable plants. There were two diminutive figures, standing by an object "about the size of a Renault."

He got within five yards of them before one of the "boys" pointed an instrument at him and he claimed to have become paralyzed. The two figures then boarded their craft, and it sped away.

It was regarded as just another sighting—until an interviewer showed the lavender grower a photograph. The man became terrified, showing all the symptoms of severe shock. It was a picture of a model, constructed from the detailed description given by Zamora, 15 months earlier in New Mexico.

On October 11, 1973, two shipyard workers out fishing in Pascagoula, Mississippi, claimed to have been taken aboard an egg-shaped UFO and examined by three silvery-skinned creatures with no eyes. Charles Hickson, then 42, and Calvin Parker, 19, said the creatures kept them for about 20 minutes, "photographed" them, and then took them back to a riverside pier.

Parker said he fainted when he first saw the humanoid creatures. Each had a slit for a mouth and three pointed protrusions instead of a nose and ears. Their vehicle had descended from the sky to hover a few feet over the Pascagoula River.

After their ordeal the two men were interviewed by Dr. J. Allen Hynek, an astronomer who investigated UFO's for the U.S. Air Force. Later, the men were questioned under hypnosis by Dr. James Harder, of the University of California.

Traumatic experience

Dr. Hynek said: "They had undergone such a shocking thing that they couldn't put it exactly into words. Whatever happened to them definitely affected their rationality."

In Holsworthy, north Devon, England, two police constables on motor patrol got involved in a high-speed chase with an object resembling a shiny cross for about 50 minutes in the cold dawn of October 24, 1967. The two constables, Roger Willey and Clifford Wycott, later held a press conference.

Willey said: "It looked like a star-spangled cross, radiating points of light from all angles. At times we drove at 90 miles an hour to keep up with it. It seemed to be watching us and would not let us catch up. It had terrific acceleration and knew we were chasing it."

The Ministry of Defense later said that the mysterious object was a giant jet tanker of the U.S. Air Force on a refueling mission. However, it was soon established that none of the tankers was airborne at the time.

UFO's appear to be attracted to western England. The town of Warminster is the UFO sightings' capital of the world. Since the mid-sixties there have been thousands of reports.

Thunderous explosion

The best substantiated incident was more a hearing than a sighting—by a whole company of Welsh Guards on Christmas morning 1964. Thirty of the men were awakened by "the sound of a thunderous explosion." The noise was repeated so many times that the men were alerted for duty. But outside there was nothing to be seen.

Later that morning a woman on her way to church was knocked down and pinned to the ground by some sort of sonic blast wave. The noise, described as a low drone with a beating rhythm, passed over several houses in the town, shaking foundations and lifting roof tiles.

Some months later there were reports that animals were suddenly and inexplicably collapsing "as if they had been hit by some sort of ray."

Sightings and strange phenomena became so prevalent in and around Warminster that local people began to refer to anything unusual as the "Warminster Thing."

It has been said that the sights and sounds are caused by experiments with new weapons at the School of Infantry, near Warminster.

Twilight zone

The objects are generally seen in rural areas, but occasionally sightings are reported over cities. Most reports are in the two twilight periods, early morning and early evening, at a time when the glare of a city would make it difficult to observe a UFO in flight.

While most UFO sightings are reported by people on the ground, there are also many sightings by airline pilots and private-plane pilots. But it is more than likely that the number of such sightings greatly exceeds the number of actual reports. Pilots, particularly those with major airlines, are understandably reluctant to be thought of as cranks.

Most pilots' reports relate to some strange object that often goes through aerial maneuvers that no manmade aircraft could execute—such as halting suddenly and hovering, after traveling at amazing speeds—and then disappears.

But in one or two cases UFO's appear to have been linked with disasters. In 1953 the pilot of a DC-6, flying from Wake Island in the Pacific to Los Angeles, reported seeing some objects in the sky. Then communications ceased. The next morning searchers found fragments of the plane and 20 bodies.

Disappeared without trace

In the same year two Air Force personnel in an F-89 jet chased a UFO over Lake Superior, on the U.S.-Canadian border. Tracked on radar, both the jet and the UFO appeared to merge on the radar screen. Then the jet disappeared, and the UFO passed out of range.

Rescue aircraft and ships were sent out, but no trace of the jet or its occupants was found, despite the rigorous searches.

There are cases in which motorists claim their cars have been immobilized by UFO's.

Other people say they were burned, put into trances, or knocked unconscious when approaching strange craft on the ground. There is even a police chief, Jeff Greenshaw, who claimed he chased a six-foot creature in a metallic suit in October 1973, at Falkville, Alabama. But, Greenshaw said, the humanoid outran the car.

But still no one has put forward a satisfactory explanation for all the strange happenings logged in UFO files, whether by amateurs or experts. Some believe that the earth is being watched by beings from another planet. If so, what is the purpose of these aliens?

Man, it seems, will simply have to wait until the extraterrestrials, if they exist, make themselves properly known to learn the answers to these and other questions. Either that or find a more plausible explanation for the strange objects seen over and on the earth.

LOOKING INTO THE FUTURE

A conversation with science writer Isaac Asimov

Prophets have been forecasting the end of the world for centuries. What sort of natural end do you envisage for this planet? Will it turn into a giant ice cube or will it burn up?
One natural end that is unavoidable, even if nothing else goes wrong, is of course the death of the sun. It will gradually use up its hydrogen fuel, and, in about 10 billion years from now, it will destroy the earth. When the hydrogen has been used up, the helium that is left will burn into carbon. In response to that, the sun will expand and become only red hot. But it will have a much larger surface, so the total amount of heat will be much greater than now, and the earth will fry.
What hope then is there? What can mankind do about it? Could we get off this world and live somewhere else in the vastness of space?

THE GREAT TREK. *Before the earth's resources are exhausted, man may capture wandering asteroids and convert them into huge spaceships in which he will set off to find inhabitable planets.*

NEW YORK, 10 BILLION A.D. *About this time the sun will burn itself out, becoming enormously enlarged in the process and turning the earth into a barren, airless, waterless desert.*

It is almost certain that before the death of the sun we will have spread through our own galaxy and perhaps others. The most practical way, barring new kinds of technical advances that are hard to foresee, is to build large ships that are self-contained ecologies—small self-contained worlds—and just send them off, not even with any special destination in mind. Every once in a while, one of them will come across a world that can be colonized.

The most logical way to do it seems to be to convert small asteroids—hollow out these small planets and supply them with whatever they are short of. Certainly in 10 billion years we have plenty of time to fill space with these ships, and, before the end of this planet, we shall have colonized probably millions of worlds all over the universe. We shall almost certainly meet other intelligences doing the same thing.

Could we set up colonies on other planets in our solar system?
None of them is habitable without heavy engineering. Some of them could be engineered—the moon, certainly, and Mars. But they will suffer the same eventual fate as the earth when the sun dies. So they do not represent any long-term solution.

How long a journey will it be? How far will we have to travel in these mobile worlds before we come to a planet on which man could live?
Eventually, these space travelers will come across another solar system with an asteroid belt. They will perhaps be able to discard their original asteroid, which by then will be in pretty bad shape, and take on a new one.

At the moment we can't say how far they will have to travel altogether to find a habitable new earth.

If we consider our galaxy alone, it has 135 billion stars, and a number of them are likely to have their own planetary systems. There could, in our galaxy, be as many as 640 million earthlike planets. In other words, the chances of our finding such planets are about 1 in 200. The odds in favor of finding such planets in the whole of the universe are even greater.

Besides, perhaps there may be more bodies than we expect between the stars. We know nothing about possible dark bodies except for those very close to our own sun. They may not be at all uncommon—let us say in the space of a thousand years, we may come across something suitable.

How feasible is all of this? What about the speed of travel? Light is the fastest thing known in the universe, traveling at more than 669 million miles an hour. Just as there is a sound barrier, there seems to be a light barrier. How long will these journeys take?

As long as the speed-of-light limit lasts, we cannot expect to communicate between the stars in any way that we know about now. If we sent some ship to the stars by any present system, it would take years to reach even the nearest star (Proxima Centauri), thousands of years to reach moderately distant stars, tens of thousands of years to span a galaxy, millions of years to reach even the nearer galaxies.

The only hope of doing anything about this is if there is some way of going faster than the speed of light—without breaking the theory of relativity, which seems to correspond to the universe as it is.

For instance, scientists now theorize that there are some kinds of particles called tachyons that always go faster than the speed of light. They have not actually been detected. If they do exist, they will be extremely difficult to detect.

However, we can speculate on the possibility of changing all the particles in a spaceship simultaneously into the corresponding tachyonic particles, taking off at many times the speed of light in an appropriate direction for an appropriate distance, and then suddenly turning everything back into ordinary particles. And there you are—no time lapse, practically, and you are at the end of the galaxy, 120 trillion miles away.

Of course, the engineering problems involved in changing all the particles in the ship, including those of the human beings, into tachyons—and of changing all of them back with such simultaneity that you do not come back missing half your heart, or just enough atoms to spoil things for you, are enormous. *You say the earth will probably last another 10 billion years. Will mankind also survive that time, or will we blow ourselves up?*
That could happen at any time—except that the longer it does not happen, the more I believe it will not. We have had opportunities for nuclear wars, and we have avoided them.
Could the earth be destroyed in a collision with another planet or huge meteor?
It is highly unlikely. Space is largely empty, and the chance of our being the target for any sizable body is very small. For example, the average distance between the stars in our own corner of the galaxy is nine light-years—about 50 million million miles.

In fact, the stars in our galaxy are in the same proportion as would be a few grains of sand in the whole of New York's Central Park.
What about a possible invasion and annihilation by people from elsewhere in the universe?
That is a very well-known science-fiction situation, but it seems to me unlikely. The nearest intelligence to us is likely to be as much as 50 light-years away, and that is not an easy distance to cross. If a people could cross it, they would be extremely advanced, and I think that a race far in advance of ourselves would probably also have advanced in humanity and would be unlikely to act like barbarians.
What then are the dangers that you see facing mankind?
I think it extremely unlikely that mankind could ever be wiped out completely, but unless we take firm action now, immediately, I believe that we could destroy civilization as we know it within 30 to 50 years. We are heading rapidly in that direction.
That seems an alarming idea and an alarmingly short space of time.

Well, that is how desperate the situation is. At the present moment the population of the world is higher by far than it has ever been—it is now about 4 billion, compared with 2 billion only 50 years ago. It has doubled in the last 50 years and is going to double again, barring some new control, in the next 35 years. So we are having trouble feeding people. A substantial proportion of mankind is in constant danger of starvation.

By the year 2009 we are going to have somewhere between 7 and 8 billion people on earth, and we are not going to double our food supply by then. This means that within 30 or 50 years famines may have become an all-too-common occurrence.

In addition, with a great many people ill-nourished, there would be an increase in disease. There would be more general unrest in the world, for even those nations that we do not usually associate with famine conditions would by then be in a bad way. They are not likely to become economically self-sufficient.
But would that necessarily spell the end of civilization as we know it?
I think that it is questionable whether our highly complicated, therefore rather rickety, technological civilization could withstand that kind of crisis.

The history of mankind has been one of advancing technology. At those times when technology declines for a period, you have what we call a dark age. In the past there have been dark ages in human history a number of times, but they have always been local.

We think of the dark age in western Europe between the 5th and 11th centuries as being enormous, but it was very local really. The only reason that we pay any attention to it is that culturally we are western European.

Actually, the Byzantine Empire was flourishing, the Arab world was at its cultural height, and there was a brilliant civilization flourishing in Spain—as near as that—through the dark ages.

It was just in the Frankish Empire that there was a dark age. In fact, when Europe started climbing out of its dark age, it was because it got rays of civilization from the rim. But if our technology is going, then we are going to have a dark age that for the first time will be worldwide. There will be no untouched portion to act as the savior of the rest.

Furthermore, it would be a dark age that

THE WORLD OF TOMORROW

would have come after we had burned up the oil, used up the easiest supplies of coal to get out, scattered the best pockets of minerals thinly over the face of the earth, perhaps rendered part of the environment radioactive, and destroyed a great deal of the earth's soil by overfarming in a desperate attempt to feed the population.

But what of new sources of power and new sources of food?

Well, of course, it is possible that we shall learn to derive much more food from the oceans, that we shall turn existing plants and trees into protein foods. This is already being done, and undoubtedly we shall develop that kind of technology.

It is true, too, that solar energy will become our principal source of power. But remarkable progress has to be made very soon if we are to avoid the eventual crisis.

Is there no hope that any other part of the universe would be able to help us?

I think the crisis is coming much too soon—in the lifetime of people who are not children even today. I would say that a person who is now 20 is going to see the crisis while he is still in the vigor of his life.

Rescue by some superior intelligence is of course possible, but, frankly, if we are rescued by something like that, life will not be worth living. We would be just a form of domestic animal.

I suppose I would not object to being saved if the alternative was destruction, but I would no longer be a member of the lords of creation. I would be a member of man, a rather intelligent domestic animal—and I would not like it!

How then can we help ourselves?

It is not enough to provide extra sources of energy or food. Supposing that, say, by A.D. 2000 we have worked out some scheme whereby we can feed 7 billion people. If we do so and everyone continues having children, then in 35 more years there will be 14 billion. And then what? Somewhere, sometime, the growth must stop.

But there are only two ways in which growth can stop. Either the death rate goes up to match the birth rate, or the birth rate comes down to match the death rate.

Have we then any right to feel optimistic in this situation?

Yes, for it is amazing how fast human beings can change, given pressure. Only 20 years ago

birth control was banned in vast areas where it is now helping to keep the size of the population under control. Perhaps as the death rate starts to go up, it will dawn on people that the birth rate must come rapidly down.

But surely this would take worldwide agreement of a kind that has never been managed before?

Yes, indeed, but the fact that we are facing global problems—declining resources, rising population, pollution, and so on—has made it very clear that no nation is an independent unit. It has made it very clear that war is impossible, not only nuclear war but ordinary war.

We in the West are now in a position of détente with Russia and China, and it was the same people in America who had been anti-Communist, and the same people in Russia and China who had been anti-American, who brought about that détente. It was forced on us by events, and as the crisis approaches each year, the whole of mankind will be forced to make more drastic efforts and do things that we now consider impossible.

Remember, too, that mankind has found ways to overcome catastrophes in the past. During the Black Death, for example, in the 14th century, perhaps one-third of all human beings were killed. That was a catastrophe, but the amazing thing is that with a disease so contagious and so fatal, and with a human race that was ignorant of the most elementary methods of hygiene, two-thirds did survive.

And if we do find a way to overcome the crisis that you outline, what then?

If we can solve the population problem, however narrowly, and we can spend the 21st century recovering and rebuilding a civilization on a philosophy of growth in quality, growth in sophistication, growth in new forms of technology—if we can do that, it seems to me that the future has the capacity to be enormously, enormously wonderful.

Man is the first creature on earth to be potentially immortal. Since we can now control evolution, control our environment—and in the future to an extent and in ways undreamed of now—we can become invulnerable.

Then we could live here for a long time, and, when scientists foresee the dangers from the sun, we could just move off?

Long before that. If we don't recklessly and needlessly commit suicide, we will almost certainly reach a point where nothing else can hurt us except the overall end of the entire universe.

Index

Page numbers in regular type refer to subjects covered in the text. Page numbers in **bold** type refer to illustrations and captions. Page numbers separated by a dash (226–228) indicate that an article (or picture) devoted to a single subject appears on this sequence of pages. Numbers separated by commas (12, 13) indicate references to or pictures of a subject appearing in a more general article.

CONTRIBUTORS

Carol Alway   Russell Ash
Isaac Asimov   Carol Barber   Raymond Baxter
Eric Beardsley   John Beattie
Richard Beckett   David Bellamy
Patrick Brown   Alan J. Charig
Erika Cheetham   John Church
John O. E. Clark   Leonard Cottrell
Nona Coxhead   Rebecca Davenport
Dr. John Douglas   Ernest Dudley
Rex Dutta   Jane Ford
Rupert Furneaux   Fernando Gay
J. C. G. George   Tony Geraghty   Sergius Golowin
Ian Grant   Nigel Hawkes
Roberto Cabral del Hoyo   Nancy Beth Jackson
Robert Jackson   Marcus Jacobson
Ken Johnson   Dr. Stephan Kaiser
Hamish Keith   George Hall Kirby
Sushma Kumar   Onni Kyster
Joan Levy   Harry Ludlam   Magnus Magnusson
Carol Mankin   Eric Maple   Ian Moffit
Patrick Moore   Nancy Elizabeth Murray
Venetia Newall   George Ordish
David Owen   Donald Pace   Cyril Pearl
Henry F. Pulitzer   Ian Ramsay
Maurice Richardson   Lynne Rogers
Charles J. M. Rondle   Peter Schirmer
Dr. Tony Smith   J. P. C. Sumption
John Taylor   Sunil Wadhwani
Royston Wells   Hugh Ross Williamson

ARTISTS AND PHOTOGRAPHERS

John Bavosi   Norman H. Burkett
A. C. Cooper Ltd.   Henry Cooper and Son
Jackson Day Design   Mike Freeman
David A. Hardy   Alex von Koettlitz
Julian Lusby   Tom McArthur   Gordon Moore
Peter Morter   Pat Oxenham
John Tebbutt   Reece Toothill   George Tuckwell
Mike Wells   Michael Woods   A. J. Wyatt

OTHER ACKNOWLEDGMENTS

The publishers express their thanks and indebtedness to the following people and organizations who have helped in the preparation of this book:

Paul Alexander; Australian Information Bureau, London; Bramah Security Equipment Ltd., London; British Airways; The British Computer Society; British Interplanetary Society; British Museum; British Museum (Natural History); British Petroleum Co. Ltd.; British Typewriter Museum; British UFO Research Association; H. H. B. Capes; Ceylon Tea Center; N. H. Chapman; Civil Aviation Authority (England); Clinical Research Center (England); College of Arms (England); L. F. E. Coombs; Courtaulds Ltd., London; Culham Research Laboratory; Daily Telegraph Information Service; The Decca Navigator Company Ltd., London; Department of the Environment for Wales; Electricité de France, Paris; EMI Ltd., London; Enfield (Automotive) Motor Engineers; R. G. Feltham; Flat Earth Society; Geological Society of London; Charles H. Gibbs-Smith; GPO Telecommunications Headquarters; P. W. Hammond; Honeywell Information Systems Ltd., London; Hovertrailers International Ltd., Southampton, England; Prof. D. E. Hughes; M. J. Humphries; Tim Hunkin; Imperial Chemical Industries Ltd., London; Imperial War Museum (England); Institute of Geological Sciences (England); F. Jaubert; Jesuit Information Office; Christopher Jordan; Kodak Ltd., London; Prof. Hubert Lamb; D. F. Lee; Joseph Lucas Industries Ltd., Birmingham, England; Medical Research Council (England); Meteorological Office (England); Metrication Board (England); NASA Center, Houston, Texas; National Army Museum (England); National Institute of Medical Research (England); National Institute of Oceanography (England); National Maritime Museum (England); Novel Protein Unit, Ministry of Agriculture (England); Alex Parker; Philips Electronics and Associated Industries Ltd., London; P. Powell; Psychic News; Richard III Society; Royal Anthropological Society; Royal Geographical Society; Royal Institute of British Architects; Royal Military School of Music; Royal Observatory; Science Museum (England); Scotland Yard; Scott Polar Research Institute; Dr. P. A. H. Seymour; Smiths Industries Ltd. (Aviation Division), London; Society for Psychical Research; Statens Sjöhistoriska Museum, Stockholm; Strangeways Laboratory; Thames Water Authority; Theosophical Society of England; Dr. D. A. Tyrell; U.S. Information Service; Robert Vincent; Waterman Pens (U.K. Ltd.); B. Waters; Wellcome Foundation Ltd.; D. Williams.

They are also grateful to the authors and publishers of the following works, which were used as sources of reference:

Abu Simbel and the Glories of Ancient Egypt by W. Macquitty (Macdonald & Janes Publishers; G. P. Putnam's Sons); *Admirals in Collision* by R. A. Hough (Hamish Hamilton Ltd.; The Viking Press, Inc.; Collins); *Aircrash Detective* by S. Barlay (Hamish Hamilton Ltd.); *All About King Arthur* by Geoffrey Ashe (W. H. Allen & Co. Ltd.); *The Amazing World of Nature* (The Reader's Digest Association Ltd.); *America* by Alistair Cooke (*The Listener*; Alfred A. Knopf, Inc.); *Ancient America* by J. N. Leonard and the Editors of Time-Life Books (Time, Inc.); *Ancient Egypt* by L. Casson and the Editors of *Life* (Time, Inc.); *Ancient Explorers* by M. Cary and E. H. Warmington (Methuen & Co. Ltd.; Dodd, Mead & Company); *Ancient Rome at Work* by P. Louis (Routledge & Kegan Paul Ltd.; Alfred A. Knopf, Inc.); *Animals My Adventure* by L. Heck (Methuen & Co. Ltd.); *The Art Stealers* by M. Esterow (George Weidenfeld & Nicolson Ltd.); *Australian Folklore* by W. Fearn-Wannan (Landsdowne Press, Pty., Ltd.; Fernhill House Ltd.); *The Autobiography of Sir Henry Morton Stanley G.C.B.* by D. Stanley (Sampson Low, Marston & Co. Ltd.); *Before Civilization* by C. Renfrew (Jonathan Cape Ltd.; Alfred A. Knopf, Inc.); *Beyond Belief* by B. Branston (George Weidenfeld & Nicolson Ltd.; Walker & Co.); *Beyond the Pillars of Hercules* by R. Carpenter (Delacorte Press); *Biofeedback: Turning on the Power of Your Mind* by M. Karlins and L. M. Andrews (Warner Books); *The Biological Time-Bomb* by G. R. Taylor (Thames & Hudson Ltd.; World Publishing Co.); *The Biology of the Algae* by F. E. Round (Edward Arnold Ltd.; St. Martin's Press, Inc.); *The Birds* by R. T. Peterson and the Editors of *Life* (Time, Inc.); *Black Holes: The End of the Universe?* by J. Taylor (Souvenir Press Ltd.; Random House, Inc.); *The Body* by A. E. Nowse and the Editors of *Life* (Time, Inc.); *The Body* by A. Smith (Penguin Books Ltd.; Walker & Co.); *Body Time* by G. G. Luce (Panther Books Ltd.; Pantheon Books); *Book of British Birds* (Drive Publications Ltd.); *A Brief History of Flying* by C. H. Gibbs-Smith (HM Stationery Office); *Call This an Opera House? Yes* by J. Pringle (*Observer*); *Camelot and the Vision of Albion* by Geoffrey Ashe (William Heinemann Ltd.; St. Martin's Press, Inc.); *A Casebook of Murder* by C. Wilson (Leslie Frewin Publishers Ltd.; Cowles Book Company, Inc.); *The Challenge of Chance* by A. Koestler, A. Hardy, and R. Harvie (Hutchinson & Co. Ltd.); *Christmas* by W. Sansom (George Weidenfeld & Nicolson Ltd.); *Christmas and Its Customs* by C. Hole (G. Bell & Sons Ltd.; Barrows Co., Inc.); *Cleopatra's Needles* by A. Noakes (H. F. and G. Witherby Ltd.); *Collins Guide to Mushrooms and Toadstools* (William Collins Sons & Co. Ltd.); *The Colosseum* by P. Quennel and the Editors of *Newsweek* (Newsweek Book Division, published by The Reader's Digest Association Ltd. in association with *Newsweek*); *The Common Cold* by C. Andrewes (George Weidenfeld & Nicolson Ltd.; W. W. Norton & Co., Inc.); *The Computer Revolution* by N. Hawkes (Thames & Hudson Ltd.; E. P. Dutton & Co., Inc.); *The Computerized Society* by J. Martin and A. Norman (Penguin Books Ltd.; Prentice-Hall, Inc.); *A Concise History of Costume* by J. Laver (Thames & Hudson Ltd.; Harry N. Abrams, Inc.); *The Conquistadors* by H. Innes (William Collins Sons & Co. Ltd.; Alfred A. Knopf, Inc.); *Cosmic Clocks* by M. Gauquelin (Peter Owen Ltd.; Henry Regnery Co.); *Counterfeits* by S. Cole (John Murray Ltd.); *Curiosities of Medicine* by B. Roueché (Victor Gollancz Ltd.; Little, Brown & Co.); *Curious Customs of Sex and Marriage* by G. R. Scott (Torchstream Books); *Curious Myths of the Middle Ages* by S. Baring-Gould (Longmans, Green & Co. Ltd.); *Dada* by K. Coutts-Smith (Studio Vista Publishers); *Dada* by H.

Richter (Thames & Hudson Ltd.; Museum of Art, Rhode Island); *The Deserts* by A. S. Leopold and the Editors of Time-Life Books (Time, Inc.); *The Development of Two Standards* by J. R. Smith (Survey Review); *A Dictionary of Fabulous Beasts* by R. Barber and A. Riches (Macmillan Publishers; Walker & Co.); *Easter and Its Customs* by C. Hole (G. Bell & Sons Ltd.; Barrows Co., Inc.); *An Egg at Easter* by V. Newall (Routledge & Kegan Paul Ltd.; Indiana University Press); *Eggs, Milk, and Cheese* by N. Lyon and P. Benton (Faber & Faber Ltd.); *Encyclopaedia of Superstitions* by F. and M. A. Radford, edited and revised by C. Hole (Hutchinson & Co. Ltd.); *Encyclopaedia of the Unexplained* edited by Richard Cavendish (Routledge & Kegan Paul Ltd.; McGraw-Hill Book Co.); *Energy* by M. Wilson and the Editors of *Life* (Time, Inc.); *The Engineer* by C. C. Furnas and T. McCarthy and the Editors of *Life* (Time, Inc.); *Enigmas of History* by H. R. Williamson (Michael Joseph Ltd.); *Everyday Life of the Pagan Celts* by A. Ross (B. T. Batsford Ltd.; G. P. Putnam's Sons); *Explorers of the World* by W. R. Clark (Aldus Books Ltd.; Doubleday & Co., Inc.); *Exploring the Planets* by I. Nicolson (The Hamlyn Publishing Group Ltd.; Grosset & Dunlap, Inc.); *Fabulous Frauds* by L. Jeppson (Arlington Books; Weybright & Talley, Inc.); *Fact, Fake, or Fable* by R. Furneaux (Cassell & Co. Ltd.); *The Fascinating Secrets of Oceans and Islands* (The Reader's Digest Association Ltd.); *The First Book of Firsts* (A Golden Hands Book published by Marshall Cavendish); *The Fishes* by F. D. Ommanney and the Editors of *Life* (Time, Inc.); *Flight* by J. J. Haggerty and the Editors of *Life* (Time, Inc.); *Geography of Strabo* by H. L. Jones (William Heinemann Ltd.); *Grand Deception* by A. Klein (Faber & Faber Ltd.; J. B. Lippincott Co.; Longmans); *Great Dramatic Stories of the 20th Century* by R. Furneaux (Odhams Books Ltd.); *The Great Orm of Loch Ness* by F. W. Holiday (Faber & Faber Ltd.; W. W. Norton & Co., Inc.); *Great Swindlers* by A. F. L. Deeson (W. Foulsham & Co. Ltd.; Drake Publishers, Inc.); *The Great Swindlers* by Judge G. Sparrow (John Long Ltd.); *The Great Travelers* by M. Rugoff (Simon & Schuster, Inc.); *Greek Calendar Customs* by G. Megas (Prime Minister's Office, Greece); *A Handbook of Medical Hypnosis* by G. Ambrose and G. Newbold (Baillière, Tindall & Cox Ltd.; Williams & Wilkins Co.); *Harvest of the Sea* by J. Bardach (George Allen & Unwin Ltd.; Harper & Row, Publishers); *Haunted England* by C. Hole (B. T. Batsford Ltd.; Clarke, Irwin & Co. Ltd.); *Historical Whodunits* by H. R. Williamson (J. M. Dent & Sons Ltd.); *Historic Oddities and Strange Events* by S. Baring-Gould (Methuen & Co. Ltd.); *Historic Tinned Foods* (International Tin Research and Development Council); *A History of Chess* by H. J. R. Murray (Clarendon Press); *A History of Flight* by C. Canby (Leisure Arts Ltd.); *A History of Playing Cards* by R. Tilley (Studio Vista Publishers; Clarkson N. Potter, Inc.); *Hoaxes* by C. D. Macdougall (Dover Publications, Inc.); *Hoaxes and Swindles* by R. Garrett (Pan Books Ltd.); *Hypnosis: Fact and Fiction* by F. L. Marcuse (Penguin Books Ltd.; Penguin Books, Inc.); *The Identity of Jack the Ripper* by D. McCormick (Arrow Books Ltd.); *The Importance of Can Openers* by W. R. Lewis (Tin Research Institute); *Innovations: Scientific, Technological, and Social* by D. Gabor (Oxford University Press); *In Search of Lake Monsters* by P. Costello (The Garnstone Press Ltd.; Coward, McCann & Geoghegan, Inc.); *Invasion 1940* by Peter Fleming (Hart-Davis, MacGibbon Ltd.); *It's a Small, Medium, and Outsize World* by J. Taylor (Hugh Evelyn Ltd.; World Publishing Co.); *Jack the Ripper* by Daniel Farson (Michael Joseph Ltd.); *Jack the Ripper in Fact and Fiction* by R. Odell (George G. Harrap & Co. Ltd.; Clarke, Irwin & Co. Ltd.); *King Henry VIII's Mary Rose* by A. McKee (Souvenir Press Ltd.; Stein & Day Publishers); *Lady Hester Stanhope* by J. Haslip (Cobden-Sanderson; Oxford); *Larousse Gastronomique* by P. Montagne (The Hamlyn Publishing Group Ltd.; Crown Publishers, Inc.); *Legend and Reality* by R. Furneaux (Allan Wingate Ltd.; Smithers and Bounellie Ltd.); *Leonardo da Vinci* (Leisure Arts Ltd.); *The Living House* by G. Ordish (Hart-Davis, MacGibbon Ltd.; J. B. Lippincott Co.); *The Living World of Animals* (The Reader's Digest Association Ltd.); *Loch Ness Monster* by Tim Dinsdale (Routledge & Kegan Paul Ltd.; Chilton Book Co.); *The Longest Day* by Cornelius Ryan (Victor Gollancz Ltd.); *Lost Discoveries* by C. Ronan (Macdonald & Janes Publishers; McGraw-Hill Book Co.); *Lotus and the Robot* by Arthur Koestler (Hutchinson & Co. Ltd.; Macmillan Publishing Co., Inc.); *Machines* by R. O'Brien and the Editors of *Life* (Time-Life International); *Magic and Superstition* by D. Hill (The Hamlyn Publishing Group Ltd.); *Making Fire* (Science Museum); *The Mammals* by R. Carrington and the Editors of *Life* (Time-Life International); *Man's Presumptuous Brain* by A. T. W. Simeons (Longman Group Ltd.; E. P. Dutton & Co., Inc.); *Mary Celeste* by J. G. Lockhart (Hart-Davis, MacGibbon Ltd.; Fernhill House Ltd.); *Masada: Herod's Fortress and the Zealot's Last Stand* by Y. Yadin (Sphere Books Ltd.; Random House, Inc.); *Mermaids and Mastodons* by R. Carrington (Chatto & Windus Ltd.; Holt, Rinehart & Winston, Inc.; Clarke, Irwin & Co. Ltd.); *The Millionth Chance* by J. Leasor (Hamish Hamilton Ltd.; Reynal & Co.); *The Mind* by J. R. Wilson and the Editors of *Life* (Time, Inc.); *The Money Pit Mystery* by R. Furneaux (Tom Stacey Ltd.; Dodd, Mead & Co.); *Mysteries of the Solar System* by R. A. Lyttleton (Oxford University Press); *The Mystery of Jack the Ripper* by L. Matters (Arrow Books Ltd.); *A Night To Remember* by Walter Lord (Longman Group Ltd.; Holt, Rinehart & Winston, Inc.); *On the Track of Unknown Animals* by B. Heuvelmans (Hart-Davis, MacGibbon Ltd.; Hill & Wang, Inc.); *Pagan Celtic Britain* by A. Ross (Routledge & Kegan Paul Ltd.; Columbia University Press); *The Parable of the Beast* by J. W. Bleibtreu (Victor Gollancz Ltd.; Macmillan Publishing Co., Inc.); *The Person in the Womb* by N. J. Berrill (Angus & Robertson Ltd.; Dodd, Mead & Co.); *A Pictorial History of Inventions* by U. Eco and G. B. Zorzoli (George Weidenfeld & Nicolson Ltd.); *Pictorial History of Magic and the Supernatural* by M. Bessy (The Hamlyn Publishing Group Ltd.); *Popular Fallacies* by A. S. E. Ackermann (Old Westminster Press); *Portugal in Quest of Prester John* by E. Sanceau (Hutchinson & Co. Ltd.); *Premonitions: A Leap Into the Future* by Herbert B. Greenhouse (Turnstone Books; Bernard Geis Associates, Inc.); *The Promise of Space* by Arthur C. Clarke (Hodder & Stoughton Ltd.; Harper & Row, Publishers); *The Prophecies of the Brahan Seer* by A. Mackenzie (Aeneas Mackay); *Purnell's Encyclopaedia of Animal Life* (BPC Publishing Ltd.); *The Pyramids and Sphinx* by D. Stewart and the Editors of the Newsweek Book Division (The Reader's Digest Association Ltd. in association with *Newsweek*); *The Pyramids of Egypt* by I. E. S. Edwards (Penguin Books Ltd.; The Viking Press, Inc.); *The Quest for Power* by M. and H. P. Vowles (Chapman & Hall Ltd.); *The Reader's Digest Pocket Guide to Nature Records* (The Reader's Digest Association Ltd. and Guinness Superlatives Ltd.); *The Real Book of Robots and Thinking Machines* by J. May (Dennis Dobson [Dobson Books] Ltd.; Doubleday & Co., Inc.); *Regent's Park: A Study of the Development of the Area From 1086 to the Present Day* by A. Saunders (David & Charles Ltd.); *Restless Earth* by Nigel Calder (BBC Publications Ltd.; The Viking Press, Inc.); *The Road to Xanadu* by J. L. Lowes (Houghton & Co. Ltd.; Houghton Mifflin Co.); *The Sea* by L. Engel and the Editors of *Life* (Time-Life International); *Sea Enchantress* by G. Benwell and A. Waugh (Hutchinson & Co. Ltd.); *The Sears Tower (Chicago)—World's Tallest Building* by L'Acier (Centre Belgo-Luxembourgeois d'Information de l'Acier, Brussels); *The Secret Life of Plants* by P. Tompkins and C. Bird (Harper & Row, Publishers); *The Secret of Mary Celeste* by G. Bradford (W. Foulsham & Co. Ltd.); *Secrets of the Great Pyramids* by P. Tompkins (Allen Lane, Penguin Books Ltd.; Harper & Row, Publishers); *Secrets of the Seas* (The Reader's Digest Association, Inc.); *Sieges of the Middle Ages* by P. Warner (G. Bell & Sons Ltd.; Clarke, Irwin & Co. Ltd.); *Space* by Patrick Moore (Lutterworth Press; Doubleday & Co., Inc.); *The Spirit of St. Louis* by C. Lindbergh (John Murray Ltd.; Charles Scribner's Sons; S. J. R. Saunders); *The Square Pegs* by I. Wallace (Hutchinson & Co. Ltd.; Alfred A. Knopf, Inc.; McClelland & Stewart); *Stonehenge* by A., A. S., and A. S. Thom (*Journal for the History of Astronomy*, edited by M. A. Hoskins—Science History Publications); *Stonehenge Decoded* by G. S. Hawkins (William Collins Sons & Co. Ltd.; Doubleday & Company, Inc.); *Stories of Famous Ships* by R. Garrett (Arthur Barker Ltd.); *The Story of Astronomy* by Patrick Moore (Macdonald & Janes Publishers; Grosset & Dunlap, Inc.); *Suez: De Lesseps' Canal* by J. Pudney (J. M. Dent & Sons Ltd.); *Sunken Cities* by F. J. North (University of Wales Press); *Superstition and the Superstitious* by E. Maple (W. H. Allen & Co. Ltd.; A. S. Barnes & Co., Inc.); *The Swedish Warship Vasa* by L. A. Kvarning and B. Ohrelius (Macmillan Publishers Ltd.); *There Could Be Light Soon at the End of the Long Bore* by T. Whiteside (*Observer*); *Time* by S. A. Goudsmit, R. Claiborne, and the Editors of *Life* (Time, Inc.); *Tomorrow's World* by Raymond Baxter and James Burke (BBC Publications Ltd.); *Travel and Travelers in the Middle Ages* by Sir E. D. Ross (Routledge & Kegan Paul Ltd.); *Treasure Seekers* by H. Roden (George G. Harrap & Co. Ltd.; Walker & Co.); *The Tuatara, Lizards, and Frogs of New Zealand* by R. Shareel (William Collins Sons & Co. Ltd.; Tri-ocean Books, c/o Western Book Service Co.); *Unbidden Guests* by W. O. Stevens (George Allen & Unwin Ltd.; Dodd, Mead & Co.); *Unfinished Symphonies* by R. Brown (Souvenir Press Ltd.; William Morrow & Co., Inc.); *The Universe* by D. Bergamini and the Editors of *Life* (Time-Life International); *Upper Pleistocene Radiocarbon Dated Artifacts From the Northern Yukon* by W. N. Irving and C. R. Harington (*Science*); *Victorian Inventions* by L. DeVries (John Murray Ltd.; McGraw-Hill Book Co.); *Welsh Folk Customs* by T. M. Owen (Welsh Folk Museum); *Where Is the Mona Lisa?* by Henry Pulitzer (Pulitzer Press); *Who Was Ann Ockenden?* by D. Bloxham (Neville Spearman Ltd.); *The Wilder Shores of Love* by Lesley Blanch (John Murray Ltd.; Simon & Schuster, Inc.); *Wild Mushrooms* by L. Zeitlmayr (Frederick Muller Ltd.); *With Intent To Deceive: Frauds Famous and Infamous* by R. A. Haldane (William Blackwood & Sons Ltd.); *The World's Great Religions* by the Editors of *Life* (William Collins Sons & Co. Ltd.; Time, Inc.); *The World's Most Intriguing Mysteries* by R. Furneaux (Odhams Books Ltd.; Arco Publishing Co., Inc.); *World's Tallest Building: Asian Building and Construction* (Far East Trade Press Ltd., Hong Kong); *The Wreck Detectives* by K. Macdonald (George G. Harrap & Co. Ltd.; A. S. Barnes & Co., Inc.); *Yearbook of Astronomy (1974)* by Patrick Moore (Sidgwick & Jackson Ltd.; W. W. Norton & Co., Inc.).

The following articles were based upon material already published:

THE ACADEMIC HOAXER—*The Theoretical Joker* by Norman Moss (reprinted by permission of A. D. Peters & Co.); ANNA'S ICE PALACE—*A Forgotten Empress: Anna Ivanovna and Her Era, 1730–1740* by Mina Curtiss (Frederick Ungar Publishing Co.); BREAD AND CIRCUSES—*Arena: The Story of the Colosseum* by J. Pearson (Thames & Hudson Ltd.; McGraw-Hill Book Co.); BUSHMAN'S PARADISE; GUARDIAN OF THE TREASURE; MOUNTAIN OF FIRE—*The Coast of Treasure* by Lawrence Green (Howard Timmins; G. P. Putnam's Sons); CHARGE OF THE RAILROAD BRIGADE—*The Railway Navvies* by Terry Coleman (Hutchinson & Co. Ltd.); CONTINENTS IN COLLISION—*The Break Up of Pangaea* by R. S. Dietz and J. C. Holder (*Scientific American*, October 1967); *Floating About on Colliding Plates* by J. Maddox (*Daily Telegraph Magazine*); THE DINOSAUR LIVES?—*The Flying Dinosaurs* by Brian Silcock (*Sunday Times*); EARLY PLANS TO TUNNEL UNDER THE CHANNEL—*Is This the Gateway to Europe?* by A. Motson (*Daily Telegraph*); EVERYTHING HAS ITS PRICE; THE MAN WHO SOLD THE EIFFEL TOWER—*The Deceivers* by Egon Larsen (John Baker Publishers Ltd.); THE FLOATING SCOTSMAN—*Alexander Mackenzie: First Across Canada* by B. Hutchinson (*Kiwanis Magazine*); GALLANTS, FIDDLERS, AND FAIRYTALES—*The Bayeux Tapestry and the Norman Invasion* by L. Thorpe (The Folio Society); GIANT WITH A JINX—*Atlantic Bridgehead* by H. Clayton (The Garnstone Press Ltd.); GIANT WITH A JINX; ON THE RIGHT LINES—*Brunel and His World* by J. Pudney (Thames & Hudson Ltd.); *Isambard Kingdom Brunel* by L. T. C. Rolt (Longman Group Ltd.; Penguin Books Ltd.); THE GREAT PALACE—*The Sun King* by Nancy Mitford (reprinted by permission of A. D. Peters and Company; Harper and Row, Publishers); *Versailles* by Ian Dunlop, © 1956, 1970 Ian Dunlop (Hamish Hamilton Ltd.; Taplinger Publishing Co.; Clarke, Irwin & Co. Ltd.); HEART OF THE VATICAN—*Saint Peter's: The Story of Saint Peter's in Rome* by James Lees-Milne (Hamish Hamilton Ltd.; Little Brown & Co.; Collins); THE HUMAN FLY (and other articles)—*Mad and Magnificent Yankees* edited by C. M. Silitch (Yankee, Inc.); HUNTING THE YETI—*Yeti-like Monster Gives Staid Town in Illinois a Fright* by A. H. Malcolm, © 1973 by the New York Times Co. (reprinted by permission); INNER FIRES—© 1967 by Emile C. Schurmacher; adapted from *Strange Unsolved Mysteries* by Emile C. Schurmacher (Warner Paperback Library); IS THIS HOW WE LEARNED TO WALK?—*How We Started* (Time, Inc.); LINCOLN'S DREAM—*Parapsychology: An Insider's View of ESP* by C. Robbins (copyright by J. Gaither Pratt; used by permission of Doubleday & Co., Inc.); THE LONG AND THE SHORT AND THE TALL (and other articles)—*The Guinness Book of Animal Facts and Feats* by N. McWhirter and R. McWhirter (Guinness Superlatives Ltd.; Doubleday & Co., Inc.); *The Guinness Book of Records* by N. McWhirter and R. McWhirter (Guinness Superlatives Ltd.); *The Guinness Book of World Records* by N. McWhirter and R. McWhirter (Sterling Publishing Co., Inc.); LOST CONTINENTS; THE PRICK OF A NEEDLE; TOP HAT, WHITE FACE—AND SKULL (and other articles)—*Man, Myth, and Magic* (BPC Publishing); THE MAGIC OF MAKE-BELIEVE—*The Oxford Book of Nursery Rhymes* by I. and P. Opie (by permission of the Clarendon Press; Oxford University Press); MAJOR WILLIAM MARTIN, ROYAL MARINE—*The Man Who Never Was* by Ewen Montagu (Evans Brothers Ltd.; J. B. Lippincott Co.); MALADIES OF FATE—*Medical Biographies: The Ailments of Thirty-three Famous Persons* by Philip Marshall Dale, M.D. (copyright 1952 by the University of Oklahoma Press); MIGHTIEST CRUSADER FORTRESS—*Castles of Europe* by G. Hindley (reproduced by permission of the Hamlyn Group Ltd.); *Crusader Castles* by R. Fedden and J. Thomson (John Murray Ltd.; F. A. Brockhaus); THE MOST VALUABLE FIND EVER—*Diving for Sunken Treasure* by Jacques-Yves Cousteau and Philip Diole (Cassell & Co. Ltd.; Doubleday & Co., Inc.).; THE MOST VALUABLE FIND EVER; PIECES OF EIGHT!—*The Treasure Diver's Guide* by John S. Potter, Jr. (copyright © by John S. Potter, Jr.; used by permission of Doubleday & Co., Inc.); NATURE'S UNDERTAKER—*Nature's Undertaker* by Alan Devol (American Mercury, Inc., 1960); NEW LIMBS FROM OLD—*Drinkers of Infinity* by Arthur Koestler (Hutchinson & Co. Ltd.; Macmillan Publishing Co., Inc.); PRIESTESS OF THE NILE—*The Cathars and Reincarnation* by Arthur Guirdham (Neville Spearman Ltd.); *Dorothy, the Nile Priestess* by Irene Beeson (*Observer Color Supplement*); RISE OF MARVIN HEWITT—*The Eight Lives of Marvin Hewitt* by Herbert Brean (*Life*, © Time, Inc., 1954); THE ROARING

U.P. TRAIL—*Union Pacific* by Garry Hogg (Hutchinson & Co. Ltd.; Walker & Co.); SHIP OF PREY—*Sea Eagle* by E. P. Hoyt (Allan Wingate Ltd.); SHIPWAY TO THE PACIFIC—*The Impossible Dream: Building of the Panama Canal* by Ian Cameron (Hodder & Stoughton Ltd.; William Morrow & Co., Inc.); SLOW TRAIN TO IZMIR—*The Dorak Treasure Mystery—Was It a Robber's Plot or a Scholars' Vendetta?* by K. Pearson and P. Conner (*Sunday Times*); SPEAKING VOLUMES IN SILENCE—*The International Dictionary of Sign Language* by Theodore Brun (Wolfe Publishing Ltd.); SUPERSCULPTURE—*Gutzon Borglum* by Willadene Price (EPM Publications, Inc.); *Statue of Liberty* by Oscar Handlin and the Editors of Newsweek Books (Newsweek); THE SUPERSENSES OF ANIMALS—*The Infrared Receptors of Snakes* by R. I. Gamow and J. F. Harris (*Scientific American*, May 1973); *The Magic of the Senses* by Vitus B. Droscher (translated by Evelyn Haggard; © 1964 E. P. Dutton and W. H. Allen & Co. Ltd.; reprinted by permission of the publishers, E. P. Dutton & Co., Inc., W. H. Allen & Co. Ltd., Paul List Verlag); THE SURVIVOR—*The Fish Named L. C. Smith* by J. Dugan (Crowell Collier Publishing Co.); THEY FEEL NO PAIN—*Book of Life* (Marshall Cavendish); THE TREASURED METAL—*Through the Crust of the Earth* by Lord Energlyn (Macdonald and Janes Publishers; McGraw-Hill Book Co.); TURNING BACK NATURE'S CLOCK—*A History of Domesticated Animals* by F. E. Zeuner (Hutchinson & Co. Ltd.; Harper & Row, Publishers); *Vanishing Animals* by Philip Street (reprinted by permission of Harold Ober Associates, Inc., copyright © 1961 Philip Street, Faber & Faber Ltd.); WINE: MAN'S ANCIENT COMFORT—*Folklore and Odysseys of Food and Medicinal Plants* by F. and J. Lehner (Tudor Publishing Co.; Farrar, Straus & Giroux, Inc.); WORDS! WORDS! WORDS!—*Brewer's Dictionary of Phrase and Fable* (Cassell & Co. Ltd.; Harper & Row, Publishers); *Word Origins and Their Romantic Stories* by Wilfred Funk; © 1950 Wilfred Funk, Inc. (Funk and Wagnall's Publishing Co., Inc.).

The publishers also acknowledge these sources of illustrations. Credits are arranged in the following sequence for each page: top left/bottom left/top right/bottom right.

12 California Institute of Technology and Carnegie Institution of Washington; Mt. Wilson Observatory 14 Photri 15 Cambridge University Press 17 NASA; Henry Grosinsky, *Life*, © Time, Inc. 18–19 NASA 22 NASA 23 California Institute of Technology and Carnegie Institution of Washington 24 California Institute of Technology and Carnegie Institution of Washington; California Institute of Technology and Carnegie Institution of Washington; Patrick Moore 26 Photo Science Museum, London; Michael Holford Library 27 Dick Kent Photography 29 Photo Science Museum, London 31 Photo Science Museum, London; Middle East Archives 32 Ronan Picture Library 33 Aerofilms 34 Photo Science Museum, London 37 Royal Astronomical Society 45 C. M. Dixon 47 Mary Evans Picture Library 57 Pictor Limited 58–59 Mats Wibe Lund; Mats Wibe Lund; G. R. Roberts; Editorial Photocolor Archives; Pictor Limited 60 Picturepoint Limited 61 David Muench 64–65 Pictor Limited; Pictor Limited; Photri; Popperfoto 66–67 Camera Press 68 Steve McCutcheon 70 Dr. B. J. Mason, CB, FRS 72 Camera Press 73 John Freeman and Company 75 Photri; Photo Trends 76 Camera Press 77 Camera Press; Dr. John Christian Jensen 79 Pictor Limited 81 Mitchell Library, Sydney 82 De Beers Consolidated Mines Limited 84 Shell International Petroleum Company Limited 86 U.S. Forest Service 88 Redwood Empire Association; K. R. Gaardern 89 Heather Angel; Heather Angel 90 Stephen Dalton/NHPA; Stephen Dalton/NHPA; Clive Wyborn; Clive Wyborn 93 Edward S. Ross 95 Tom McHugh/Photo Researchers 97 David Houston/Bruce Coleman Limited; Jane Burton/Bruce Coleman Limited; Peter M. David/Seaphot; J. M. Bassot/Jacana 98 Peter M. David/Seaphot; Oxford Scientific Films/Bruce Coleman Limited 99 Anthony Bannister/NHPA; David Hughes/Bruce Coleman Limited; David Hughes/Bruce Coleman Limited 100 Jane Burton/Bruce Coleman Limited 101 Scientific American, Inc. (February 1966) 102 A. G. Wells/NHPA; Dr. H. C. Bennet Clark 103 Jane Burton/Bruce Coleman Limited 104 French Government Tourist Office; Jane Burton/Bruce Coleman Limited; Toni Angermayer 105 Scientific American, Inc. (December 1955) 106 A. van den Nieuwenhuizen 108 Mansell Collection 111 Dr. Masao Kawai 112 Roger Perry/NHPA; Peter M. David/Seaphot; Karl W. Kenyon 113 Axel Poignant 115 Harry Titcombe 116 Trustees of the British Museum (Natural History) 118 Scientific American, Inc. (August 1961) 120 George Ordish 125 NASA; NASA 127 R. Sanders/Mt. Vernon Hospital 128 GE Research and Development Center 129 Harold E. Edgerton, MIT; Middlesex Hospital, London 130 Palestine Archeological Museum of Jerusalem/Kodak 132 Keystone 133 Stan Wayman, *Life*, © Time, Inc., 1974 134 Miles Laboratories, Inc. 137 Camera Press 138 Bell Telephone Laboratories 139 Microfilm Reprographics 140 Fritz Goro, *Life*, © Time, Inc., 1974; Fritz Goro, *Life*, © Time, Inc., 1974 141 *Daily Telegraph* 142 J. R. Eyerman, *Life*, © Time, Inc., 1974 143 Henry Groskinsky, *Life*, © Time, Inc., 1974 144 Photographie Giraudon 146 Cliché Musées Nationaux 150 Associated Press 151 Michael Holford Library; Emil Muench/Ostman Agency 152 Mondadoripress, Milan 154 Mansell Collection 155 J. Powell, Rome 156 Aerofilms 158 Trustees of the British Museum; Roubier-Rapho 160–161 Culver Pictures 161 Brown Brothers; Culver Pictures; Brown Brothers 162 Mansell Collection 165 Mansell Collection; Mary Evans Picture Library; Mansell Collection 167 Mansell Collection; Mary Evans Picture Library 168 Photo Science Museum, London 169 Imperial War Museum; Imperial War Museum 171 Mansell Collection 172 Mansell Collection 174 Mansell Collection 175 Picturepoint Ltd. 176 Mansell Collection; Mansell Collection 177 Lucille Handberg/Photo Trends; Sears Roebuck & Co. 178 Mary Evans Picture Library 180 Radio Times Hulton Picture Library 181 Trustees of the Pierpont Morgan Library; *New York Times* 182 John Freeman; crown copyright 183 John Freeman; Photo Science Museum, London; John Freeman 184 Thames and Hudson Limited; Thames and Hudson Limited 185 Imperial War Museum 186 John Murray Limited 187 Photo Science Museum, London; Photo Science Museum, London; Photo Science Museum, London; London Council Print Collection; Ardea Photographic 188 Photo Science Museum, London 189 John Murray Limited; Photo Science Museum, London; Photographie Giraudon 191 Photri 193 Radio Times Hulton Picture Library 194 Radio Times Hulton Picture Library 196 Mary Evans Picture Library; John Murray Limited 197 Collection Audouin Dollfus; John Murray Limited 199 *Illustrated London News*/The Post Office 200 Photo Science Museum, London 202 Culver Pictures 203 Photo Science Museum, London 204 *Illustrated London News* 205 Mary Evans Picture Library 206 Mary Evans Picture Library 207 Tin Research Institute 209 Photo Science Museum, London 213 Bodleian Library 214 Bodleian Library 216 Helge Ingstad; Per Meurtredt 219 *New York Times*; *New York Times* 222 Radio Times Hulton Picture Library 225 Associated Press 226 J. Allan Cash 227 *Illustrated London News* 231 Denver Public Library; Historical Pictures Service, Chicago; Denver Public Library 232 Harrah's Automobile Collection, Reno, Nevada 234 Brown Brothers 235 Brown Brothers 236 Royal Geographical Society 237 Royal Geographical Society 238 New York Public Library 239 Trustees of the British Museum 241 Steve McCutcheon 242–243 Time-Life, Inc./Dean Brown 245 Mary Evans Picture Library 248 Afrique Photos 249 Mary Evans Picture Library 252–253 *The Times*; Robert Harding Associates; Ashmolean Museum 254 Ashmolean Museum 257 Susan Griggs Agency 258 Israel Press 260 John Hillelson Agency 263 Mansell Collection 264 Lee Battaglia 265 Robert Harding Associates 267 John Hillelson Agency 270 Magnum Photos, Inc.; Magnum Photos, Inc. 272 Stockholm Marine Museum 274–275 National Maritime Museum, Greenwich 278 Camera Press 281 Radio Times Hulton Picture Library 282 Maltese Government Tourist Office 283 Hallmark Cards 284 Camera Press 285 Henry Monroe/DPI 288 National Museum of Wales 289 Camera Press 290 John Deakin 291 City of Plymouth Museum and Art Gallery; Mark Edwards 292 Maltese Government Tourist Office 293 Keystone 294 Paramount Pictures 296 Mary Evans Picture Library; Associated Press; Mary Evans Picture Library 298 Mary Evans Picture Library 299 Theo Dennet 300 Michael Pinney 302–303 Rider and Company 306–307 Camera Press; Camera Press 308 Magnum 310 British Tourist Authority 311 Aldus Books 313 Mary Evans Picture Library; Bodleian Library 317 City of Birmingham Museum Art Gallery 319 Süddeutscher Verlag; Mansell Collection; Mansell Collection 320 Popperfoto; Mary Evans Picture Library 321 Essex County Newspapers 323 Mary Evans Picture Library 324 Douglas Dickens 325 Kobal Collection; Bruce Coleman Limited 326 Mary Evans Picture Library; Mary Evans Picture Library 327 Mansell Collection; Mary Evans Picture Library 328 Amon Carter Museum, Fort Worth, Texas; Michael Holford Library 329 Mansell Collection; Frank Phillips; Mansell Collection 330 Mary Evans Picture Library 332 Mary Evans Picture Library 333 Kobal Collection; Kobal Collection; The Cinema Bookshop 335 U.S. National Park Service 337 Novosti 339 Miguel Rubio 341 California Historical Society 345 Photographie Giraudon 346 Mansell Collection 347 Photographie Giraudon/Bibliothèque des Arts Decoratifs 349 Nova Scotia Communications and Information Center; Bob Brookes Photos 351 Popperfoto 353 Popperfoto 354 *Illustrated London News*; *Illustrated London News*; *Illustrated London News* 356 Photographie Giraudon 358 Radio Times Hulton Picture Library 359 Mansell Collection 362 Granger Collection 367 Fox Photos; Keystone 371 Associated Press; Associated Press 375 Mary Evans Picture Library 376 Michael Holford Library 377 *Illustrated London News* 380 Mansell Collection 383 Abresch Federico/*Man, Myth, and Magic* 385 Süddeutscher Verlag 386 Transworld Feature Syndicate 391 Agencia Europa Press, Madrid; Agencia Europa Press, Madrid 393 Mary Evans Picture Library 396 Mary Evans Picture Library 397 Paxton Music Limited, 1974; *Psychic News* 398 Mary Evans Picture Library 399 Mary Evans Picture Library 400 Mary Evans Picture Library 401 Mary Evans Picture Library 402 Bettmann Archive 403 Richard Hough, from *Admirals in Collision*; Mary Evans Picture Library 404 *Illustrated London News* 405 *Illustrated London News* 406 *Illustrated London News* 407 *Illustrated London News* 410 Peter Underwood 416 Scala; Wawel Castle, Krakow 417 Trustees of the British Museum (Natural History) 418 Luton Museum and Art Gallery 419 St. Bride's Library; Royal Danish Ministry of Foreign Affairs 421 Bodleian Library 422 Radio Times Hulton Picture Library 423 National Library of Wales; National Library of Wales 424 Syndication International 425 Kenneth Wilson; London Express 427 Rapho-Guillumette 428 Bodleian Library 430 Michael Holford Library 433 Radio Times Hulton Picture Library 434 *Man, Myth, and Magic* 435 *Man, Myth, and Magic* 436 Roger Patterson 438 Michael Holford Library 441 Trustees of the British Library 442–443 Gordon Moore 444 Crown copyright, Victoria and Albert Museum; Archivo MAS 445 Michael Holford Library; Philadelphia Museum of Art 446 Michael Holford Library; Horniman Museum, London; Mary Evans Picture Library 447 Scala 448 Wallraf-Richartz Museum, Cologne 451 Mary Evans Picture Library 454 Süddeutscher Verlag; Radio Times Hulton Picture Library 456 Radio Times Hulton Picture Library; Radio Times Hulton Picture Library 458 Mary Evans Picture Library 459 Mary Evans Picture Library; Mansell Collection 460 Wiener Library; Wiener Library 462 Süddeutscher Verlag 463 From *The Man Who Never Was* by Ewen Montagu, © 1953 by Walter D'Arcy Hart and O. H. Frost by permission of J. B. Lippincott Company 465 Süddeutscher Verlag; Süddeutscher Verlag; Süddeutscher Verlag 469 New York State Historical Association, Cooperstown 474 Trustees of the British Museum (Natural History) 475 *Sunday Times*/Geological Society of London 477 Radio Times Hulton Picture Library; Public Record Office, London 478 Metropolitan Museum of Art (1915) 482 Musée de Louvre/Colorphoto Hans Hinz 483 Cliché Musées Nationaux, Paris; The Earl Spencer 484 Swiss Art Research Institute 485 Museum Boymans-van Beuningen, Rotterdam 488 Trustees of the British Library 489 Mansell Collection 490 John T. Hopf; Neiman-Marcus Christmas Catalog 491 Morris Rosenfeld and Sons, Inc.; Culver Pictures 492 Brighton Central Art Gallery and Museum 493 Michael Holford Library 496 Radio Times Hulton Picture Library 498 Mansell Collection 499 Reproduced from *Dada*, Willi Verkauf/Tiranti 500 Mary Evans Picture Library 501 Trustees of the British Library 503 Wide World Photos 504 Mary Evans Picture Library 506 Mary Evans Picture Library; Radio Times Hulton Picture Library 507 Richard W. O'Donnell, Derry, New Hampshire 508 *Yankee Magazine*/N. H. Polley 509 Mary Evans Picture Library 510 Radio Times Hulton Picture Library 512 Mansell Collection; Mansell Collection 513 Mansell Collection; Mansell Collection; Mansell Collection 514 Mansell Collection; Popperfoto; Popperfoto 515 Camera Press; Popperfoto 516 Mary Evans Picture Library 517 Mary Evans Picture Library 518 Mary Evans Picture Library 521 Mary Evans Picture Library 526 London Electrotype Agency 527 Paramount Pictures 528 Mary Evans Picture Library; Bettmann Archive 529 King Features Syndicate 530 Mark Edwards 531 Mansell Collection 532 John Webb 533 Mansell Collection 535 London Electrotype Agency 540 Mary Evans Picture Library 541 Mansell Collection; *Illustrated London News* 542–543 National Portrait Gallery; Mary Evans Picture Library; Mary Evans Picture Library 545 Kodak 546 Shell Photographic Unit 547 C. M. Dixon 548 W. S. Lewis, Farmington, Connecticut 549 Mary Evans Picture Library 550 Mary Evans Picture Library 552 Mary Evans Picture Library 553 Mary Evans Picture Library; Bettmann Archive 554 Mary Evans Picture Library; Mary Evans Picture Library 556 Mander and Mitchenson Collection; Hammer Films 557 Mary Evans Picture Library 558 Radio Times Hulton Picture Library; Mansell Collection 559 Mansell Collection; Süddeutscher Verlag; Mansell Collection 560 Mansell Collection 561 Crown copyright, Victoria and Albert Museum Library 562 Bettmann Archive 563 Mary Evans Picture Library; Ardea 567 Graham Finlayson 569 Derek Bayes/Aspect 575 Ardea 576 Ley Kenyon 577 Ley Kenyon 579 Middle East Archive 580 Middle East Archive; Middle East Archive 581 Popperfoto 586 *Flying Saucer Viewpoint*/Rex Dutta 587 Worldwide Photos.